TRANSFORMERS

THE WRECKERS SAGA

Become our fan on Facebook **facebook.com/idwpublishing**
Follow us on Twitter **@idwpublishing**
Subscribe to us on YouTube **youtube.com/idwpublishing**
See what's new on Tumblr **tumblr.idwpublishing.com**
Check us out on Instagram **instagram.com/idwpublishing**

Special thanks to Ben Montano,
Josh Feldman, Ed Lane,
Beth Artale, and Michael Kelly
for their invaluable assistance.

Licensed By:

ISBN: 978-1-68405-221-9   21 20 19 18   1 2 3 4

Originally published as TRANSFORMERS: LAST STAND OF THE
WRECKERS issues #1–5, TRANSFORMERS: SINS OF THE WRECKERS
issues #1–5, and TRANSFORMERS: REQUIEM OF THE WRECKERS.

Greg Goldstein, President & Publisher
Robbie Robbins, EVP & Sr. Art Director
Matthew Ruzicka, CPA, Chief Financial Officer
David Hedgecock, Associate Publisher
Lorelei Bunjes, VP of Digital Services
Jerry Bennington, VP of New Product Development
Eric Moss, Sr. Director, Licensing & Business Development

Ted Adams, Founder & CEO of IDW Media Holdings

For international rights, please contact
licensing@idwpublishing.com

LAST STAND OF THE WRECKERS

STORY **NICK ROCHE & JAMES ROBERTS**
PENCILS **NICK ROCHE & GUIDO GUIDI**
INKS **NICK ROCHE, JOHN WYCOUGH, GUIDO GUIDI, AND ANDREW GRIFFITH**
COLORS **JOSH BURCHAM AND JOANA LAFUENTE**
LETTERS **NEIL UYETAKE AND CHRIS MOWRY**
SERIES EDITS **ANDY SCHMIDT**
ASSOCIATE SERIES EDITS **DENTON J. TIPTON**

SINS OF THE WRECKERS

STORY AND ART **NICK ROCHE**
COLORS **JOSH BURCHAM**
ADDITIONAL COLORS **JOANA LAFUENTE**
LETTERS **TOM B. LONG**
SERIES EDITS **JOHN BARBER**

REQUIEM OF THE WRECKERS

STORY **NICK ROCHE**
ART **NICK ROCHE, GEOFF SENIOR, AND BRENDAN CAHILL**
COLORS **JOSH BURCHAM AND JOSH PEREZ**
LETTERS **SHAWN LEE AND TOM B. LONG**
SERIES EDITS **DAVID MARIOTTE**

COVER ART **NICK ROCHE**
COVER COLORS **JOSH BURCHAM**
COLLECTION EDITS **JUSTIN EISINGER AND ALONZO SIMON**
COLLECTION DESIGN **SHAWN LEE**
PUBLISHER **GREG GOLDSTEIN**

LAST STAND OF THE WRECKERS

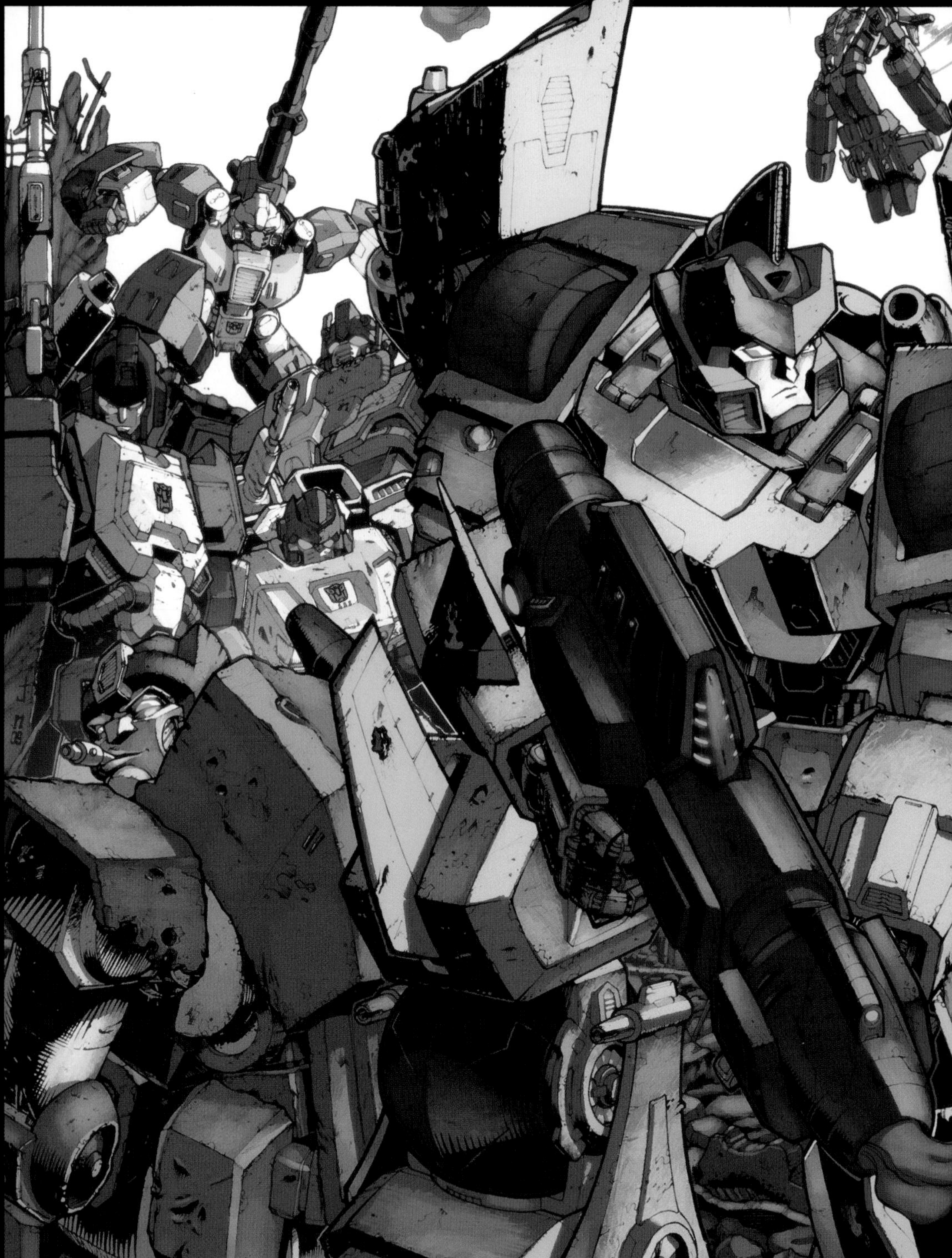

ART NICK ROCHE COLORS JOSH BURCHAM

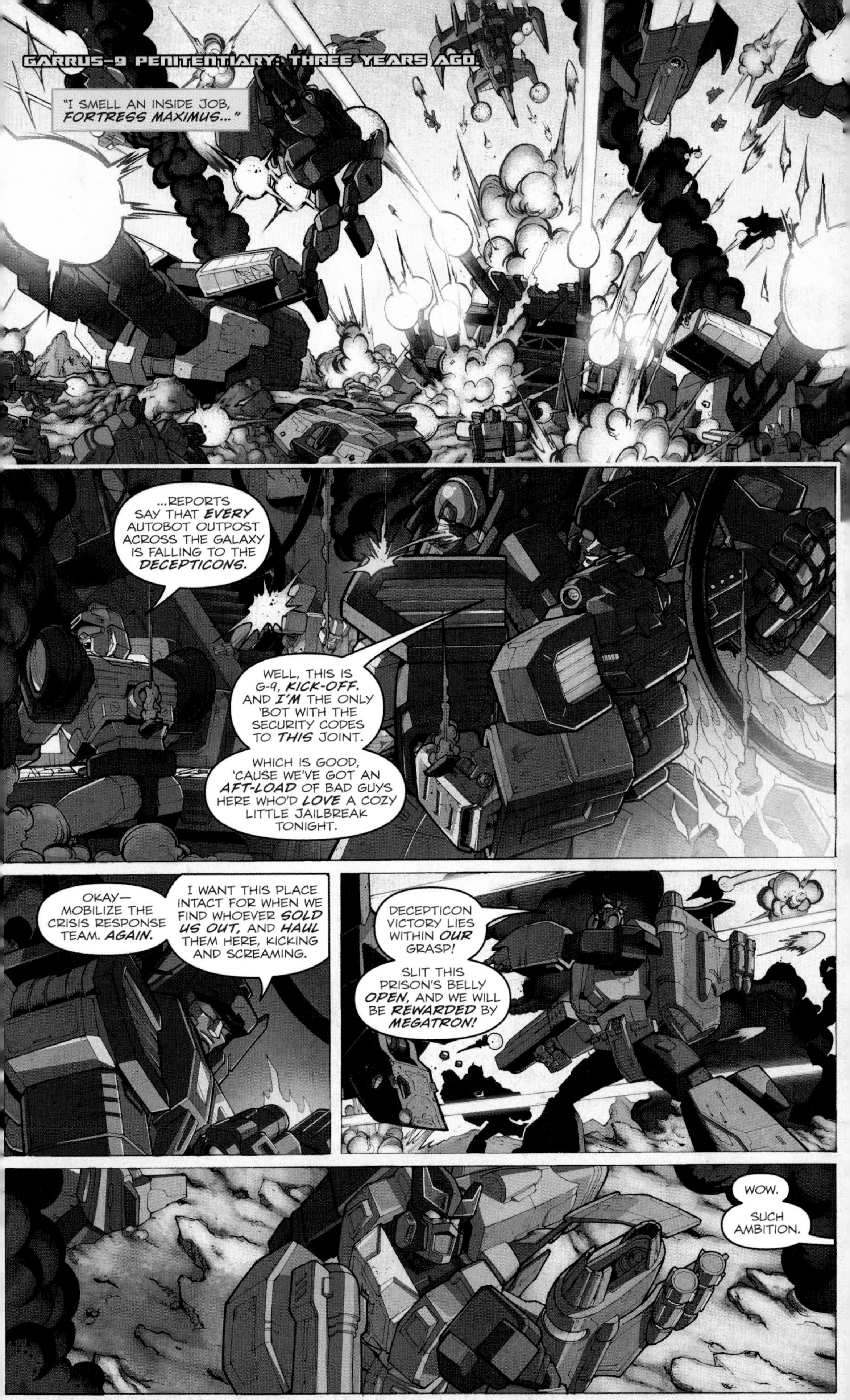
GARRUS-9 PENITENTIARY: THREE YEARS AGO.
"I SMELL AN INSIDE JOB, FORTRESS MAXIMUS..."
...REPORTS SAY THAT EVERY AUTOBOT OUTPOST ACROSS THE GALAXY IS FALLING TO THE DECEPTICONS.
WELL, THIS IS G-9, KICK-OFF. AND I'M THE ONLY 'BOT WITH THE SECURITY CODES TO THIS JOINT.
WHICH IS GOOD, 'CAUSE WE'VE GOT AN AFT-LOAD OF BAD GUYS HERE WHO'D LOVE A COZY LITTLE JAILBREAK TONIGHT.
OKAY— MOBILIZE THE CRISIS RESPONSE TEAM. AGAIN.
I WANT THIS PLACE INTACT FOR WHEN WE FIND WHOEVER SOLD US OUT, AND HAUL THEM HERE, KICKING AND SCREAMING.
DECEPTICON VICTORY LIES WITHIN OUR GRASP!
SLIT THIS PRISON'S BELLY OPEN, AND WE WILL BE REWARDED BY MEGATRON!
WOW.
SUCH AMBITION.

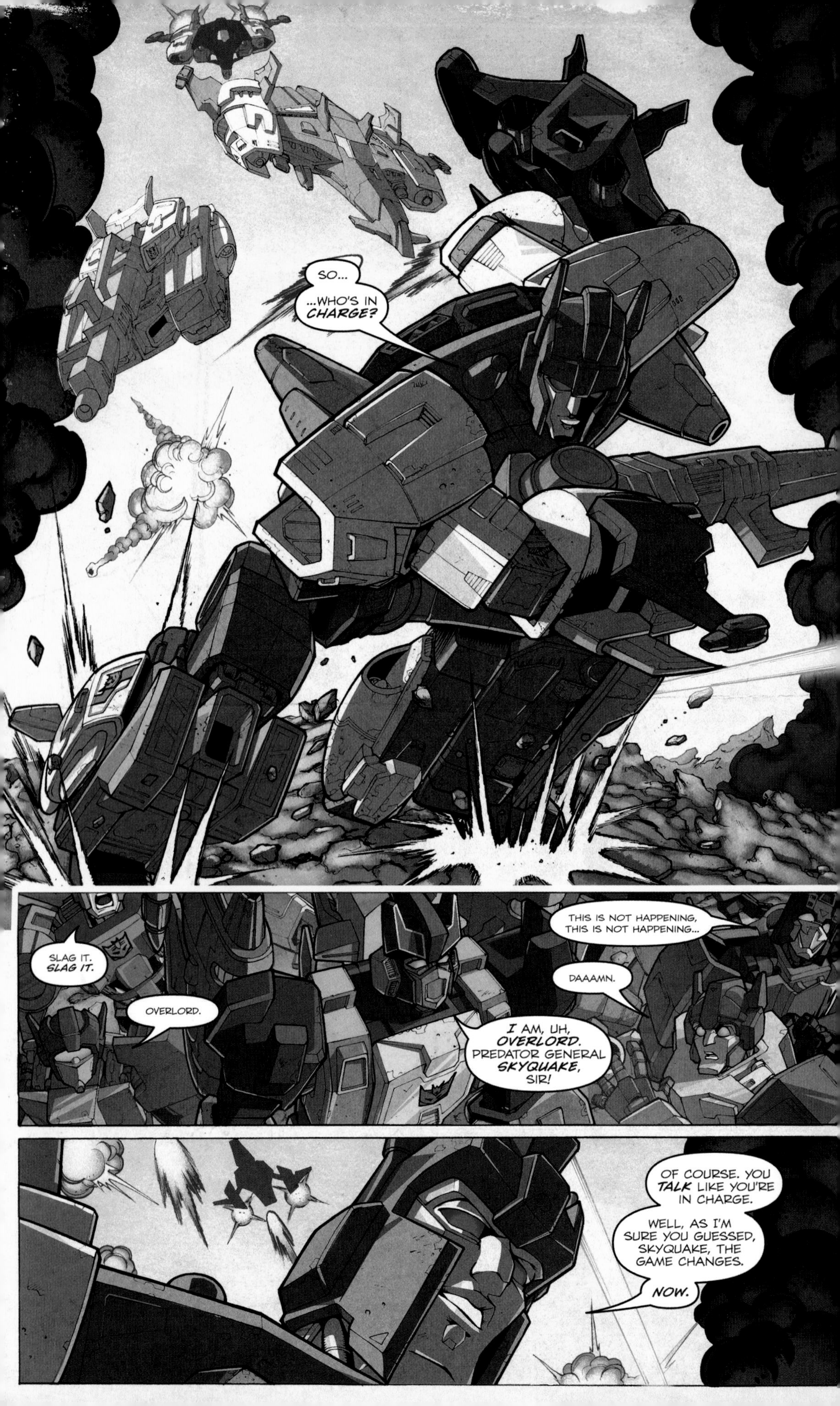
SO...
...WHO'S IN CHARGE?
SLAG IT. SLAG IT.
OVERLORD.
THIS IS NOT HAPPENING, THIS IS NOT HAPPENING...
DAAAMN.
I AM, UH, OVERLORD. PREDATOR GENERAL SKYQUAKE, SIR!
OF COURSE. YOU TALK LIKE YOU'RE IN CHARGE.
WELL, AS I'M SURE YOU GUESSED, SKYQUAKE, THE GAME CHANGES.
NOW.

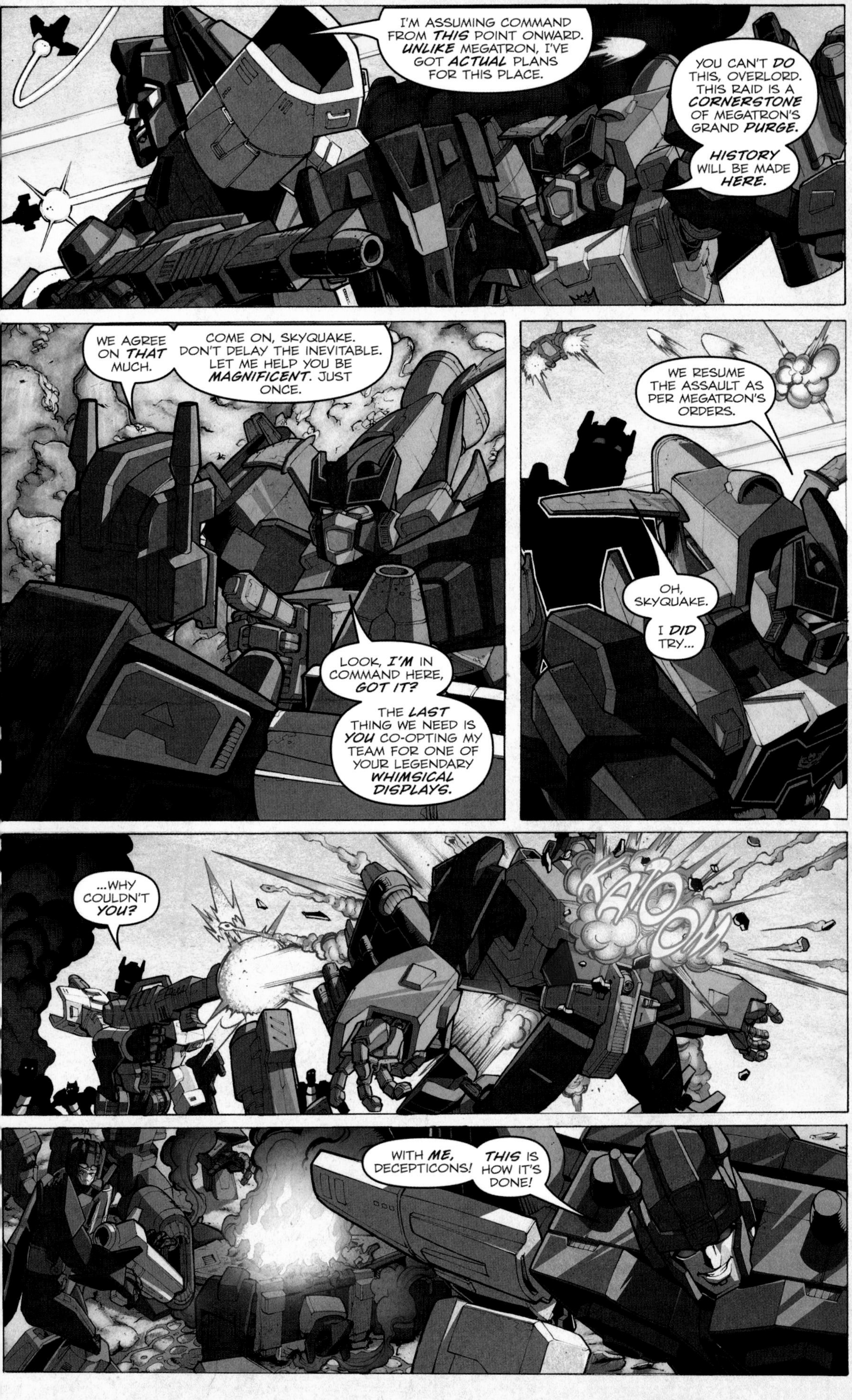

I'M ASSUMING COMMAND FROM THIS POINT ONWARD. UNLIKE MEGATRON, I'VE GOT ACTUAL PLANS FOR THIS PLACE.
YOU CAN'T DO THIS, OVERLORD. THIS RAID IS A CORNERSTONE OF MEGATRON'S GRAND PURGE.
HISTORY WILL BE MADE HERE.
WE AGREE ON THAT MUCH.
COME ON, SKYQUAKE. DON'T DELAY THE INEVITABLE. LET ME HELP YOU BE MAGNIFICENT. JUST ONCE.
LOOK, I'M IN COMMAND HERE, GOT IT?
THE LAST THING WE NEED IS YOU CO-OPTING MY TEAM FOR ONE OF YOUR LEGENDARY WHIMSICAL DISPLAYS.
WE RESUME THE ASSAULT AS PER MEGATRON'S ORDERS.
OH, SKYQUAKE.
I DID TRY...
...WHY COULDN'T YOU?
KA-BOOM
WITH ME, DECEPTICONS!
THIS IS HOW IT'S DONE!

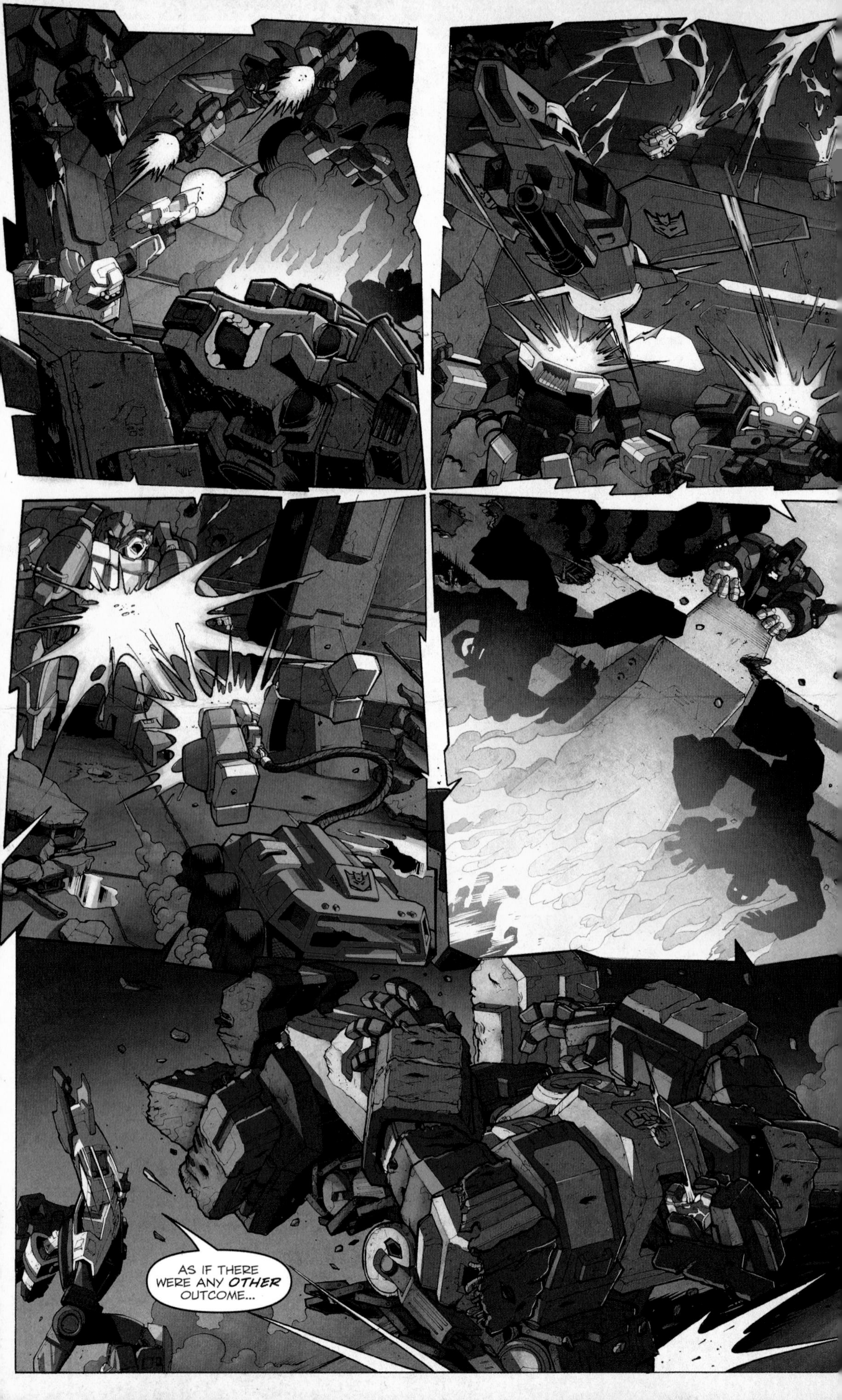
AS IF THERE WERE ANY OTHER OUTCOME...

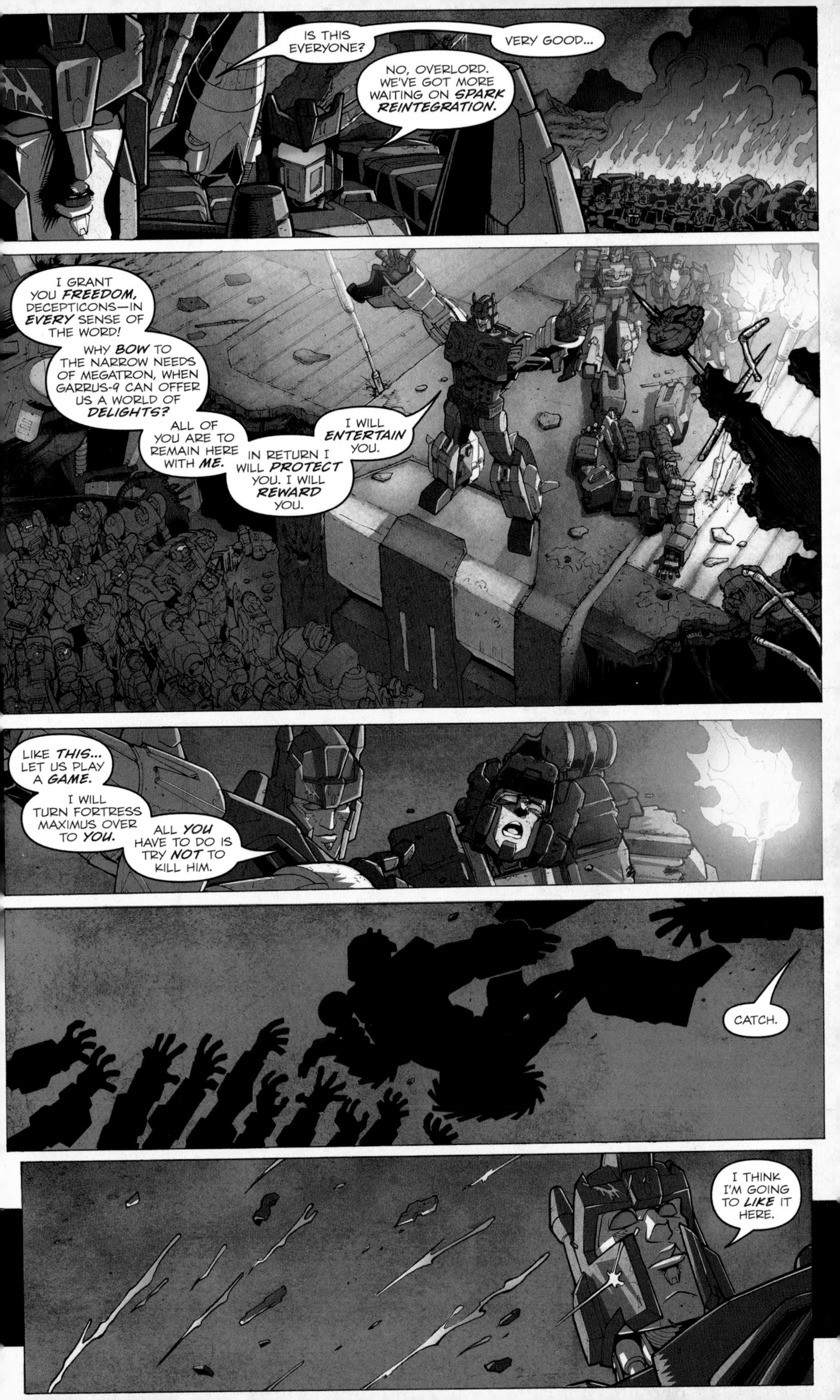
IS THIS EVERYONE?
NO, OVERLORD. WE'VE GOT MORE WAITING ON SPARK REINTEGRATION.
VERY GOOD...
I GRANT YOU FREEDOM, DECEPTICONS—IN EVERY SENSE OF THE WORD!
WHY BOW TO THE NARROW NEEDS OF MEGATRON, WHEN GARRUS-9 CAN OFFER US A WORLD OF DELIGHTS?
ALL OF YOU ARE TO REMAIN HERE WITH ME.
IN RETURN I WILL PROTECT YOU. I WILL REWARD YOU.
I WILL ENTERTAIN YOU.
LIKE THIS... LET US PLAY A GAME.
I WILL TURN FORTRESS MAXIMUS OVER TO YOU.
ALL YOU HAVE TO DO IS TRY NOT TO KILL HIM.
CATCH.
I THINK I'M GOING TO LIKE IT HERE.

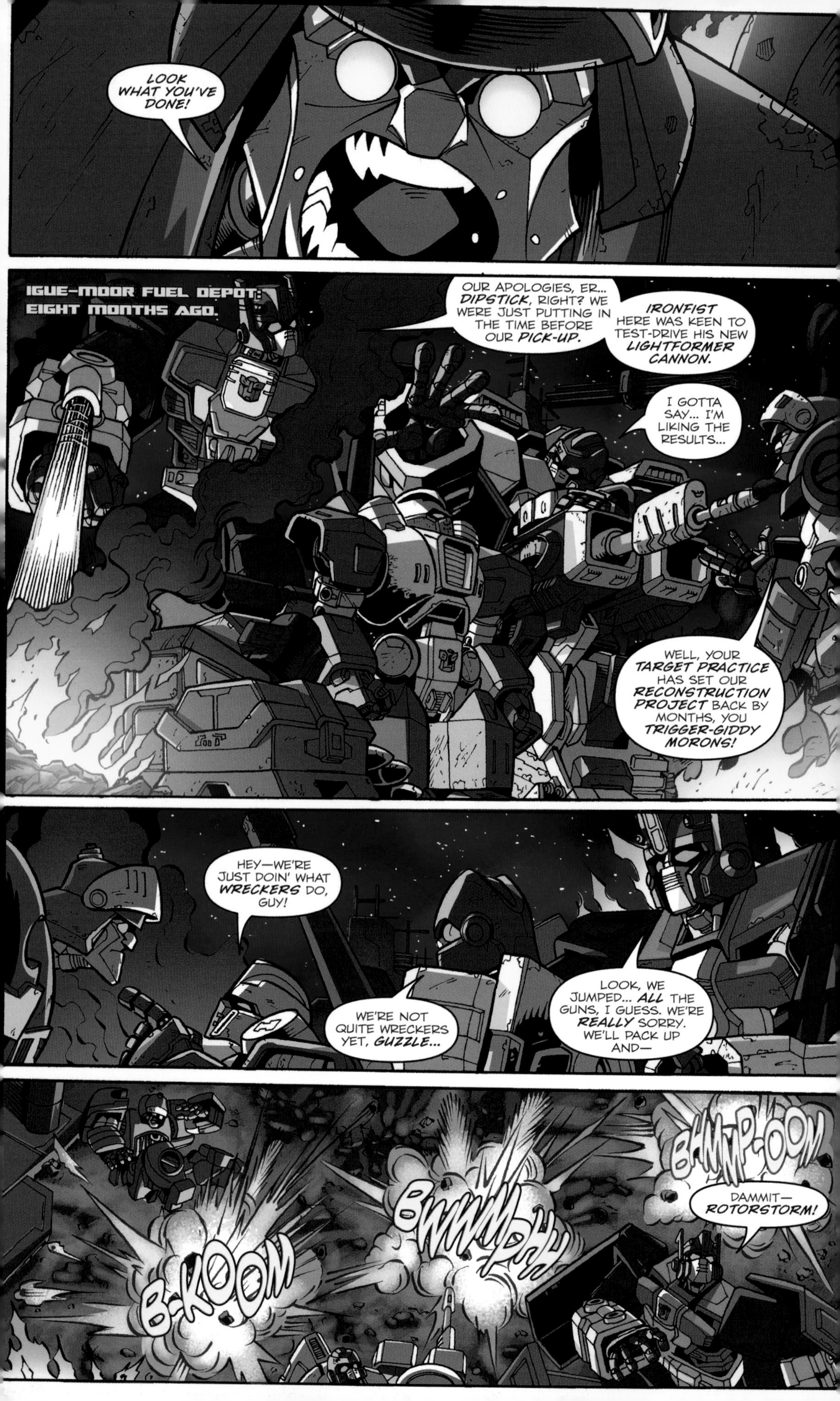
LOOK WHAT YOU'VE DONE!
IGUE-MOOR FUEL DEPOT: EIGHT MONTHS AGO.
OUR APOLOGIES, ER... DIPSTICK, RIGHT? WE WERE JUST PUTTING IN THE TIME BEFORE OUR PICK-UP.
IRONFIST HERE WAS KEEN TO TEST-DRIVE HIS NEW LIGHTFORMER CANNON.
I GOTTA SAY... I'M LIKING THE RESULTS...
WELL, YOUR TARGET PRACTICE HAS SET OUR RECONSTRUCTION PROJECT BACK BY MONTHS, YOU TRIGGER-GIDDY MORONS!
HEY—WE'RE JUST DOIN' WHAT WRECKERS DO, GUY!
WE'RE NOT QUITE WRECKERS YET, GUZZLE...
LOOK, WE JUMPED... ALL THE GUNS, I GUESS. WE'RE REALLY SORRY. WE'LL PACK UP AND—
B-KOOM
BWWMPH
BHMMP-OOM
DAMMIT—ROTORSTORM!

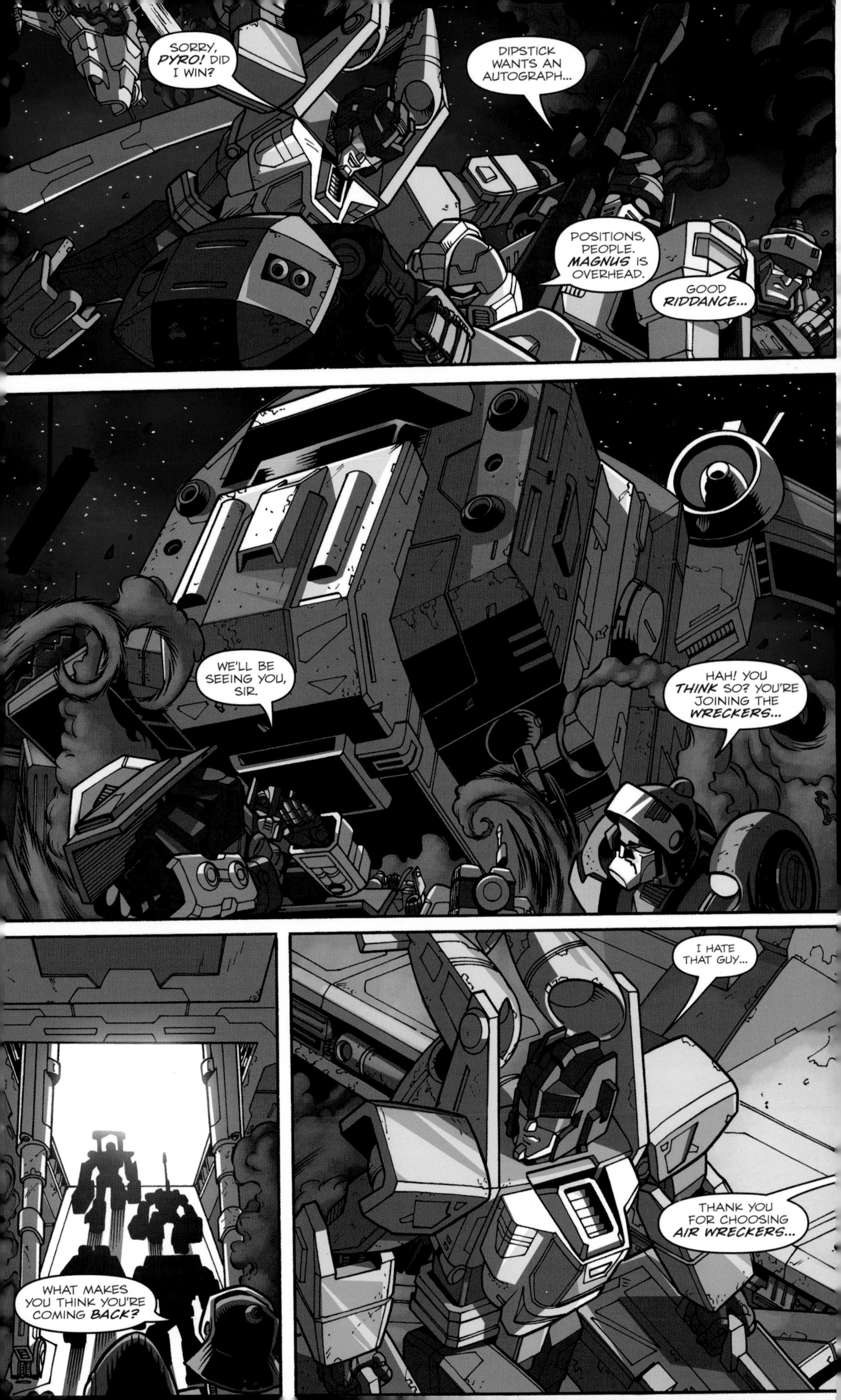
SORRY, PYRO! DID I WIN?
DIPSTICK WANTS AN AUTOGRAPH...
POSITIONS, PEOPLE. MAGNUS IS OVERHEAD.
GOOD RIDDANCE...
WE'LL BE SEEING YOU, SIR.
HAH! YOU THINK SO? YOU'RE JOINING THE WRECKERS...
WHAT MAKES YOU THINK YOU'RE COMING BACK?
I HATE THAT GUY...
THANK YOU FOR CHOOSING AIR WRECKERS...

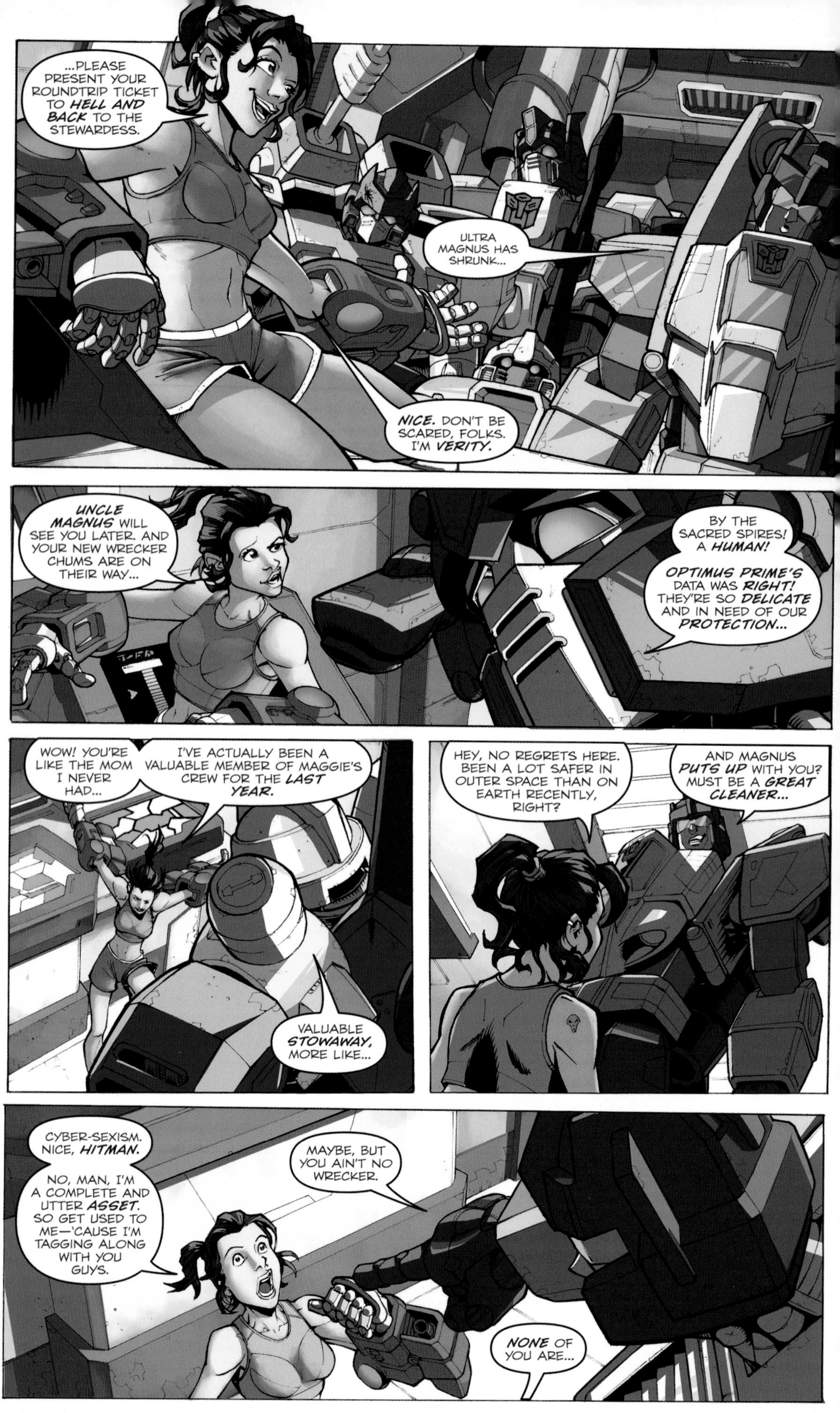
...PLEASE PRESENT YOUR ROUNDTRIP TICKET TO *HELL AND BACK* TO THE STEWARDESS.
ULTRA MAGNUS HAS SHRUNK...
NICE. DON'T BE SCARED, FOLKS. I'M *VERITY.*
UNCLE MAGNUS WILL SEE YOU LATER. AND YOUR NEW WRECKER CHUMS ARE ON THEIR WAY...
BY THE SACRED SPIRES! A *HUMAN!*
OPTIMUS PRIME'S DATA WAS *RIGHT!* THEY'RE SO *DELICATE* AND IN NEED OF OUR *PROTECTION...*
WOW! YOU'RE LIKE THE MOM I NEVER HAD...
I'VE ACTUALLY BEEN A VALUABLE MEMBER OF MAGGIE'S CREW FOR THE *LAST YEAR.*
VALUABLE *STOWAWAY,* MORE LIKE...
HEY, NO REGRETS HERE. BEEN A LOT SAFER IN OUTER SPACE THAN ON EARTH RECENTLY, RIGHT?
AND MAGNUS *PUTS UP* WITH YOU? MUST BE A *GREAT CLEANER...*
CYBER-SEXISM. NICE, *HITMAN.*
MAYBE, BUT YOU AIN'T NO WRECKER.
NO, MAN, I'M A COMPLETE AND UTTER *ASSET.* SO GET USED TO ME—'CAUSE I'M TAGGING ALONG WITH YOU GUYS.
NONE OF YOU ARE...

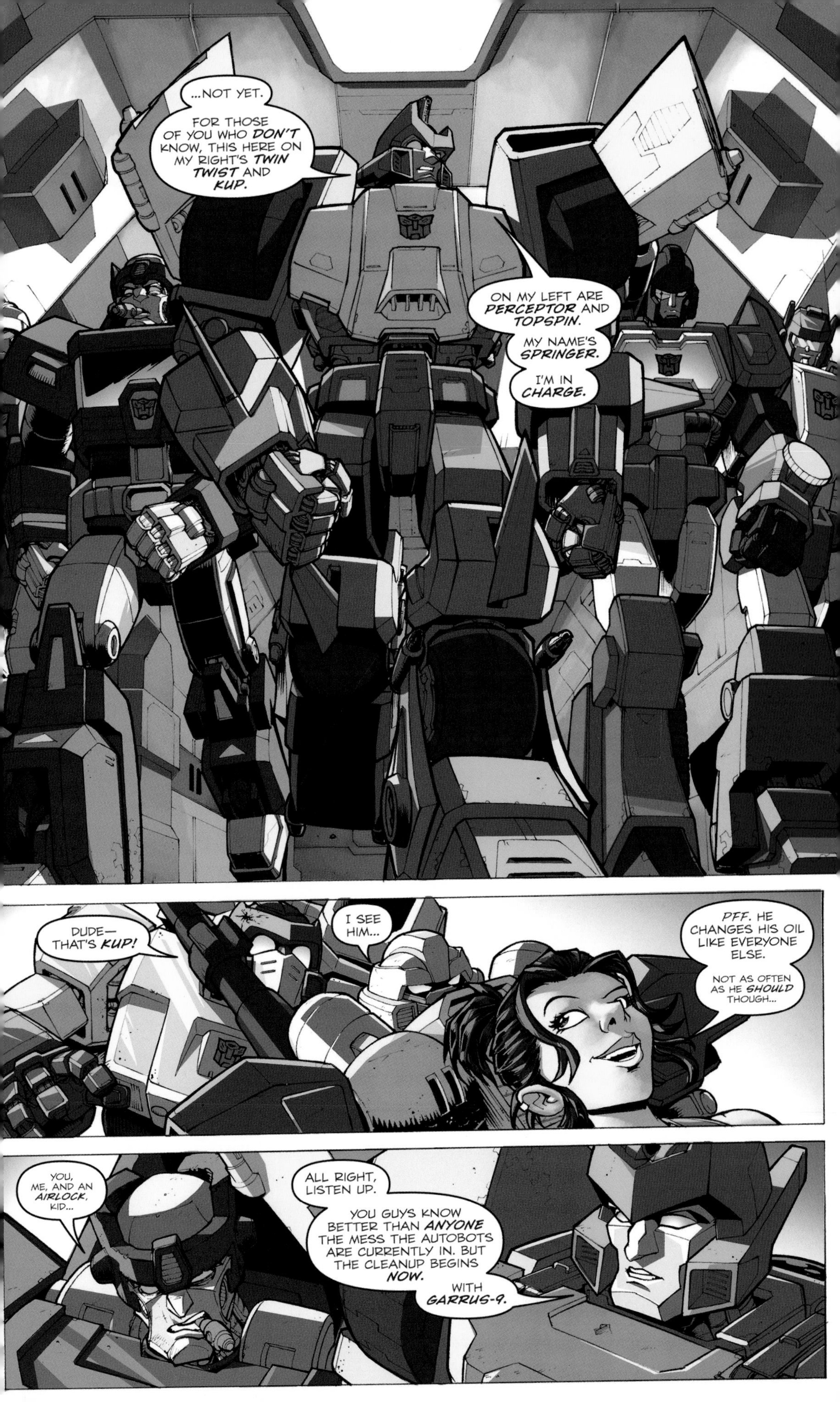

...NOT YET.
FOR THOSE OF YOU WHO DON'T KNOW, THIS HERE ON MY RIGHT'S TWIN TWIST AND KUP.
ON MY LEFT ARE PERCEPTOR AND TOPSPIN.
MY NAME'S SPRINGER.
I'M IN CHARGE.
DUDE— THAT'S KUP!
I SEE HIM...
PFF. HE CHANGES HIS OIL LIKE EVERYONE ELSE.
NOT AS OFTEN AS HE SHOULD THOUGH...
YOU, ME, AND AN AIRLOCK, KID...
ALL RIGHT, LISTEN UP.
YOU GUYS KNOW BETTER THAN ANYONE THE MESS THE AUTOBOTS ARE CURRENTLY IN. BUT THE CLEANUP BEGINS NOW.
WITH GARRUS-9.

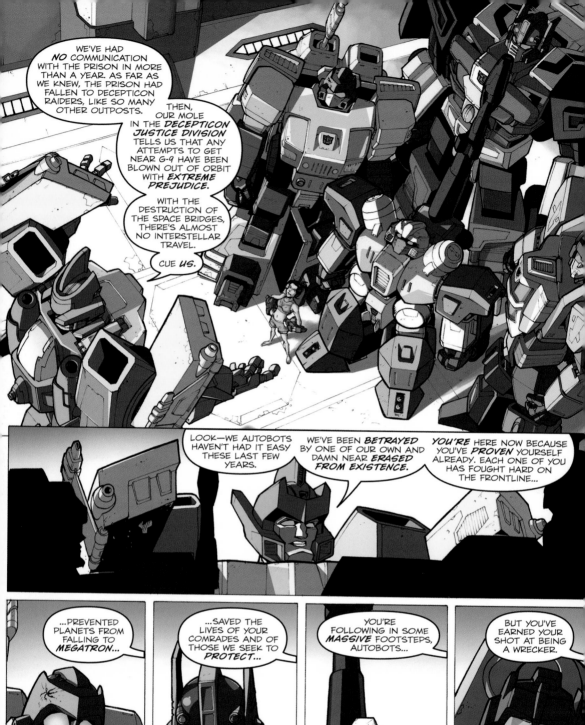

WE'VE HAD *NO* COMMUNICATION WITH THE PRISON IN MORE THAN A YEAR. AS FAR AS WE KNEW, THE PRISON HAD FALLEN TO DECEPTICON RAIDERS, LIKE SO MANY OTHER OUTPOSTS.

THEN, OUR MOLE IN THE *DECEPTICON JUSTICE DIVISION* TELLS US THAT ANY ATTEMPTS TO GET NEAR G-9 HAVE BEEN BLOWN OUT OF ORBIT WITH *EXTREME PREJUDICE.*

WITH THE DESTRUCTION OF THE SPACE BRIDGES, THERE'S ALMOST NO INTERSTELLAR TRAVEL.

CUE *US.*

LOOK—WE AUTOBOTS HAVEN'T HAD IT EASY THESE LAST FEW YEARS.

WE'VE BEEN *BETRAYED* BY ONE OF OUR OWN AND DAMN NEAR *ERASED FROM EXISTENCE.*

YOU'RE HERE NOW BECAUSE YOU'VE *PROVEN* YOURSELF ALREADY. EACH ONE OF YOU HAS FOUGHT HARD ON THE FRONTLINE...

...PREVENTED PLANETS FROM FALLING TO *MEGATRON...*

...SAVED THE LIVES OF YOUR COMRADES AND OF THOSE WE SEEK TO *PROTECT...*

YOU'RE FOLLOWING IN SOME *MASSIVE* FOOTSTEPS, AUTOBOTS...

BUT YOU'VE EARNED YOUR SHOT AT BEING A WRECKER.

WELCOME TO THE TEAM.

JUST BE PREPARED: SOMETIMES IN THE WRECKERS, YOUR *FIRST* DAY IS YOUR *LAST.*

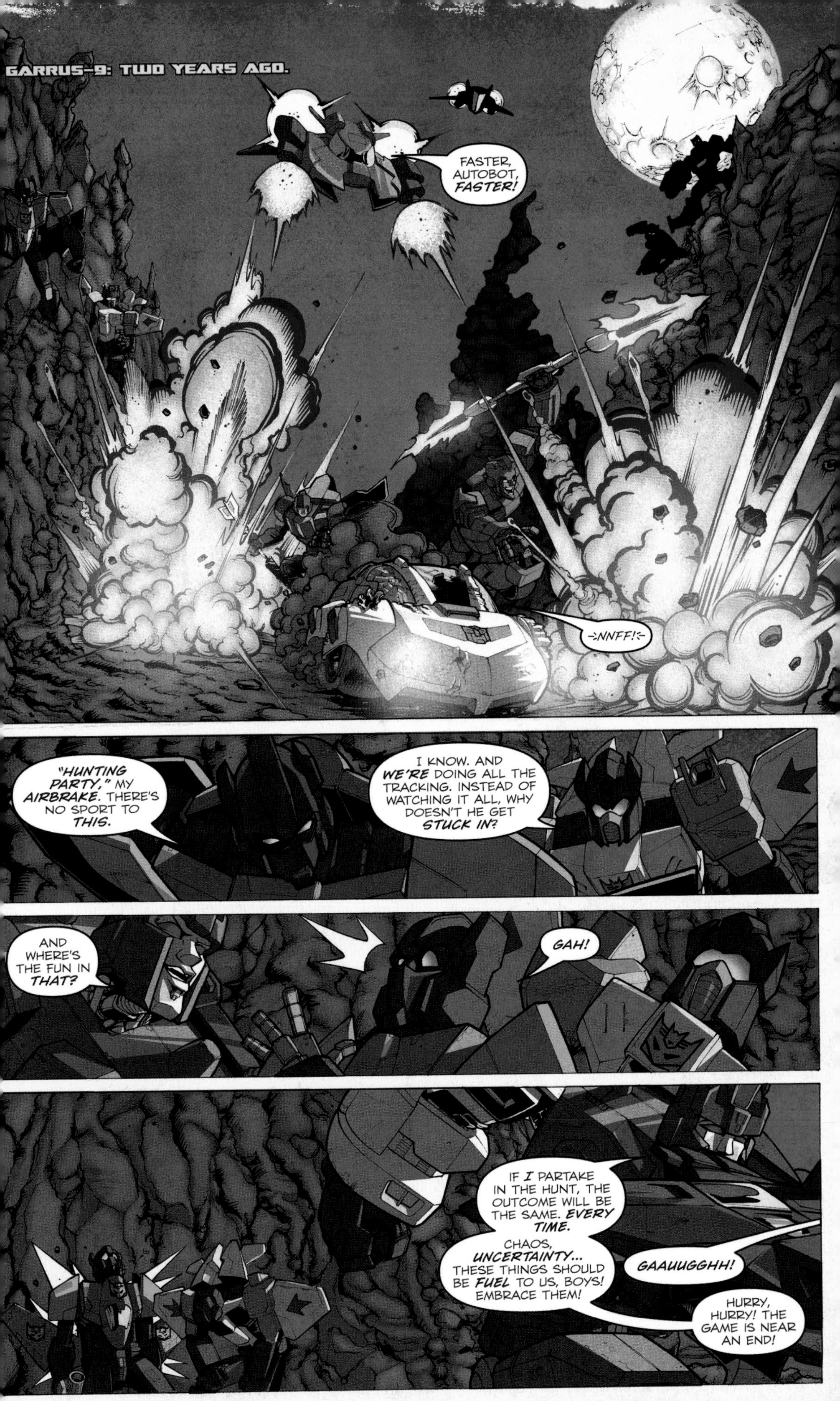
GARRUS-9: TWO YEARS AGO.
FASTER, AUTOBOT, FASTER!
-NNFF!-
"HUNTING PARTY," MY AIRBRAKE. THERE'S NO SPORT TO THIS.
I KNOW. AND WE'RE DOING ALL THE TRACKING. INSTEAD OF WATCHING IT ALL, WHY DOESN'T HE GET STUCK IN?
AND WHERE'S THE FUN IN THAT?
GAH!
IF I PARTAKE IN THE HUNT, THE OUTCOME WILL BE THE SAME. EVERY TIME.
CHAOS, UNCERTAINTY... THESE THINGS SHOULD BE FUEL TO US, BOYS! EMBRACE THEM!
GAAUUGGHH!
HURRY, HURRY! THE GAME IS NEAR AN END!

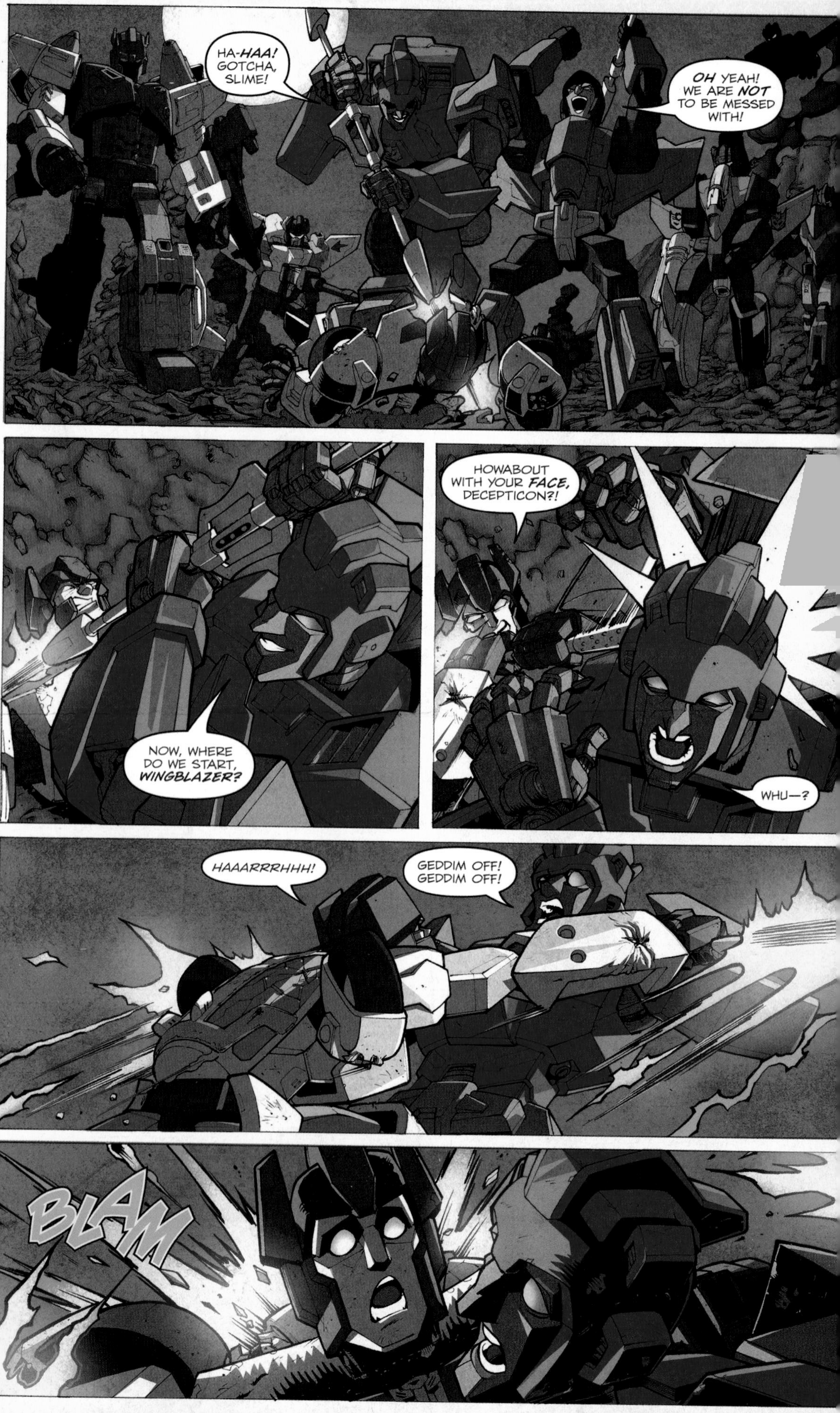
HA-HAA! GOTCHA, SLIME!
OH YEAH! WE ARE NOT TO BE MESSED WITH!
NOW, WHERE DO WE START, WINGBLAZER?
HOWABOUT WITH YOUR FACE, DECEPTICON?!
WHU—?
HAAARRRHHH!
GEDDIM OFF! GEDDIM OFF!
BLAM

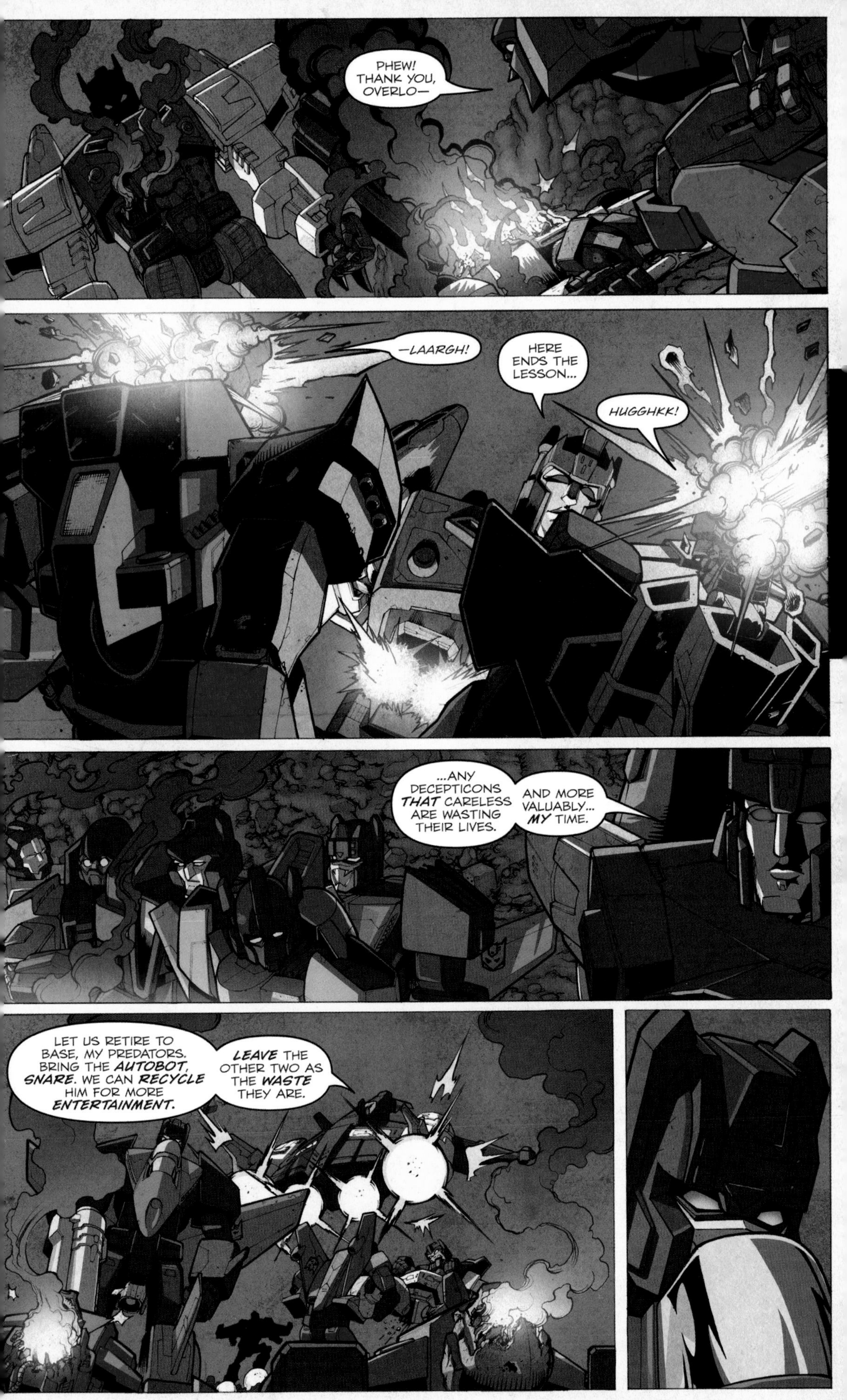
PHEW! THANK YOU, OVERLO—
—LAARGH!
HERE ENDS THE LESSON...
HUGGHKK!
...ANY DECEPTICONS THAT CARELESS ARE WASTING THEIR LIVES.
AND MORE VALUABLY... MY TIME.
LET US RETIRE TO BASE, MY PREDATORS. BRING THE AUTOBOT, SNARE. WE CAN RECYCLE HIM FOR MORE ENTERTAINMENT.
LEAVE THE OTHER TWO AS THE WASTE THEY ARE.

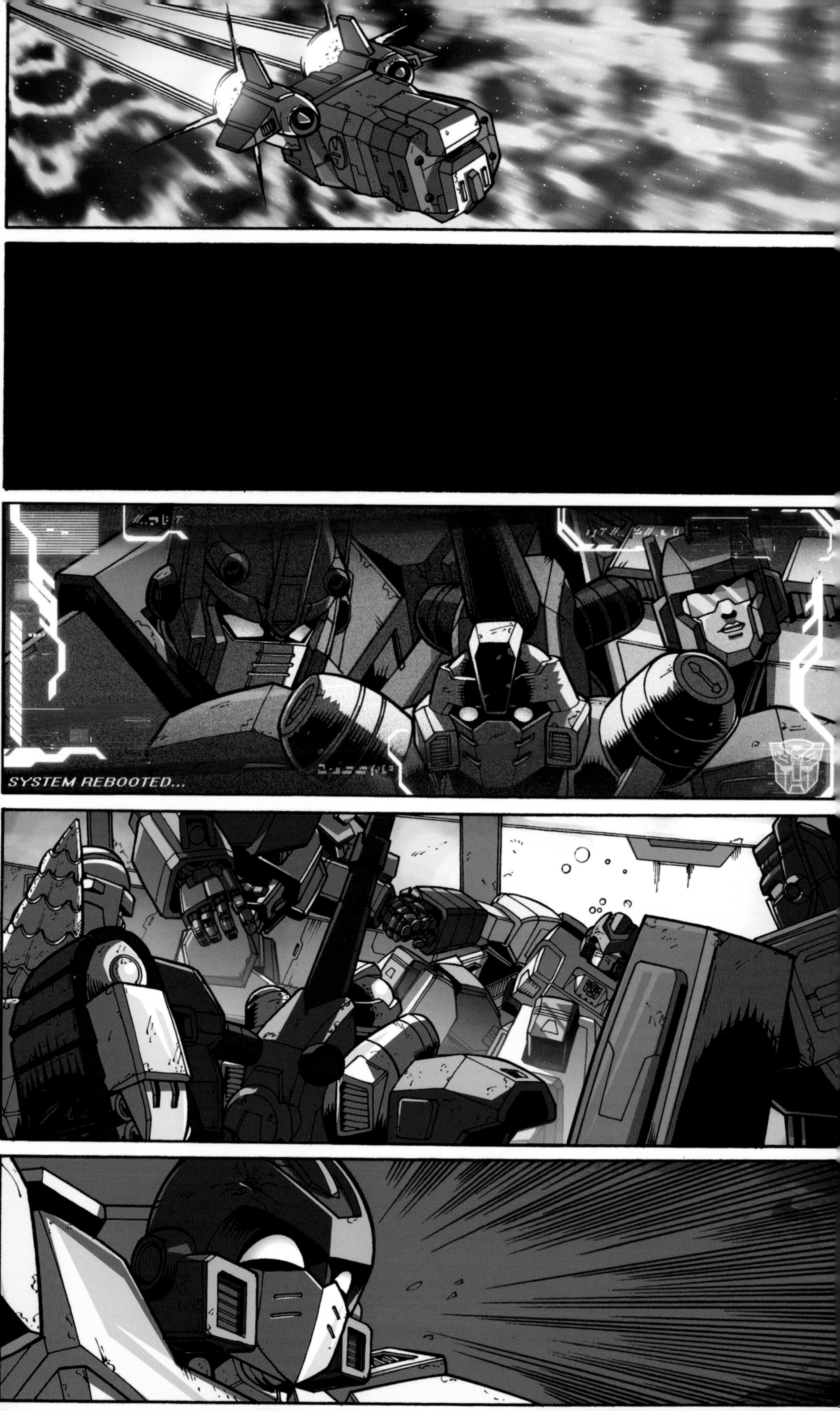
SYSTEM REBOOTED...

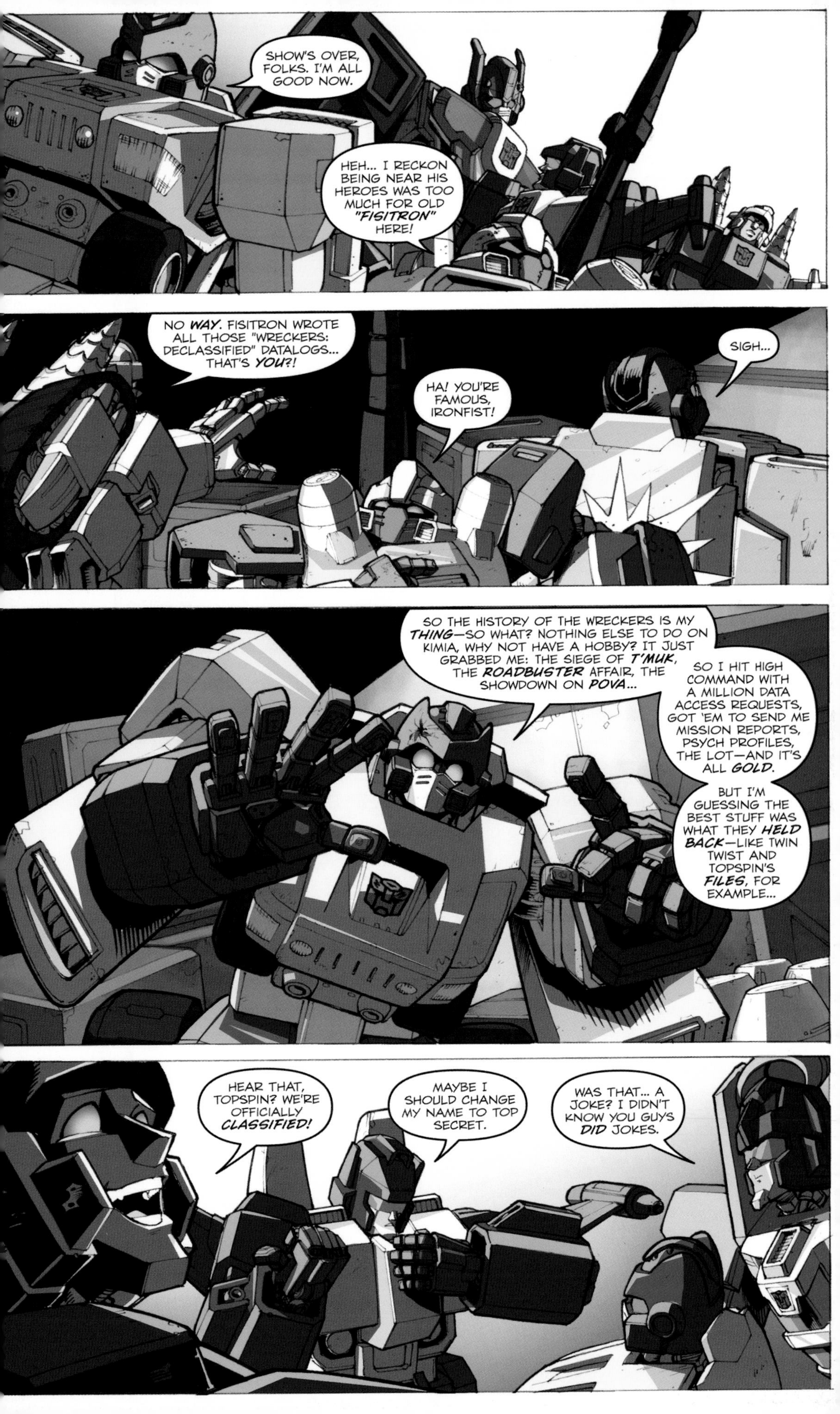
SHOW'S OVER, FOLKS. I'M ALL GOOD NOW.
HEH... I RECKON BEING NEAR HIS HEROES WAS TOO MUCH FOR OLD "FISITRON" HERE!
NO WAY. FISITRON WROTE ALL THOSE "WRECKERS: DECLASSIFIED" DATALOGS... THAT'S YOU?!
HA! YOU'RE FAMOUS, IRONFIST!
SIGH...
SO THE HISTORY OF THE WRECKERS IS MY THING—SO WHAT? NOTHING ELSE TO DO ON KIMIA, WHY NOT HAVE A HOBBY? IT JUST GRABBED ME: THE SIEGE OF T'MUK, THE ROADBUSTER AFFAIR, THE SHOWDOWN ON POVA...
SO I HIT HIGH COMMAND WITH A MILLION DATA ACCESS REQUESTS, GOT 'EM TO SEND ME MISSION REPORTS, PSYCH PROFILES, THE LOT—AND IT'S ALL GOLD.
BUT I'M GUESSING THE BEST STUFF WAS WHAT THEY HELD BACK—LIKE TWIN TWIST AND TOPSPIN'S FILES, FOR EXAMPLE...
HEAR THAT, TOPSPIN? WE'RE OFFICIALLY CLASSIFIED!
MAYBE I SHOULD CHANGE MY NAME TO TOP SECRET.
WAS THAT... A JOKE? I DIDN'T KNOW YOU GUYS DID JOKES.

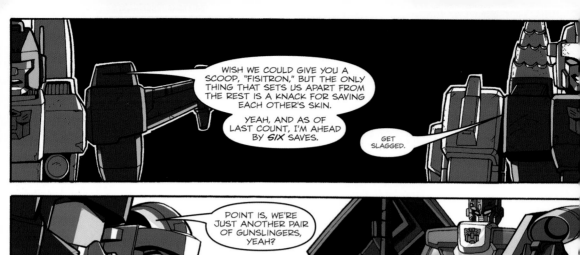

WISH WE COULD GIVE YOU A SCOOP, "FISITRON," BUT THE ONLY THING THAT SETS US APART FROM THE REST IS A KNACK FOR SAVING EACH OTHER'S SKIN.

YEAH, AND AS OF LAST COUNT, I'M AHEAD BY SIX SAVES.

GET SLAGGED.

POINT IS, WE'RE JUST ANOTHER PAIR OF GUNSLINGERS, YEAH?

SO NO MORE DATA ACCESS REQUESTS, NO MORE PRYING. UNDERSTOOD?

YEAH, ENOUGH ABOUT YOU TWO!

PYRO, ANY REASON WHY YOU'VE STOLEN OPTIMUS PRIME'S LOOK?

IRONFIST! EVERYTHING... OKAY?

OF COURSE.

WHY WOULDN'T IT BE?

NEED TO KEEP AN EYE OUT FOR HIM...

NEED TO KEEP ONE OUT FER YERSELF, KID.

SOMETHIN'S ON YER MIND...

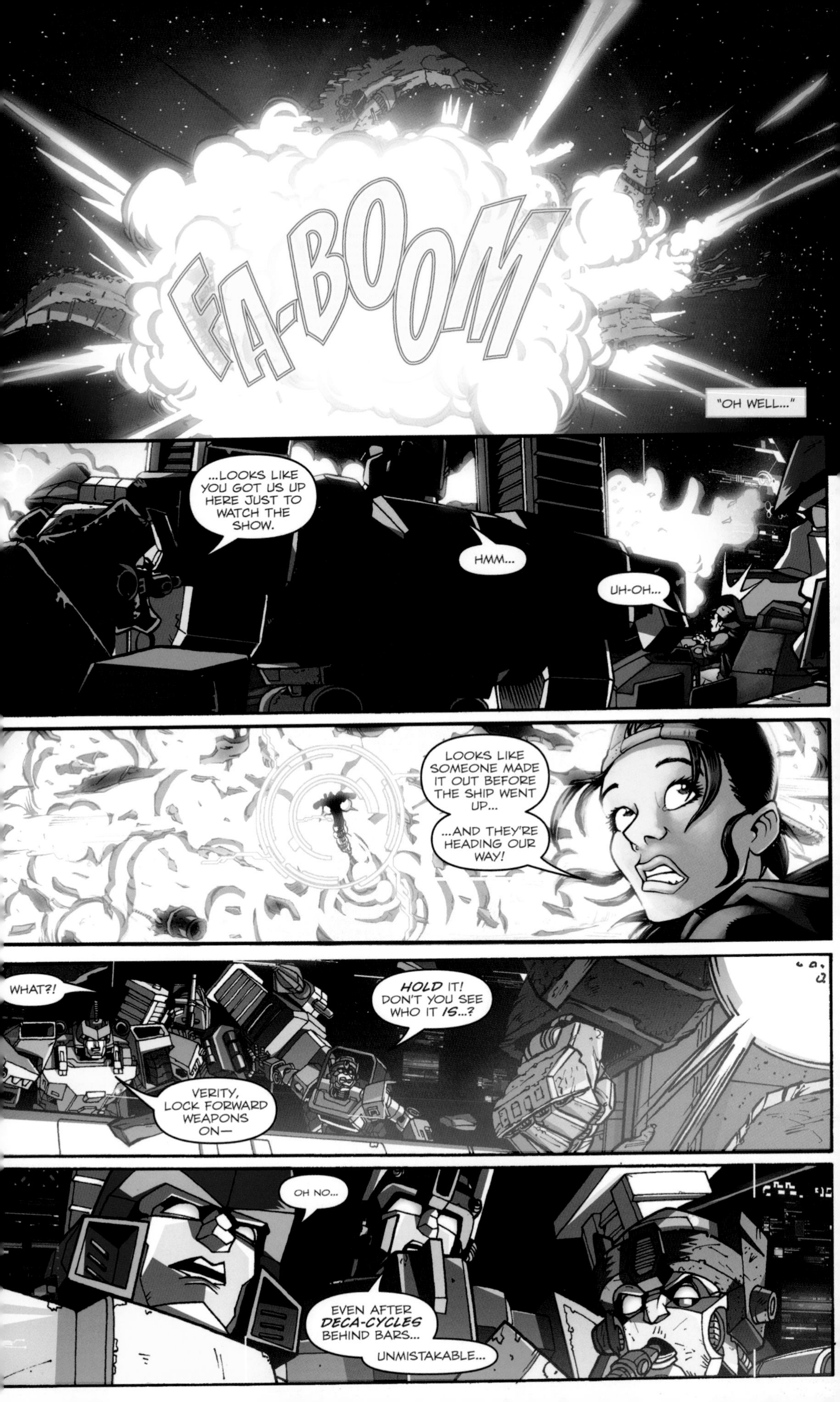
FA-BOOM
"OH WELL..."
...LOOKS LIKE YOU GOT US UP HERE JUST TO WATCH THE SHOW.
HMM...
UH-OH...
LOOKS LIKE SOMEONE MADE IT OUT BEFORE THE SHIP WENT UP...
...AND THEY'RE HEADING OUR WAY!
WHAT?!
HOLD IT! DON'T YOU SEE WHO IT IS...?
VERITY, LOCK FORWARD WEAPONS ON—
OH NO...
EVEN AFTER DECA-CYCLES BEHIND BARS...
UNMISTAKABLE...

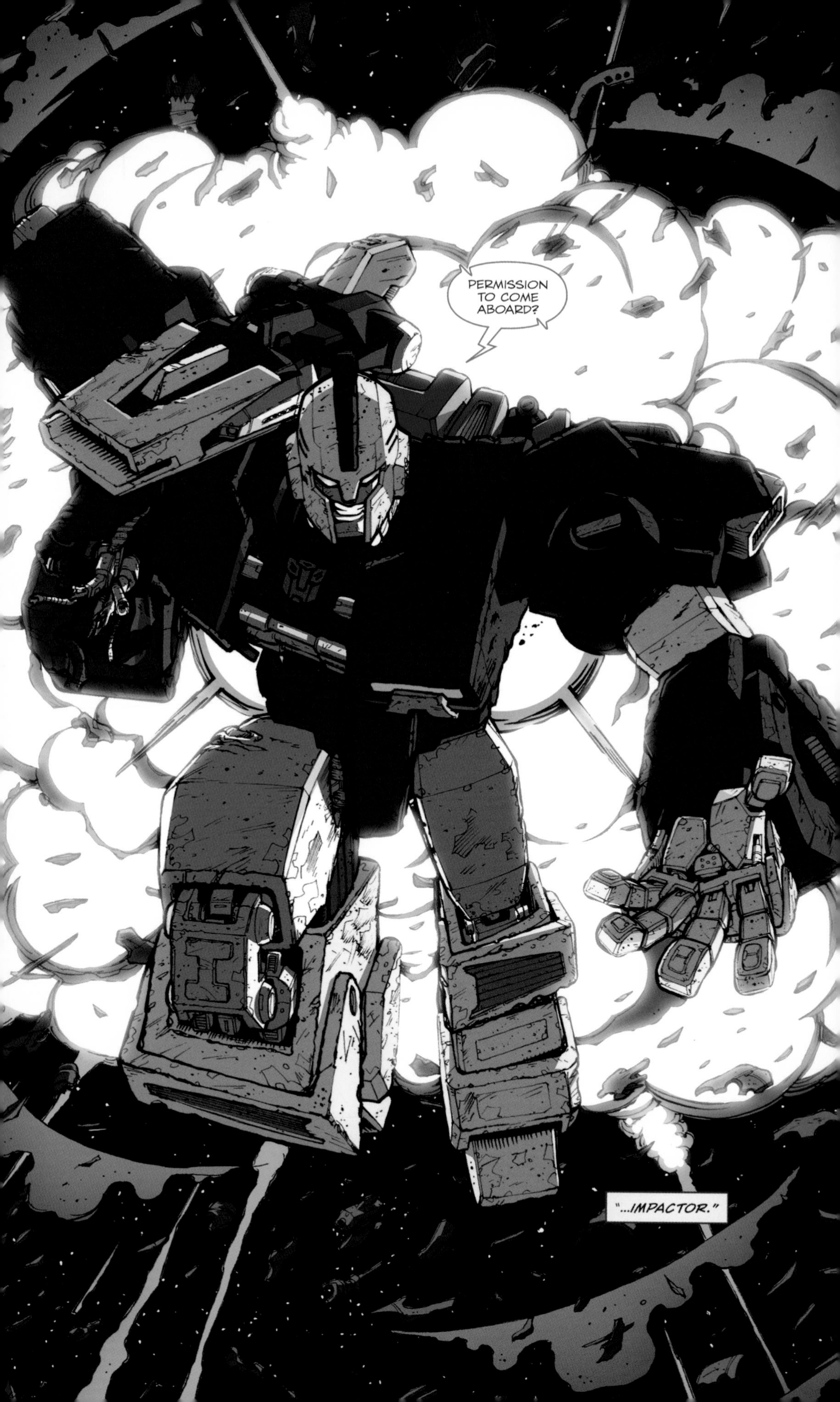
PERMISSION TO COME ABOARD?
"...IMPACTOR."

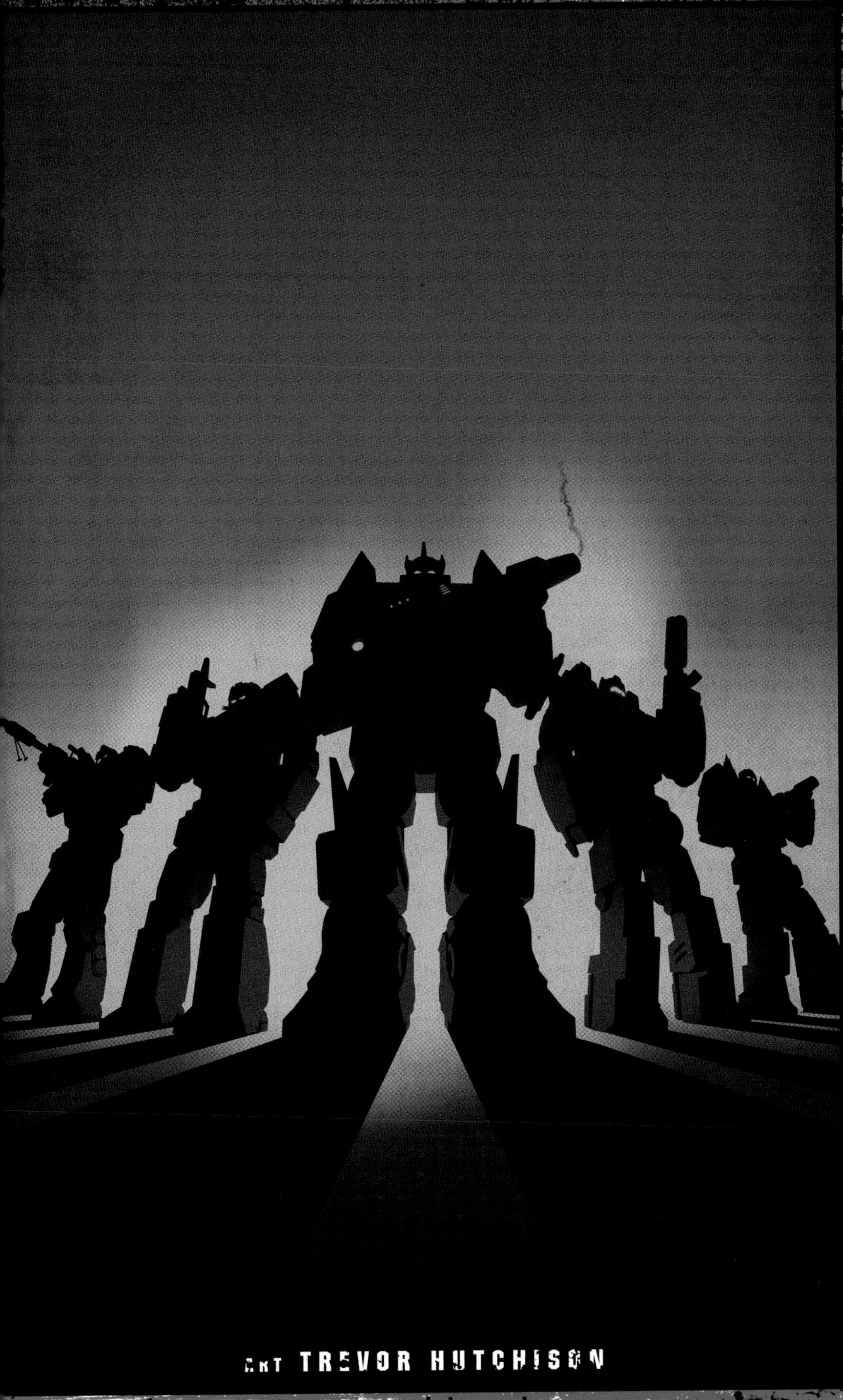

ART TREVOR HUTCHISON

ART NICK ROCHE COLORS JOSH BURCHAM

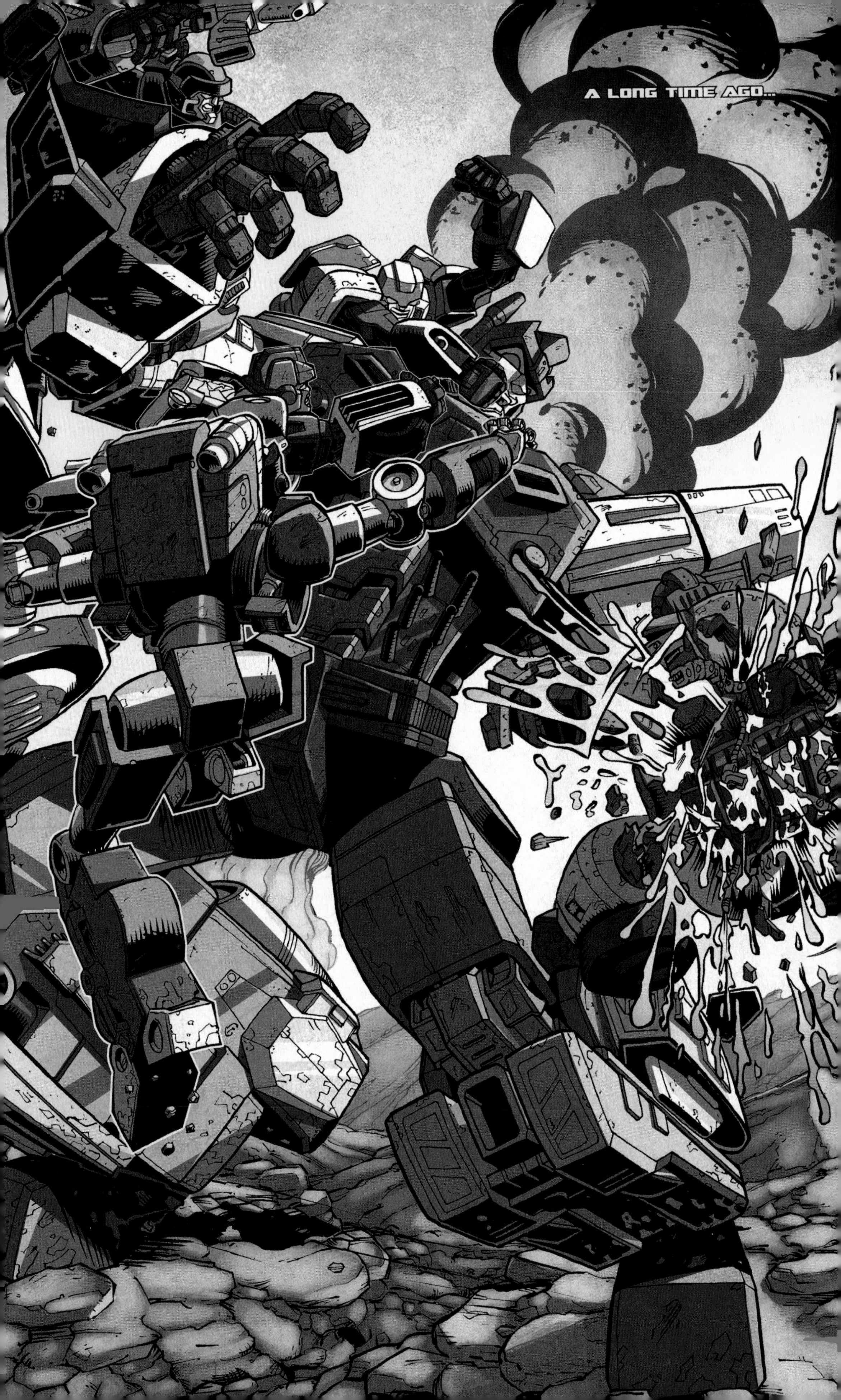
A LONG TIME AGO...

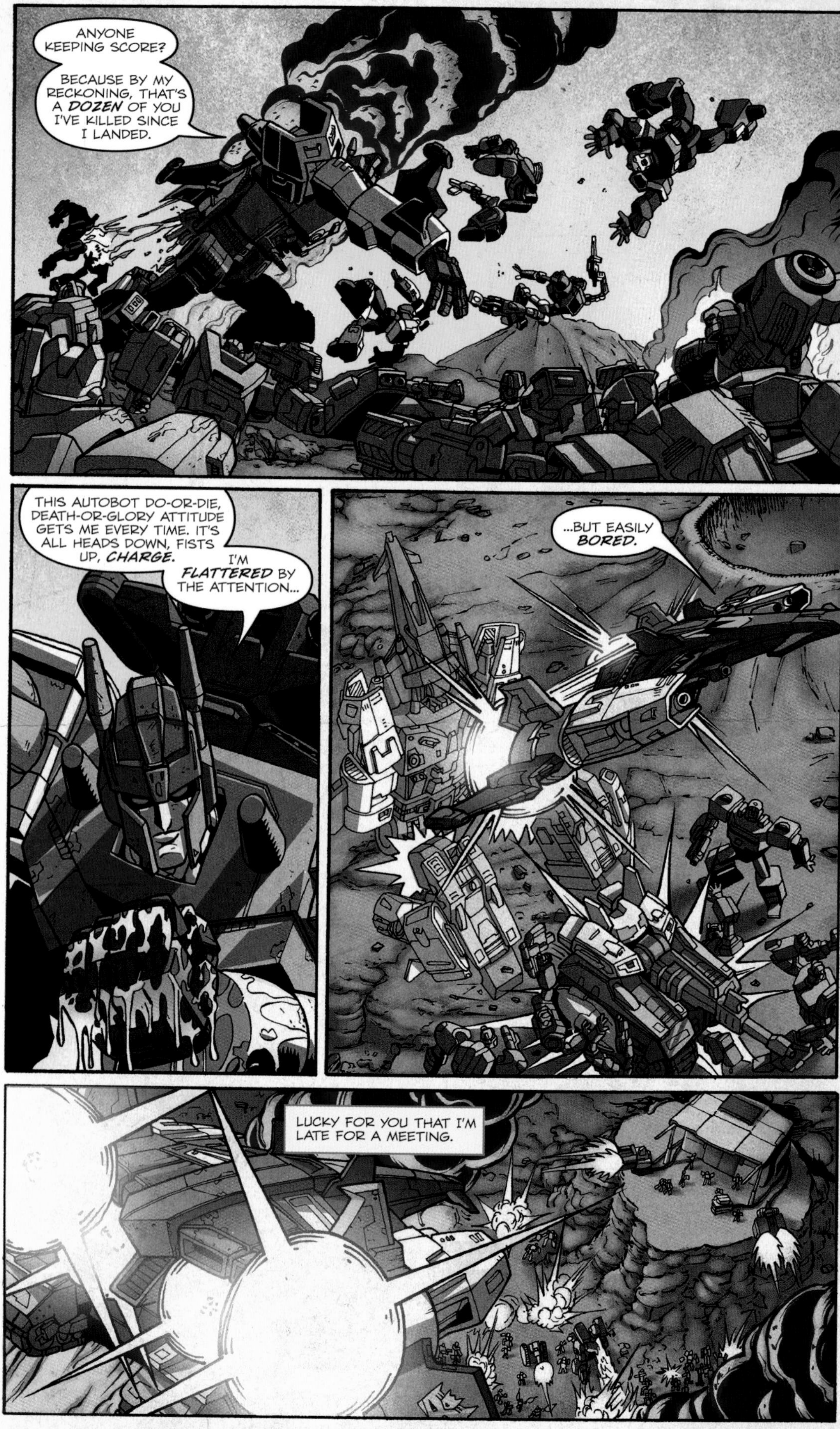
ANYONE KEEPING SCORE?
BECAUSE BY MY RECKONING, THAT'S A DOZEN OF YOU I'VE KILLED SINCE I LANDED.
THIS AUTOBOT DO-OR-DIE, DEATH-OR-GLORY ATTITUDE GETS ME EVERY TIME. IT'S ALL HEADS DOWN, FISTS UP, CHARGE.
I'M FLATTERED BY THE ATTENTION...
...BUT EASILY BORED.
LUCKY FOR YOU THAT I'M LATE FOR A MEETING.

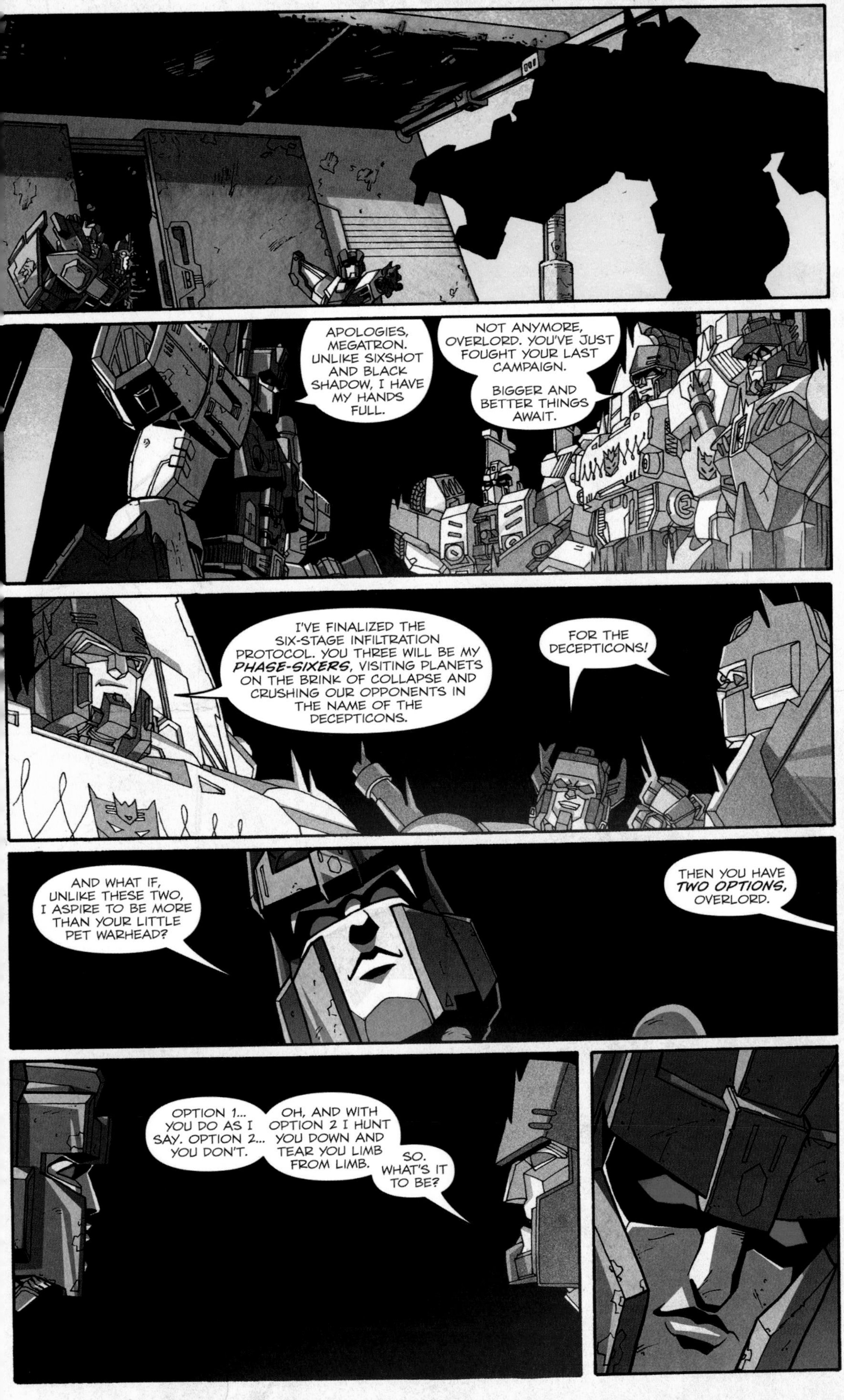

APOLOGIES, MEGATRON. UNLIKE SIXSHOT AND BLACK SHADOW, I HAVE MY HANDS FULL.
NOT ANYMORE, OVERLORD. YOU'VE JUST FOUGHT YOUR LAST CAMPAIGN.
BIGGER AND BETTER THINGS AWAIT.
I'VE FINALIZED THE SIX-STAGE INFILTRATION PROTOCOL. YOU THREE WILL BE MY PHASE-SIXERS, VISITING PLANETS ON THE BRINK OF COLLAPSE AND CRUSHING OUR OPPONENTS IN THE NAME OF THE DECEPTICONS.
FOR THE DECEPTICONS!
AND WHAT IF, UNLIKE THESE TWO, I ASPIRE TO BE MORE THAN YOUR LITTLE PET WARHEAD?
THEN YOU HAVE TWO OPTIONS, OVERLORD.
OPTION 1... YOU DO AS I SAY. OPTION 2... YOU DON'T.
OH, AND WITH OPTION 2 I HUNT YOU DOWN AND TEAR YOU LIMB FROM LIMB.
SO. WHAT'S IT TO BE?

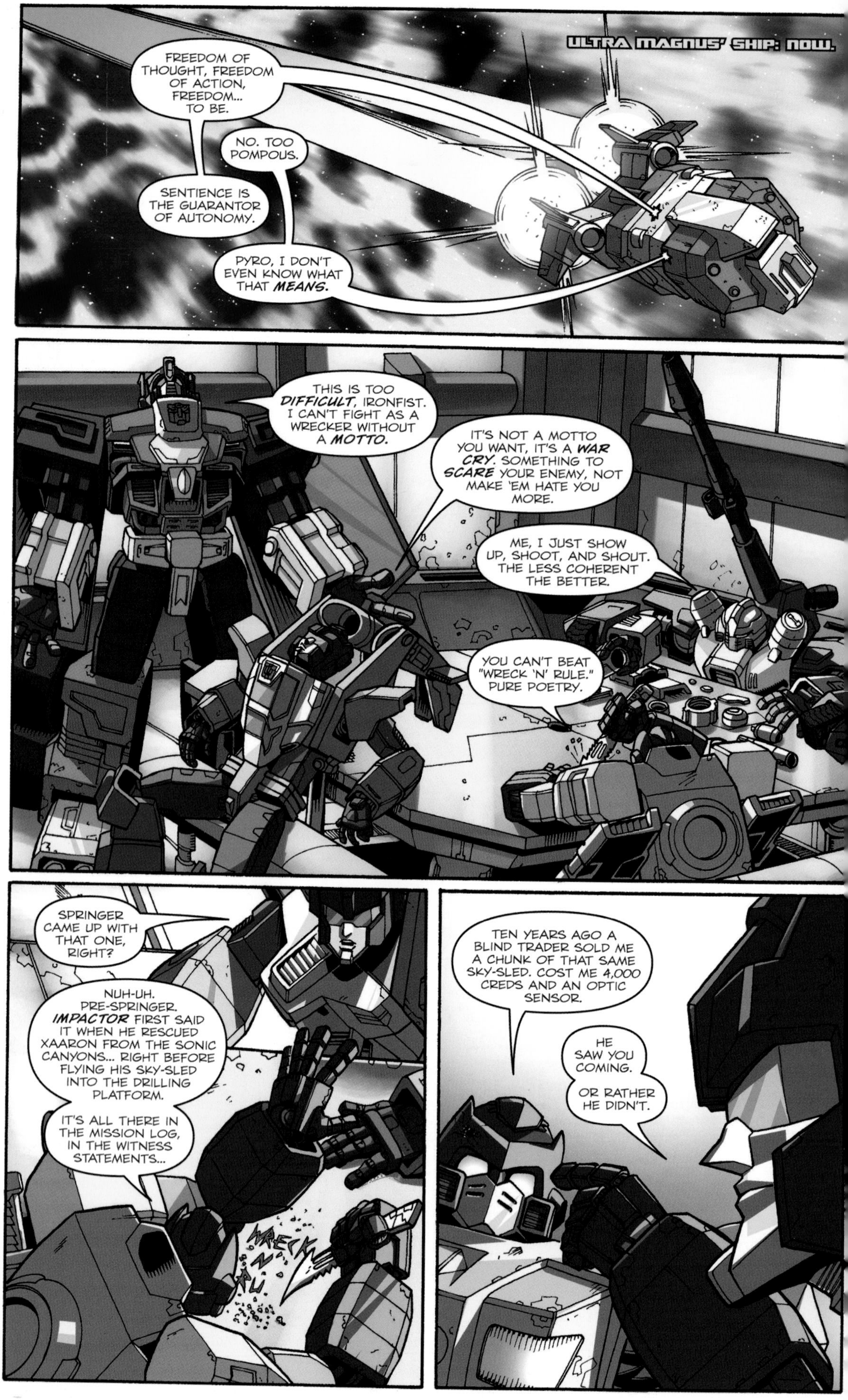

ULTRA MAGNUS' SHIP: NOW.
FREEDOM OF THOUGHT, FREEDOM OF ACTION, FREEDOM... TO BE.
NO. TOO POMPOUS.
SENTIENCE IS THE GUARANTOR OF AUTONOMY.
PYRO, I DON'T EVEN KNOW WHAT THAT MEANS.
THIS IS TOO DIFFICULT, IRONFIST. I CAN'T FIGHT AS A WRECKER WITHOUT A MOTTO.
IT'S NOT A MOTTO YOU WANT, IT'S A WAR CRY. SOMETHING TO SCARE YOUR ENEMY, NOT MAKE 'EM HATE YOU MORE.
ME, I JUST SHOW UP, SHOOT, AND SHOUT. THE LESS COHERENT THE BETTER.
YOU CAN'T BEAT "WRECK 'N' RULE." PURE POETRY.
SPRINGER CAME UP WITH THAT ONE, RIGHT?
NUH-UH. PRE-SPRINGER. IMPACTOR FIRST SAID IT WHEN HE RESCUED XAARON FROM THE SONIC CANYONS... RIGHT BEFORE FLYING HIS SKY-SLED INTO THE DRILLING PLATFORM.
IT'S ALL THERE IN THE MISSION LOG, IN THE WITNESS STATEMENTS...
WRECK N RU
TEN YEARS AGO A BLIND TRADER SOLD ME A CHUNK OF THAT SAME SKY-SLED. COST ME 4,000 CREDS AND AN OPTIC SENSOR.
HE SAW YOU COMING.
OR RATHER HE DIDN'T.

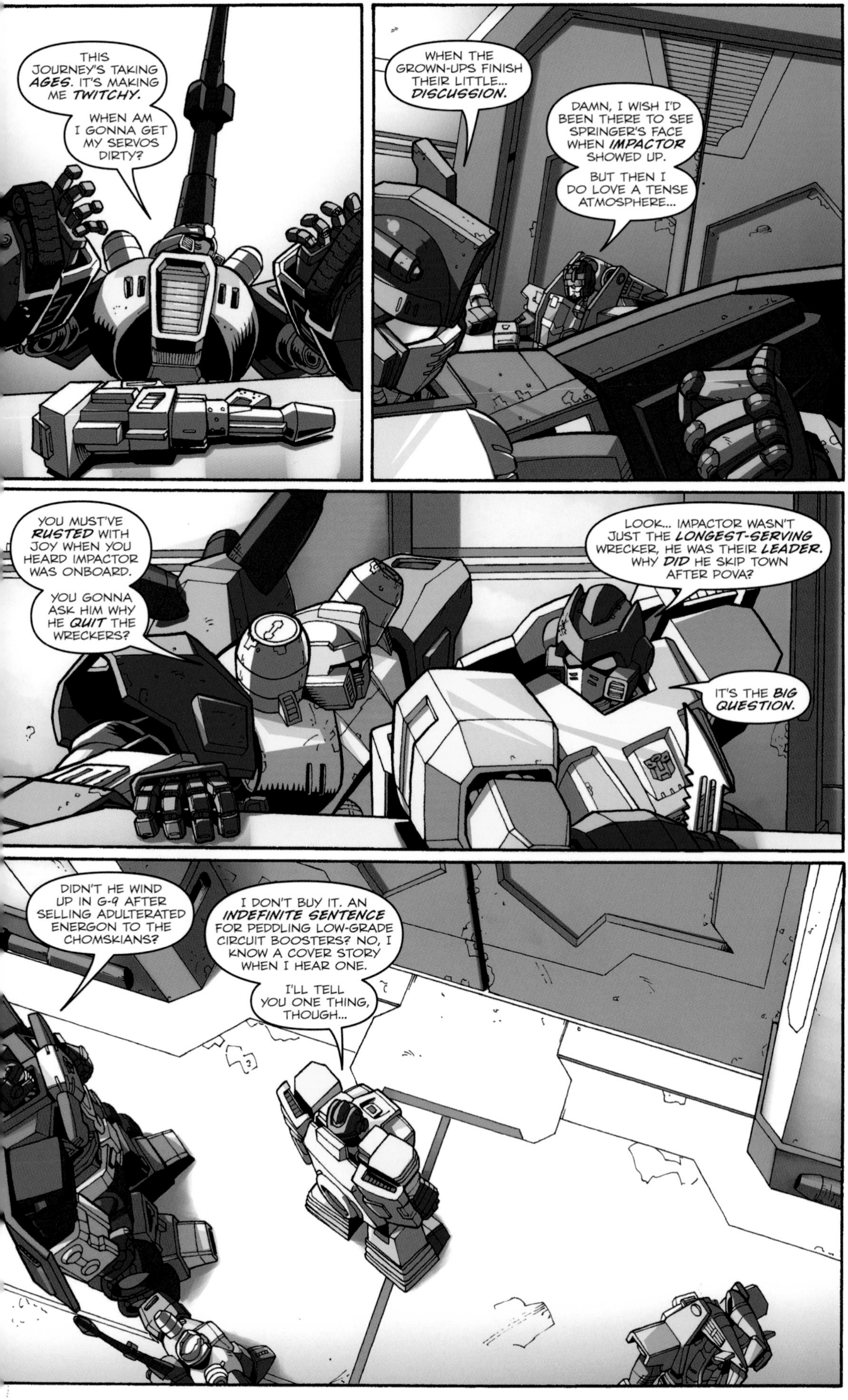

THIS JOURNEY'S TAKING *AGES*. IT'S MAKING ME *TWITCHY*.
WHEN AM I GONNA GET MY SERVOS DIRTY?
WHEN THE GROWN-UPS FINISH THEIR LITTLE... *DISCUSSION*.
DAMN, I WISH I'D BEEN THERE TO SEE SPRINGER'S FACE WHEN *IMPACTOR* SHOWED UP.
BUT THEN I DO LOVE A TENSE ATMOSPHERE...
YOU MUST'VE *RUSTED* WITH JOY WHEN YOU HEARD IMPACTOR WAS ONBOARD.
YOU GONNA ASK HIM WHY HE *QUIT* THE WRECKERS?
LOOK... IMPACTOR WASN'T JUST THE *LONGEST-SERVING* WRECKER, HE WAS THEIR *LEADER*. WHY *DID* HE SKIP TOWN AFTER POVA?
IT'S THE *BIG QUESTION*.
DIDN'T HE WIND UP IN G-9 AFTER SELLING ADULTERATED ENERGON TO THE CHOMSKIANS?
I DON'T BUY IT. AN *INDEFINITE SENTENCE* FOR PEDDLING LOW-GRADE CIRCUIT BOOSTERS? NO, I KNOW A COVER STORY WHEN I HEAR ONE.
I'LL TELL YOU ONE THING, THOUGH...

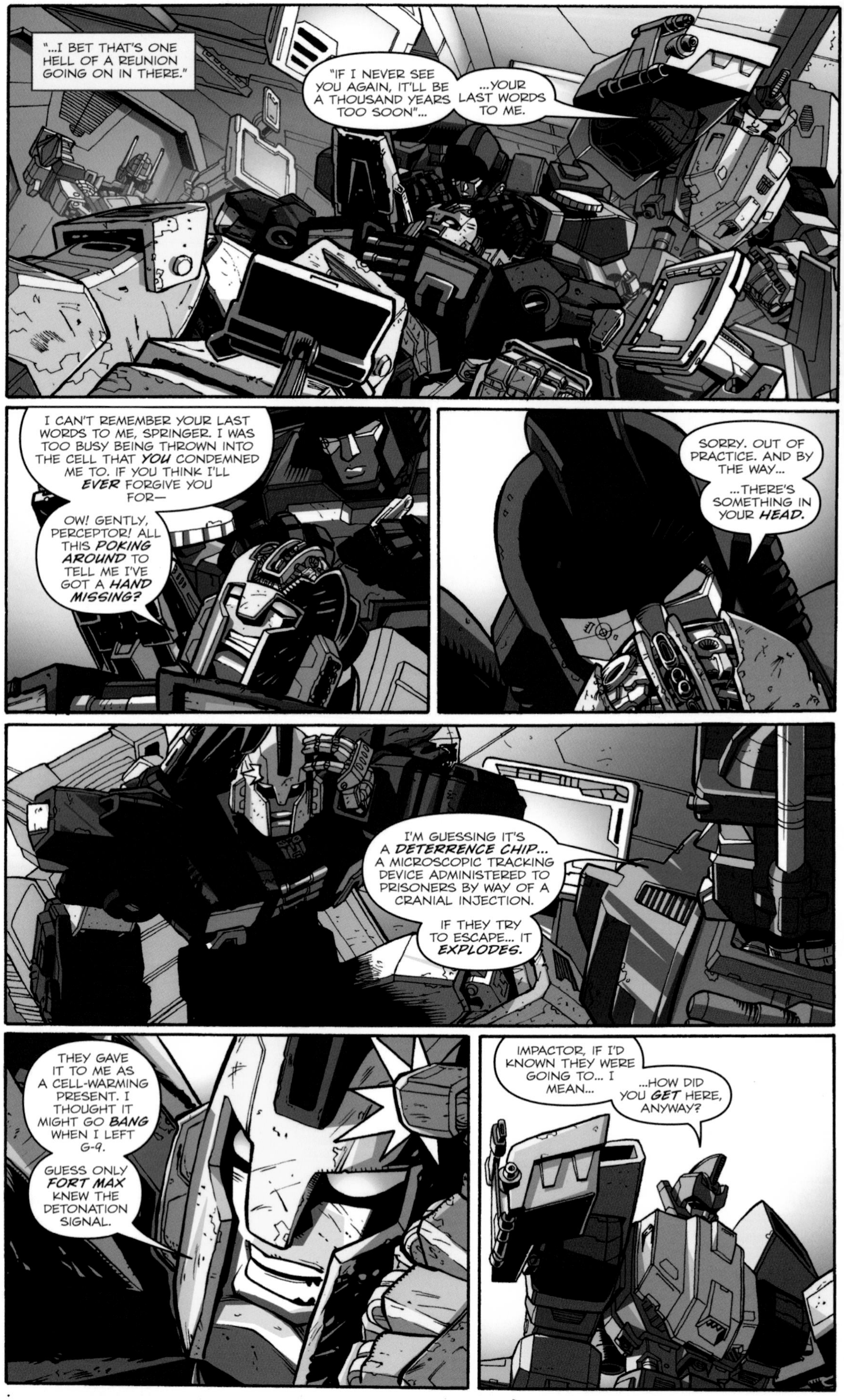
"...I BET THAT'S ONE HELL OF A REUNION GOING ON IN THERE."
"IF I NEVER SEE YOU AGAIN, IT'LL BE A THOUSAND YEARS TOO SOON"...
...YOUR LAST WORDS TO ME.
I CAN'T REMEMBER YOUR LAST WORDS TO ME, SPRINGER. I WAS TOO BUSY BEING THROWN INTO THE CELL THAT YOU CONDEMNED ME TO. IF YOU THINK I'LL EVER FORGIVE YOU FOR—
OW! GENTLY, PERCEPTOR! ALL THIS POKING AROUND TO TELL ME I'VE GOT A HAND MISSING?
SORRY. OUT OF PRACTICE. AND BY THE WAY...
...THERE'S SOMETHING IN YOUR HEAD.
I'M GUESSING IT'S A DETERRENCE CHIP... A MICROSCOPIC TRACKING DEVICE ADMINISTERED TO PRISONERS BY WAY OF A CRANIAL INJECTION.
IF THEY TRY TO ESCAPE... IT EXPLODES.
THEY GAVE IT TO ME AS A CELL-WARMING PRESENT. I THOUGHT IT MIGHT GO BANG WHEN I LEFT G-9.
GUESS ONLY FORT MAX KNEW THE DETONATION SIGNAL.
IMPACTOR, IF I'D KNOWN THEY WERE GOING TO... I MEAN...
...HOW DID YOU GET HERE, ANYWAY?

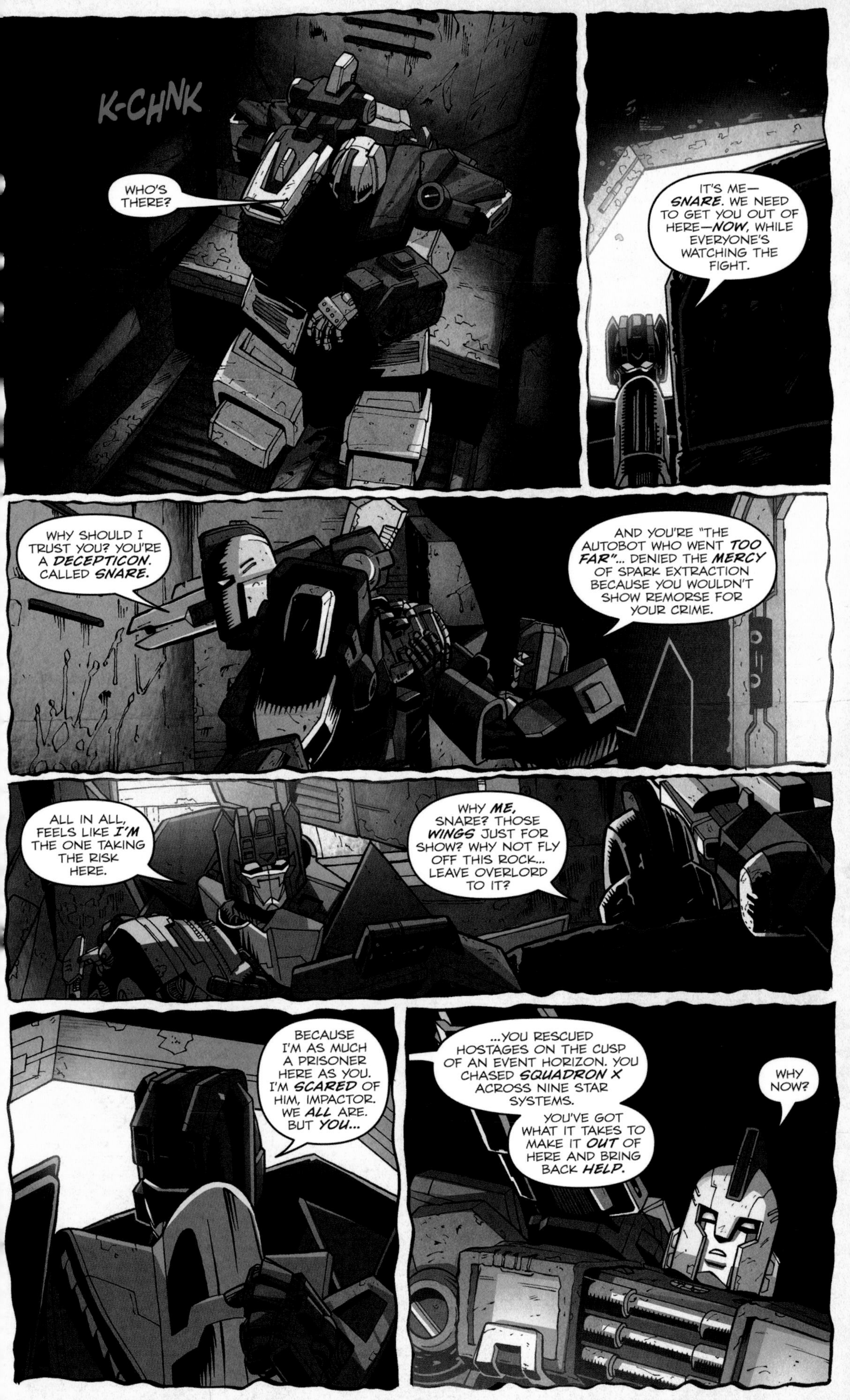
K-CHNK
WHO'S THERE?
IT'S ME— SNARE. WE NEED TO GET YOU OUT OF HERE—NOW, WHILE EVERYONE'S WATCHING THE FIGHT.
WHY SHOULD I TRUST YOU? YOU'RE A DECEPTICON. CALLED SNARE.
AND YOU'RE "THE AUTOBOT WHO WENT TOO FAR"... DENIED THE MERCY OF SPARK EXTRACTION BECAUSE YOU WOULDN'T SHOW REMORSE FOR YOUR CRIME.
ALL IN ALL, FEELS LIKE I'M THE ONE TAKING THE RISK HERE.
WHY ME, SNARE? THOSE WINGS JUST FOR SHOW? WHY NOT FLY OFF THIS ROCK... LEAVE OVERLORD TO IT?
BECAUSE I'M AS MUCH A PRISONER HERE AS YOU. I'M SCARED OF HIM, IMPACTOR. WE ALL ARE. BUT YOU...
...YOU RESCUED HOSTAGES ON THE CUSP OF AN EVENT HORIZON. YOU CHASED SQUADRON X ACROSS NINE STAR SYSTEMS.
YOU'VE GOT WHAT IT TAKES TO MAKE IT OUT OF HERE AND BRING BACK HELP.
WHY NOW?

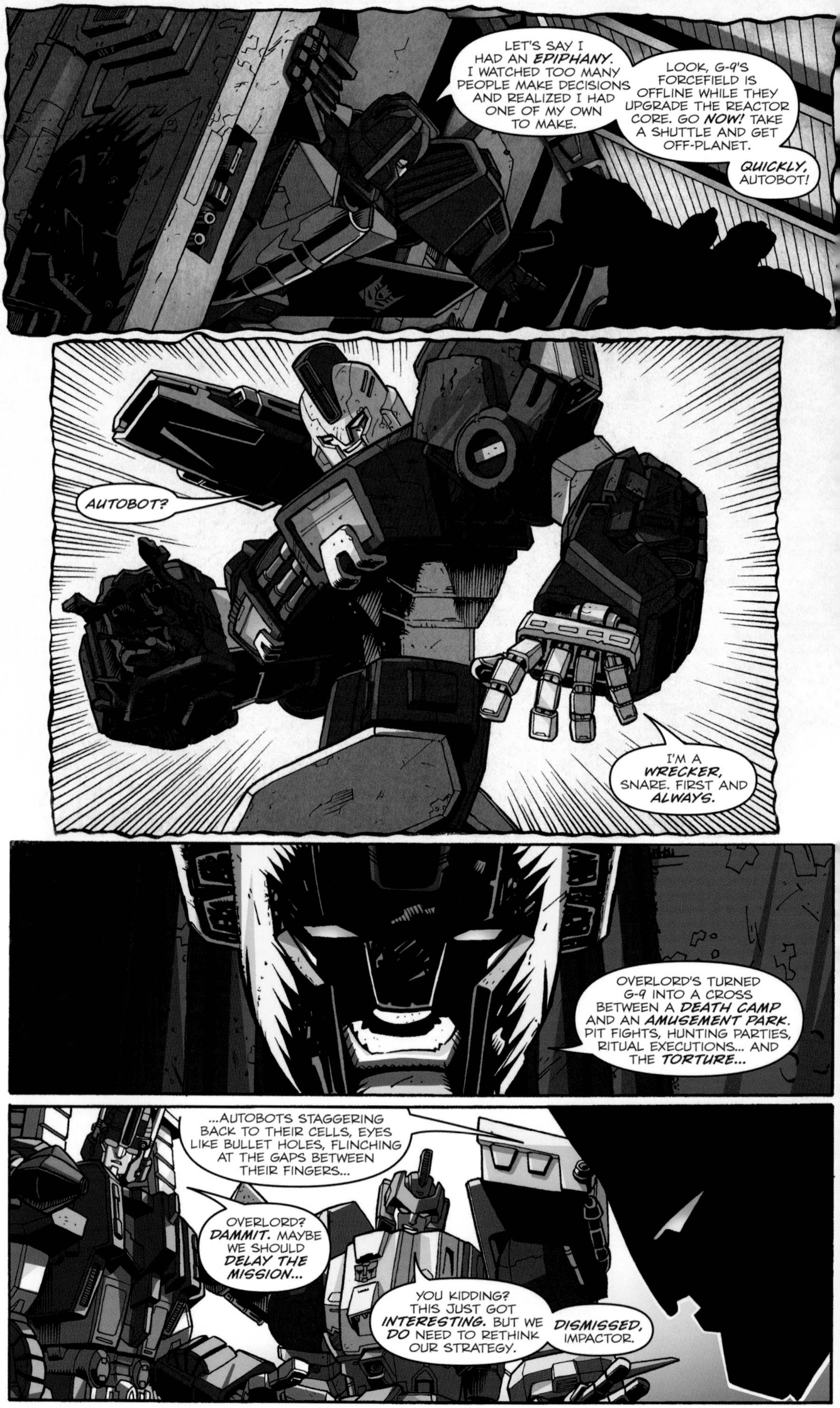
LET'S SAY I HAD AN EPIPHANY. I WATCHED TOO MANY PEOPLE MAKE DECISIONS AND REALIZED I HAD ONE OF MY OWN TO MAKE.
LOOK, G-9'S FORCEFIELD IS OFFLINE WHILE THEY UPGRADE THE REACTOR CORE. GO NOW! TAKE A SHUTTLE AND GET OFF-PLANET.
QUICKLY, AUTOBOT!
AUTOBOT?
I'M A WRECKER, SNARE. FIRST AND ALWAYS.
OVERLORD'S TURNED G-9 INTO A CROSS BETWEEN A DEATH CAMP AND AN AMUSEMENT PARK. PIT FIGHTS, HUNTING PARTIES, RITUAL EXECUTIONS... AND THE TORTURE...
...AUTOBOTS STAGGERING BACK TO THEIR CELLS, EYES LIKE BULLET HOLES, FLINCHING AT THE GAPS BETWEEN THEIR FINGERS...
OVERLORD? DAMMIT. MAYBE WE SHOULD DELAY THE MISSION...
YOU KIDDING? THIS JUST GOT INTERESTING. BUT WE DO NEED TO RETHINK OUR STRATEGY.
DISMISSED, IMPACTOR.

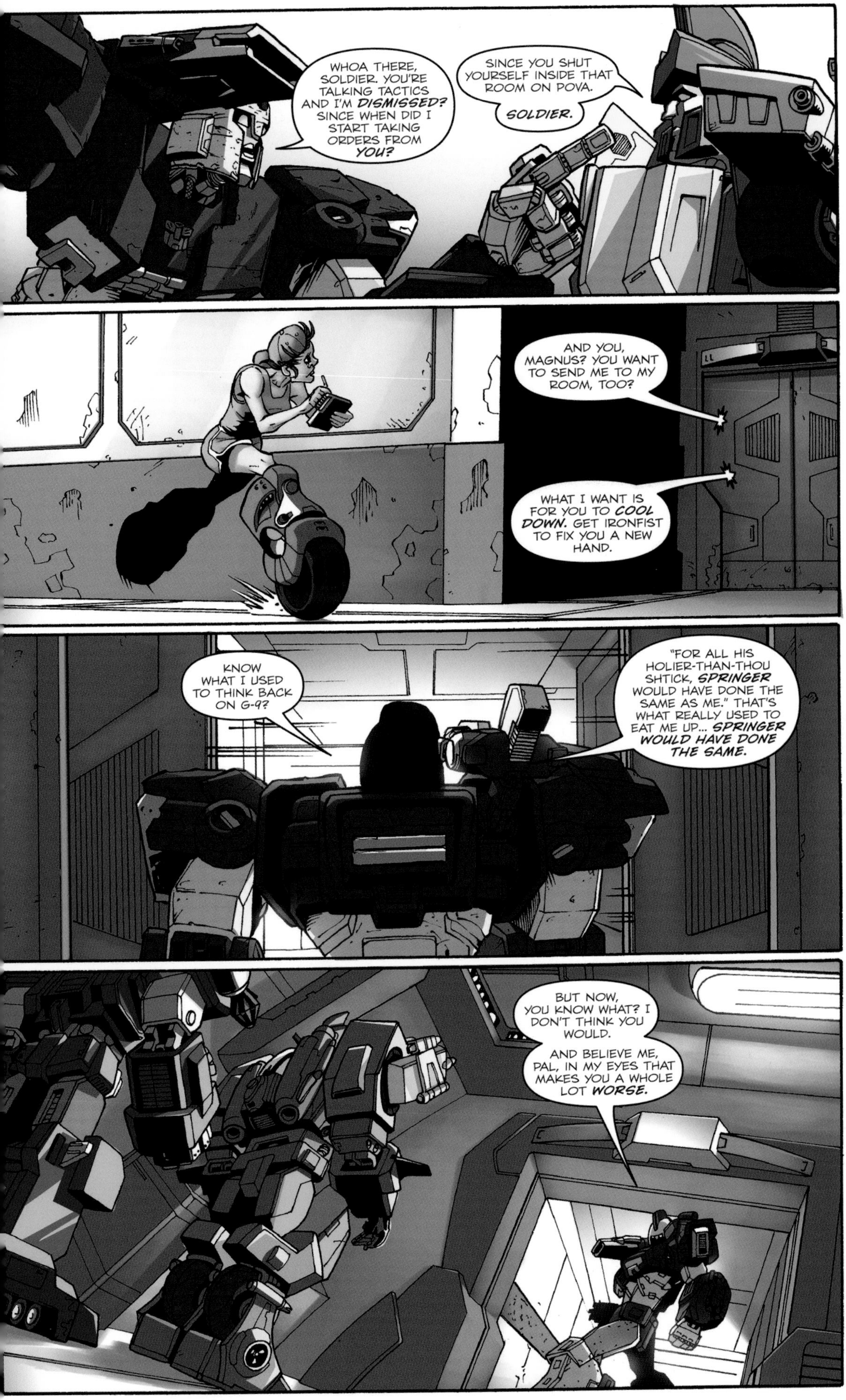
WHOA THERE, SOLDIER. YOU'RE TALKING TACTICS AND I'M DISMISSED? SINCE WHEN DID I START TAKING ORDERS FROM YOU?
SINCE YOU SHUT YOURSELF INSIDE THAT ROOM ON POVA.
SOLDIER.
AND YOU, MAGNUS? YOU WANT TO SEND ME TO MY ROOM, TOO?
WHAT I WANT IS FOR YOU TO COOL DOWN. GET IRONFIST TO FIX YOU A NEW HAND.
KNOW WHAT I USED TO THINK BACK ON G-9?
"FOR ALL HIS HOLIER-THAN-THOU SHTICK, SPRINGER WOULD HAVE DONE THE SAME AS ME." THAT'S WHAT REALLY USED TO EAT ME UP... SPRINGER WOULD HAVE DONE THE SAME.
BUT NOW, YOU KNOW WHAT? I DON'T THINK YOU WOULD.
AND BELIEVE ME, PAL, IN MY EYES THAT MAKES YOU A WHOLE LOT WORSE.

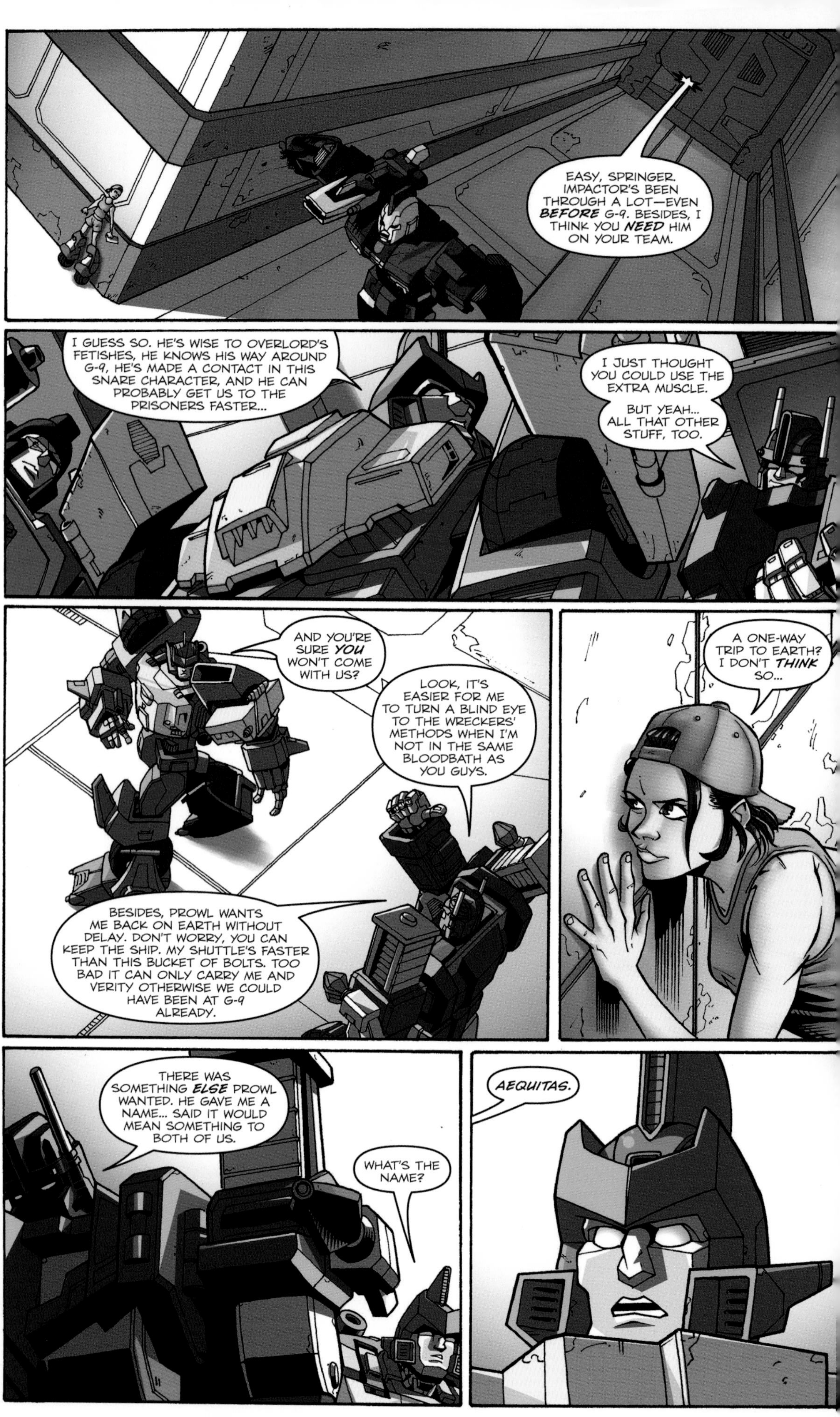
EASY, SPRINGER. IMPACTOR'S BEEN THROUGH A LOT—EVEN BEFORE G-9. BESIDES, I THINK YOU NEED HIM ON YOUR TEAM.
I GUESS SO. HE'S WISE TO OVERLORD'S FETISHES, HE KNOWS HIS WAY AROUND G-9, HE'S MADE A CONTACT IN THIS SNARE CHARACTER, AND HE CAN PROBABLY GET US TO THE PRISONERS FASTER...
I JUST THOUGHT YOU COULD USE THE EXTRA MUSCLE.
BUT YEAH... ALL THAT OTHER STUFF, TOO.
AND YOU'RE SURE YOU WON'T COME WITH US?
LOOK, IT'S EASIER FOR ME TO TURN A BLIND EYE TO THE WRECKERS' METHODS WHEN I'M NOT IN THE SAME BLOODBATH AS YOU GUYS.
BESIDES, PROWL WANTS ME BACK ON EARTH WITHOUT DELAY. DON'T WORRY, YOU CAN KEEP THE SHIP. MY SHUTTLE'S FASTER THAN THIS BUCKET OF BOLTS. TOO BAD IT CAN ONLY CARRY ME AND VERITY OTHERWISE WE COULD HAVE BEEN AT G-9 ALREADY.
A ONE-WAY TRIP TO EARTH? I DON'T THINK SO...
THERE WAS SOMETHING ELSE PROWL WANTED. HE GAVE ME A NAME... SAID IT WOULD MEAN SOMETHING TO BOTH OF US.
WHAT'S THE NAME?
AEQUITAS.

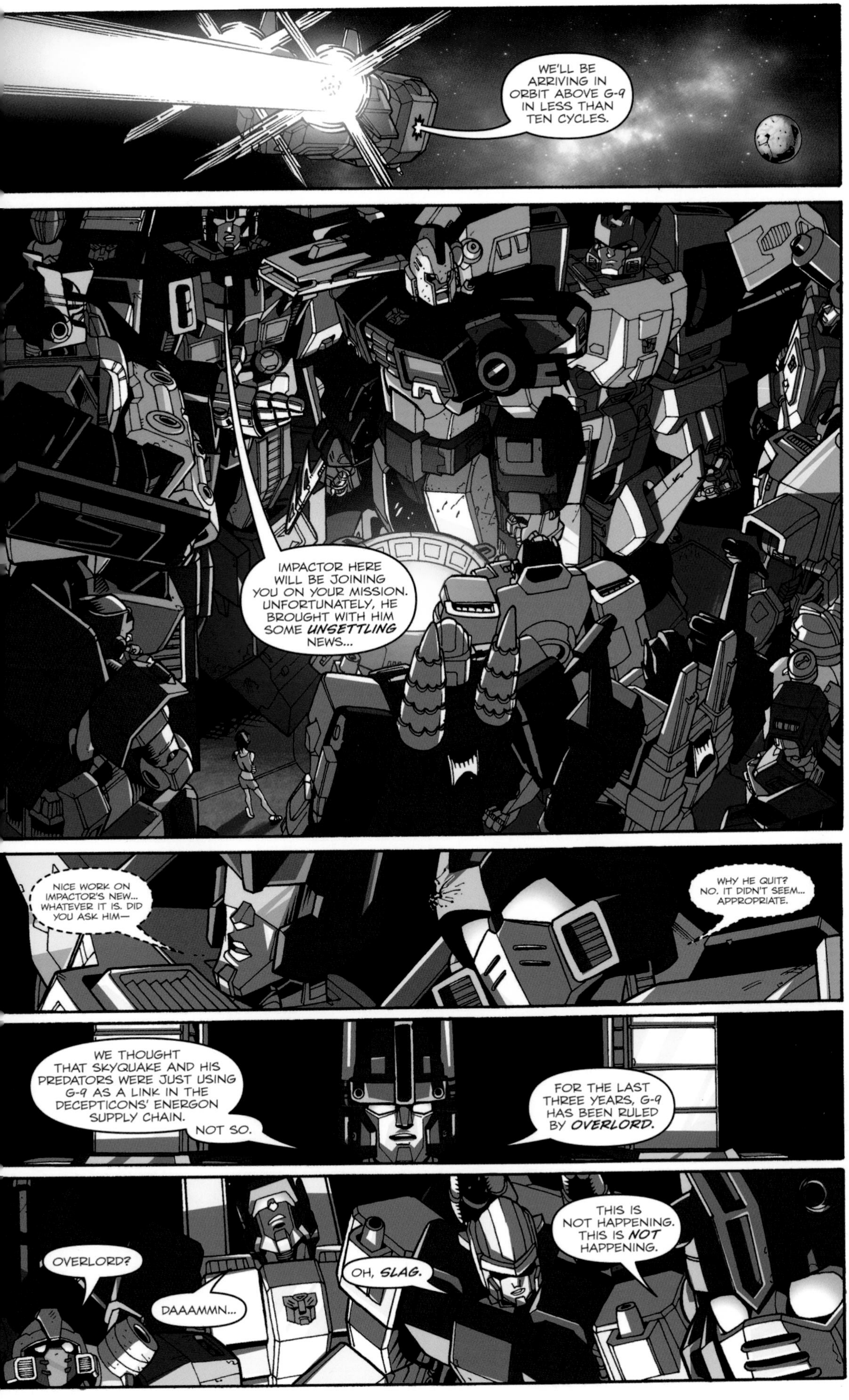
WE'LL BE ARRIVING IN ORBIT ABOVE G-9 IN LESS THAN TEN CYCLES.
IMPACTOR HERE WILL BE JOINING YOU ON YOUR MISSION. UNFORTUNATELY, HE BROUGHT WITH HIM SOME UNSETTLING NEWS...
NICE WORK ON IMPACTOR'S NEW... WHATEVER IT IS. DID YOU ASK HIM—
WHY HE QUIT? NO. IT DIDN'T SEEM... APPROPRIATE.
WE THOUGHT THAT SKYQUAKE AND HIS PREDATORS WERE JUST USING G-9 AS A LINK IN THE DECEPTICONS' ENERGON SUPPLY CHAIN.
NOT SO.
FOR THE LAST THREE YEARS, G-9 HAS BEEN RULED BY OVERLORD.
OVERLORD?
DAAAMMN...
OH, SLAG.
THIS IS NOT HAPPENING. THIS IS NOT HAPPENING.

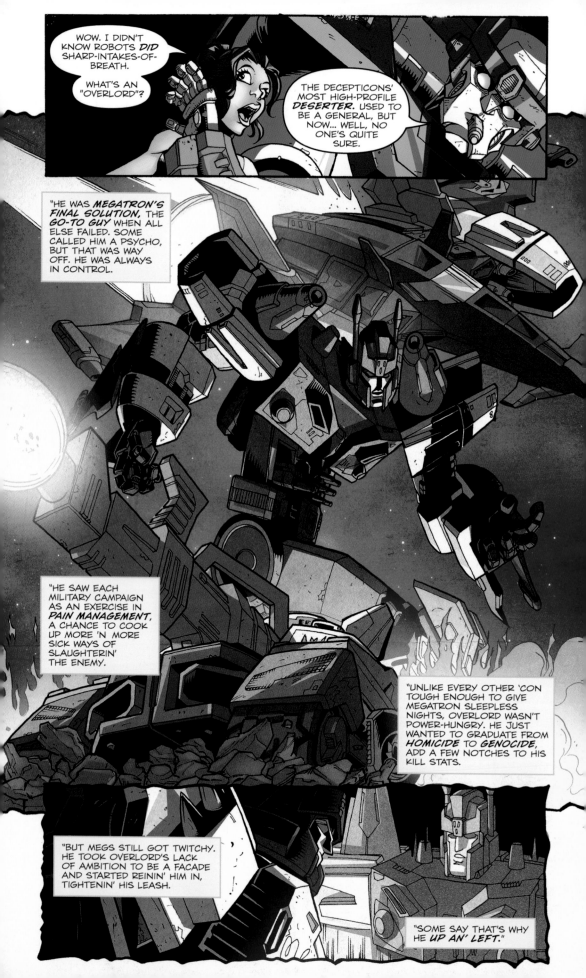

WOW. I DIDN'T KNOW ROBOTS *DID* SHARP-INTAKES-OF-BREATH.

WHAT'S AN "OVERLORD"?

THE DECEPTICONS' MOST HIGH-PROFILE *DESERTER*. USED TO BE A GENERAL, BUT NOW... WELL, NO ONE'S QUITE SURE.

"HE WAS *MEGATRON'S FINAL SOLUTION,* THE *GO-TO GUY* WHEN ALL ELSE FAILED. SOME CALLED HIM A PSYCHO, BUT THAT WAS WAY OFF. HE WAS ALWAYS IN CONTROL.

"HE SAW EACH MILITARY CAMPAIGN AS AN EXERCISE IN *PAIN MANAGEMENT,* A CHANCE TO COOK UP MORE 'N MORE SICK WAYS OF SLAUGHTERIN' THE ENEMY.

"UNLIKE EVERY OTHER 'CON TOUGH ENOUGH TO GIVE MEGATRON SLEEPLESS NIGHTS, OVERLORD WASN'T POWER-HUNGRY. HE JUST WANTED TO GRADUATE FROM *HOMICIDE* TO *GENOCIDE,* ADD A FEW NOTCHES TO HIS KILL STATS.

"BUT MEGS STILL GOT TWITCHY. HE TOOK OVERLORD'S LACK OF AMBITION TO BE A FACADE AND STARTED REININ' HIM IN, TIGHTENIN' HIS LEASH.

"SOME SAY THAT'S WHY HE *UP AN' LEFT.*"

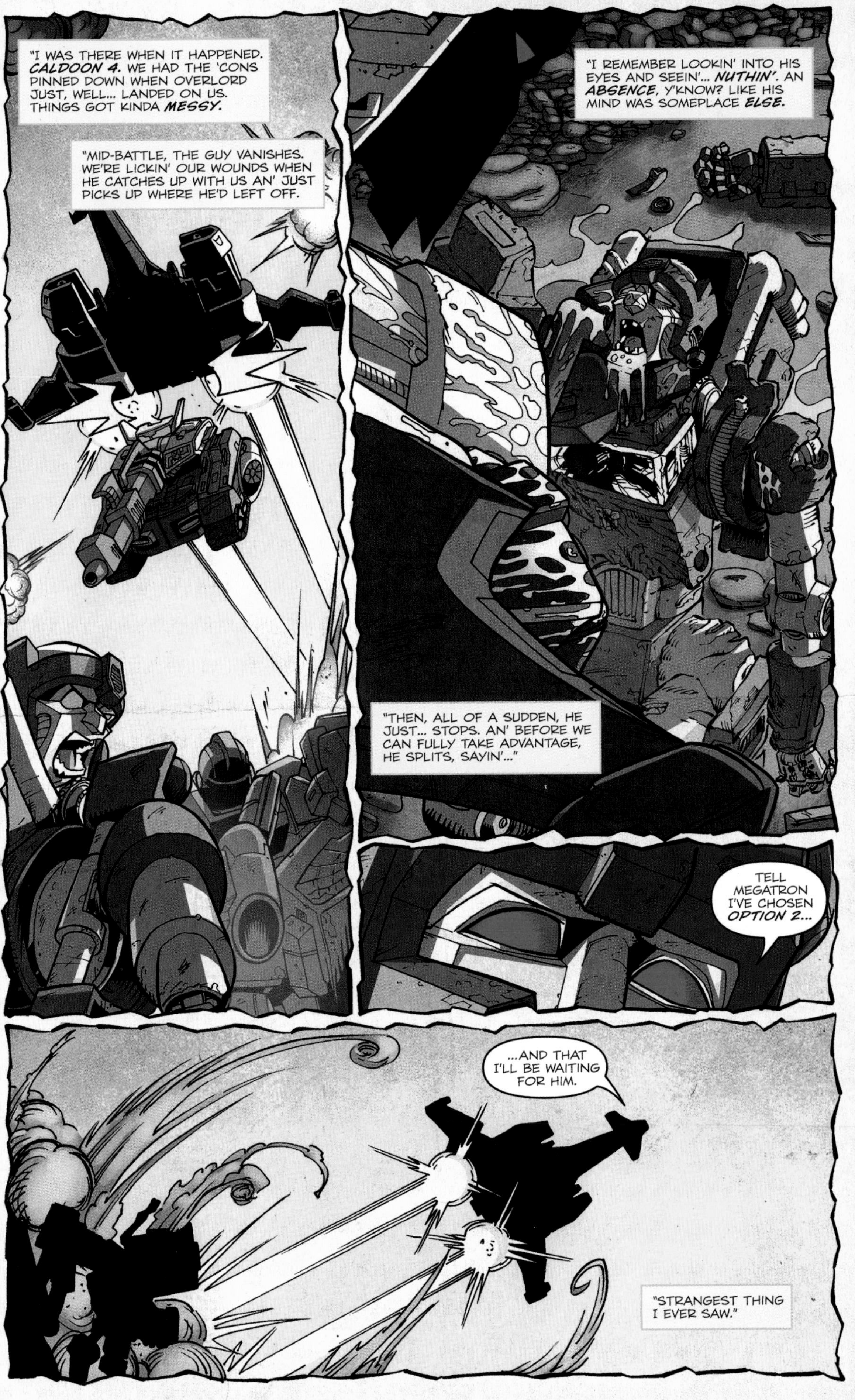
"I WAS THERE WHEN IT HAPPENED. CALDOON 4. WE HAD THE 'CONS PINNED DOWN WHEN OVERLORD JUST, WELL... LANDED ON US. THINGS GOT KINDA MESSY.
"MID-BATTLE, THE GUY VANISHES. WE'RE LICKIN' OUR WOUNDS WHEN HE CATCHES UP WITH US AN' JUST PICKS UP WHERE HE'D LEFT OFF.
"I REMEMBER LOOKIN' INTO HIS EYES AND SEEIN'... NUTHIN'. AN ABSENCE, Y'KNOW? LIKE HIS MIND WAS SOMEPLACE ELSE.
"THEN, ALL OF A SUDDEN, HE JUST... STOPS. AN' BEFORE WE CAN FULLY TAKE ADVANTAGE, HE SPLITS, SAYIN'..."
TELL MEGATRON I'VE CHOSEN OPTION 2...
...AND THAT I'LL BE WAITING FOR HIM.
"STRANGEST THING I EVER SAW."

ME AN' EVERYONE ELSE KINDA THOUGHT HE WAS *DEAD.* GUESS NOT...

ER... KUP?

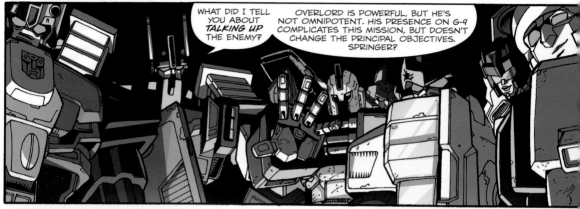

WHAT DID I TELL YOU ABOUT *TALKING UP* THE ENEMY?

OVERLORD IS POWERFUL, BUT HE'S NOT OMNIPOTENT. HIS PRESENCE ON G-9 COMPLICATES THIS MISSION, BUT DOESN'T CHANGE THE PRINCIPAL OBJECTIVES. SPRINGER?

IMPACTOR SAYS THERE ARE *FIFTY AUTOBOTS* DOWN THERE, MOSTLY EX-GUARDS, HELD IN CELL BLOCKS IN THE *SOUTHERN DOME.* RESCUING THEM IS OUR FIRST OBJECTIVE. OUR SECOND OBJECTIVE IS—

KILL OVERLORD!

THANK YOU, GUZZLE, FOR REMINDING ME WHY I RECRUITED YOU. BUT NO, THE SECOND OBJECTIVE IS TO FIND *AEQUITAS.*

SOME OF YOU WILL *RECOGNIZE* THE NAME...

...BUT MOST OF YOU *WON'T.*

ALL THAT MATTERS IS THAT AEQUITAS IS *DOWN THERE* AMONGST HUNDREDS OF DECEPTICONS, AND THAT'S *NOT* GOOD.

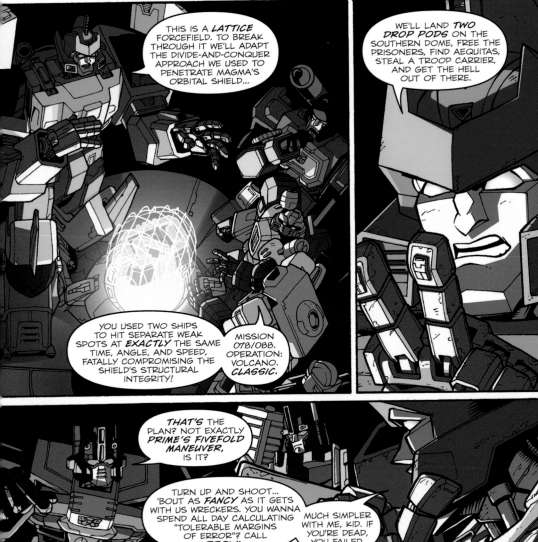

THIS IS A *LATTICE* FORCEFIELD. TO BREAK THROUGH IT WE'LL ADAPT THE DIVIDE-AND-CONQUER APPROACH WE USED TO PENETRATE MAGMA'S ORBITAL SHIELD...

YOU USED TWO SHIPS TO HIT SEPARATE WEAK SPOTS AT *EXACTLY* THE SAME TIME, ANGLE, AND SPEED, FATALLY COMPROMISING THE SHIELD'S STRUCTURAL INTEGRITY!

MISSION 078/088. OPERATION: VOLCANO. *CLASSIC.*

WE'LL LAND *TWO DROP PODS* ON THE SOUTHERN DOME, FREE THE PRISONERS, FIND AEQUITAS, STEAL A TROOP CARRIER, AND GET THE HELL OUT OF THERE.

THAT'S THE PLAN? NOT EXACTLY *PRIME'S FIVEFOLD MANEUVER,* IS IT?

TURN UP AND SHOOT... 'BOUT AS *FANCY* AS IT GETS WITH US WRECKERS. YOU WANNA SPEND ALL DAY CALCULATING "TOLERABLE MARGINS OF ERROR"? CALL *PROWL.*

MUCH SIMPLER WITH ME, KID. IF YOU'RE DEAD, YOU FAILED.

HANG ON. ONLY ROTORSTORM'S GOT WHAT IT TAKES TO HIT A WEAK SPOT ON A LATTICE FORCEFIELD. HE'S GOT *ONE* OF THE PODS UNDER CONTROL. WHO'S GOT THE OTHER?

ME *AGAIN,* OLD MAN. *REMOTE CONTROL.*

AND YES, I *AM* THAT GOOD.

SO THAT'S THE PLAN, WRECKERS.

WHAT COULD POSSIBLY GO *RIGHT?*

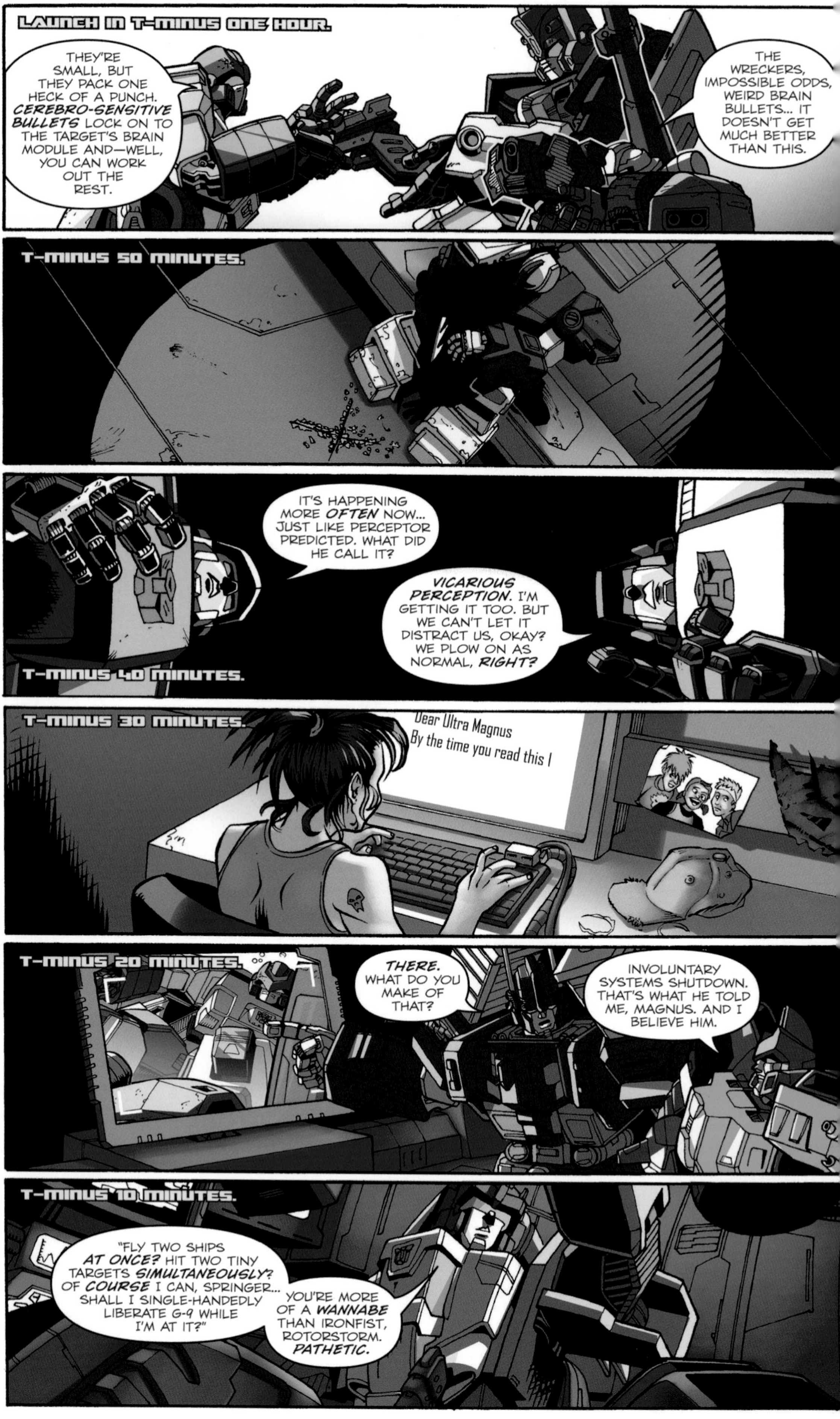
LAUNCH IN T-MINUS ONE HOUR.
THEY'RE SMALL, BUT THEY PACK ONE HECK OF A PUNCH. *CEREBRO-SENSITIVE BULLETS* LOCK ON TO THE TARGET'S BRAIN MODULE AND—WELL, YOU CAN WORK OUT THE REST.
THE WRECKERS, IMPOSSIBLE ODDS, WEIRD BRAIN BULLETS... IT DOESN'T GET MUCH BETTER THAN THIS.
T-MINUS 50 MINUTES.
IT'S HAPPENING MORE *OFTEN* NOW... JUST LIKE PERCEPTOR PREDICTED. WHAT DID HE CALL IT?
VICARIOUS PERCEPTION. I'M GETTING IT TOO. BUT WE CAN'T LET IT DISTRACT US, OKAY? WE PLOW ON AS NORMAL, *RIGHT?*
T-MINUS 40 MINUTES.
T-MINUS 30 MINUTES.
Dear Ultra Magnus
By the time you read this I
T-MINUS 20 MINUTES.
THERE. WHAT DO YOU MAKE OF THAT?
INVOLUNTARY SYSTEMS SHUTDOWN. THAT'S WHAT HE TOLD ME, MAGNUS. AND I BELIEVE HIM.
T-MINUS 10 MINUTES.
"FLY TWO SHIPS *AT ONCE?* HIT TWO TINY TARGETS *SIMULTANEOUSLY?* OF *COURSE* I CAN, SPRINGER... SHALL I SINGLE-HANDEDLY LIBERATE G-9 WHILE I'M AT IT?"
YOU'RE MORE OF A *WANNABE* THAN IRONFIST, ROTORSTORM. *PATHETIC.*

OKAY, MAGNUS. TIME TO CUT US LOOSE.

GOOD LUCK, PEOPLE...

...MAY YOUR WIRES NEVER CROSS AND YOUR LUSTER NEVER DULL.

SPRINGER, I'LL TAKE CONTROL OF YOUR POD AFTER ATMOSPHERIC ENTRY, OKAY?

ROGER THAT, ROTORSTORM.

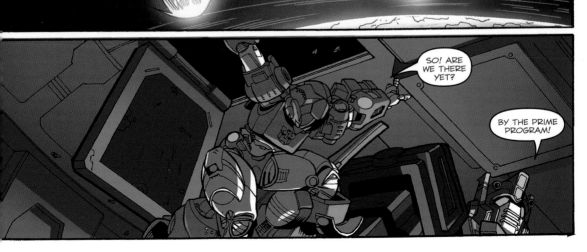

SO! ARE WE THERE YET?

BY THE PRIME PROGRAM!

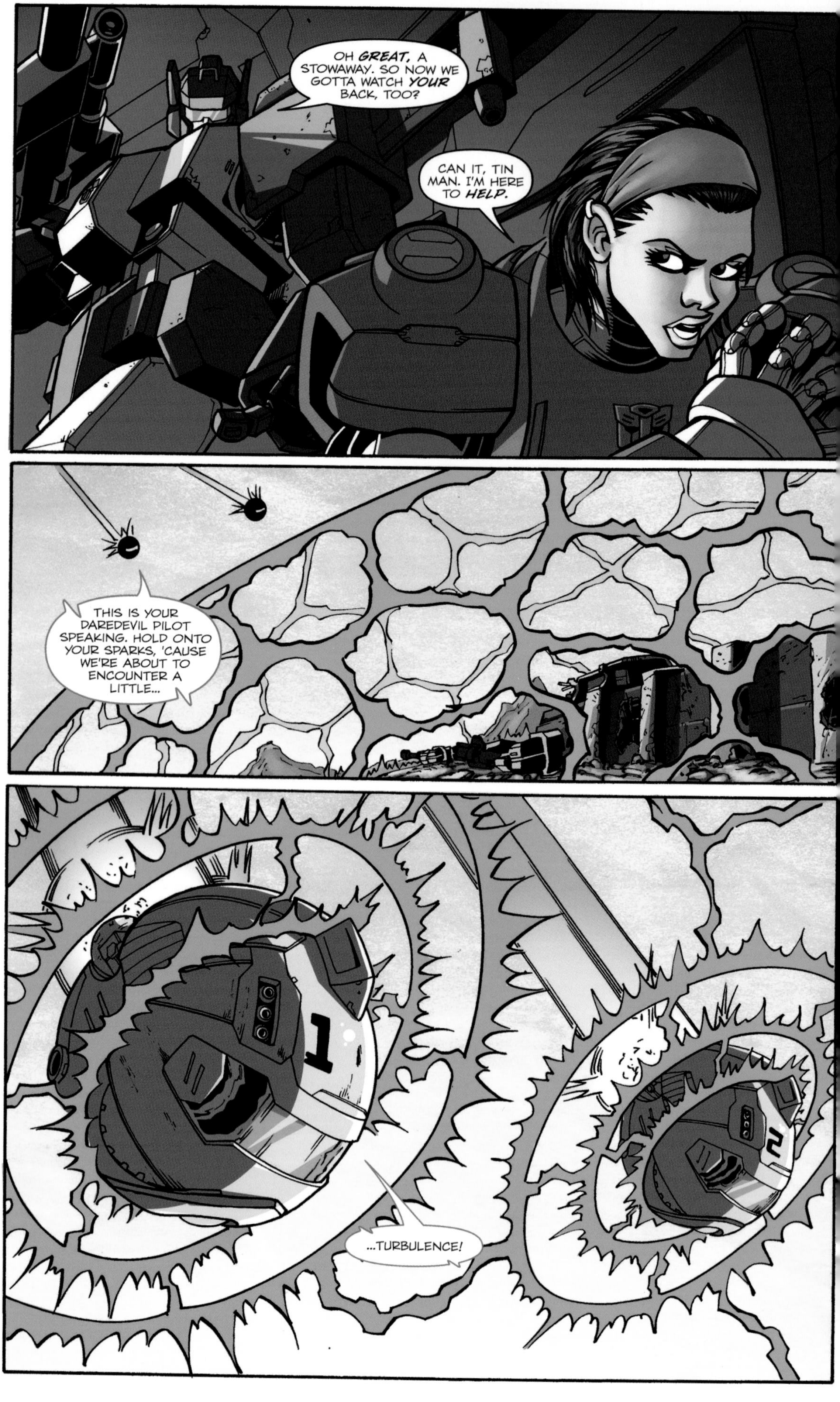
OH GREAT, A STOWAWAY. SO NOW WE GOTTA WATCH YOUR BACK, TOO?
CAN IT, TIN MAN. I'M HERE TO HELP.
THIS IS YOUR DAREDEVIL PILOT SPEAKING. HOLD ONTO YOUR SPARKS, 'CAUSE WE'RE ABOUT TO ENCOUNTER A LITTLE...
...TURBULENCE!

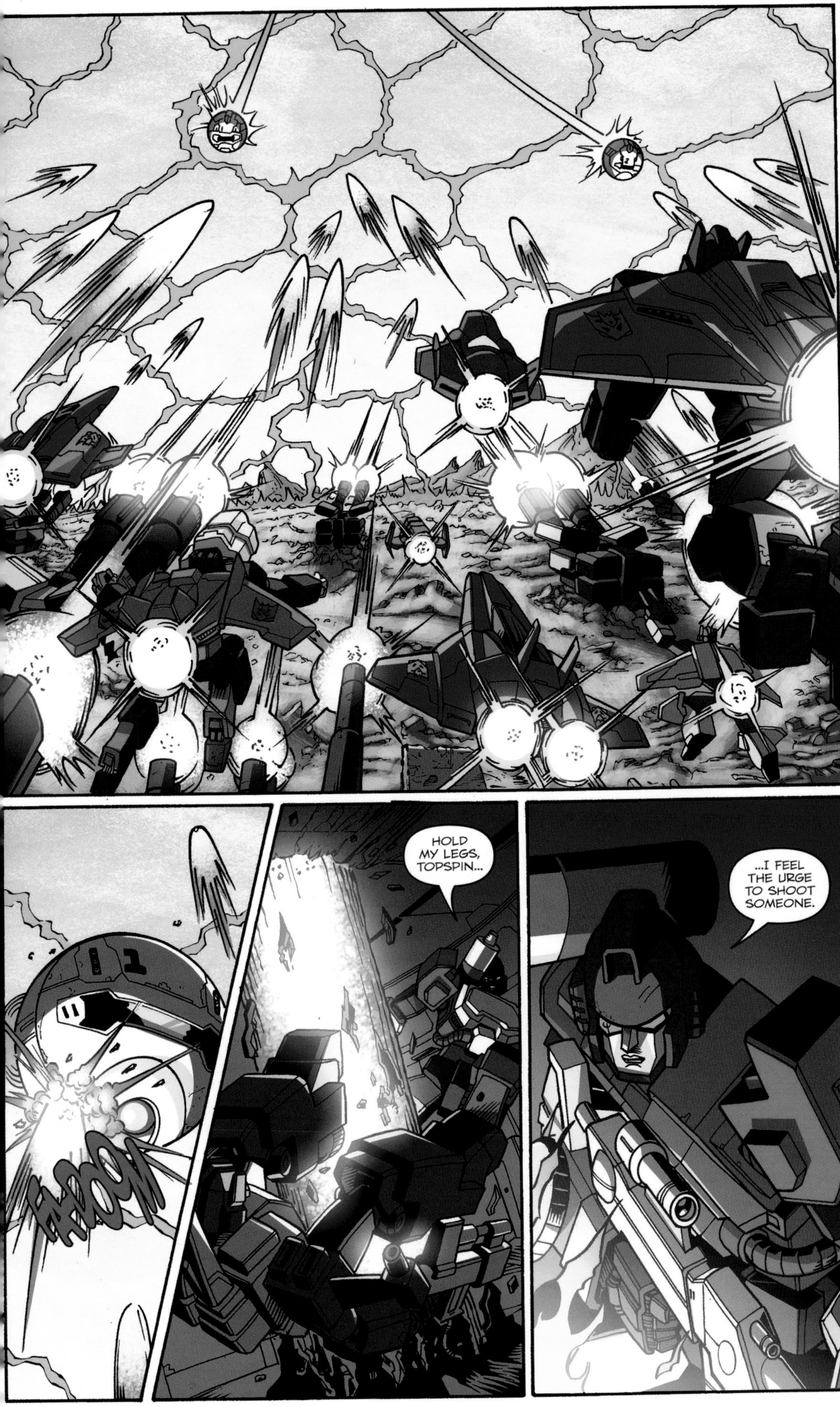
HOLD MY LEGS, TOPSPIN...
...I FEEL THE URGE TO SHOOT SOMEONE.

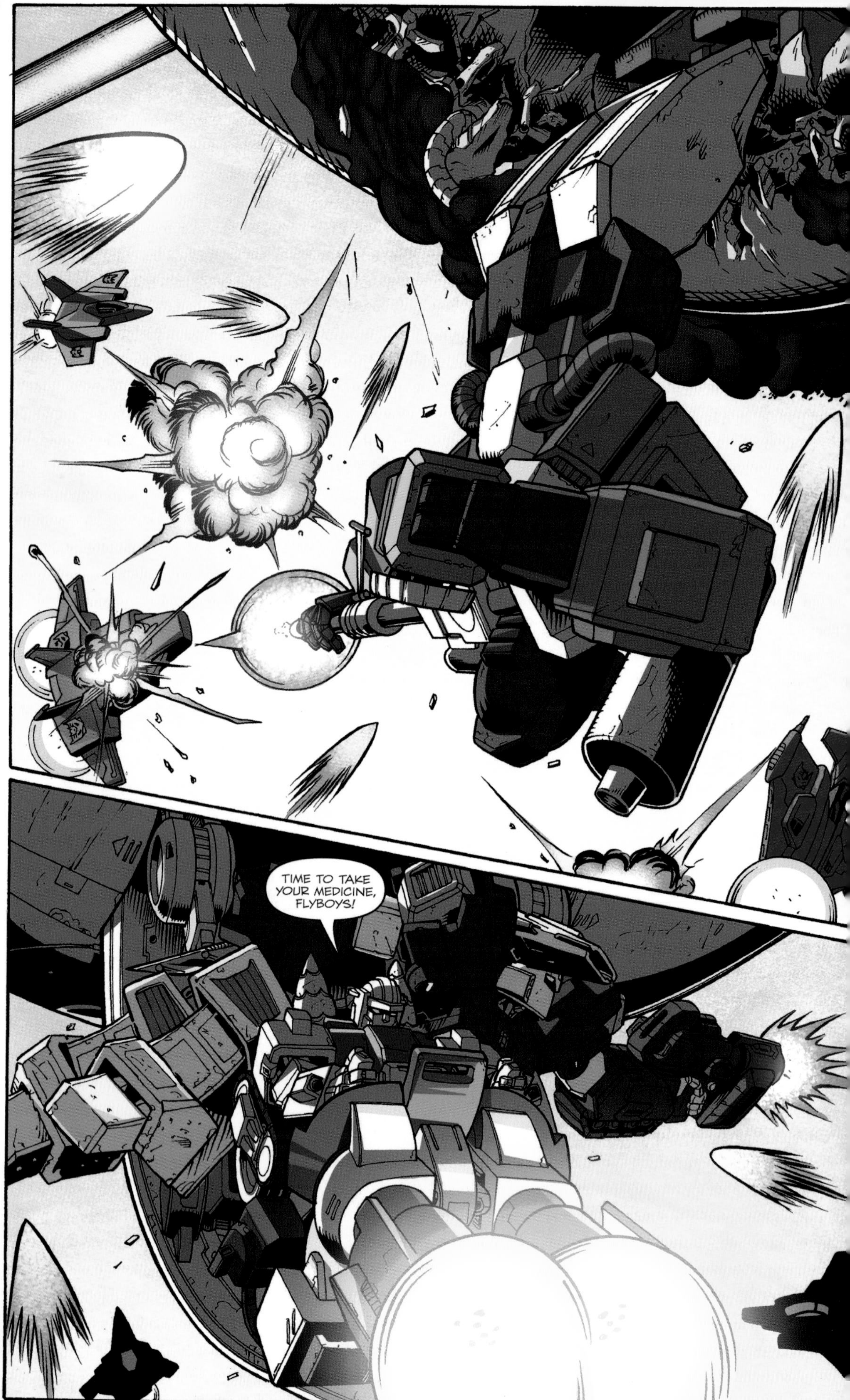
TIME TO TAKE YOUR MEDICINE, FLYBOYS!

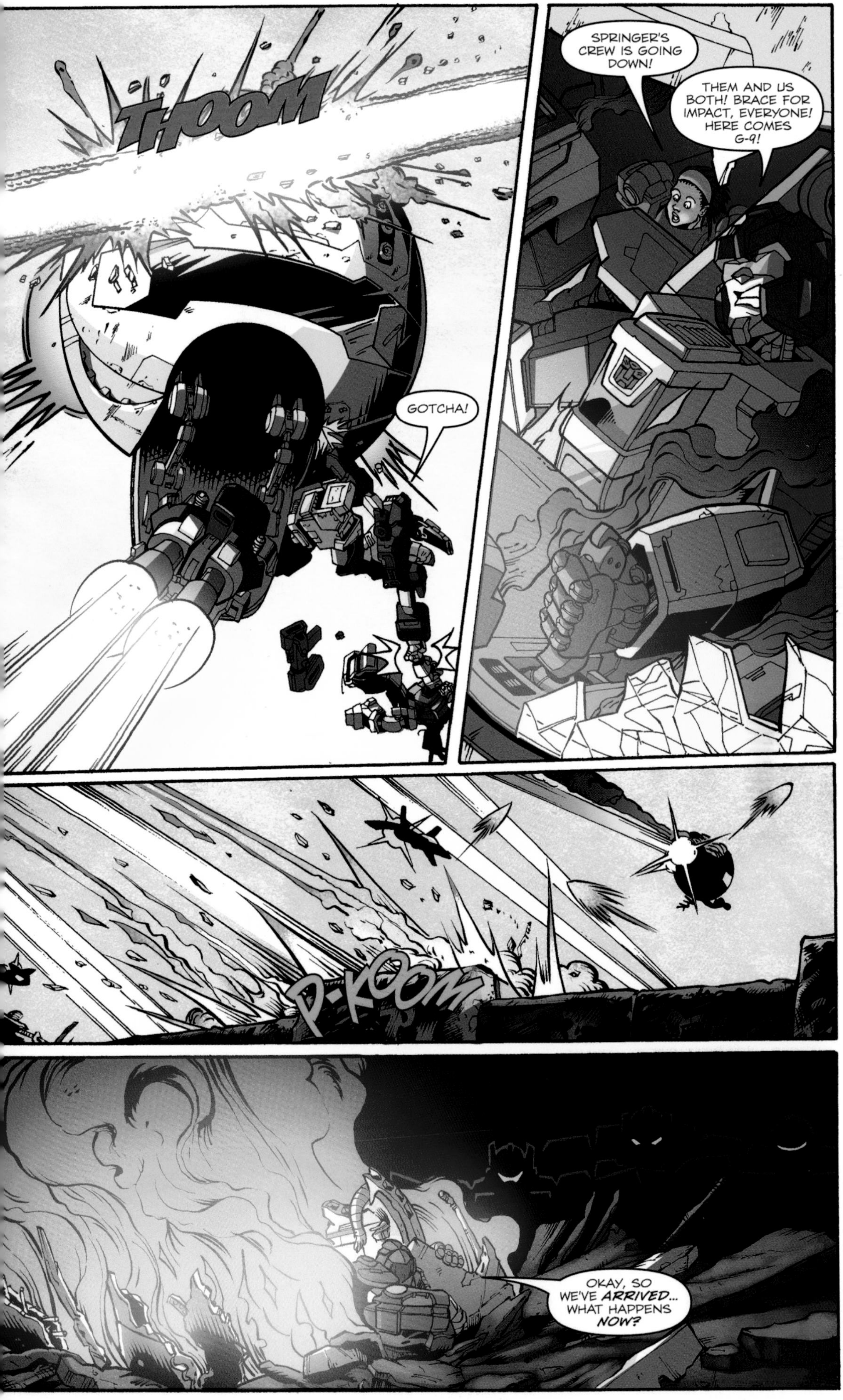
THOOM
GOTCHA!
SPRINGER'S CREW IS GOING DOWN!
THEM AND US BOTH! BRACE FOR IMPACT, EVERYONE! HERE COMES G-9!
P-KOOM
OKAY, SO WE'VE *ARRIVED*... WHAT HAPPENS *NOW?*

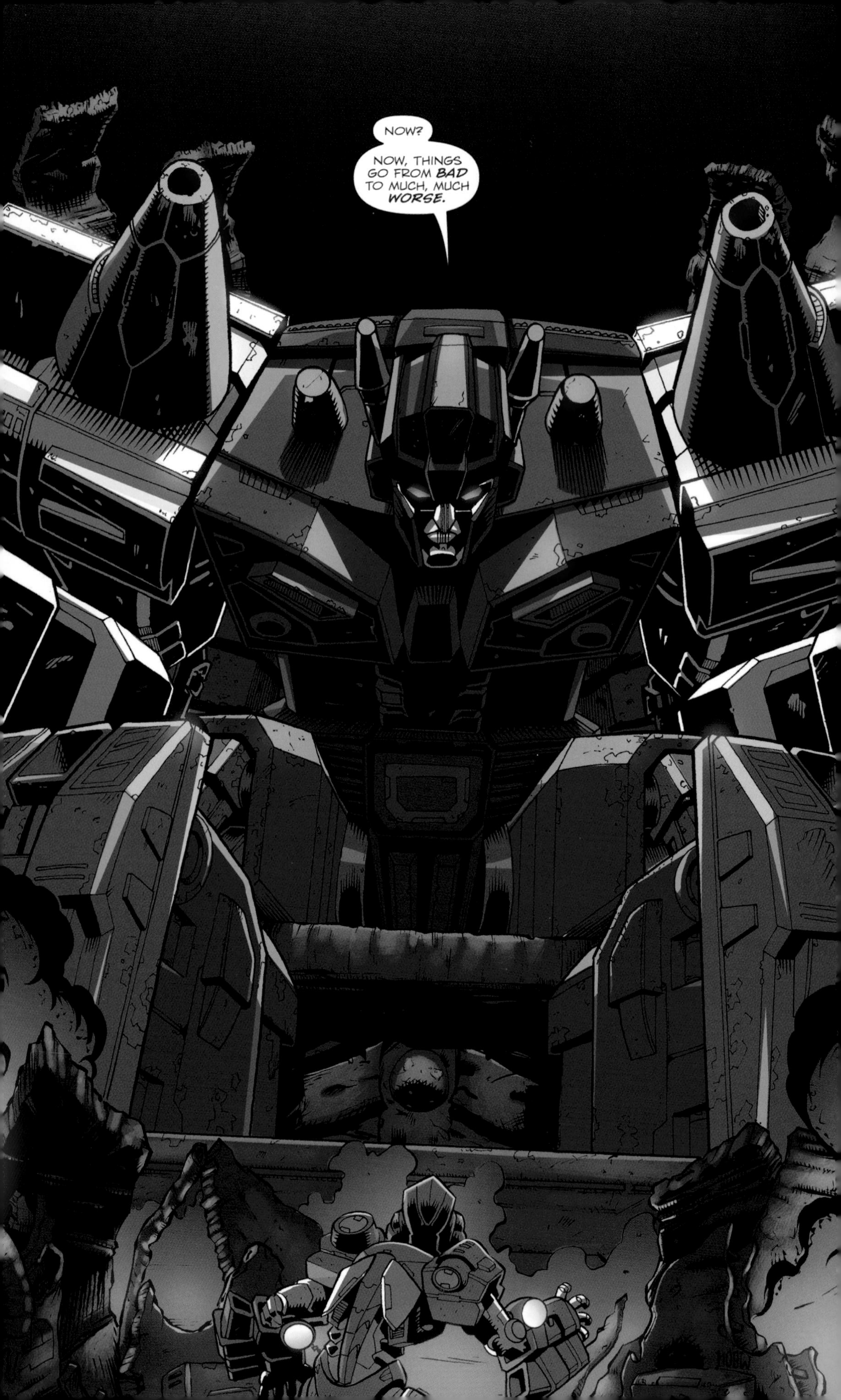
NOW?
NOW, THINGS GO FROM BAD TO MUCH, MUCH WORSE.

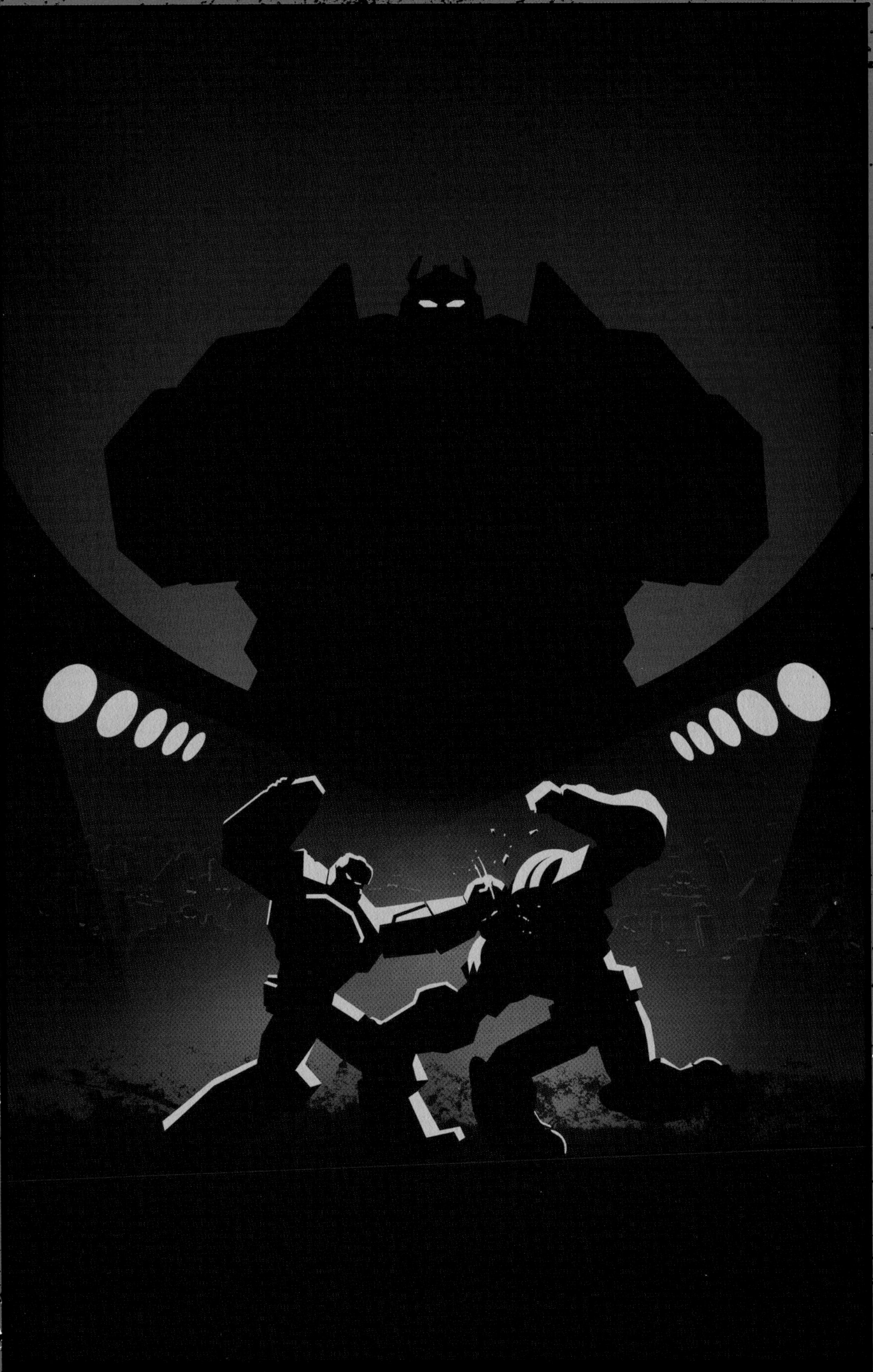

ART TREVOR HUTCHISON

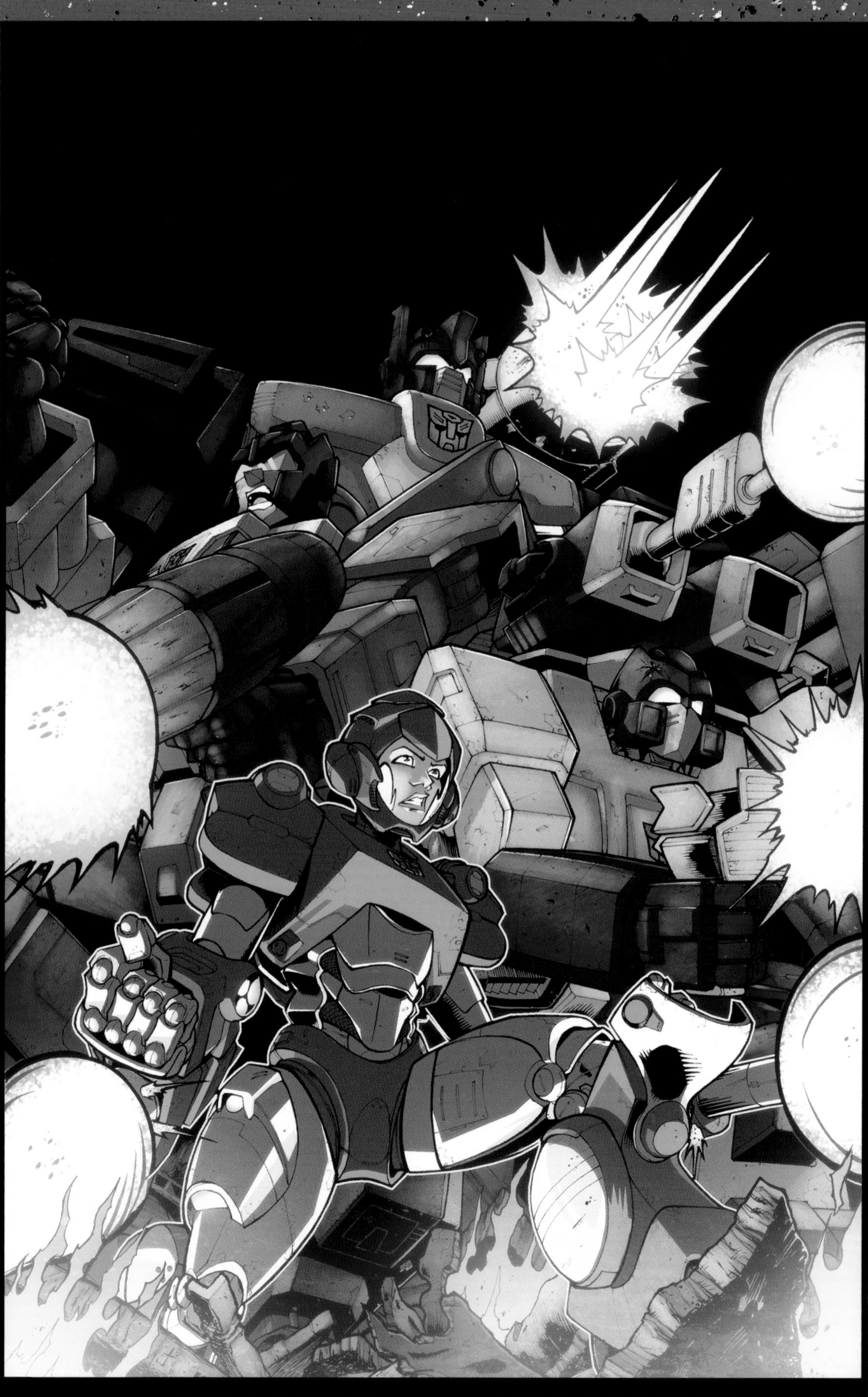

ART NICK ROCHE COLORS JOSH BURCHAM

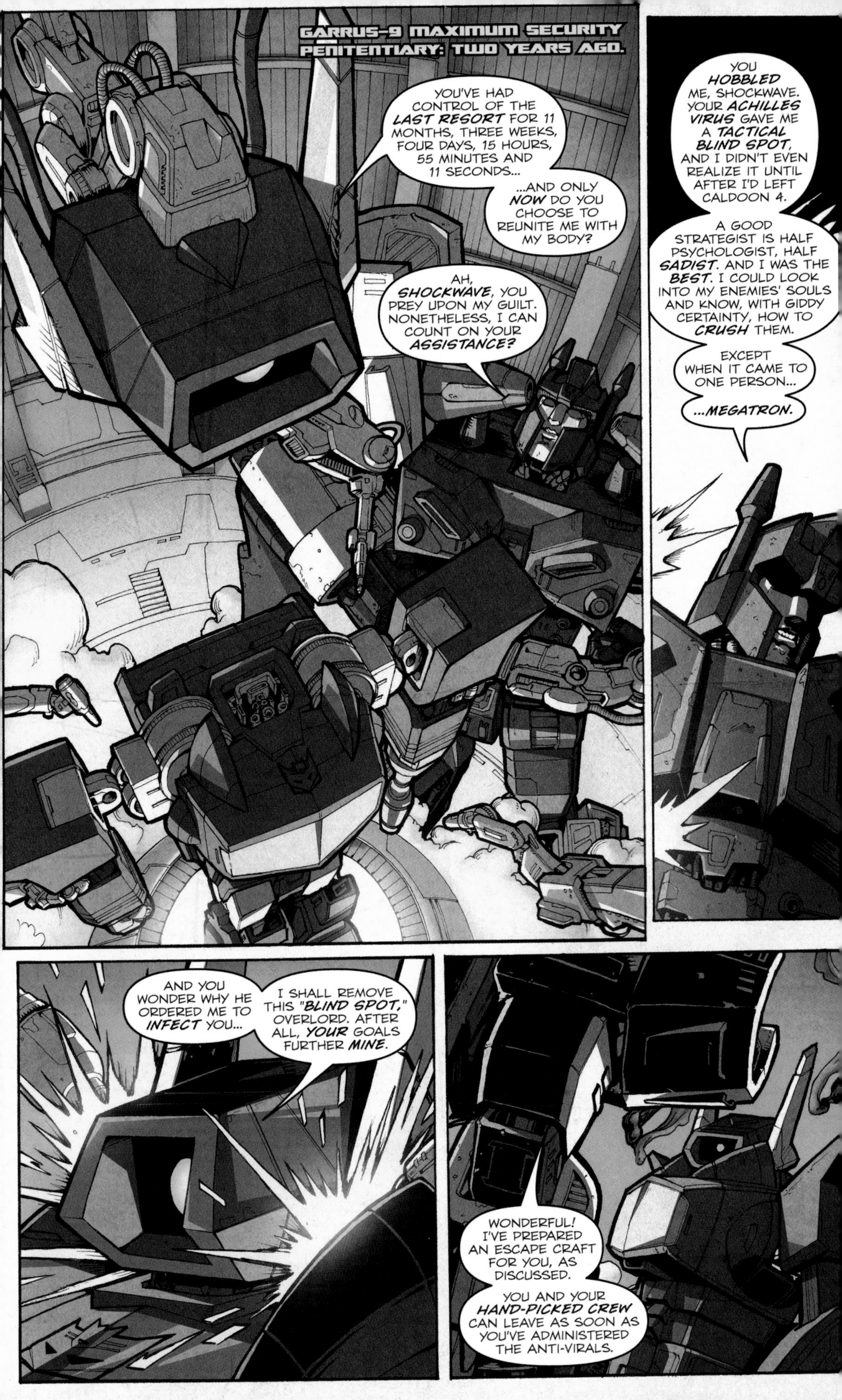
GARRUS-9 MAXIMUM SECURITY PENITENTIARY: TWO YEARS AGO.
YOU'VE HAD CONTROL OF THE LAST RESORT FOR 11 MONTHS, THREE WEEKS, FOUR DAYS, 15 HOURS, 55 MINUTES AND 11 SECONDS...
...AND ONLY NOW DO YOU CHOOSE TO REUNITE ME WITH MY BODY?
AH, SHOCKWAVE, YOU PREY UPON MY GUILT. NONETHELESS, I CAN COUNT ON YOUR ASSISTANCE?
YOU HOBBLED ME, SHOCKWAVE. YOUR ACHILLES VIRUS GAVE ME A TACTICAL BLIND SPOT, AND I DIDN'T EVEN REALIZE IT UNTIL AFTER I'D LEFT CALDOON 4.
A GOOD STRATEGIST IS HALF PSYCHOLOGIST, HALF SADIST. AND I WAS THE BEST. I COULD LOOK INTO MY ENEMIES' SOULS AND KNOW, WITH GIDDY CERTAINTY, HOW TO CRUSH THEM.
EXCEPT WHEN IT CAME TO ONE PERSON...
...MEGATRON.
AND YOU WONDER WHY HE ORDERED ME TO INFECT YOU...
I SHALL REMOVE THIS "BLIND SPOT," OVERLORD. AFTER ALL, YOUR GOALS FURTHER MINE.
WONDERFUL! I'VE PREPARED AN ESCAPE CRAFT FOR YOU, AS DISCUSSED.
YOU AND YOUR HAND-PICKED CREW CAN LEAVE AS SOON AS YOU'VE ADMINISTERED THE ANTI-VIRALS.

AND WHEN I'VE GONE—WHAT THEN FOR YOU, OVERLORD? MORE TERROR EXPERIMENTS IN THIS BUBBLE YOU'VE BUILT FOR YOURSELF?

NO DOUBT. I'M CURRENTLY ENCOURAGING MY "GUESTS" TO BELIEVE THAT THEY CAN FIGHT THEIR WAY TO FREEDOM. HILARIOUS.

YOU THINK YOU'RE ENJOYING THIS, BUT YOU'RE NOT.

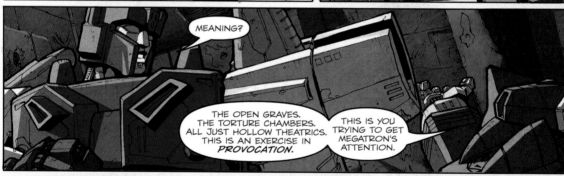

MEANING?

THE OPEN GRAVES. THE TORTURE CHAMBERS. ALL JUST HOLLOW THEATRICS. THIS IS AN EXERCISE IN PROVOCATION.

THIS IS YOU TRYING TO GET MEGATRON'S ATTENTION.

HAVING ONE EYE MAKES YOU SEE THE WORLD IN UNUSUAL WAYS, SHOCKWAVE...

THANKFULLY.

YOU'RE NOT THE FIRST PHASE SIXER TO BAIT MEGATRON, OVERLORD...

TRUE. BUT I ONLY HAVE TO BE THE LAST...

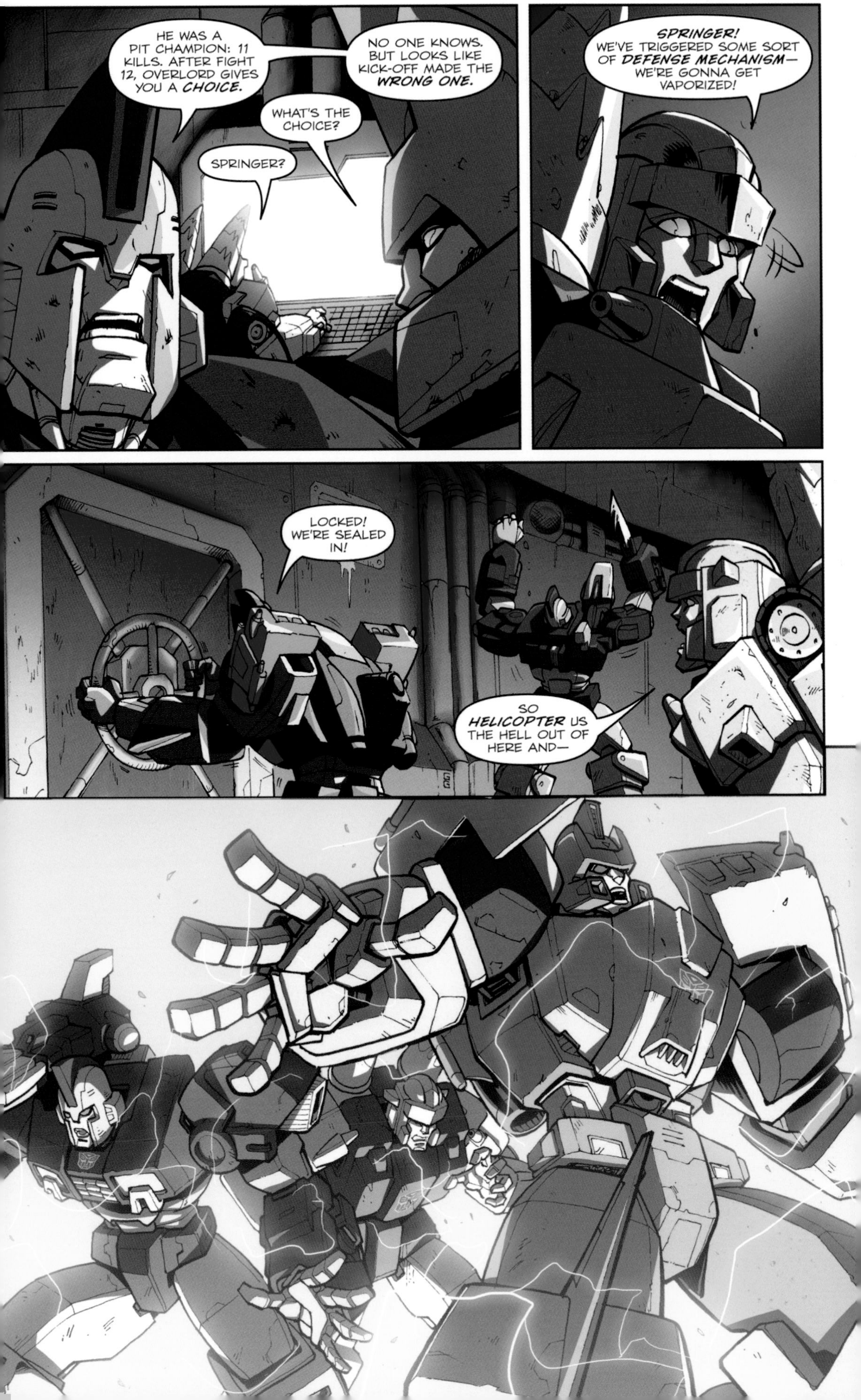
HE WAS A PIT CHAMPION: 11 KILLS. AFTER FIGHT 12, OVERLORD GIVES YOU A *CHOICE*.
WHAT'S THE CHOICE?
NO ONE KNOWS. BUT LOOKS LIKE KICK-OFF MADE THE *WRONG ONE*.
SPRINGER?
SPRINGER! WE'VE TRIGGERED SOME SORT OF *DEFENSE MECHANISM*— WE'RE GONNA GET VAPORIZED!
LOCKED! WE'RE SEALED IN!
SO *HELICOPTER* US THE HELL OUT OF HERE AND—

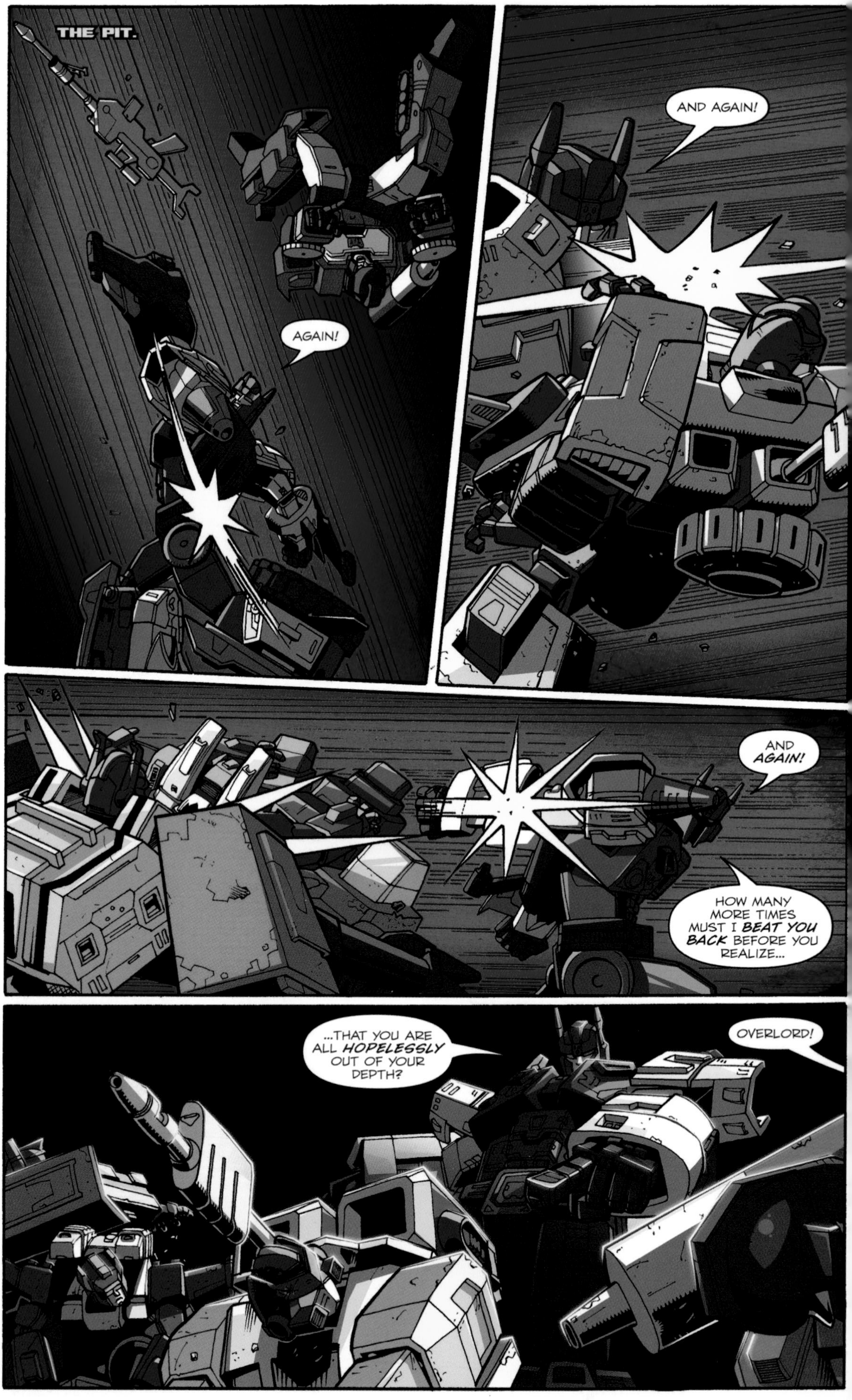
THE PIT.
AGAIN!
AND AGAIN!
AND AGAIN!
HOW MANY MORE TIMES MUST I BEAT YOU BACK BEFORE YOU REALIZE...
...THAT YOU ARE ALL HOPELESSLY OUT OF YOUR DEPTH?
OVERLORD!

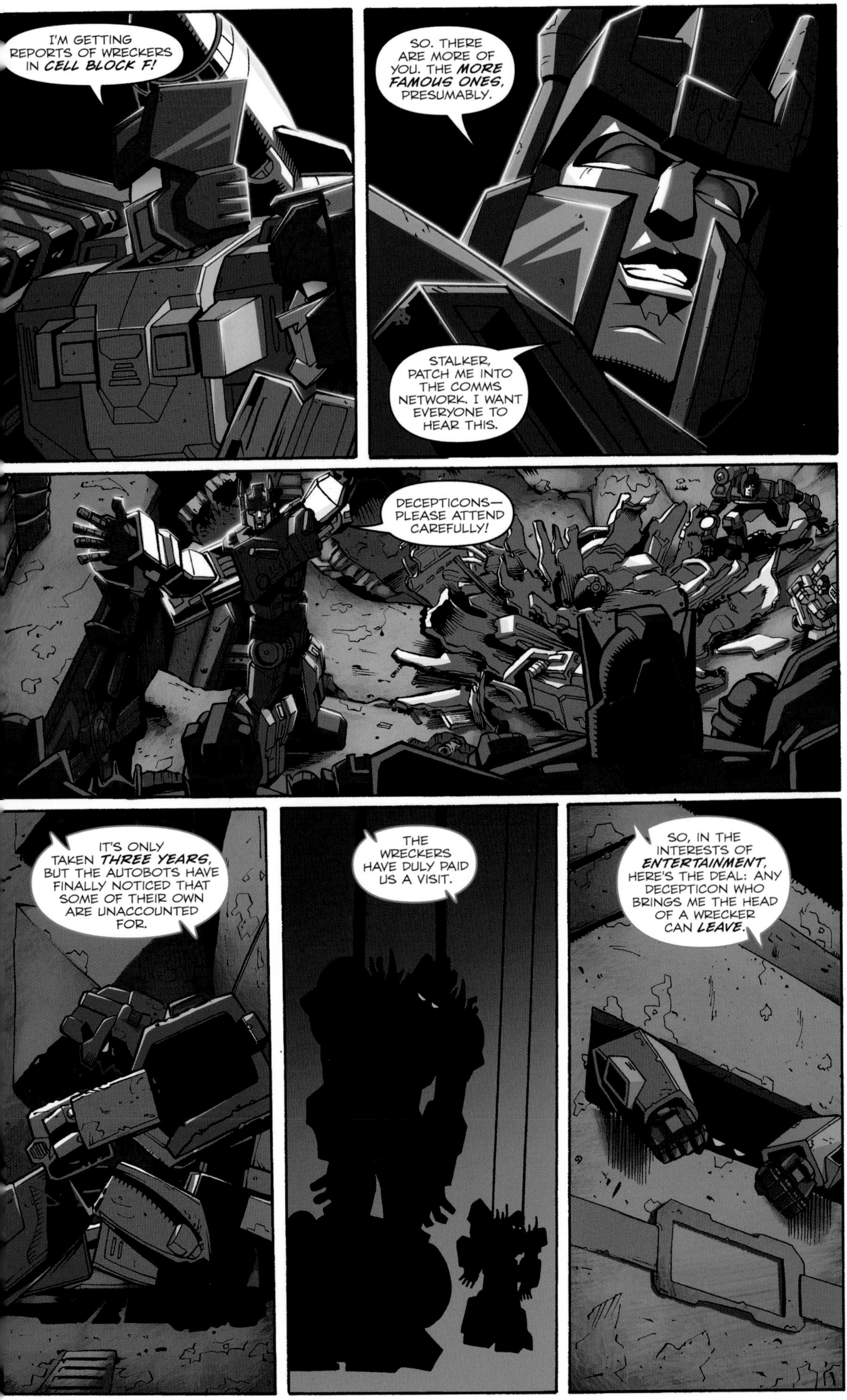

I'M GETTING REPORTS OF WRECKERS IN CELL BLOCK F!
SO. THERE ARE MORE OF YOU. THE MORE FAMOUS ONES, PRESUMABLY.
STALKER, PATCH ME INTO THE COMMS NETWORK. I WANT EVERYONE TO HEAR THIS.
DECEPTICONS— PLEASE ATTEND CAREFULLY!
IT'S ONLY TAKEN THREE YEARS, BUT THE AUTOBOTS HAVE FINALLY NOTICED THAT SOME OF THEIR OWN ARE UNACCOUNTED FOR.
THE WRECKERS HAVE DULY PAID US A VISIT.
SO, IN THE INTERESTS OF ENTERTAINMENT, HERE'S THE DEAL: ANY DECEPTICON WHO BRINGS ME THE HEAD OF A WRECKER CAN LEAVE.

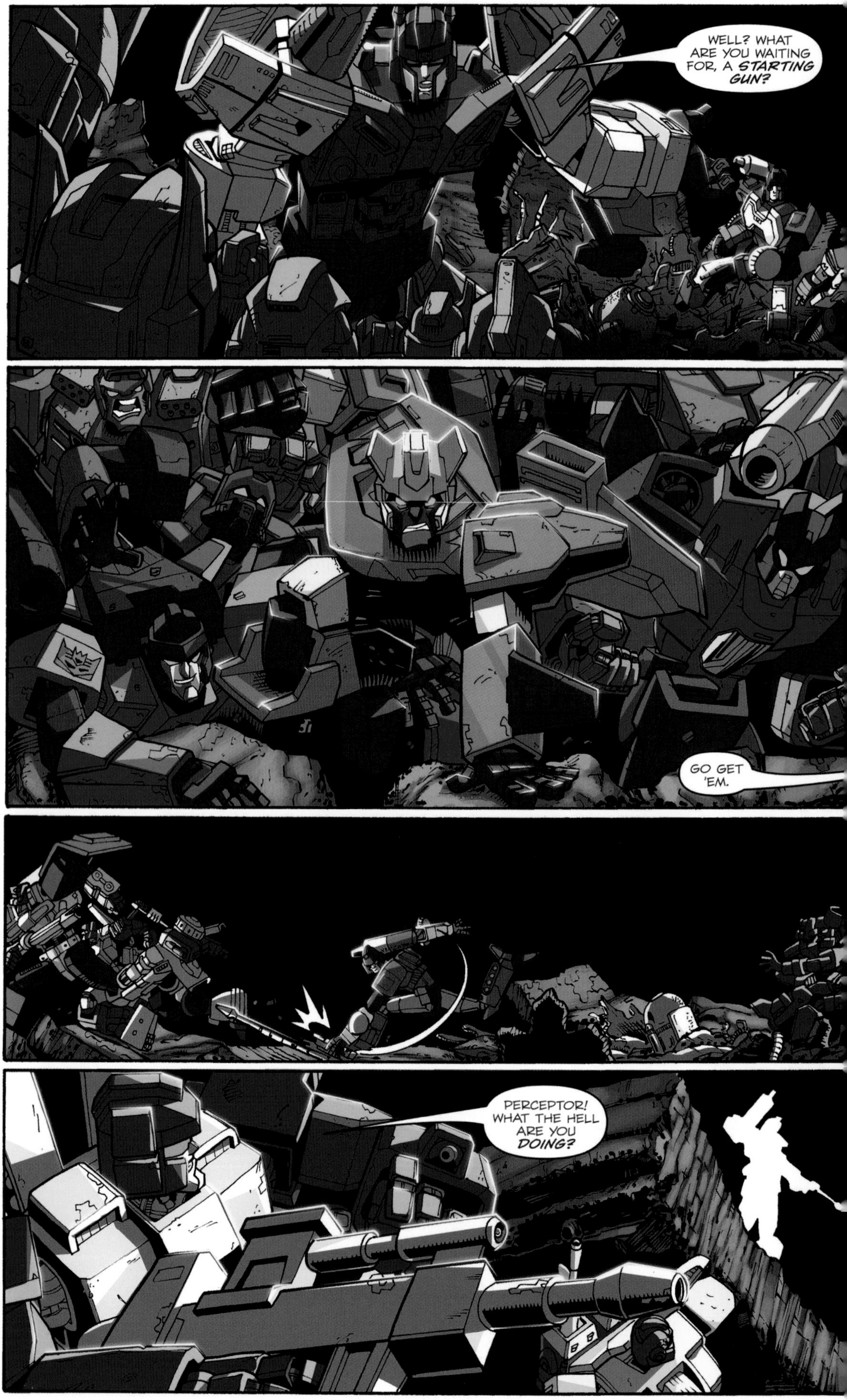
WELL? WHAT ARE YOU WAITING FOR, A STARTING GUN?
GO GET 'EM.
PERCEPTOR! WHAT THE HELL ARE YOU DOING?

BUYING US SOME TIME...

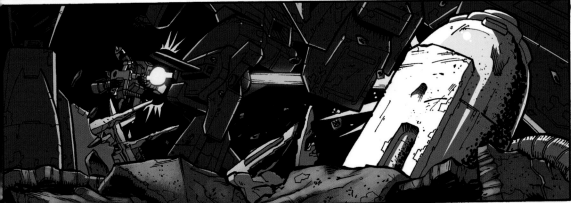

BRAK-A-DOOM

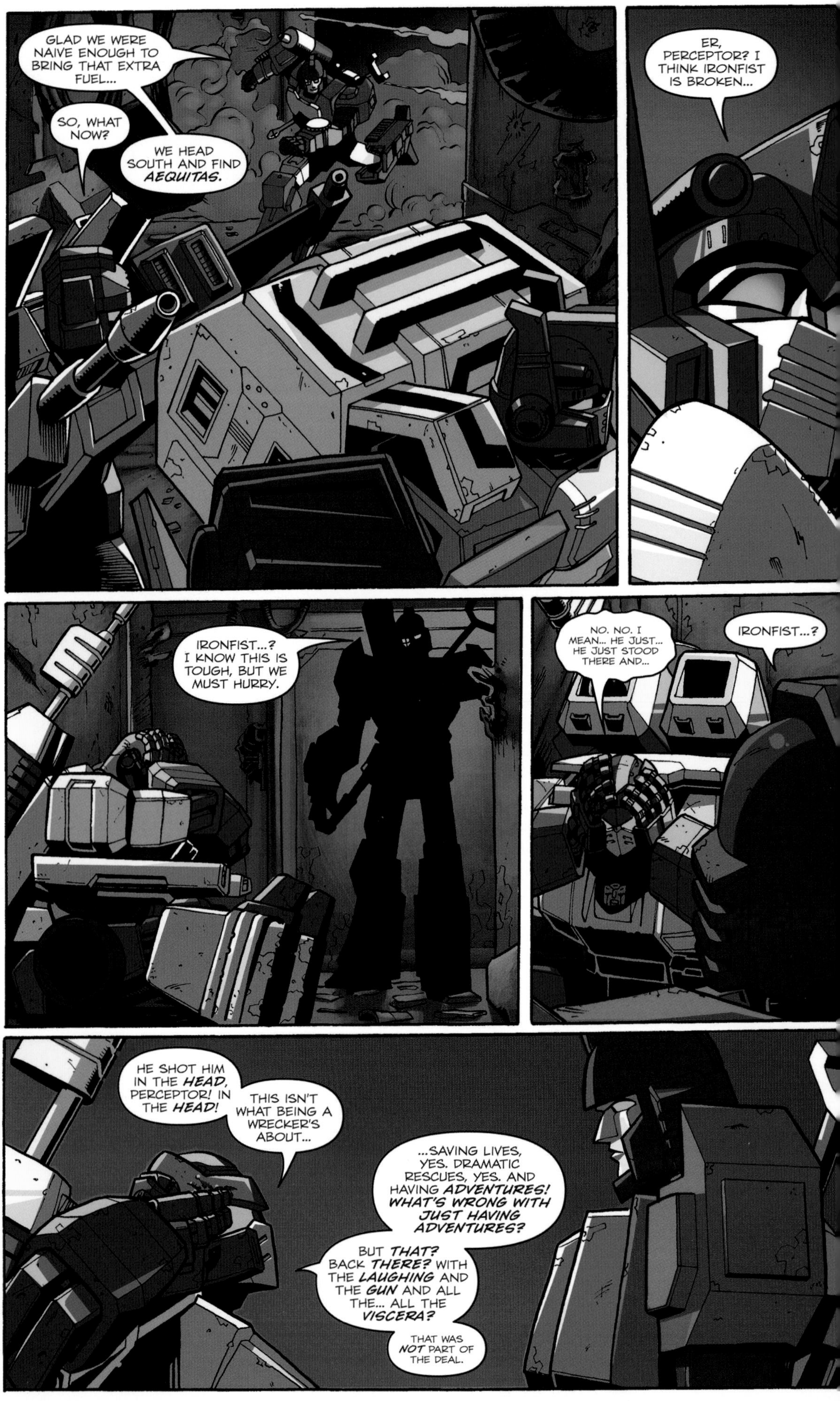

GLAD WE WERE NAIVE ENOUGH TO BRING THAT EXTRA FUEL...
SO, WHAT NOW?
WE HEAD SOUTH AND FIND *AEQUITAS.*
ER, PERCEPTOR? I THINK IRONFIST IS BROKEN...
IRONFIST...? I KNOW THIS IS TOUGH, BUT WE MUST HURRY.
NO. NO. I MEAN... HE JUST... HE JUST STOOD THERE AND...
IRONFIST...?
HE SHOT HIM IN THE *HEAD*, PERCEPTOR! IN THE *HEAD*!
THIS ISN'T WHAT BEING A WRECKER'S ABOUT...
...SAVING LIVES, YES. DRAMATIC RESCUES, YES. AND HAVING *ADVENTURES! WHAT'S WRONG WITH JUST HAVING ADVENTURES?*
BUT *THAT?* BACK *THERE?* WITH THE *LAUGHING* AND THE *GUN* AND ALL THE... ALL THE *VISCERA?*
THAT WAS *NOT* PART OF THE DEAL.

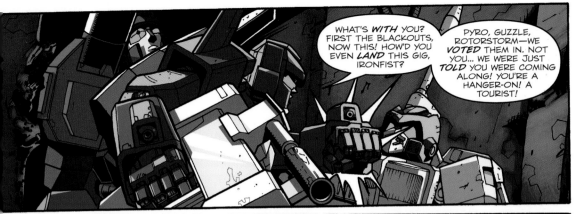

WHAT'S *WITH* YOU? FIRST THE BLACKOUTS, NOW THIS! HOW'D YOU EVEN *LAND* THIS GIG, IRONFIST?

PYRO, GUZZLE, ROTORSTORM—WE *VOTED* THEM IN. NOT YOU... WE WERE JUST *TOLD* YOU WERE COMING ALONG! YOU'RE A HANGER-ON! A TOURIST!

THIS ISN'T *ROLE-PLAY*. PEOPLE *DIE* IN STUPID, POINTLESS WAYS. *DEAL* WITH IT.

DON'T YOU *DARE* TALK TO ME ABOUT DEATH.

ENOUGH.

WE MOURN ROTORSTORM LATER. RIGHT NOW...

"...WE CAN'T AFFORD TO GET PERSONAL."

YOU SURE HE'S GONNA BE ALL THE WAY DOWN HERE?

TRUST ME, KID. THE *MAXIMUM SECURITY CELLS* ARE ALWAYS IN THE BASEMENT.

JUST WATCH YER STEP. YOU'RE NO USE TO ANYONE IF YOU DIE DURIN' A RESCUE ATTEMPT.

THAT HAPPENED TO SOME *GOOD FRIENDS* OF MINE...

...THEY WERE KILLED TRYING TO SAVE ANOTHER 'BOT'S TAILPIPE.*

HOPE THE GUY WAS WORTH IT.

*SEEN IN TF SPOTLIGHT: KUP.

DEPENDS WHO YOU ASK...

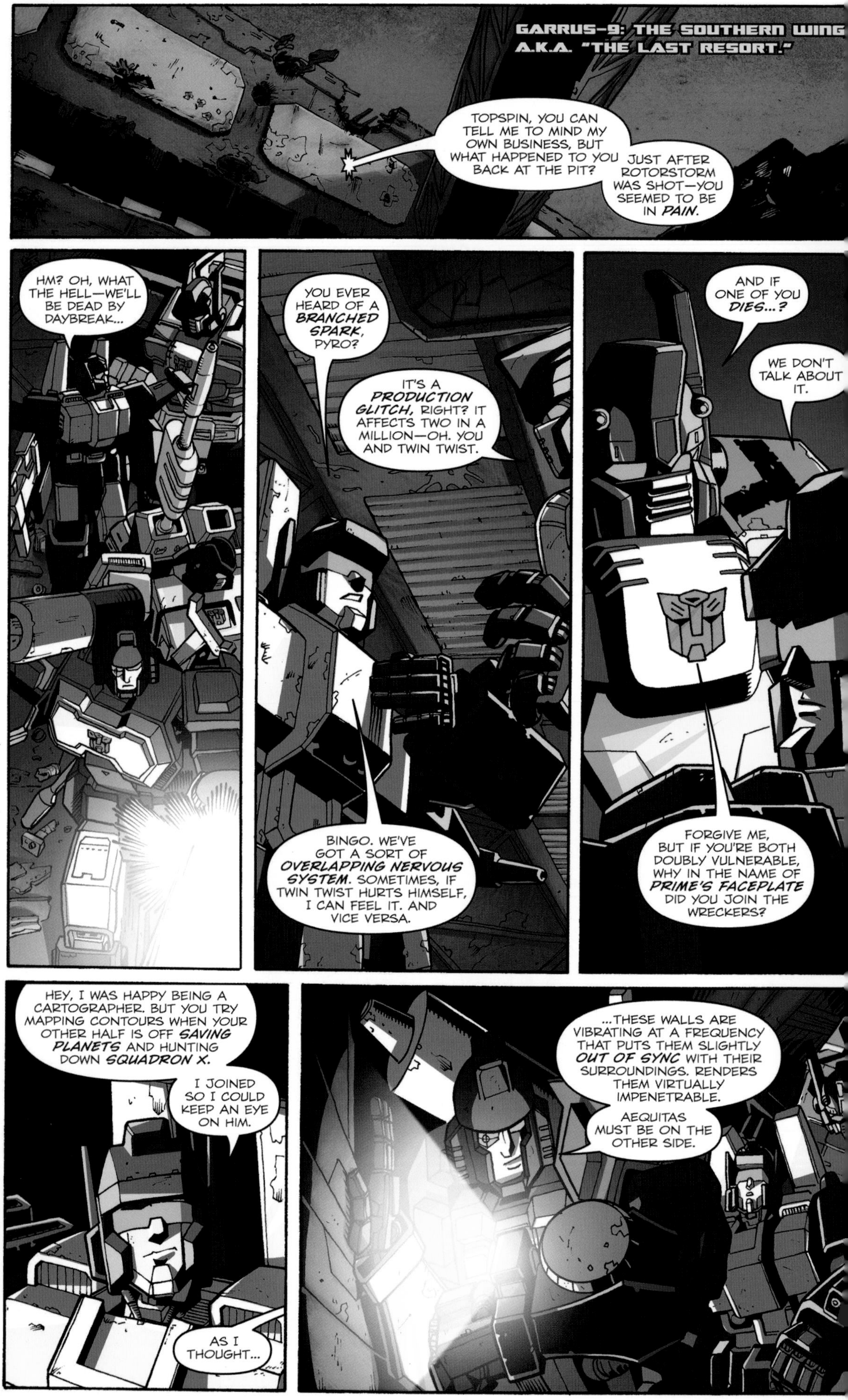
GARRUS-9: THE SOUTHERN WING
A.K.A. "THE LAST RESORT."
TOPSPIN, YOU CAN TELL ME TO MIND MY OWN BUSINESS, BUT WHAT HAPPENED TO YOU BACK AT THE PIT?
JUST AFTER ROTORSTORM WAS SHOT—YOU SEEMED TO BE IN PAIN.
HM? OH, WHAT THE HELL—WE'LL BE DEAD BY DAYBREAK...
YOU EVER HEARD OF A BRANCHED SPARK, PYRO?
IT'S A PRODUCTION GLITCH, RIGHT? IT AFFECTS TWO IN A MILLION—OH. YOU AND TWIN TWIST.
BINGO. WE'VE GOT A SORT OF OVERLAPPING NERVOUS SYSTEM. SOMETIMES, IF TWIN TWIST HURTS HIMSELF, I CAN FEEL IT. AND VICE VERSA.
AND IF ONE OF YOU DIES...?
WE DON'T TALK ABOUT IT.
FORGIVE ME, BUT IF YOU'RE BOTH DOUBLY VULNERABLE, WHY IN THE NAME OF PRIME'S FACEPLATE DID YOU JOIN THE WRECKERS?
HEY, I WAS HAPPY BEING A CARTOGRAPHER. BUT YOU TRY MAPPING CONTOURS WHEN YOUR OTHER HALF IS OFF SAVING PLANETS AND HUNTING DOWN SQUADRON X.
I JOINED SO I COULD KEEP AN EYE ON HIM.
AS I THOUGHT...
...THESE WALLS ARE VIBRATING AT A FREQUENCY THAT PUTS THEM SLIGHTLY OUT OF SYNC WITH THEIR SURROUNDINGS. RENDERS THEM VIRTUALLY IMPENETRABLE.
AEQUITAS MUST BE ON THE OTHER SIDE.

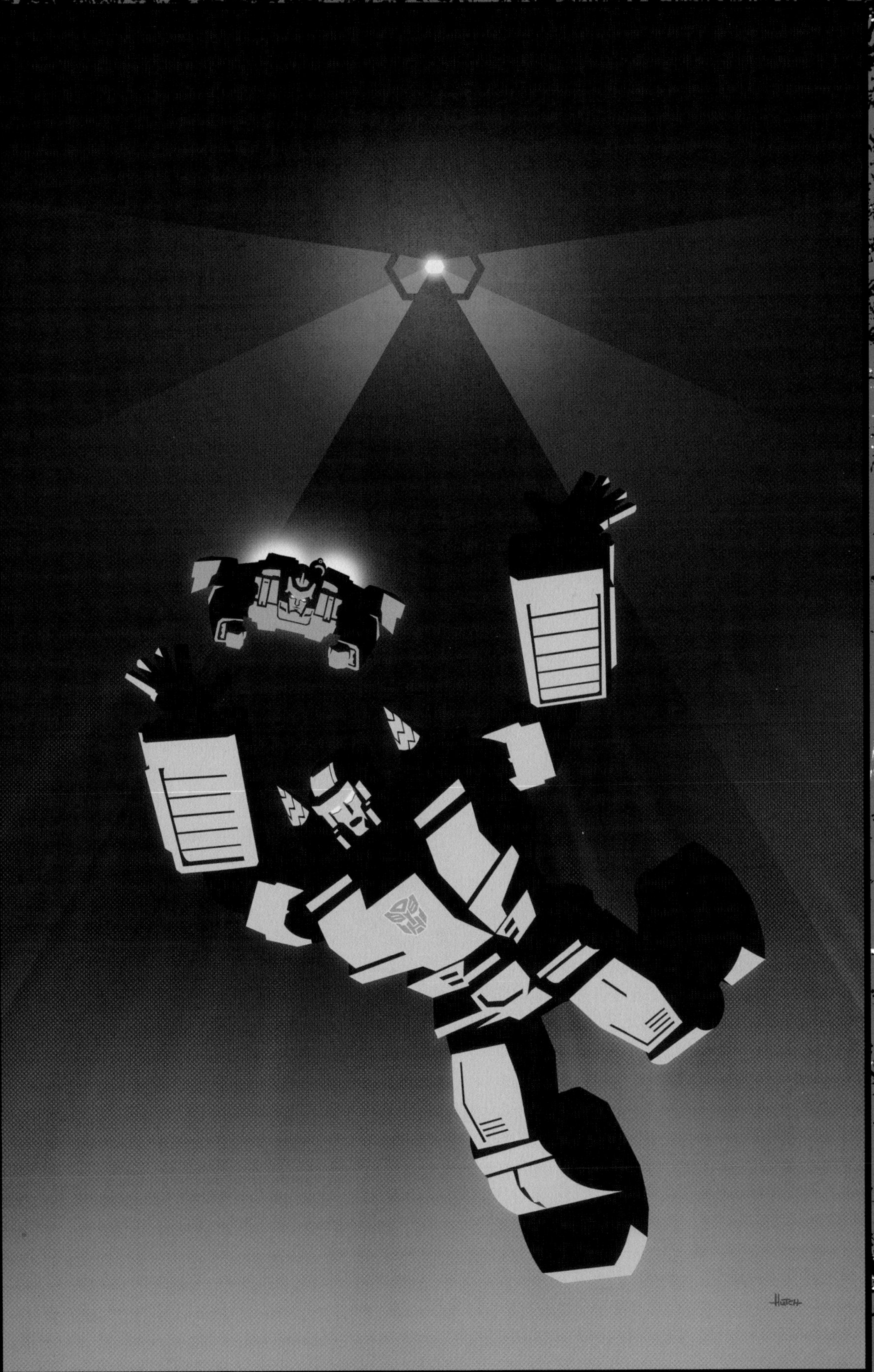
HUTCH

ART TREVOR HUTCHISON

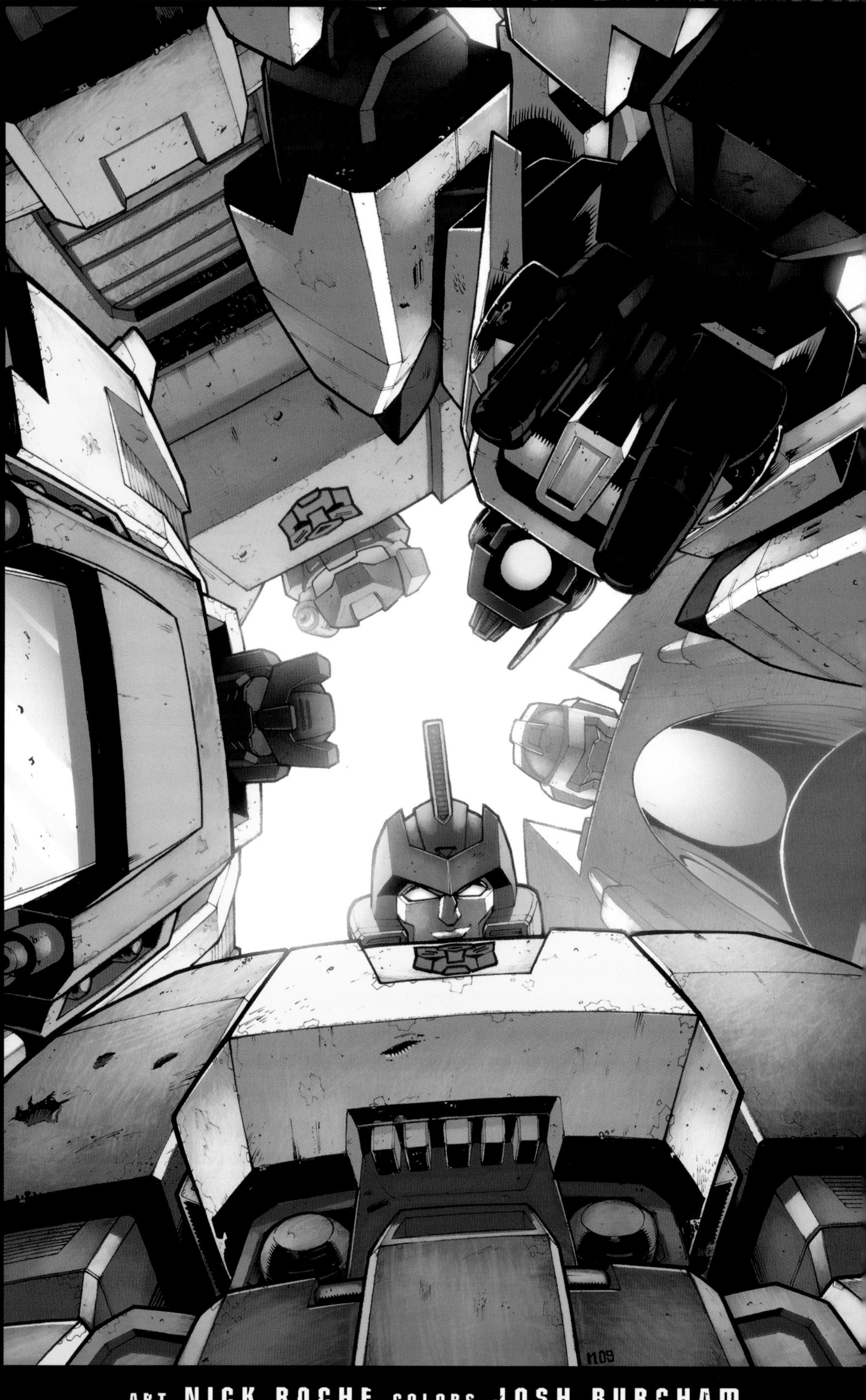
M09

ART **NICK ROCHE** COLORS **JOSH BURCHAM**

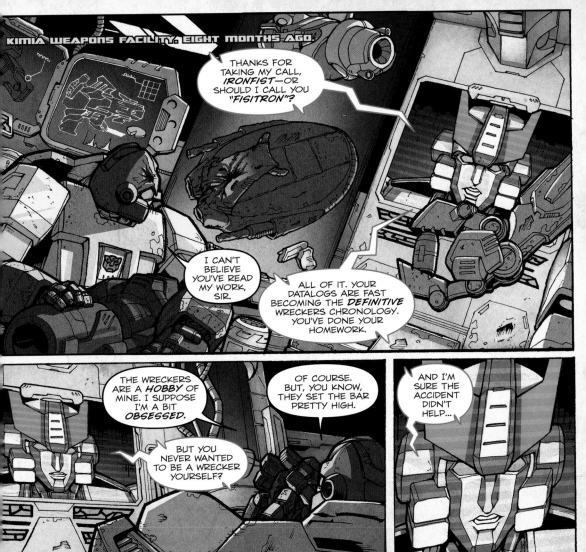

THANKS FOR TAKING MY CALL, *IRONFIST*—OR SHOULD I CALL YOU *"FISITRON"?*

I CAN'T BELIEVE YOU'VE READ MY WORK, SIR.

ALL OF IT. YOUR DATALOGS ARE FAST BECOMING THE *DEFINITIVE* WRECKERS CHRONOLOGY. YOU'VE DONE YOUR HOMEWORK.

THE WRECKERS ARE A *HOBBY* OF MINE. I SUPPOSE I'M A BIT *OBSESSED.*

OF COURSE. BUT, YOU KNOW, THEY SET THE BAR PRETTY HIGH.

AND I'M SURE THE ACCIDENT DIDN'T HELP...

BUT YOU NEVER WANTED TO BE A WRECKER YOURSELF?

YOU *KNOW* ABOUT THAT?

The first rule of being a Wrecker is "stic always greater than the sum of its par seperated, finding your teammates ain priority. The second rule is" e each mission with th

IRONFIST, I HAVE A *PROPOSITION* FOR YOU.

SPRINGER'S PUTTING TOGETHER A NEW TEAM OF WRECKERS, BUT I HAD TO *OVERRULE* ONE OF HIS SELECTIONS. THERE'S ROOM ON THE BENCH FOR ONE MORE—A *WEAPONS EXPERT.*

BUT FIRST I HAVE TO ASK YOU—JUST HOW *BADLY* DO YOU WANT THIS?

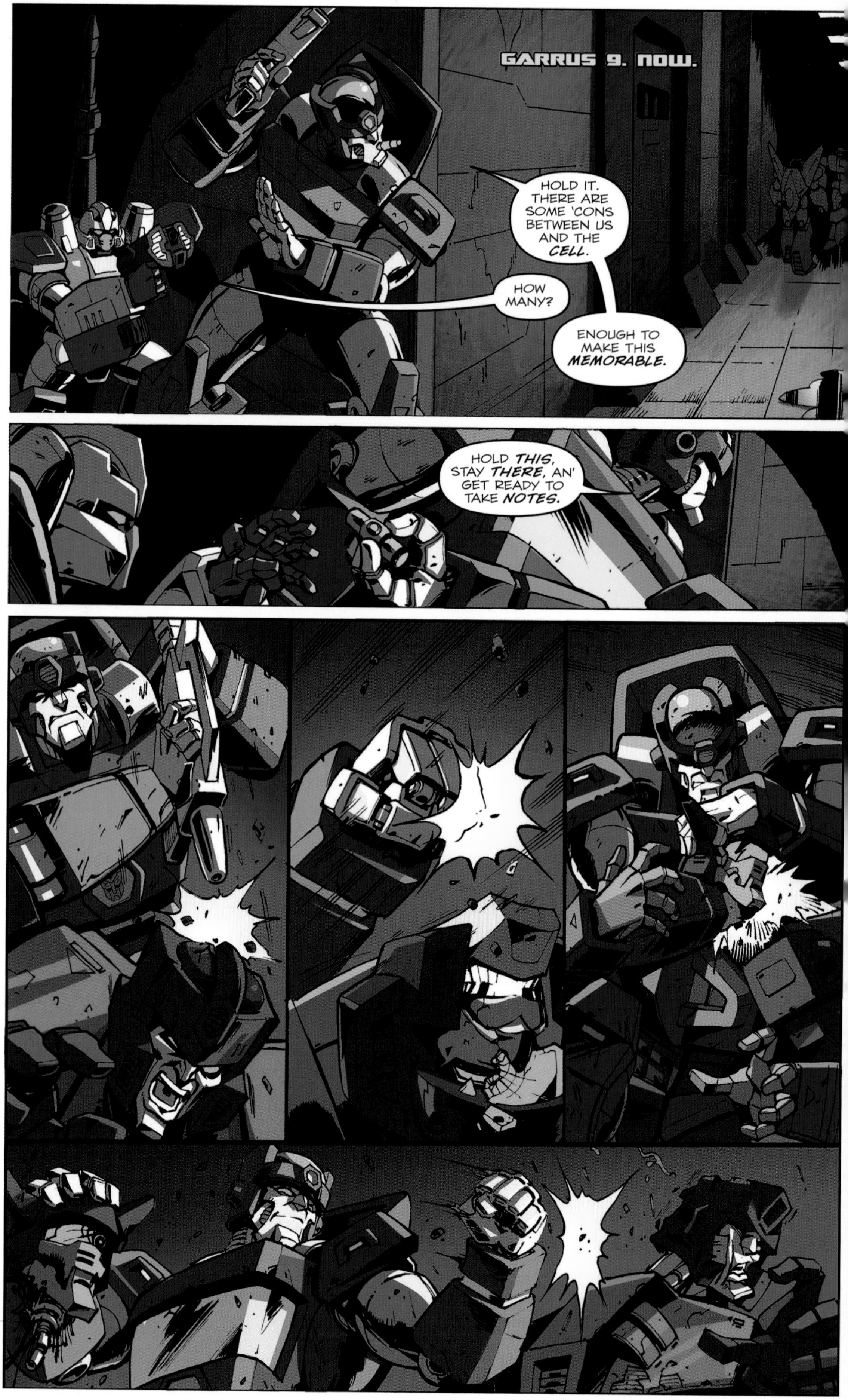
GARRUS 9. NOW.
HOLD IT. THERE ARE SOME 'CONS BETWEEN US AND THE CELL.
HOW MANY?
ENOUGH TO MAKE THIS MEMORABLE.
HOLD THIS, STAY THERE, AN' GET READY TO TAKE NOTES.

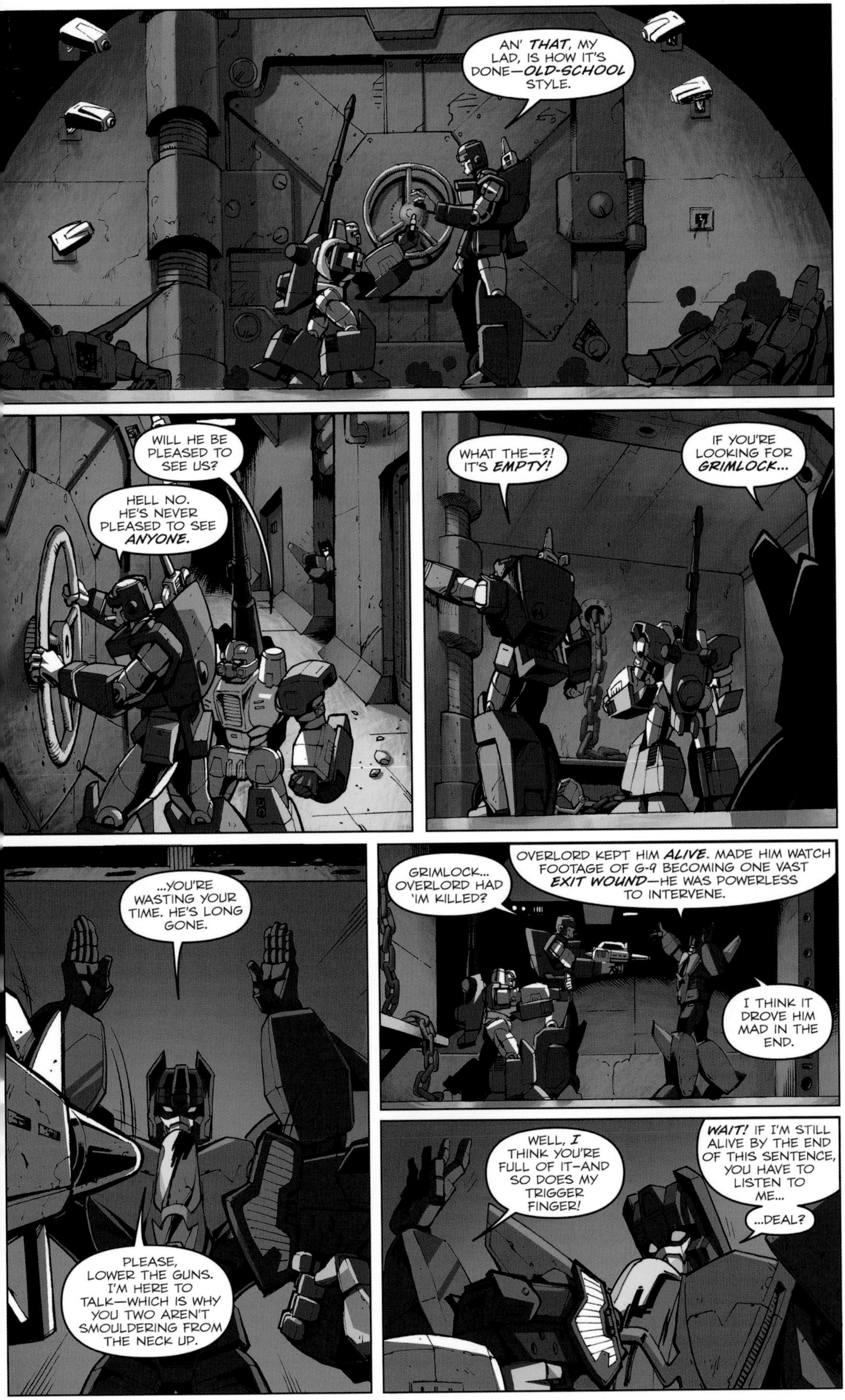
AN' THAT, MY LAD, IS HOW IT'S DONE—OLD-SCHOOL STYLE.
WILL HE BE PLEASED TO SEE US?
HELL NO. HE'S NEVER PLEASED TO SEE ANYONE.
WHAT THE—?! IT'S EMPTY!
IF YOU'RE LOOKING FOR GRIMLOCK...
...YOU'RE WASTING YOUR TIME. HE'S LONG GONE.
PLEASE, LOWER THE GUNS. I'M HERE TO TALK—WHICH IS WHY YOU TWO AREN'T SMOULDERING FROM THE NECK UP.
GRIMLOCK... OVERLORD HAD 'IM KILLED?
OVERLORD KEPT HIM ALIVE. MADE HIM WATCH FOOTAGE OF G-9 BECOMING ONE VAST EXIT WOUND—HE WAS POWERLESS TO INTERVENE.
I THINK IT DROVE HIM MAD IN THE END.
WELL, I THINK YOU'RE FULL OF IT—AND SO DOES MY TRIGGER FINGER!
WAIT! IF I'M STILL ALIVE BY THE END OF THIS SENTENCE, YOU HAVE TO LISTEN TO ME...
...DEAL?

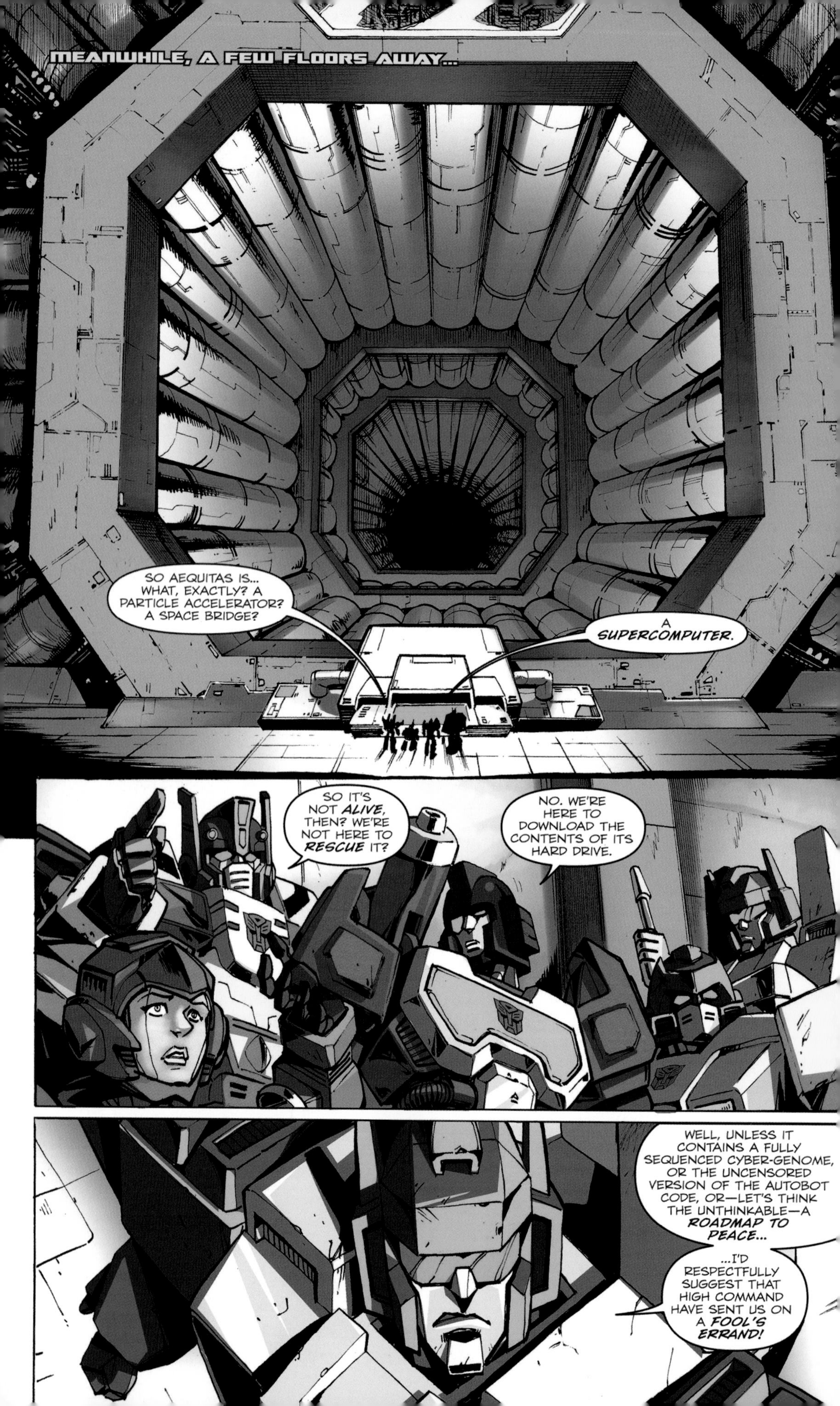
MEANWHILE, A FEW FLOORS AWAY...
SO AEQUITAS IS... WHAT, EXACTLY? A PARTICLE ACCELERATOR? A SPACE BRIDGE?
A *SUPERCOMPUTER*.
SO IT'S NOT *ALIVE*, THEN? WE'RE NOT HERE TO *RESCUE* IT?
NO. WE'RE HERE TO DOWNLOAD THE CONTENTS OF ITS HARD DRIVE.
WELL, UNLESS IT CONTAINS A FULLY SEQUENCED CYBER-GENOME, OR THE UNCENSORED VERSION OF THE AUTOBOT CODE, OR—LET'S THINK THE UNTHINKABLE—A *ROADMAP TO PEACE*...
...I'D RESPECTFULLY SUGGEST THAT HIGH COMMAND HAVE SENT US ON A *FOOL'S ERRAND!*

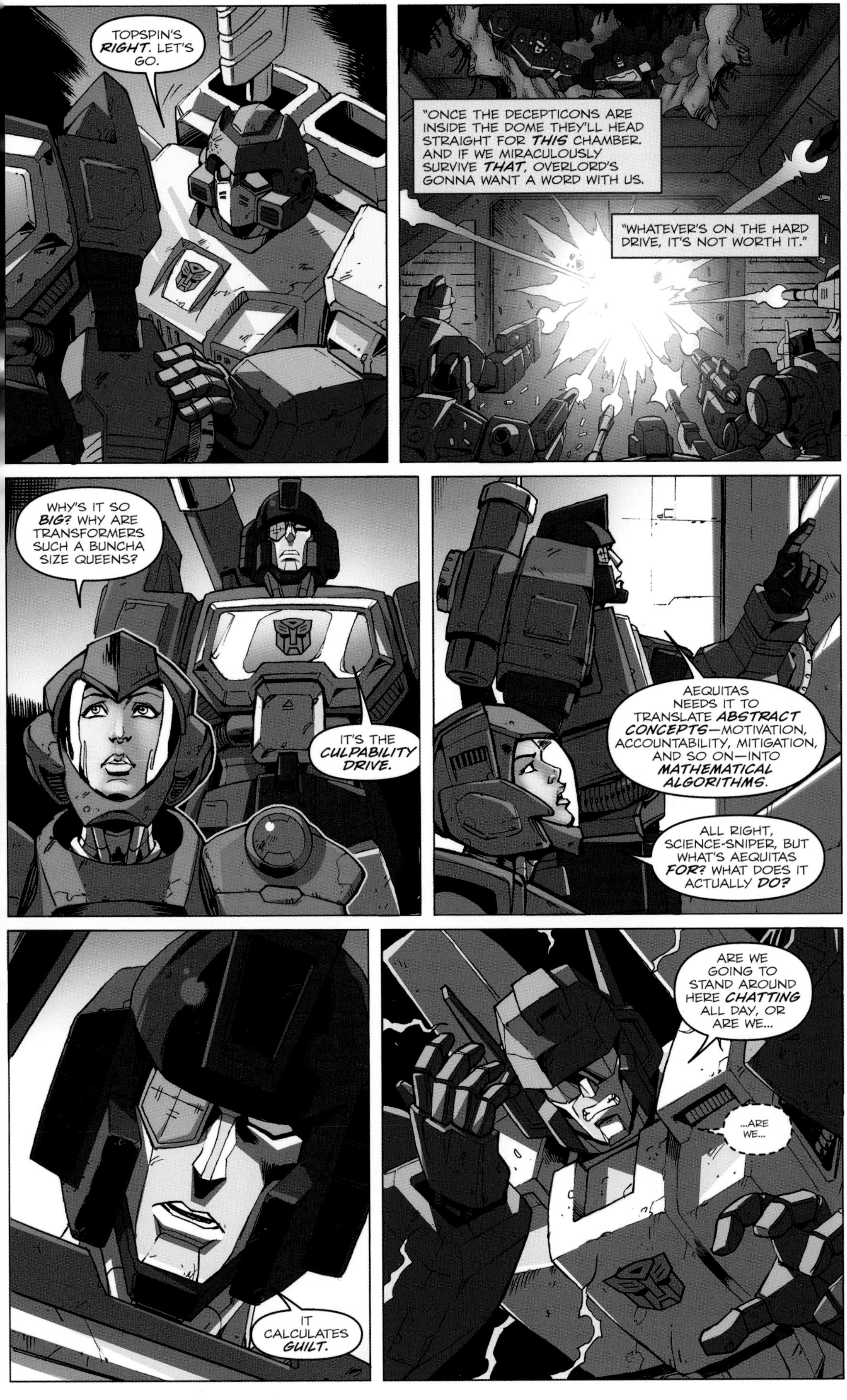

TOPSPIN'S RIGHT. LET'S GO.
"ONCE THE DECEPTICONS ARE INSIDE THE DOME THEY'LL HEAD STRAIGHT FOR THIS CHAMBER. AND IF WE MIRACULOUSLY SURVIVE THAT, OVERLORD'S GONNA WANT A WORD WITH US.
"WHATEVER'S ON THE HARD DRIVE, IT'S NOT WORTH IT."
WHY'S IT SO BIG? WHY ARE TRANSFORMERS SUCH A BUNCHA SIZE QUEENS?
IT'S THE CULPABILITY DRIVE.
AEQUITAS NEEDS IT TO TRANSLATE ABSTRACT CONCEPTS—MOTIVATION, ACCOUNTABILITY, MITIGATION, AND SO ON—INTO MATHEMATICAL ALGORITHMS.
ALL RIGHT, SCIENCE-SNIPER, BUT WHAT'S AEQUITAS FOR? WHAT DOES IT ACTUALLY DO?
IT CALCULATES GUILT.
ARE WE GOING TO STAND AROUND HERE CHATTING ALL DAY, OR ARE WE...
...ARE WE...

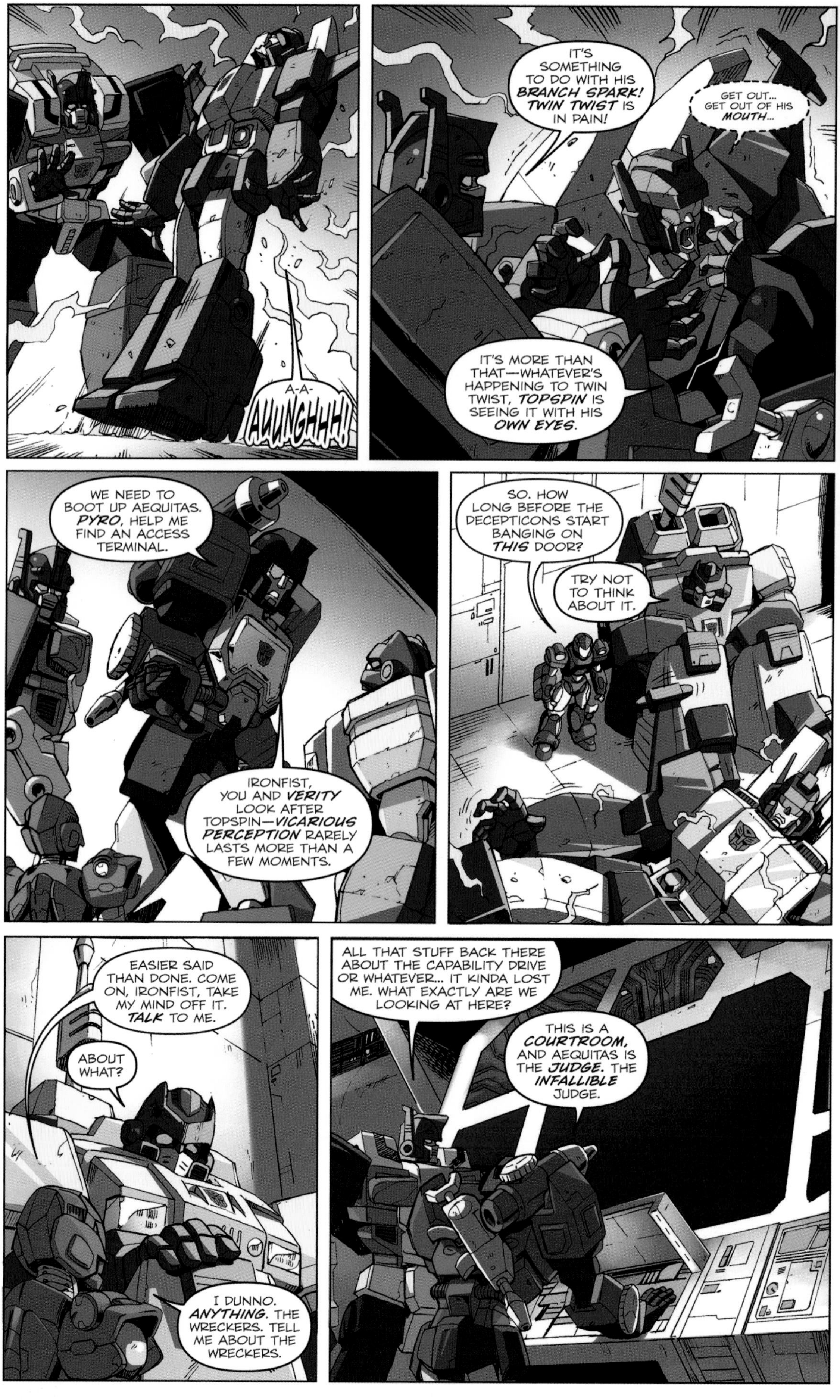

A-A-
AUUNGHHH!
IT'S SOMETHING TO DO WITH HIS BRANCH SPARK! TWIN TWIST IS IN PAIN!
GET OUT... GET OUT OF HIS MOUTH...
IT'S MORE THAN THAT—WHATEVER'S HAPPENING TO TWIN TWIST, TOPSPIN IS SEEING IT WITH HIS OWN EYES.
WE NEED TO BOOT UP AEQUITAS. PYRO, HELP ME FIND AN ACCESS TERMINAL.
IRONFIST, YOU AND VERITY LOOK AFTER TOPSPIN—VICARIOUS PERCEPTION RARELY LASTS MORE THAN A FEW MOMENTS.
SO. HOW LONG BEFORE THE DECEPTICONS START BANGING ON THIS DOOR?
TRY NOT TO THINK ABOUT IT.
EASIER SAID THAN DONE. COME ON, IRONFIST, TAKE MY MIND OFF IT. TALK TO ME.
ABOUT WHAT?
I DUNNO. ANYTHING. THE WRECKERS. TELL ME ABOUT THE WRECKERS.
ALL THAT STUFF BACK THERE ABOUT THE CAPABILITY DRIVE OR WHATEVER... IT KINDA LOST ME. WHAT EXACTLY ARE WE LOOKING AT HERE?
THIS IS A COURTROOM, AND AEQUITAS IS THE JUDGE. THE INFALLIBLE JUDGE.

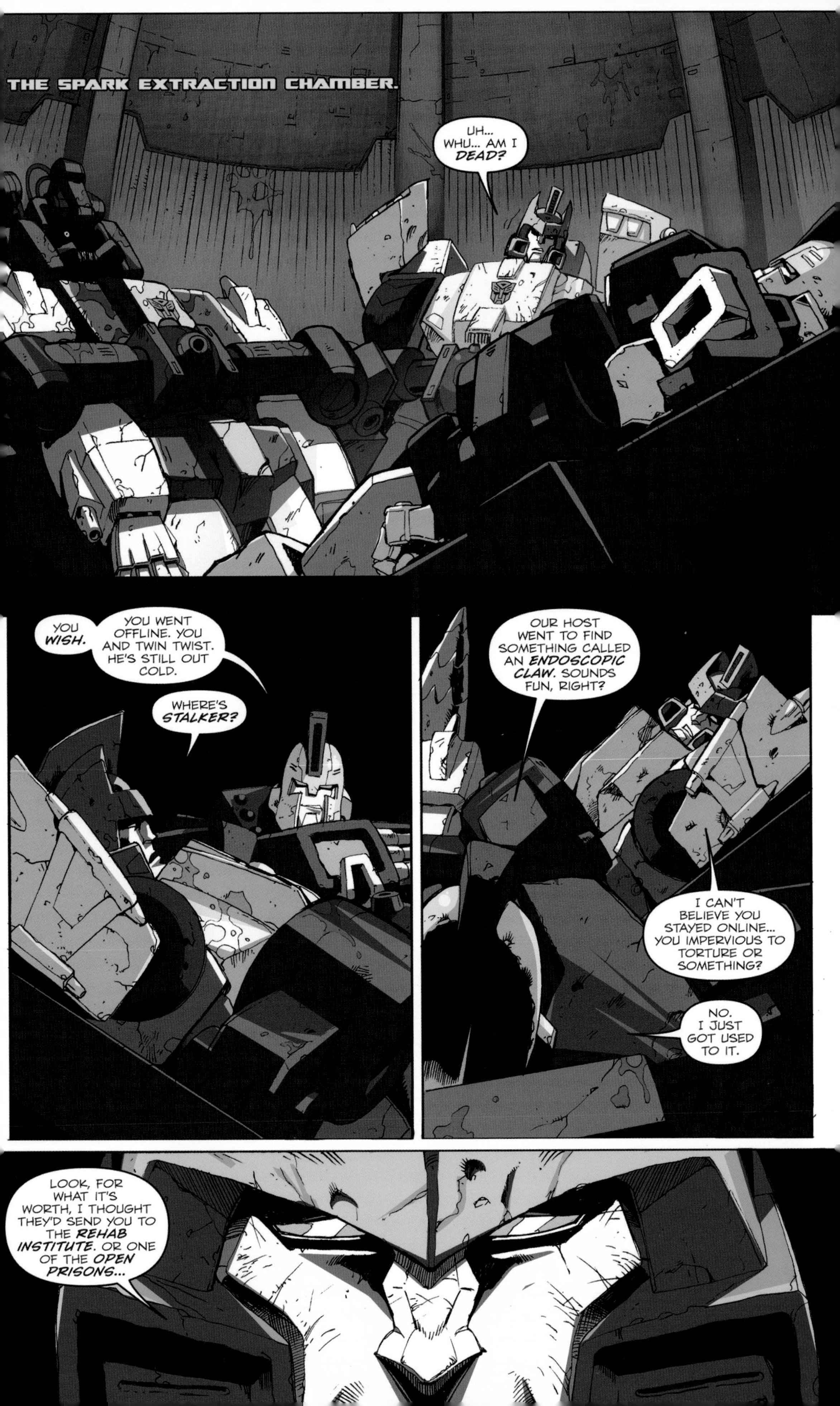
THE SPARK EXTRACTION CHAMBER.
UH... WHU... AM I DEAD?
YOU WISH.
YOU WENT OFFLINE. YOU AND TWIN TWIST. HE'S STILL OUT COLD.
WHERE'S STALKER?
OUR HOST WENT TO FIND SOMETHING CALLED AN ENDOSCOPIC CLAW. SOUNDS FUN, RIGHT?
I CAN'T BELIEVE YOU STAYED ONLINE... YOU IMPERVIOUS TO TORTURE OR SOMETHING?
NO. I JUST GOT USED TO IT.
LOOK, FOR WHAT IT'S WORTH, I THOUGHT THEY'D SEND YOU TO THE REHAB INSTITUTE. OR ONE OF THE OPEN PRISONS...

AFTER *YOUR* TESTIMONY?! THEY PLUGGED YOU INTO *AEQUITAS* AND THE FIRST THING YOU SAID WAS, "I SAW HIM DO IT."

THE DECEPTICONS TRIED FOR HUNDREDS OF YEARS TO RIP THE WRECKERS APART. YOU MANAGED IT IN *FIVE WORDS*.

IF YOU KNEW YOU'D BE A TARGET IN G-9, WHY DIDN'T YOU OPT FOR *SPARK EXTRACTION?*

YOU MEAN YOU STILL *DON'T?*

BECAUSE UNLESS YOU'RE *THREAT LEVEL NINE*, YOU ONLY GET THAT CHOICE IF YOU ACCEPT WHAT YOU DID WAS WRONG.

LOOK, I HATE MYSELF FOR REPORTING YOU TO HIGH COMMAND. BUT IF YOU *STILL* CAN'T UNDERSTAND WHY I DID IT, IT'S NO WONDER YOU DETEST ME.

I NEVER SAID I DETESTED—

I WANT TO FORGIVE YOU, IMPACTOR. HELL, I WANT TO FORGIVE *MYSELF*. BUT I CAN'T DO *EITHER* UNTIL YOU REALIZE THAT WHAT YOU DID VIOLATED EVERY TENET OF THE AUTOBOT CODE.

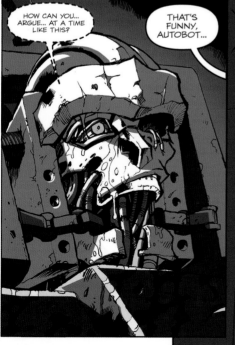

HOW CAN YOU... ARGUE... AT A TIME LIKE THIS?

THAT'S FUNNY, AUTOBOT...

...I WAS ASKING MYSELF THE SAME THING.

NOW, I REALLY THINK IT'S TIME THAT ONE OF YOU *DIED*.

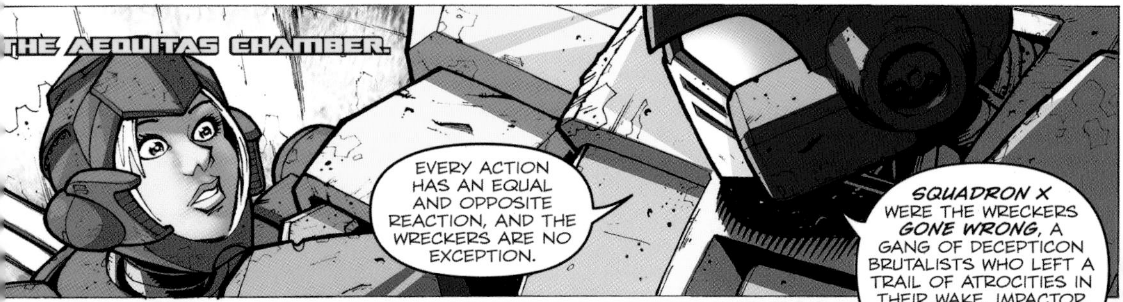
THE AEQUITAS CHAMBER.
EVERY ACTION HAS AN EQUAL AND OPPOSITE REACTION, AND THE WRECKERS ARE NO EXCEPTION.
SQUADRON X WERE THE WRECKERS GONE WRONG, A GANG OF DECEPTICON BRUTALISTS WHO LEFT A TRAIL OF ATROCITIES IN THEIR WAKE. IMPACTOR WAS OBSESSED WITH TRACKING THEM DOWN.

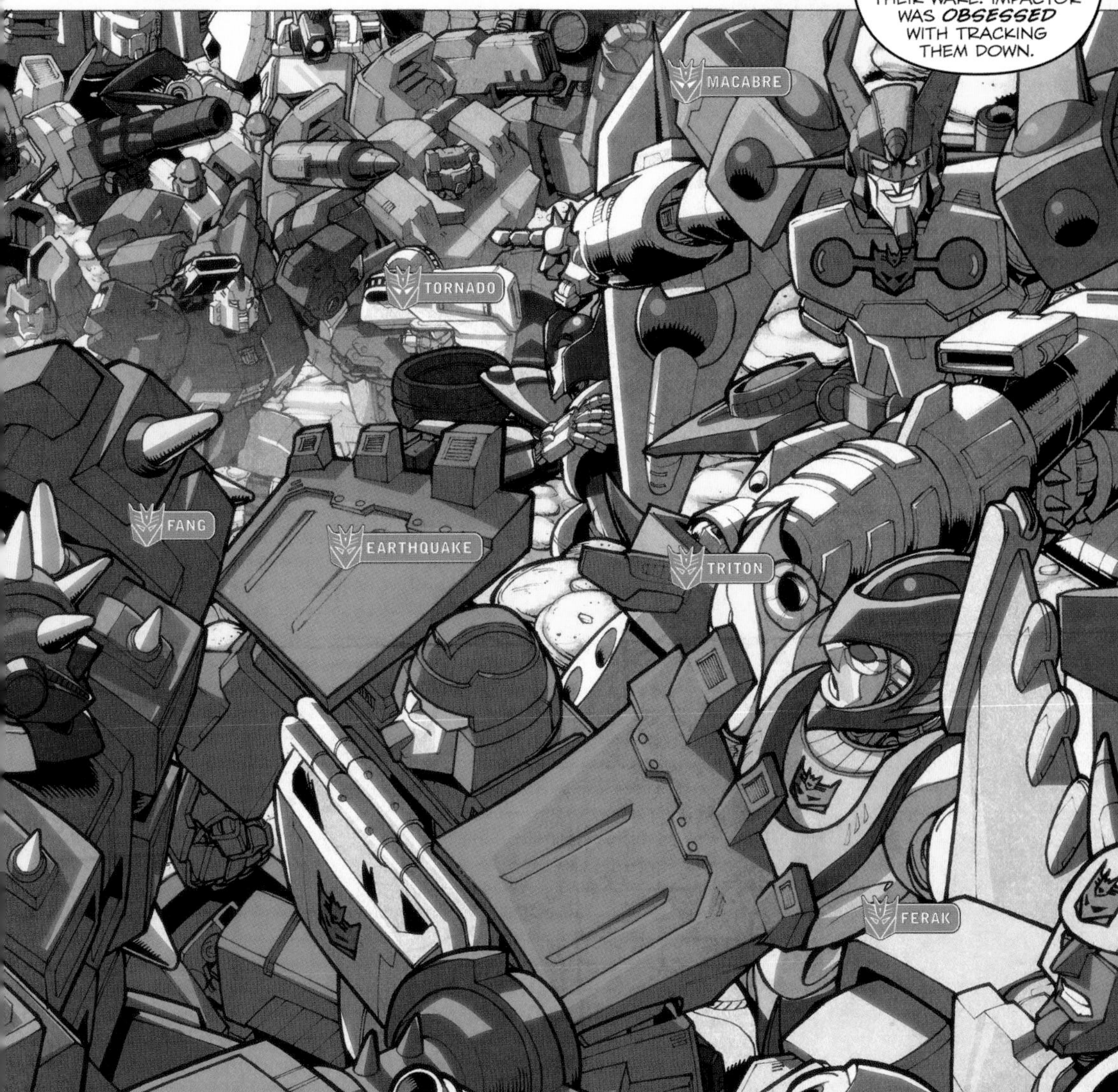
MACABRE
TORNADO
FANG
EARTHQUAKE
TRITON
FERAK
CROSSCUT

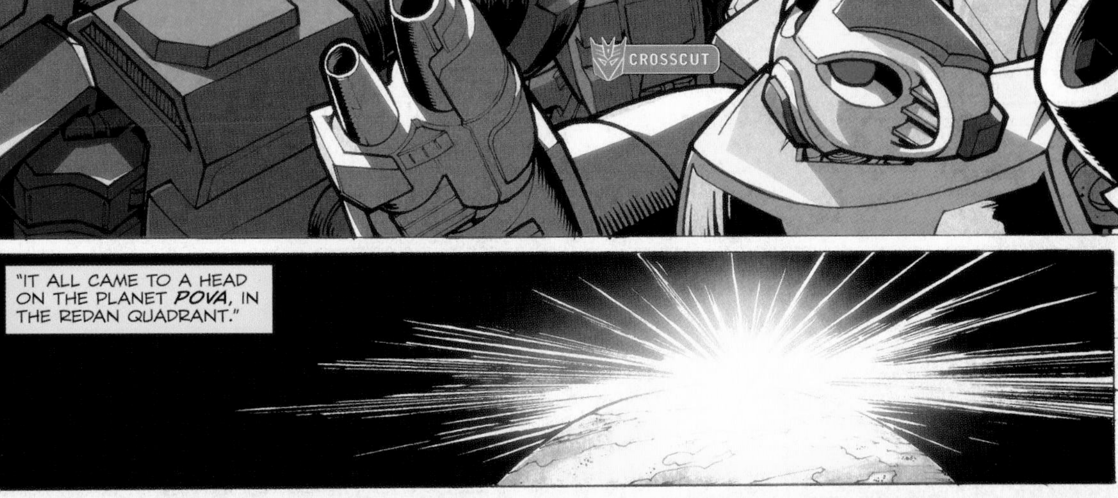
"IT ALL CAME TO A HEAD ON THE PLANET POVA, IN THE REDAN QUADRANT."

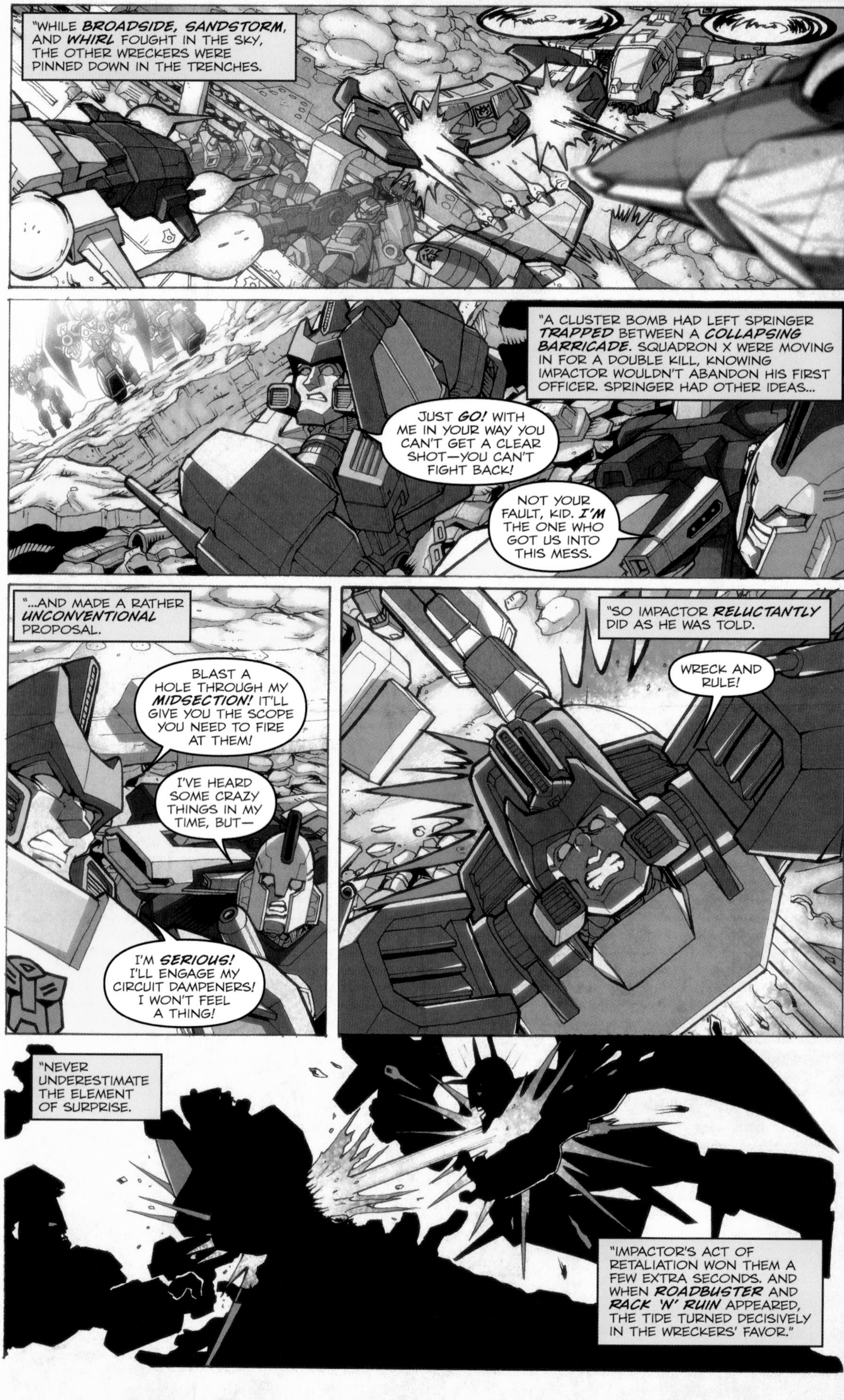
"WHILE BROADSIDE, SANDSTORM, AND WHIRL FOUGHT IN THE SKY, THE OTHER WRECKERS WERE PINNED DOWN IN THE TRENCHES.
"A CLUSTER BOMB HAD LEFT SPRINGER TRAPPED BETWEEN A COLLAPSING BARRICADE. SQUADRON X WERE MOVING IN FOR A DOUBLE KILL, KNOWING IMPACTOR WOULDN'T ABANDON HIS FIRST OFFICER. SPRINGER HAD OTHER IDEAS...
JUST GO! WITH ME IN YOUR WAY YOU CAN'T GET A CLEAR SHOT—YOU CAN'T FIGHT BACK!
NOT YOUR FAULT, KID. I'M THE ONE WHO GOT US INTO THIS MESS.
"...AND MADE A RATHER UNCONVENTIONAL PROPOSAL.
BLAST A HOLE THROUGH MY MIDSECTION! IT'LL GIVE YOU THE SCOPE YOU NEED TO FIRE AT THEM!
I'VE HEARD SOME CRAZY THINGS IN MY TIME, BUT—
I'M SERIOUS! I'LL ENGAGE MY CIRCUIT DAMPENERS! I WON'T FEEL A THING!
"SO IMPACTOR RELUCTANTLY DID AS HE WAS TOLD.
WRECK AND RULE!
"NEVER UNDERESTIMATE THE ELEMENT OF SURPRISE.
"IMPACTOR'S ACT OF RETALIATION WON THEM A FEW EXTRA SECONDS. AND WHEN ROADBUSTER AND RACK 'N' RUIN APPEARED, THE TIDE TURNED DECISIVELY IN THE WRECKERS' FAVOR."

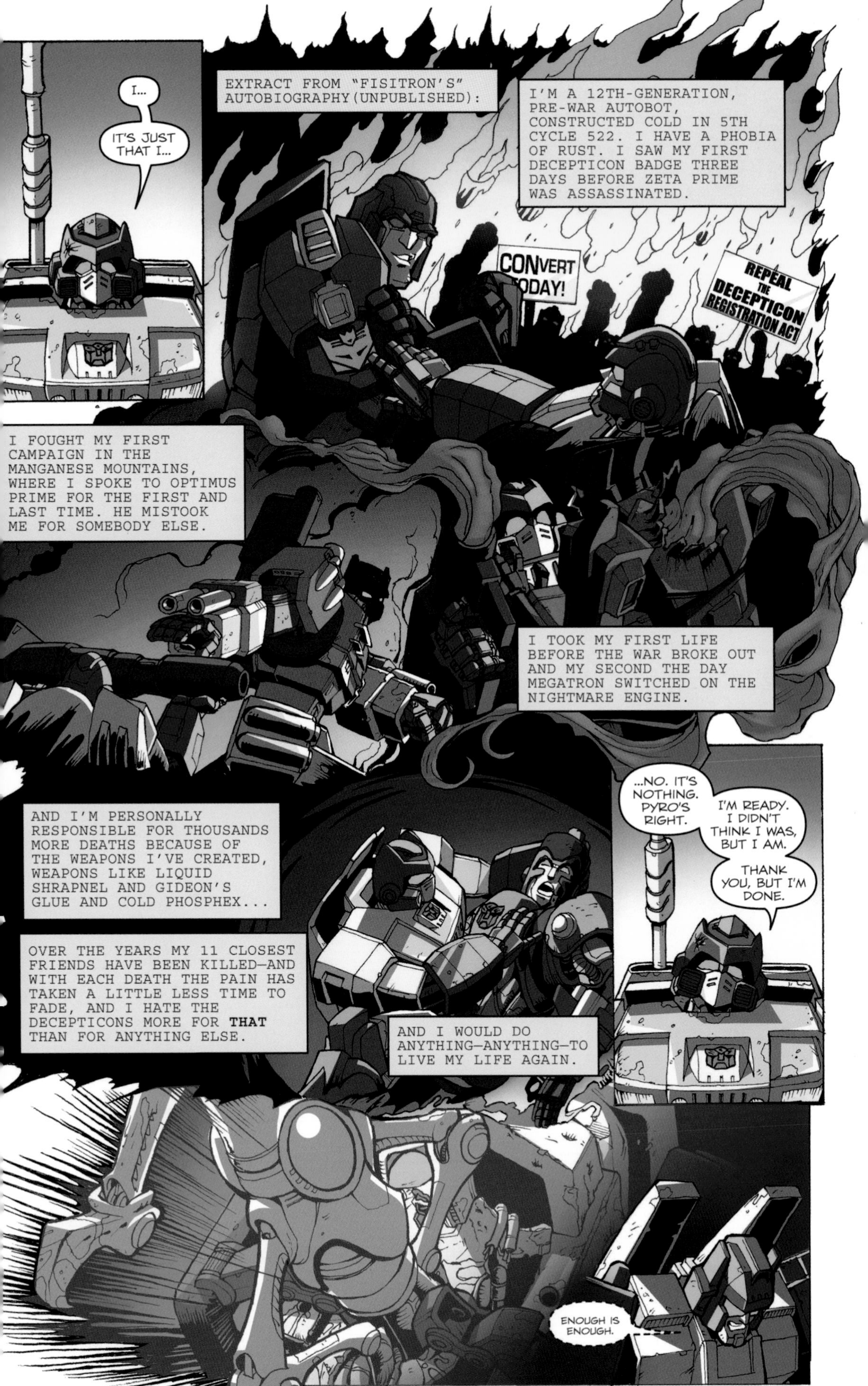
I...
IT'S JUST THAT I...
EXTRACT FROM "FISITRON'S" AUTOBIOGRAPHY(UNPUBLISHED):
I'M A 12TH-GENERATION, PRE-WAR AUTOBOT, CONSTRUCTED COLD IN 5TH CYCLE 522. I HAVE A PHOBIA OF RUST. I SAW MY FIRST DECEPTICON BADGE THREE DAYS BEFORE ZETA PRIME WAS ASSASSINATED.
CONVERT TODAY!
REPEAL THE DECEPTICON REGISTRATION ACT
I FOUGHT MY FIRST CAMPAIGN IN THE MANGANESE MOUNTAINS, WHERE I SPOKE TO OPTIMUS PRIME FOR THE FIRST AND LAST TIME. HE MISTOOK ME FOR SOMEBODY ELSE.
I TOOK MY FIRST LIFE BEFORE THE WAR BROKE OUT AND MY SECOND THE DAY MEGATRON SWITCHED ON THE NIGHTMARE ENGINE.
AND I'M PERSONALLY RESPONSIBLE FOR THOUSANDS MORE DEATHS BECAUSE OF THE WEAPONS I'VE CREATED, WEAPONS LIKE LIQUID SHRAPNEL AND GIDEON'S GLUE AND COLD PHOSPHEX...
OVER THE YEARS MY 11 CLOSEST FRIENDS HAVE BEEN KILLED—AND WITH EACH DEATH THE PAIN HAS TAKEN A LITTLE LESS TIME TO FADE, AND I HATE THE DECEPTICONS MORE FOR **THAT** THAN FOR ANYTHING ELSE.
AND I WOULD DO ANYTHING—ANYTHING—TO LIVE MY LIFE AGAIN.
...NO. IT'S NOTHING. PYRO'S RIGHT.
I'M READY. I DIDN'T THINK I WAS, BUT I AM.
THANK YOU, BUT I'M DONE.
ENOUGH IS ENOUGH.

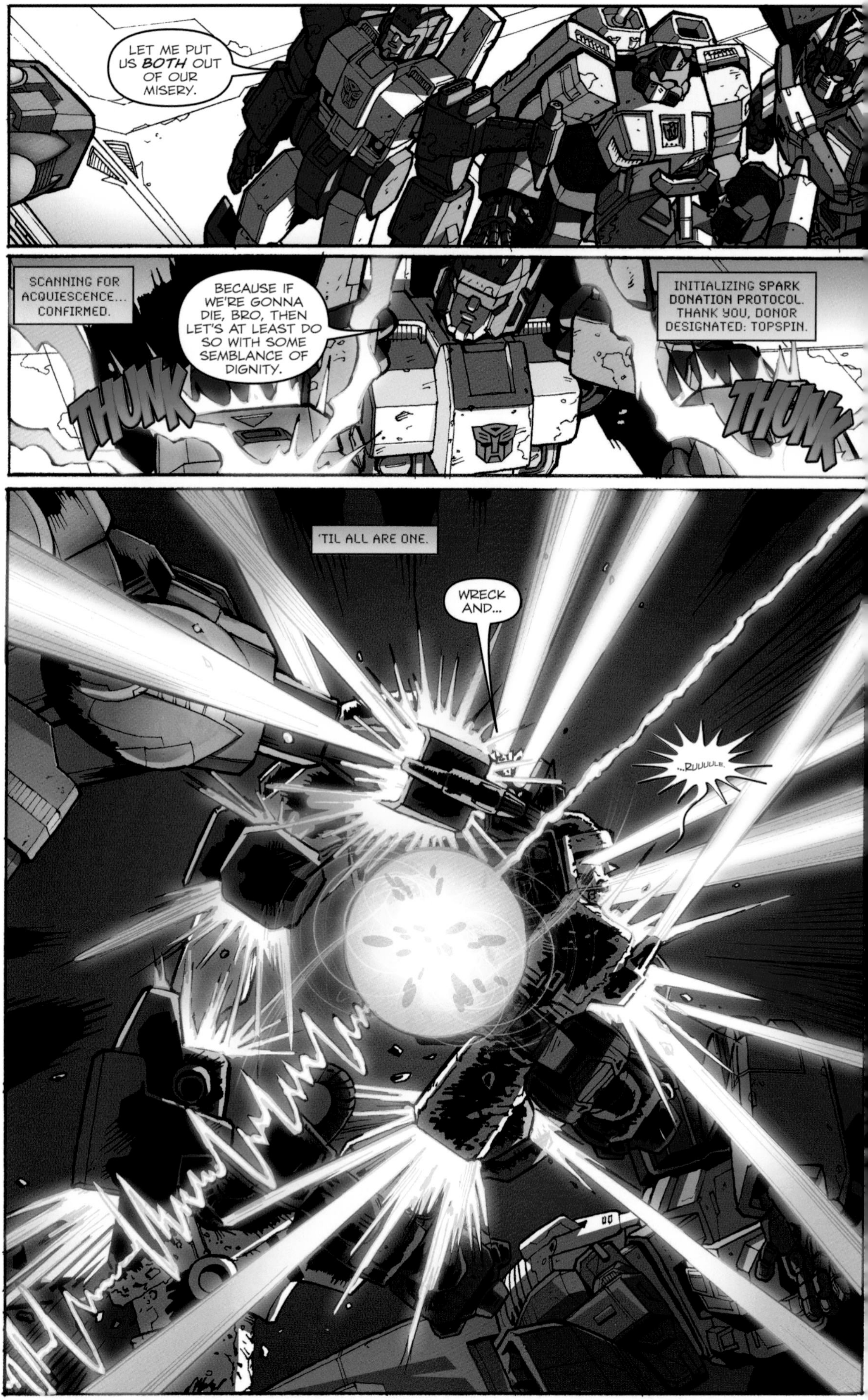
LET ME PUT US BOTH OUT OF OUR MISERY.
SCANNING FOR ACQUIESCENCE... CONFIRMED.
BECAUSE IF WE'RE GONNA DIE, BRO, THEN LET'S AT LEAST DO SO WITH SOME SEMBLANCE OF DIGNITY.
INITIALIZING SPARK DONATION PROTOCOL. THANK YOU, DONOR DESIGNATED: TOPSPIN.
THUNK
THUNK
'TIL ALL ARE ONE.
WRECK AND...
...RUUUULE.

WHAT... THE *HELL* HAPPENED? I WAS *JUST* STARTING TO GET INTO THAT!

I THINK WE JUST WITNESSED AN *ASSISTED SUICIDE.*

ALL RIGHT THEN—SO WHO'S FOR TWIN TWIST'S PORTION OF SADISM?

THE AEQUITAS CHAMBER.

AS I SUSPECTED: AEQUITAS IS LINKED TO ALL OF G-9'S *SURVEILLANCE CAMERAS.*

LOOK! THERE'S *IMPACTOR!* WHAT'S THAT DECEPTICON *DOING* TO HIM?

AND WHAT ABOUT THOSE DECEPTICONS THERE? WHERE'S *THAT?*

THAT, IRONFIST, WOULD BE THE *DOOR...*

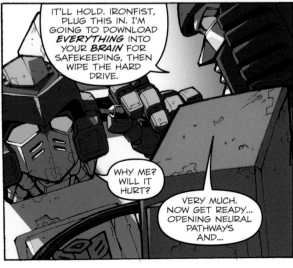

IT'LL HOLD. IRONFIST, PLUG THIS IN. I'M GOING TO DOWNLOAD *EVERYTHING* INTO YOUR *BRAIN* FOR SAFEKEEPING, THEN WIPE THE HARD DRIVE.

WHY ME? WILL IT HURT?

VERY MUCH. NOW GET READY... OPENING NEURAL PATHWAYS AND...

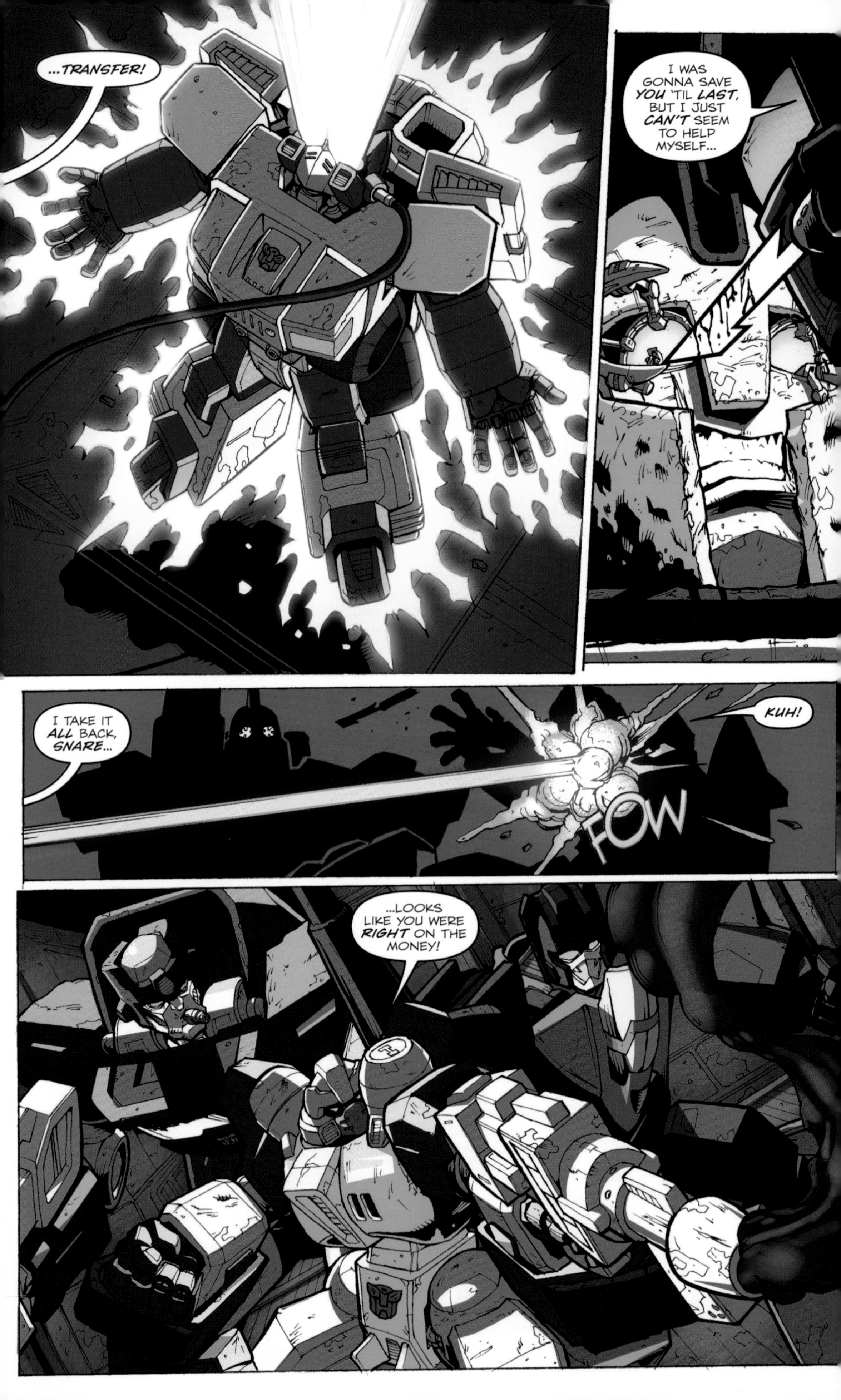
...TRANSFER!
I WAS GONNA SAVE YOU 'TIL LAST, BUT I JUST CAN'T SEEM TO HELP MYSELF...
I TAKE IT ALL BACK, SNARE...
KUH!
FOW
...LOOKS LIKE YOU WERE RIGHT ON THE MONEY!

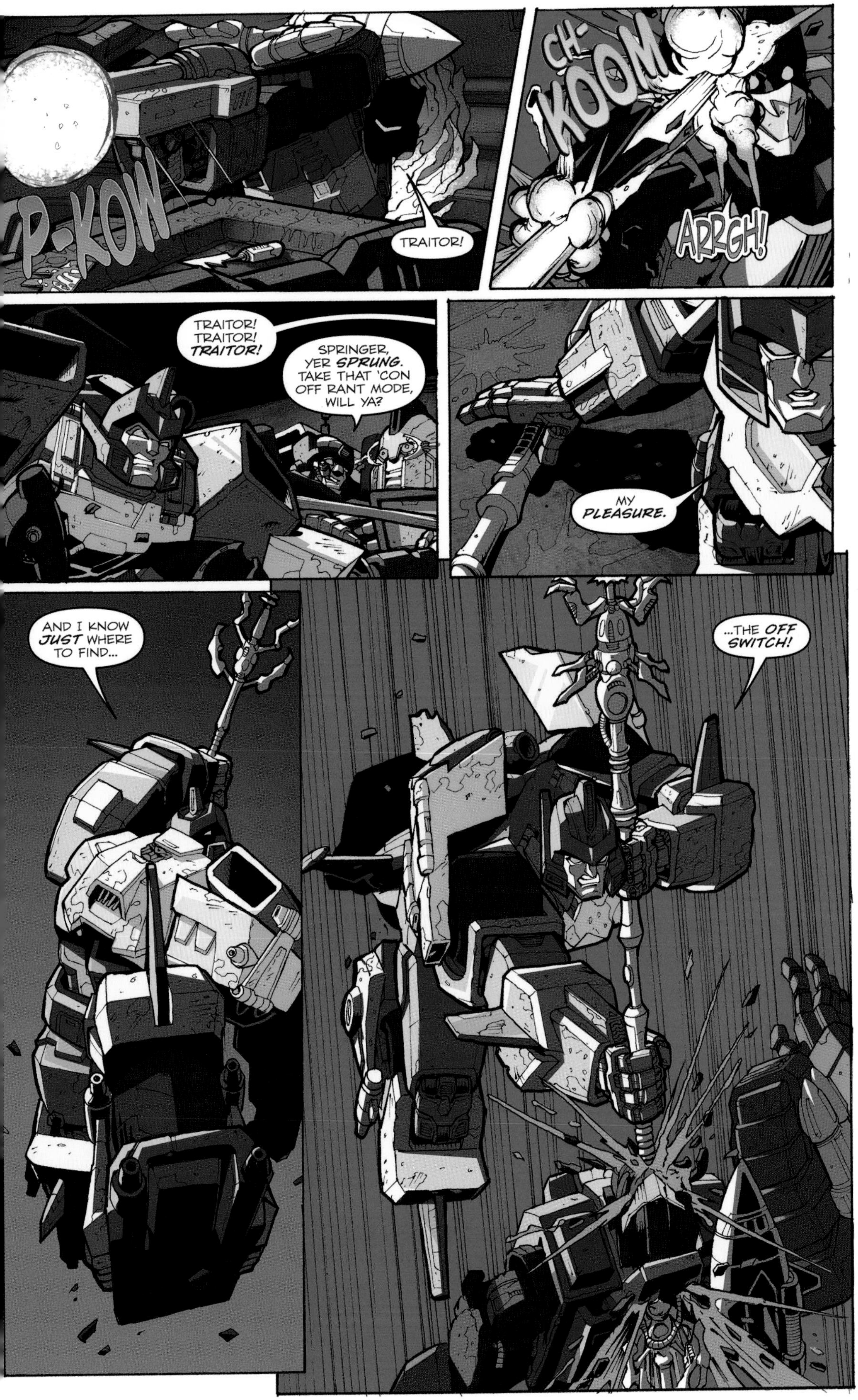
P-KOW
TRAITOR!
CH-KOOM
ARRGH!
TRAITOR! TRAITOR! TRAITOR!
SPRINGER, YER SPRUNG. TAKE THAT 'CON OFF RANT MODE, WILL YA?
MY PLEASURE.
AND I KNOW JUST WHERE TO FIND...
...THE OFF SWITCH!

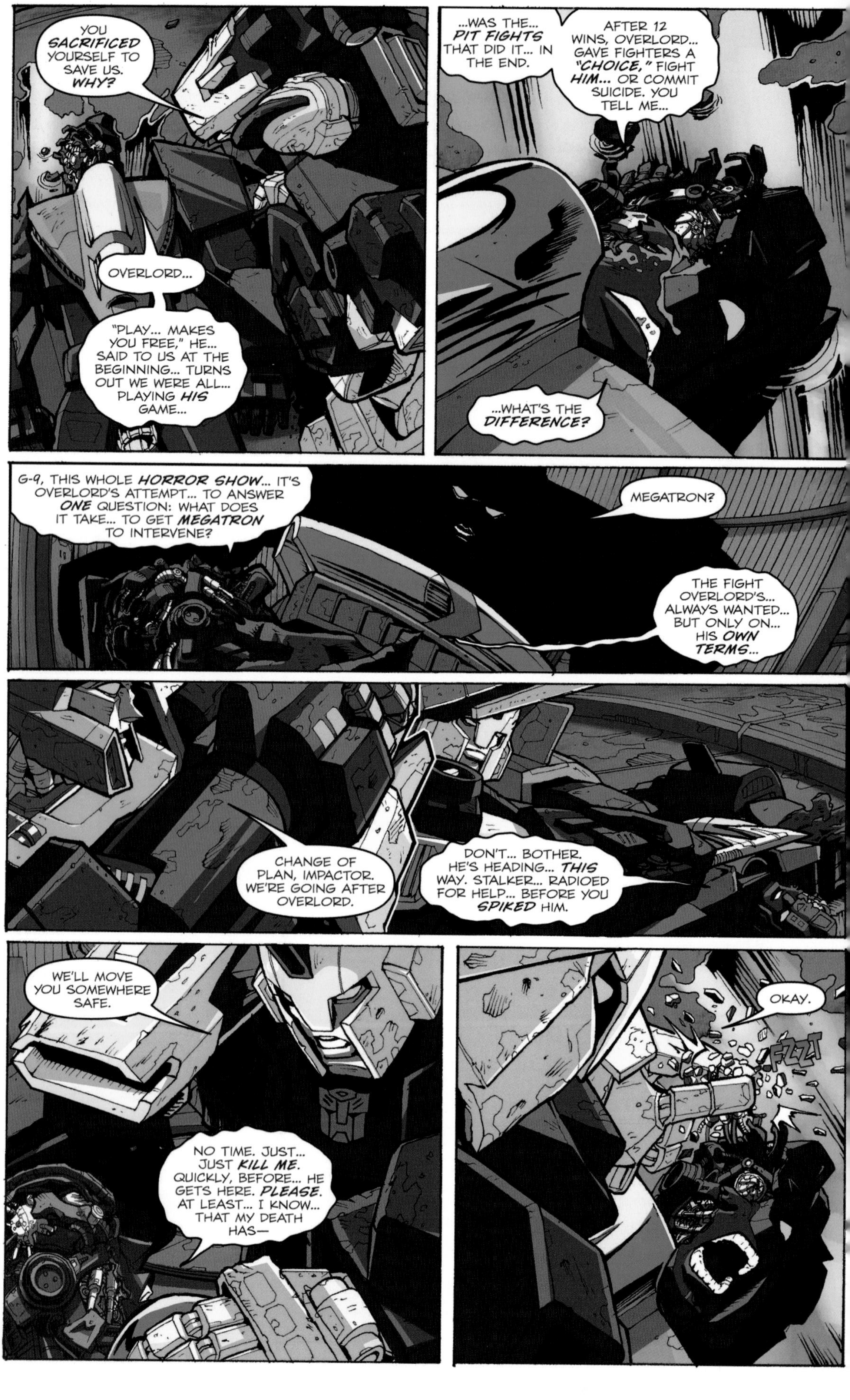
YOU SACRIFICED YOURSELF TO SAVE US. WHY?
OVERLORD...
"PLAY... MAKES YOU FREE," HE... SAID TO US AT THE BEGINNING... TURNS OUT WE WERE ALL... PLAYING HIS GAME...
...WAS THE... PIT FIGHTS THAT DID IT... IN THE END.
AFTER 12 WINS, OVERLORD... GAVE FIGHTERS A "CHOICE," FIGHT HIM... OR COMMIT SUICIDE. YOU TELL ME...
...WHAT'S THE DIFFERENCE?
G-9, THIS WHOLE HORROR SHOW... IT'S OVERLORD'S ATTEMPT... TO ANSWER ONE QUESTION: WHAT DOES IT TAKE... TO GET MEGATRON TO INTERVENE?
MEGATRON?
THE FIGHT OVERLORD'S... ALWAYS WANTED... BUT ONLY ON... HIS OWN TERMS...
CHANGE OF PLAN, IMPACTOR. WE'RE GOING AFTER OVERLORD.
DON'T... BOTHER. HE'S HEADING... THIS WAY. STALKER... RADIOED FOR HELP... BEFORE YOU SPIKED HIM.
WE'LL MOVE YOU SOMEWHERE SAFE.
NO TIME. JUST... JUST KILL ME. QUICKLY, BEFORE... HE GETS HERE. PLEASE. AT LEAST... I KNOW... THAT MY DEATH HAS—
OKAY.
FZZT

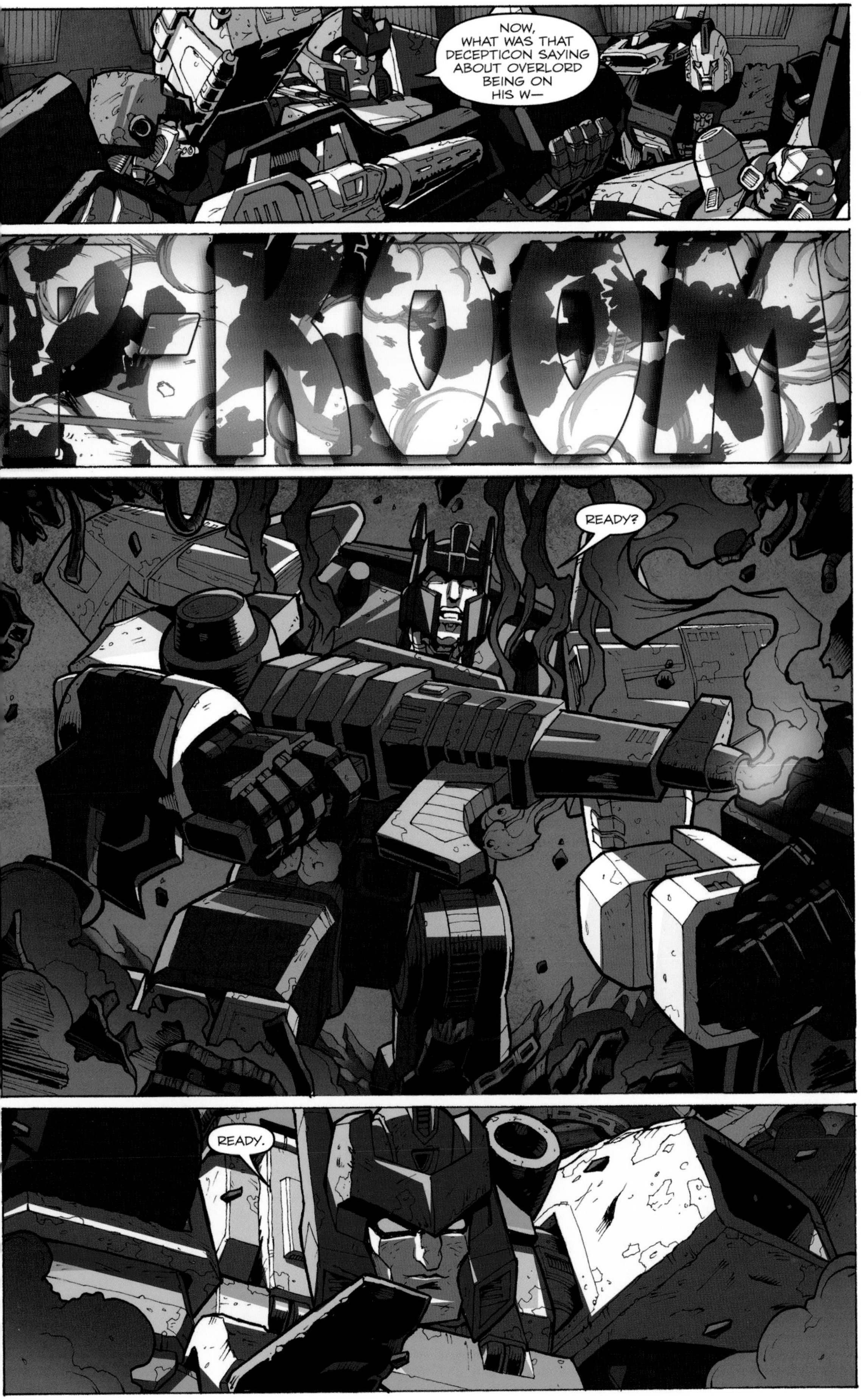
NOW, WHAT WAS THAT DECEPTICON SAYING ABOUT OVERLORD BEING ON HIS W—
KROOM
READY?
READY.

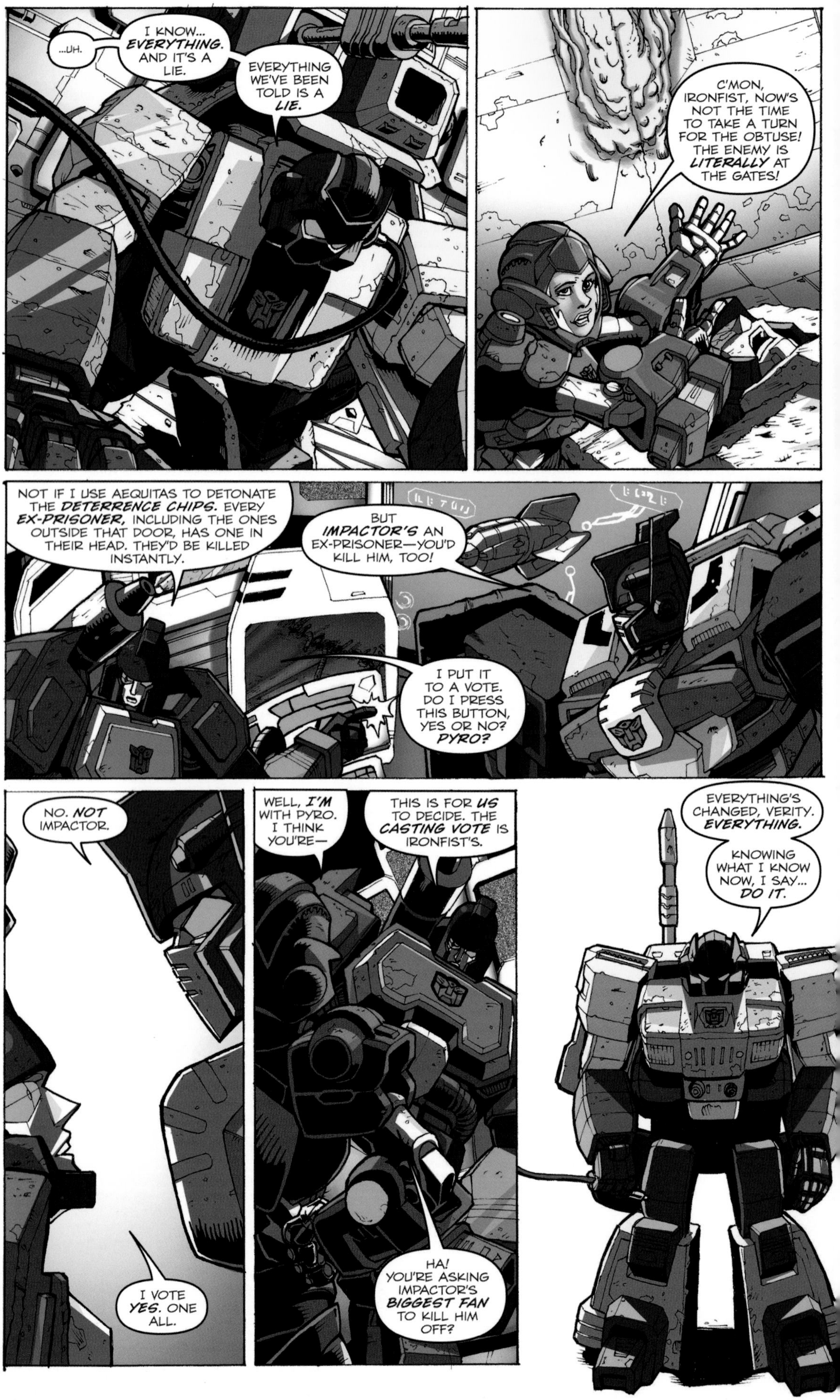
...UH.
I KNOW... EVERYTHING. AND IT'S A LIE.
EVERYTHING WE'VE BEEN TOLD IS A LIE.
C'MON, IRONFIST, NOW'S NOT THE TIME TO TAKE A TURN FOR THE OBTUSE! THE ENEMY IS LITERALLY AT THE GATES!
NOT IF I USE AEQUITAS TO DETONATE THE DETERRENCE CHIPS. EVERY EX-PRISONER, INCLUDING THE ONES OUTSIDE THAT DOOR, HAS ONE IN THEIR HEAD. THEY'D BE KILLED INSTANTLY.
BUT IMPACTOR'S AN EX-PRISONER—YOU'D KILL HIM, TOO!
I PUT IT TO A VOTE. DO I PRESS THIS BUTTON, YES OR NO? PYRO?
NO. NOT IMPACTOR.
I VOTE YES. ONE ALL.
WELL, I'M WITH PYRO. I THINK YOU'RE—
THIS IS FOR US TO DECIDE. THE CASTING VOTE IS IRONFIST'S.
HA! YOU'RE ASKING IMPACTOR'S BIGGEST FAN TO KILL HIM OFF?
EVERYTHING'S CHANGED, VERITY. EVERYTHING.
KNOWING WHAT I KNOW NOW, I SAY... DO IT.

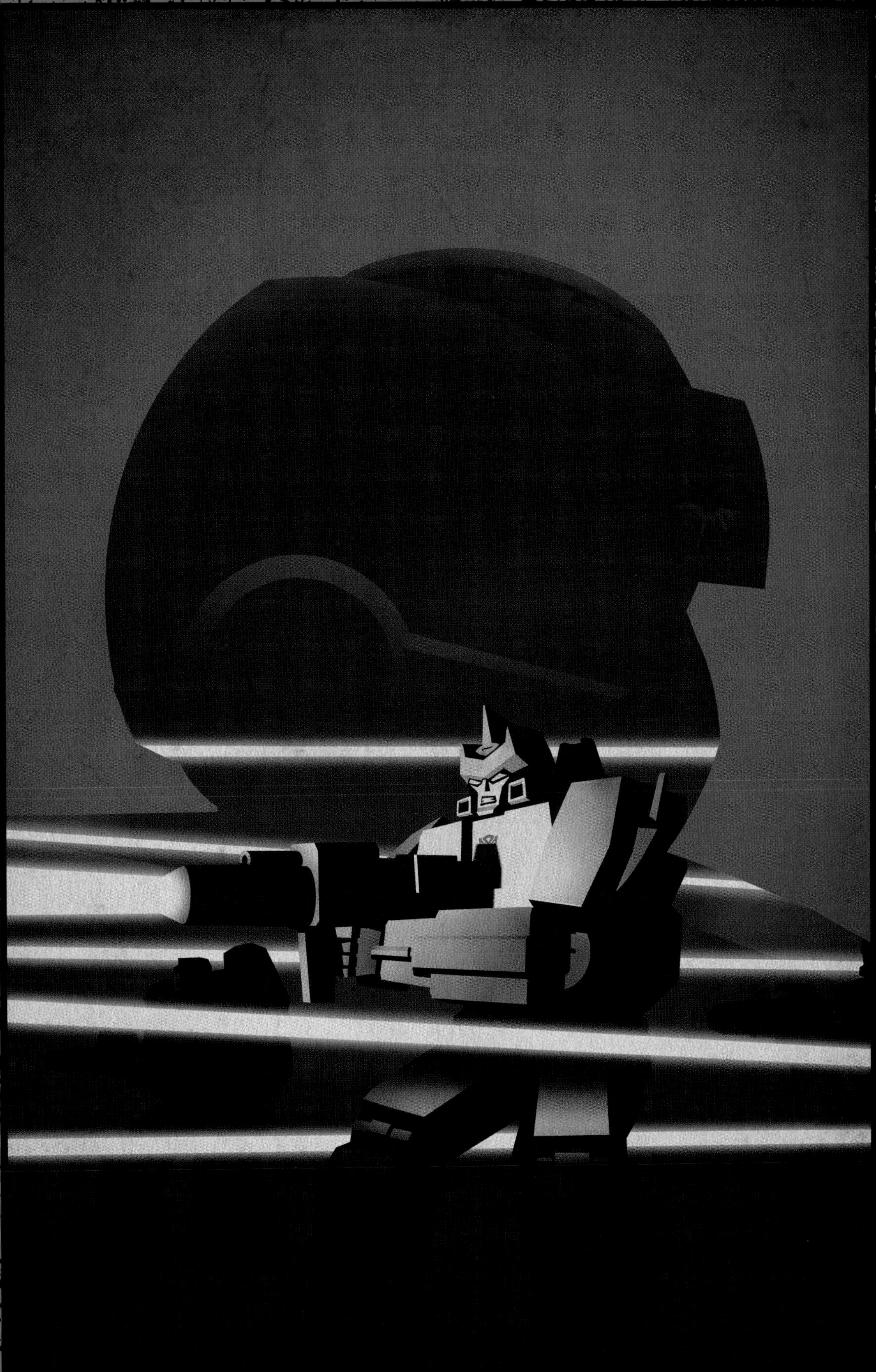

ART TREVOR HUTCHISON

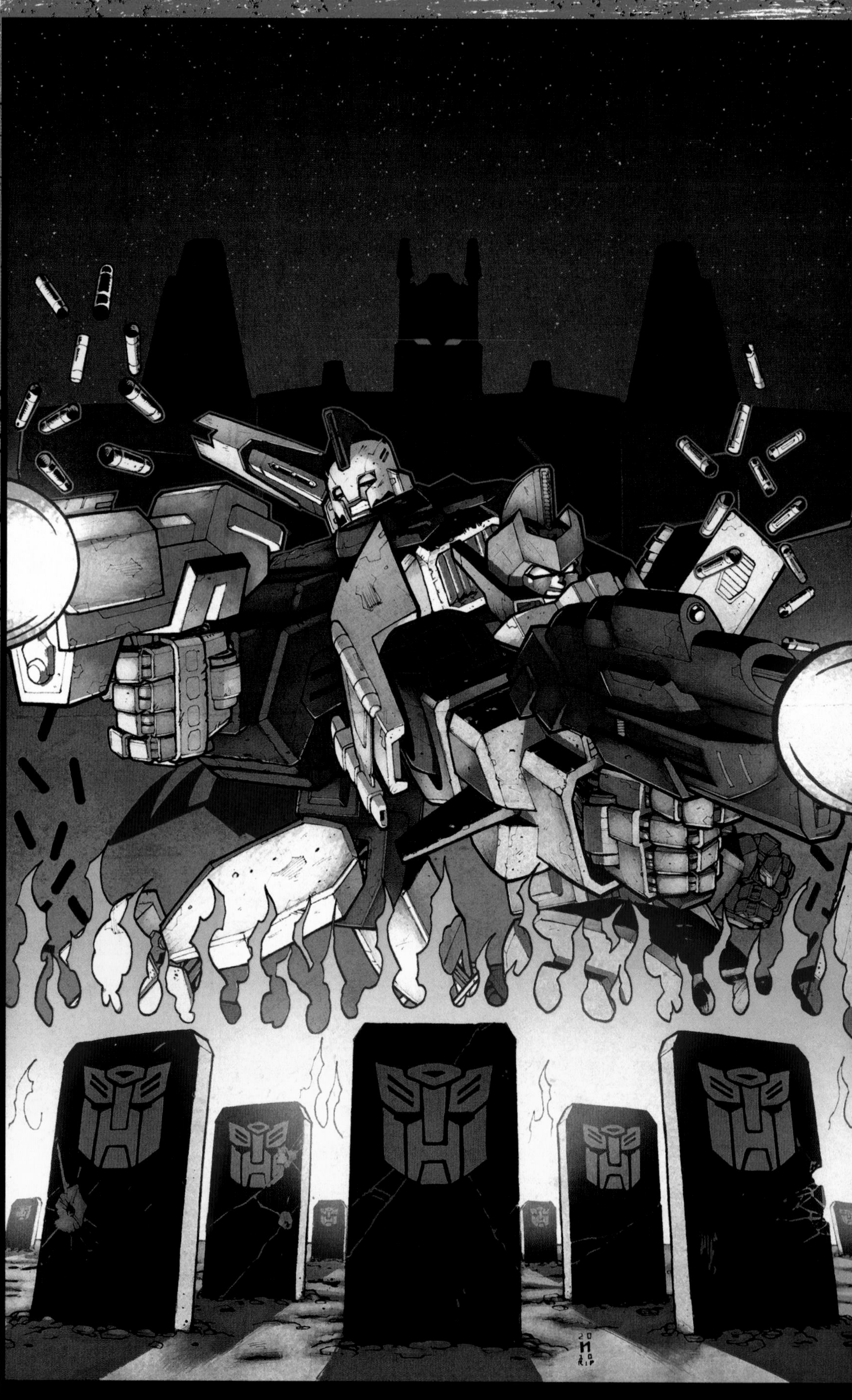
20
RIP

ART NICK ROCHE COLORS JOSH BURCHAM

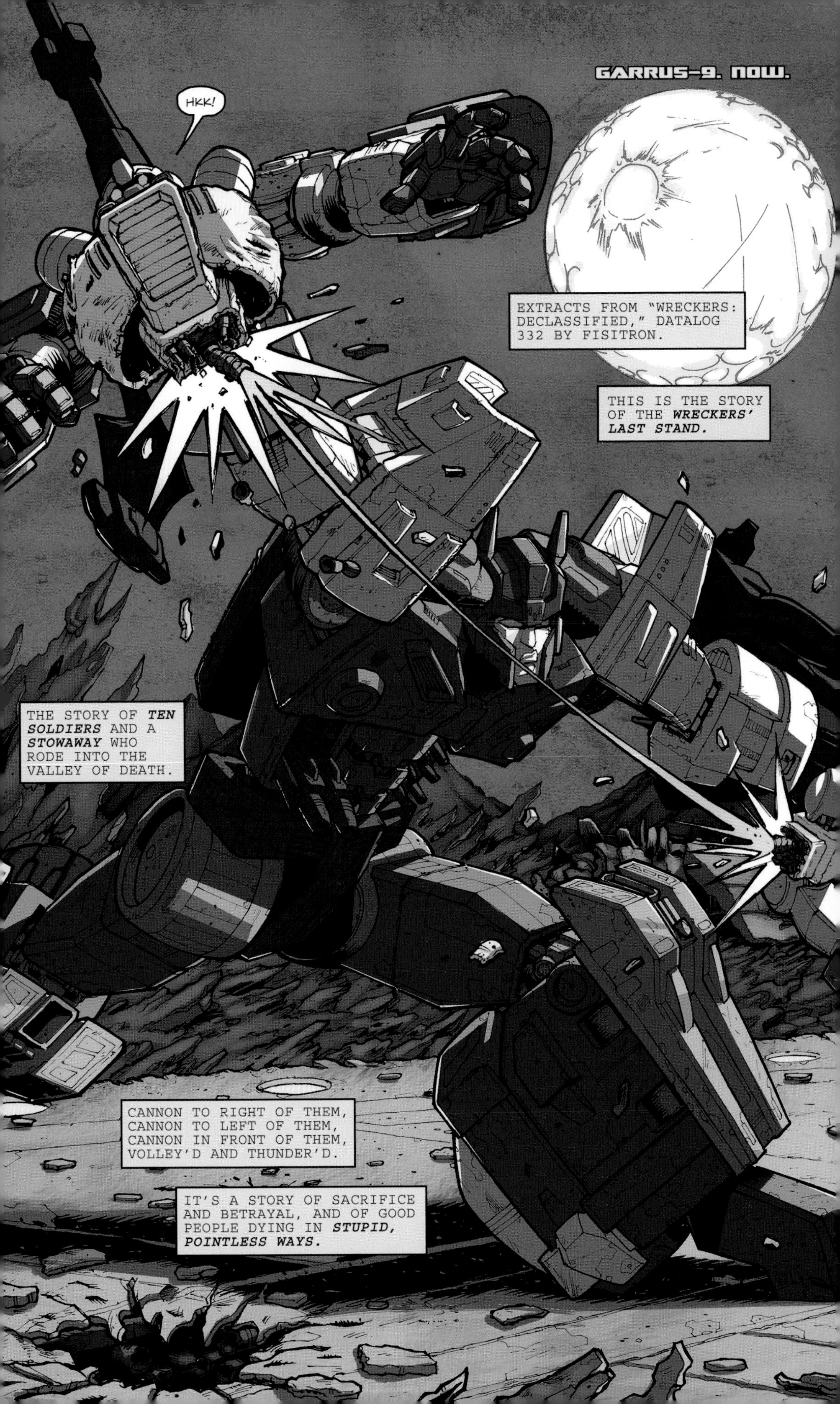
GARRUS-9. NOW.
HKK!
EXTRACTS FROM "WRECKERS: DECLASSIFIED," DATALOG 332 BY FISITRON.
THIS IS THE STORY OF THE WRECKERS' LAST STAND.
THE STORY OF TEN SOLDIERS AND A STOWAWAY WHO RODE INTO THE VALLEY OF DEATH.
CANNON TO RIGHT OF THEM, CANNON TO LEFT OF THEM, CANNON IN FRONT OF THEM, VOLLEY'D AND THUNDER'D.
IT'S A STORY OF SACRIFICE AND BETRAYAL, AND OF GOOD PEOPLE DYING IN STUPID, POINTLESS WAYS.

IT'S THE STORY OF THE DECEPTICON WHO CHOSE *OPTION 2,* AND PAID FOR IT WITH HIS *SANITY...*

OH, DON'T LOOK SO *SURPRISED.* YOU DIDN'T EXPECT THIS STUNTED LITTLE *WRETCH* TO *SURVIVE,* DID YOU?

YOU'RE A *MANIAC!*

AND YOU WRECKERS ARE LITTLE MORE THAN A *DISTRACTION.*

AT BEST, YOU'RE A *STARTER* BEFORE THE *MAIN COURSE.*

HISH

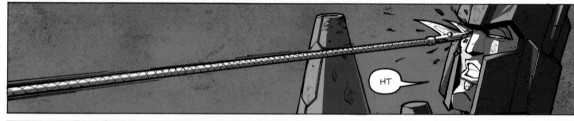

HT

YOU *TALK* TOO MUCH.

...AND OF THE AUTOBOT WHO WENT TOO FAR.

COME *HERE* AND SAY THAT.

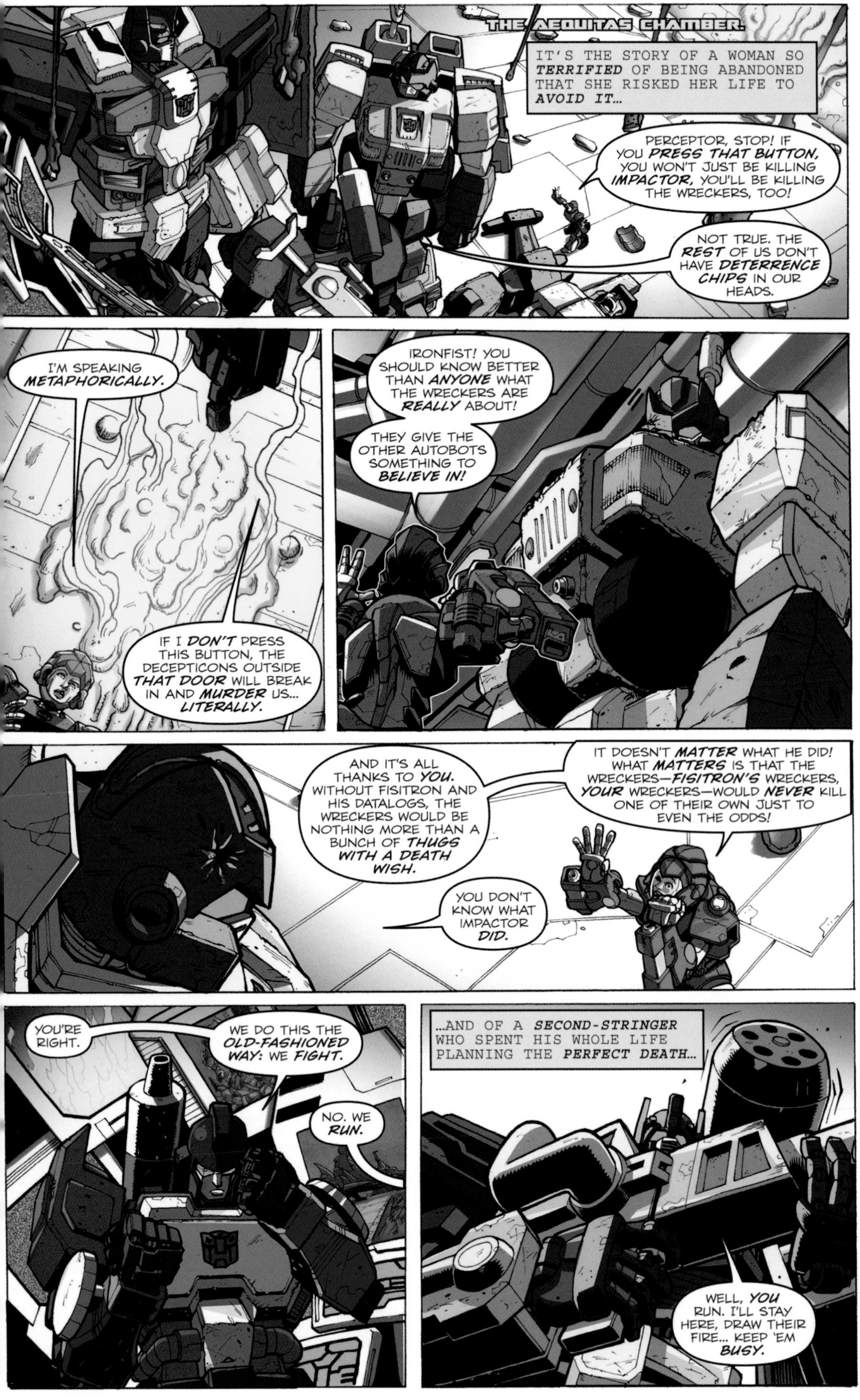
THE AEQUITAS CHAMBER.
IT'S THE STORY OF A WOMAN SO TERRIFIED OF BEING ABANDONED THAT SHE RISKED HER LIFE TO AVOID IT...
PERCEPTOR, STOP! IF YOU PRESS THAT BUTTON, YOU WON'T JUST BE KILLING IMPACTOR, YOU'LL BE KILLING THE WRECKERS, TOO!
NOT TRUE. THE REST OF US DON'T HAVE DETERRENCE CHIPS IN OUR HEADS.
I'M SPEAKING METAPHORICALLY.
IF I DON'T PRESS THIS BUTTON, THE DECEPTICONS OUTSIDE THAT DOOR WILL BREAK IN AND MURDER US... LITERALLY.
IRONFIST! YOU SHOULD KNOW BETTER THAN ANYONE WHAT THE WRECKERS ARE REALLY ABOUT!
THEY GIVE THE OTHER AUTOBOTS SOMETHING TO BELIEVE IN!
AND IT'S ALL THANKS TO YOU. WITHOUT FISITRON AND HIS DATALOGS, THE WRECKERS WOULD BE NOTHING MORE THAN A BUNCH OF THUGS WITH A DEATH WISH.
IT DOESN'T MATTER WHAT HE DID! WHAT MATTERS IS THAT THE WRECKERS—FISITRON'S WRECKERS, YOUR WRECKERS—WOULD NEVER KILL ONE OF THEIR OWN JUST TO EVEN THE ODDS!
YOU DON'T KNOW WHAT IMPACTOR DID.
YOU'RE RIGHT.
WE DO THIS THE OLD-FASHIONED WAY: WE FIGHT.
NO. WE RUN.
...AND OF A SECOND-STRINGER WHO SPENT HIS WHOLE LIFE PLANNING THE PERFECT DEATH...
WELL, YOU RUN. I'LL STAY HERE, DRAW THEIR FIRE... KEEP 'EM BUSY.

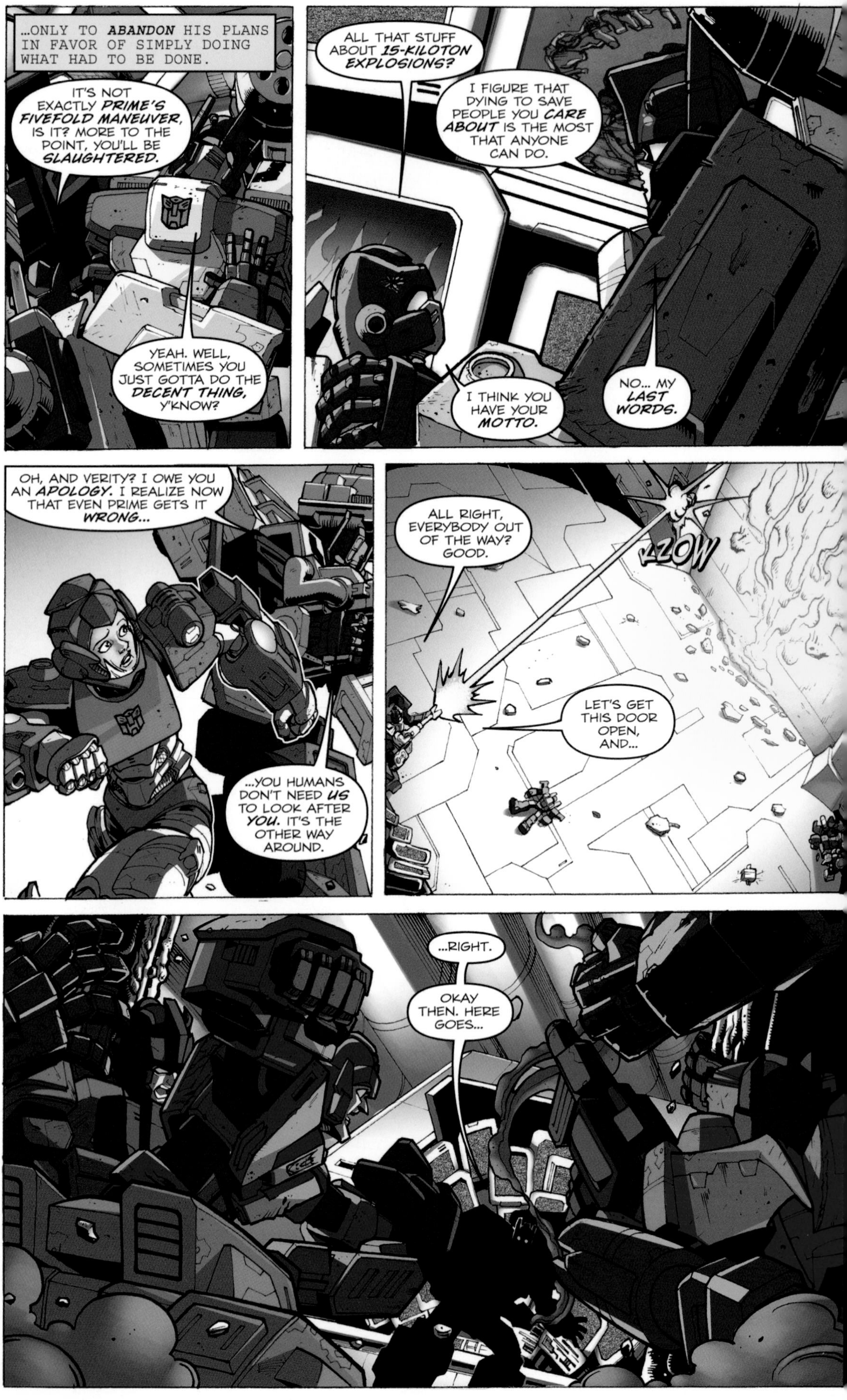
...ONLY TO ABANDON HIS PLANS IN FAVOR OF SIMPLY DOING WHAT HAD TO BE DONE.
IT'S NOT EXACTLY PRIME'S FIVEFOLD MANEUVER, IS IT? MORE TO THE POINT, YOU'LL BE SLAUGHTERED.
YEAH. WELL, SOMETIMES YOU JUST GOTTA DO THE DECENT THING, Y'KNOW?
ALL THAT STUFF ABOUT 15-KILOTON EXPLOSIONS?
I FIGURE THAT DYING TO SAVE PEOPLE YOU CARE ABOUT IS THE MOST THAT ANYONE CAN DO.
I THINK YOU HAVE YOUR MOTTO.
NO... MY LAST WORDS.
OH, AND VERITY? I OWE YOU AN APOLOGY. I REALIZE NOW THAT EVEN PRIME GETS IT WRONG...
...YOU HUMANS DON'T NEED US TO LOOK AFTER YOU. IT'S THE OTHER WAY AROUND.
ALL RIGHT, EVERYBODY OUT OF THE WAY? GOOD.
KZOW
LET'S GET THIS DOOR OPEN, AND...
...RIGHT.
OKAY THEN. HERE GOES...

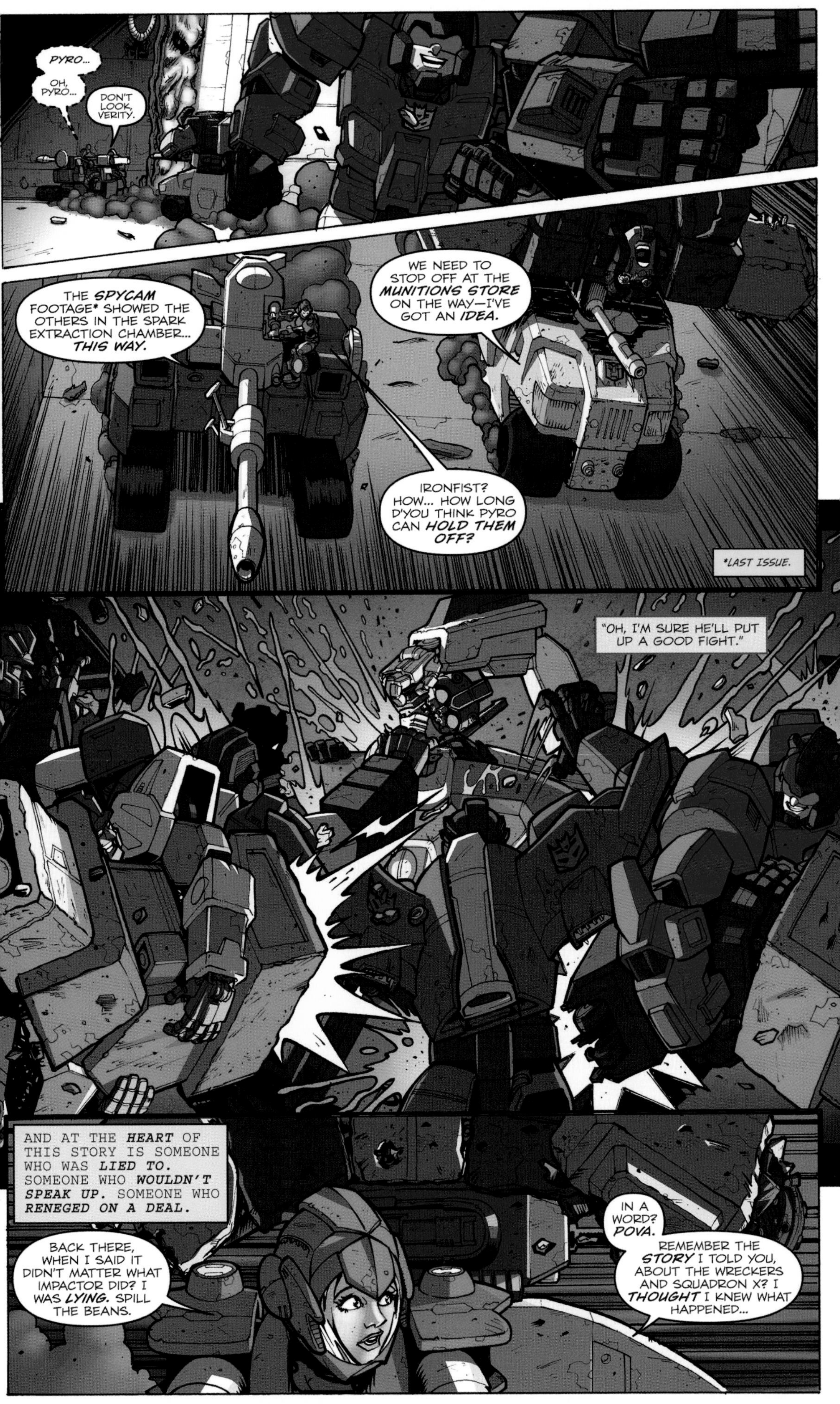
PYRO...
OH, PYRO...
DON'T LOOK, VERITY.
THE SPYCAM FOOTAGE* SHOWED THE OTHERS IN THE SPARK EXTRACTION CHAMBER... THIS WAY.
WE NEED TO STOP OFF AT THE MUNITIONS STORE ON THE WAY—I'VE GOT AN IDEA.
IRONFIST? HOW... HOW LONG D'YOU THINK PYRO CAN HOLD THEM OFF?
*LAST ISSUE.
"OH, I'M SURE HE'LL PUT UP A GOOD FIGHT."
AND AT THE HEART OF THIS STORY IS SOMEONE WHO WAS LIED TO. SOMEONE WHO WOULDN'T SPEAK UP. SOMEONE WHO RENEGED ON A DEAL.
BACK THERE, WHEN I SAID IT DIDN'T MATTER WHAT IMPACTOR DID? I WAS LYING. SPILL THE BEANS.
IN A WORD? POVA.
REMEMBER THE STORY I TOLD YOU, ABOUT THE WRECKERS AND SQUADRON X? I THOUGHT I KNEW WHAT HAPPENED...

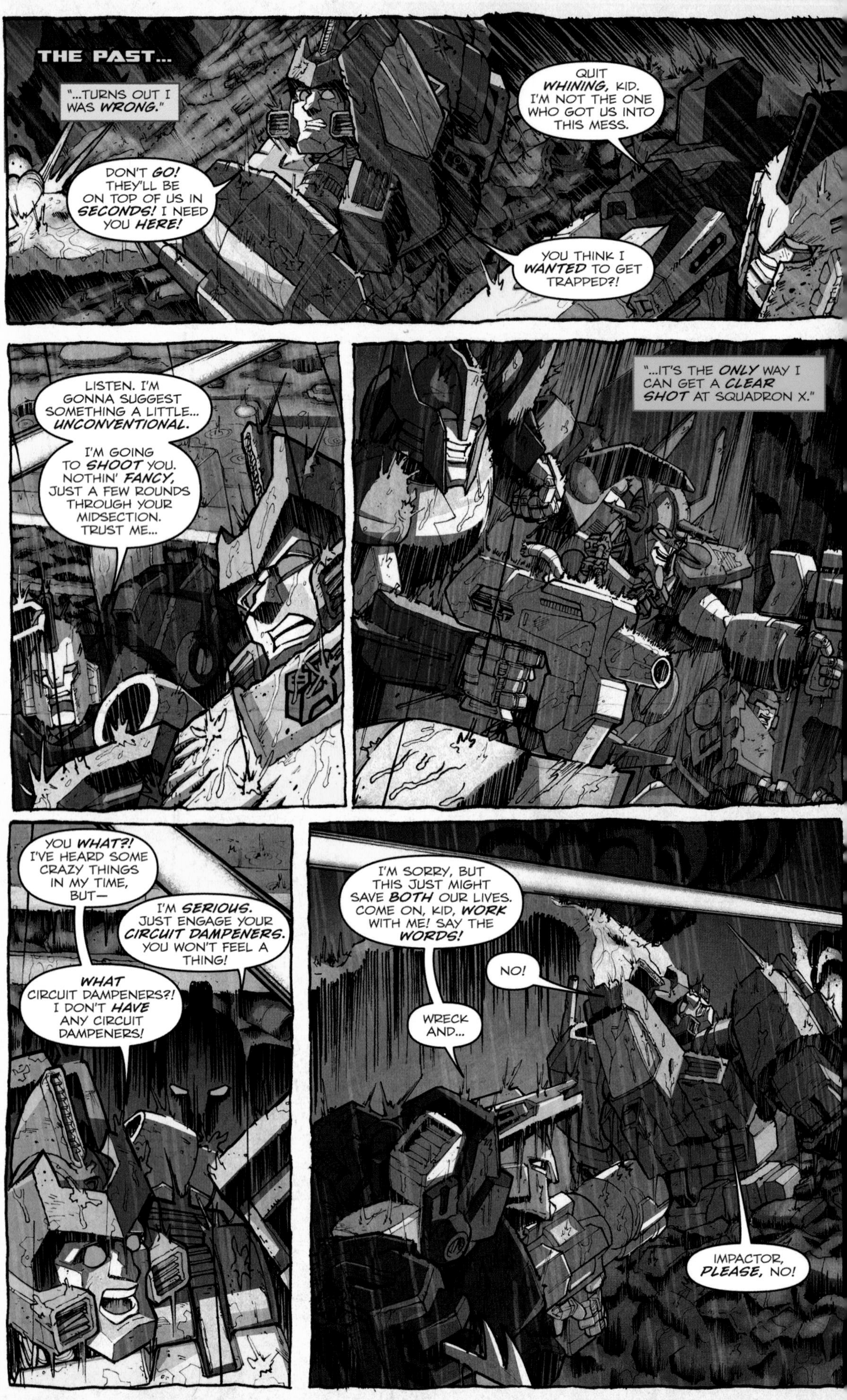
THE PAST...
"...TURNS OUT I WAS WRONG."
DON'T GO! THEY'LL BE ON TOP OF US IN SECONDS! I NEED YOU HERE!
QUIT WHINING, KID. I'M NOT THE ONE WHO GOT US INTO THIS MESS.
YOU THINK I WANTED TO GET TRAPPED?!
LISTEN. I'M GONNA SUGGEST SOMETHING A LITTLE... UNCONVENTIONAL.
I'M GOING TO SHOOT YOU. NOTHIN' FANCY, JUST A FEW ROUNDS THROUGH YOUR MIDSECTION. TRUST ME...
"...IT'S THE ONLY WAY I CAN GET A CLEAR SHOT AT SQUADRON X."
YOU WHAT?! I'VE HEARD SOME CRAZY THINGS IN MY TIME, BUT—
I'M SERIOUS. JUST ENGAGE YOUR CIRCUIT DAMPENERS. YOU WON'T FEEL A THING!
WHAT CIRCUIT DAMPENERS?! I DON'T HAVE ANY CIRCUIT DAMPENERS!
I'M SORRY, BUT THIS JUST MIGHT SAVE BOTH OUR LIVES. COME ON, KID, WORK WITH ME! SAY THE WORDS!
NO!
WRECK AND...
IMPACTOR, PLEASE, NO!

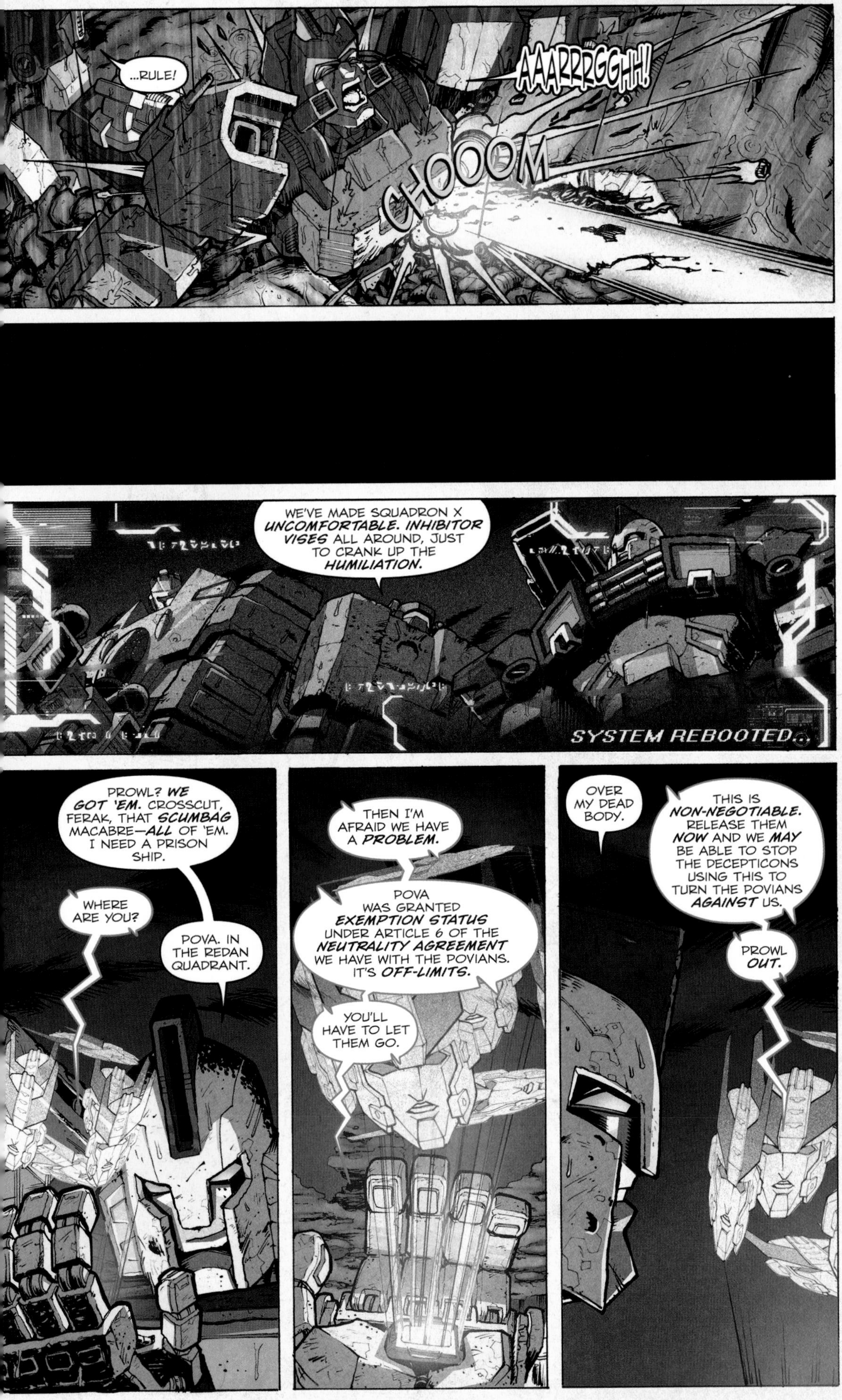
...RULE!
AAARRRGGHH!
CHOOOM
WE'VE MADE SQUADRON X UNCOMFORTABLE. INHIBITOR VISES ALL AROUND, JUST TO CRANK UP THE HUMILIATION.
SYSTEM REBOOTED.
PROWL? WE GOT 'EM. CROSSCUT, FERAK, THAT SCUMBAG MACABRE—ALL OF 'EM. I NEED A PRISON SHIP.
WHERE ARE YOU?
POVA. IN THE REDAN QUADRANT.
THEN I'M AFRAID WE HAVE A PROBLEM.
POVA WAS GRANTED EXEMPTION STATUS UNDER ARTICLE 6 OF THE NEUTRALITY AGREEMENT WE HAVE WITH THE POVIANS. IT'S OFF-LIMITS.
YOU'LL HAVE TO LET THEM GO.
OVER MY DEAD BODY.
THIS IS NON-NEGOTIABLE. RELEASE THEM NOW AND WE MAY BE ABLE TO STOP THE DECEPTICONS USING THIS TO TURN THE POVIANS AGAINST US.
PROWL OUT.

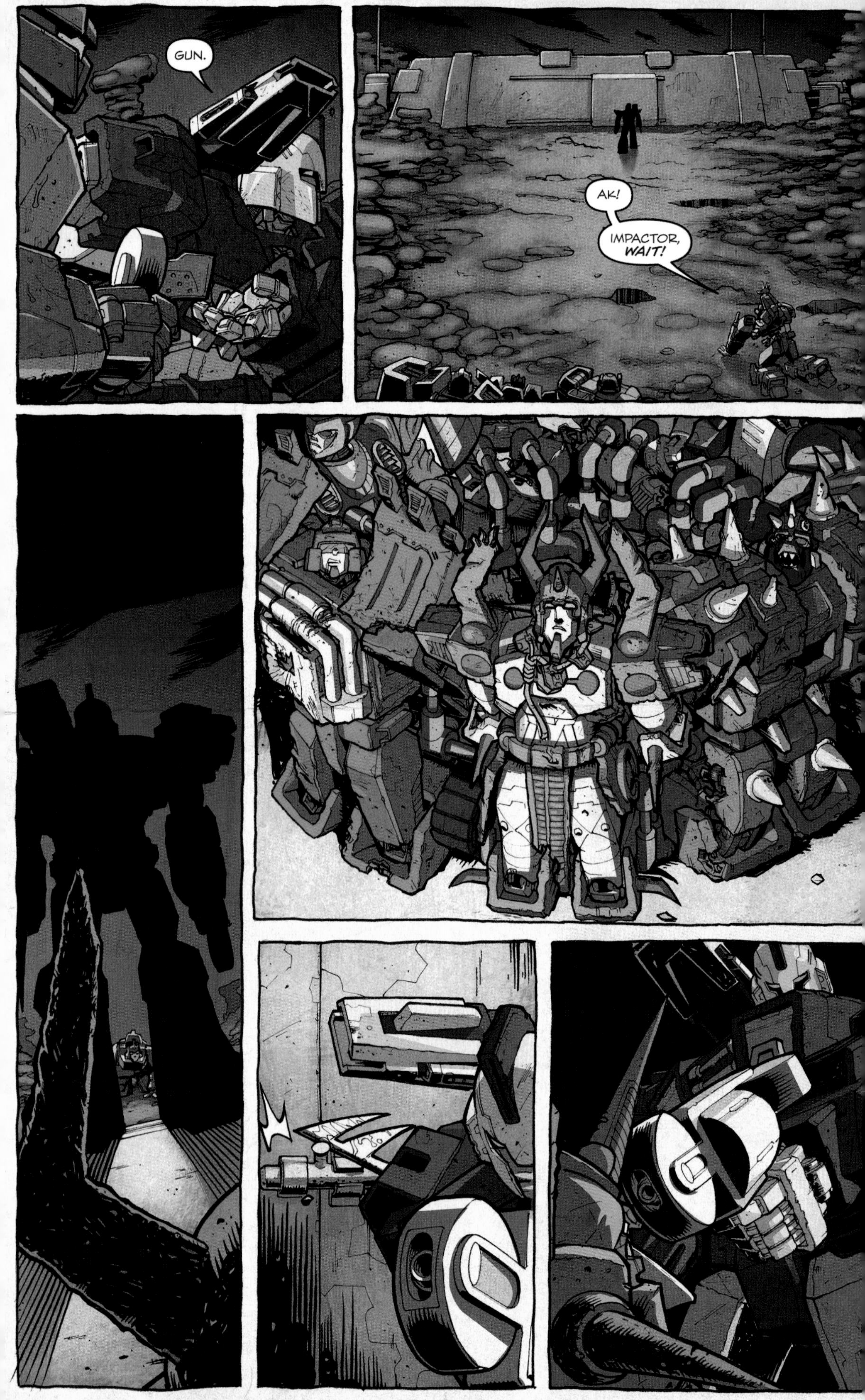
GUN.
AK!
IMPACTOR, WAIT!

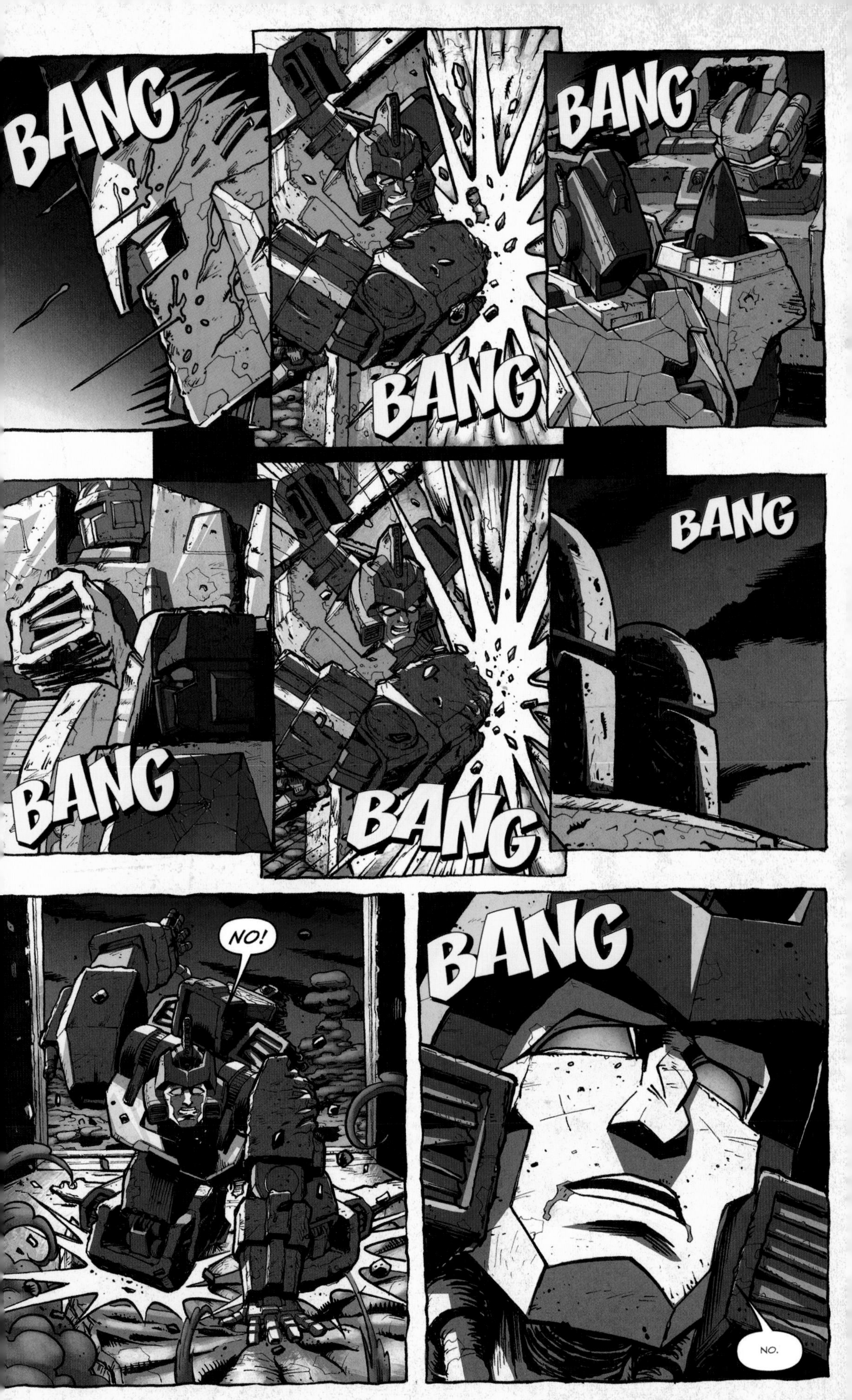

BANG
BANG
BANG
BANG
BANG
BANG
NO!
BANG
NO.

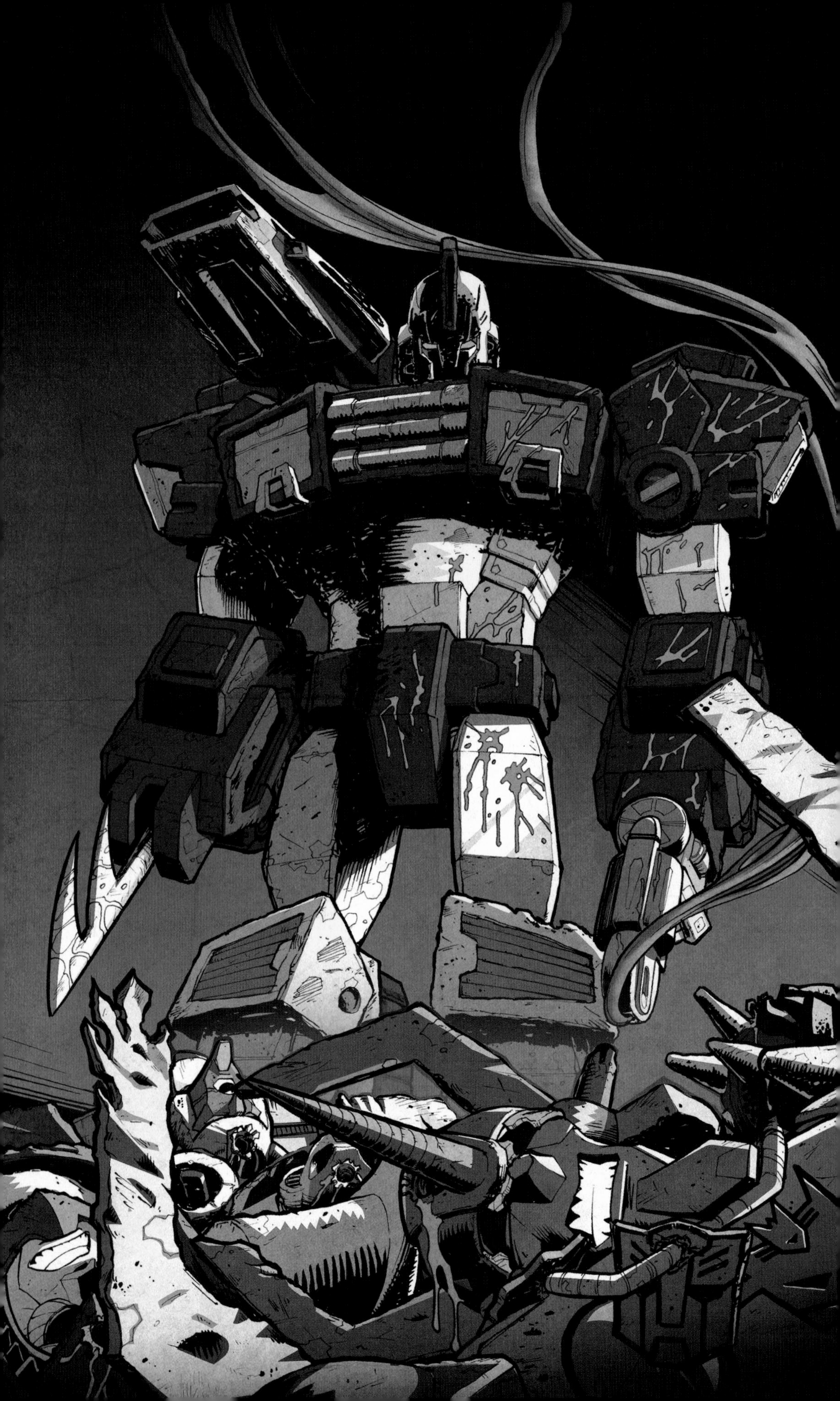

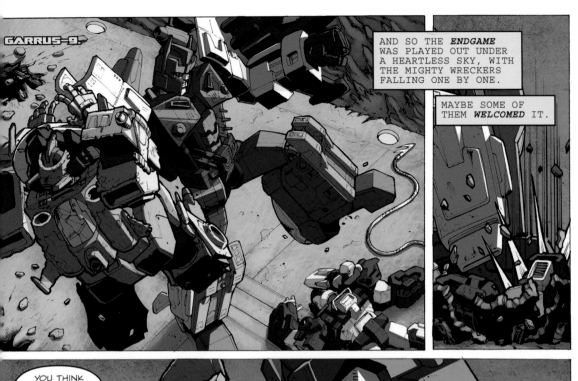

AND SO THE *ENDGAME* WAS PLAYED OUT UNDER A HEARTLESS SKY, WITH THE MIGHTY WRECKERS FALLING ONE BY ONE.

MAYBE SOME OF THEM *WELCOMED* IT.

YOU THINK THIS IS *IT*, OVERLORD? YOU THINK YOU'VE *WON?*

MY WRECKERS ARE THE *BEST*. THEY'LL HAVE FREED THE AUTOBOT PRISONERS BY NOW... AND ALL OF THEM WILL BE *HEADING THIS WAY*, READY TO FEED YOU YOUR FUSELAGE.

I DOUBT THAT *VERY* MUCH. YOU SEE, SHORTLY AFTER I HEARD YOU WRECKERS WERE ON MY *PATCH*, I GAVE A SIMPLE *ORDER*:

"KILL.

"EVERY.

"PRISONER."

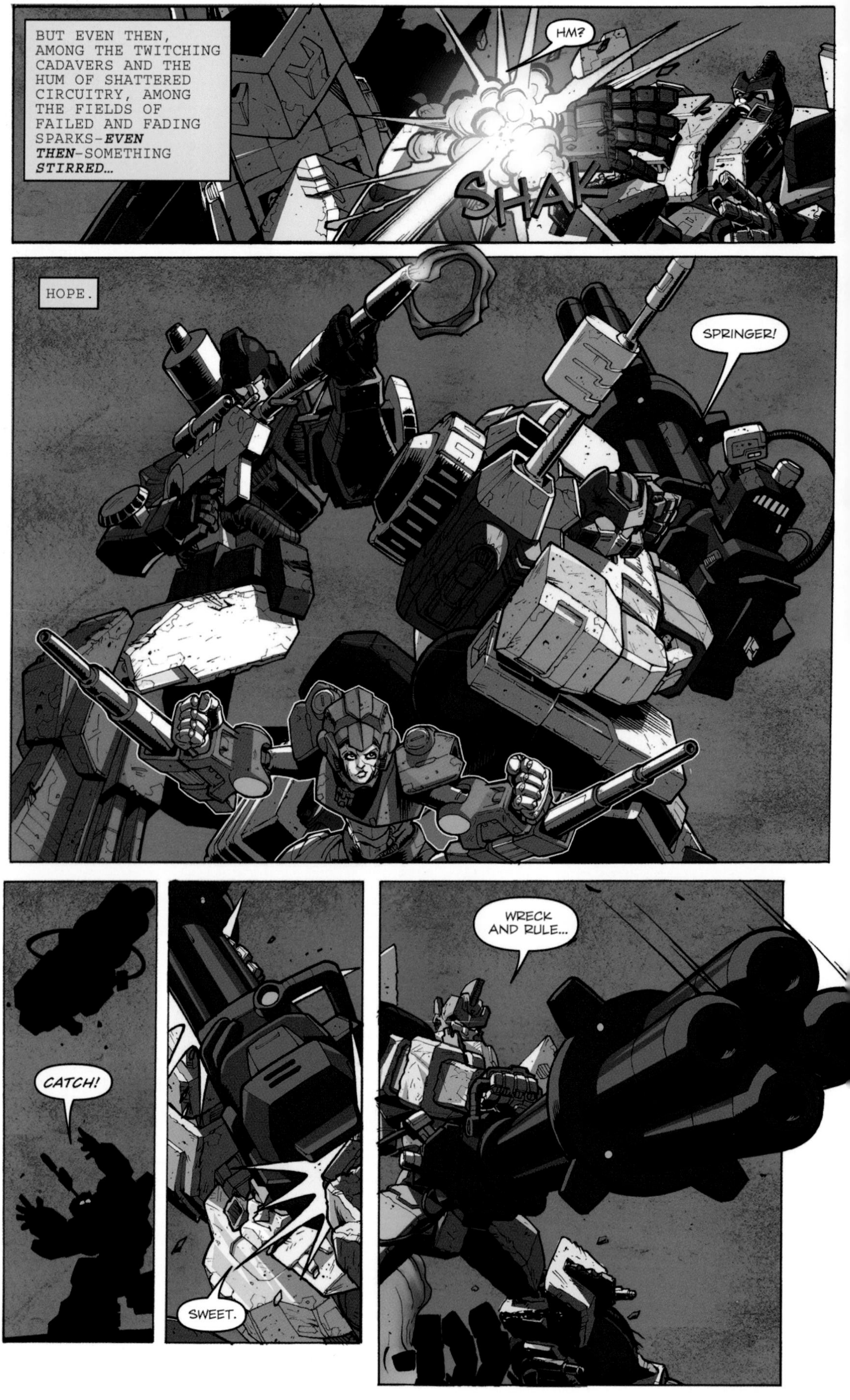

BUT EVEN THEN, AMONG THE TWITCHING CADAVERS AND THE HUM OF SHATTERED CIRCUITRY, AMONG THE FIELDS OF FAILED AND FADING SPARKS-*EVEN THEN*-SOMETHING *STIRRED*...
HM?
SHAK
HOPE.
SPRINGER!
CATCH!
SWEET.
WRECK AND RULE...

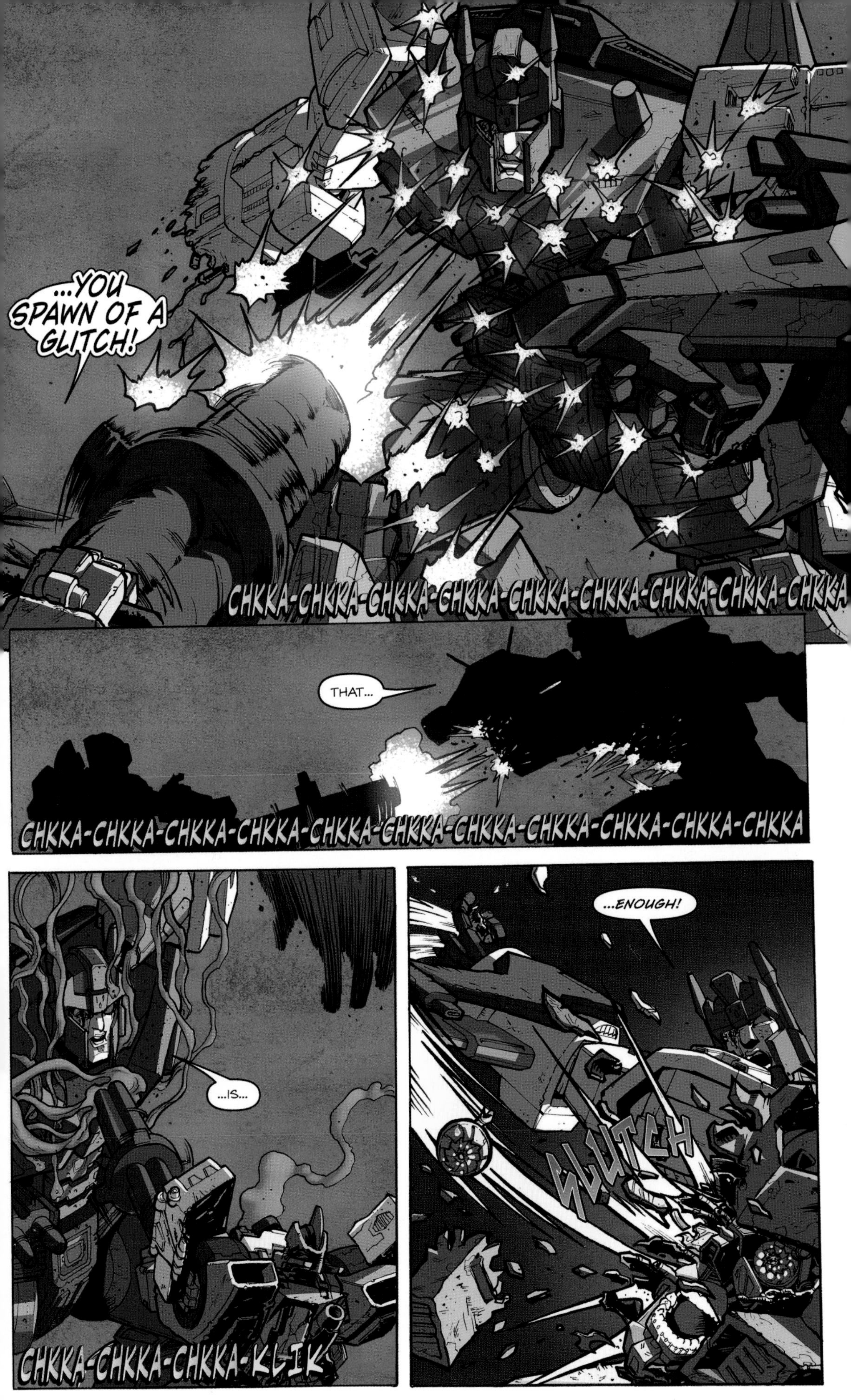
...YOU SPAWN OF A GLITCH!
CHKKA-CHKKA-CHKKA-CHKKA-CHKKA-CHKKA-CHKKA-CHKKA-CHKKA
THAT...
CHKKA-CHKKA-CHKKA-CHKKA-CHKKA-CHKKA-CHKKA-CHKKA-CHKKA-CHKKA-CHKKA
...IS...
CHKKA-CHKKA-CHKKA-KLIK
...ENOUGH!
SLUTCH

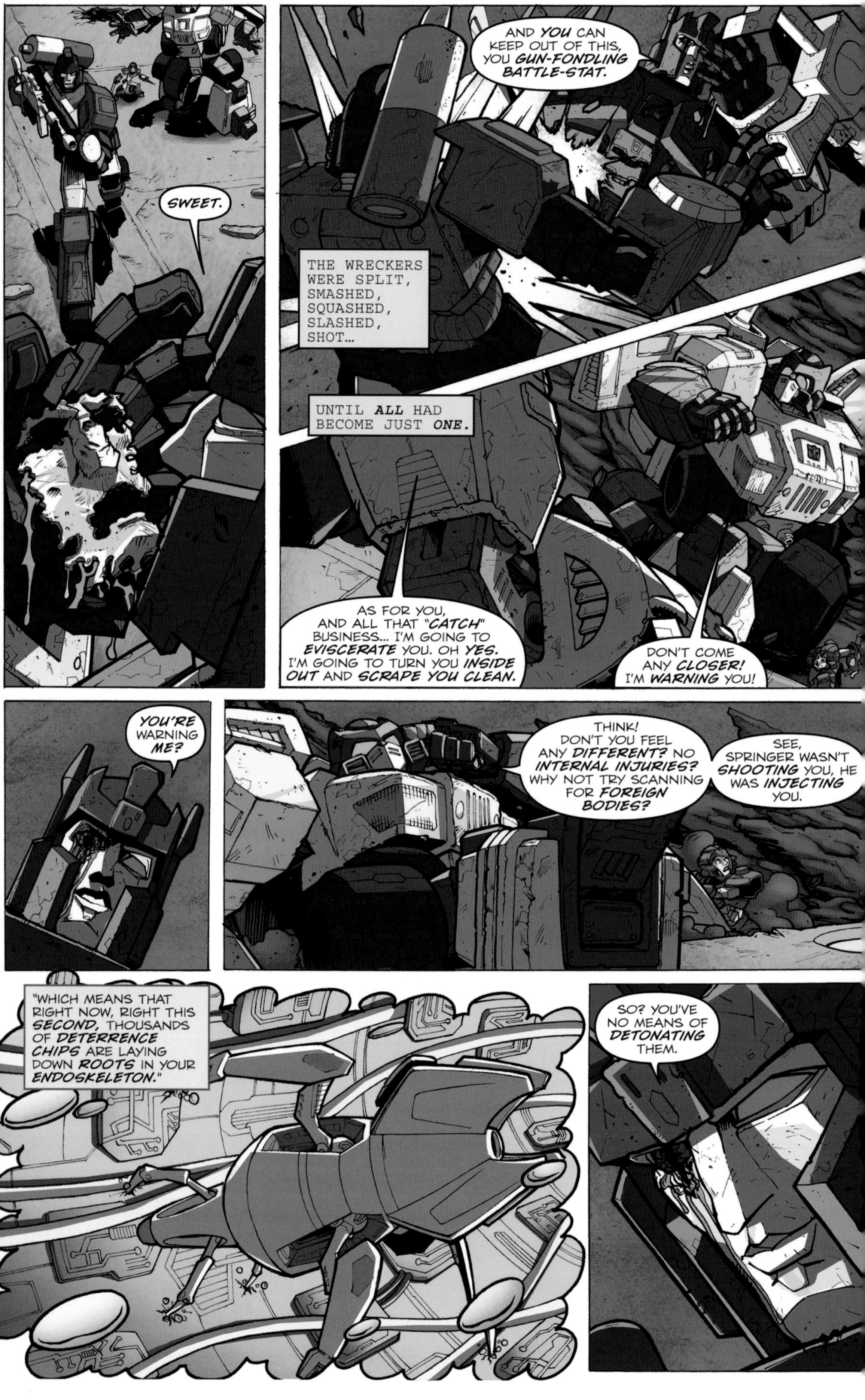
SWEET.
AND YOU CAN KEEP OUT OF THIS, YOU GUN-FONDLING BATTLE-STAT.
THE WRECKERS WERE SPLIT, SMASHED, SQUASHED, SLASHED, SHOT...
UNTIL ALL HAD BECOME JUST ONE.
AS FOR YOU, AND ALL THAT "CATCH" BUSINESS... I'M GOING TO EVISCERATE YOU. OH YES. I'M GOING TO TURN YOU INSIDE OUT AND SCRAPE YOU CLEAN.
DON'T COME ANY CLOSER! I'M WARNING YOU!
YOU'RE WARNING ME?
THINK! DON'T YOU FEEL ANY DIFFERENT? NO INTERNAL INJURIES? WHY NOT TRY SCANNING FOR FOREIGN BODIES?
SEE, SPRINGER WASN'T SHOOTING YOU, HE WAS INJECTING YOU.
"WHICH MEANS THAT RIGHT NOW, RIGHT THIS SECOND, THOUSANDS OF DETERRENCE CHIPS ARE LAYING DOWN ROOTS IN YOUR ENDOSKELETON."
SO? YOU'VE NO MEANS OF DETONATING THEM.

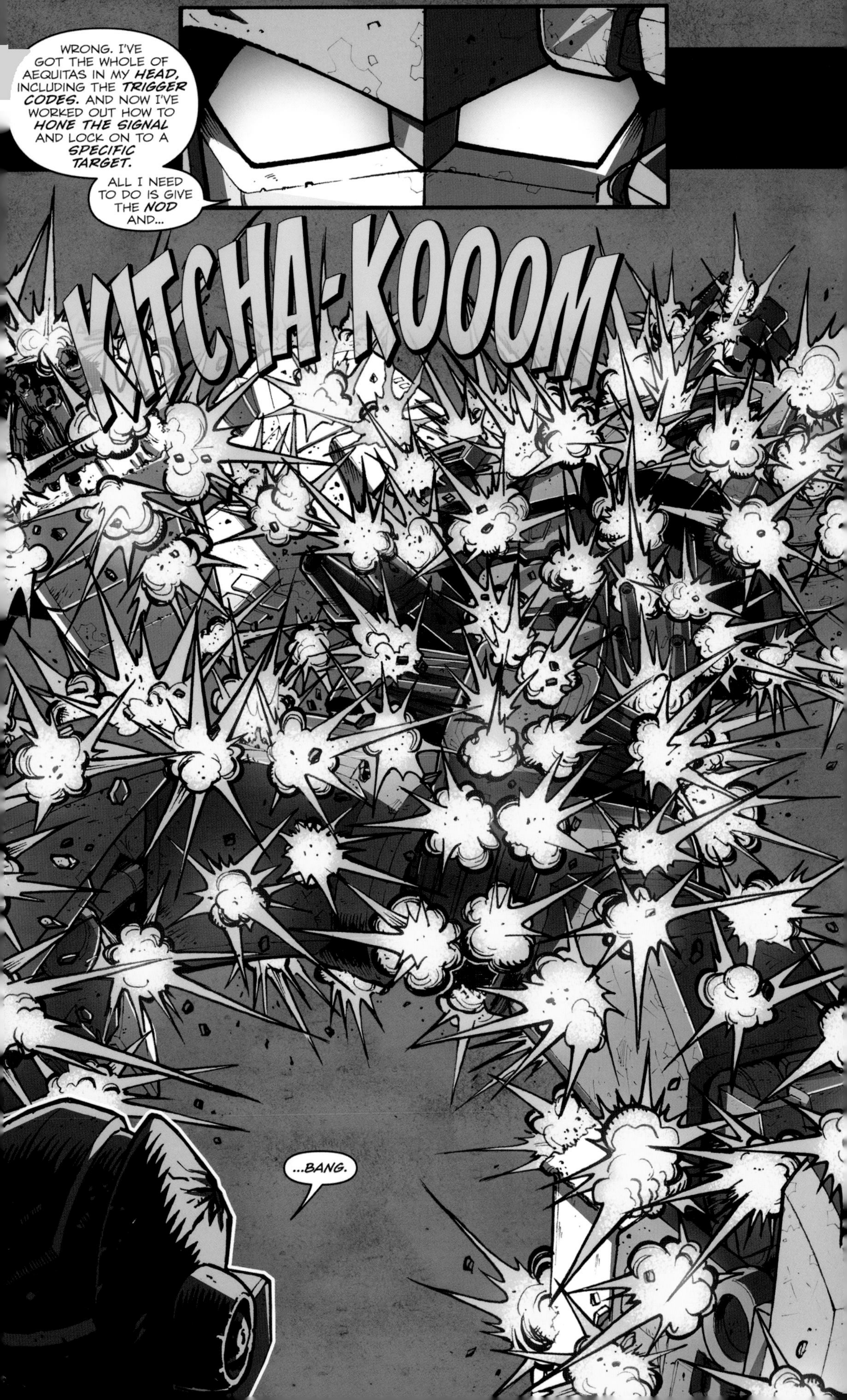

WRONG. I'VE GOT THE WHOLE OF AEQUITAS IN MY *HEAD,* INCLUDING THE *TRIGGER CODES.* AND NOW I'VE WORKED OUT HOW TO *HONE THE SIGNAL* AND LOCK ON TO A *SPECIFIC TARGET.*
ALL I NEED TO DO IS GIVE THE *NOD* AND...
KITCHA-KOOOM
...BANG.

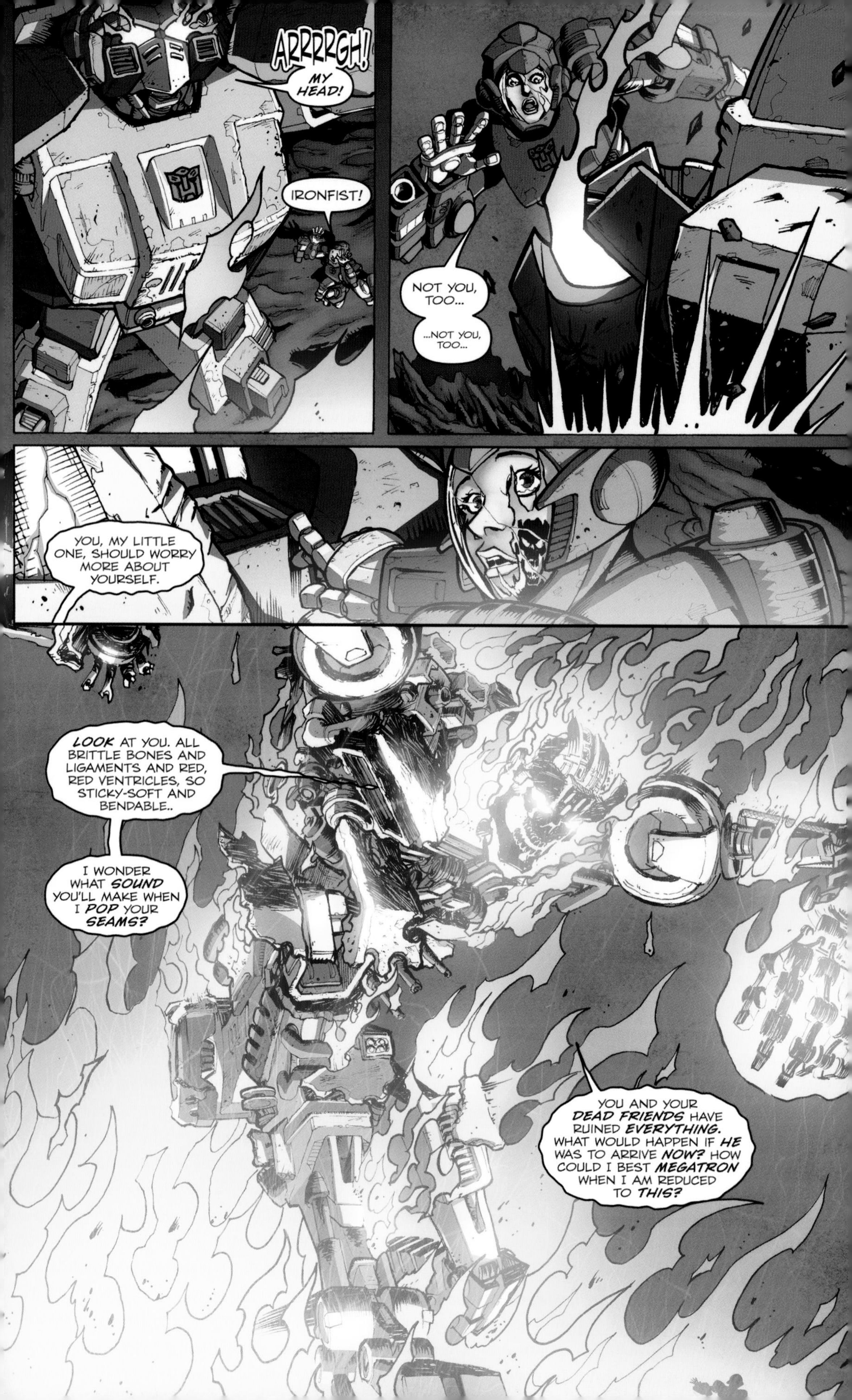
ARRRRGH!
MY HEAD!
IRONFIST!
NOT YOU, TOO...
...NOT YOU, TOO...
YOU, MY LITTLE ONE, SHOULD WORRY MORE ABOUT YOURSELF.
LOOK AT YOU. ALL BRITTLE BONES AND LIGAMENTS AND RED, RED VENTRICLES, SO STICKY-SOFT AND BENDABLE..
I WONDER WHAT SOUND YOU'LL MAKE WHEN I POP YOUR SEAMS?
YOU AND YOUR DEAD FRIENDS HAVE RUINED EVERYTHING. WHAT WOULD HAPPEN IF HE WAS TO ARRIVE NOW? HOW COULD I BEST MEGATRON WHEN I AM REDUCED TO THIS?

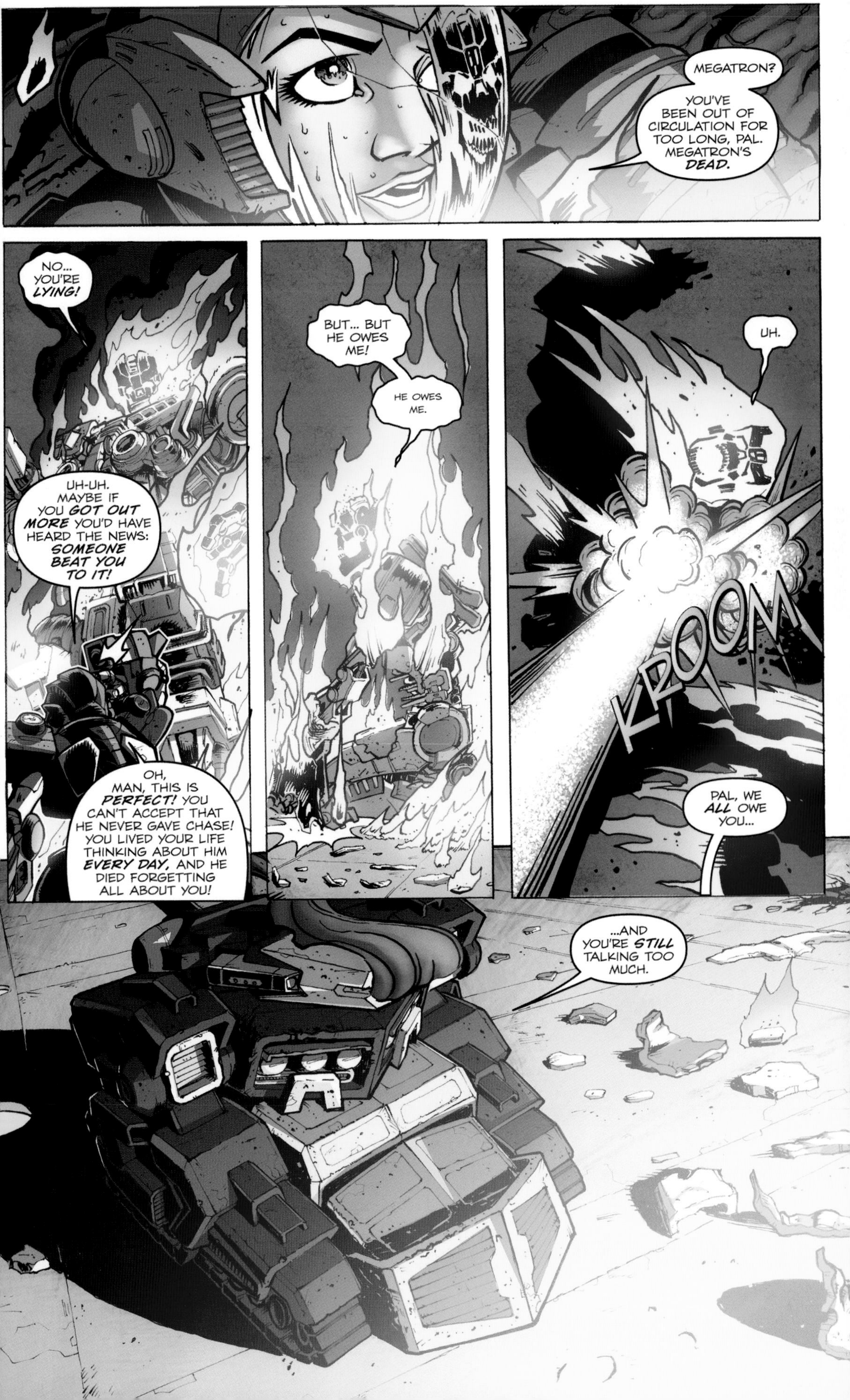
MEGATRON?
YOU'VE BEEN OUT OF CIRCULATION FOR TOO LONG, PAL. MEGATRON'S DEAD.
NO... YOU'RE LYING!
UH-UH. MAYBE IF YOU GOT OUT MORE YOU'D HAVE HEARD THE NEWS: SOMEONE BEAT YOU TO IT!
OH, MAN, THIS IS PERFECT! YOU CAN'T ACCEPT THAT HE NEVER GAVE CHASE! YOU LIVED YOUR LIFE THINKING ABOUT HIM EVERY DAY, AND HE DIED FORGETTING ALL ABOUT YOU!
BUT... BUT HE OWES ME!
HE OWES ME.
UH.
KROOM
PAL, WE ALL OWE YOU...
...AND YOU'RE STILL TALKING TOO MUCH.

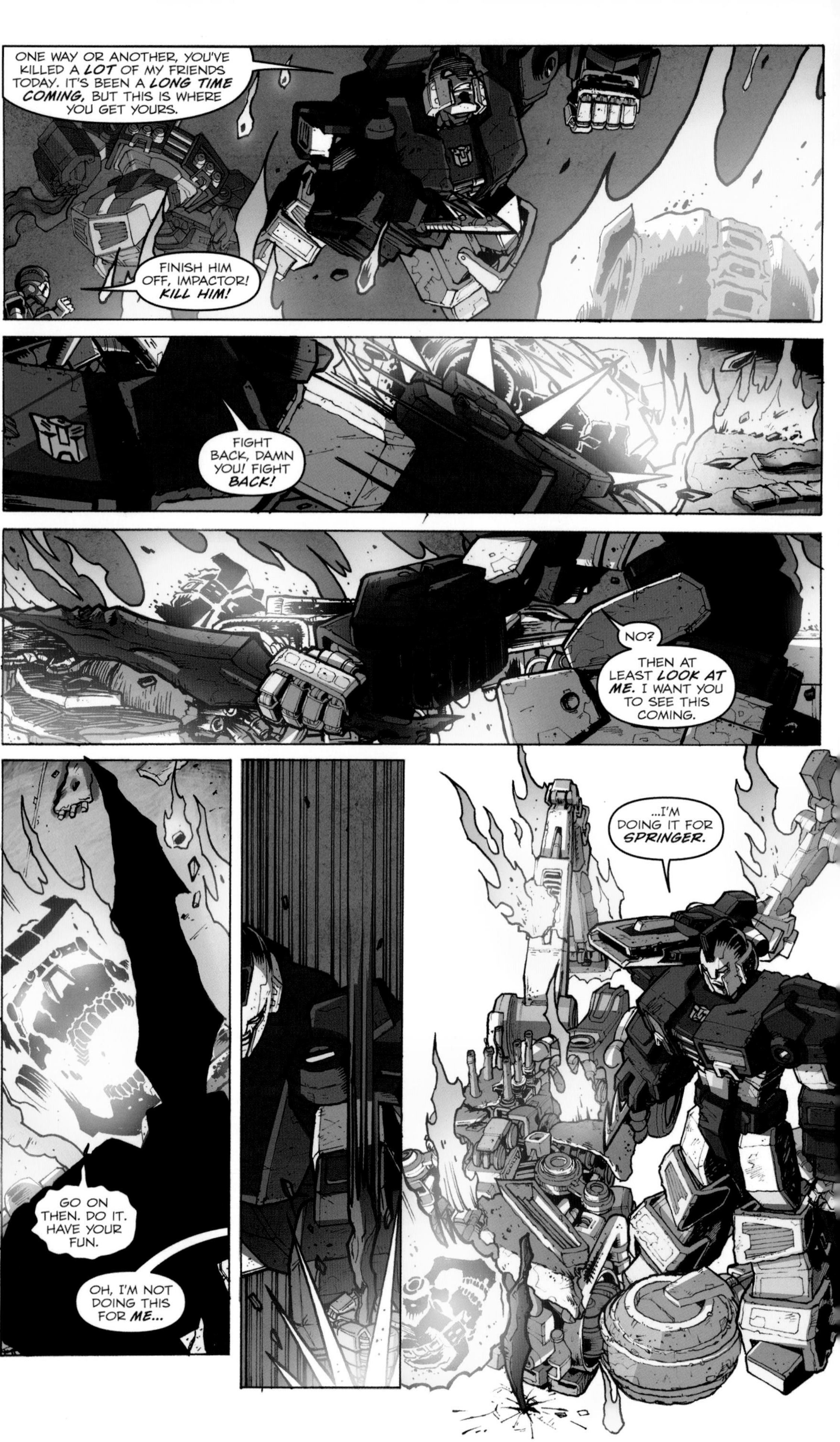

ONE WAY OR ANOTHER, YOU'VE KILLED A LOT OF MY FRIENDS TODAY. IT'S BEEN A LONG TIME COMING, BUT THIS IS WHERE YOU GET YOURS.
FINISH HIM OFF, IMPACTOR! KILL HIM!
FIGHT BACK, DAMN YOU! FIGHT BACK!
NO?
THEN AT LEAST LOOK AT ME. I WANT YOU TO SEE THIS COMING.
GO ON THEN. DO IT. HAVE YOUR FUN.
OH, I'M NOT DOING THIS FOR ME...
...I'M DOING IT FOR SPRINGER.

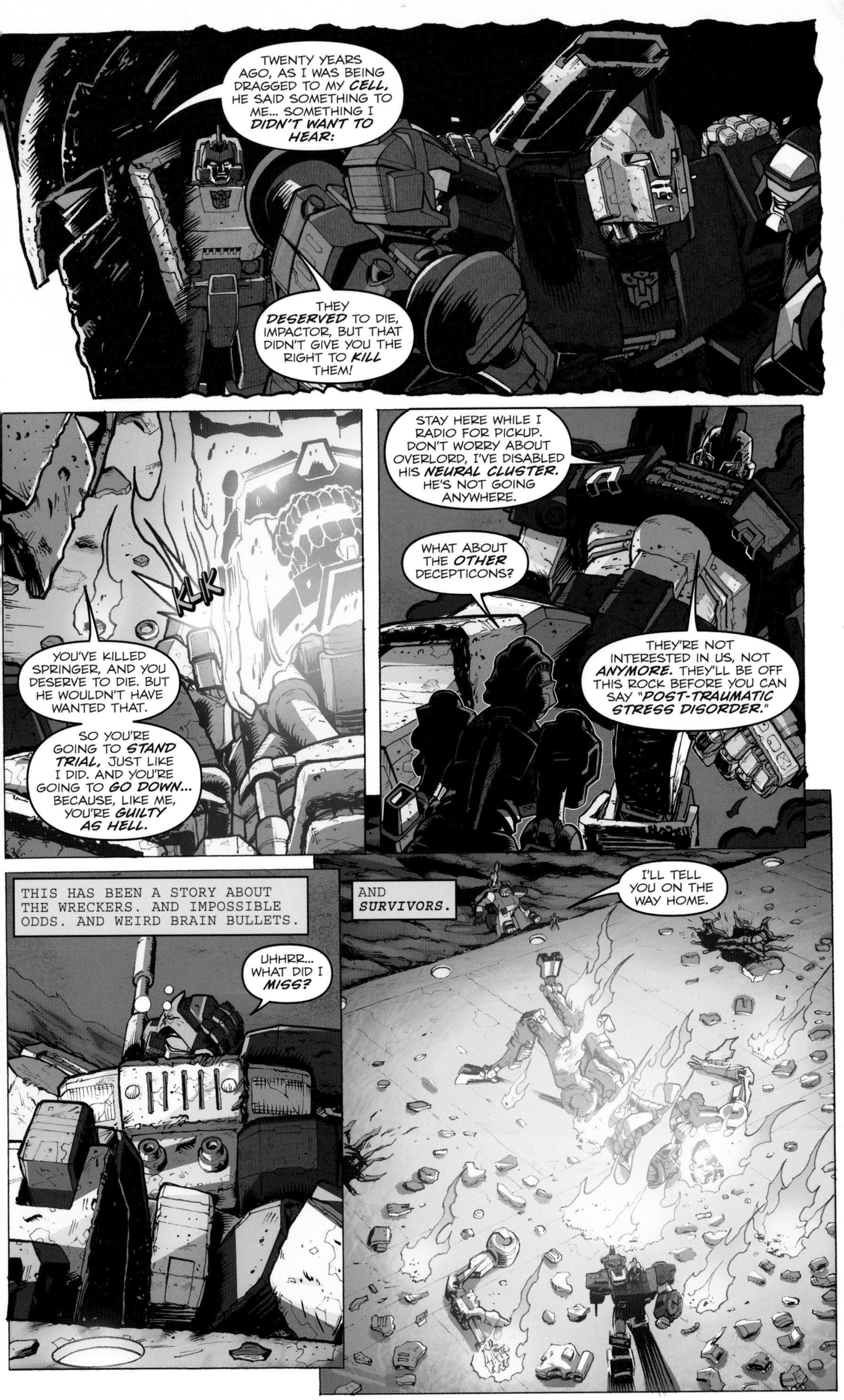

TWENTY YEARS AGO, AS I WAS BEING DRAGGED TO MY CELL, HE SAID SOMETHING TO ME... SOMETHING I DIDN'T WANT TO HEAR:
THEY DESERVED TO DIE, IMPACTOR, BUT THAT DIDN'T GIVE YOU THE RIGHT TO KILL THEM!
KLIK
YOU'VE KILLED SPRINGER, AND YOU DESERVE TO DIE. BUT HE WOULDN'T HAVE WANTED THAT.
SO YOU'RE GOING TO STAND TRIAL, JUST LIKE I DID. AND YOU'RE GOING TO GO DOWN... BECAUSE, LIKE ME, YOU'RE GUILTY AS HELL.
STAY HERE WHILE I RADIO FOR PICKUP. DON'T WORRY ABOUT OVERLORD, I'VE DISABLED HIS NEURAL CLUSTER. HE'S NOT GOING ANYWHERE.
WHAT ABOUT THE OTHER DECEPTICONS?
THEY'RE NOT INTERESTED IN US, NOT ANYMORE. THEY'LL BE OFF THIS ROCK BEFORE YOU CAN SAY "POST-TRAUMATIC STRESS DISORDER."
THIS HAS BEEN A STORY ABOUT THE WRECKERS. AND IMPOSSIBLE ODDS. AND WEIRD BRAIN BULLETS.
UHHRR... WHAT DID I MISS?
AND SURVIVORS.
I'LL TELL YOU ON THE WAY HOME.

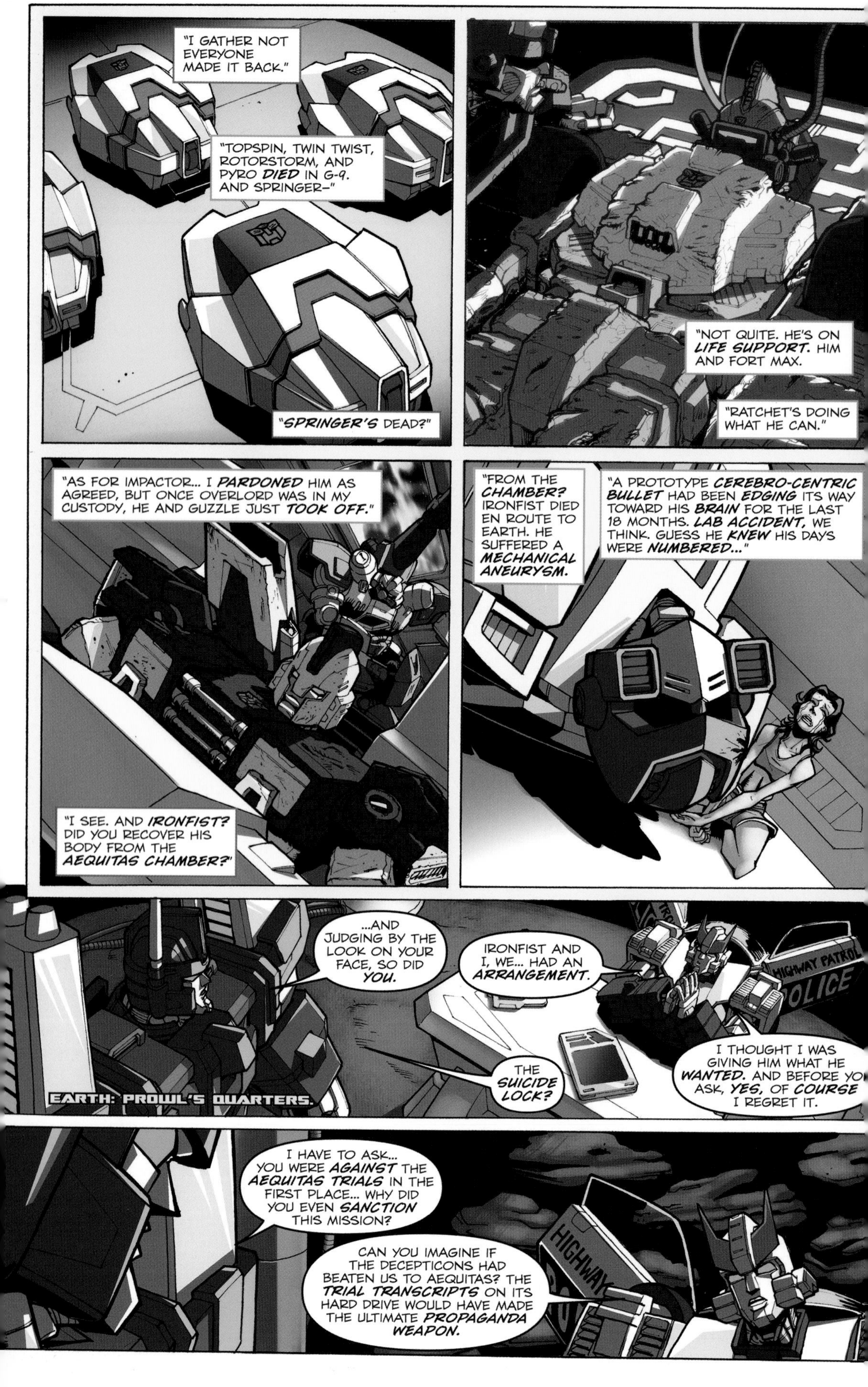
"I GATHER NOT EVERYONE MADE IT BACK."
"TOPSPIN, TWIN TWIST, ROTORSTORM, AND PYRO DIED IN G-9. AND SPRINGER–"
"SPRINGER'S DEAD?"
"NOT QUITE. HE'S ON LIFE SUPPORT. HIM AND FORT MAX.
"RATCHET'S DOING WHAT HE CAN."
"AS FOR IMPACTOR... I PARDONED HIM AS AGREED, BUT ONCE OVERLORD WAS IN MY CUSTODY, HE AND GUZZLE JUST TOOK OFF."
"I SEE. AND IRONFIST? DID YOU RECOVER HIS BODY FROM THE AEQUITAS CHAMBER?"
"FROM THE CHAMBER? IRONFIST DIED EN ROUTE TO EARTH. HE SUFFERED A MECHANICAL ANEURYSM.
"A PROTOTYPE CEREBRO-CENTRIC BULLET HAD BEEN EDGING ITS WAY TOWARD HIS BRAIN FOR THE LAST 18 MONTHS. LAB ACCIDENT, WE THINK. GUESS HE KNEW HIS DAYS WERE NUMBERED..."
EARTH: PROWL'S QUARTERS.
...AND JUDGING BY THE LOOK ON YOUR FACE, SO DID YOU.
IRONFIST AND I, WE... HAD AN ARRANGEMENT.
HIGHWAY PATROL
POLICE
THE SUICIDE LOCK?
I THOUGHT I WAS GIVING HIM WHAT HE WANTED. AND BEFORE YO ASK, YES, OF COURSE I REGRET IT.
I HAVE TO ASK... YOU WERE AGAINST THE AEQUITAS TRIALS IN THE FIRST PLACE... WHY DID YOU EVEN SANCTION THIS MISSION?
HIGHWAY
CAN YOU IMAGINE IF THE DECEPTICONS HAD BEATEN US TO AEQUITAS? THE TRIAL TRANSCRIPTS ON ITS HARD DRIVE WOULD HAVE MADE THE ULTIMATE PROPAGANDA WEAPON.

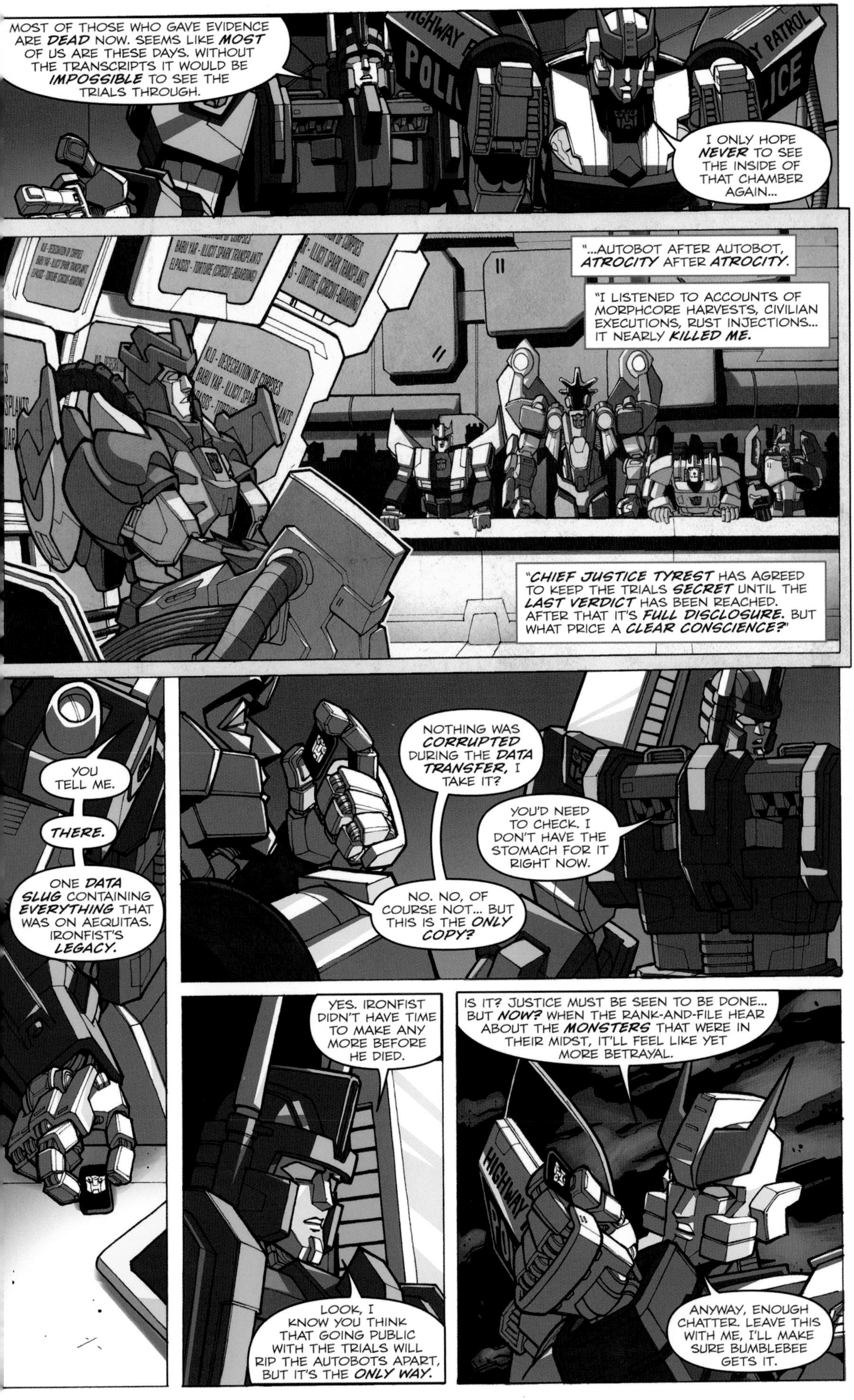

MOST OF THOSE WHO GAVE EVIDENCE ARE DEAD NOW. SEEMS LIKE MOST OF US ARE THESE DAYS. WITHOUT THE TRANSCRIPTS IT WOULD BE IMPOSSIBLE TO SEE THE TRIALS THROUGH.
I ONLY HOPE NEVER TO SEE THE INSIDE OF THAT CHAMBER AGAIN...
KLO - DESECRATION OF CORPSES
BABU YAR - ILLICIT SPARK TRANSPLANTS
ELPASOS - TORTURE (CIRCUIT-BOARDING)
"...AUTOBOT AFTER AUTOBOT, ATROCITY AFTER ATROCITY.
"I LISTENED TO ACCOUNTS OF MORPHCORE HARVESTS, CIVILIAN EXECUTIONS, RUST INJECTIONS... IT NEARLY KILLED ME.
"CHIEF JUSTICE TYREST HAS AGREED TO KEEP THE TRIALS SECRET UNTIL THE LAST VERDICT HAS BEEN REACHED. AFTER THAT IT'S FULL DISCLOSURE. BUT WHAT PRICE A CLEAR CONSCIENCE?"
YOU TELL ME.
THERE.
ONE DATA SLUG CONTAINING EVERYTHING THAT WAS ON AEQUITAS. IRONFIST'S LEGACY.
NOTHING WAS CORRUPTED DURING THE DATA TRANSFER, I TAKE IT?
YOU'D NEED TO CHECK. I DON'T HAVE THE STOMACH FOR IT RIGHT NOW.
NO. NO, OF COURSE NOT... BUT THIS IS THE ONLY COPY?
YES. IRONFIST DIDN'T HAVE TIME TO MAKE ANY MORE BEFORE HE DIED.
LOOK, I KNOW YOU THINK THAT GOING PUBLIC WITH THE TRIALS WILL RIP THE AUTOBOTS APART, BUT IT'S THE ONLY WAY.
IS IT? JUSTICE MUST BE SEEN TO BE DONE... BUT NOW? WHEN THE RANK-AND-FILE HEAR ABOUT THE MONSTERS THAT WERE IN THEIR MIDST, IT'LL FEEL LIKE YET MORE BETRAYAL.
ANYWAY, ENOUGH CHATTER. LEAVE THIS WITH ME, I'LL MAKE SURE BUMBLEBEE GETS IT.

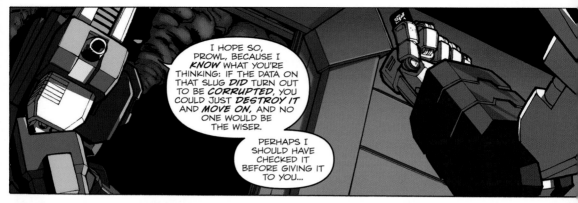

I HOPE SO, PROWL, BECAUSE I KNOW WHAT YOU'RE THINKING: IF THE DATA ON THAT SLUG DID TURN OUT TO BE CORRUPTED, YOU COULD JUST DESTROY IT AND MOVE ON, AND NO ONE WOULD BE THE WISER.
PERHAPS I SHOULD HAVE CHECKED IT BEFORE GIVING IT TO YOU...
"...BUT THAT WOULD HAVE DONE US BOTH A DISSERVICE."
MAYBE GARRUS-9 MARKS THE END OF THE ROAD FOR THE WRECKERS. AFTER ALL, THERE HAS TO BE A LIMIT.
MISSION AFTER MISSION, FATALITY AFTER FATALITY... SURELY EVERYTHING—EVERYONE—HAS A BREAKING POINT...
...IT'S JUST A QUESTION OF HOW MUCH PRESSURE IS APPLIED.
BUT MAYBE THIS ISN'T THE END OF THE ROAD, MAYBE IT'S A STOP-OFF, A MOMENT TO REFLECT BEFORE MOVING ON.
Mister O's
BECAUSE THAT'S HOW WE HONOR THOSE WE'VE LOST: BY LOOKING FORWARD, NOT BACK.
MENU
YOU SEE, THIS IS ONE OF THOSE STORIES WITH A MORAL.
AND THE MORAL IS SIMPLY THIS:
WHITTLE WONDER
TENNYSON
life persists.
THE END

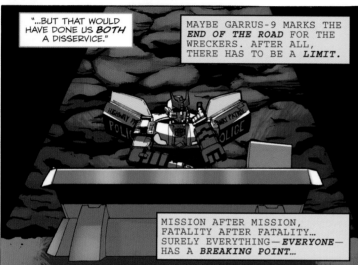

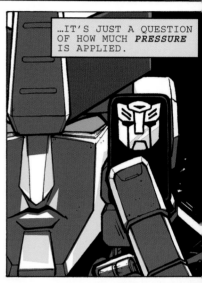

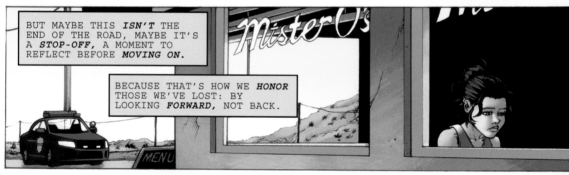

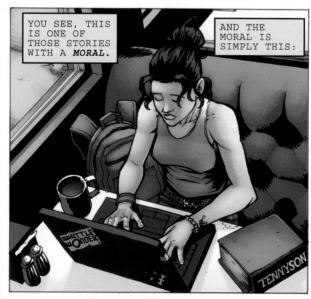

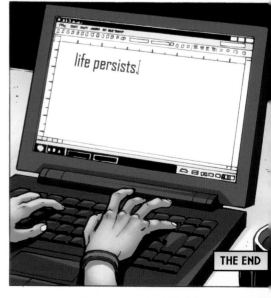

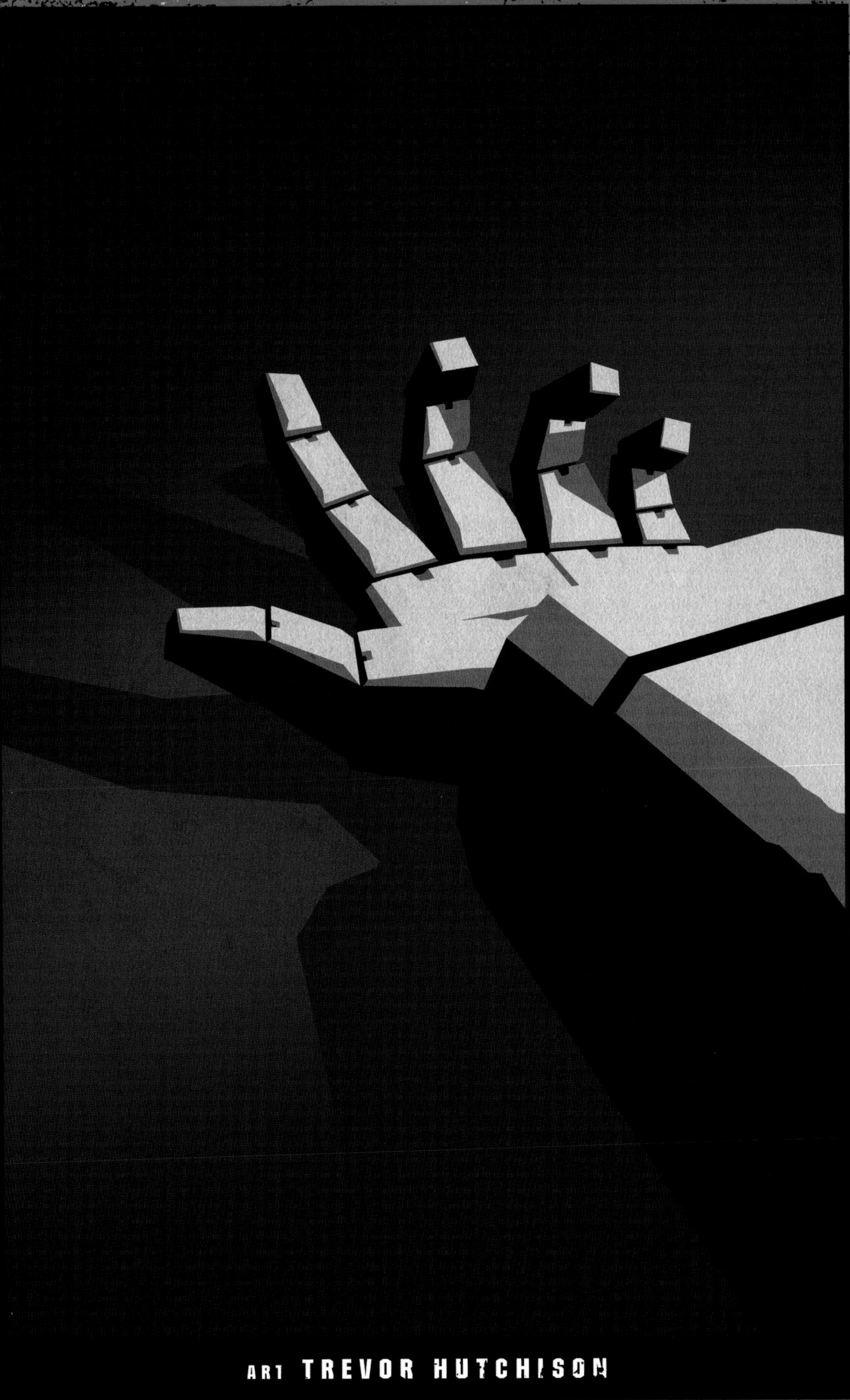

ART TREVOR HUTCHISON

BULLETS

BY JAMES ROBERTS

Pova, and the Wreckers were in a whole world of pain.

Positions had been taken, battle lines drawn; one way or another, this was the end of the road for the Autobot commandoes and their arch-enemies, Squadron X.

When Impactor spoke to his battle-hardened brigade there was no mistaking the sense of finality in his voice. "It's over - finished," he said tersely. "Squadron X are evil, pure and simple, and it falls to us to put a stop to their reign of terror."

Springer pointed to the silhouette disfiguring the moon. "That's them," he said gravely. "They've fixed the Pale Fire." The Decepticons' fearsome spaceship hung in the air like some predatory bird, waiting for the right moment to strike.

"Face it, Impactor," said Rack n' Ruin in unison. "We're way out of our depth! Eight of us against a battlecruiser? Let's split while we still have the chance."

"That's where we differ," Impactor growled. "Because I'd rather fight and die than live with the knowledge that I ran."

The others yelled their agreement.

"Then it's decided," said Impactor solemnly. "And if this really is our last stand, there's something I have to say. The truth is, I–"

First Aid stopped reading as he sensed someone approaching him from behind. He tapped the keyboard and Fisitron's 113th datalog–The Wreckers: Showdown on Pova–was replaced by a picture of a fractured elbow joint. Okay, so he was still sitting at a computer terminal when he should have been walking the ward, administering energon boosters and propex swabs to the patients downstairs, but at least he was now looking at something vaguely medical instead of reading Fisitron's account of how Impactor and his hardbitten heroes had brought down Squadron X once and for all. He made sure he was frowning in concentration when Pharma strode past.

"So Fisitron's writing about the Wreckers' elbows now, is he?" said Delphi's Chief Medical Officer. "Come on, First Aid - get to it. You've got a Fader in Row 2 downstairs." He squeezed the air with his finger and thumb. "He's about this far from shutdown."

"I'm on it." For First Aid, life on Delphi - a military hospital on the planet Messatine, on the fringes of the Cybertronians' galactic battleground–was a series of fits and starts. He'd been stationed there for 10 years, on and off, and he still couldn't call it home. As he headed downstairs he thought about Pova, and about bullets and trenches and circuit dampeners. There was no denying it: he loved datalog 113. As a subscriber to Wreckers: Declassified, 113 had been beamed directly into his brain upon its release, enabling him to digest it instantaneously. But he often read it in the more conventional sense, the better to savour its contents.

And what thrilling contents! Broadside's desperate gamble with the psychic explosives; Rack n' Ruin finally coming clean to Impactor about the tragic nature of their prognosis; Roadbuster bringing down Pale Fire with a single shot. But the best bit was when Springer and Impactor were in the trench. As Fisitron says in his commentary, their mutual affection has never been more apparent, more poignant, than when Springer asks–no, demands–that Impactor shoot him so that they both have a chance of survival.

First Aid could boast his own connection with the Wreckers–or with Springer, anyway. Five years ago, the leader of the Wreckers had cornered him at a medical conference at Kimia, the space station that doubled as a weapons research facility.

"I need your help," Springer had said, grinning that grin of his. First Aid remembered his physique more than anything else. With a chest big enough to accommodate ten Matrixes and shoulders that would put Metroplex to shame, his entire upper body was a bold visual testament to the power of unchecked width.

First Aid's eyes had loitered on Springer's infamous midsection (there was no scar, no souvenir from Pova) before he'd replied. "What can I do for you? Straighten your olfactory unit? Upgrade your circuit dampeners? Maybe your center of balance is causing you problems. Are you a bit top heavy?"

"I'm not looking for that kind of help. I'm looking for helpers. Up-and-coming medics like you who have that little extra to give."

For a terrifying moment First Aid had thought that Springer wanted him to be a Wrecker. The panic had made his vocal synthesizer misbehave, aborting every sentence after the first syllable: "But - but - I - I - why - "

"Relax. I'm not looking for new recruits. You think I'm gonna find another Roadbuster among all these Ratchets? No, this is about being the Wreckers' eyes and ears." Springer had passed him a thin rectangle of metal, one side of which was engraved with a single letter.

"What does the 'M' stand for?" First Aid had asked.

"You're holding it upside down... Listen, First Aid - that's your name, right? On the other side of that card is my personal hailing frequency. Give me a buzz sometime and we can talk some more."

Seemed like a long time ago now.

First Aid reached the ward and started moving from circuit slab to circuit slab, checking on his patients–all of whom had been powered down to minimum operating status so as to conserve energy: all non-essential functions, including those pertaining to movement and speech, were on hold pending recovery. The enforced silence spooked him; sometimes, despite himself, he imagined that they were screaming. Their mouths may have been closed, their limbs frozen at the joint, and their optics glossy with disuse, but inside their heads they were screaming.

He found the Fader and started replacing frayed energon leads. Poor Roulette. Here was one robot who was unlikely to make it until morning. He touched his forearm, moved by a need to make physical contact (he'd have put his hand on Roulette's forehead if there'd been one, but north of the neck there was only a knuckle of scorched metal).

He went to fetch more leads, knowing that when he stepped into the corridor the lights would go out behind him—after all, what was the point of illumination when the patients' eyes were switched off?

The ward doors suddenly slammed open, knocking him over. He reached instinctively for his photon pistol, then relaxed: this was an emergency situation, not an attack. Four paramedics were pushing a mobile circuit slab into the ward and trying to stop a greying, groaning robot from falling off. He watched as they fired up the Cryogenic Regeneration Chamber.

"Don't just stand there, First Aid!" yelled the chief paramedic, a skinny-limbed robot named Ambulon. "Pass me those energon swabs!"

First Aid looked down at the writhing robot. "Is that... is that Schema?"

"Yeah. Dogfight's recon team ran into the DJD as they were returning from the Serp Mines."

The ward doors swung open a second time and Dogfight stormed in, followed by Dodger and Backstreet. He scanned the rows of patients suspiciously, as if he expected Decepticons to be hiding under the circuit slabs. "Where is he?"

"You're injured," said First Aid, pointing to the sparks escaping from Dogfight's shoulder. "Let me take a look."

"It's nothing. Forget it... Hey! What are you doing?"

"Ignore me," said First Aid, examining the wings on Dogfight's upper arms and running his fingers over two Autobot symbols. After a cursory look at the shoulder wound (just a minor graze) he moved on to Backstreet.

"Leave me be, doc!"

"Just ignore him," said Ambulon, who was busy placing Schema's body inside the CR Chamber. "He does that to everyone. It's a thing of yours, isn't it First Aid?"

"Yep. Whatever. Just making sure everyone's OK. Dammit, Backstreet, where's your—ah! There it is!" First Aid scrutinized the Autobot badge on Backstreet's hip.

Dodger knew it was his turn and didn't protest. "I took a few blasts," he shrugged, letting First Aid pore over his bodywork. "This one guy hit me right—"

"Here." First Aid pointed with trembling fingers to Dodger's midsection. "On your badge." He rubbed the symbol with his thumb. "Oh my. Oh yes."

Dodger looked at Ambulon for guidance. "Is this part of his thing too?"

"Nope. Never seen this before."

First Aid dragged Dodger towards a tray of surgical instruments then let go of the bewildered Autobot and jogged for the exit. "Don't go anywhere, Dodger! I need to operate on you! This is brilliant!"

He raced upstairs to his computer terminal and typed in a certain frequency code for the second time in his life. A face appeared on the screen and grinned.

"It's me," said First Aid. "And you're never gonna guess what I've got for you!"

"I know this is difficult to talk about, Flattop, but that's actually a good sign. It means we're getting somewhere. Think of this as a positive experience. Today could be life changing!"

Rung looked at his patient. Flattop was sitting cross-legged underneath the relaxation table, hugging his knees and... well, it wasn't quite whimpering, but it was certainly a good approximation.

It was the war's fault, of course: the dynamics of perpetual combat did not make for good mental health. The number of patients complaining of cerebral malfunctions had increased a thousandfold since that fateful afternoon, all those years ago, when a Decepticon's bullet had comprehensively emptied the back of an Autobot's head and the whole world had started to unravel.

Some recent cases sprang to mind: the paranoid cadet who thought that someone had hacked into his optic sensors so that he only saw what "They" wanted to him to see; and the data processor, obsessed with gestalt technology, who suffered from a variation of phantom limb syndrome and refused to go indoors because he was convinced that he formed the right leg of a colossal super-warrior. In recent months he'd also diagnosed several cases of primus apotheosis, which made ordinary robots try to emulate Optimus Prime, and treated a medic who'd been found obsessively examining Autobot badges. (The medic had denied doing this.)

Compared to some of his patients, Flattop here hadn't presented as too much of a challenge. Rung had first assumed that he was dealing with a manic depressive or a soldier grappling with his conscience. Textbook stuff. But everything had changed when Flattop had admitted that he had been at Babu Yar on the day it rained.

"I'm so sorry," Rung had said, as Flattop's pristine bodywork had taken on a new and terrible significance. "I wouldn't have guessed that you were a Survivor."

Most Survivors, like Flattop, had accepted High Command's offer of a brand-new body, but there were those who refused on point of principle. They were the ones who would stand on street corners in front of hastily erected neon signs that said, "I was at Babu Yar." No elaboration was necessary: you just had to look at the way the light poured through their perforated bodies, like water through a sieve.

Rung crouched down and tried to make eye contact with the Babu Yar veteran who, by seeking shelter (albeit under a table), was very much conforming to type. And yet Flattop wasn't here to talk about the day he'd become a Survivor. No, he was here to discuss something else, something that had happened only a few months ago.

Rung offered Flattop his hand. "Tell me what you saw," he said softly.

Flattop climbed sheepishly to his feet. "I was on Hydrus 5, serving under Silverstreak."

Rung nodded at the mention of his longest-standing patient.

"We were stationed in the mountains, watching some 'Cons below. It was a routine mission. Well, routine for everyone else."

"It was your first tour of duty since... since it rained."

"Yeah. I was twitchy. I'd not long had my new..." He gestured to his body. "I was still breaking this in. Anyway, we were perched on this ledge and Silverstreak asks me to check the southwest vantage point. It's getting dark and I'm aching all over and I look up and I see it. Right in front of me."

"The Shimmer. What was it like?"

"It was. . . well, it was just like they say. A green light that just hangs in the air. Kinda spectral, I guess. I'm not good at describing things."

Rung helped Flattop lay down on the relaxation table. "So. What did you do?"

"I. . . I short-circuited. I passed out. I mean, I was terrified. I'd heard all the stories. I knew what the Shimmer meant."

"Hmm. Tell me, what do you think it means."

"Death! It means I'm going to die!"

Rung walked to his desk and picked up the model of Ark-1. Flattop was right - in a sense. The Shimmer was a piece of modern folklore. According to legend, anyone who saw it was destined to die in the near future. Being a rationalist at heart, Rung thought the Shimmer was a myth; being a psychoanalyst, he thought it was a projection of the subconscious, the fear of death made manifest. But soldiers were a superstitious lot, and robots like Flattop—poor, traumatized Flattop—had started taking the so-called Shimmer Stories seriously.

"You are not going to die," he said, putting down Ark-1. "I can give you two explanations for what you saw, a scientific one and a psychoanalytical one. Which would you prefer?"

Flattop stared at the ceiling.

"Okay. Well, the scientific explanation is pretty straightforward. You'd not long been in your new body. After a spark transplant it takes time for the neural processor to find its bearings. All those sensor-nets to recalibrate. So the simplest explanation is that you experienced a good old-fashioned visual hallucination."

Rung started pacing around his desk, talking to his hands. "And the psychoanalytical explanation? You were suffering from post-traumatic stress disorder. You may have inherited a new body, but Babu Yar left a trace. You don't feel you've properly cheated death." He looked up. "I hope that puts you at ease."

He walked over to his patient, frowning. "Flattop? Is everything okay?"

He was about to wave his hand in front of Flattop's face when he realized that the robot in front of him was dead.

Ironfist looked around Room 113, with its white walls and its featureless surfaces. Buried in the depths of Kimia, it couldn't have been more ordinary—far removed from the high-octane adventures of his beloved Wreckers, with their battles atop disintegrating star freighters and their skirmishes with The Anguished.

And yet as he took his seat in front of the Ethics Committee he knew that it was in nondescript rooms like this one that the important battles would be fought: heated discussions about pacts and treaties, sanctions and reparations. Forget vast armies of heavily armed robots tearing into each other until the last one standing surrendered to his mortal wounds; the Autobot/Decepticon war would only reach its end when two robots sat opposite each other in a room much like this one, forgot about the color of their badges, and started to talk.

"Thank you for your patience," said Xaaron from the table at the front of the room. Seated on either side of him were Animus and Trailbreaker. "Sometimes the Committee can reach a decision quickly, but on this occasion it was necessary to examine your submission from several angles. I will summarize the case before delivering the Committee's verdict."

Ironfist reached into his waist compartment and pulled out his trusty data slug. A black rectangle of metal stamped with a white Autobot symbol, he only needed it when nervous. As Xaaron began reading from prepared notes he flipped the slug between his fingers and took another look around. When the Ethics Committee had finished for the day, Room 113 would no doubt play host to another tableful of bureaucrats with glassy eyes and a thousand ways of apportioning blame.

The rush to convene committees was symptomatic of life after what had become known as the Surge. After a betrayal within the Autobot ranks, Megatron had acquired the access codes to all of the major Autobot outposts. Waves of Decepticons had attacked on multiple fronts, gripped by a terrifying desire to win. Prime had turned the tide—Prime always turned the tide - but the Autobot army that was left to pick up the pieces was decidedly ill-at-ease with itself. Now, every sullen soldier was a potential turncoat; anyone who raised their voice was another one to watch; you'd loiter in a doorway to avoid a ranting comrade-in-arms before quietly passing on their name to Someone Higher Up. Plagued by mutual mistrust and desperate for ideological certainty, for fixity of purpose, the Autobots looked to those in charge to lay down some ground rules. And if that meant extra scrutiny, extra checks and balances, so be it.

Ironfist refocused as Xaaron held up a bullet.

"Your testimony, Ironfist, was crucial in helping the Committee decide whether to sanction the use of these 'cerebro-sensitive bullets' in general combat situations."

Ironfist was tired of the sterile language, of the qualifiers and the caveats. Everything was carefully considered these days: tactical decisions were made only after month-long strategy meetings, while official pronouncements were equivocal and gently shaded, lest they be undermined by unforeseen events. The more he thought about it, the more he realized that the hunger for accountability had begun before the Surge. It had begun, in fact, the moment it had stopped raining on Babu Yar. There was horror at what Gideon's Decepticons had done to Flame's Autobots, but after the horror came the questions: just what was it that had fallen from that bright, cloudless sky and all but eaten the Autobots below? A few days later an anonymous informant had alerted High Command to the similarities between "Gideon's Glue," the nickname given to this ravenous chemical weapon, and a hyper-toxic vesicant that had allegedly been developed on Kimia. Prowl had ordered an inquiry and all of Kimia's weapons engineers, from Brainstorm down, had given evidence before a panel appointed by Chief Justice Tyrest himself. A panel, chaired by Ultra Magnus, that had sat in this very room.

To Ironfist, who like everyone else had denied playing any part in the creation of the vesicant, the Magnus Inquiry had felt like a trial. Throughout, Skyfall had been a tremendous source of strength. A confidant and a trusted advisor, his best friend had sensed the depths of his anguish and arranged for him to be ferried away from Kimia so that he could start a new life elsewhere. In the end that hadn't been necessary: Magnus had ruled that it was impossible to establish a definite link between the massacre on Babu Yar and any chemical weapon developed on Kimia. But the seeds of suspicion had been planted, and the Ethics Committee was just one of several ways of keeping tabs on Brainstorm and the rest of them.

Xaaron continued: "The Committee understands that, when fired, these bullets exhibit something you describe as 'cranial bias.' They abandon their natural trajectory in favour of the nearest... well, the nearest head."

"Yes," said Ironfist, sensing that he was expected to elaborate. "Each bullet has a simple onboard computer which is activated when the bullet is fired. The computer immediately locks on to its target's neural processor."

"Tell me, Ironfist," said Trailbreaker, picking up the bullet and guiding it in slow motion towards his own head. "Are you proud of what you've done?"

Ironfist dropped his data slug. "I'm sorry?"

"Most weapons can be used to wound. To disarm. To neutralize a threat. Your weapon kills. Every time. And I wondered whether, in your world, that counted as a success."

"Trailbreaker's question will be struck from the record," said Xaaron. "The moral issues raised by the existence of these bullets are for the Committee to consider, not you." He raised a hand to silence Trailbreaker's objection. "And the Committee has reached a decision. Ironfist, please stand.

"This Committee is charged with upholding Section 19 of the Autobot Code, and to that end we have considered whether to sanction the use of this ammunition. We have decided that to use cerebro-sensitive bullets against enemy combatants would in all but the most exceptional cases constitute a war crime. The manufacture of these bullets is henceforth banned under Protocol III of the Non-Conventional Weapons Act. You have 36 hours to surrender the bullets and any specially adapted firing mechanism."

Xaaron and the others walked out, leaving Ironfist standing and staring into space.

"Hey."

Ironfist jumped as he felt a hand on his shoulder. He turned to see Skyfall holding up his hands apologetically.

"Relax buddy, it's me. How'd it go?"

"Protocol III."

"Aww, no. I'm sorry. Who was chairing? Xaaron? Well, that explains it. The guy lost his bearings decades ago. He's older than most mineral deposits."

Skyfall detected a smile behind Ironfist's faceplate. "See, that's what makes you better than me, Fiz. If I'd just been humiliated by a bunch of pacifists—if I'd just seen months of work go up in smoke—I'd be mad as hell."

Ironfist shrugged, stepped into the corridor, and closed the door behind them.

"Room 113, of all places," said Skyfall. "I still get flashbacks to the Inquiry. Sitting there in front of Magnus, listening to Nightbeat talk about scar patterns and droplet craters."

"Let's not go there."

"No, you're right. I know I had it bad, but it was nothing compared to the grilling they gave you. I'd have buckled. After the third day of questioning, I'd have buckled." Skyfall steered Ironfist towards The Exit Rooms, a warren of recharge booths next to the shuttle bays and the one place where Kimia's staff could take a break from their duties and ingest energon or engex. "But you, my friend, are made of sterner stuff. The strong and silent type... A little bit Impactor-esque, if you don't mind me saying so."

"Stop it," grinned Ironfist, struggling to contain a spark surge.

"Uh-oh, here comes Perceptor's brainier spark brother," said Skyfall. "Hi, Brainstorm. Don't tell me: Room 113?"

Kimia's foremost weapons engineer held up a slim case that was handcuffed to his wrist. "How'd you guess?"

Brainstorm was a legend among Kimia's engineering community, mainly because his weapons were so horrendously over the top. More often than not, whatever exotic gun Ironfist or Crosshairs or Tripwire unveiled, Brainstorm had not only developed a more extreme version but had seen it rejected by a scandalized Ethics Committee who had found the weapon so morally reprehensible that to even contemplate its use in all but the most extreme combat situations (such as the imminent destruction of Cybertron) was utterly unconscionable. Brainstorm rather gleefully referred to these weapons as the Unmentionables.

"What's in the case?" asked Skyfall.

Brainstorm leaned forward conspiratorially. "I call it an MCP. A Malevolent Counterintuitive Pathogen. It's based on the Uncertainty Principle. When you open this case you'll find whatever you least expect - and then it'll kill you."

"Very funny," said Ironfist. "You are joking, right?"

Skyfall tugged his arm. "Come on, Fiz. Exit Rooms."

"I'm going to need that cerebro-gun back, Brainstorm," Ironfist called out as he was dragged away. "Don't worry about giving it the once over. I managed to iron out the kinks. Not that it mattered, in the end."

The sky above Hydrus 5 was losing it, no question. Subjected to a variety of rare and recherche weaponry, the browbeaten firmament was now suffering something of a meteorological panic attack: horizontal rain, banks of scalding vapor, clouds that collapsed in on themselves. That sort of thing.

The Decepticons were to blame. And the Autobots. For months the two sides had battled enthusiastically on the ground below, throwing everything they had at each other. Now that the battle was over it was time for quiet soul-searching, contemplation and private reflection.

"Will you get a load of that!" exclaimed Pyro, surveying the landscape from the top of a mountain created only that morning by the Tremorcons and their tectonic cannon. The remains of a displaced Hydrusian temple smoldered nearby. "Look around you, Afterburner! What do you see? Freedom! A world liberated from the Decepticon menace! I mean, yes, the planet has sustained minor collateral damage, but that's to be expected when you're up against an infiltration unit on the brink of Phase 4." He paused. "Or is it Phase 5? I find it hard to tell them apart."

"We fought hard and we came through," said Afterburner. "And if I may say so, Commander, I think you tipped the balance. Taking on Seizor single-handed and all that."

"Oh, I don't deserve to be singled out." Pyro puffed out his chest. "Which bit did you like best?"

"Definitely the bit when you were driving towards Seizor's bunker and the Tremorcons were in your way." Afterburner sketched out the action with his hands. "You ram-raided Aftershock and Fracture—bam!—and then activated the boosters under your cab so you could transform. In midair."

"Yes, well, that's a rather famous maneuver. Go on."

"After you put down Tectonix and the others, you found Seizor in the bunker. I think you sensed it was going to be your final battle and wanted to say something to mark the occasion. You must've accidentally switched on inter-Autobot radio because we all heard you say—"

"Anyway!" said Pyro. "Moving on..."

"You said—and I don't think I'll ever forget the sheer sense of gravity in your voice—you said, 'You're late for a meeting with my fists, Decepticreep!'"

Pyro winced. He'd been working on a more memorable line, something to do with standing and/or falling.

"Anyway," said Afterburner, "I'd better go and see how the rest of the troops are coping. Will you be giving a speech?"

"Yes. Just give me a moment to compose something."

He watched Afterburner turn into a motorcycle and speed down the mountainside, then started to replay Optimus Prime's greatest speeches in his head. As he searched his memory-net under keywords like "courage," "resolve," and "fortitude," he was reminded of how any problem could be solved by asking one question: what would Prime do?

Pulling a soldering gun from a chest compartment he'd had re-sized to accommodate the Matrix (you know, just in case…), he climbed down into the remains of the temple and started patching things up. He was distracted by an odd feeling, as if something was brushing against his spark. For a second he thought he was about to experience a vision, something Prime always seemed to be doing. "Bring it on," he thought, steeling himself. "The more apocalyptic the better."

He sensed a movement on the periphery of his optic field and turned, afraid of what he might see. Partway down the mountain was a faint green flicker of heat-rippled air. He knew at once that he was looking at The Shimmer.

Springer stood alone on the command deck of Debris, a crumbling Autobot space station in orbit around Klo, and stared at 12 names on a computer screen.

In his right hand he was holding an Autobot bullet (of sorts) that had been fired by a Decepticon (of sorts). The bullet was, in fact, a benign projectile: inside there was no vein of combustible energon, just a data chip containing the latest report from Agent 113, an Autobot working undercover at the Decepticon Justice Division. The name was misleading: it was the DJD's job to scour their own ranks for dissidents and turncoats and then, very publicly, murder them. Information provided by Agent 113 often led the Autobots to Decepticons who, being dissidents and turncoats, were willing to betray their ex-comrades in exchange for protection against reprisals.

"Your friend has a funny way of making contact," First Aid had said when he'd got in touch three days earlier, and he was right. Terrified of being detected, the increasingly eccentric Agent 113 had developed a unique way of reporting his findings. Instead of, say, a midnight rendezvous on the steps of the Chomskian Embassy, he would wait until the DJD attacked some Autobots and then shoot the "enemy" with a data-laced bullet. Springer had recruited medics at key facilities so that someone was always on the lookout for Agent 113's calling card: a single bullet hole in the right "eye" of an Autobot symbol.

With his latest communiqué, Agent 113 had relayed concerns within the DJD that nothing had been heard of Garrus-9 since the Autobot prison had been overrun by Sky Quake's Predators during the early stages of the Surge. The DJD had despatched an exploratory force to investigate. They'd never come back.

Springer had shared this information with High Command, who - on the basis of an earlier report from Agent 113 - had originally concluded that G-9 had been utterly destroyed. They were now faced with the possibility that Fortress Maximus and Co. had not only survived the Surge, but were repelling Decepticon invasion parties whilst waiting to be rescued. All of which had led Prowl to contact Springer to discuss plans for Operation: Retrieval.

Springer would have preferred a more inspiring name, but it was typical of Prowl to opt for something clinical and detached. Fort Max and his team didn't need "retrieving," they needed rescuing. Nonetheless, drab name aside, Operation: Retrieval was why he was doing what Impactor and Crest and Hyperion before him had done: staring at names on a screen and deciding who he would ask to join the Wreckers.

Guzzle had never held the Matrix before.

The object in his hand was the perfect weight: heavy enough to matter, to tug on the wire sinews in his forearm, but easy to carry. A good size, too: portable, but big enough to stop Decepticons in their tracks. Best of all was the way it felt: the perfect union of holder and held, it sang in his grip.

Guzzle had never held the Matrix before and probably never would, but surely it could never feel as satisfying, as fundamentally right, as it felt when he picked up The Judge, his favorite handgun.

He'd lived an itinerant life of late, latching onto a succession of Autobot squads in the hope of recapturing the sense of belonging that he'd felt when serving in his old platoon. He'd decided to help with Dipstick's reconstruction project until he could find something better suited to his talents (those talents chiefly consisting of the ability to insert various deadly projectiles into various deadly Decepticons). And while the thrill of close combat hadn't entirely deserted him, this most unreflective of robots had recently identified a certain… hollowness inside him. His first reaction, of course, had been to seek medical help. Fixit had carried out a full body search and, finding no internal cavities, suggested that the hollow feeling was not an early indication of corrodia gravis but "an emotional response." Guzzle had pondered this at length, until a pang of acute discomfort had heralded the arrival of bona fide insight: he was in mourning. Most of his old platoon had died trying to rescue Kup, and he was still struggling to accept their deaths and the circumstances surrounding them.

His new life on Igue Moor–a fuel depot on the outskirts of Babu Yar–had now settled into a reassuring rhythm. Every day, a few hours before dawn, he and The Judge would go outside and shoot statues. If he'd felt a flicker of guilt when he'd first started using the remains of the Sacred Debating Chamber as a firing range, he hadn't recognized it as such.

He loaded a handful of tracer bullets into his gun and looked around for today's first target. On the statue of Babu Fost, the Great Pacifist, he found it: a forehead scar. He slid his green targeting visor over his optics and was beginning to squeeze the trigger when the unthinkable happened: he stopped. He'd always seen a gunshot through. He wondered whether his overworked trigger finger had seized up, but no, Fixit had only last week given him new digits. Which meant that this was something else entirely: another "feeling." Something, he sensed, to do with his own mortality.

Thankfully the moment passed quickly, and he felt sufficiently at ease with himself to unload an entire magazine of tracers into the Great Pacifist's head.

For some reason the luminous green tracer trails did not fade away. Instead, they hovered over the floor of the Sacred Debating Chamber, gathered themselves up and started to flicker. No, it wasn't a flicker. It was more of… more of a shimmer. The Judge slipped from Guzzle's new fingers.

Ironfist was safe in the womb that was his workshop. It was small, yes, and it smelt of cordite and coolant, but it was home. The workbench in the middle of the room, worn out but well loved, glistened like brown sugar under the filtered light.

The workshop doubled as a museum of Wreckers memorabilia. The main attraction, on permanent display, was Impactor's sky sled. Above the doorway was the broadsword that Springer had used to (literally) disarm Soundwave. Mounted on the wall was a grainy picture of Rack that had been taken hours before the operation that saved two lives. Best of all was something the casual visitor never noticed: if you transformed the workbench into a command chair and repositioned a few monitors, the workshop resembled the bridge of the Wreckers' one-time spaceship, the Xantium.

Ironfist sat in front of his computer and studied an image that was by now as familiar to him as the backs of his hands: a schematic of his own head. Every circuit board and nano-piston was exposed, every muscle wire and actuator made explicit. And there, close to the centre of the skull, was his own Unmentionable: a cerebro-sensitive bullet. Whenever this dark invader annexed another part of his headspace, he would pass out. His first thought upon waking up was always, "I'm alive!" His second thought was always, "I'm dead." Because the bullet—the damn bullet—was still moving closer to its target.

Three people knew about the accident: Crosshairs, who ten months ago had found him on the floor of his workshop, the cerebro-gun inches from his open hand; Kaput, the surgeon who had concluded (rather too quickly for Ironfist's liking) that it was impossible to safely remove the bullet; and Skyfall - poor, traumatized Skyfall—whom he'd told in the Exit Rooms and who, rather touchingly, had asked permission to personally rip the cerebro-gun to shreds.

Ironfist knew he was lucky to be alive. If the prototype bullet had been at a more advanced stage, things would have been different. In the spirit of making the most of his remaining days he'd considered giving his workshop to Skyfall—thus keeping a promise he'd made when the two of them had first arrived on Kimia - and setting off to have his first and last adventure. He'd decided to stay behind and perfect the cerebro-sensitive bullets for one simple reason: it gave him power over them. It meant that he controlled them and not the other way round.

Skyfall had been frustrated by Ironfist's failure to act, telling him he needed his head examined.

Ironfist smiled at the thought of his friend's knack for making inappropriate remarks. The two of them had met in the Manganese Mountains and were both, initially, of equal rank. They had different styles of working: Ironfist was slow and methodical, happy to test and tinker until everything was in its right place, while Skyfall was the opposite. In those days the success of one had spurred the other on. Ironfist had emerged as a clear winner when he'd developed an ion blaster capable of burning a hole in the nose cone of a Decepticon jet fighter from 30 miles away. Although he'd handed it to Optimus Prime in person, Optimus—distracted by reports of an attack on a convoy of refugees in the Neutral Territories—later told senior officers that Skyfall was behind its creation. Skyfall, for his part, kept quiet for fear of embarrassing Prime.

Although Skyfall had received a run of special commissions on the back of "Blastergate" it was Ironfist who later made history by inventing cold phosphex, a chemical agent that made anything it came into contact with as brittle as glass. Skyfall had joked that Ironfist had "stolen" molecular research that he had begun years earlier, something that Ironfist had denied. The next day Skyfall was among those ambushed by the Decepticons outside the Yussian territories. He'd ended up in the infamous Grindcore prison camp and had not seen Ironfist again until his escape a hundred years later. Shortly afterwards, Ironfist had been offered a place at the prestigious Kimia facility, where there was a 60-year waiting list for workshops. Ironfist had accepted on the condition that Skyfall, who was still adjusting to life outside Grindcore, came with him.

Sensing that Skyfall was unhappy with life in Kimia's manufacturing division, Ironfist had allowed him use of the equipment in his workshop. Black phosphex was the result. A more potent version of the original, it later became apparent that Skyfall had skipped several stages of the testing process in a rush to see it used in the field. The result: 14 Autobots on maneuver near Gorlam Prime had been left exposed when their weapons, loaded with black phosphex, had turned to dust in their hands. Skyfall had been sent to Garrus 9—not as an inmate, but as a guard. "An enforced change of career," Prowl had said at the time.

Skyfall had spent several years at G-9. On one occasion, much to the

envy of Ironfist, he'd even helped the Wreckers thwart a jailbreak. Ironfist had campaigned tirelessly for his friend to be reassigned to Kimia. Demonstrating the type of bad luck that had characterized his career, Skyfall had returned just in time to be caught up in the Magnus Inquiry.

Ironfist touched the scar on his forehead. Sometimes, when he got sick of life on the knife edge, he would think about pushing. And what stopped him was not the thought of Skyfall collapsing with grief, or of work left unfinished in his lab. No, what stopped him—what stopped him every time—was the thought of a robot with a harpoon for a hand.

"C'mon, everyone, let's hear it! Three cheers for Rotorstorm!"

Landfill looked up at the robot being carried on the shoulders of his adoring troops. "Er, excuse me, commander. . . but aren't we the ones who are supposed to say that?"

"What, the three cheers thing? Oh, don't be so conventional." He smiled. The battle for Karashi Delta was over and the Autobots, largely due to his strategic prowess and peerless flying skills, had won. "Put me down," he said eventually. "I need to stretch my blades."

Seconds later he was flying through the Morobishi Canyons, enjoying the solitude. Away from his troops there was no pressure to perform or impress. Besides, eschewing the aeronautical maneuvers that had made him famous meant he didn't have to think about Jetstream. That was the idea, anyway; in practice, his instructor at the Iaconian Aerial Academy was never far from his mind.

Jetstream had taught him to recognize his inherent worthlessness. In front of the other cadets he'd always been supportive, but in private he would berate him for showing off and for getting ideas above his station. "You think you're something special?" he would say. "You think you're better than the rest, better than me, just because you can turn a few tricks? On a good day—on your best day—I'd say you were unremarkable."

Rotorstorm's only response to Jetstream's verbal abuse was to make jokes. If you can make light of the situation, he'd think, it can't be as bad as it seems.

Over time, Jetstream's verbal abuse... evolved. On one occasion, Rotorstorm was pushed against a wall. On another, he was pushed to the floor. On yet another, he was punched to the floor. Before long, he was on the receiving end of sustained and entirely unprovoked beatings.

The worst day of Rotorstorm's life—worse than the day war was declared; worse than the day of the Simanzi Massacre—was the day the IAA installed a Cryogenic Regeneration Chamber. He couldn't remember what he'd done to deserve that night's battering, but as he lay on the floor of the aircraft hangar, his torso freshly pummeled, his spinal strut bent at a right angle and his face reduced to a shallow bowl of oil and splinters, he saw something he would never forget: Jetstream was standing over him, fists clenched and head cocked, coolly appraising his options. And the most terrifying thing of all was the look of exhilaration on his face as he'd wondered where to place the next punch.

Rotorstorm had passed out while Jetstream was shoveling him into the CR Chamber. He'd woken up the next day without a single scratch on his body. Jetstream, meanwhile, was gone: he'd moved to a training facility in another province and some time after that changed his name. Since then, Rotorstorm had only seen him once: he'd been sitting in the front row when Rotorstorm had been awarded the Novic Medal for Outstanding Valor, and he'd been clapping and cheering more loudly than anyone else.

Rotorstorm was dragged back to the present by the sight of something up ahead: a movement on the top of a canyon. As he got closer he realized, with a start, what it was. He panicked. He ran. He pushed his thrusters to maximum burn and hurtled away from the canyons, kicking up dust in his wake and slowing down only when he'd reached open space. Exhausted, he transformed and leaned against a rock, his head in his hands. When he looked up it was there again–the Shimmer–right in front of him. Screaming, he opened fire.

Springer looked at the four names on the screen in front of him.

Four names: four new Wreckers. Four new robots to replace Roadbuster, who was still caught up in that Sparkeater business; Whirl, who had proven himself something of a liability of late; Sandstorm, who was deep behind enemy lines; and Broadside, who was all but lost to them now.

Four names: an aerial strategist, a soldier, a field commander, and a weapons expert. Just what he needed. He'd send his recommendations to Prowl for final approval before convening a meeting of the existing Wreckers and putting his choices to the vote.

Four names: Rotorstorm, Guzzle, Pyro, and Skyfall.

Skyfall sauntered into the workshop and slumped into a chair opposite Ironfist, who was working at his computer.

"So I'm sitting in the Exit Rooms, and guess what? I overhear Brainstorm's crew talking about datalog 330."

Ironfist stopped typing. "Really? And?"

"They love it! They were trying to work out who 'Fisitron' is. I thought, good job no one except me ever visits you, otherwise your secret would be out."

"But they liked it."

"Oh, definitely. I mean, they had a few niggles. Totally minor stuff. But overall they really liked it."

"I'm glad it was well received," said Ironfist, returning to his keyboard.

"Like, one of them… what's his name? Atomizer? Atomizer said that you - I mean Fisitron - writes like he's actually inside the Wreckers' heads? You know, all that interior monologue stuff? Now you once told me that was called Technique, and I like it. I get it. But Atomizer was saying that it 'detracted from a powerful historical account.'"

Ironfist gave up trying to type and looked at his friend. "Well, Fisitron's never put himself forward as a straight historian. He's more of a chronicler–"

"–and dramatist, yeah, so you've said. And that's what I almost said to these guys. But by then they'd started quoting all these Fisitronisms."

"Fisi-what?"

"You know, those phrases you use a lot. 'It's over, finished!' That was one. 'The end of the road' crops up a lot too, apparently."

"Well, perhaps Atomizer should try writing 330 datalogs without repeating himself."

"Anyway, so then Swerve calls Fisitron a hag–a hagio–what's the name for a writer who idealizes his subjects?"

"A hagiographer. Swerve called me a hagiographer."

"That's it! He said the datalogs were like… what's the other word he

used? Oh yeah, 'fan-fiction.' I know! Totally out of order. But don't worry, 'cos Tripwire said that downloading Wreckers: Declassified was, like, the highlight of his work-cycle. Even if…" Skyfall trailed off, smiling to himself.

"Even if what?"

"Nothing, nothing. It's just a style thing. Look, I really like how you write."

"What did they say, Skyfall? I know you try to protect me from these things, but I'm big enough to take criticism."

"Adverbs," said Skyfall, shaking his head at the absurdity of it all. "You know, bits like, 'This war should have been over aeons ago, Springer said ruefully.' Or, 'You'll have to count the Wreckers out of Operation: Volcano,' Impactor growled threateningly.'"

Ironfist looked at the first draft of datalog 331. Every other word ended in -ly. He reached for the delete key and called up another document he'd been working on: the Unofficial Wreckers' Training Guide. He started typing.

"Where have you got to, anyway? With the datalogs."

"Me?" Skyfall frowned. "Er… 113. The Pova one. Still got another, like, million to go. I'm a slow reader."

"You should just download them all directly to your neural processor. Save you a lot of time."

"Yeah, but getting it beamed into your head feels like cheating. Besides, I wouldn't be able to spot the typos."

Ironfist stood up. "Is there anything else you wanted?"

"Not really. I'm just bored… When are you going to write about the Wreckers putting down that jailbreak on G-9 a few years ago? I'm in that! You can build the story around a proper firsthand account instead of all those dodgy dossiers that High Command send you."

"Datalog 332, maybe. Right now I've got to get all the cerebro-guns packed up. You can help if you want."

Skyfall headed for the door. "Thanks for the offer, buddy, but I've got to… you know. Stuff. All that stuff I do all day."

Alone again, Ironfist started dismantling a cerebro-cannon. He was interrupted by a sound he'd not heard in years: a comms alert. He looked up and said, "Accept."

Prowl's face appeared on a monitor screen. "Thanks for taking my call, Ironfist. Or should I call you 'Fisitron'?"

Springer turned Kup's handshake into a hug. "Been a while since you visited Debris," he smiled.

Kup took his cygar out of his mouth and looked his protege up and down. "There's something different about you, lad… Ah! You've polished. An' that can only mean one thing: new recruits. Anyone I know?"

"You know three of them, definitely. The fourth… well, between you and me, he wasn't my first choice."

Kup sat down at the conference table. "Not up to scratch, eh? Or did your conscience get the better of you?"

"Only if my conscience looks and sounds like Prowl." Springer pulled up a chair. "He vetoed my original choice. Skyfall. You know, the gun guy."

"Came up with Prime's shootin' stick. An' that black perspex stuff."

"Phosphex. But he made up for that, as far as I'm concerned. Did some good work on G-9. Impressed me. Thought he deserved a second chance."

"Hm. Garrus-9 an' second chances. Two don't often go together."

Springer shot him a look. "Anyway. So Prowl tells me that Skyfall's not quite up to standard. Says he wants to 'parachute someone in'–I know, he actually said that. Apparently he can vouch for the replacement personally."

"One of Prowl's friends, eh? Bet he's a laugh a minute. Probably some calculator on legs. Oh hell, it's not Calculus, is it?" Kup chewed on the cygar. "Jeez, why doesn't he just take charge of the entire mission? Can you imagine? It'd be two years before you set off. The guy can't disconnect himself from his circuit slab without makin' sure it doesn't contravene some new legislation he made up the night before. Hey, I ever tell you about the time him and me an' the Heliobots raided the Fatal Consequence? Y'know, the Decepticon deep spacer, the one with Violator and his crew? We arrested everyone, an' Prowl insists on reading Violator his charge sheet. Not just the crimes, but the actual sections of the Tyrest Accord that he's contravened. In full. Have I not told you this?"

Springer stood up to get the door. "No, but go on."

"It took forever. Picture it. The two of them, either side of the table, Violator chained to the floor, Prowl doing that voice he does when he's telling you off. By the end of day two, Violator couldn't take it anymore. He was literally beggin' to be beaten up. Anything to break the monotony. Prowl's havin' none of it. Starts quoting Cybertronian law–in the original laconian program code. Halfway through day three, Violator's optics start trickling down his face."

"No way."

"Yup. He'd done himself in. Flicked his own kill-switch. Prowl had chapter 'n versed him to death."

"That," said Springer, shaking his head as he opened the door, "is the best story ever."

Twin Twist was in the corridor, in drill mode, revving his engines.

"That's just his way of telling you he was getting impatient," said Topspin, stepping over Twin Twist and into the conference room. Perceptor followed him.

The vote did not take long. Springer didn't mention Skyfall or Prowl's intervention, but he could tell that Topspin in particular was puzzled as to why they were being given a chance to veto three of the candidates but not the fourth. "It's just the way it is," said Springer, heading into the science lab with Kup. "I'll just go and tell our new recruits the good news."

Perceptor turned to Twin Twist and Topspin. "As I was saying, it's called vicarious perception. And it may very well change your lives." It was, quite literally, too much for Ironfist to process. Prowl's request that he become a Wrecker–and his decision to accept–were such life-changing events that he'd had to employ discrete subsections of his neural processor in order to better analyze their ramifications: his central processor handled the big cause-and-effect stuff while a support processor at the rear explored the more subtle implications.

Of course there was more to it than just becoming a Wrecker. Prowl had mentioned a name, Aequitas, and explained how there were certain "expectations" involved if Ironfist joined Springer and his crew.

Ironfist stopped tidying up his workshop and tapped his forehead scar.

It was more than a scar now: it was his ticket to adventure. He still hated it. "You're not going to get me," he said quietly. "I'll decide when I die, not you." And if a little voice at the back of his head said, "You're being exploited. Don't do it, don't do it, don't do it," that voice was ignored.

Ironfist saw movement reflected in a monitor screen and turned to find its source. There it was, in front of the sky sled: an anomaly in the air; a visual typo; a shimmer. It grew in size, soaking the workshop in green light as it became more defined and precise. He reached out to touch it but shrank back at the last moment, suddenly afraid. It was only once the Shimmer had settled into a definitive pattern that Ironfist realized what–who–he was looking at.

"Hello," said Springer.

Ironfist went to speak but found that nerves had got the better of him: his vocal synthesizer was malfunctioning, making his voice sound like a detuned radio. He noticed that Springer cast no shadow, that his feet were hovering fractionally above the floor, and that his gestures were sluggish and approximate. You're a hologram, he thought. A remote projection.

"You must be Ironfist. You know why I'm here. It's time."

Ironfist rose to his full height. "I've waited all my life for this moment, Springer, ever since I watched Impactor leap from an exploding hover-bike onto the roof of the Vosian Citadel. I remember dead Decepticons crashing out of the windows on the sixth floor, then the fifth, then the fourth. I remember him walking out of the front doors, firing his harpoon into a low-flying shuttle pod and disappearing into the sunset. From that moment on, the Wreckers were one of the few constants in my bit part, back room life. They spoke to me. They resonated. So yes, Springer, I do know why you're here: you're here to ask me to fight alongside you. And my answer is yes. A thousand times yes. Because if this is the final act in my sorry life story, if this is my swan song, then at least I'll know that I died the robot I always wanted to be."

Springer frowned and pointed to his throat. "Sorry Ironfist, I didn't catch any of that. Something's wrong with your vocal synthesizer. You sound like a detuned radio."

Ironfist transformed into vehicle mode and back again, hoping the jolt would kick his systems back into line. "Is that better?" he asked.

"Much. Now, where were we? Ah yes. Your name is top of the list. I'm obliged to tell you that as of the 11th Cycle 987, the Wreckers' survival rate is 42%."

"Are you sure? I make it 38%. I suppose if you count Rack n' Ruin as one robot..." He caught the look on Springer's face. "Sorry, sir. Nerves. Can we start this conversation again?"

"You can turn down this opportunity. No questions asked. What do you say?"

"The answer's yes. It's always been yes."

"Excellent. Report to Rung for a pre-ops screening, then rendezvous with the other recruits at the Igue Moor Fuel Depot outside Babu Yar. 48 hours, Ironfist. Use them wisely." Springer pressed a button on his waist. "Nice place you've got here," he said, looking around as he started to fade away. "Reminds me of...the bridge of the Xantium."

Springer watched the science room solidify around him and reached for a communicube bearing Twin Twist's image. "I've finished my house calls, Twin Twist. Only Guzzle turned me down. Said he had certain things to do before he died."

It had been his first wasted journey since the time he'd dropped in on one of Silverstreak's company on Hydrus 5. The robot in question–Flatpack?–had collapsed in shock before the holo-projection had even asserted itself. He'd made a quick exit and removed Flatline's name from the list of reservists: someone who short-circuited at the sight of a green light wouldn't last two seconds with the Wreckers.

"Guzzle turned you down?" said Twin Twist. "The same Guzzle who's holding on line two? He wants to talk to you about Kup. Dunno why, boss, but I think someone's had a change of heart..."

"Wait. Wait. What did you just say?"

"The Wreckers. I'm on the team! Springer just sort of projected himself inside the workshop and--you don't have to look quite so surprised, Skyfall."

"No. No, I mean... The Wreckers! That's impossible!" He looked up sharply. "Did I say impossible? I meant incredible. Absolutely incredible."

"I don't think I'll be coming back."

Skyfall put his hands on Ironfist's shoulders and looked him squarely in the eye, as if he was about to disclose a profound universal truth. "What's gonna happen to the workshop?"

"The workshop? It's all yours," said Ironfist. "A promise is a promise."

"Wow... wow." Skyfall started running his hands over hard surfaces, tapping monitors and testing switches. "I've often pictured myself in here, carrying on your work. You'll keep in touch, right? We can meet up for a quart of engex in the Exit Rooms once you've got your first mission under your belt, hmm? Doesn't have to be the Exit Rooms. Anywhere'll do."

"Like I said, I don't think I'll be coming back."

Skyfall turned around. "Say what? Sorry, buddy, I was miles away. Where are your field modulators?"

"Over there, next to the display cabinet with the harpoon heads in. No, next to the sky sled. Look, give me a couple of hours and then you can move your stuff in. OK?"

"Sure. No problem. Wow! Big day!" Skyfall shook Ironfist's hand. "Be seeing you, Fiz. When you're done saving the world I want you to get in touch, yeah? Promise?"

"I promise."

Ironfist waited until his friend had gone before turning to the two identical carry cases on his workbench. Inside the first were weapons he could work on during the long journey to wherever it was the Wreckers were going. Inside the second was everything that related to the cerebro-bullet project, including the prototype weapon that Brainstorm had left on his workbench a few hours earlier. He'd leave the second case for Xaaron to collect.

It was a good time to go. News had just reached Kimia of another death linked to Gideon's Glue. Despite being given a new body, a robot called Flattop had belatedly succumbed to brain melt, which suggested that the damage had literally run deeper than anyone had imagined. Flattop's death would drag everything back out into the open.

He put his hand on the first carry case and looked at the second. His first and only mission with the Wreckers. His one opportunity to make an impression. No doubt his new teammates had all lived lives that resembled one big action sequence. But him? What did he have to offer except a spark that could be put to better use?

Funny how the second case was identical to the first. It would be so easy to mix up the two...

A noise made him jump. He had another call. "Accept."

A face appeared on screen. "Thank goodness I caught you, Ironfist. There's something you should know."

The tiny shuttlepod landed outside Igue Moor Fuel Depot. Ironfist pushed open the cockpit canopy, threw a carry case and a backpack-shaped lightformer cannon onto the ground, and climbed out. He scanned the deserted construction site and spotted a lone figure sitting at the base of a crane, a colossal gun turret protruding from his back. Ironfist walked over to him. "Hi. Are you here for the..."

"For the pick-up? Yeah. I'm Guzzle." The robot climbed to his feet and proffered his handgun. "And this is The Judge."

"Nice to meet you both," said Ironfist, turning the gun over in his hands. "Hmm. Supercooled base cylinders, partly tensioned pin lock, detuned kickback cushions... Good job on the hammer spur. Bet the recoil is crisp as hell." He handed it back. "Very nice."

"You must be Ironfist. So, you ready for the suicide mission?"

"Who told you--Prowl? I thought I was supposed to keep it--ah. Wait. You don't mean it literally... In which case, to answer your question, Guzzle, no, I don't think I am ready."

"Me neither. Wasn't sure whether to say yes at first. Then I thought 'Come on Guzzle, this is a once-in-a-lifetime opportunity.'"

Or an end-of-a-lifetime opportunity, thought Ironfist.

"But you knew about the Wreckers, though? Before the call."

Ironfist weighed up the pros and cons of what he was about to say and thought to hell with it. "I know more about them than just about anybody else." He picked up a length of steel piping and wrote his name in the dirt, arranging the letters in a circle. "I don't know if you read Wreckers: Declassified...?"

"Religiously. That Fisitron guy is a legend."

"He's very flattered to hear you say that."

Guzzle looked blank. "Sorry?"

"Fisitron." Ironfist used the pipe to point at the letters. "F. I. S... No?"

"I don't follow," said Guzzle.

Ironfist dragged his hands over his face and looked his companion in the eye. "It's me. I'm Fisitron."

"You're Fisitron?! Ha! Your name--it's an anagram!" He turned serious. "Was that deliberate?"

They froze as they each felt a gun against the back of their head.

"A head shot at close range..." said a voice behind them. "Not a pleasant way to go."

Rotorstorm somersaulted over their heads, landed in front of them, and holstered his weapons. "What is this, the Cannon Fodder Convention? Let me see... Guzzle I recognize from all the Body Augmentation controversy. Which means that you must be Ironfist. Weapons expert. From Kimia, yeah? About as far away from the frontline as you can get without sitting in Omega Supreme's lap. Nice battle scar you got there, Goggles. What happened? You slip on a spanner and hit your head on your workbench?"

"You're Rotorstorm," said Ironfist, standing up.

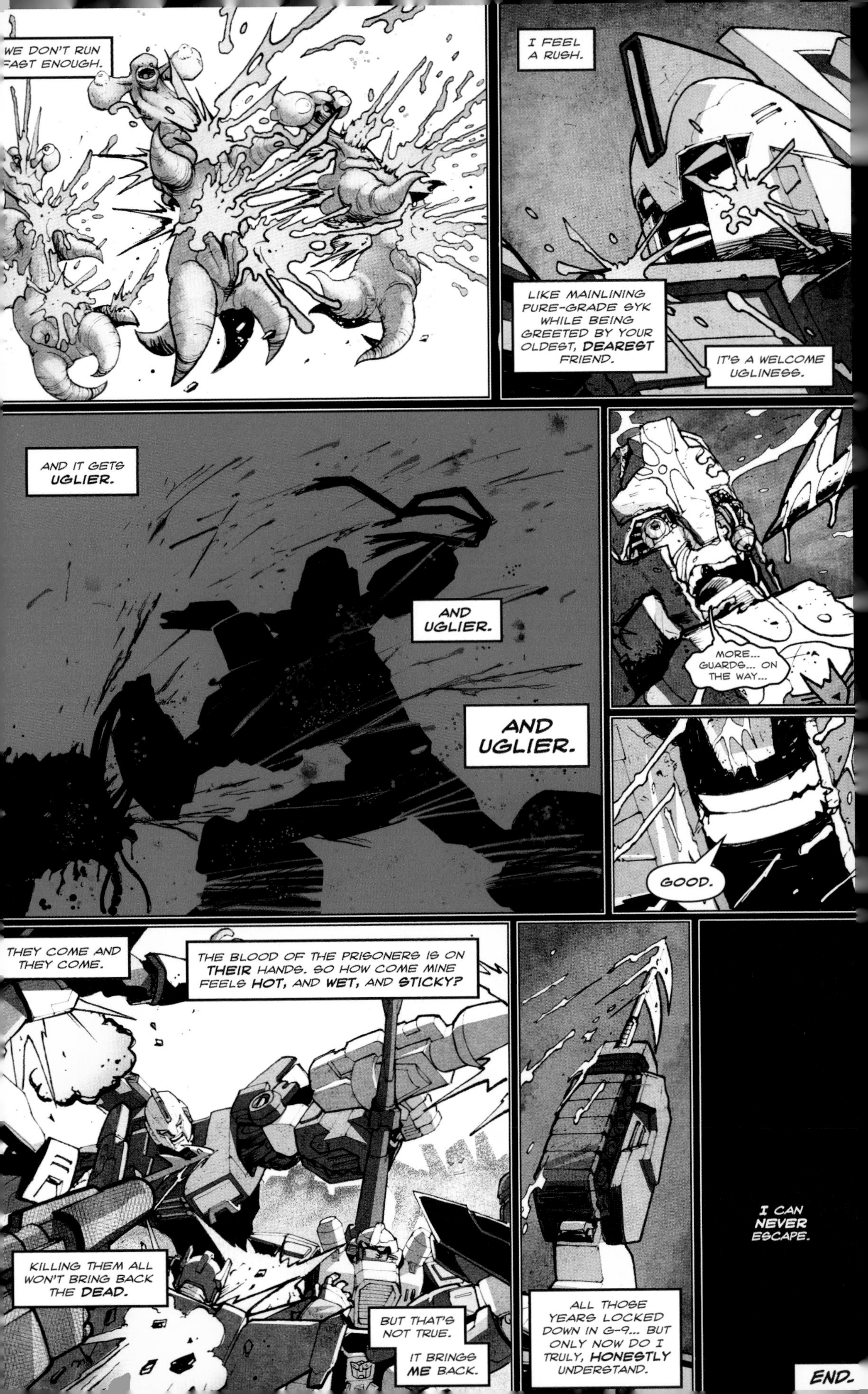
WE DON'T RUN FAST ENOUGH.
I FEEL A RUSH.
LIKE MAINLINING PURE-GRADE SYK WHILE BEING GREETED BY YOUR OLDEST, DEAREST FRIEND.
IT'S A WELCOME UGLINESS.
AND IT GETS UGLIER.
AND UGLIER.
AND UGLIER.
MORE... GUARDS... ON THE WAY...
GOOD.
THEY COME AND THEY COME.
THE BLOOD OF THE PRISONERS IS ON THEIR HANDS. SO HOW COME MINE FEELS HOT, AND WET, AND STICKY?
KILLING THEM ALL WON'T BRING BACK THE DEAD.
BUT THAT'S NOT TRUE.
IT BRINGS ME BACK.
ALL THOSE YEARS LOCKED DOWN IN G-9... BUT ONLY NOW DO I TRULY, HONESTLY UNDERSTAND.
I CAN NEVER ESCAPE.
END.

ZERO POINT

BY JAMES ROBERTS

Every day, at midnight, when the stars best held their shape and the world below was steady on the turn, he polished Springer's eyes.

He didn't need to; not really. The air in the medibay was triple-filtered and cryo-controlled, and therefore entirely free from dust, pollutants, particulate matter, and any of the Decepticons' airborne micro-assassins (although he wasn't sure if he'd made the Nanocons up; loneliness could play hideous tricks on the mind)—but that wasn't really the point.

No, Roadbuster polished Springer's eyes because he cared.

Soon after volunteering to keep watch on his comatose leader, Roadbuster had realised that the key to staving off the excruciating boredom was routine. And so, in the morning, he would check that Debris—the all-but deserted containment facility, high in orbit above Hydrus 5, that had once been the Wreckers' base of operations—was safe and secure. He would test the locks, walk the corridors, throw some torchlight around and talk to the coffins in the of Zone of Remembrance ("Hello Top Spin, hello Twin Twist. Morning, Rotorstorm. How you doing, Ironfist? Just saying hi, Pyro"). And in the afternoon he would switch on his datapad and read as best he could, congratulating himself if he finished a sentence without moving his faceplate. And in the evening—his favorite part of the 120-hour day—he would invent new weaponry, cannibalizing his extensive personal arsenal to produce ever larger and more fearsomely elaborate creations. And finally, when it was nearly midnight, he would put down or unplug or climb out of his latest weapon, reach for a spray-duster, lean over Springer's resolutely expressionless face—a collision of right angles and hard shadow—and set to work sluicing out the Triple Changer's optical gutters, sterilizing his retinal filaments, and cleansing his dilated photoreceptors.

Springer didn't move, of course. He hadn't moved of his own accord for nearly nine months. A fixed point in space, he lay on the circuit slab and braved the weight of the exterior world, blind to the interplay of ambient forces, oblivious to the silent realignment of shape and mass and pressure.

Roadbuster knew very little about other cultures, but he'd heard that many organic races believed that the eyes were the windows to the soul. In a Cybertronian's case, that was, in fact, true: thanks to a complex network of internal apertures and diaphragms, your optics were illuminated by your Spark. The brighter your eyes, the healthier your Spark. And of course the converse was true, which was why Roadbuster rarely looked at Springer while cleaning his eyes: it was too depressing. Before the incident on Garrus 9—before Overlord had forced five fingers into his frowning face—Springer's optics had been an arresting, thousand-watt blue; and not just any blue, either, but Matrix blue—something which apparently suggested he was Compatible. Now all that light was gone, hurriedly recalled home to the Spark itself in an effort to bolster the dim, diminishing core. Now, no matter how often Roadbuster polished them, Springer's eyes were variously the color of low cloud or smoked glass or rain-soaked concrete.

All of which meant that despite the best efforts of the nearby life-support machines (and there were dozens of them, and they were huge, and the energy they consumed in a day would have illuminated the dark side of Luna 2), Springer was very nearly dead. Roadbuster knew very little about persistent vegetative states, but he was sure of one thing: if Springer had any life left, if his coffin-shaped body harbored even the slightest animating force, then it was confined to the circuits of his brain.

Forget last words; Springer was now onto his last thoughts.

Springer lay there, not knowing where 'there' was, not knowing if he was alive, or dead, or poised between the two, reaching in both directions for balance.

His mind fled to the past, to a long, long time ago, when The War had yet to acquire capital letters. Back then, when both sides maintained that civilian causalities would never break the one million mark, and when people still said things like, "This'll all blow over in a century or two," Springer had seen the world in binary terms. Right or wrong, good or bad, black or white; everything lent itself to explicit categorization. The Autobot Code was nothing less than a set of instructions for life, and it was up to Autobots like him—broad-chested and stout of spirit—to uphold the Code in word and deed.

And for many years that was how he'd shouldered his way through life, satisfied that he was fundamentally a decent 'bot, strong and surefooted, forever confident in his ability to negotiate a clearly-mapped moral terrain. There were Evil Decepticons and there were Heroic Autobots, and the two factions were reassuringly distinct. And he used to think: 'Good. I can define myself by what I am not; and I am not, and never will be, a Decepticon.'

But after years on the front line, pushing forward, pulling back, gaining and conceding ground, he concluded that being a decent 'bot wasn't enough. Being a decent 'bot held him back, slowed him down, boxed him in. He wanted to do more. He wanted to leave his mark. He wanted to become a Wrecker.

Not much was known about the Wreckers in those days. They didn't even have a name. They were referred to euphemistically, or in the abstract, their existence confirmed by the occasional sideways glance between those in the know. There was no Fisitron dutifully chronicling their exploits, just rumors spread by word of mouth: a friend of a friend would overhear a conversation between two Autobot high-ups; or a cadet trying to fix a shortwave radio would accidentally intercept details of a secret mission; or a Decepticon would be seen staggering through the streets in a suicidal haze, fretful and undone, babbling hysterically about harpoons before hooking his mouth over the barrel of his gun and finishing what Impactor and Co. had started.

He remembered the first time he'd seen Impactor. He'd been standing at the bottom of Sherma Bridge, trying to guess how tall it was before testing out his newly-upgraded thigh hydraulics, when a flaming Decepticon shuttle pod had dropped out of a transmat portal and bounced between the arches. Riding the pod was a yellow and purple robot with a retractable drill for a hand; a robot who punched his way inside the cockpit, jettisoned the headless Decepticon pilot and set the pod down safely at the foot of Zeta Prime's memorial statue.

Impactor and the Wreckers.

The third faction.

The dividing line between Autobot and Decepticon.

He knew he should've stayed away, but he couldn't help it. As far as he was concerned, Impactor's gang of bullet-battered, flame-scorched, energon-drenched malcontents mattered. They crashed into your life with the force of a rampaging Phase Sixer and they made a difference. They taught the Decepticons the error of their ways; and if in so doing they had to use a certain degree of force—if they had to press the point—well, it was for everyone's own good. No apologies.

A few months after the Sherma Bridge incident he'd asked Kup to add his name to the list of Wreckers reservists—a request which, even then, was seen as an admission not simply that you were willing to die for the Autobot Cause, but that you were actively seeking to bring about, ahead of time, your own fantastically violent demise.

For a long time he'd heard no more about it, that being the way it worked: you didn't even know whether you were under consideration until Impactor himself turned up on your doorstep—or battlefield, in Springer's case. He remembered their first meeting as clearly as the day he was Autobranded: he'd been with the Heliobots, tracking a distress signal through the Toxic Sludge Swamps—deep into Slicer territory—when Impactor had dropped out of the sky, taken out the eight blade-wielding Decepticons that had been hiding in the mist, held out a mighty hand, and said:

"You must be Springer. You know why I'm here. It's time."

And then, with a single handshake from a single hand, his pre-Wreckers life—his black and white life—was over.

"His life isn't over," Kaput had said to Roadbuster on the day he'd delivered Springer to Debris. "But from a medical perspective—physiologically speaking—his death has begun."

Roadbuster helped the diminutive Kaput carry Springer to the circuit slab and watched him plug crayon-colored energon feeds into a lattice of power points that had been drilled into his body to maximise incoming energy flow.

Kup was there too, chewing on his cygar, circling the slab, treading a trench into the floor and saying nothing.

"You managed to save his face, then," Roadbuster said, touching Springer's chin and looking for telltale signs of reattachment.

Kaput nodded, and turned circles on the wheel that carried him everywhere. "Thanks to Impactor, yes. He was holding it when we got to G9. Strong grip he has, too."

"Well, you've put it back on perfectly. He looks as good as new."

"He's better than new. Fixit and I repaired everything, inside and out. Full body renovation. You know how he used to hum? When he got up too quickly, or stopped running? That humming noise?"

Roadbuster looked up, suddenly aware of Kup's grief, and then turned his attention back to Springer.

"He used to get embarrassed by that, but—yeah. Something to do with his legs, right? Overactive rotors."

"Well, we even fixed them. C'mere." Kaput pulled Roadbuster close to the body. "See? Silent running."

Roadbuster straightened up. "Come on, then. Say it. I've heard it second-hand, but I want to hear it from you. What's wrong with him? Why can't he wake up?"

Kaput preoccupied himself by reconnecting a loose energon feed. "Prowl sends his condolences," he mumbled.

"Oh, does he now? And what did he say, exactly? What were his exact words?"

Silence.

Kaput removed an imaginary speck of dirt from Springer's chest and kept his eyes on the patient when he said: "He can't wake up because we can't find the zero point."

There was a crash as Kup kicked a chair across the room.

Roadbuster stared at Kaput. "I'm sure you did your best," he said at last, adding mentally, 'Because if I find out that you didn't— if I find out that you gave up a fraction of a second earlier than was absolutely necessary—I will strap myself into the Eviscerator and demolish you.'

That was then.

That was before he'd spent six months watching someone he'd come to admire die a little more each day. Now, Roadbuster wished he had grabbed Kaput by the shoulders, stared into his one good eye, and spoken his mind.

Organic races typically took too reductionist a view of Cybertronian physiology. Just because the Autobots and Decepticons were mechanical, just because they could be taken apart and reassembled, the uninitiated assumed that there was no scope in the realm of technomedical science for mystery. But there was a reason why the likes of Ratchet and Fixit and Pharma and Kaput called themselves doctors and surgeons rather than mechanics and engineers, and that reason could be found buried in the chest of every Cybertronian. The Spark—regarded by the Higher Races as a bona fide miracle phenomena—transformed a mechanical body from a rough rectangle of moving parts into something more. Something far less predictable. Sentience, it seemed, complicated everything.

The zero point was the name given to an infinitesimally small cavity between two nervecircuits—a cavity that prevented a Spark from completing its vital journey around the body. Roadbuster knew very little about technomedical science, but he knew that certain injuries could open up a fatal gap inside the chest or brain—a tiny sinus of warm space between two all-important energy conductors that was invisible to even the most sophisticated sensors. The micro-vacuum would force the Spark to veer off course and, ultimately, rob the body of life.

Occasionally you'd hear of a freak recovery—Ultra Magnus sprang to mind—and the experts would say that a medic or a mourner had accidentally pressed an invisible pressure point and the resultant jolt had somehow closed the gap.

He picked up a datapad. The Complete Works of Fisitron contained all 332 of the Wreckers: Declassified datalogs, and more besides. The deluxe data-pack had been released to coincide with the unveiling of Ironfist's statue at Kimia, and was padded out with extras including a 'heartfelt' foreword, written by Prowl, that had all the warmth and sensitivity of a subpoena.

Roadbuster had never subscribed to Fisitron's datalogs: just as some people hated the sound of their own voice, he hated the sound of his own character. Was he really that one-dimensional, that relentlessly gung-ho? As depicted by Fisitron, his every utterance related to the fact that he was in need of, or had just acquired, or was marveling at the damage caused by, a weapon.

He scrolled down the page with his trigger-finger, trying to find where he'd left off the night before.

Picking up a datapad and reading to Springer had, in the beginning, presented Roadbuster with a number of challenges; he'd had to learn to read, for starters. Like being able to look at Bumblebee without wanting to pat him on the head, or hold a conversation with Optimus Prime without trying to catch a glimpse of the Matrix through the windows of his chest plate, the ability to read had been one of those things—one of those handy little life skills—that he'd only recently acquired.

It was Kup's fault, the reading thing—Kup having been the one who, soon after Springer was moved to Debris, had asked one of his oldest friends, Rung, to give a psychological account for Springer's condition.

"It's not an interruption of the body," Rung had concluded, referring to the suspected presence of the zero point. "It's an interruption of the mind. No one really understands the properties of a Spark, but I think it's psychosensitive. I think it responds to certain triggers…"

Roadbuster had at that point stopped staring at Rung's oversized eyebrows and taken an active interest in the conversation. "Triggers?"

"Emotional triggers, yes. If you could elicit a powerful enough emotional response—love, hate, anger, pride—it might encourage Springer, subconsciously of course, to will his Spark across the synaptic cavity. You just need to connect with him in some way."

"Connect with him?"

"Talk to him."

"Talk to him? What about?"

"I don't know—reminisce about the good old days. All those people you've killed together."

"The thing is, Rung, I kind of struggle with, um… with…"

"With conversation?"

"…yeah."

Rung had pulled a datapad out of his chest compartment and handed it to Roadbuster. "The Complete Works. 332 War Stories. Give him a couple of these every night and see what happens."

Roadbuster had now read all but one datalog. Actually, he'd read each of the remaining 331 datalogs twice (the second time round he'd attacked the difficult words from which he'd originally retreated).

"Okay, Springer," he muttered as he found chapter seven of 'The Wreckers' Air Attack.' "Where were we? Oh yeah, the aerial drilling platform. Wow. That was a hell of an afternoon. Now, let's see… Megatron's just crushed Impactor's arm and is about to shoot him in the head… 'never did want to live forever'…'reap the whirlwind'…'all the dirty jobs'…'power beyond measure'… ah yes, here we are…

"A dazed Impactor tried to pull himself off the floor of the drilling platform as it tilted towards the Manganese Mountains far below. As he lifted up his head he realized that he'd left something behind, something very important: his mouth. As his chin slid out of reach he felt something touch the back of his head: the barrel of Megatron's second generation micro-calibrated antimatter-catalyzed full-spectrum Mk II fusion cannon.

"Megatron stared down at him, a look of pure evil in his eyes. "It's over, Impactor," the leader of the Decepticons smiled "mavel—mavelo—malevo—"

Roadbuster pulled the datapad closer to his face. "Malevolently?" He showed the datapad to Springer. "Is that what that says? Hmm. Anyway…

'It's over, Impactor,' the leader of the Decepticons smiled mavelolently. 'Consider the world one last time, and know that

sweet death beckons. Evade not its tender embrace but run, open-armed, into its smothering folds. When the darkness plays at the edge of your consciousness, cherish it.'

"Impactor channelled the last of his strength into his mangled right arm. He couldn't lift his harpoon from the floor, but he didn't need to. He scraped the blade across the metal, carving out one letter, then another, until he'd written three small words:

'NOT MORE POETRY'

"Megatron paused. Perhaps he was caught off guard by the random nature of Impactor's final words; perhaps his fusion cannon had seized up (a common fault with the Mk II); perhaps he thought there was more of the message to come. Whatever the reason he hesitated—just for a second.

"A second was all Springer needed.

"Impactor's trusty second-in-command rammed his sky sled into the small of Megatron's back and kept going, carrying the Decepticon off the edge of the platform. In a blur, Springer backflipped off the sled, switched to helicopter mode, and watched Megatron fall thousands of feet towards the Manganese Mountains below.

"'Nice going, kid,' said Impactor, reattaching his vocal synthesizer. 'Now, by my reckoning we've got four minutes to save Xaaron, rescue Sandstorm from his antimatter duplicate, deactivate Bludgeon's necrocannon, and—what's the last thing…?—oh yeah, stop this platform from crashing into that nucleon reactor and triggering a chain reaction that will destroy half of Cybertron.'

"Springer landed beside him in robot mode. 'You expect us to do all that in four minutes?'

"'Two minutes, actually. I lied to make you feel better. But don't worry, I have a plan.' He pulled something from his waist compartment. 'When I give the signal, I want you to take this authentically detailed scale model of Omega Supreme and very, very carefully—'"

Roadbuster stopped, shook his head, and checked how much there was left to read. This was chapter seven. Chapter seven of 40. He wondered if he could make it to the end; there was only so many times he could read about Impactor saying something "grimly," or Springer "leaping to the rescue," or Whirl "stepping out of line." And he really couldn't face Datalog 98, with its extended dream sequence, a third time.

This reading business would be far less of a chore, he decided, if his efforts were bearing fruit; if something he'd said had made Springer… well, he wasn't expecting him to sit bolt upright, punch the air and shout "Wreck 'n Rule!," but a twitch would have been nice. Something small but significant: a finger finding a thumb, or a mouth widening at the hinge. Something.

Rung had spoken of a window of opportunity—a chance to pull Springer back from the brink—but the window was surely close to closing. In that sense, for all their size (and they were so big they had their own stairwells, their own antechambers, and mezzanines), the nearby life-support machines were little more than chronometers. Actually, no, not even that; they were metronomes, marking out the slow deceleration of a long life long lived at speed.

Tick.

Tock.

His fingers danced over the datapad and he jumped to Datalog 113. "Showdown on Pova." The only datalog he'd not read out loud. The other 331 were full of embellishments and fabrications, but at least they were true to the essence of the adventures they

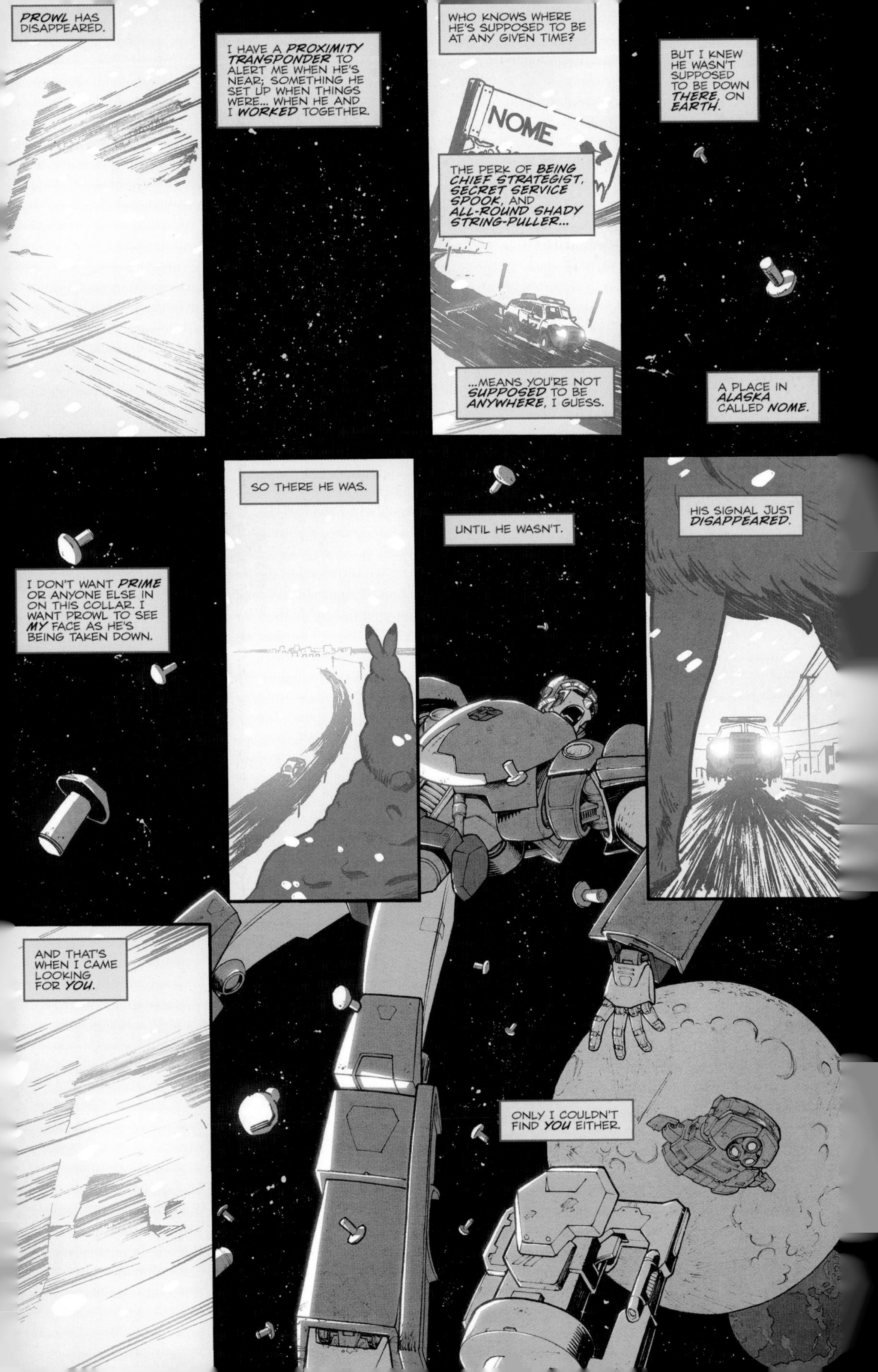
PROWL HAS DISAPPEARED.
I HAVE A PROXIMITY TRANSPONDER TO ALERT ME WHEN HE'S NEAR; SOMETHING HE SET UP WHEN THINGS WERE... WHEN HE AND I WORKED TOGETHER.
WHO KNOWS WHERE HE'S SUPPOSED TO BE AT ANY GIVEN TIME?
NOME
THE PERK OF BEING CHIEF STRATEGIST, SECRET SERVICE SPOOK, AND ALL-ROUND SHADY STRING-PULLER...
...MEANS YOU'RE NOT SUPPOSED TO BE ANYWHERE, I GUESS.
BUT I KNEW HE WASN'T SUPPOSED TO BE DOWN THERE, ON EARTH.
A PLACE IN ALASKA CALLED NOME.
I DON'T WANT PRIME OR ANYONE ELSE IN ON THIS COLLAR. I WANT PROWL TO SEE MY FACE AS HE'S BEING TAKEN DOWN.
SO THERE HE WAS.
UNTIL HE WASN'T.
HIS SIGNAL JUST DISAPPEARED.
AND THAT'S WHEN I CAME LOOKING FOR YOU.
ONLY I COULDN'T FIND YOU EITHER.

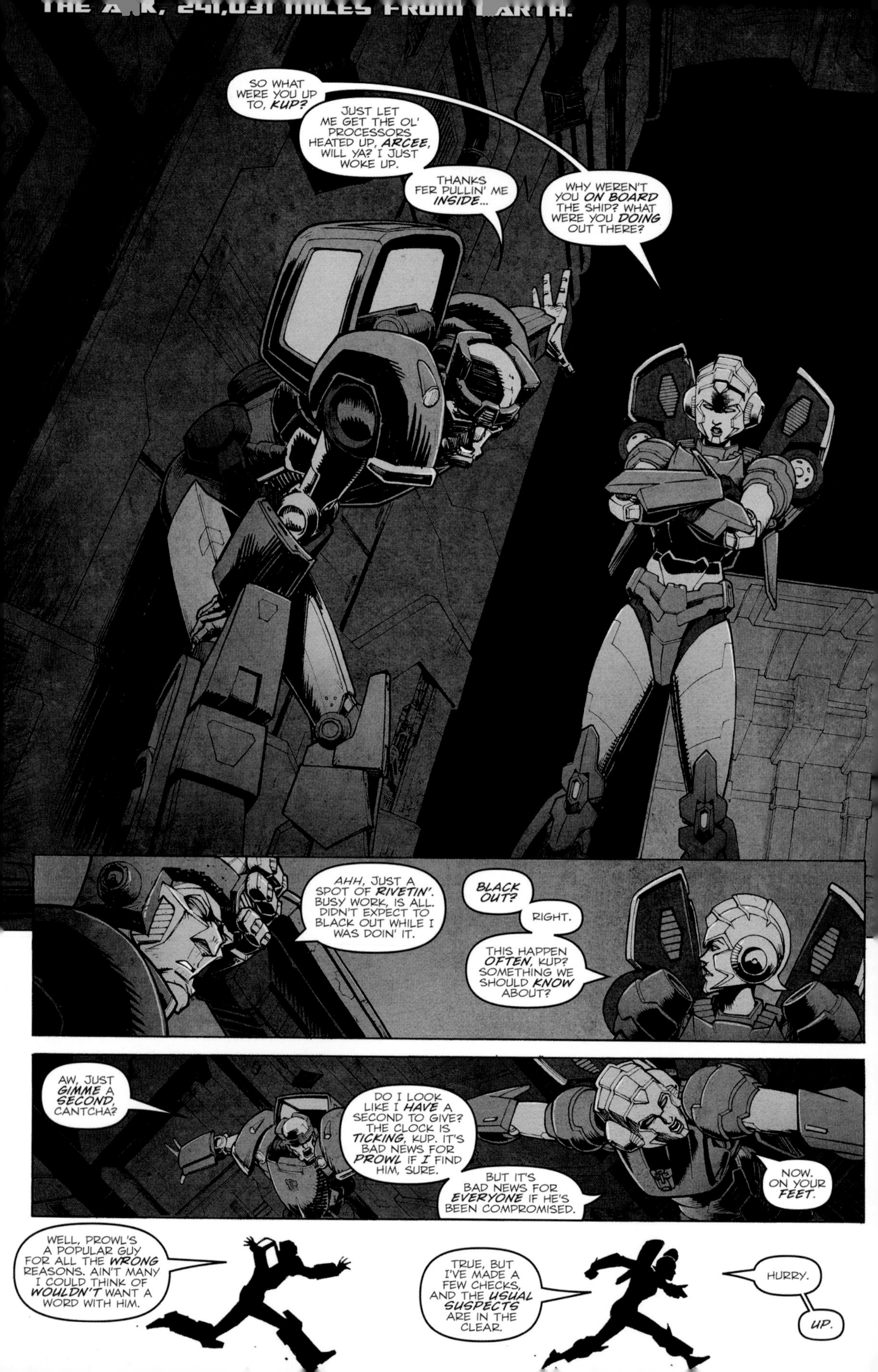
THE 241,031 MILES FROM
SO WHAT WERE YOU UP TO, KUP?
JUST LET ME GET THE OL' PROCESSORS HEATED UP, ARCEE, WILL YA? I JUST WOKE UP.
THANKS FER PULLIN' ME INSIDE...
WHY WEREN'T YOU ON BOARD THE SHIP? WHAT WERE YOU DOING OUT THERE?
AHH, JUST A SPOT OF RIVETIN'. BUSY WORK, IS ALL. DIDN'T EXPECT TO BLACK OUT WHILE I WAS DOIN' IT.
BLACK OUT?
RIGHT.
THIS HAPPEN OFTEN, KUP? SOMETHING WE SHOULD KNOW ABOUT?
AW, JUST GIMME A SECOND, CANTCHA?
DO I LOOK LIKE I HAVE A SECOND TO GIVE? THE CLOCK IS TICKING, KUP. IT'S BAD NEWS FOR PROWL IF I FIND HIM, SURE.
BUT IT'S BAD NEWS FOR EVERYONE IF HE'S BEEN COMPROMISED.
NOW. ON YOUR FEET.
WELL, PROWL'S A POPULAR GUY FOR ALL THE WRONG REASONS. AIN'T MANY I COULD THINK OF WOULDN'T WANT A WORD WITH HIM.
TRUE, BUT I'VE MADE A FEW CHECKS, AND THE USUAL SUSPECTS ARE IN THE CLEAR.
HURRY.
UP.

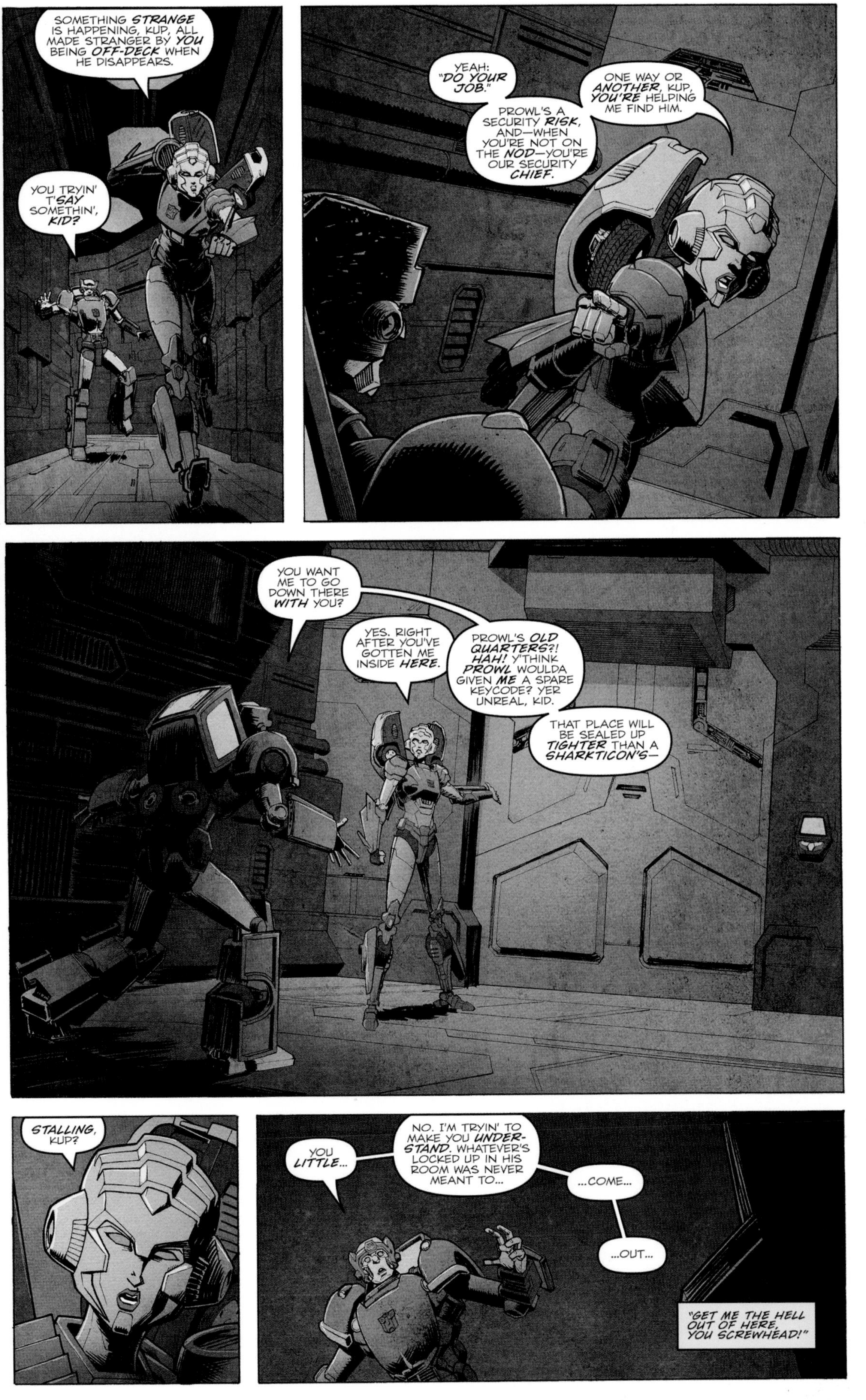
SOMETHING STRANGE IS HAPPENING, KUP, ALL MADE STRANGER BY YOU BEING OFF-DECK WHEN HE DISAPPEARS.
YOU TRYIN' T'SAY SOMETHIN', KID?
YEAH: "DO YOUR JOB."
PROWL'S A SECURITY RISK, AND—WHEN YOU'RE NOT ON THE NOD—YOU'RE OUR SECURITY CHIEF.
ONE WAY OR ANOTHER, KUP, YOU'RE HELPING ME FIND HIM.
YOU WANT ME TO GO DOWN THERE WITH YOU?
YES. RIGHT AFTER YOU'VE GOTTEN ME INSIDE HERE.
PROWL'S OLD QUARTERS?! HAH! Y'THINK PROWL WOULDA GIVEN ME A SPARE KEYCODE? YER UNREAL, KID.
THAT PLACE WILL BE SEALED UP TIGHTER THAN A SHARKTICON'S—
STALLING, KUP?
YOU LITTLE...
NO. I'M TRYIN' TO MAKE YOU UNDER-STAND. WHATEVER'S LOCKED UP IN HIS ROOM WAS NEVER MEANT TO...
...COME...
...OUT...
"GET ME THE HELL OUT OF HERE, YOU SCREWHEAD!"

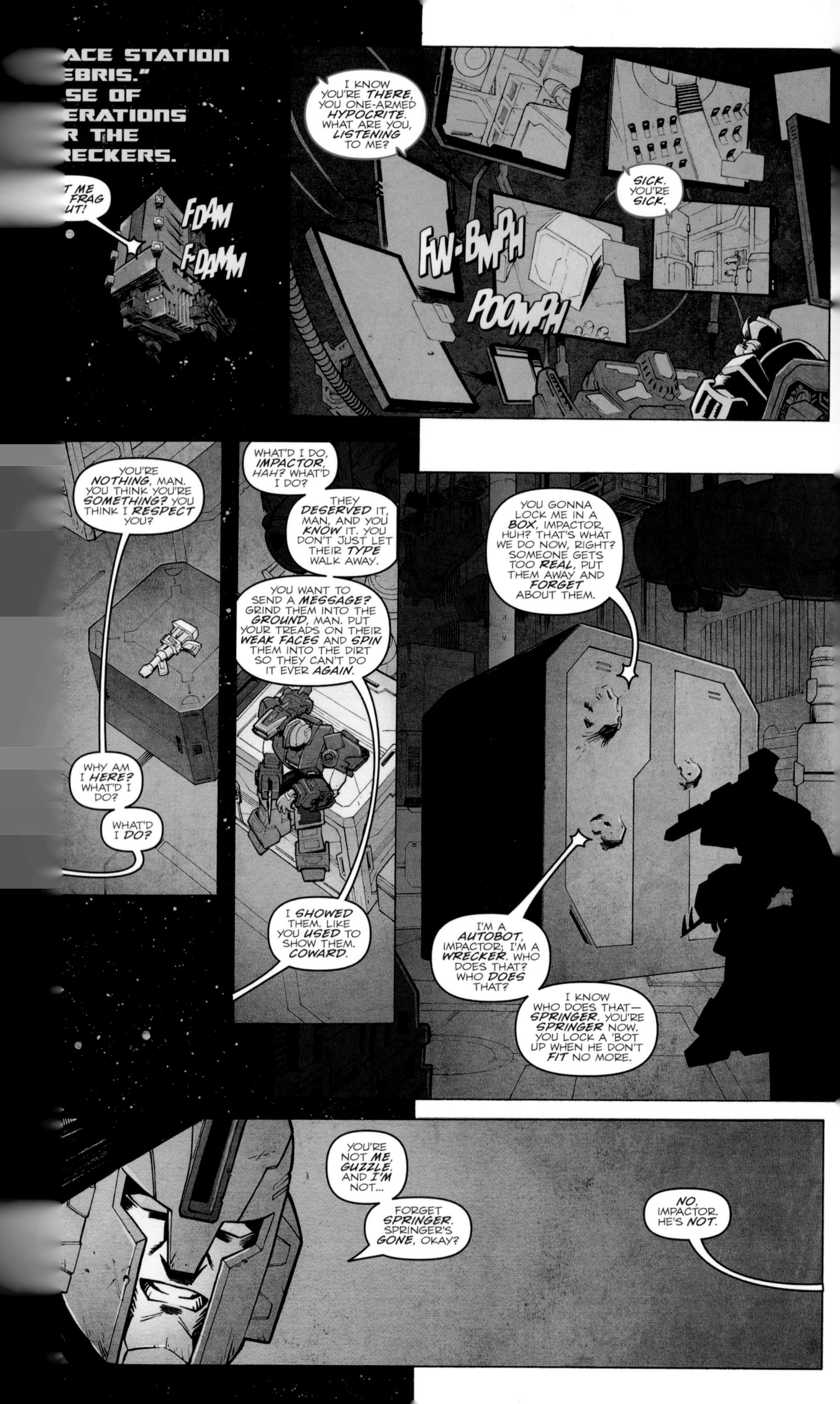
ACE STATION
EBRIS."
SE OF
ERATIONS
R THE
RECKERS.
T ME
FRAG
UT!
FDAM
F-DAMM
I KNOW YOU'RE THERE, YOU ONE-ARMED HYPOCRITE. WHAT ARE YOU, LISTENING TO ME?
SICK. YOU'RE SICK.
FW-BMPH
POOMPH
YOU'RE NOTHING, MAN. YOU THINK YOU'RE SOMETHING? YOU THINK I RESPECT YOU?
WHY AM I HERE? WHAT'D I DO?
WHAT'D I DO?
WHAT'D I DO, IMPACTOR, HAH? WHAT'D I DO?
THEY DESERVED IT, MAN, AND YOU KNOW IT. YOU DON'T JUST LET THEIR TYPE WALK AWAY.
YOU WANT TO SEND A MESSAGE? GRIND THEM INTO THE GROUND, MAN. PUT YOUR TREADS ON THEIR WEAK FACES AND SPIN THEM INTO THE DIRT SO THEY CAN'T DO IT EVER AGAIN.
I SHOWED THEM. LIKE YOU USED TO SHOW THEM. COWARD.
YOU GONNA LOCK ME IN A BOX, IMPACTOR, HUH? THAT'S WHAT WE DO NOW, RIGHT? SOMEONE GETS TOO REAL, PUT THEM AWAY AND FORGET ABOUT THEM.
I'M A AUTOBOT, IMPACTOR; I'M A WRECKER. WHO DOES THAT? WHO DOES THAT?
I KNOW WHO DOES THAT— SPRINGER. YOU'RE SPRINGER NOW. YOU LOCK A 'BOT UP WHEN HE DON'T FIT NO MORE.
YOU'RE NOT ME, GUZZLE. AND I'M NOT...
FORGET SPRINGER. SPRINGER'S GONE, OKAY?
NO, IMPACTOR. HE'S NOT.

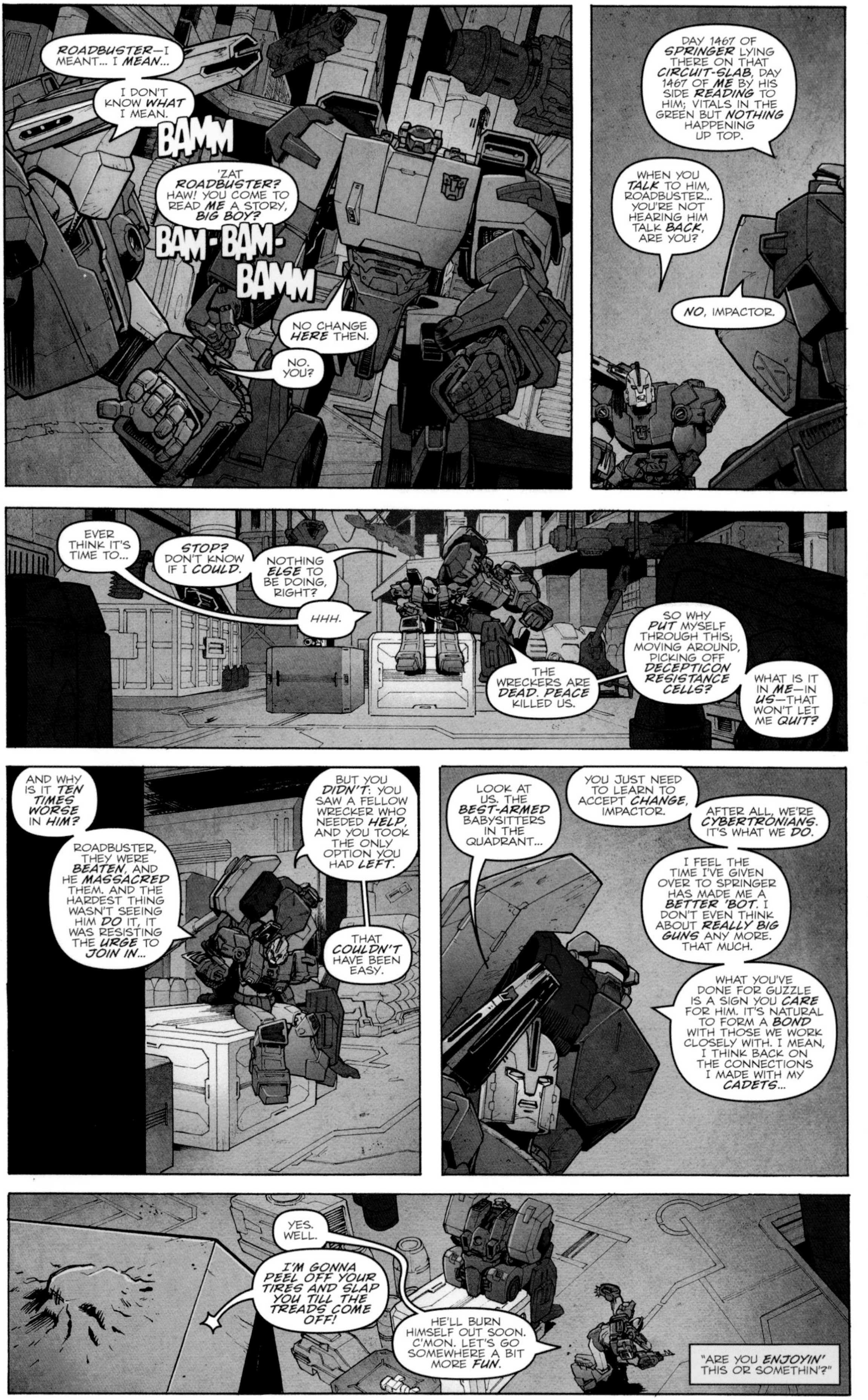
ROADBUSTER—I MEANT... I MEAN...
I DON'T KNOW WHAT I MEAN.
BAMM
'ZAT ROADBUSTER? HAW! YOU COME TO READ ME A STORY, BIG BOY?
BAM-BAM-BAMM
NO CHANGE HERE THEN.
NO. YOU?
DAY 1467 OF SPRINGER LYING THERE ON THAT CIRCUIT-SLAB, DAY 1467 OF ME BY HIS SIDE READING TO HIM; VITALS IN THE GREEN BUT NOTHING HAPPENING UP TOP.
WHEN YOU TALK TO HIM, ROADBUSTER... YOU'RE NOT HEARING HIM TALK BACK, ARE YOU?
NO, IMPACTOR.
EVER THINK IT'S TIME TO...
STOP? DON'T KNOW IF I COULD.
NOTHING ELSE TO BE DOING, RIGHT?
HHH.
THE WRECKERS ARE DEAD. PEACE KILLED US.
SO WHY PUT MYSELF THROUGH THIS; MOVING AROUND, PICKING OFF DECEPTICON RESISTANCE CELLS?
WHAT IS IT IN ME—IN US—THAT WON'T LET ME QUIT?
AND WHY IS IT TEN TIMES WORSE IN HIM?
ROADBUSTER, THEY WERE BEATEN, AND HE MASSACRED THEM. AND THE HARDEST THING WASN'T SEEING HIM DO IT, IT WAS RESISTING THE URGE TO JOIN IN...
BUT YOU DIDN'T: YOU SAW A FELLOW WRECKER WHO NEEDED HELP, AND YOU TOOK THE ONLY OPTION YOU HAD LEFT.
THAT COULDN'T HAVE BEEN EASY.
LOOK AT US. THE BEST-ARMED BABYSITTERS IN THE QUADRANT...
YOU JUST NEED TO LEARN TO ACCEPT CHANGE, IMPACTOR.
AFTER ALL, WE'RE CYBERTRONIANS. IT'S WHAT WE DO.
I FEEL THE TIME I'VE GIVEN OVER TO SPRINGER HAS MADE ME A BETTER 'BOT. I DON'T EVEN THINK ABOUT REALLY BIG GUNS ANY MORE. THAT MUCH.
WHAT YOU'VE DONE FOR GUZZLE IS A SIGN YOU CARE FOR HIM. IT'S NATURAL TO FORM A BOND WITH THOSE WE WORK CLOSELY WITH. I MEAN, I THINK BACK ON THE CONNECTIONS I MADE WITH MY CADETS...
YES. WELL.
I'M GONNA PEEL OFF YOUR TIRES AND SLAP YOU TILL THE TREADS COME OFF!
HE'LL BURN HIMSELF OUT SOON. C'MON. LET'S GO SOMEWHERE A BIT MORE FUN.
"ARE YOU ENJOYIN' THIS OR SOMETHIN'?"

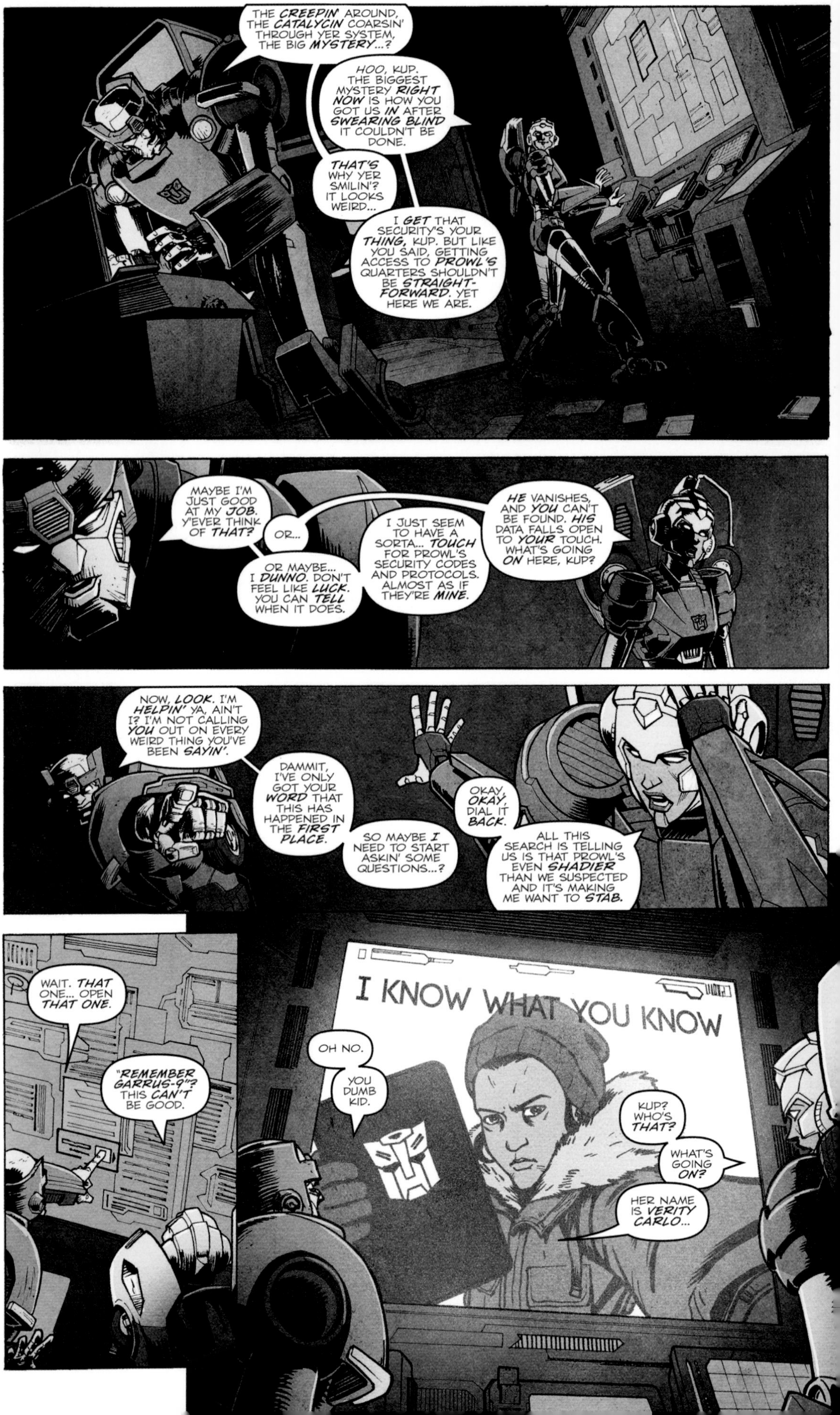
THE CREEPIN' AROUND, THE CATALYCIN COARSIN' THROUGH YER SYSTEM, THE BIG MYSTERY...?
HOO, KUP. THE BIGGEST MYSTERY RIGHT NOW IS HOW YOU GOT US IN AFTER SWEARING BLIND IT COULDN'T BE DONE.
THAT'S WHY YER SMILIN'? IT LOOKS WEIRD...
I GET THAT SECURITY'S YOUR THING, KUP. BUT LIKE YOU SAID, GETTING ACCESS TO PROWL'S QUARTERS SHOULDN'T BE STRAIGHT-FORWARD. YET HERE WE ARE.
MAYBE I'M JUST GOOD AT MY JOB. Y'EVER THINK OF THAT?
OR...
OR MAYBE... I DUNNO. DON'T FEEL LIKE LUCK. YOU CAN TELL WHEN IT DOES.
I JUST SEEM TO HAVE A SORTA... TOUCH FOR PROWL'S SECURITY CODES AND PROTOCOLS. ALMOST AS IF THEY'RE MINE.
HE VANISHES, AND YOU CAN'T BE FOUND. HIS DATA FALLS OPEN TO YOUR TOUCH. WHAT'S GOING ON HERE, KUP?
NOW, LOOK. I'M HELPIN' YA, AIN'T I? I'M NOT CALLING YOU OUT ON EVERY WEIRD THING YOU'VE BEEN SAYIN'.
DAMMIT, I'VE ONLY GOT YOUR WORD THAT THIS HAS HAPPENED IN THE FIRST PLACE.
SO MAYBE I NEED TO START ASKIN' SOME QUESTIONS...?
OKAY, OKAY, DIAL IT BACK.
ALL THIS SEARCH IS TELLING US IS THAT PROWL'S EVEN SHADIER THAN WE SUSPECTED AND IT'S MAKING ME WANT TO STAB.
WAIT. THAT ONE... OPEN THAT ONE.
"REMEMBER GARRUS-9"? THIS CAN'T BE GOOD.
I KNOW WHAT YOU KNOW
OH NO.
YOU DUMB KID.
KUP? WHO'S THAT?
WHAT'S GOING ON?
HER NAME IS VERITY CARLO...

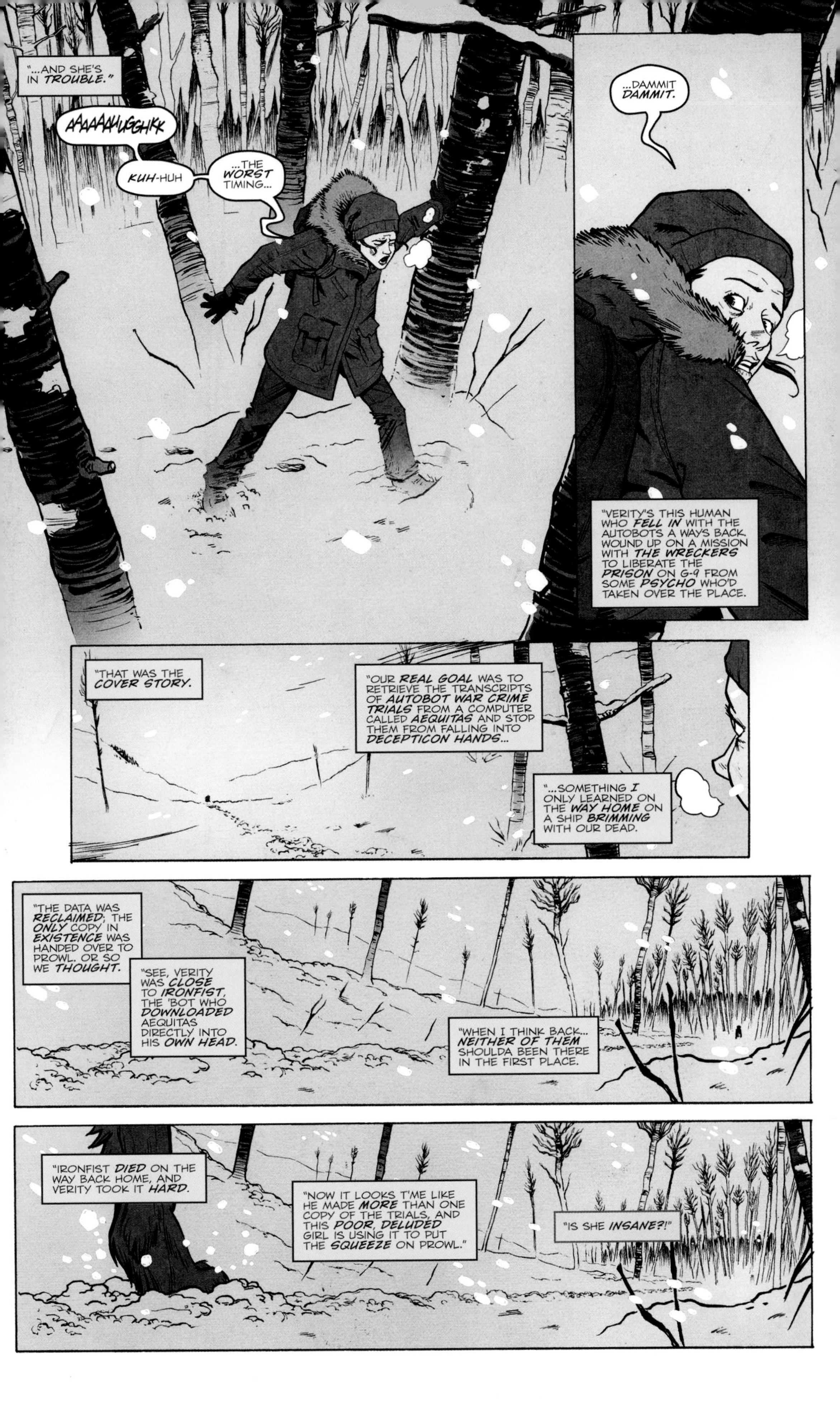
"...AND SHE'S IN TROUBLE."
AAAAAAHUGGHKK
KUH-HUH
...THE WORST TIMING...
...DAMMIT DAMMIT.
"VERITY'S THIS HUMAN WHO FELL IN WITH THE AUTOBOTS A WAYS BACK. WOUND UP ON A MISSION WITH THE WRECKERS TO LIBERATE THE PRISON ON G-9 FROM SOME PSYCHO WHO'D TAKEN OVER THE PLACE.
"THAT WAS THE COVER STORY.
"OUR REAL GOAL WAS TO RETRIEVE THE TRANSCRIPTS OF AUTOBOT WAR CRIME TRIALS FROM A COMPUTER CALLED AEQUITAS AND STOP THEM FROM FALLING INTO DECEPTICON HANDS...
"...SOMETHING I ONLY LEARNED ON THE WAY HOME ON A SHIP BRIMMING WITH OUR DEAD.
"THE DATA WAS RECLAIMED; THE ONLY COPY IN EXISTENCE WAS HANDED OVER TO PROWL. OR SO WE THOUGHT.
"SEE, VERITY WAS CLOSE TO IRONFIST, THE 'BOT WHO DOWNLOADED AEQUITAS DIRECTLY INTO HIS OWN HEAD.
"WHEN I THINK BACK... NEITHER OF THEM SHOULDA BEEN THERE IN THE FIRST PLACE.
"IRONFIST DIED ON THE WAY BACK HOME, AND VERITY TOOK IT HARD.
"NOW IT LOOKS T'ME LIKE HE MADE MORE THAN ONE COPY OF THE TRIALS, AND THIS POOR, DELUDED GIRL IS USING IT TO PUT THE SQUEEZE ON PROWL."
"IS SHE INSANE?!"

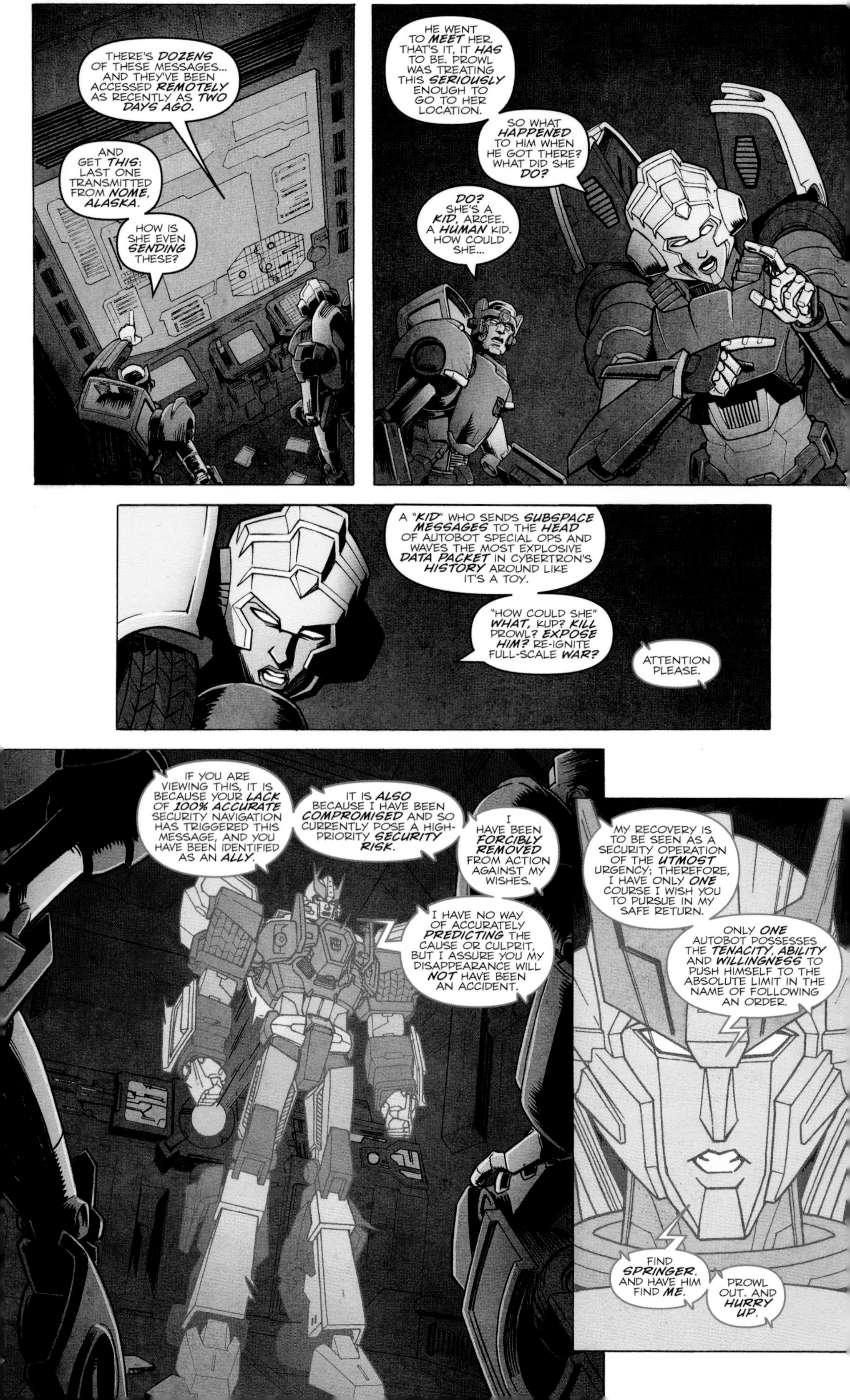

THERE'S DOZENS OF THESE MESSAGES... AND THEY'VE BEEN ACCESSED REMOTELY AS RECENTLY AS TWO DAYS AGO.
AND GET THIS: LAST ONE TRANSMITTED FROM NOME, ALASKA.
HOW IS SHE EVEN SENDING THESE?
HE WENT TO MEET HER. THAT'S IT, IT HAS TO BE. PROWL WAS TREATING THIS SERIOUSLY ENOUGH TO GO TO HER LOCATION.
SO WHAT HAPPENED TO HIM WHEN HE GOT THERE? WHAT DID SHE DO?
DO? SHE'S A KID, ARCEE. A HUMAN KID. HOW COULD SHE...
A "KID" WHO SENDS SUBSPACE MESSAGES TO THE HEAD OF AUTOBOT SPECIAL OPS AND WAVES THE MOST EXPLOSIVE DATA PACKET IN CYBERTRON'S HISTORY AROUND LIKE IT'S A TOY.
"HOW COULD SHE" WHAT, KUP? KILL PROWL? EXPOSE HIM? RE-IGNITE FULL-SCALE WAR?
ATTENTION PLEASE.
IF YOU ARE VIEWING THIS, IT IS BECAUSE YOUR LACK OF 100% ACCURATE SECURITY NAVIGATION HAS TRIGGERED THIS MESSAGE, AND YOU HAVE BEEN IDENTIFIED AS AN ALLY.
IT IS ALSO BECAUSE I HAVE BEEN COMPROMISED AND SO CURRENTLY POSE A HIGH-PRIORITY SECURITY RISK.
I HAVE BEEN FORCIBLY REMOVED FROM ACTION AGAINST MY WISHES.
I HAVE NO WAY OF ACCURATELY PREDICTING THE CAUSE OR CULPRIT, BUT I ASSURE YOU MY DISAPPEARANCE WILL NOT HAVE BEEN AN ACCIDENT.
MY RECOVERY IS TO BE SEEN AS A SECURITY OPERATION OF THE UTMOST URGENCY; THEREFORE, I HAVE ONLY ONE COURSE I WISH YOU TO PURSUE IN MY SAFE RETURN.
ONLY ONE AUTOBOT POSSESSES THE TENACITY, ABILITY AND WILLINGNESS TO PUSH HIMSELF TO THE ABSOLUTE LIMIT IN THE NAME OF FOLLOWING AN ORDER.
FIND SPRINGER. AND HAVE HIM FIND ME.
PROWL OUT. AND HURRY UP.

SPRINGER.

SPRINGER?!

YEAH *SPRINGER* WAS...

I *KNOW* WHO SPRINGER WAS—HARD CASE; TENACIOUS; MAVERICK-TYPE. PROWL *HATED* HIM AND STILL...

NAMES HIM AS THE 'BOT FOR THE JOB. GOTTA *STING*, KID.

DAMN YOU, PROWL. WHAT WAS THE *POINT* IN HAVING *ME* AROUND IF YOU'RE JUST GOING TO...

KUP, WHAT DO YOU *THINK* YOU'RE DOING?!

I'M PUTTIN' IN A CALL TO *DEBRIS*, SEE IF I CAN GET *PATCHED THROUGH* TO *SPRINGER*.

HANG ON; AM I WRONG, OR ISN'T THE *GREAT* SPRINGER ROTTING AWAY ON A *LIFE-SUPPORT*, JUST A GREAT BIG *DRAIN* ON RESOURCES AND GOODWILL?

IF YOUR *BOND* WITH THIS GUY IS SO *STRONG*, KUP, WHY DIDN'T YOU *MAGIC* HIM BACK TO LIFE *BEFORE* NOW?

ARCEE, WHAT? JUST *ME* AND YOU HANDLE THIS?

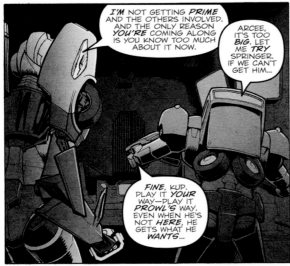

I'M NOT GETTING *PRIME* AND THE OTHERS INVOLVED. AND THE ONLY REASON *YOU'RE* COMING ALONG IS YOU KNOW TOO MUCH ABOUT IT NOW.

ARCEE, IT'S TOO *BIG*. LET ME *TRY* SPRINGER. IF WE CAN'T GET HIM...

FINE, KUP, PLAY IT *YOUR* WAY—PLAY IT *PROWL'S* WAY. EVEN WHEN HE'S NOT *HERE*, HE GETS WHAT HE *WANTS*...

I'LL MAKE IT *QUICK*. I'LL...

KLONK

ANOTHER NASTY *BLACKOUT*, KUP. YOU SHOULD GET THAT *SEEN TO*.

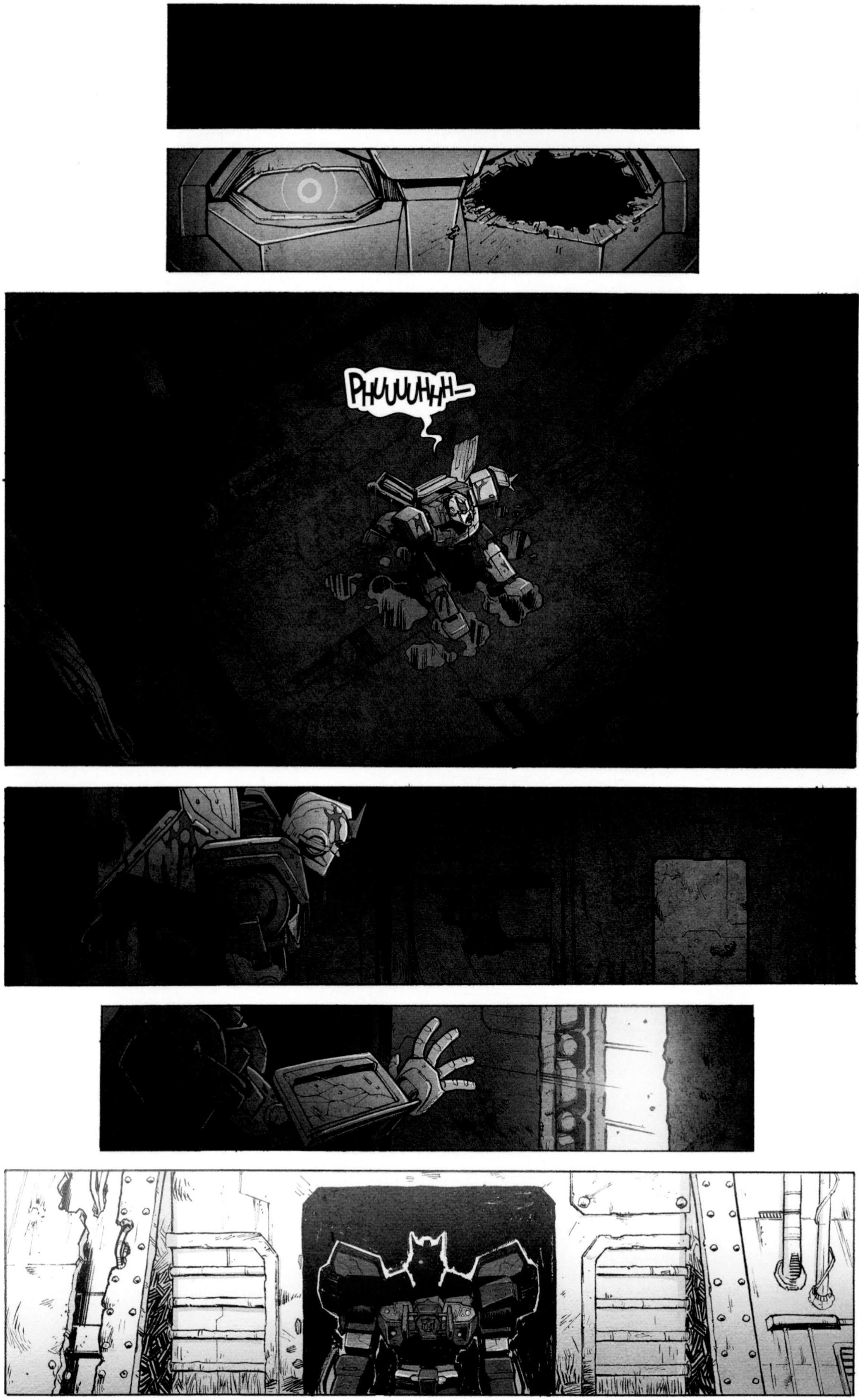
PHUUUUHHH—

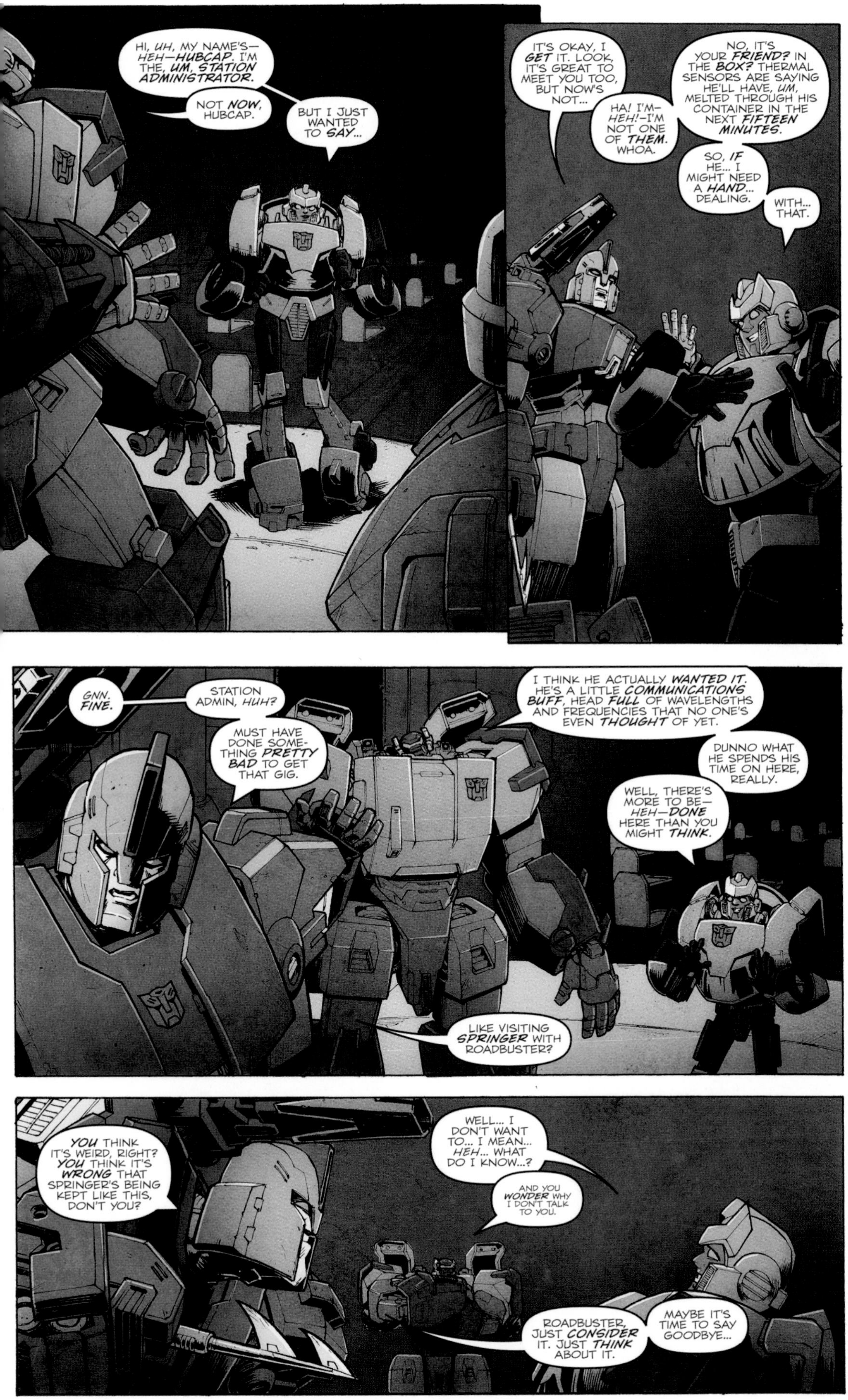
HI, UH, MY NAME'S— HEH—HUBCAP. I'M THE, UM, STATION ADMINISTRATOR.
NOT NOW, HUBCAP.
BUT I JUST WANTED TO SAY...
IT'S OKAY, I GET IT. LOOK, IT'S GREAT TO MEET YOU TOO, BUT NOW'S NOT...
HA! I'M— HEH!—I'M NOT ONE OF THEM. WHOA.
NO, IT'S YOUR FRIEND? IN THE BOX? THERMAL SENSORS ARE SAYING HE'LL HAVE, UM, MELTED THROUGH HIS CONTAINER IN THE NEXT FIFTEEN MINUTES.
SO, IF HE... I MIGHT NEED A HAND... DEALING.
WITH... THAT.
GNN. FINE.
STATION ADMIN, HUH?
MUST HAVE DONE SOMETHING PRETTY BAD TO GET THAT GIG.
I THINK HE ACTUALLY WANTED IT. HE'S A LITTLE COMMUNICATIONS BUFF, HEAD FULL OF WAVELENGTHS AND FREQUENCIES THAT NO ONE'S EVEN THOUGHT OF YET.
DUNNO WHAT HE SPENDS HIS TIME ON HERE, REALLY.
WELL, THERE'S MORE TO BE— HEH—DONE HERE THAN YOU MIGHT THINK.
LIKE VISITING SPRINGER WITH ROADBUSTER?
YOU THINK IT'S WEIRD, RIGHT? YOU THINK IT'S WRONG THAT SPRINGER'S BEING KEPT LIKE THIS, DON'T YOU?
WELL... I DON'T WANT TO... I MEAN... HEH... WHAT DO I KNOW...?
AND YOU WONDER WHY I DON'T TALK TO YOU.
ROADBUSTER, JUST CONSIDER IT. JUST THINK ABOUT IT.
MAYBE IT'S TIME TO SAY GOODBYE...

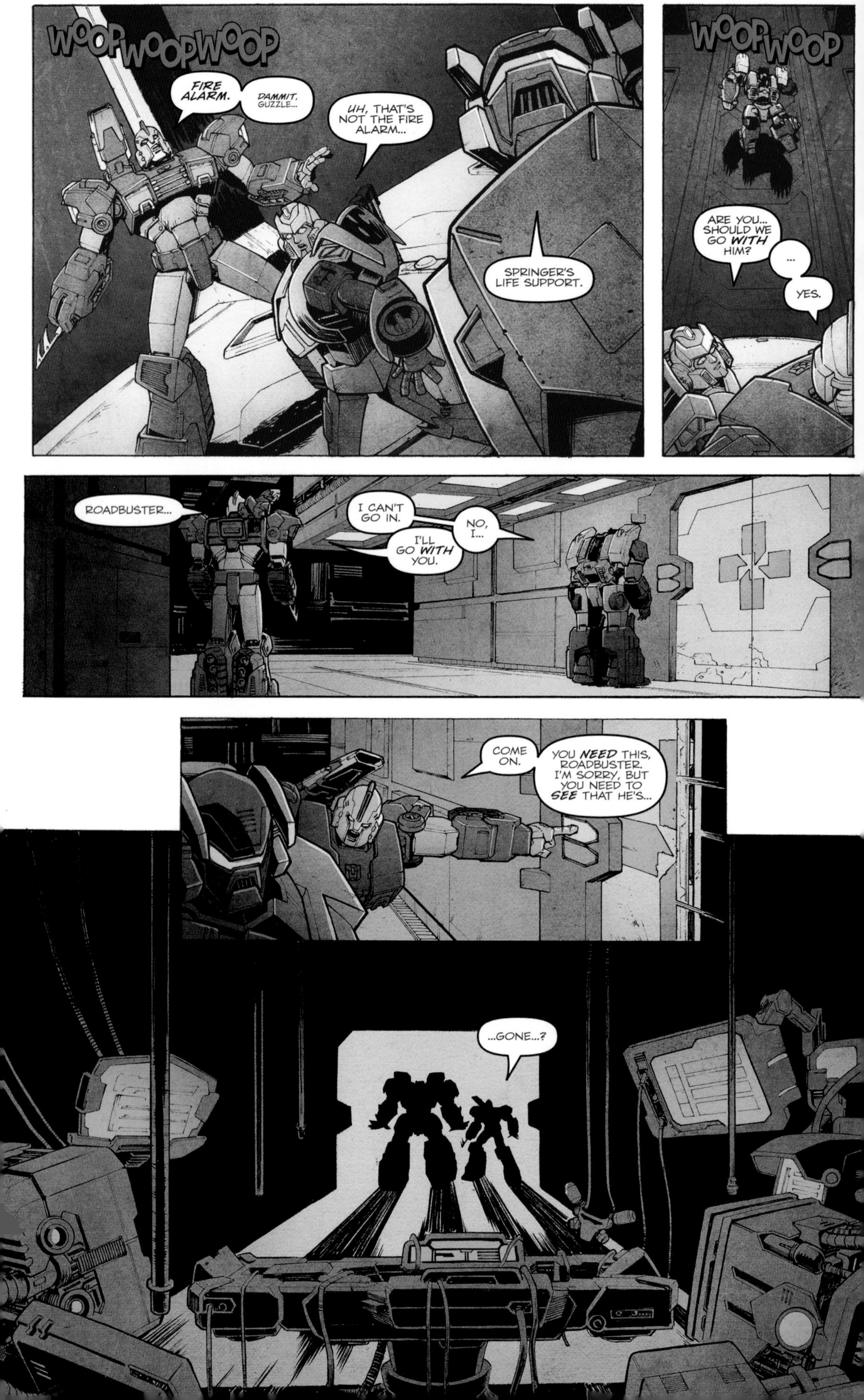
WOOPWOOPWOOP
FIRE ALARM.
DAMMIT, GUZZLE...
UH, THAT'S NOT THE FIRE ALARM...
SPRINGER'S LIFE SUPPORT.
WOOPWOOP
ARE YOU... SHOULD WE GO WITH HIM?
...
YES.
ROADBUSTER...
I CAN'T GO IN.
NO, I...
I'LL GO WITH YOU.
COME ON.
YOU NEED THIS, ROADBUSTER. I'M SORRY, BUT YOU NEED TO SEE THAT HE'S...
...GONE...?

PROWL HAS DISAPPEARED.

NOW, I *KNOW* YOU SENT HIM *THOSE MESSAGES*, VERITY CARLO, AND I *KNOW* YOU INTENDED TO COMPROMISE *CLASSIFIED DATA* IN ORDER TO SERVE YOUR AMOEBIC VIEW OF *JUSTICE*.

WHAT I DON'T KNOW IS, *WHY* ARE YOU LYING *NOW*?

I HAVE NO *CLUE* WHERE PROWL IS, *ALRIGHT*? SORRY YOU *MISPLACED* HIM, BUT I AIN'T GONNA SQUEEZE ANY *TEARS* OVER IT.

EVERYTHING LEADS BACK TO *YOU*, VERITY CARLO. YOU EXPECT ME TO *BELIEVE* THAT YOU DON'T KNOW WHERE HE *IS*?

I EXPECT *NOTHING* FROM *YOU* OR *ANYONE ELSE*, PINK LADY. AND I *DEFINITELY* DON'T EXPECT ANYONE WHO WEARS *THAT BADGE* TO UNDERSTAND MY REASONS FOR CALLING PROWL OUT ON EVERYTHING HE'S *DONE*.

BUT I KNOW *I'M RIGHT*.

THIS DISK CONTAINS THE *TESTIMONY* OF AUTOBOTS CHARGED WITH *WAR CRIMES*, ONLY IT'S *WEIRD*—PROWL *HIMSELF* ONLY APPEARS AS A *WITNESS*. HE WAS NEVER *CHARGED* WITH *ANYTHING*.

I *GET* IT. I GET *WAR*. A *THIRD* OF MY LIFE HAS BEEN *RUINED* BY *YOURS*.

PROWL DOESN'T *PLAY* WAR THOUGH; HE *MANIPULATES* AND *CONTROLS* THEM INTO DOING HORRIBLE THINGS IN *HIS* NAME.

I DON'T KNOW WHERE HE IS. *GOOD LUCK* FINDING HIM. NO DOUBT YOU *WILL*. LACKEY COMES TO THE *RESCUE*; BACON IS *SAVED*; BAD COP *GETS AWAY AGAIN*.

MAYBE, HUMAN, *MY NEED* TO FIND HIM HAS *VERY LITTLE* TO DO WITH *HIS* WELL-BEING...

NOW, I'M *CONSTANTLY* REMINDED THAT *YOUR KIND* DESERVES *OUR PROTECTION*, BUT I FEEL THAT THE *RESPONSE* TO ANY THREAT SHOULD BE *PROPORTIONAL*...

DO IT, *RIZZO*. YOU THINK I HAVEN'T BEEN SCHOOLED TO RESIST "*REFINED METHODS OF QUESTIONING*" FROM YOUR TYPE? I'VE GOT *NOTHING* TO LOSE.

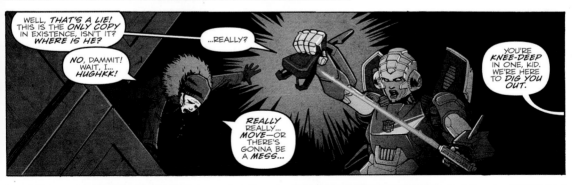

WELL, *THAT'S A LIE!* THIS IS THE *ONLY COPY* IN EXISTENCE, ISN'T IT? *WHERE IS HE?*

NO, DAMMIT! WAIT, I... HUGHKK!

...REALLY?

REALLY REALLY... MOVE—OR THERE'S GONNA BE A *MESS*...

YOU'RE *KNEE-DEEP* IN ONE, KID. WE'RE HERE TO *DIG YOU OUT.*

KUP? AND... *WELL*, DECIDED TO *WAKE UP?*

CAN'T STAY ASLEEP FOREVER.

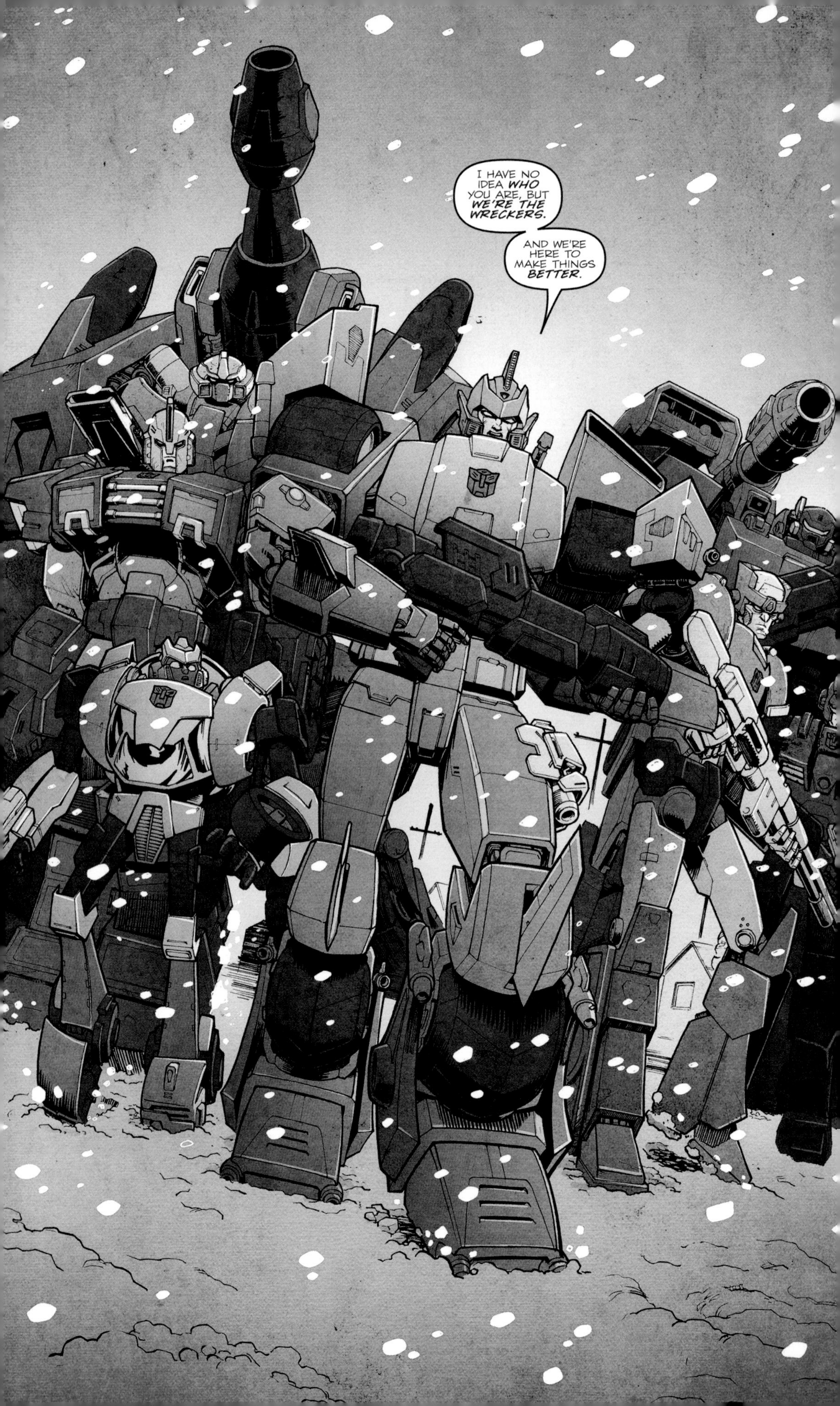
I HAVE NO IDEA WHO YOU ARE, BUT WE'RE THE WRECKERS.
AND WE'RE HERE TO MAKE THINGS BETTER.

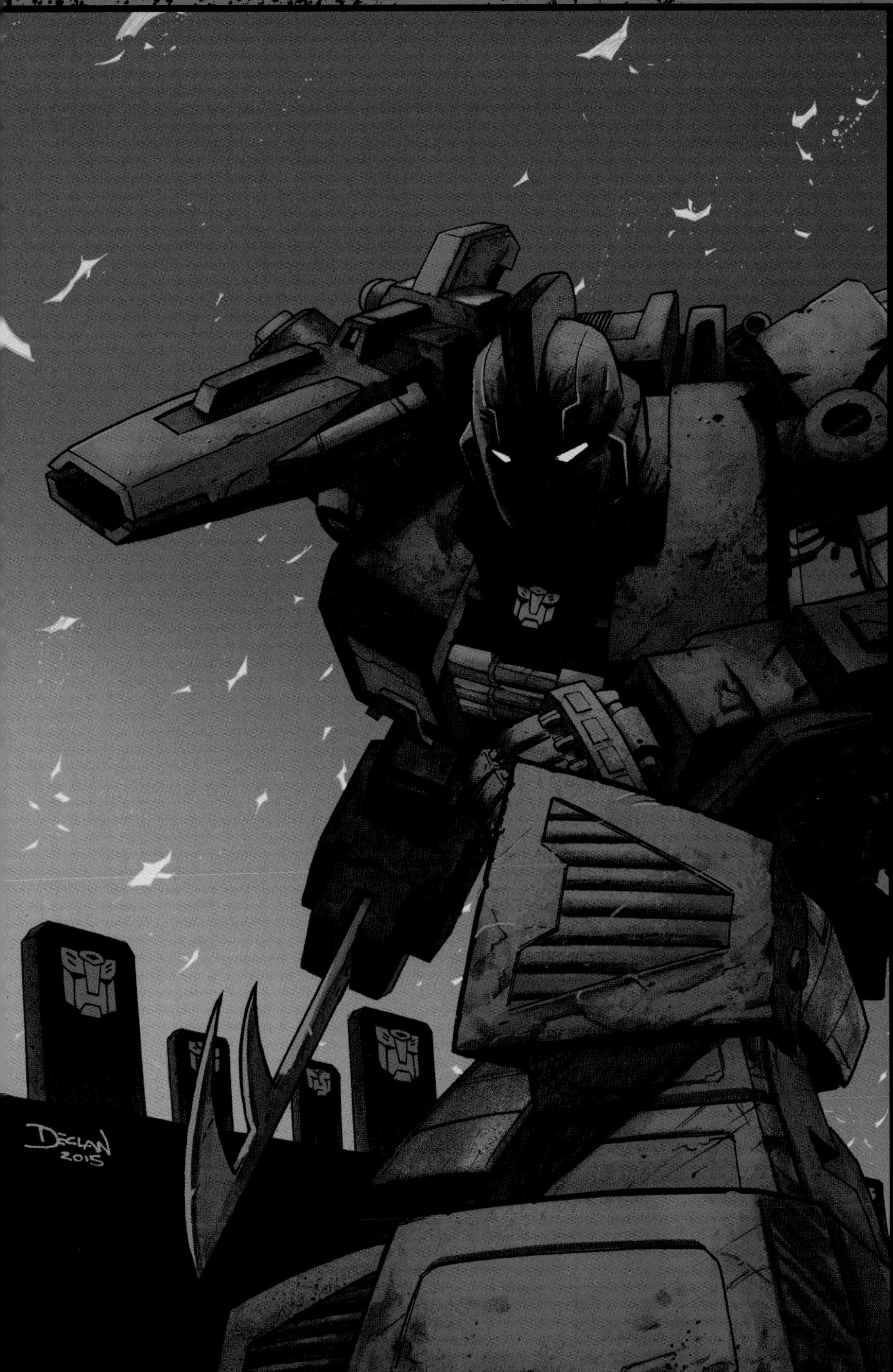
DECLAN
2015

ART **DECLAN SHALVEY** COLORS **JORDIE BELLAIRE**

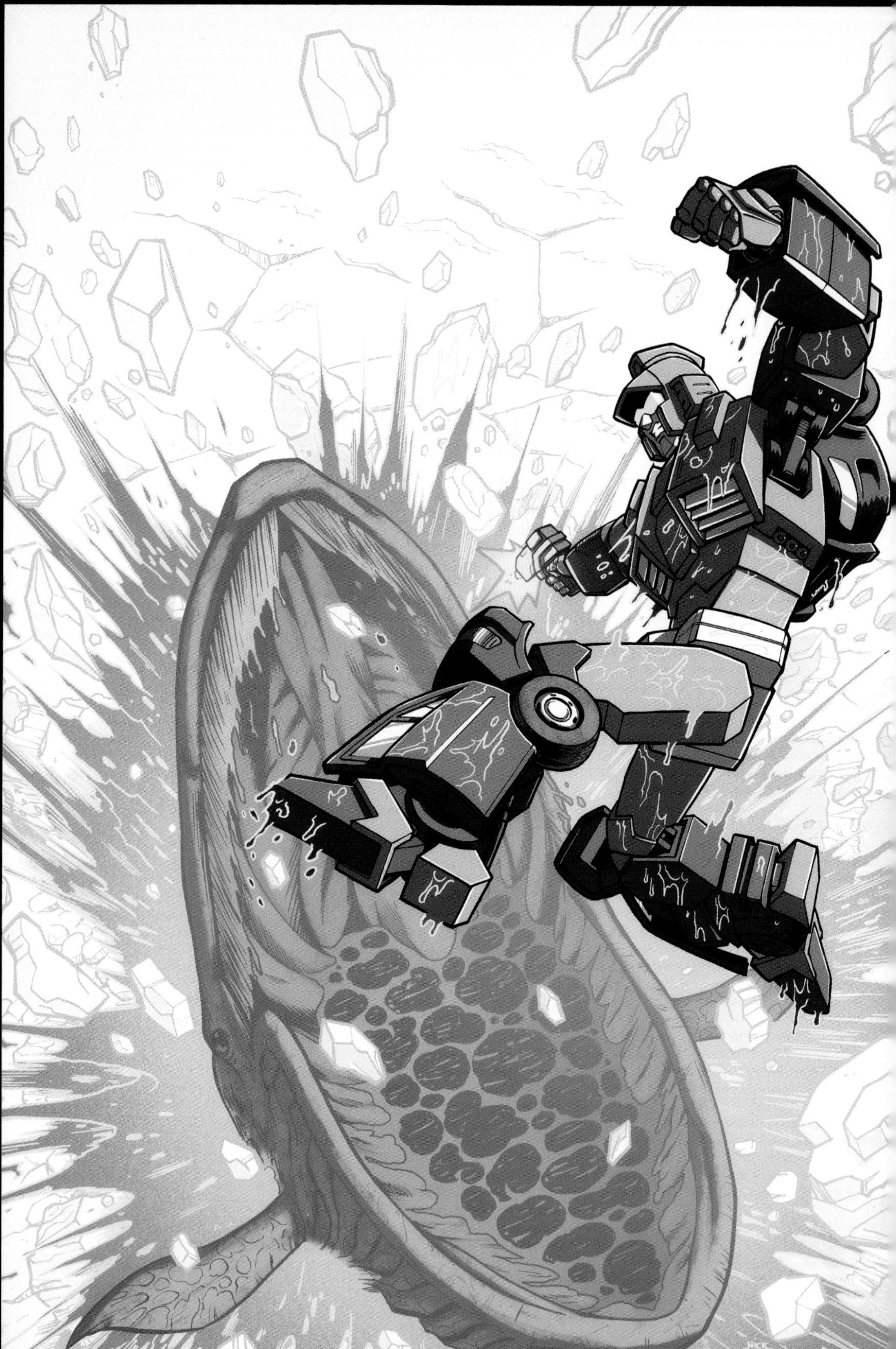

ART NICK ROCHE COLORS JOSH BURCHAM

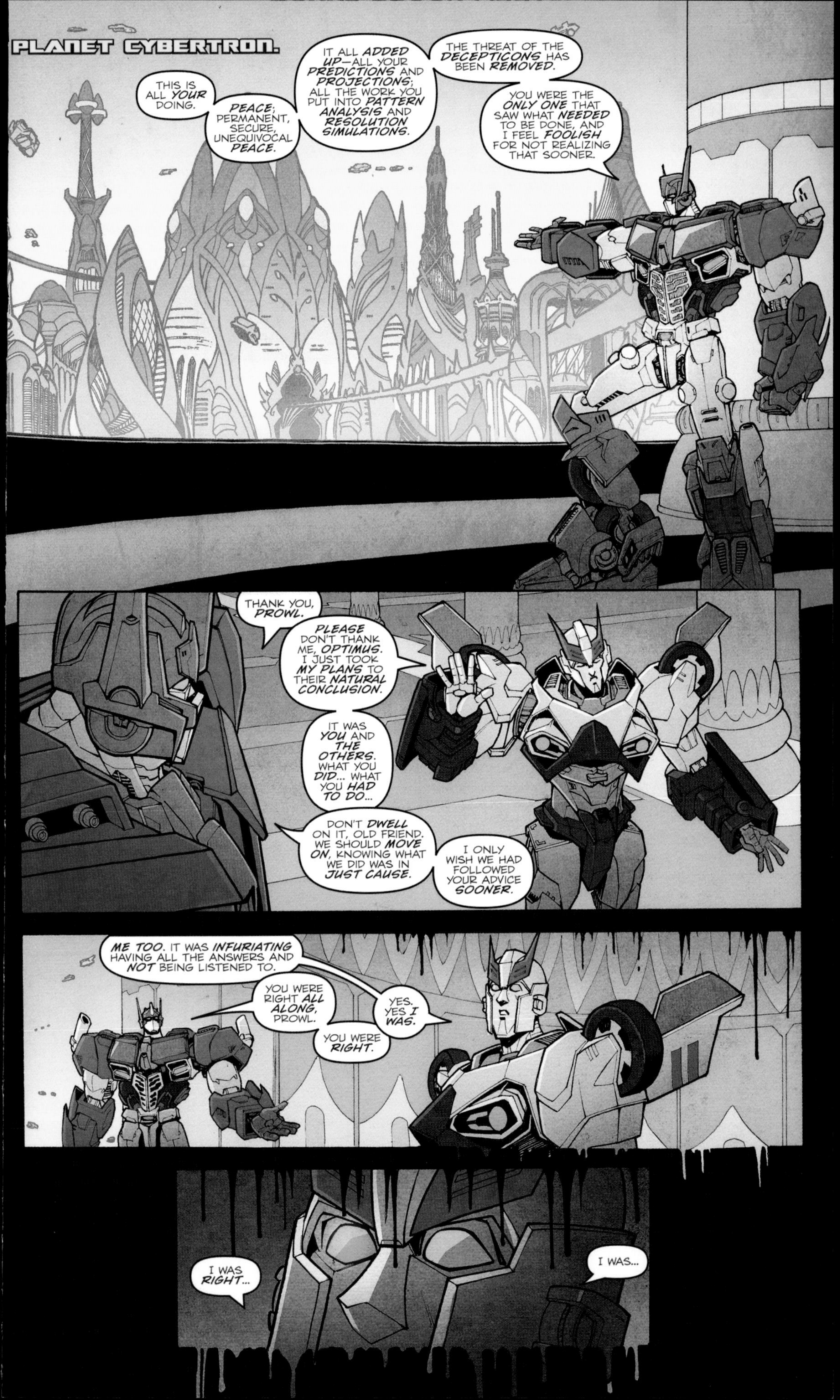
PLANET CYBERTRON.
THIS IS ALL YOUR DOING.
PEACE; PERMANENT, SECURE, UNEQUIVOCAL PEACE.
IT ALL ADDED UP—ALL YOUR PREDICTIONS AND PROJECTIONS; ALL THE WORK YOU PUT INTO PATTERN ANALYSIS AND RESOLUTION SIMULATIONS.
THE THREAT OF THE DECEPTICONS HAS BEEN REMOVED.
YOU WERE THE ONLY ONE THAT SAW WHAT NEEDED TO BE DONE, AND I FEEL FOOLISH FOR NOT REALIZING THAT SOONER.
THANK YOU, PROWL.
PLEASE DON'T THANK ME, OPTIMUS. I JUST TOOK MY PLANS TO THEIR NATURAL CONCLUSION.
IT WAS YOU AND THE OTHERS. WHAT YOU DID... WHAT YOU HAD TO DO...
DON'T DWELL ON IT, OLD FRIEND. WE SHOULD MOVE ON, KNOWING WHAT WE DID WAS IN JUST CAUSE.
I ONLY WISH WE HAD FOLLOWED YOUR ADVICE SOONER.
ME TOO. IT WAS INFURIATING HAVING ALL THE ANSWERS AND NOT BEING LISTENED TO.
YOU WERE RIGHT ALL ALONG, PROWL.
YES. YES I WAS.
YOU WERE RIGHT.
I WAS RIGHT...
I WAS...

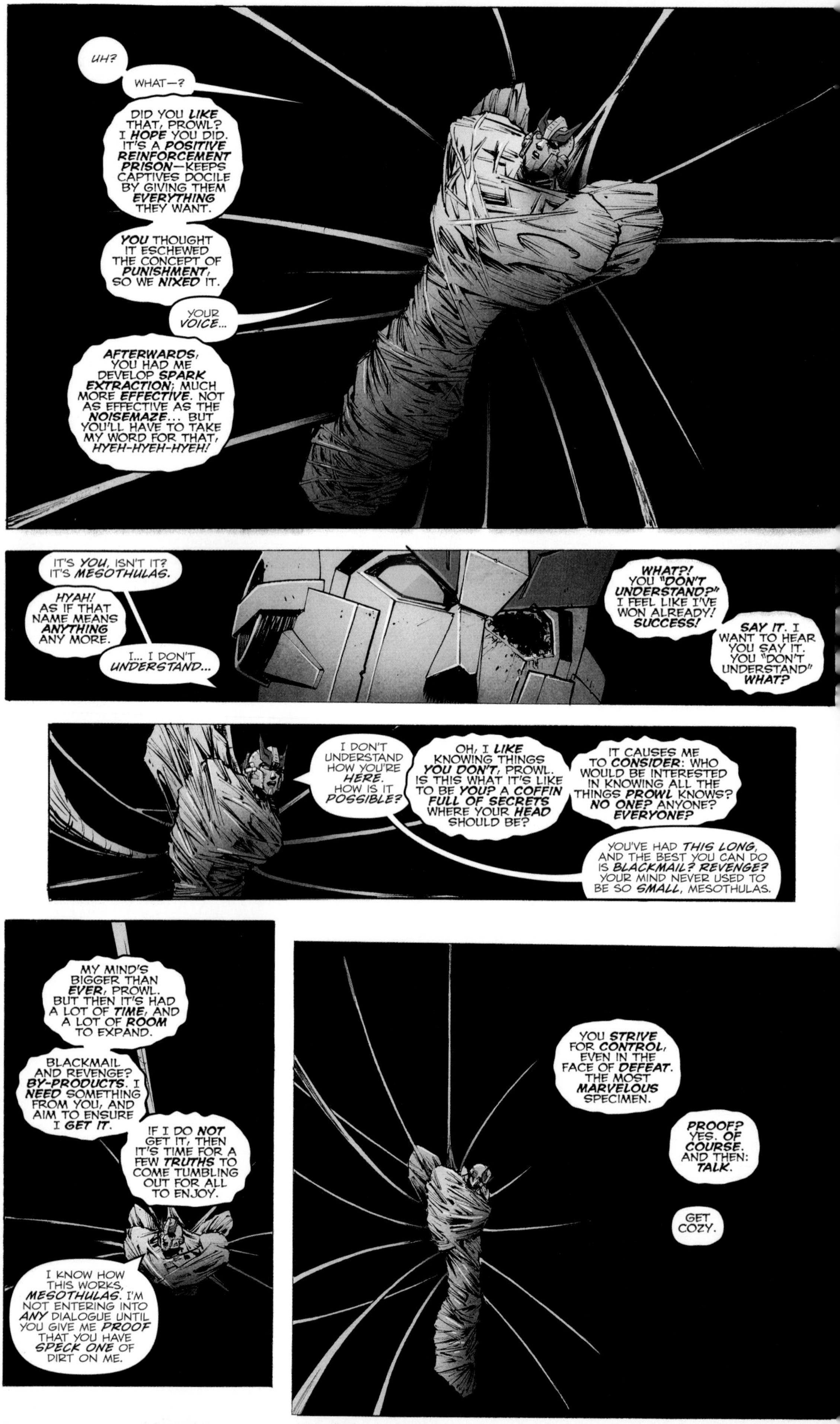
UH?
WHAT—?
DID YOU LIKE THAT, PROWL? I HOPE YOU DID. IT'S A POSITIVE REINFORCEMENT PRISON—KEEPS CAPTIVES DOCILE BY GIVING THEM EVERYTHING THEY WANT.
YOU THOUGHT IT ESCHEWED THE CONCEPT OF PUNISHMENT, SO WE NIXED IT.
YOUR VOICE...
AFTERWARDS, YOU HAD ME DEVELOP SPARK EXTRACTION; MUCH MORE EFFECTIVE. NOT AS EFFECTIVE AS THE NOISEMAZE... BUT YOU'LL HAVE TO TAKE MY WORD FOR THAT, HYEH-HYEH-HYEH!
IT'S YOU, ISN'T IT? IT'S MESOTHULAS.
HYAH! AS IF THAT NAME MEANS ANYTHING ANY MORE.
I... I DON'T UNDERSTAND...
WHAT?! YOU "DON'T UNDERSTAND?" I FEEL LIKE I'VE WON ALREADY! SUCCESS!
SAY IT. I WANT TO HEAR YOU SAY IT. YOU "DON'T UNDERSTAND" WHAT?
I DON'T UNDERSTAND HOW YOU'RE HERE. HOW IS IT POSSIBLE?
OH, I LIKE KNOWING THINGS YOU DON'T, PROWL. IS THIS WHAT IT'S LIKE TO BE YOU? A COFFIN FULL OF SECRETS WHERE YOUR HEAD SHOULD BE?
IT CAUSES ME TO CONSIDER: WHO WOULD BE INTERESTED IN KNOWING ALL THE THINGS PROWL KNOWS? NO ONE? ANYONE? EVERYONE?
YOU'VE HAD THIS LONG, AND THE BEST YOU CAN DO IS BLACKMAIL? REVENGE? YOUR MIND NEVER USED TO BE SO SMALL, MESOTHULAS.
MY MIND'S BIGGER THAN EVER, PROWL. BUT THEN IT'S HAD A LOT OF TIME, AND A LOT OF ROOM TO EXPAND.
BLACKMAIL AND REVENGE? BY-PRODUCTS. I NEED SOMETHING FROM YOU, AND AIM TO ENSURE I GET IT.
IF I DO NOT GET IT, THEN IT'S TIME FOR A FEW TRUTHS TO COME TUMBLING OUT FOR ALL TO ENJOY.
I KNOW HOW THIS WORKS, MESOTHULAS. I'M NOT ENTERING INTO ANY DIALOGUE UNTIL YOU GIVE ME PROOF THAT YOU HAVE SPECK ONE OF DIRT ON ME.
YOU STRIVE FOR CONTROL, EVEN IN THE FACE OF DEFEAT. THE MOST MARVELOUS SPECIMEN.
PROOF? YES. OF COURSE. AND THEN: TALK.
GET COZY.

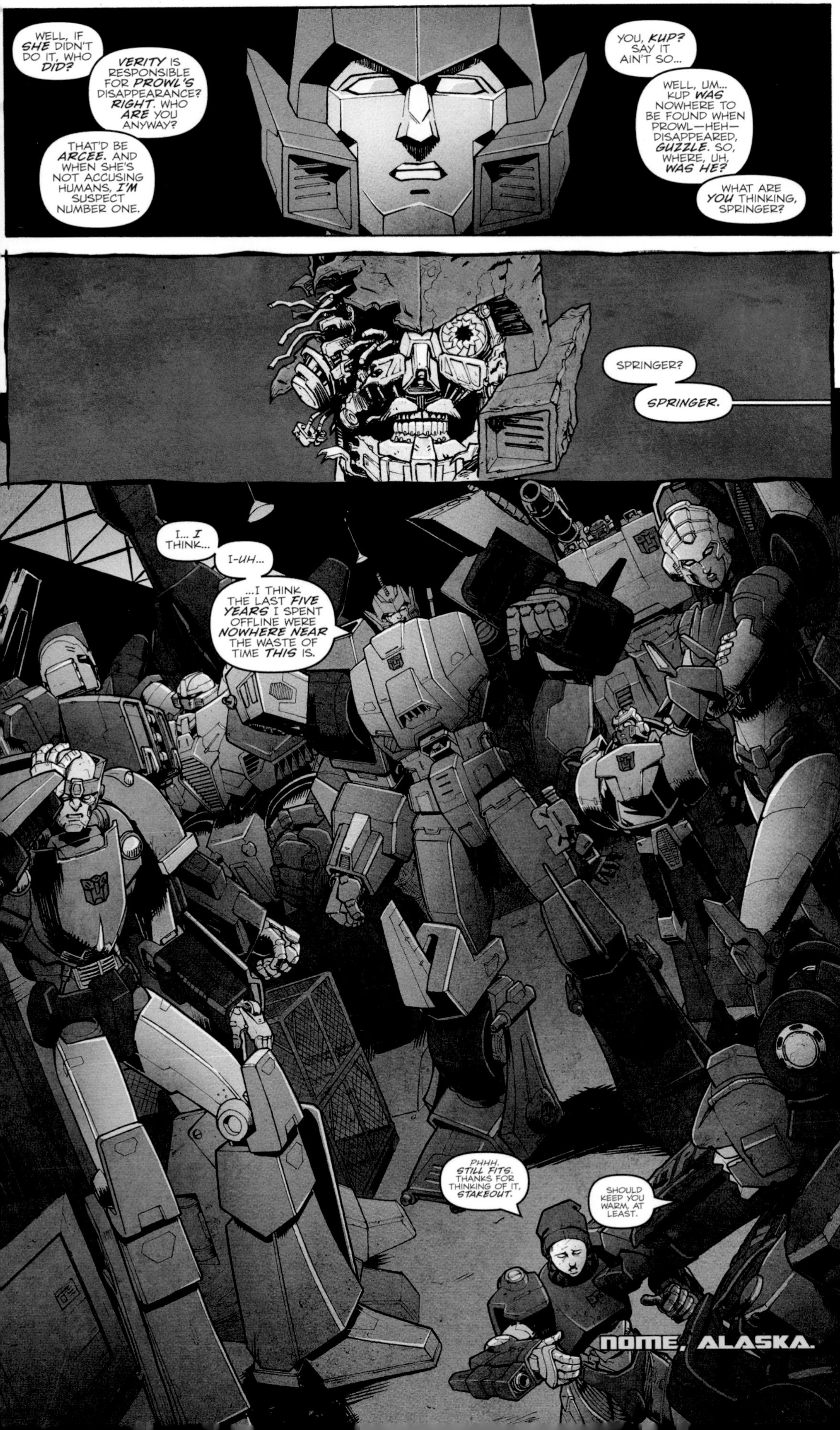

WELL, IF SHE DIDN'T DO IT, WHO DID?
VERITY IS RESPONSIBLE FOR PROWL'S DISAPPEARANCE? RIGHT. WHO ARE YOU ANYWAY?
THAT'D BE ARCEE. AND WHEN SHE'S NOT ACCUSING HUMANS, I'M SUSPECT NUMBER ONE.
YOU, KUP? SAY IT AIN'T SO...
WELL, UM... KUP WAS NOWHERE TO BE FOUND WHEN PROWL—HEH—DISAPPEARED, GUZZLE. SO, WHERE, UH, WAS HE?
WHAT ARE YOU THINKING, SPRINGER?
SPRINGER?
SPRINGER.
I... I THINK...
I-UH...
...I THINK THE LAST FIVE YEARS I SPENT OFFLINE WERE NOWHERE NEAR THE WASTE OF TIME THIS IS.
PHHH. STILL FITS. THANKS FOR THINKING OF IT, STAKEOUT.
SHOULD KEEP YOU WARM, AT LEAST.
NOME, ALASKA.

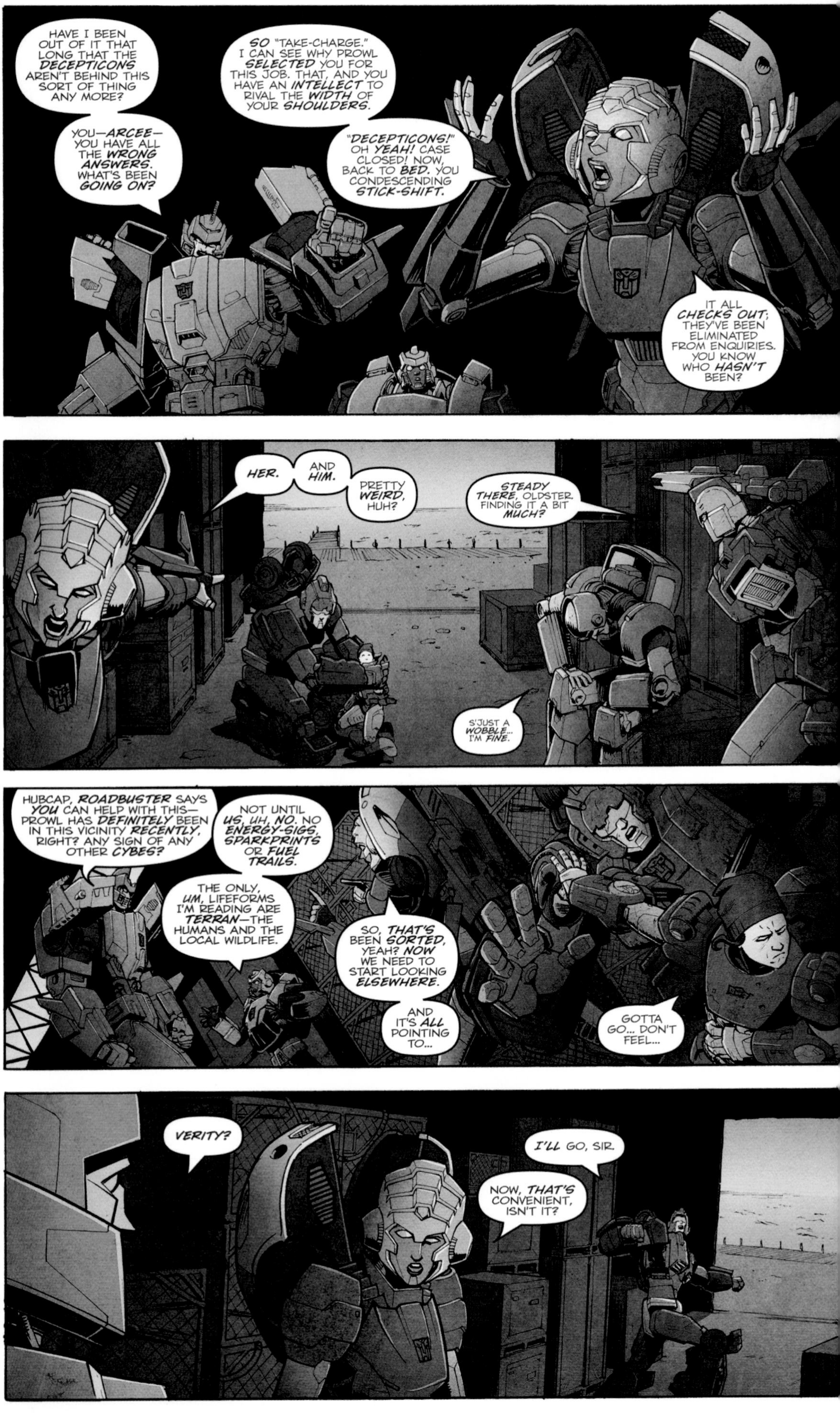
HAVE I BEEN OUT OF IT THAT LONG THAT THE DECEPTICONS AREN'T BEHIND THIS SORT OF THING ANY MORE?
YOU—ARCEE—YOU HAVE ALL THE WRONG ANSWERS. WHAT'S BEEN GOING ON?
SO "TAKE-CHARGE." I CAN SEE WHY PROWL SELECTED YOU FOR THIS JOB. THAT, AND YOU HAVE AN INTELLECT TO RIVAL THE WIDTH OF YOUR SHOULDERS.
"DECEPTICONS!" OH YEAH! CASE CLOSED! NOW, BACK TO BED, YOU CONDESCENDING STICK-SHIFT.
IT ALL CHECKS OUT; THEY'VE BEEN ELIMINATED FROM ENQUIRIES. YOU KNOW WHO HASN'T BEEN?
HER.
AND HIM.
PRETTY WEIRD, HUH?
STEADY THERE, OLDSTER. FINDING IT A BIT MUCH?
S'JUST A WOBBLE... I'M FINE.
HUBCAP, ROADBUSTER SAYS YOU CAN HELP WITH THIS—PROWL HAS DEFINITELY BEEN IN THIS VICINITY RECENTLY, RIGHT? ANY SIGN OF ANY OTHER CYBES?
NOT UNTIL US, UH, NO. NO ENERGY-SIGS, SPARKPRINTS OR FUEL TRAILS.
THE ONLY, UM, LIFEFORMS I'M READING ARE TERRAN—THE HUMANS AND THE LOCAL WILDLIFE.
SO, THAT'S BEEN SORTED, YEAH? NOW WE NEED TO START LOOKING ELSEWHERE.
AND IT'S ALL POINTING TO...
GOTTA GO... DON'T FEEL...
VERITY?
I'LL GO, SIR.
NOW, THAT'S CONVENIENT, ISN'T IT?

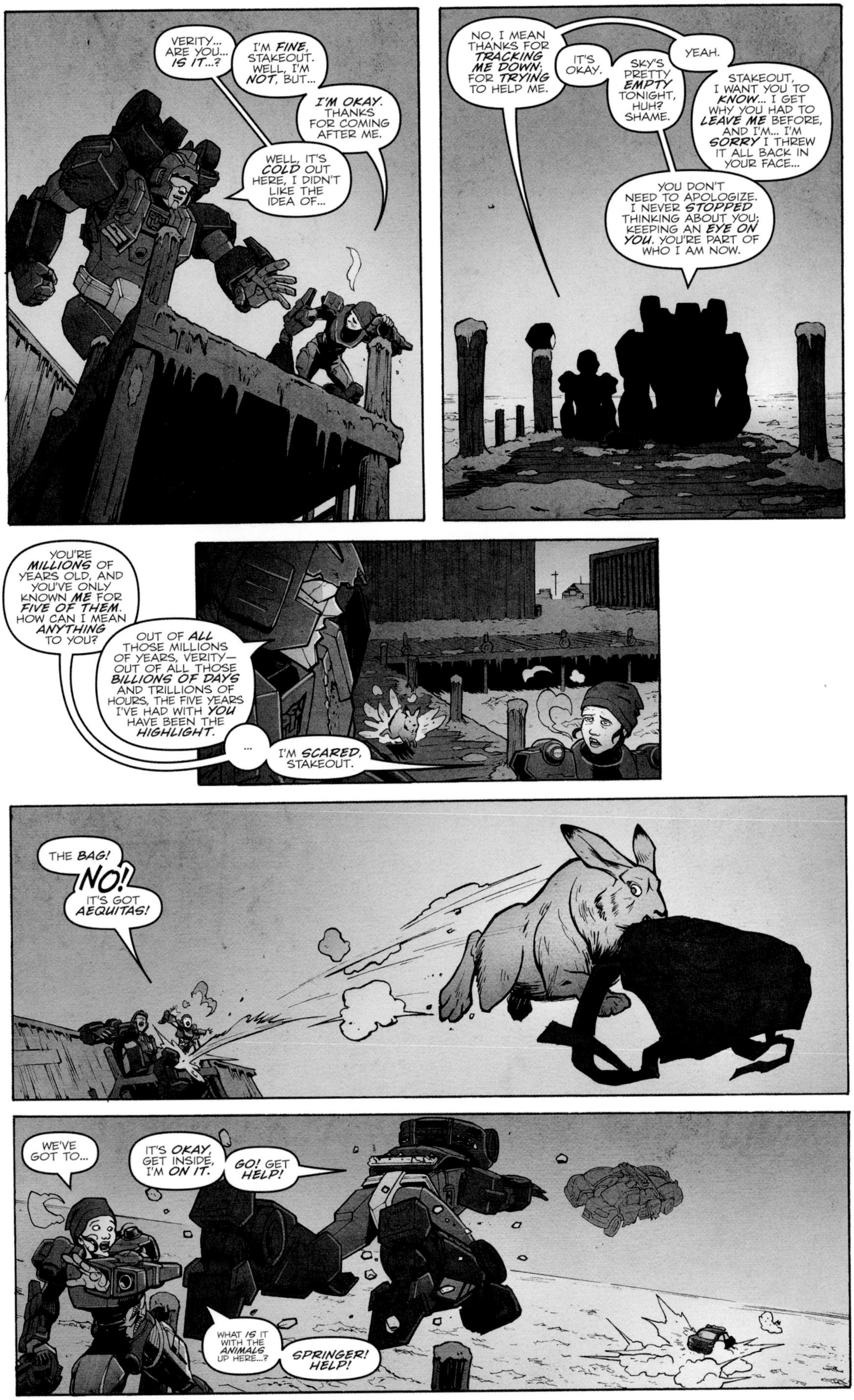
VERITY... ARE YOU... IS IT...?
I'M FINE, STAKEOUT. WELL, I'M NOT, BUT...
I'M OKAY. THANKS FOR COMING AFTER ME.
WELL, IT'S COLD OUT HERE, I DIDN'T LIKE THE IDEA OF...
NO, I MEAN THANKS FOR TRACKING ME DOWN; FOR TRYING TO HELP ME.
IT'S OKAY.
SKY'S PRETTY EMPTY TONIGHT, HUH? SHAME.
YEAH.
STAKEOUT, I WANT YOU TO KNOW... I GET WHY YOU HAD TO LEAVE ME BEFORE, AND I'M... I'M SORRY I THREW IT ALL BACK IN YOUR FACE...
YOU DON'T NEED TO APOLOGIZE. I NEVER STOPPED THINKING ABOUT YOU; KEEPING AN EYE ON YOU. YOU'RE PART OF WHO I AM NOW.
YOU'RE MILLIONS OF YEARS OLD, AND YOU'VE ONLY KNOWN ME FOR FIVE OF THEM. HOW CAN I MEAN ANYTHING TO YOU?
OUT OF ALL THOSE MILLIONS OF YEARS, VERITY— OUT OF ALL THOSE BILLIONS OF DAYS AND TRILLIONS OF HOURS, THE FIVE YEARS I'VE HAD WITH YOU HAVE BEEN THE HIGHLIGHT.
...
I'M SCARED, STAKEOUT.
THE BAG!
NO!
IT'S GOT AEQUITAS!
WE'VE GOT TO...
IT'S OKAY, GET INSIDE, I'M ON IT.
GO! GET HELP!
WHAT IS IT WITH THE ANIMALS UP HERE...?
SPRINGER! HELP!

AEQUITAS... AEQUITAS IS GONE... A *RABBIT*... OR *HARE*—I DUNNO... IT TOOK THE BAG.

STAKEOUT WENT AFTER IT... *FOLLOWED* THE LITTLE PIECE OF CRAP...

PROWL'S DIRT FILE *DISAPPEARS* AND SO DOES PO-PO?

NEVER TRUST A COP.

SHUT UP. COME ON, LET'S CHECK IT OUT.

SHOOTIN' AND HUNTIN'! WOO-EE!

THIS THING... THIS *WHOLE* SITUATION IS GETTING *AWAY* FROM US.

WE NEED TO GET *OUT* THERE AND GET THAT *DATASLUG* BACK. EVERYONE, LET'S...

KUP?!

KERRASH

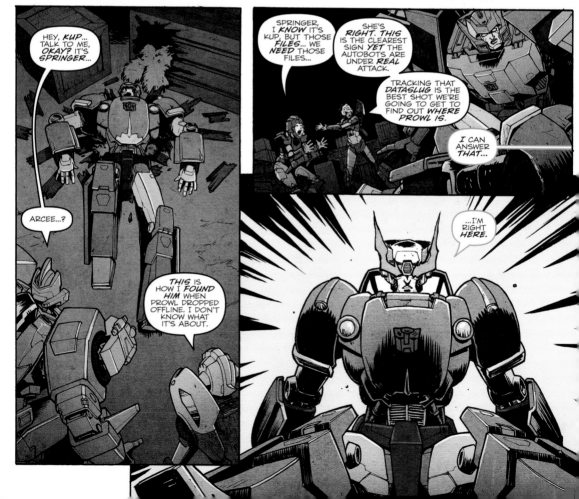

HEY, *KUP*... TALK TO ME, *OKAY?* IT'S *SPRINGER*...

ARCEE...?

THIS IS HOW I *FOUND HIM* WHEN PROWL DROPPED OFFLINE. I DON'T KNOW WHAT IT'S ABOUT.

SPRINGER, I *KNOW* IT'S KUP, BUT THOSE *FILES*... WE *NEED* THOSE FILES...

SHE'S *RIGHT. THIS* IS THE CLEAREST SIGN *YET* THE AUTOBOTS ARE UNDER *REAL* ATTACK.

TRACKING THAT *DATASLUG* IS THE BEST SHOT WE'RE GOING TO GET TO FIND OUT *WHERE PROWL IS.*

I CAN ANSWER *THAT...*

...I'M *RIGHT HERE.*

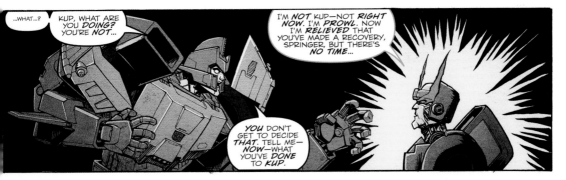

...WHAT...?

KUP, WHAT ARE YOU *DOING?* YOU'RE *NOT...*

I'M *NOT* KUP—NOT *RIGHT NOW.* I'M *PROWL.* NOW I'M *RELIEVED* THAT YOU'VE MADE A RECOVERY, SPRINGER, BUT THERE'S *NO TIME...*

YOU DON'T GET TO DECIDE *THAT.* TELL ME— *NOW*—WHAT YOU'VE *DONE* TO KUP.

MIND CONTROL. A PROTOCOL I HAD PLACED IN KUP'S *CEREBRAL NETWORK* TO ALLOW ME TO INFLUENCE HIS WORDS AND THOUGHTS.

KUP REQUIRED *EXTENSIVE ATTENTION* FOLLOWING HIS *RADIATION SICKNESS* ON *TSIEHCHI.* REMEMBER? WHERE HE KILLED *DOZENS* OF AUTOBOTS *YOU* SENT TO RESCUE HIM? SO I HAD *PERCEPTOR* INSTALL THIS LITTLE... *EXTRA.*

WHY? WHY WOULD YOU *NEED* TO...?

OUR WAR WAS AT A *CRITICAL POINT,* AND ALL MY *CAREFULLY-CALCULATED* SOLUTIONS WERE BEING IGNORED. A *CHARISMATIC FIGUREHEAD* LIKE *KUP* COULD GET MY MESSAGE ACROSS. I NEEDED THE AUTOBOTS—I NEED *PRIME*—TO *LISTEN.*

AND *DID* THEY?

THE OPPORTUNITY NEVER AROSE. ULTIMATELY, I WAS FORCED TO USE *THIS* CONNECTION TO *URGE* KUP TO SEAL A *PORTAL* TO THE *DEAD UNIVERSE.* HE WAS *STRANDED* THERE FOR *FOURTEEN BILLION YEARS,* BUT ALL EXISTENCE WAS *SAVED,* SO YOU'RE WELCOME.

THERE. HAPPY?

BUT *YOU'RE... WE'RE* AUTOBOTS...

YOU'RE A MONSTER, PROWL.

NOTED. NOW, NO MORE *QUESTIONS.*

A *FORMER ASSOCIATE* KNOWN AS *MESOTHULAS* HAS ABDUCTED ME. WE PARTED *UNPLEASANTLY* AND HIS RETURN SEEMED... *UNLIKELY.* I HAVE *NO IDEA* WHAT HE WANTS, AND IT'S *BUGGING* ME.

I'M BEING HELD IN SOME PLACE CALLED THE *NOISEMAZE.* I WAS RENDERED UNCONSCIOUS DURING MY *EXTRACTION,* SO HAVE NO CLUE AS TO THE LOCATION OF MY PRISON.

HUBCAP *SCANNED...* WE COULDN'T DETECT *ANY* CYBERTRONIAN SIGNALS HERE...

NO. NOR COULD I. NOW *SHUSH.* THIS NEXT BIT'S *IMPORTANT.*

WHEN I CAME *BACK ONLINE,* I WAS COATED IN *RESIDUAL TRACES* OF *EARTHEN SALTWATER.*

I HYPOTHESIZE THERE TO BE AN *OFF-SHORE UNDERSEA FACILITY* BELONGING TO MESOTHULAS THAT I WAS TAKEN TO *BEFORE* MY ARRIVAL *HERE.*

FIND *IT,* AND YOU MAY HAVE *SOME* HOPE OF LOCATING ME. BUT *BE WARNED:* THE NOISEMAZE ITSELF IS—

ARGGHHH

PROWL!

DAMMIT —KUP!

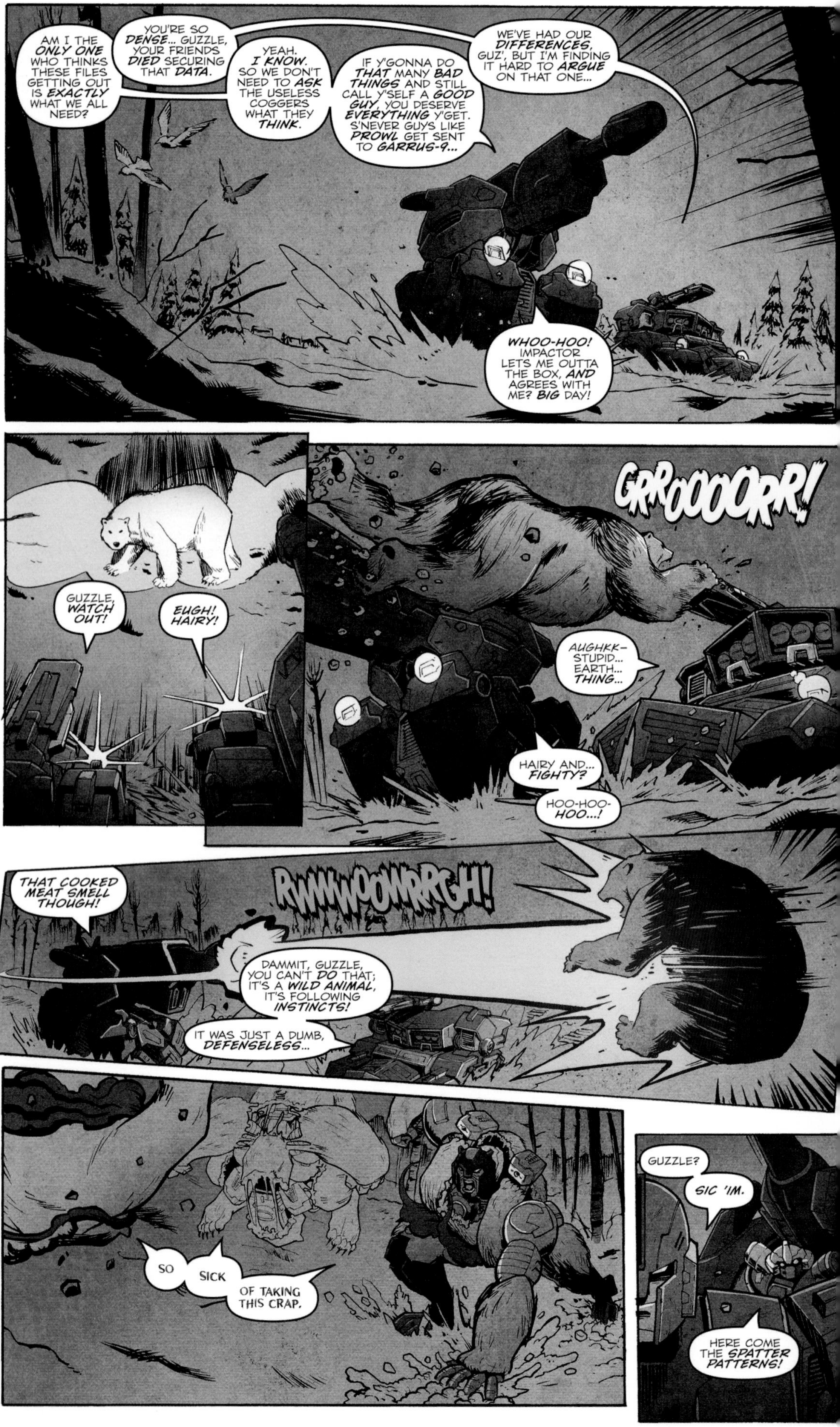
AM I THE ONLY ONE WHO THINKS THESE FILES GETTING OUT IS EXACTLY WHAT WE ALL NEED?
YOU'RE SO DENSE... GUZZLE, YOUR FRIENDS DIED SECURING THAT DATA.
YEAH. I KNOW. SO WE DON'T NEED TO ASK THE USELESS COGGERS WHAT THEY THINK.
IF Y'GONNA DO THAT MANY BAD THINGS AND STILL CALL Y'SELF A GOOD GUY, YOU DESERVE EVERYTHING Y'GET. S'NEVER GUYS LIKE PROWL GET SENT TO GARRUS-9...
WE'VE HAD OUR DIFFERENCES, GUZ', BUT I'M FINDING IT HARD TO ARGUE ON THAT ONE...
WHOO-HOO! IMPACTOR LETS ME OUTTA THE BOX, AND AGREES WITH ME? BIG DAY!
GRROOOOORR!
GUZZLE, WATCH OUT!
EUGH! HAIRY!
AUGHKK-STUPID... EARTH... THING...
HAIRY AND... FIGHTY?
HOO-HOO-HOO...!
THAT COOKED MEAT SMELL THOUGH!
RWWWOOWRRGH!
DAMMIT, GUZZLE, YOU CAN'T DO THAT; IT'S A WILD ANIMAL, IT'S FOLLOWING INSTINCTS!
IT WAS JUST A DUMB, DEFENSELESS...
SO
SICK
OF TAKING THIS CRAP.
GUZZLE?
SIC 'IM.
HERE COME THE SPATTER PATTERNS!

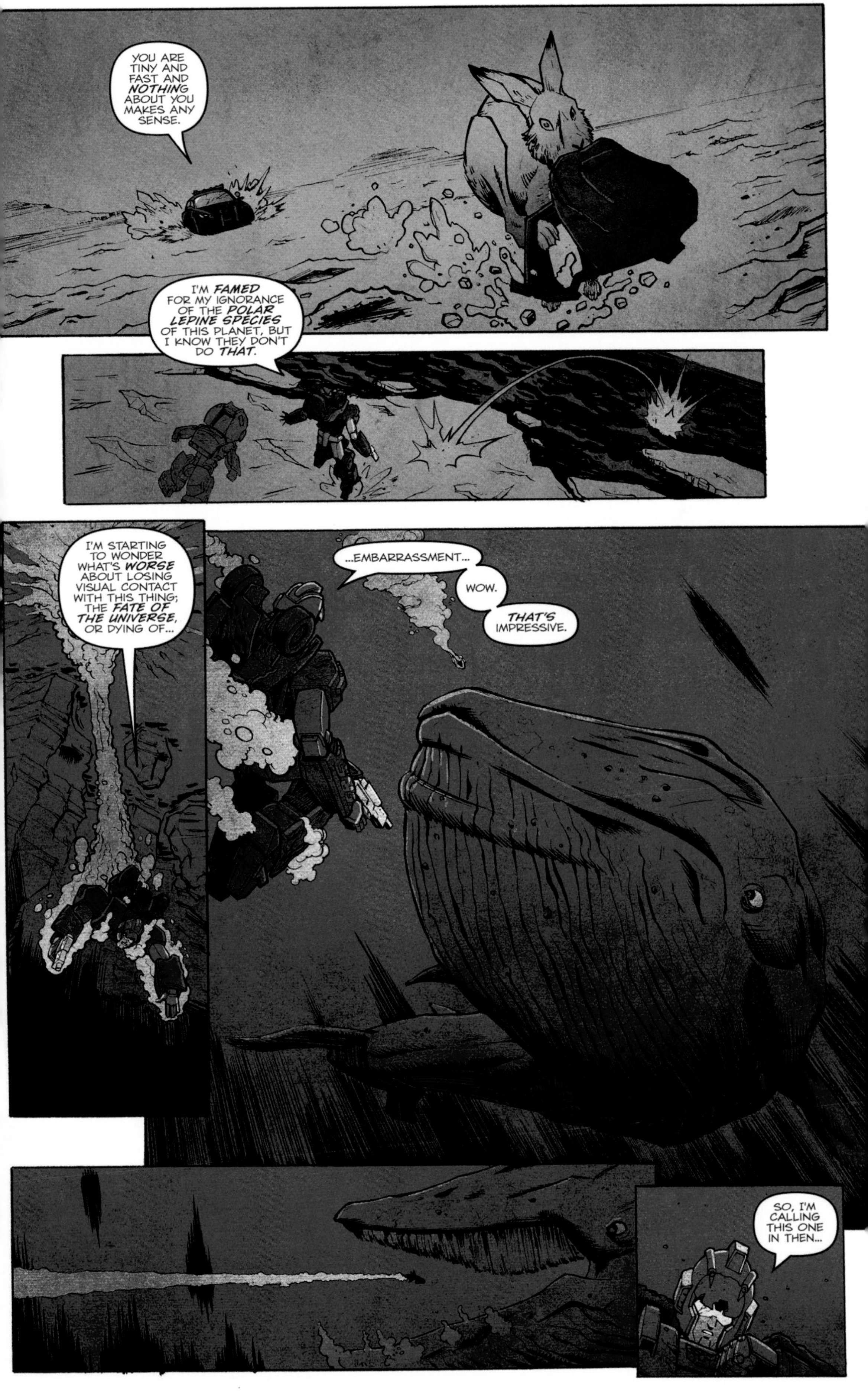
YOU ARE TINY AND FAST AND NOTHING ABOUT YOU MAKES ANY SENSE.
I'M FAMED FOR MY IGNORANCE OF THE POLAR LEPINE SPECIES OF THIS PLANET, BUT I KNOW THEY DON'T DO THAT.
I'M STARTING TO WONDER WHAT'S WORSE ABOUT LOSING VISUAL CONTACT WITH THIS THING; THE FATE OF THE UNIVERSE, OR DYING OF...
...EMBARRASSMENT...
WOW.
THAT'S IMPRESSIVE.
SO, I'M CALLING THIS ONE IN THEN...

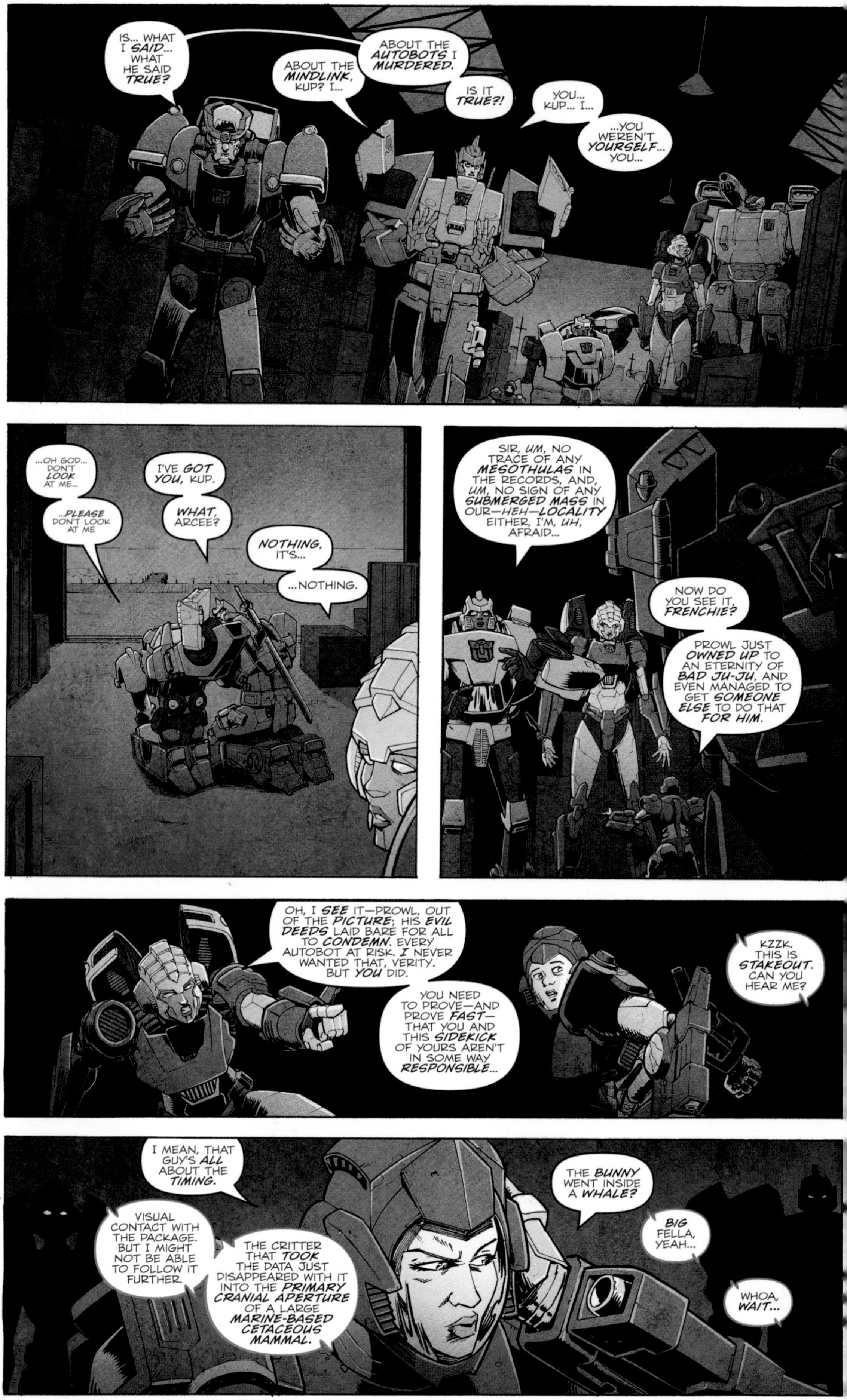
IS... WHAT I SAID... WHAT HE SAID TRUE?
ABOUT THE MINDLINK, KUP? I...
ABOUT THE AUTOBOTS I MURDERED.
IS IT TRUE?!
YOU... KUP... I...
...YOU WEREN'T YOURSELF... YOU...
...OH GOD... DON'T LOOK AT ME...
...PLEASE DON'T LOOK AT ME
I'VE GOT YOU, KUP.
WHAT, ARCEE?
NOTHING, IT'S...
...NOTHING.
SIR, UM, NO TRACE OF ANY MESOTHULAS IN THE RECORDS, AND, UM, NO SIGN OF ANY SUBMERGED MASS IN OUR—HEH—LOCALITY EITHER, I'M, UH, AFRAID...
NOW DO YOU SEE IT, FRENCHIE?
PROWL JUST OWNED UP TO AN ETERNITY OF BAD JU-JU, AND EVEN MANAGED TO GET SOMEONE ELSE TO DO THAT FOR HIM.
OH, I SEE IT—PROWL, OUT OF THE PICTURE; HIS EVIL DEEDS LAID BARE FOR ALL TO CONDEMN. EVERY AUTOBOT AT RISK. I NEVER WANTED THAT, VERITY. BUT YOU DID.
YOU NEED TO PROVE—AND PROVE FAST—THAT YOU AND THIS SIDEKICK OF YOURS AREN'T IN SOME WAY RESPONSIBLE...
KZZK. THIS IS STAKEOUT. CAN YOU HEAR ME?
I MEAN, THAT GUY'S ALL ABOUT THE TIMING.
VISUAL CONTACT WITH THE PACKAGE. BUT I MIGHT NOT BE ABLE TO FOLLOW IT FURTHER.
THE CRITTER THAT TOOK THE DATA JUST DISAPPEARED WITH IT INTO THE PRIMARY CRANIAL APERTURE OF A LARGE MARINE-BASED CETACEOUS MAMMAL.
THE BUNNY WENT INSIDE A WHALE?
BIG FELLA, YEAH...
WHOA, WAIT...

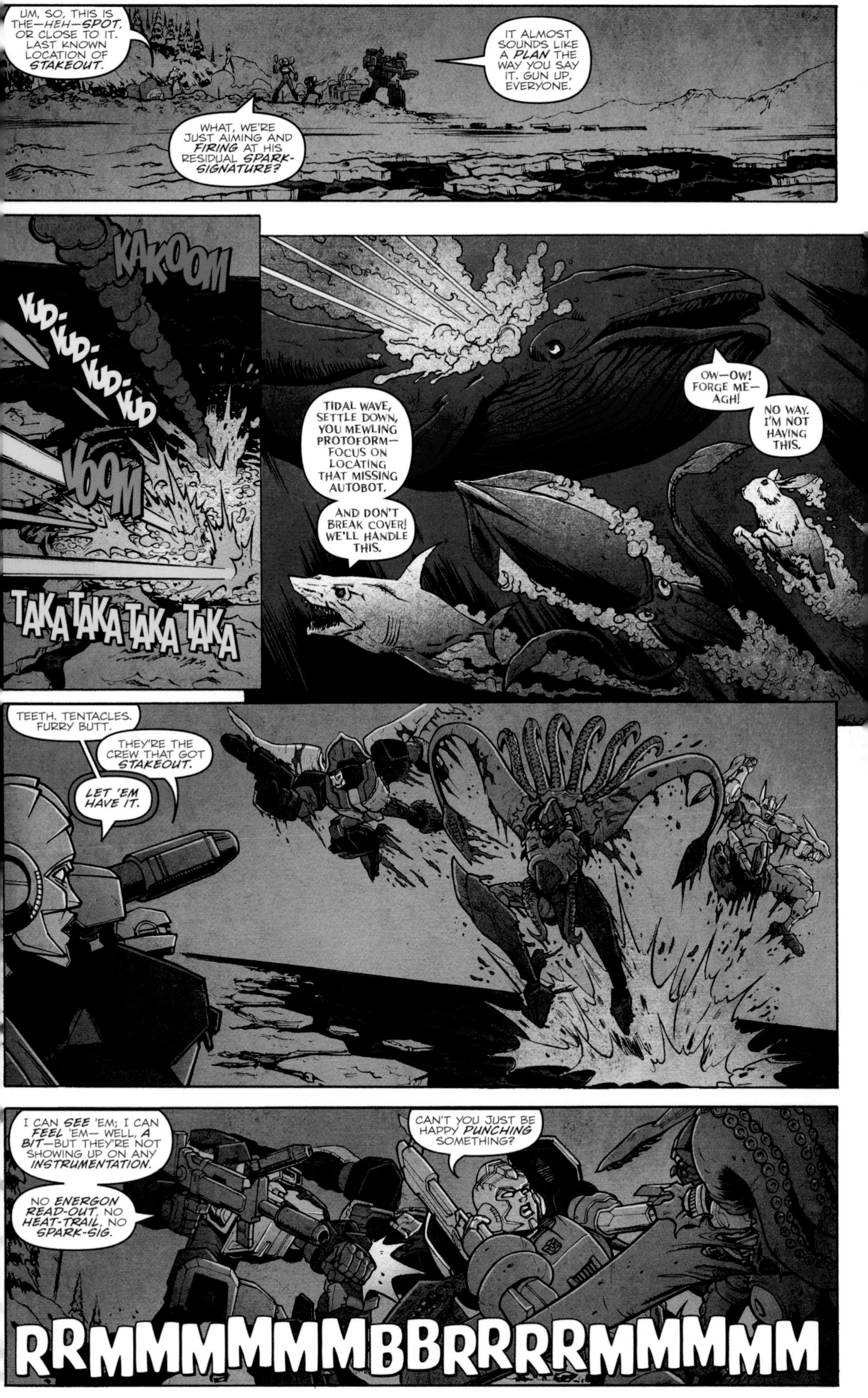

UM, SO, THIS IS THE—HEH—SPOT, OR CLOSE TO IT. LAST KNOWN LOCATION OF STAKEOUT.
WHAT, WE'RE JUST AIMING AND FIRING AT HIS RESIDUAL SPARK-SIGNATURE?
IT ALMOST SOUNDS LIKE A PLAN THE WAY YOU SAY IT. GUN UP, EVERYONE.
KAKOOM
VUD-VUD-VUD-VUD
VOOM
TAKA TAKA TAKA TAKA
TIDAL WAVE, SETTLE DOWN, YOU MEWLING PROTOFORM— FOCUS ON LOCATING THAT MISSING AUTOBOT.
AND DON'T BREAK COVER! WE'LL HANDLE THIS.
OW—OW! FORGE ME— AGH!
NO WAY. I'M NOT HAVING THIS.
TEETH. TENTACLES. FURRY BUTT.
THEY'RE THE CREW THAT GOT STAKEOUT.
LET 'EM HAVE IT.
I CAN SEE 'EM; I CAN FEEL 'EM— WELL, A BIT—BUT THEY'RE NOT SHOWING UP ON ANY INSTRUMENTATION.
NO ENERGON READ-OUT, NO HEAT-TRAIL, NO SPARK-SIG.
CAN'T YOU JUST BE HAPPY PUNCHING SOMETHING?
RRMMMMMMMBRRRRRMMMMMM

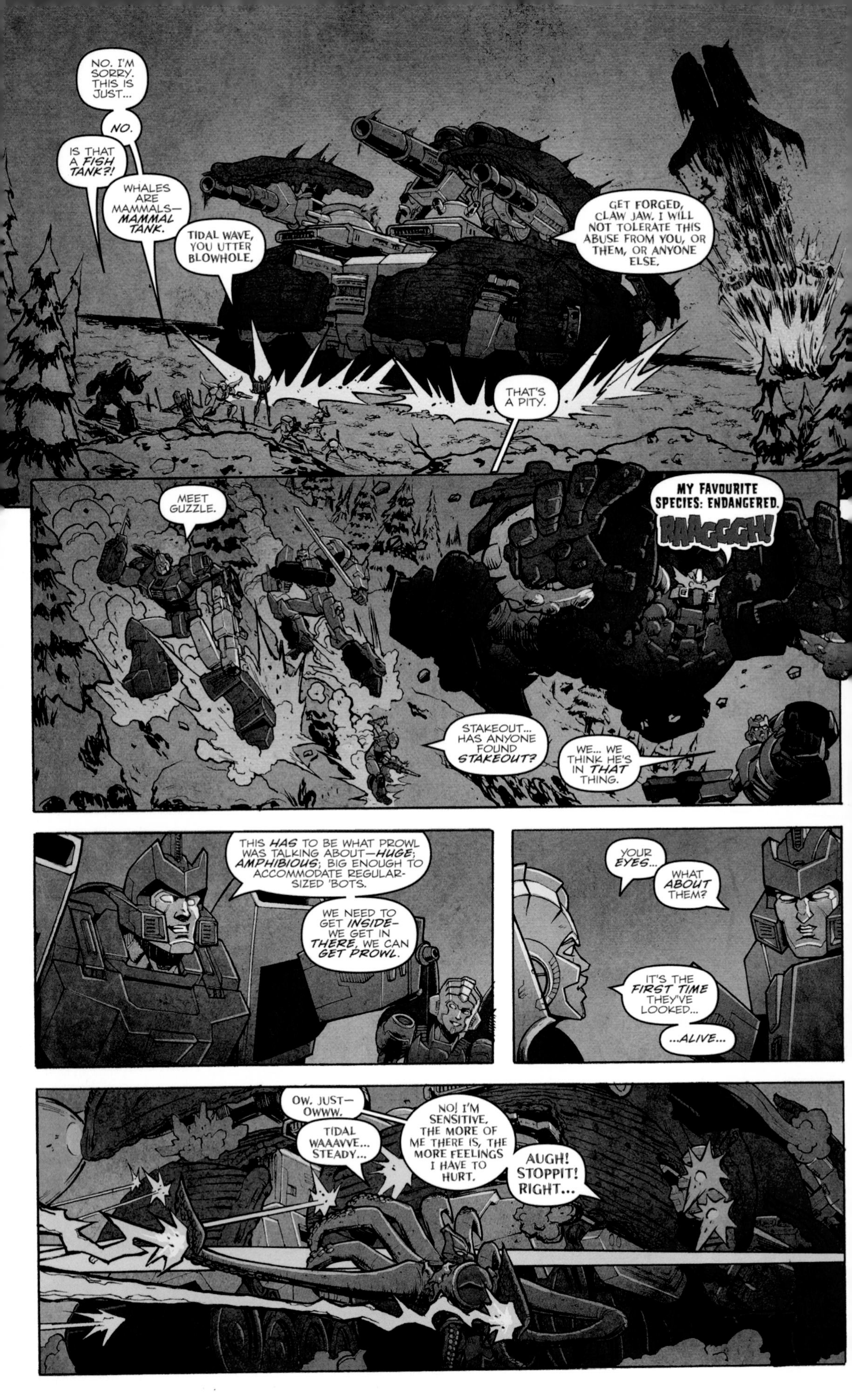
NO. I'M SORRY. THIS IS JUST...
NO.
IS THAT A FISH TANK?!
WHALES ARE MAMMALS—MAMMAL TANK.
TIDAL WAVE, YOU UTTER BLOWHOLE.
GET FORGED, CLAW JAW. I WILL NOT TOLERATE THIS ABUSE FROM YOU, OR THEM, OR ANYONE ELSE.
THAT'S A PITY.
MEET GUZZLE.
MY FAVOURITE SPECIES: ENDANGERED.
RAAGGGH!
STAKEOUT... HAS ANYONE FOUND STAKEOUT?
WE... WE THINK HE'S IN THAT THING.
THIS HAS TO BE WHAT PROWL WAS TALKING ABOUT—HUGE; AMPHIBIOUS; BIG ENOUGH TO ACCOMMODATE REGULAR-SIZED 'BOTS.
WE NEED TO GET INSIDE—WE GET IN THERE, WE CAN GET PROWL.
YOUR EYES...
WHAT ABOUT THEM?
IT'S THE FIRST TIME THEY'VE LOOKED...
...ALIVE...
OW. JUST—OWWW.
TIDAL WAAAVVE... STEADY...
NO! I'M SENSITIVE. THE MORE OF ME THERE IS, THE MORE FEELINGS I HAVE TO HURT.
AUGH! STOPPIT! RIGHT...

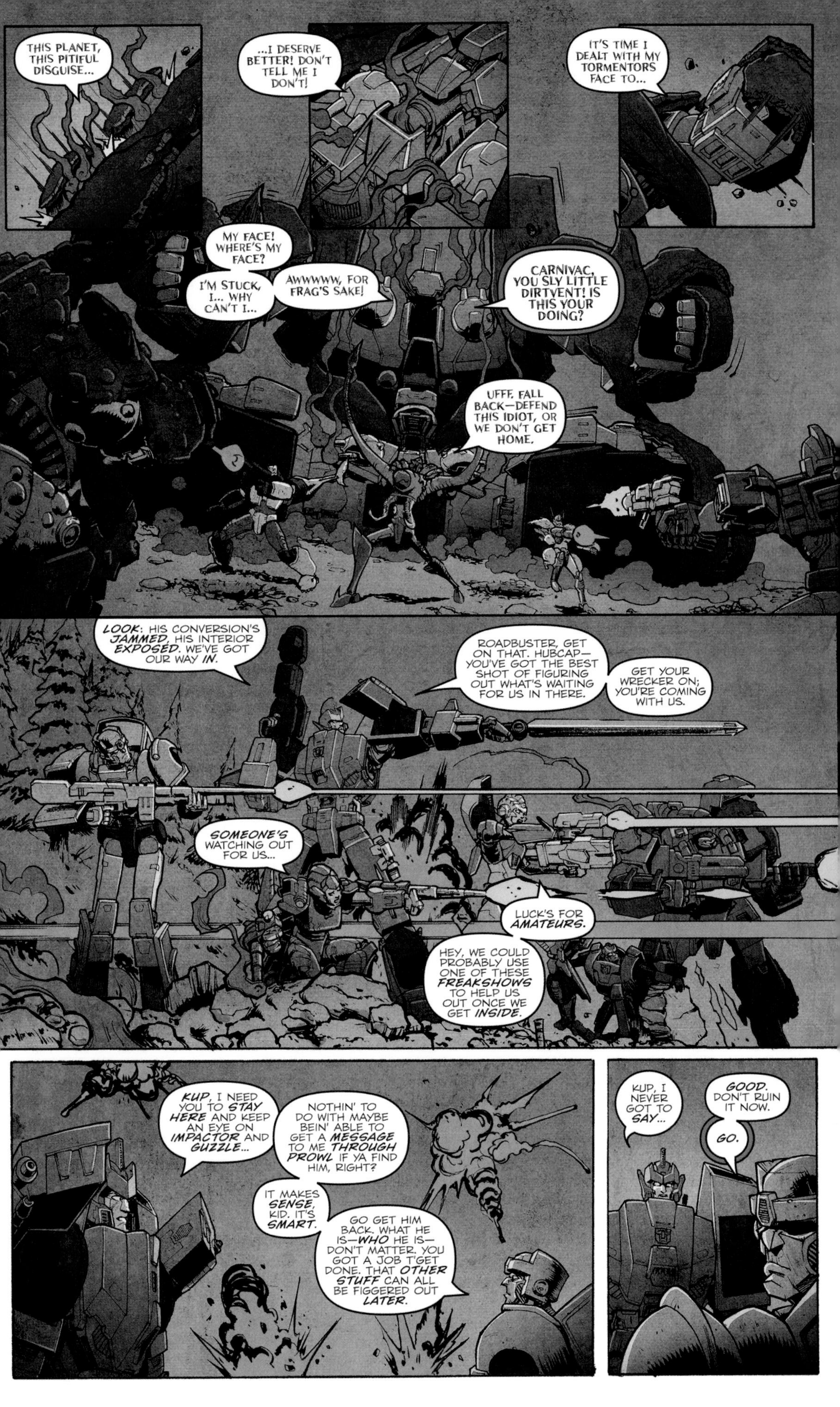
THIS PLANET, THIS PITIFUL DISGUISE...
...I DESERVE BETTER! DON'T TELL ME I DON'T!
IT'S TIME I DEALT WITH MY TORMENTORS FACE TO...
MY FACE! WHERE'S MY FACE?
I'M STUCK, I... WHY CAN'T I...
AWWWWW, FOR FRAG'S SAKE!
CARNIVAC, YOU SLY LITTLE DIRTVENT! IS THIS YOUR DOING?
UFFF. FALL BACK—DEFEND THIS IDIOT, OR WE DON'T GET HOME.
LOOK: HIS CONVERSION'S JAMMED, HIS INTERIOR EXPOSED. WE'VE GOT OUR WAY IN.
ROADBUSTER, GET ON THAT. HUBCAP—YOU'VE GOT THE BEST SHOT OF FIGURING OUT WHAT'S WAITING FOR US IN THERE.
GET YOUR WRECKER ON; YOU'RE COMING WITH US.
SOMEONE'S WATCHING OUT FOR US...
LUCK'S FOR AMATEURS.
HEY, WE COULD PROBABLY USE ONE OF THESE FREAKSHOWS TO HELP US OUT ONCE WE GET INSIDE.
KUP, I NEED YOU TO STAY HERE AND KEEP AN EYE ON IMPACTOR AND GUZZLE...
NOTHIN' TO DO WITH MAYBE BEIN' ABLE TO GET A MESSAGE TO ME THROUGH PROWL IF YA FIND HIM, RIGHT?
IT MAKES SENSE, KID. IT'S SMART.
GO GET HIM BACK. WHAT HE IS—WHO HE IS—DON'T MATTER. YOU GOT A JOB T'GET DONE. THAT OTHER STUFF CAN ALL BE FIGGERED OUT LATER.
KUP, I NEVER GOT TO SAY...
GOOD. DON'T RUIN IT NOW.
GO.

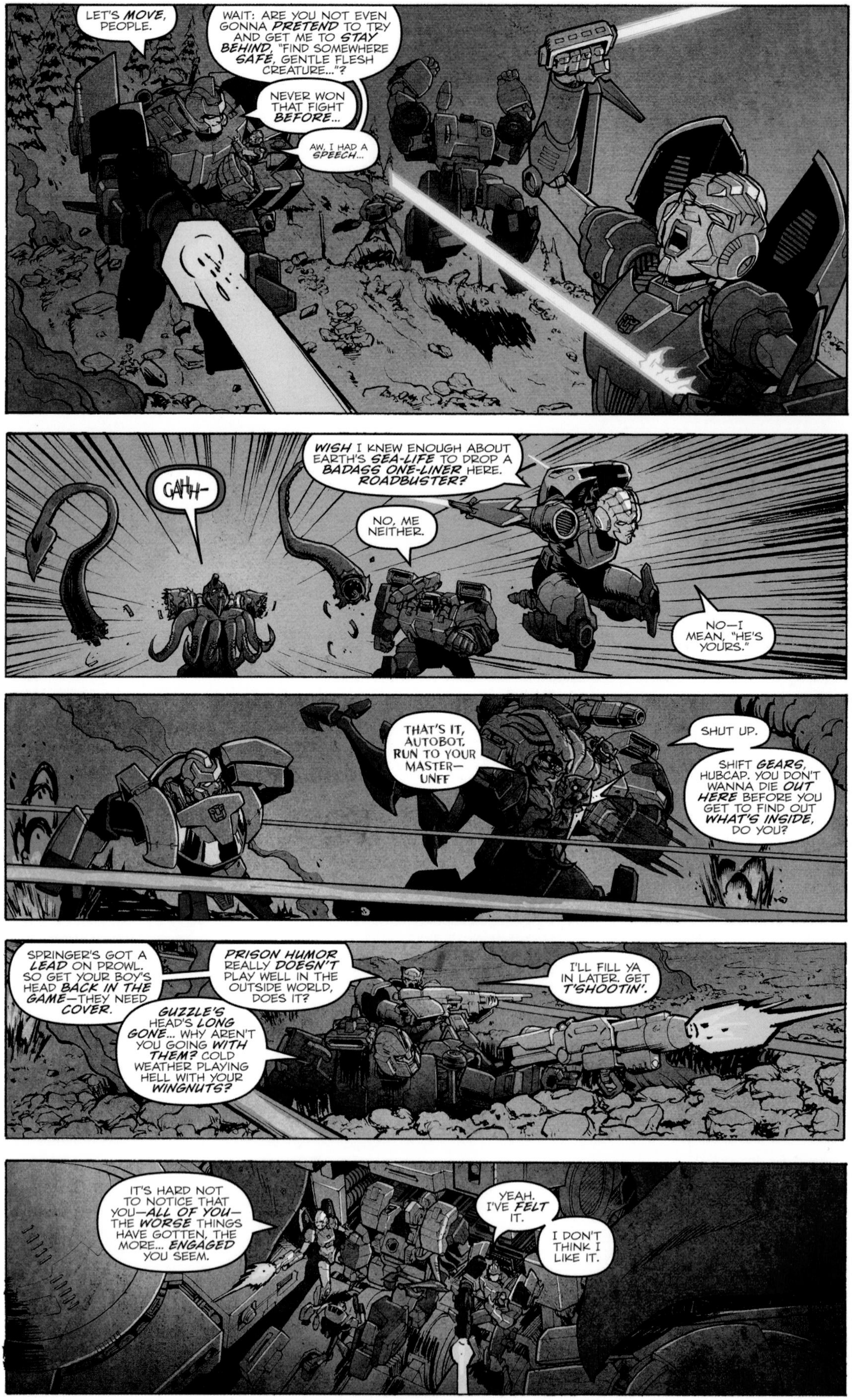
LET'S MOVE, PEOPLE.
WAIT: ARE YOU NOT EVEN GONNA PRETEND TO TRY AND GET ME TO STAY BEHIND, "FIND SOMEWHERE SAFE, GENTLE FLESH CREATURE..."?
NEVER WON THAT FIGHT BEFORE...
AW, I HAD A SPEECH...
GAHH-
WISH I KNEW ENOUGH ABOUT EARTH'S SEA-LIFE TO DROP A BADASS ONE-LINER HERE. ROADBUSTER?
NO, ME NEITHER.
NO—I MEAN, "HE'S YOURS."
THAT'S IT, AUTOBOT. RUN TO YOUR MASTER— UNFF
SHUT UP.
SHIFT GEARS, HUBCAP. YOU DON'T WANNA DIE OUT HERE BEFORE YOU GET TO FIND OUT WHAT'S INSIDE, DO YOU?
SPRINGER'S GOT A LEAD ON PROWL. SO GET YOUR BOY'S HEAD BACK IN THE GAME—THEY NEED COVER.
PRISON HUMOR REALLY DOESN'T PLAY WELL IN THE OUTSIDE WORLD, DOES IT?
I'LL FILL YA IN LATER. GET T'SHOOTIN'.
GUZZLE'S HEAD'S LONG GONE... WHY AREN'T YOU GOING WITH THEM? COLD WEATHER PLAYING HELL WITH YOUR WINGNUTS?
IT'S HARD NOT TO NOTICE THAT YOU—ALL OF YOU—THE WORSE THINGS HAVE GOTTEN, THE MORE... ENGAGED YOU SEEM.
YEAH. I'VE FELT IT.
I DON'T THINK I LIKE IT.

ROADBUSTER!

YOU *HEAR* ME, YOU LITTLE *RUST-STREAK?* TAKE *US* TO THE *NOISEMAZE.*

ROADBUSTER. *BACK OFF*—THAT'S AN *ORDER.*

GHUKK-GUKK

ARE YOU FOR *REAL?* WE'RE *THE WRECKERS*— WE'VE ALL DONE *FAR WORSE* FOR *FAR LESS.*

SO WHY NOT *STOP?* I DON'T WANT TO BELIEVE THE SAME 'BOT WHO *SAT WITH ME* FOR *FIVE YEARS* STILL DOES... *THIS.*

THE TWO THINGS AREN'T *MUTUALLY EXCLUSIVE*— THEY DON'T *CANCEL* EACH OTHER *OUT.*

LET HIM *UP,* ROADBUSTER.

SURE THING.

WHAAMMM

...THE *NOISEMAZE*... IT'S A *PLACE*... THERE'S A *GATE*...

ROADBUSTER... *DAMMIT*...

THAT YOU'LL *TAKE US* TO? *LOVELY.*

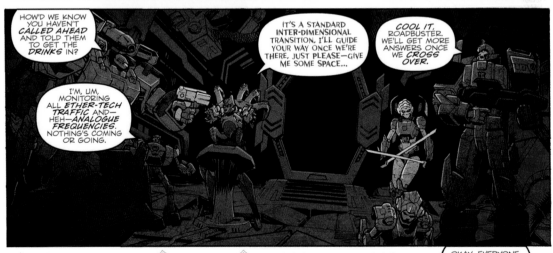

HOW'D WE *KNOW* YOU HAVEN'T *CALLED AHEAD* AND TOLD THEM TO GET THE *DRINKS IN?*

I'M, UM, MONITORING ALL *ETHER-TECH TRAFFIC* AND— HEH—*ANALOGUE FREQUENCIES.* NOTHING'S COMING OR GOING.

IT'S A STANDARD *INTER-DIMENSIONAL TRANSITION.* I'LL GUIDE YOUR WAY ONCE WE'RE THERE, JUST PLEASE— GIVE ME SOME SPACE...

COOL IT, ROADBUSTER. WE'LL GET MORE *ANSWERS* ONCE WE *CROSS OVER.*

OKAY, EVERYONE. JUST *LIE* AND TELL YOURSELVES, "HE'D DO THE *SAME* FOR *ME.*"

LET'S GO.

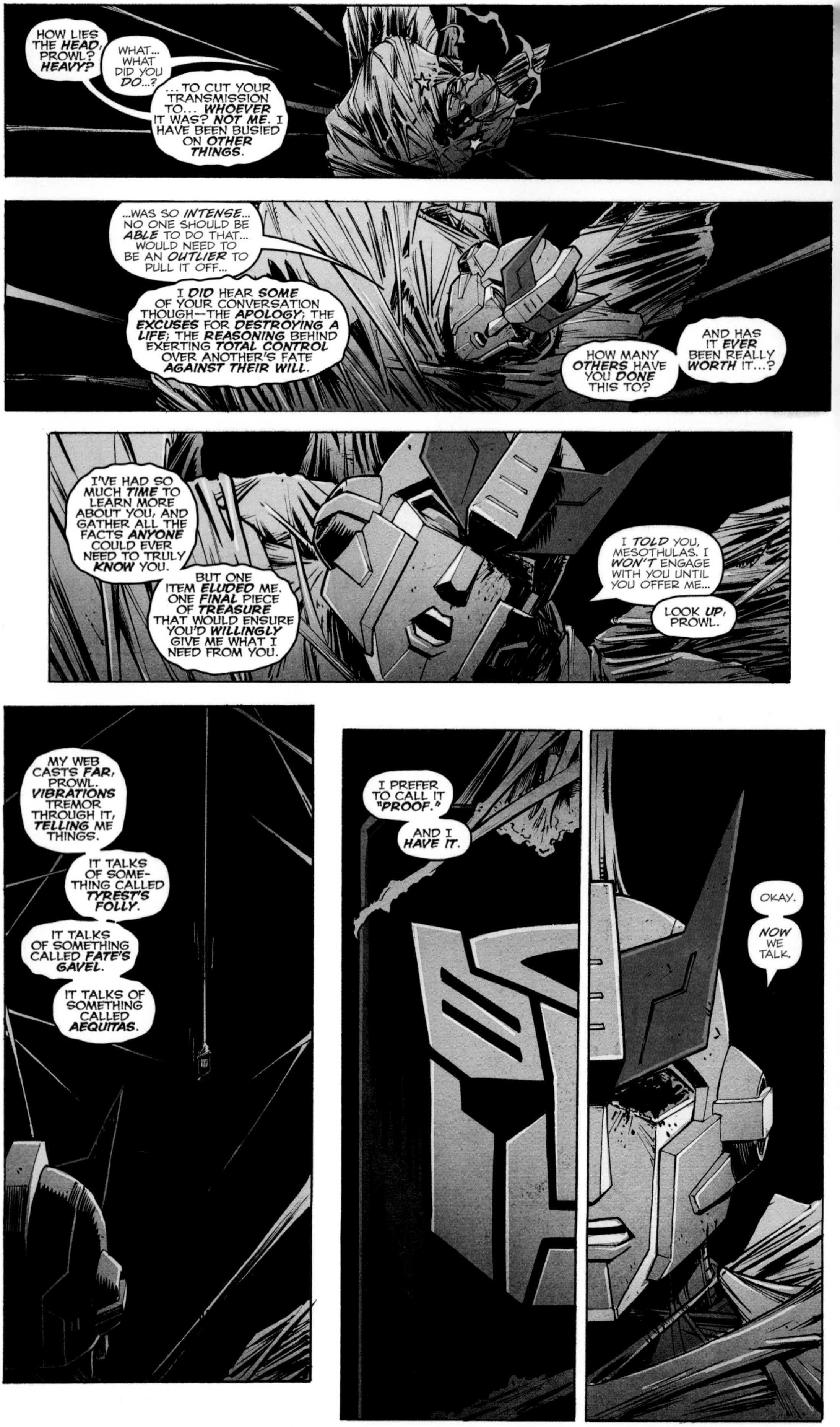
HOW LIES THE HEAD, PROWL? HEAVY?
WHAT... WHAT DID YOU DO...?
...TO CUT YOUR TRANSMISSION TO... WHOEVER IT WAS? NOT ME. I HAVE BEEN BUSIED ON OTHER THINGS.
...WAS SO INTENSE... NO ONE SHOULD BE ABLE TO DO THAT... WOULD NEED TO BE AN OUTLIER TO PULL IT OFF...
I DID HEAR SOME OF YOUR CONVERSATION THOUGH—THE APOLOGY; THE EXCUSES FOR DESTROYING A LIFE; THE REASONING BEHIND EXERTING TOTAL CONTROL OVER ANOTHER'S FATE AGAINST THEIR WILL.
HOW MANY OTHERS HAVE YOU DONE THIS TO?
AND HAS IT EVER BEEN REALLY WORTH IT...?
I'VE HAD SO MUCH TIME TO LEARN MORE ABOUT YOU, AND GATHER ALL THE FACTS ANYONE COULD EVER NEED TO TRULY KNOW YOU.
BUT ONE ITEM ELUDED ME. ONE FINAL PIECE OF TREASURE THAT WOULD ENSURE YOU'D WILLINGLY GIVE ME WHAT I NEED FROM YOU.
I TOLD YOU, MESOTHULAS. I WON'T ENGAGE WITH YOU UNTIL YOU OFFER ME...
LOOK UP, PROWL.
MY WEB CASTS FAR, PROWL. VIBRATIONS TREMOR THROUGH IT, TELLING ME THINGS.
IT TALKS OF SOME-THING CALLED TYREST'S FOLLY.
IT TALKS OF SOMETHING CALLED FATE'S GAVEL.
IT TALKS OF SOMETHING CALLED AEQUITAS.
I PREFER TO CALL IT "PROOF."
AND I HAVE IT.
OKAY.
NOW WE TALK.

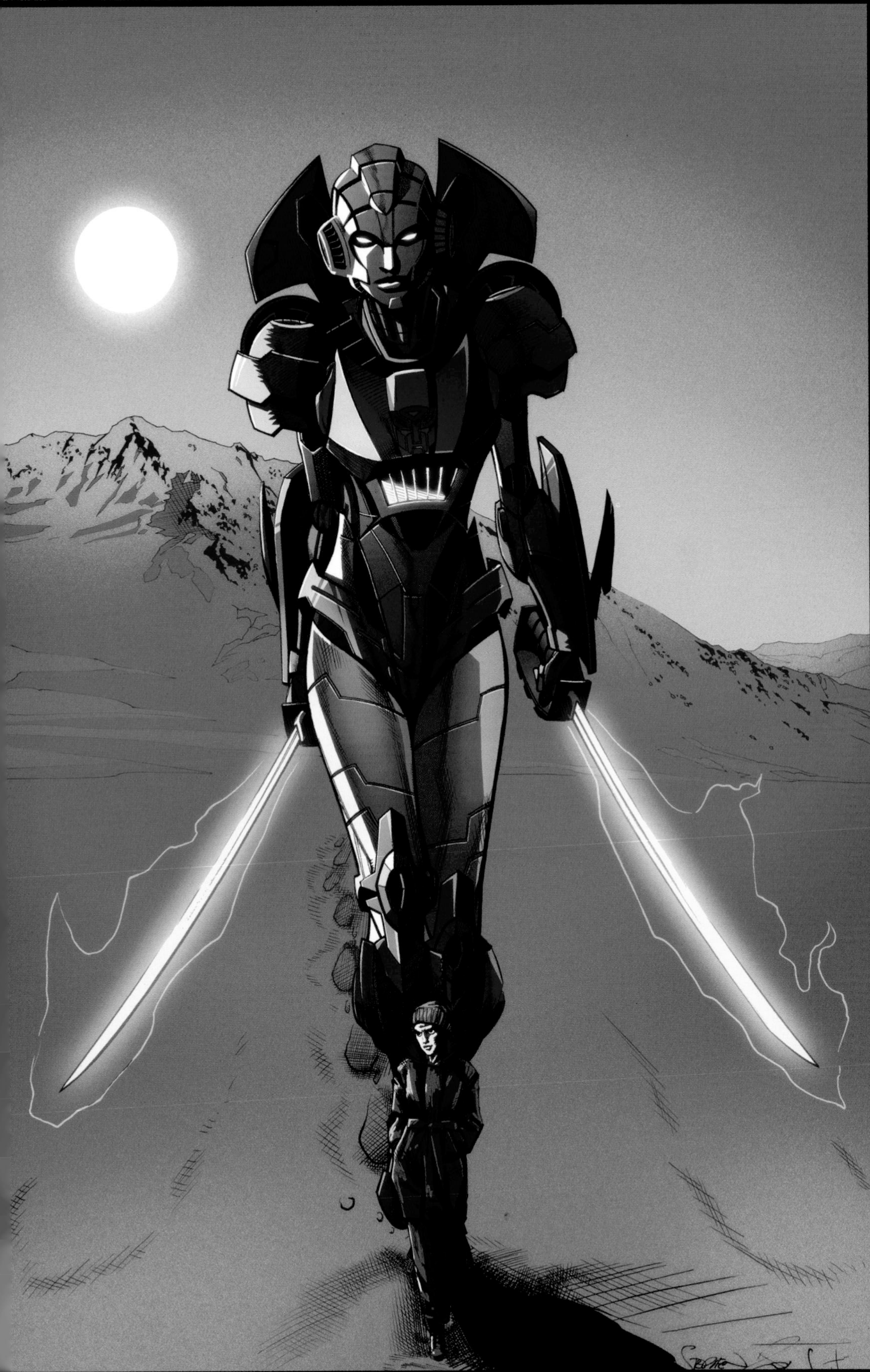

ART STEPHEN MOONEY COLORS JOSH BURCHAM

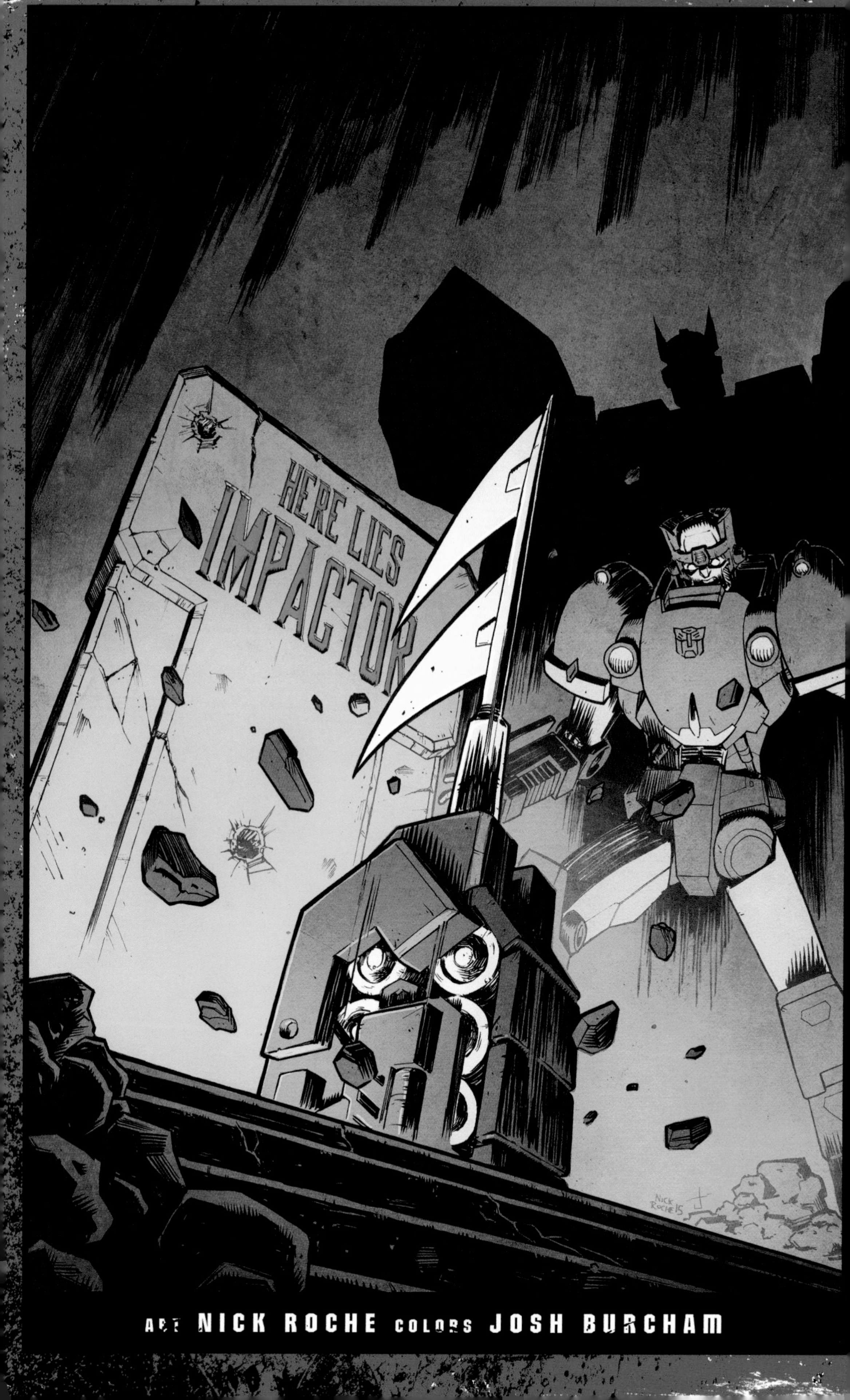

HERE LIES
IMPACTOR
NICK ROCHE 15

ART NICK ROCHE COLORS JOSH BURCHAM

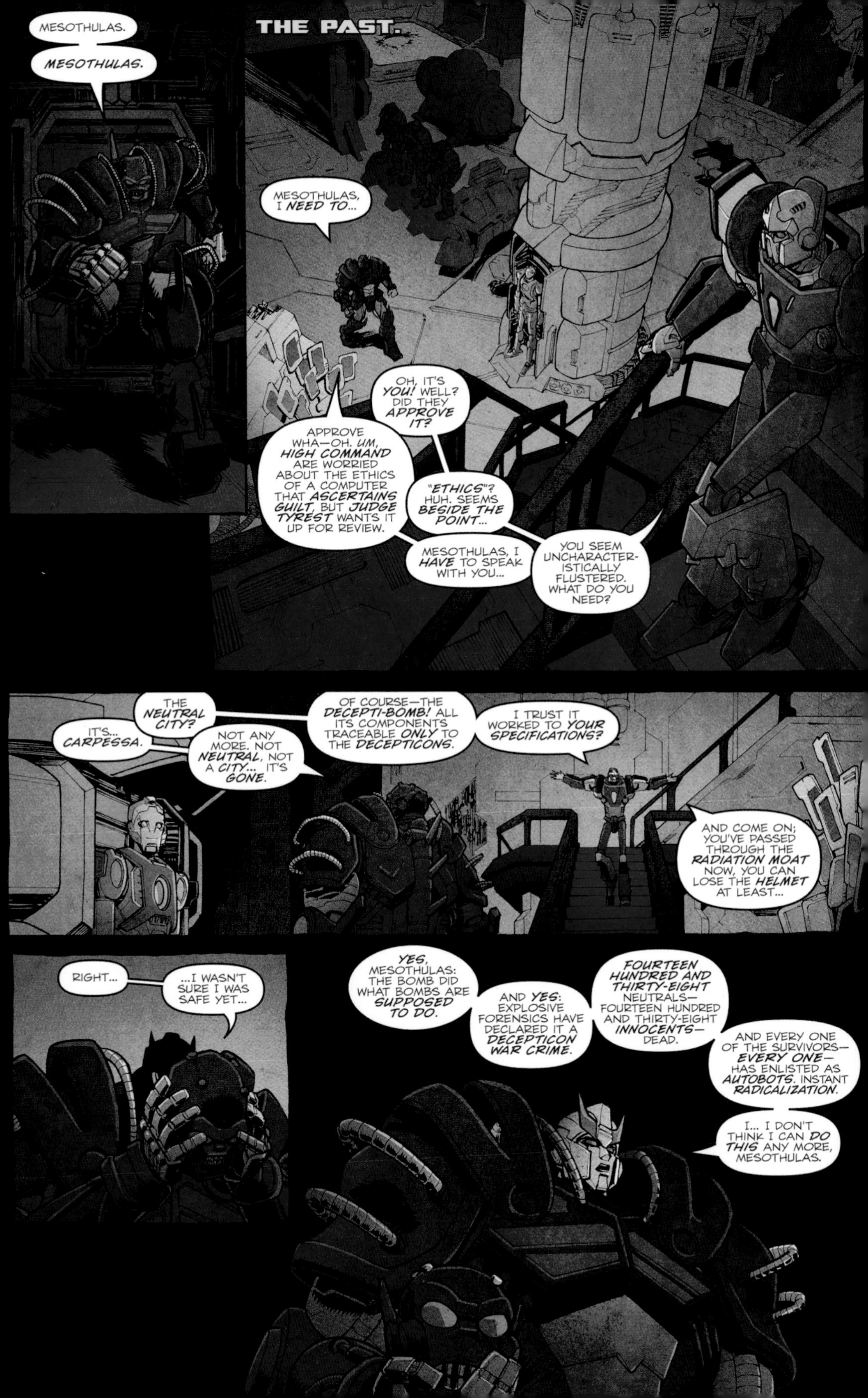
MESOTHULAS.
MESOTHULAS.
THE PAST...
MESOTHULAS, I NEED TO...
OH, IT'S YOU! WELL? DID THEY APPROVE IT?
APPROVE WHA—OH. UM, HIGH COMMAND ARE WORRIED ABOUT THE ETHICS OF A COMPUTER THAT ASCERTAINS GUILT, BUT JUDGE TYREST WANTS IT UP FOR REVIEW.
"ETHICS"? HUH. SEEMS BESIDE THE POINT...
MESOTHULAS, I HAVE TO SPEAK WITH YOU...
YOU SEEM UNCHARACTER-ISTICALLY FLUSTERED. WHAT DO YOU NEED?
IT'S... CARPESSA.
THE NEUTRAL CITY?
NOT ANY MORE. NOT NEUTRAL, NOT A CITY... IT'S GONE.
OF COURSE—THE DECEPTI-BOMB! ALL ITS COMPONENTS TRACEABLE ONLY TO THE DECEPTICONS.
I TRUST IT WORKED TO YOUR SPECIFICATIONS?
AND COME ON; YOU'VE PASSED THROUGH THE RADIATION MOAT NOW, YOU CAN LOSE THE HELMET AT LEAST...
RIGHT...
...I WASN'T SURE I WAS SAFE YET...
YES, MESOTHULAS: THE BOMB DID WHAT BOMBS ARE SUPPOSED TO DO.
AND YES: EXPLOSIVE FORENSICS HAVE DECLARED IT A DECEPTICON WAR CRIME.
FOURTEEN HUNDRED AND THIRTY-EIGHT NEUTRALS— FOURTEEN HUNDRED AND THIRTY-EIGHT INNOCENTS— DEAD.
AND EVERY ONE OF THE SURVIVORS— EVERY ONE— HAS ENLISTED AS AUTOBOTS. INSTANT RADICALIZATION.
I... I DON'T THINK I CAN DO THIS ANY MORE, MESOTHULAS.

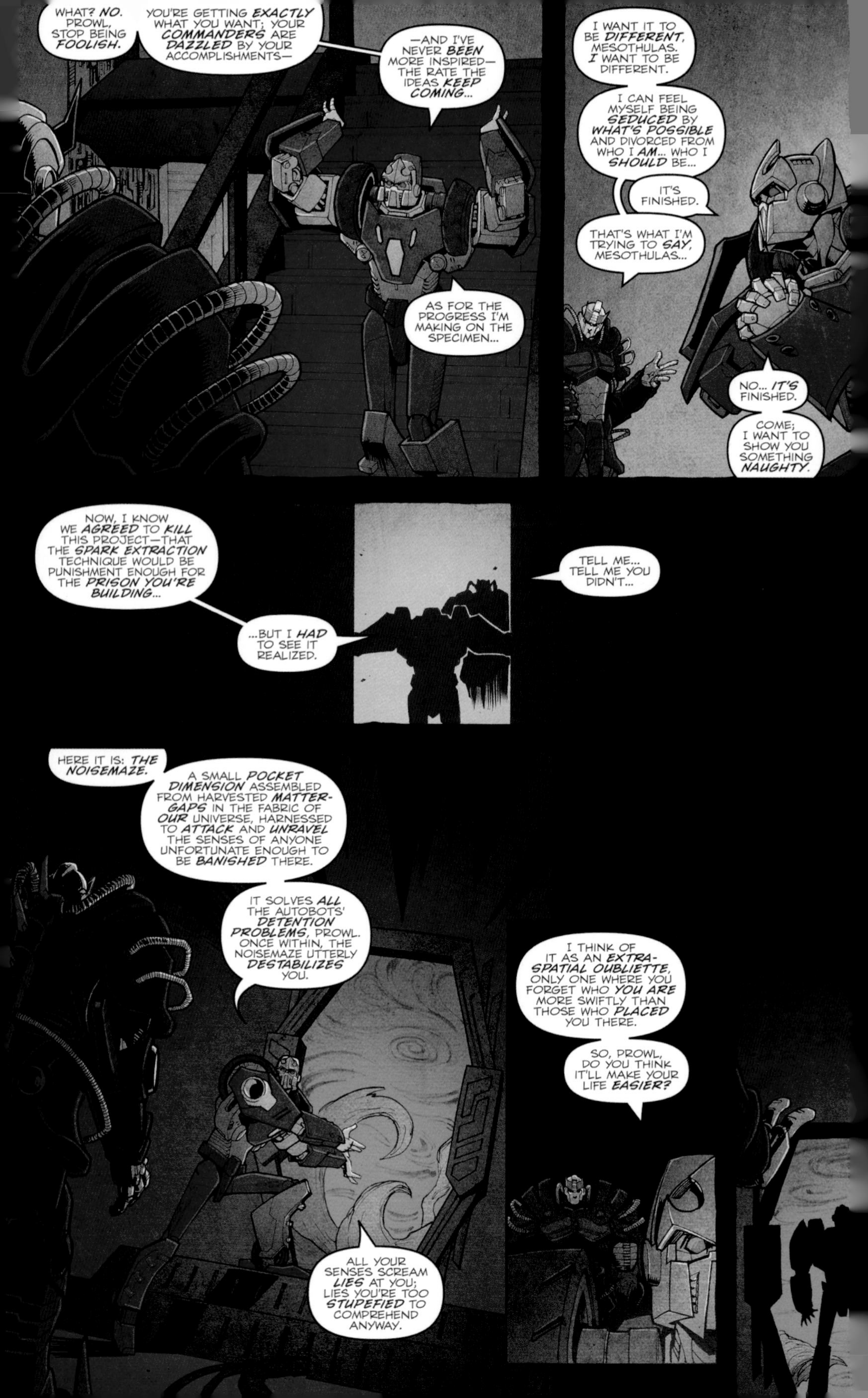
WHAT? NO. PROWL, STOP BEING FOOLISH.
YOU'RE GETTING EXACTLY WHAT YOU WANT; YOUR COMMANDERS ARE DAZZLED BY YOUR ACCOMPLISHMENTS—
—AND I'VE NEVER BEEN MORE INSPIRED—THE RATE THE IDEAS KEEP COMING...
AS FOR THE PROGRESS I'M MAKING ON THE SPECIMEN...
I WANT IT TO BE DIFFERENT, MESOTHULAS. I WANT TO BE DIFFERENT.
I CAN FEEL MYSELF BEING SEDUCED BY WHAT'S POSSIBLE AND DIVORCED FROM WHO I AM... WHO I SHOULD BE...
IT'S FINISHED.
THAT'S WHAT I'M TRYING TO SAY, MESOTHULAS...
NO... IT'S FINISHED.
COME; I WANT TO SHOW YOU SOMETHING NAUGHTY.
NOW, I KNOW WE AGREED TO KILL THIS PROJECT—THAT THE SPARK EXTRACTION TECHNIQUE WOULD BE PUNISHMENT ENOUGH FOR THE PRISON YOU'RE BUILDING...
...BUT I HAD TO SEE IT REALIZED.
TELL ME... TELL ME YOU DIDN'T...
HERE IT IS: THE NOISEMAZE.
A SMALL POCKET DIMENSION ASSEMBLED FROM HARVESTED MATTER-GAPS IN THE FABRIC OF OUR UNIVERSE, HARNESSED TO ATTACK AND UNRAVEL THE SENSES OF ANYONE UNFORTUNATE ENOUGH TO BE BANISHED THERE.
IT SOLVES ALL THE AUTOBOTS' DETENTION PROBLEMS, PROWL. ONCE WITHIN, THE NOISEMAZE UTTERLY DESTABILIZES YOU.
ALL YOUR SENSES SCREAM LIES AT YOU; LIES YOU'RE TOO STUPEFIED TO COMPREHEND ANYWAY.
I THINK OF IT AS AN EXTRA-SPATIAL OUBLIETTE, ONLY ONE WHERE YOU FORGET WHO YOU ARE MORE SWIFTLY THAN THOSE WHO PLACED YOU THERE.
SO, PROWL, DO YOU THINK IT'LL MAKE YOUR LIFE EASIER?

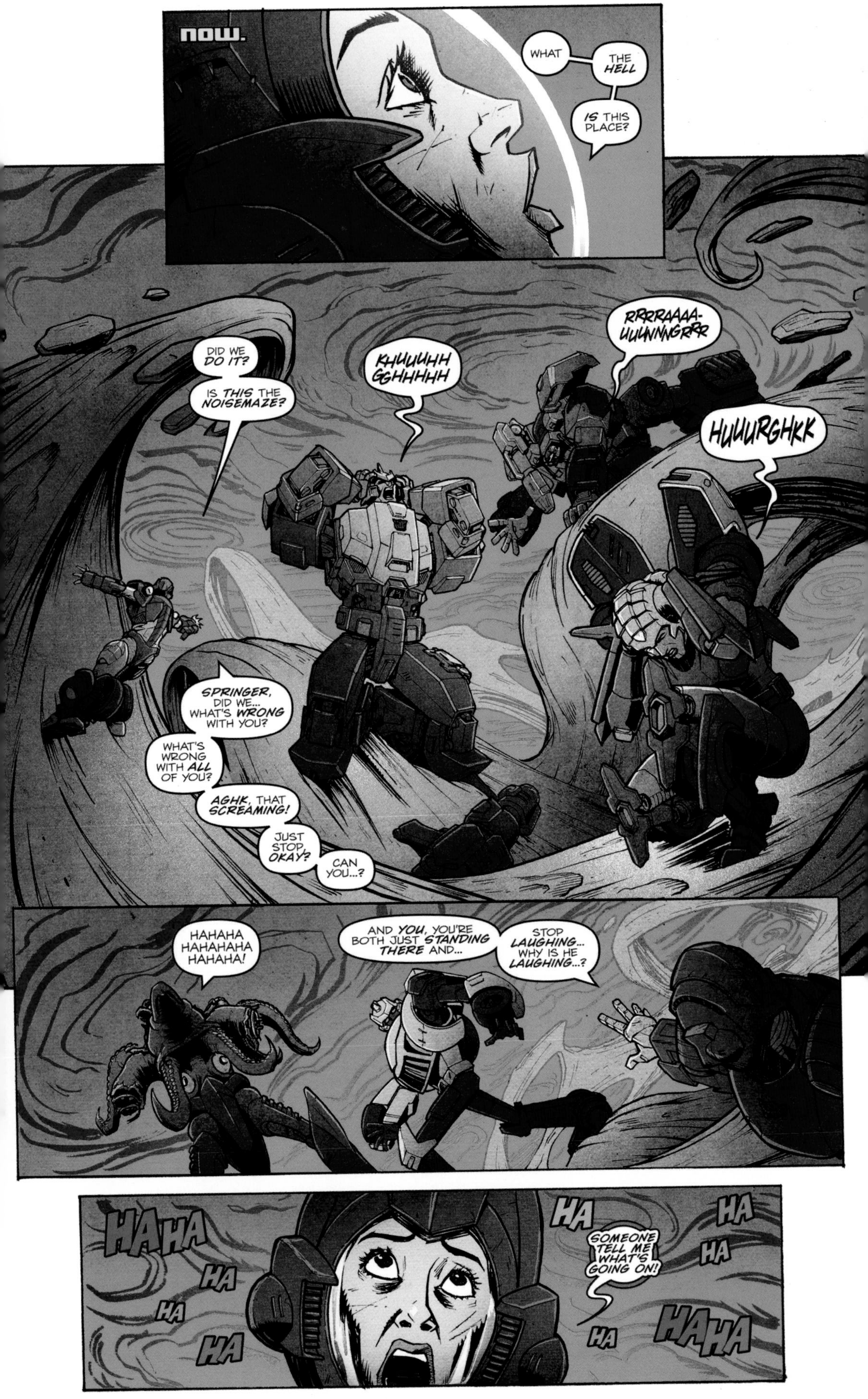
NOW.
WHAT
THE HELL
IS THIS PLACE?
DID WE DO IT?
IS THIS THE NOISEMAZE?
KHUUUHH GGHHHHH
RRRRAAAA-UUUNNNGRRR
HUUURGHKK
SPRINGER, DID WE... WHAT'S WRONG WITH YOU?
WHAT'S WRONG WITH ALL OF YOU?
AGHK, THAT SCREAMING!
JUST STOP, OKAY?
CAN YOU...?
HAHAHA HAHAHAHA HAHAHA!
AND YOU, YOU'RE BOTH JUST STANDING THERE AND...
STOP LAUGHING... WHY IS HE LAUGHING...?
HAHA
HA
HA
HA
HA
HA
HA
SOMEONE TELL ME WHAT'S GOING ON!
HA
HAHA

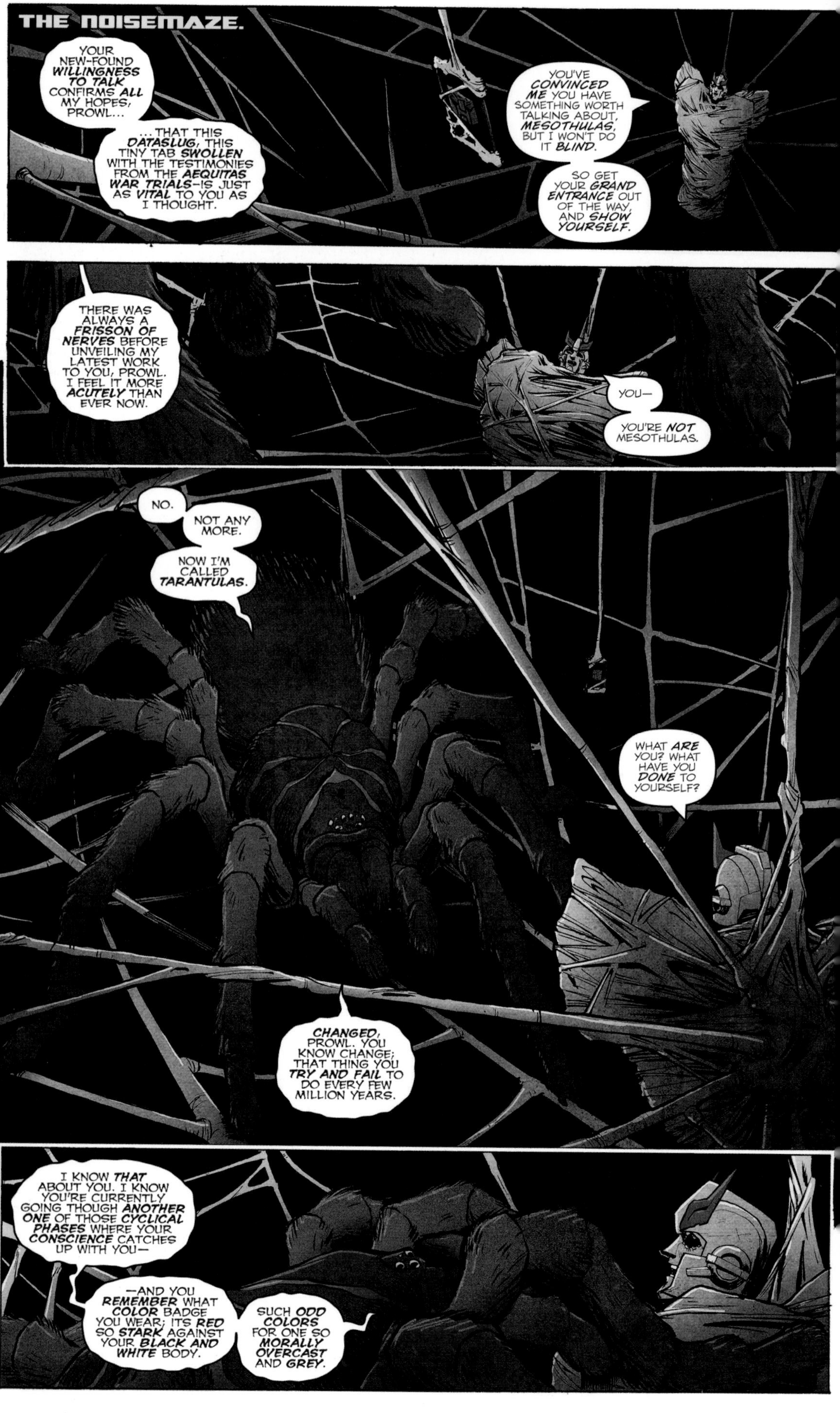
THE NOISEMAZE.
YOUR NEW-FOUND WILLINGNESS TO TALK CONFIRMS ALL MY HOPES, PROWL...
...THAT THIS DATASLUG, THIS TINY TAB SWOLLEN WITH THE TESTIMONIES FROM THE AEQUITAS WAR TRIALS--IS JUST AS VITAL TO YOU AS I THOUGHT.
YOU'VE CONVINCED ME YOU HAVE SOMETHING WORTH TALKING ABOUT, MESOTHULAS, BUT I WON'T DO IT BLIND.
SO GET YOUR GRAND ENTRANCE OUT OF THE WAY, AND SHOW YOURSELF.
THERE WAS ALWAYS A FRISSON OF NERVES BEFORE UNVEILING MY LATEST WORK TO YOU, PROWL. I FEEL IT MORE ACUTELY THAN EVER NOW.
YOU—
YOU'RE NOT MESOTHULAS.
NO.
NOT ANY MORE.
NOW I'M CALLED TARANTULAS.
WHAT ARE YOU? WHAT HAVE YOU DONE TO YOURSELF?
CHANGED, PROWL. YOU KNOW CHANGE; THAT THING YOU TRY AND FAIL TO DO EVERY FEW MILLION YEARS.
I KNOW THAT ABOUT YOU. I KNOW YOU'RE CURRENTLY GOING THOUGH ANOTHER ONE OF THOSE CYCLICAL PHASES WHERE YOUR CONSCIENCE CATCHES UP WITH YOU—
—AND YOU REMEMBER WHAT COLOR BADGE YOU WEAR; ITS RED SO STARK AGAINST YOUR BLACK AND WHITE BODY.
SUCH ODD COLORS FOR ONE SO MORALLY OVERCAST AND GREY.

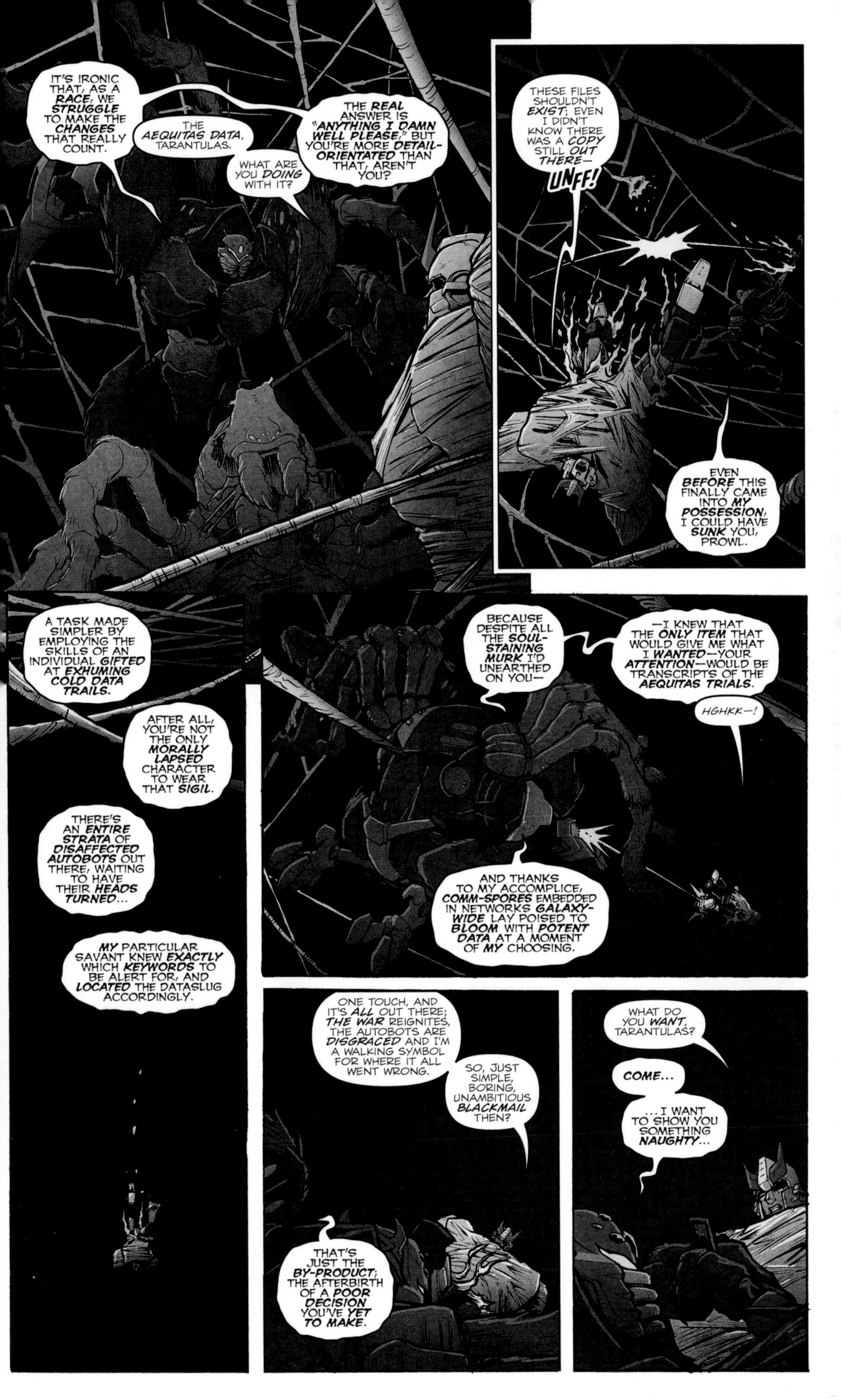
IT'S IRONIC THAT, AS A RACE, WE STRUGGLE TO MAKE THE CHANGES THAT REALLY COUNT.
THE AEQUITAS DATA, TARANTULAS.
WHAT ARE YOU DOING WITH IT?
THE REAL ANSWER IS "ANYTHING I DAMN WELL PLEASE," BUT YOU'RE MORE DETAIL-ORIENTATED THAN THAT, AREN'T YOU?
THESE FILES SHOULDN'T EXIST; EVEN I DIDN'T KNOW THERE WAS A COPY STILL OUT THERE—
UNFF!
EVEN BEFORE THIS FINALLY CAME INTO MY POSSESSION, I COULD HAVE SUNK YOU, PROWL.
A TASK MADE SIMPLER BY EMPLOYING THE SKILLS OF AN INDIVIDUAL GIFTED AT EXHUMING COLD DATA TRAILS.
AFTER ALL, YOU'RE NOT THE ONLY MORALLY LAPSED CHARACTER TO WEAR THAT SIGIL.
THERE'S AN ENTIRE STRATA OF DISAFFECTED AUTOBOTS OUT THERE, WAITING TO HAVE THEIR HEADS TURNED...
MY PARTICULAR SAVANT KNEW EXACTLY WHICH KEYWORDS TO BE ALERT FOR, AND LOCATED THE DATASLUG ACCORDINGLY.
BECAUSE DESPITE ALL THE SOUL-STAINING MURK I'D UNEARTHED ON YOU—
—I KNEW THAT THE ONLY ITEM THAT WOULD GIVE ME WHAT I WANTED—YOUR ATTENTION—WOULD BE TRANSCRIPTS OF THE AEQUITAS TRIALS.
HGHKK—!
AND THANKS TO MY ACCOMPLICE, COMM-SPORES EMBEDDED IN NETWORKS GALAXY-WIDE LAY POISED TO BLOOM WITH POTENT DATA AT A MOMENT OF MY CHOOSING.
ONE TOUCH, AND IT'S ALL OUT THERE; THE WAR REIGNITES, THE AUTOBOTS ARE DISGRACED AND I'M A WALKING SYMBOL FOR WHERE IT ALL WENT WRONG.
SO, JUST SIMPLE, BORING, UNAMBITIOUS BLACKMAIL THEN?
THAT'S JUST THE BY-PRODUCT; THE AFTERBIRTH OF A POOR DECISION YOU'VE YET TO MAKE.
WHAT DO YOU WANT, TARANTULAS?
COME...
...I WANT TO SHOW YOU SOMETHING NAUGHTY...

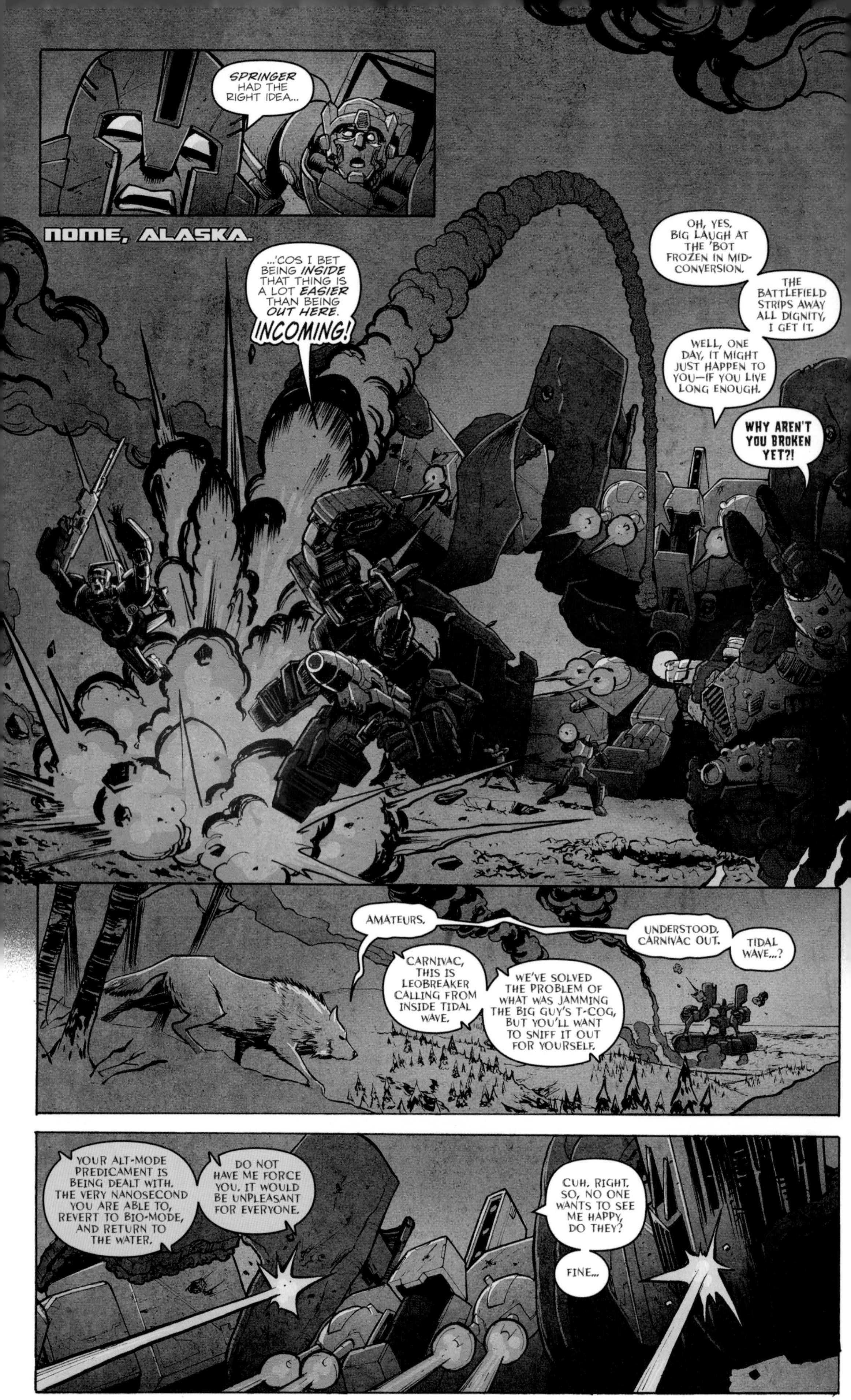
SPRINGER HAD THE RIGHT IDEA...
NOME, ALASKA.
...'COS I BET BEING INSIDE THAT THING IS A LOT EASIER THAN BEING OUT HERE.
INCOMING!
OH, YES, BIG LAUGH AT THE 'BOT FROZEN IN MID-CONVERSION.
THE BATTLEFIELD STRIPS AWAY ALL DIGNITY, I GET IT.
WELL, ONE DAY, IT MIGHT JUST HAPPEN TO YOU—IF YOU LIVE LONG ENOUGH.
WHY AREN'T YOU BROKEN YET?!
AMATEURS.
CARNIVAC, THIS IS LEOBREAKER CALLING FROM INSIDE TIDAL WAVE.
WE'VE SOLVED THE PROBLEM OF WHAT WAS JAMMING THE BIG GUY'S T-COG, BUT YOU'LL WANT TO SNIFF IT OUT FOR YOURSELF.
UNDERSTOOD. CARNIVAC OUT.
TIDAL WAVE...?
YOUR ALT-MODE PREDICAMENT IS BEING DEALT WITH. THE VERY NANOSECOND YOU ARE ABLE TO, REVERT TO BIO-MODE, AND RETURN TO THE WATER.
DO NOT HAVE ME FORCE YOU. IT WOULD BE UNPLEASANT FOR EVERYONE.
CUH, RIGHT. SO, NO ONE WANTS TO SEE ME HAPPY, DO THEY?
FINE...

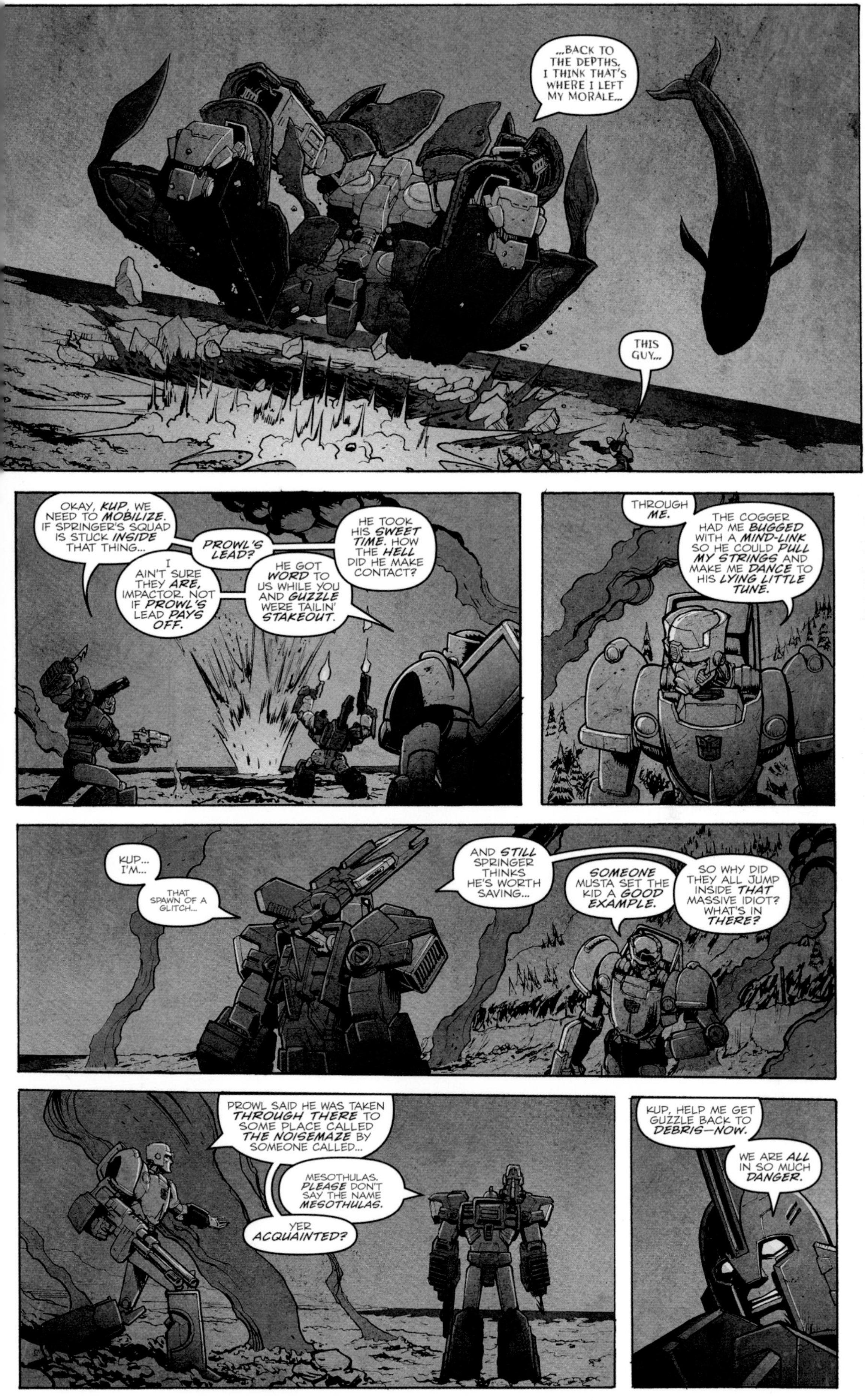
...BACK TO THE DEPTHS. I THINK THAT'S WHERE I LEFT MY MORALE...
THIS GUY...
OKAY, KUP, WE NEED TO MOBILIZE. IF SPRINGER'S SQUAD IS STUCK INSIDE THAT THING...
I AIN'T SURE THEY ARE, IMPACTOR. NOT IF PROWL'S LEAD PAYS OFF.
PROWL'S LEAD?
HE GOT WORD TO US WHILE YOU AND GUZZLE WERE TAILIN' STAKEOUT.
HE TOOK HIS SWEET TIME. HOW THE HELL DID HE MAKE CONTACT?
THROUGH ME.
THE COGGER HAD ME BUGGED WITH A MIND-LINK SO HE COULD PULL MY STRINGS AND MAKE ME DANCE TO HIS LYING LITTLE TUNE.
KUP... I'M...
THAT SPAWN OF A GLITCH...
AND STILL SPRINGER THINKS HE'S WORTH SAVING...
SOMEONE MUSTA SET THE KID A GOOD EXAMPLE.
SO WHY DID THEY ALL JUMP INSIDE THAT MASSIVE IDIOT? WHAT'S IN THERE?
PROWL SAID HE WAS TAKEN THROUGH THERE TO SOME PLACE CALLED THE NOISEMAZE BY SOMEONE CALLED...
MESOTHULAS. PLEASE DON'T SAY THE NAME MESOTHULAS.
YER ACQUAINTED?
KUP, HELP ME GET GUZZLE BACK TO DEBRIS—NOW.
WE ARE ALL IN SO MUCH DANGER.

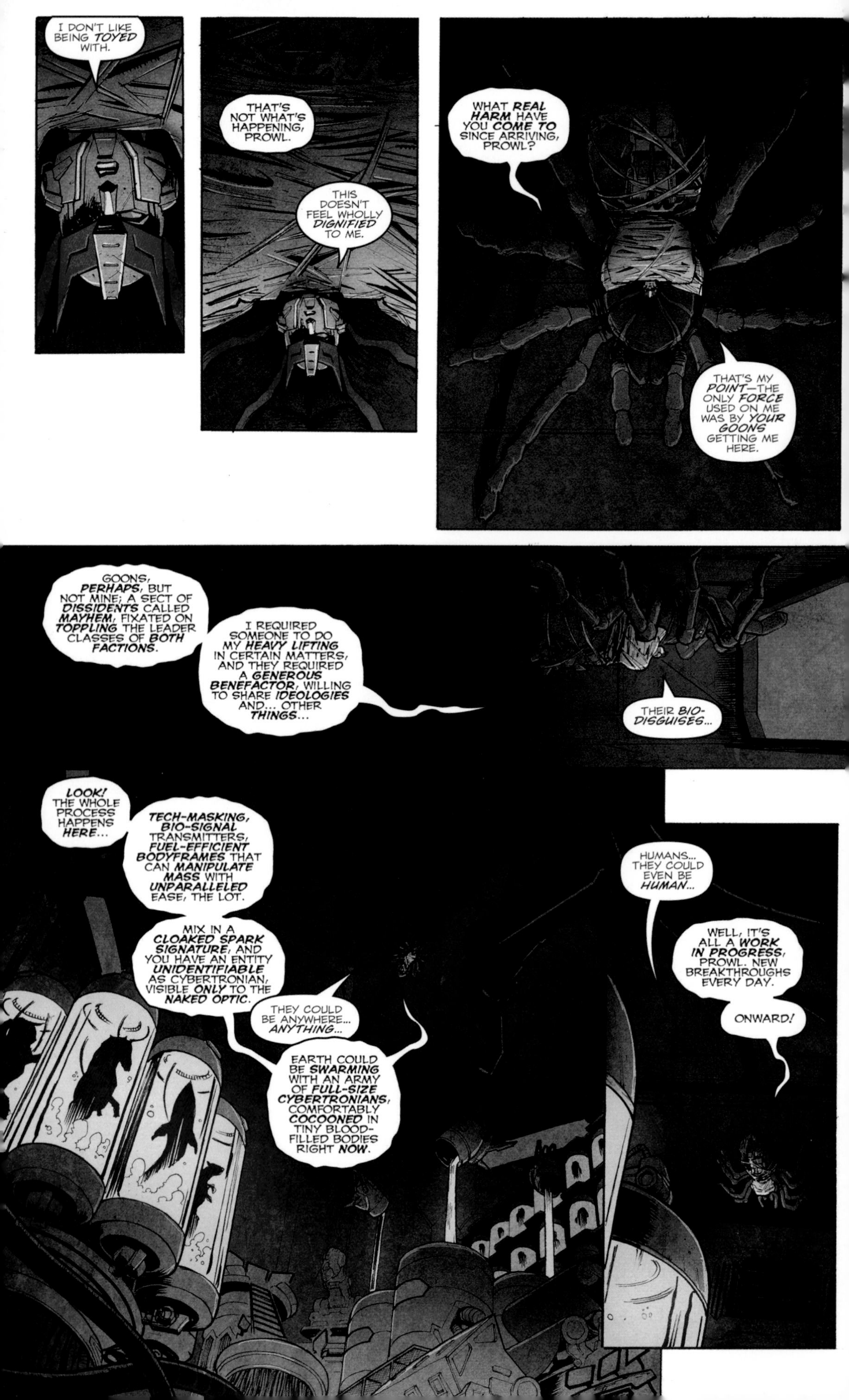
I DON'T LIKE BEING TOYED WITH.
THAT'S NOT WHAT'S HAPPENING, PROWL.
THIS DOESN'T FEEL WHOLLY DIGNIFIED TO ME.
WHAT REAL HARM HAVE YOU COME TO SINCE ARRIVING, PROWL?
THAT'S MY POINT—THE ONLY FORCE USED ON ME WAS BY YOUR GOONS GETTING ME HERE.
GOONS, PERHAPS, BUT NOT MINE; A SECT OF DISSIDENTS CALLED MAYHEM, FIXATED ON TOPPLING THE LEADER CLASSES OF BOTH FACTIONS.
I REQUIRED SOMEONE TO DO MY HEAVY LIFTING IN CERTAIN MATTERS, AND THEY REQUIRED A GENEROUS BENEFACTOR, WILLING TO SHARE IDEOLOGIES AND... OTHER THINGS...
THEIR BIO-DISGUISES...
LOOK! THE WHOLE PROCESS HAPPENS HERE...
TECH-MASKING, BIO-SIGNAL TRANSMITTERS, FUEL-EFFICIENT BODYFRAMES THAT CAN MANIPULATE MASS WITH UNPARALLELED EASE, THE LOT.
MIX IN A CLOAKED SPARK SIGNATURE, AND YOU HAVE AN ENTITY UNIDENTIFIABLE AS CYBERTRONIAN, VISIBLE ONLY TO THE NAKED OPTIC.
THEY COULD BE ANYWHERE... ANYTHING...
EARTH COULD BE SWARMING WITH AN ARMY OF FULL-SIZE CYBERTRONIANS, COMFORTABLY COCOONED IN TINY BLOOD-FILLED BODIES RIGHT NOW.
HUMANS... THEY COULD EVEN BE HUMAN...
WELL, IT'S ALL A WORK IN PROGRESS, PROWL. NEW BREAKTHROUGHS EVERY DAY.
ONWARD!

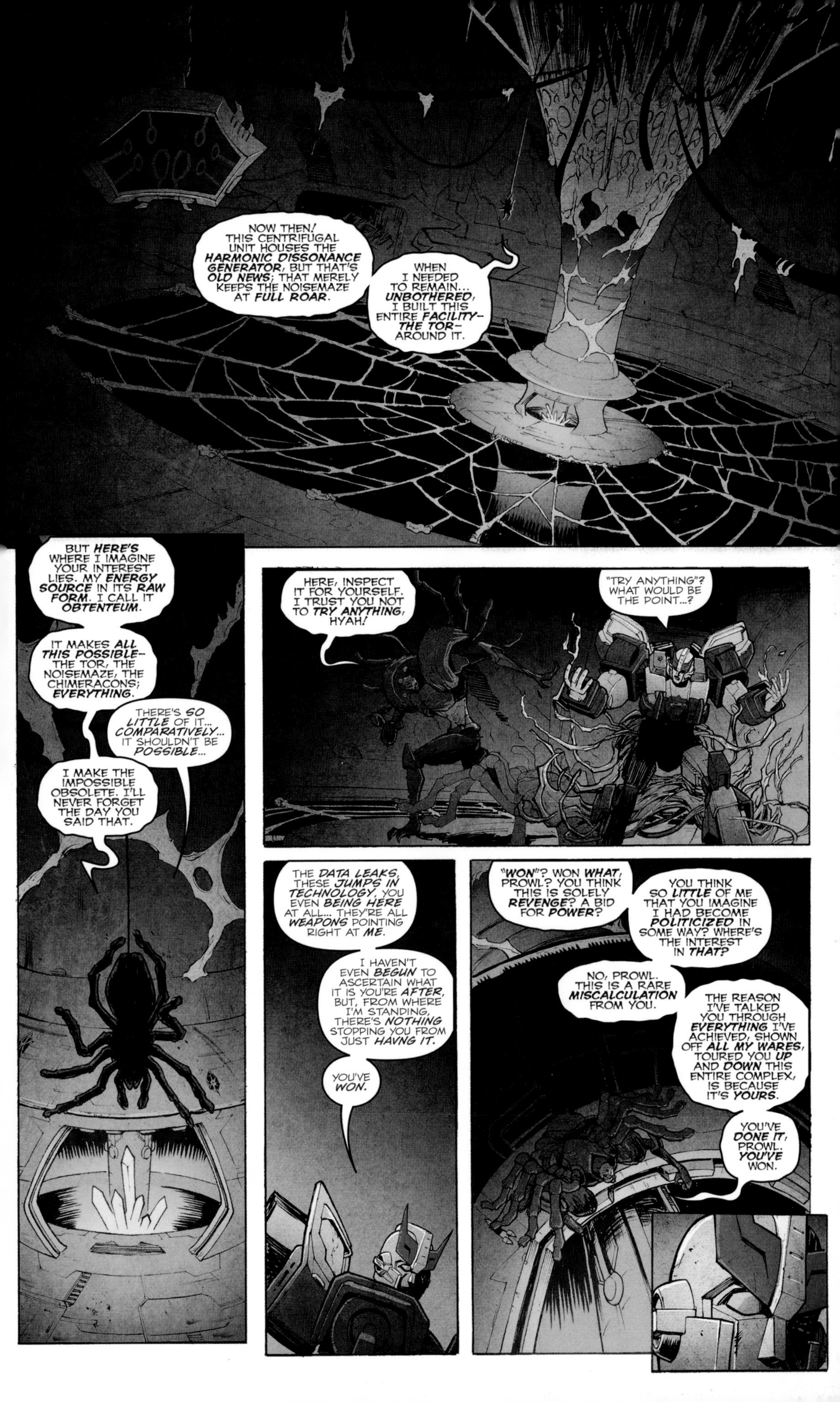
NOW THEN! THIS CENTRIFUGAL UNIT HOUSES THE HARMONIC DISSONANCE GENERATOR, BUT THAT'S OLD NEWS; THAT MERELY KEEPS THE NOISEMAZE AT FULL ROAR.
WHEN I NEEDED TO REMAIN... UNBOTHERED, I BUILT THIS ENTIRE FACILITY- THE TOR- AROUND IT.
BUT HERE'S WHERE I IMAGINE YOUR INTEREST LIES. MY ENERGY SOURCE IN ITS RAW FORM. I CALL IT OBTENTEUM.
IT MAKES ALL THIS POSSIBLE- THE TOR, THE NOISEMAZE, THE CHIMERACONS; EVERYTHING.
THERE'S SO LITTLE OF IT... COMPARATIVELY... IT SHOULDN'T BE POSSIBLE...
I MAKE THE IMPOSSIBLE OBSOLETE. I'LL NEVER FORGET THE DAY YOU SAID THAT.
HERE, INSPECT IT FOR YOURSELF. I TRUST YOU NOT TO TRY ANYTHING, HYAH!
"TRY ANYTHING"? WHAT WOULD BE THE POINT...?
THE DATA LEAKS, THESE JUMPS IN TECHNOLOGY, YOU EVEN BEING HERE AT ALL... THEY'RE ALL WEAPONS POINTING RIGHT AT ME.
I HAVEN'T EVEN BEGUN TO ASCERTAIN WHAT IT IS YOU'RE AFTER, BUT, FROM WHERE I'M STANDING, THERE'S NOTHING STOPPING YOU FROM JUST HAVING IT.
YOU'VE WON.
"WON"? WON WHAT, PROWL? YOU THINK THIS IS SOLELY REVENGE? A BID FOR POWER?
YOU THINK SO LITTLE OF ME THAT YOU IMAGINE I HAD BECOME POLITICIZED IN SOME WAY? WHERE'S THE INTEREST IN THAT?
NO, PROWL. THIS IS A RARE MISCALCULATION FROM YOU.
THE REASON I'VE TALKED YOU THROUGH EVERYTHING I'VE ACHIEVED, SHOWN OFF ALL MY WARES, TOURED YOU UP AND DOWN THIS ENTIRE COMPLEX, IS BECAUSE IT'S YOURS.
YOU'VE DONE IT, PROWL. YOU'VE WON.

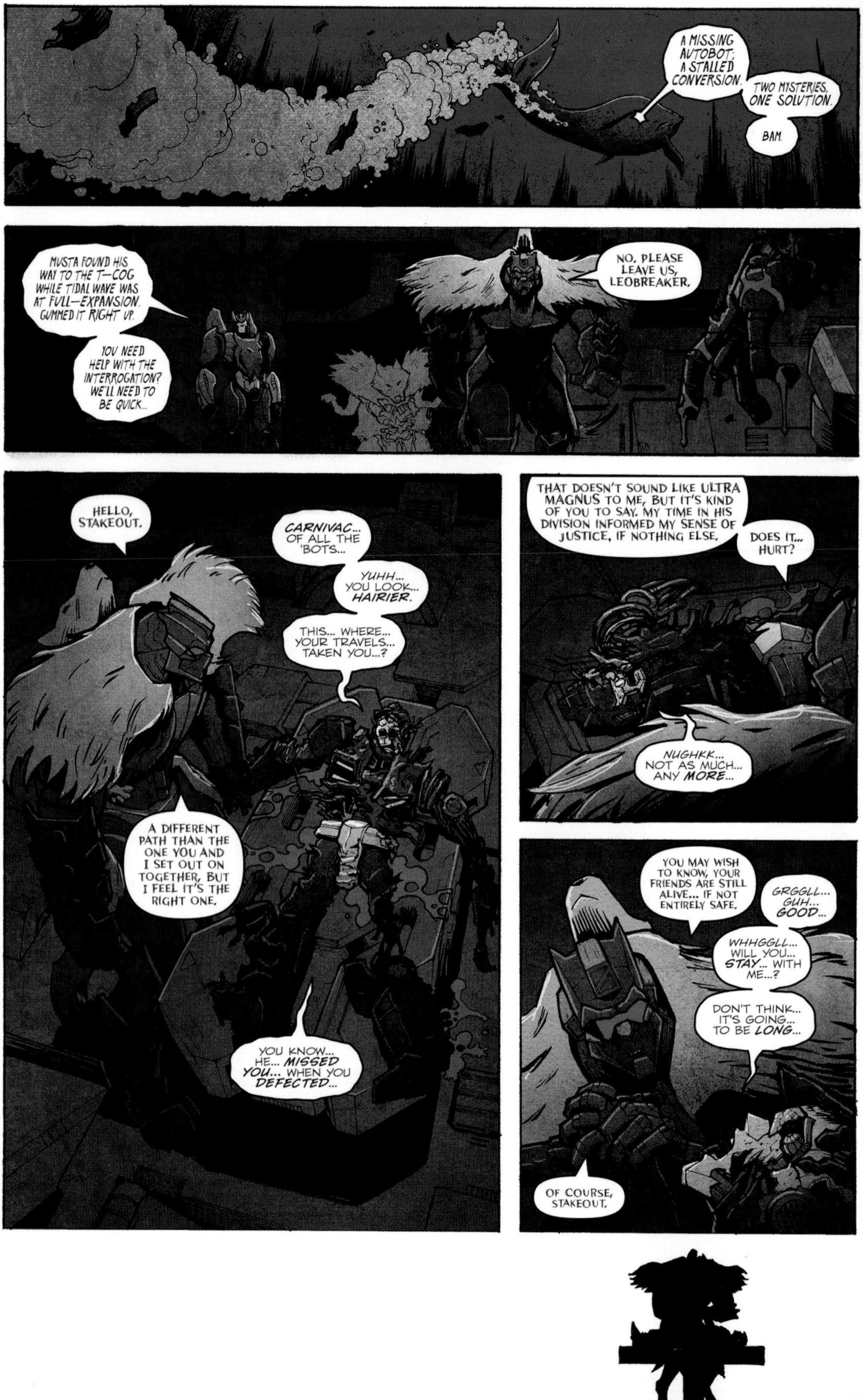
A MISSING AUTOBOT; A STALLED CONVERSION.
TWO MYSTERIES, ONE SOLUTION.
BAM.
MUSTA FOUND HIS WAY TO THE T—COG WHILE TIDAL WAVE WAS AT FULL—EXPANSION. GUMMED IT RIGHT UP.
YOU NEED HELP WITH THE INTERROGATION? WE'LL NEED TO BE QUICK...
NO, PLEASE LEAVE US, LEOBREAKER.
HELLO, STAKEOUT.
CARNIVAC... OF ALL THE 'BOTS...
YUHH... YOU LOOK... HAIRIER.
THIS... WHERE... YOUR TRAVELS... TAKEN YOU...?
A DIFFERENT PATH THAN THE ONE YOU AND I SET OUT ON TOGETHER, BUT I FEEL IT'S THE RIGHT ONE.
YOU KNOW... HE... MISSED YOU... WHEN YOU DEFECTED...
THAT DOESN'T SOUND LIKE ULTRA MAGNUS TO ME, BUT IT'S KIND OF YOU TO SAY. MY TIME IN HIS DIVISION INFORMED MY SENSE OF JUSTICE, IF NOTHING ELSE.
DOES IT... HURT?
NUGHKK... NOT AS MUCH... ANY MORE...
YOU MAY WISH TO KNOW, YOUR FRIENDS ARE STILL ALIVE... IF NOT ENTIRELY SAFE.
GRGGLL... GUH... GOOD...
WHHGGLL... WILL YOU... STAY... WITH ME...?
DON'T THINK... IT'S GOING... TO BE LONG...
OF COURSE, STAKEOUT.

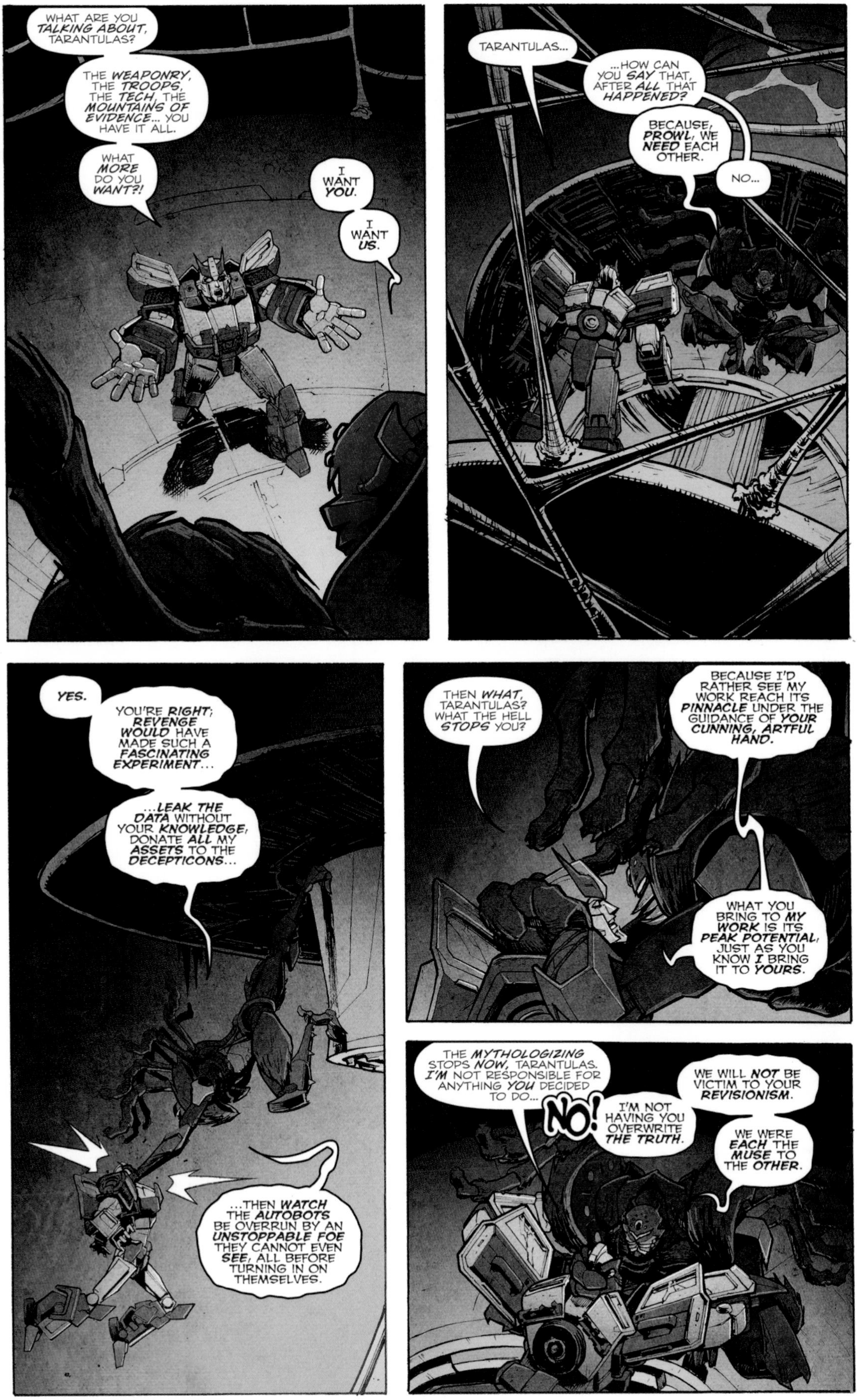
WHAT ARE YOU TALKING ABOUT, TARANTULAS?
THE WEAPONRY, THE TROOPS, THE TECH, THE MOUNTAINS OF EVIDENCE... YOU HAVE IT ALL.
WHAT MORE DO YOU WANT?!
I WANT YOU.
I WANT US.
TARANTULAS...
...HOW CAN YOU SAY THAT, AFTER ALL THAT HAPPENED?
BECAUSE, PROWL, WE NEED EACH OTHER.
NO...
YES.
YOU'RE RIGHT; REVENGE WOULD HAVE MADE SUCH A FASCINATING EXPERIMENT...
...LEAK THE DATA WITHOUT YOUR KNOWLEDGE, DONATE ALL MY ASSETS TO THE DECEPTICONS...
...THEN WATCH THE AUTOBOTS BE OVERRUN BY AN UNSTOPPABLE FOE THEY CANNOT EVEN SEE, ALL BEFORE TURNING IN ON THEMSELVES.
THEN WHAT, TARANTULAS? WHAT THE HELL STOPS YOU?
BECAUSE I'D RATHER SEE MY WORK REACH ITS PINNACLE UNDER THE GUIDANCE OF YOUR CUNNING, ARTFUL HAND.
WHAT YOU BRING TO MY WORK IS ITS PEAK POTENTIAL, JUST AS YOU KNOW I BRING IT TO YOURS.
THE MYTHOLOGIZING STOPS NOW, TARANTULAS. I'M NOT RESPONSIBLE FOR ANYTHING YOU DECIDED TO DO...
WE WILL NOT BE VICTIM TO YOUR REVISIONISM.
NO!
I'M NOT HAVING YOU OVERWRITE THE TRUTH.
WE WERE EACH THE MUSE TO THE OTHER.

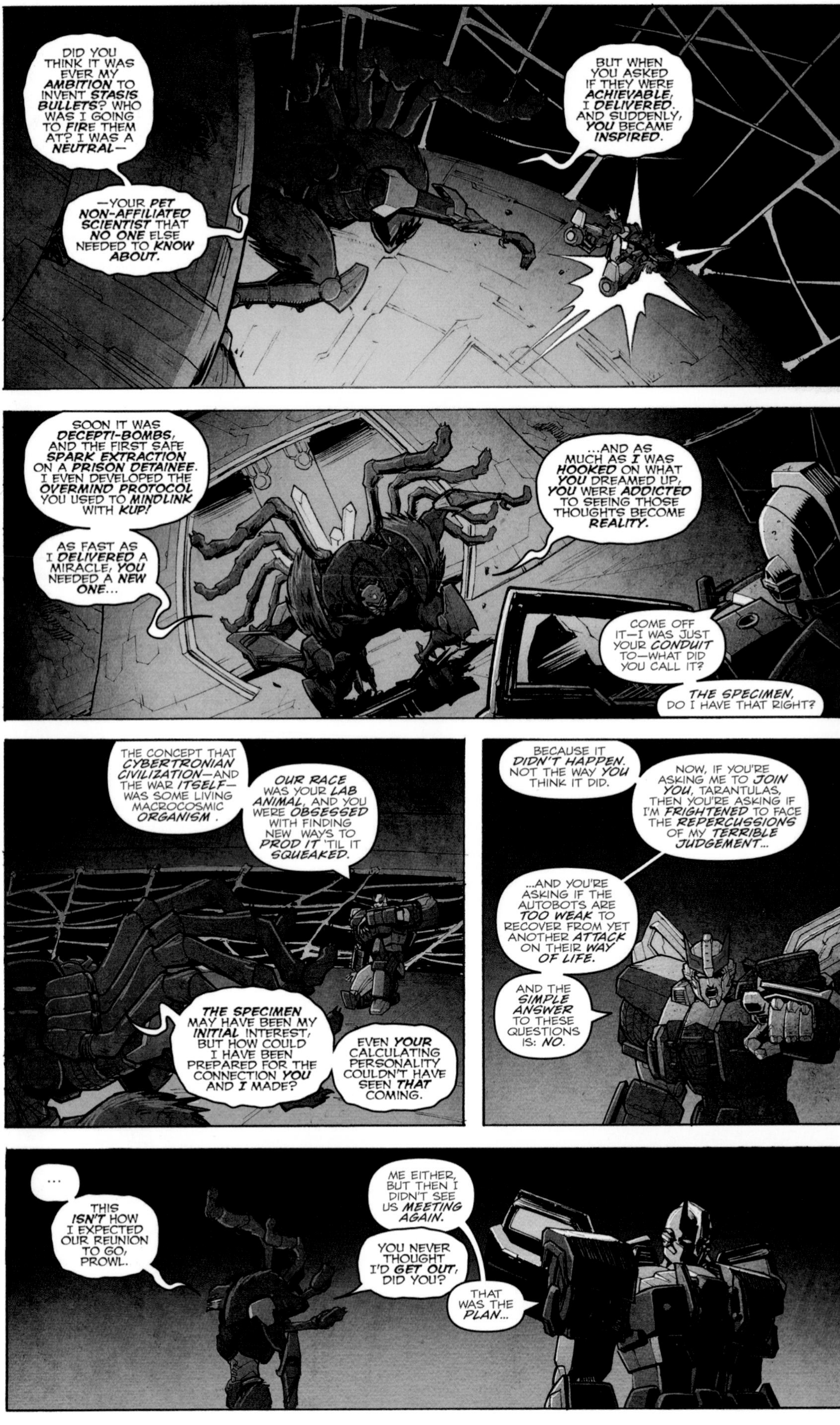
DID YOU THINK IT WAS EVER MY AMBITION TO INVENT STASIS BULLETS? WHO WAS I GOING TO FIRE THEM AT? I WAS A NEUTRAL—
—YOUR PET NON-AFFILIATED SCIENTIST THAT NO ONE ELSE NEEDED TO KNOW ABOUT.
BUT WHEN YOU ASKED IF THEY WERE ACHIEVABLE, I DELIVERED. AND SUDDENLY, YOU BECAME INSPIRED.
SOON IT WAS DECEPTI-BOMBS, AND THE FIRST SAFE SPARK EXTRACTION ON A PRISON DETAINEE. I EVEN DEVELOPED THE OVERMIND PROTOCOL YOU USED TO MINDLINK WITH KUP!
AS FAST AS I DELIVERED A MIRACLE, YOU NEEDED A NEW ONE...
...AND AS MUCH AS I WAS HOOKED ON WHAT YOU DREAMED UP, YOU WERE ADDICTED TO SEEING THOSE THOUGHTS BECOME REALITY.
COME OFF IT—I WAS JUST YOUR CONDUIT TO—WHAT DID YOU CALL IT?
THE SPECIMEN, DO I HAVE THAT RIGHT?
THE CONCEPT THAT CYBERTRONIAN CIVILIZATION—AND THE WAR ITSELF—WAS SOME LIVING MACROCOSMIC ORGANISM.
OUR RACE WAS YOUR LAB ANIMAL, AND YOU WERE OBSESSED WITH FINDING NEW WAYS TO PROD IT 'TIL IT SQUEAKED.
THE SPECIMEN MAY HAVE BEEN MY INITIAL INTEREST, BUT HOW COULD I HAVE BEEN PREPARED FOR THE CONNECTION YOU AND I MADE?
EVEN YOUR CALCULATING PERSONALITY COULDN'T HAVE SEEN THAT COMING.
BECAUSE IT DIDN'T HAPPEN. NOT THE WAY YOU THINK IT DID.
NOW, IF YOU'RE ASKING ME TO JOIN YOU, TARANTULAS, THEN YOU'RE ASKING IF I'M FRIGHTENED TO FACE THE REPERCUSSIONS OF MY TERRIBLE JUDGEMENT...
...AND YOU'RE ASKING IF THE AUTOBOTS ARE TOO WEAK TO RECOVER FROM YET ANOTHER ATTACK ON THEIR WAY OF LIFE.
AND THE SIMPLE ANSWER TO THESE QUESTIONS IS: NO.
...
THIS ISN'T HOW I EXPECTED OUR REUNION TO GO, PROWL.
ME EITHER, BUT THEN I DIDN'T SEE US MEETING AGAIN.
YOU NEVER THOUGHT I'D GET OUT, DID YOU?
THAT WAS THE PLAN...

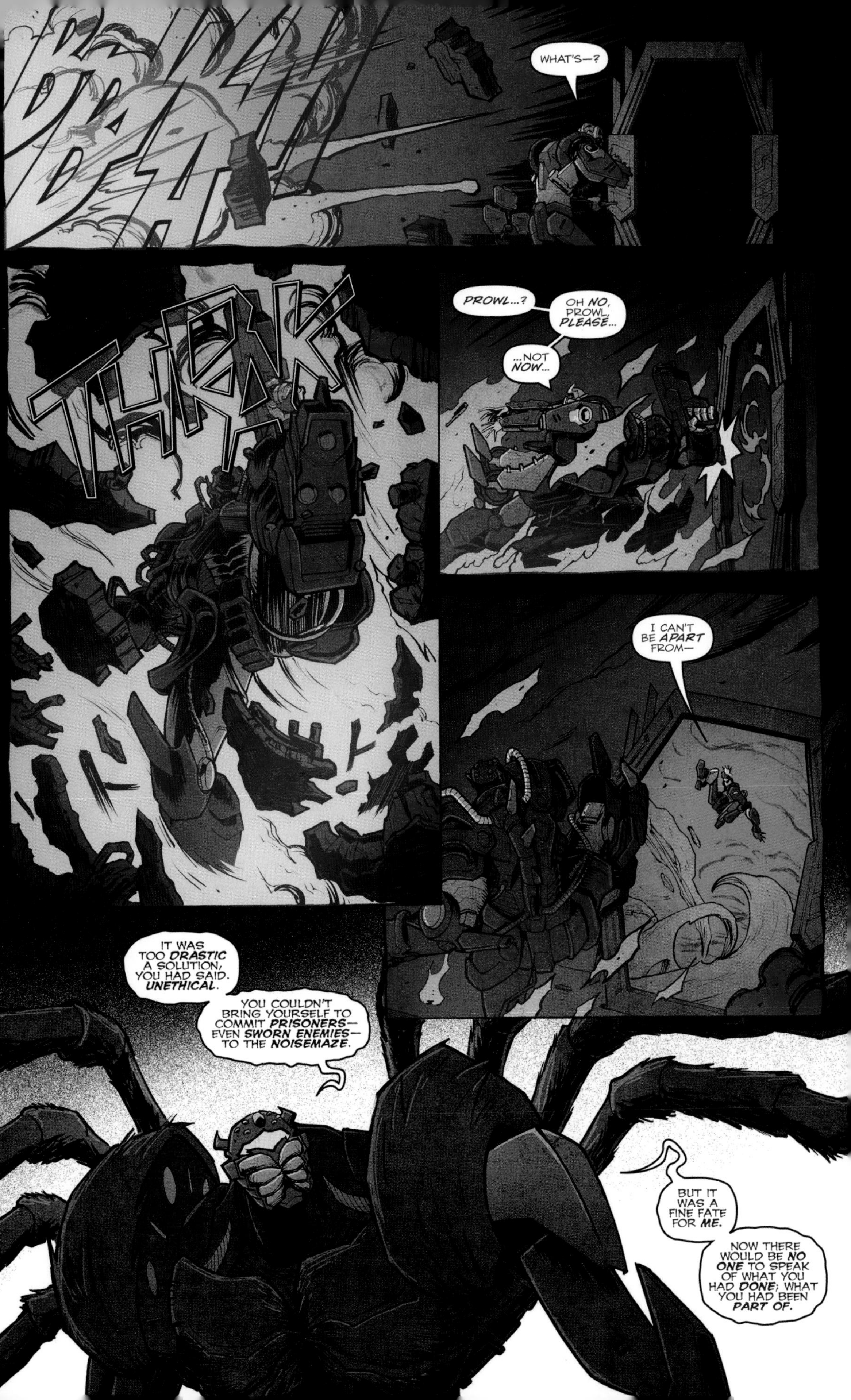
WHAT'S—?
THRAK!
PROWL...?
OH NO, PROWL, PLEASE...
...NOT NOW...
I CAN'T BE APART FROM—
IT WAS TOO DRASTIC A SOLUTION, YOU HAD SAID. UNETHICAL.
YOU COULDN'T BRING YOURSELF TO COMMIT PRISONERS— EVEN SWORN ENEMIES— TO THE NOISEMAZE.
BUT IT WAS A FINE FATE FOR ME.
NOW THERE WOULD BE NO ONE TO SPEAK OF WHAT YOU HAD DONE; WHAT YOU HAD BEEN PART OF.

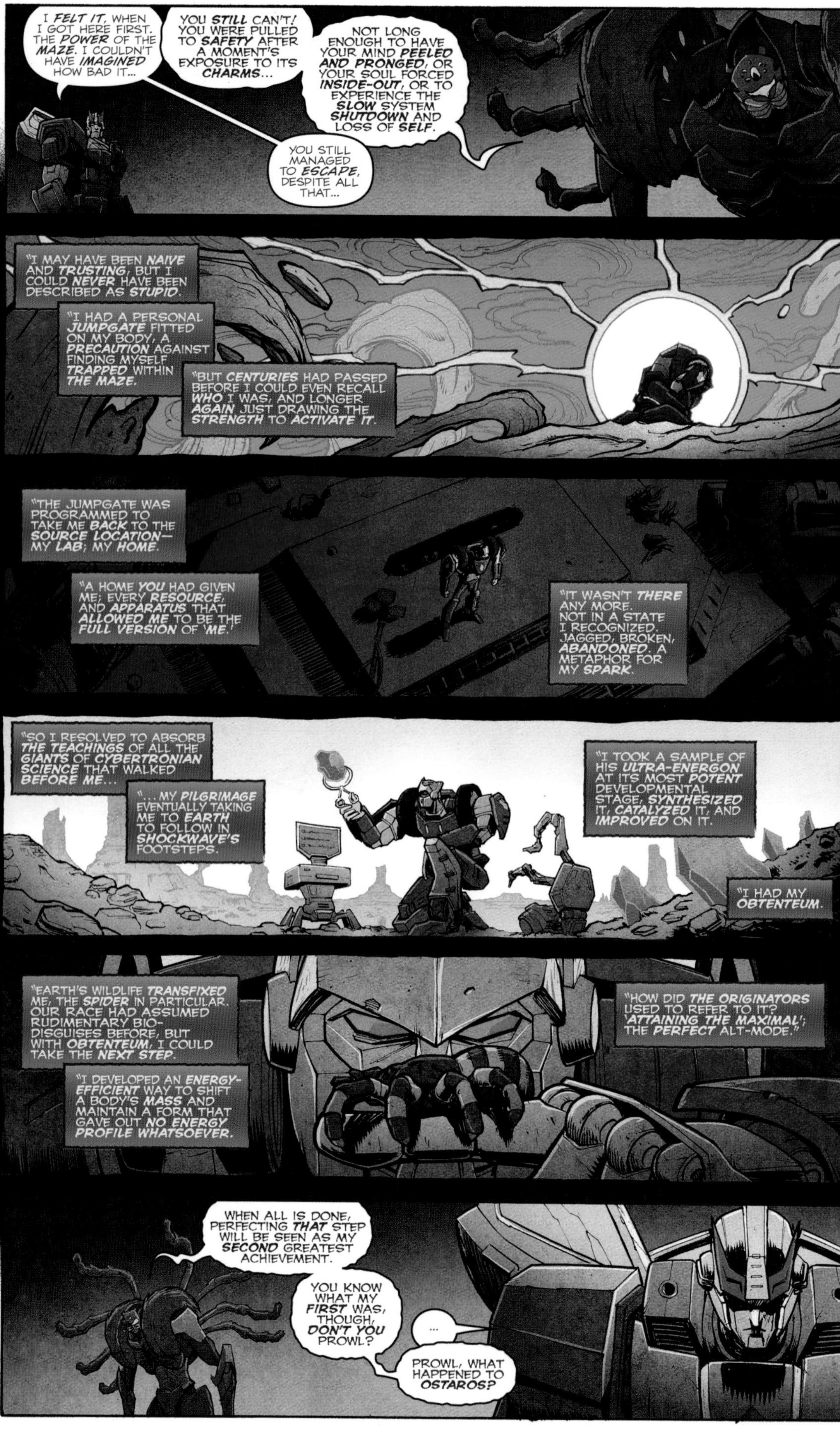
I FELT IT, WHEN I GOT HERE FIRST. THE POWER OF THE MAZE. I COULDN'T HAVE IMAGINED HOW BAD IT...
YOU STILL CAN'T! YOU WERE PULLED TO SAFETY AFTER A MOMENT'S EXPOSURE TO ITS CHARMS...
NOT LONG ENOUGH TO HAVE YOUR MIND PEELED AND PRONGED, OR YOUR SOUL FORCED INSIDE-OUT, OR TO EXPERIENCE THE SLOW SYSTEM SHUTDOWN AND LOSS OF SELF.
YOU STILL MANAGED TO ESCAPE, DESPITE ALL THAT...
"I MAY HAVE BEEN NAIVE AND TRUSTING, BUT I COULD NEVER HAVE BEEN DESCRIBED AS STUPID.
"I HAD A PERSONAL JUMPGATE FITTED ON MY BODY, A PRECAUTION AGAINST FINDING MYSELF TRAPPED WITHIN THE MAZE.
"BUT CENTURIES HAD PASSED BEFORE I COULD EVEN RECALL WHO I WAS, AND LONGER AGAIN JUST DRAWING THE STRENGTH TO ACTIVATE IT.
"THE JUMPGATE WAS PROGRAMMED TO TAKE ME BACK TO THE SOURCE LOCATION—MY LAB; MY HOME.
"A HOME YOU HAD GIVEN ME; EVERY RESOURCE, AND APPARATUS THAT ALLOWED ME TO BE THE FULL VERSION OF 'ME.'
"IT WASN'T THERE ANY MORE. NOT IN A STATE I RECOGNIZED. JAGGED, BROKEN, ABANDONED. A METAPHOR FOR MY SPARK.
"SO I RESOLVED TO ABSORB THE TEACHINGS OF ALL THE GIANTS OF CYBERTRONIAN SCIENCE THAT WALKED BEFORE ME...
"...MY PILGRIMAGE EVENTUALLY TAKING ME TO EARTH TO FOLLOW IN SHOCKWAVE'S FOOTSTEPS.
"I TOOK A SAMPLE OF HIS ULTRA-ENERGON AT ITS MOST POTENT DEVELOPMENTAL STAGE, SYNTHESIZED IT, CATALYZED IT, AND IMPROVED ON IT.
"I HAD MY OBTENTEUM.
"EARTH'S WILDLIFE TRANSFIXED ME, THE SPIDER IN PARTICULAR. OUR RACE HAD ASSUMED RUDIMENTARY BIO-DISGUISES BEFORE, BUT WITH OBTENTEUM, I COULD TAKE THE NEXT STEP.
"I DEVELOPED AN ENERGY-EFFICIENT WAY TO SHIFT A BODY'S MASS AND MAINTAIN A FORM THAT GAVE OUT NO ENERGY PROFILE WHATSOEVER.
"HOW DID THE ORIGINATORS USED TO REFER TO IT? 'ATTAINING THE MAXIMAL'; THE PERFECT ALT-MODE."
WHEN ALL IS DONE, PERFECTING THAT STEP WILL BE SEEN AS MY SECOND GREATEST ACHIEVEMENT.
YOU KNOW WHAT MY FIRST WAS, THOUGH, DON'T YOU PROWL?
...
PROWL, WHAT HAPPENED TO OSTAROS?

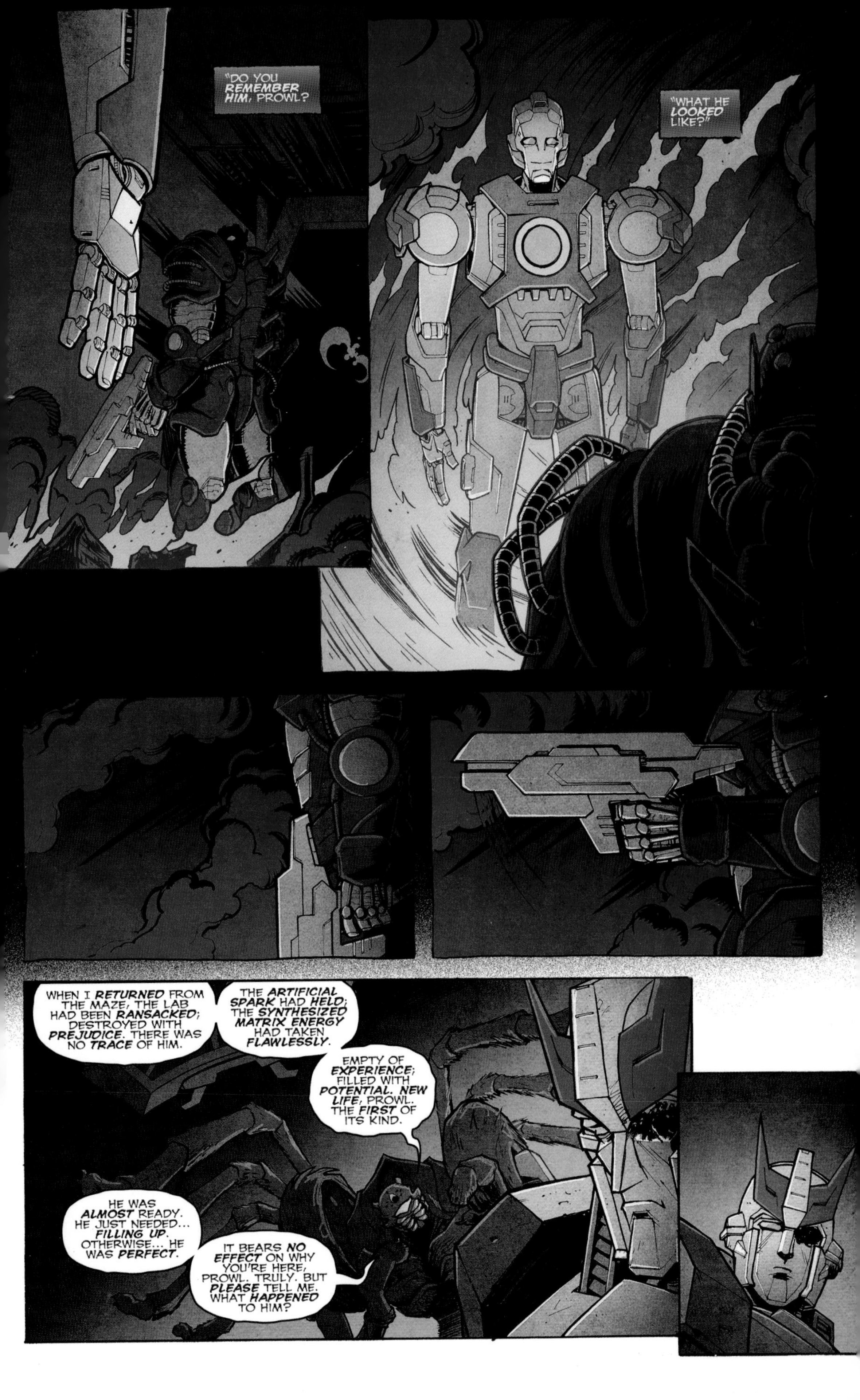
"DO YOU REMEMBER HIM, PROWL?
"WHAT HE LOOKED LIKE?"
WHEN I RETURNED FROM THE MAZE, THE LAB HAD BEEN RANSACKED; DESTROYED WITH PREJUDICE. THERE WAS NO TRACE OF HIM.
THE ARTIFICIAL SPARK HAD HELD; THE SYNTHESIZED MATRIX ENERGY HAD TAKEN FLAWLESSLY.
EMPTY OF EXPERIENCE; FILLED WITH POTENTIAL. NEW LIFE, PROWL. THE FIRST OF ITS KIND.
HE WAS ALMOST READY. HE JUST NEEDED... FILLING UP. OTHERWISE... HE WAS PERFECT.
IT BEARS NO EFFECT ON WHY YOU'RE HERE, PROWL. TRULY. BUT PLEASE TELL ME. WHAT HAPPENED TO HIM?

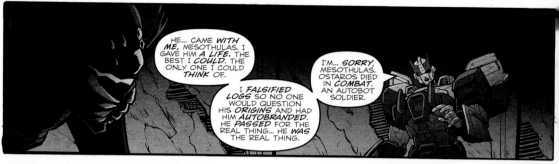

HE... CAME *WITH ME*, MESOTHULAS. I GAVE HIM *A LIFE*. THE BEST I *COULD*. THE ONLY ONE I COULD *THINK* OF.

I *FALSIFIED LOGS* SO NO ONE WOULD QUESTION HIS *ORIGINS* AND HAD HIM *AUTOBRANDED*. HE *PASSED* FOR THE REAL THING... HE *WAS* THE REAL THING.

I'M... *SORRY*, MESOTHULAS. OSTAROS DIED IN *COMBAT*. AN AUTOBOT SOLDIER.

...

I WANT... TO *ASK* YOU... *THE QUESTION*... ONE MORE TIME.

MY ANSWER'S NOT GOING TO...

IF YOU SAY *NO*, I WILL SEE YOU *DESTROYED*, AS *I* WAS. NOT *PHYSICALLY*, BUT MENTALLY, *EMOTIONALLY*.

ALL YOU'VE *WORKED FOR*— ALL YOU'VE *LIVED FOR*, TOPPLED OVER FOR THE VULTURES TO *FEAST* ON, JUST BECAUSE YOU DENIED ME.

I HAVE FELT *TRUE LOSS*, PROWL. AND I WANT *YOU* TO BE *ALIVE* AND *AWARE* AND *COGENT* TO FEEL IT, TOO.

OSTAROS I MISS *TERRIBLY*, BUT HE COULD *NEVER* HAVE HAPPENED *WITHOUT* YOU, AND NOTHING *LIKE HIM* WILL HAPPEN AGAIN *WITHOUT* YOU EITHER.

MY GOD, TARANTULAS...

WILL YOU JOIN *ME*?

... MY ANSWER... IS STILL *NO*...

I HOPE YOU'RE TELLING THE *TRUTH* TO ME, PROWL.

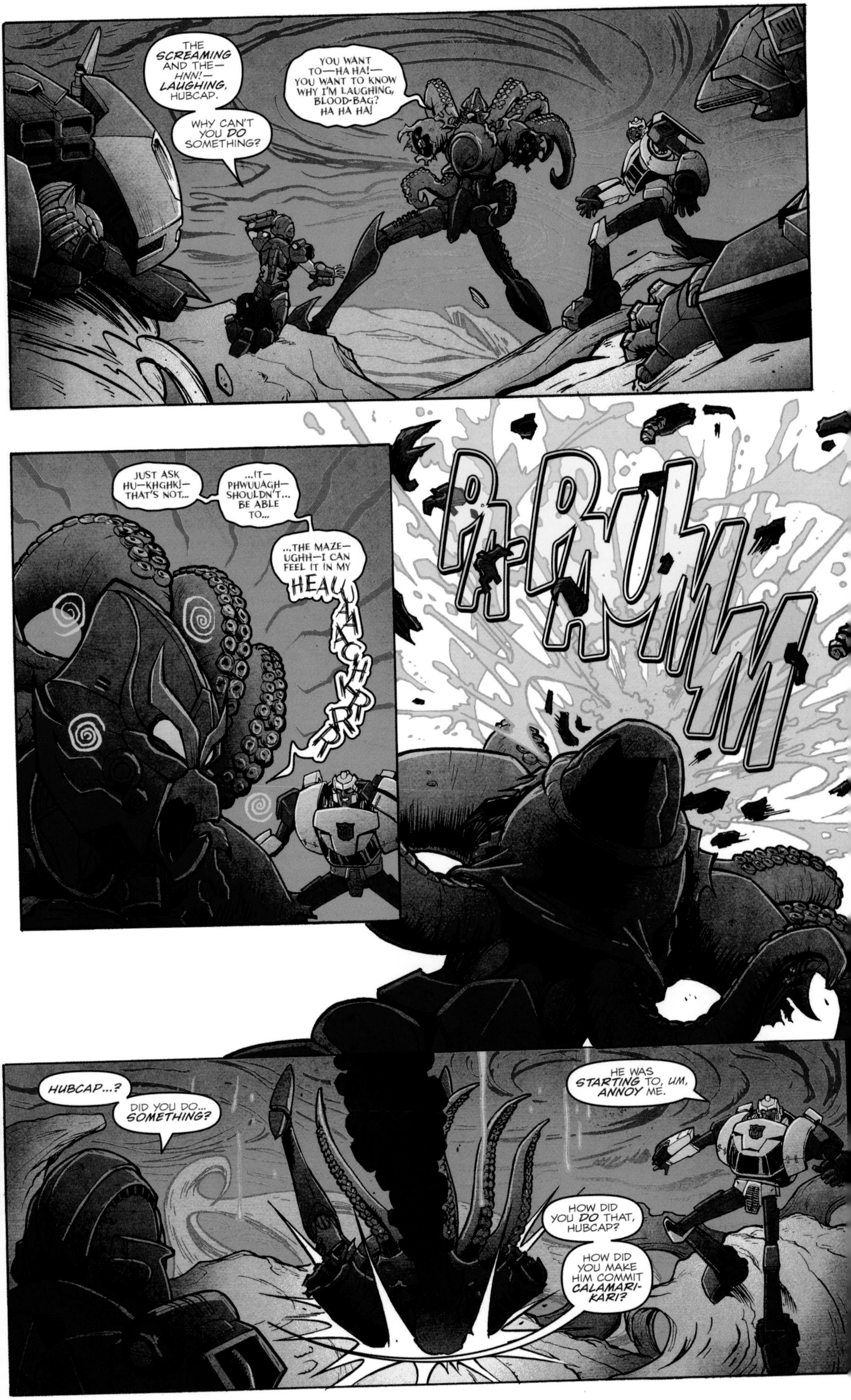

THE SCREAMING AND THE— HNN!— LAUGHING, HUBCAP.
WHY CAN'T YOU DO SOMETHING?
YOU WANT TO—HA HA!— YOU WANT TO KNOW WHY I'M LAUGHING, BLOOD-BAG? HA HA HA!
JUST ASK HU–KHGHK!— THAT'S NOT...
...IT— PHWUUAGH— SHOULDN'T... BE ABLE TO...
...THE MAZE— UGHH–I CAN FEEL IT IN MY
HEAUUHACHKRRRT
BRROOM
HUBCAP...?
DID YOU DO... SOMETHING?
HE WAS STARTING TO, UM, ANNOY ME.
HOW DID YOU DO THAT, HUBCAP?
HOW DID YOU MAKE HIM COMMIT CALAMARI-KARI?

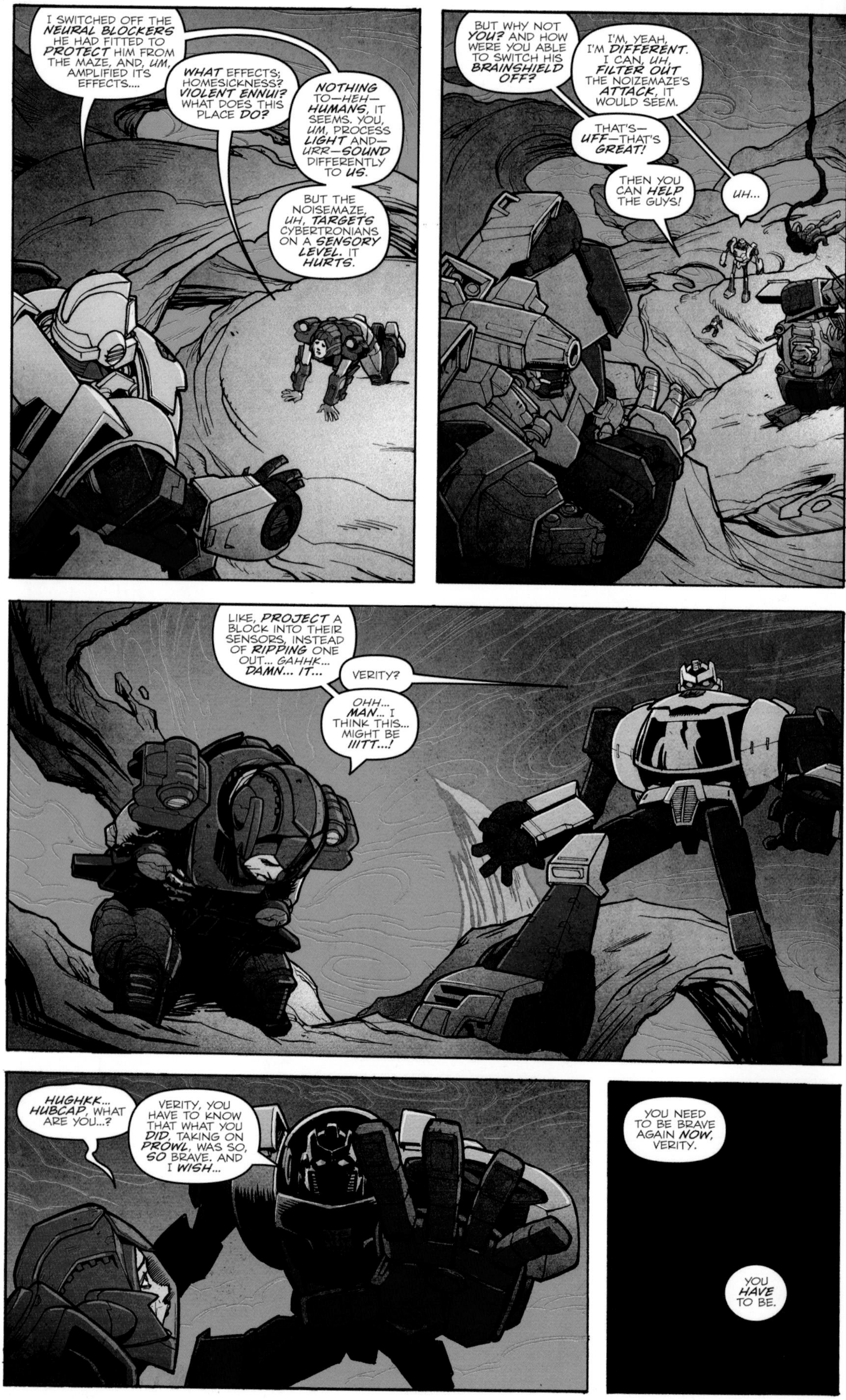

I SWITCHED OFF THE NEURAL BLOCKERS HE HAD FITTED TO PROTECT HIM FROM THE MAZE, AND, UM, AMPLIFIED ITS EFFECTS....
WHAT EFFECTS; HOMESICKNESS? VIOLENT ENNUI? WHAT DOES THIS PLACE DO?
NOTHING TO—HEH—HUMANS, IT SEEMS. YOU, UM, PROCESS LIGHT AND—URR—SOUND DIFFERENTLY TO US.
BUT THE NOISEMAZE, UH, TARGETS CYBERTRONIANS ON A SENSORY LEVEL. IT HURTS.
BUT WHY NOT YOU? AND HOW WERE YOU ABLE TO SWITCH HIS BRAINSHIELD OFF?
I'M, YEAH, I'M DIFFERENT. I CAN, UH, FILTER OUT THE NOIZEMAZE'S ATTACK, IT WOULD SEEM.
THAT'S—UFF—THAT'S GREAT!
THEN YOU CAN HELP THE GUYS!
UH...
LIKE, PROJECT A BLOCK INTO THEIR SENSORS, INSTEAD OF RIPPING ONE OUT... GAHHK... DAMN... IT...
VERITY?
OHH... MAN... I THINK THIS... MIGHT BE IIITT...!
HUGHKK... HUBCAP, WHAT ARE YOU...?
VERITY, YOU HAVE TO KNOW THAT WHAT YOU DID, TAKING ON PROWL, WAS SO, SO BRAVE. AND I WISH...
YOU NEED TO BE BRAVE AGAIN NOW, VERITY.
YOU HAVE TO BE.

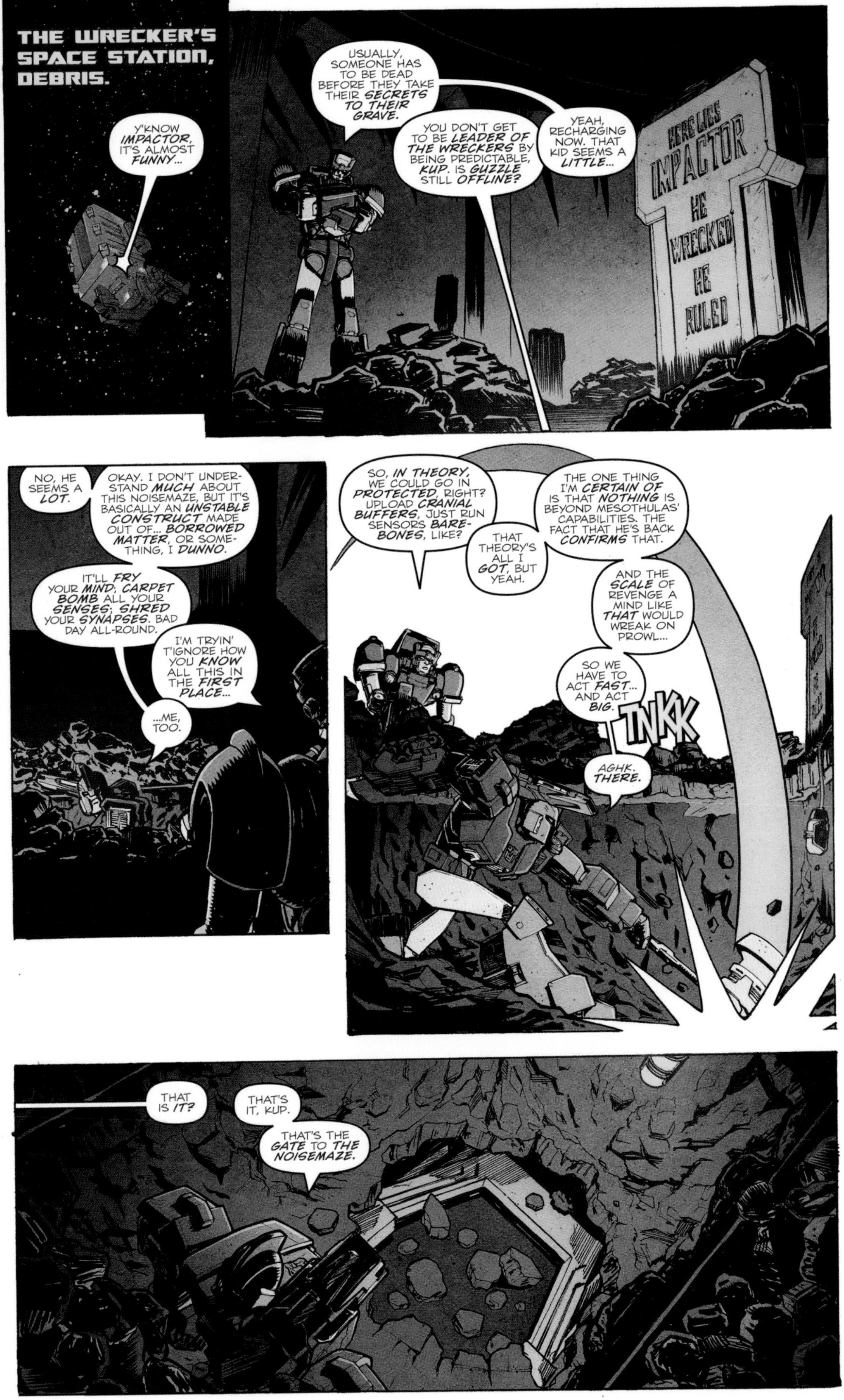
THE WRECKER'S SPACE STATION, DEBRIS.
Y'KNOW IMPACTOR, IT'S ALMOST FUNNY...
USUALLY, SOMEONE HAS TO BE DEAD BEFORE THEY TAKE THEIR SECRETS TO THEIR GRAVE.
YOU DON'T GET TO BE LEADER OF THE WRECKERS BY BEING PREDICTABLE, KUP. IS GUZZLE STILL OFFLINE?
YEAH, RECHARGING NOW. THAT KID SEEMS A LITTLE...
HERE LIES IMPACTOR HE WRECKED HE RULED
NO, HE SEEMS A LOT.
OKAY. I DON'T UNDERSTAND MUCH ABOUT THIS NOISEMAZE, BUT IT'S BASICALLY AN UNSTABLE CONSTRUCT MADE OUT OF... BORROWED MATTER, OR SOMETHING, I DUNNO.
IT'LL FRY YOUR MIND; CARPET BOMB ALL YOUR SENSES; SHRED YOUR SYNAPSES. BAD DAY ALL-ROUND.
I'M TRYIN' T'IGNORE HOW YOU KNOW ALL THIS IN THE FIRST PLACE...
...ME, TOO.
SO, IN THEORY, WE COULD GO IN PROTECTED, RIGHT? UPLOAD CRANIAL BUFFERS, JUST RUN SENSORS BARE-BONES, LIKE?
THAT THEORY'S ALL I GOT, BUT YEAH.
THE ONE THING I'M CERTAIN OF IS THAT NOTHING IS BEYOND MESOTHULAS' CAPABILITIES. THE FACT THAT HE'S BACK CONFIRMS THAT.
AND THE SCALE OF REVENGE A MIND LIKE THAT WOULD WREAK ON PROWL...
SO WE HAVE TO ACT FAST... AND ACT BIG.
TNKK
AGHK. THERE.
THAT IS IT?
THAT'S IT, KUP.
THAT'S THE GATE TO THE NOISEMAZE.

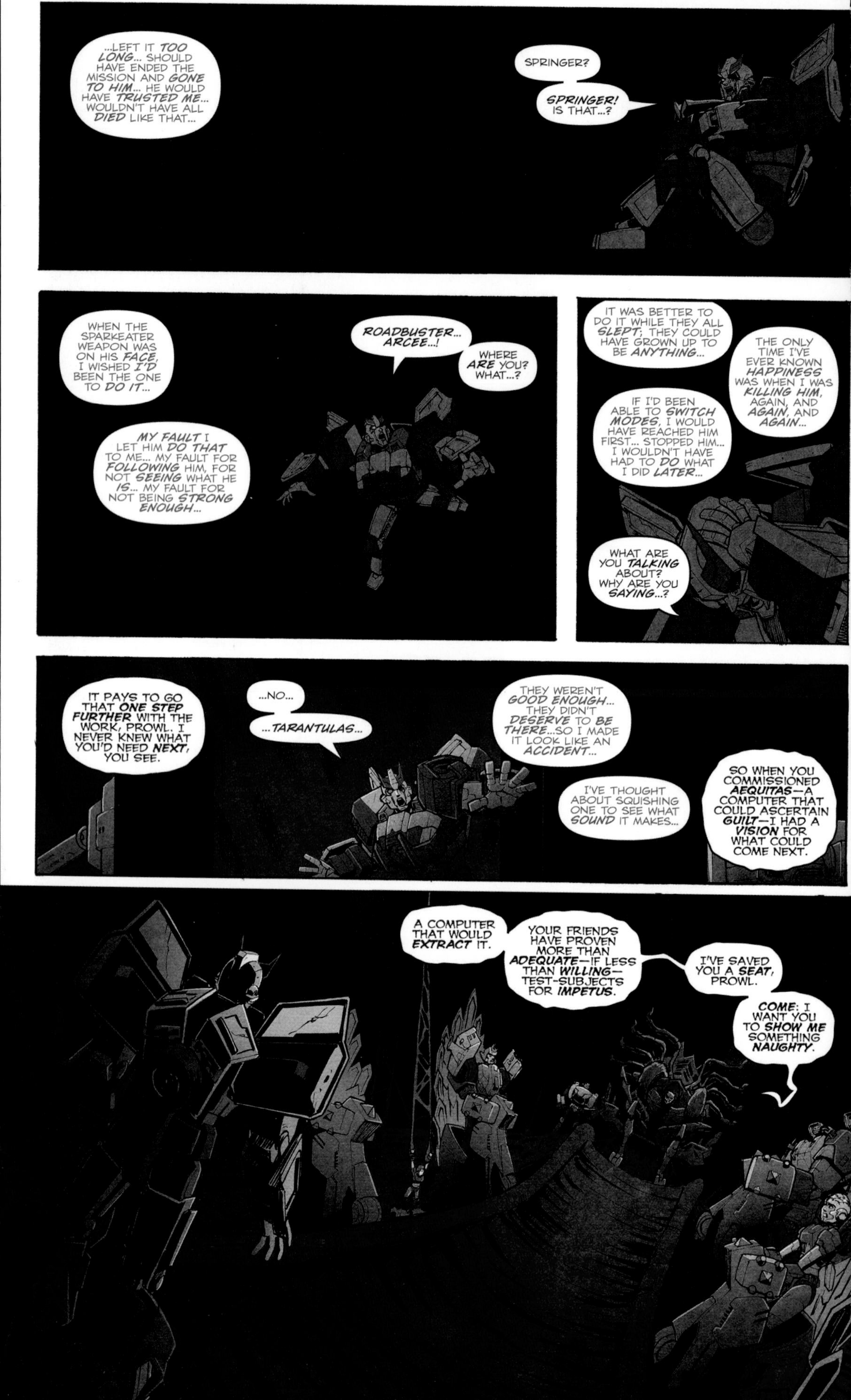
...LEFT IT TOO LONG... SHOULD HAVE ENDED THE MISSION AND GONE TO HIM... HE WOULD HAVE TRUSTED ME... WOULDN'T HAVE ALL DIED LIKE THAT...
SPRINGER?
SPRINGER! IS THAT...?
WHEN THE SPARKEATER WEAPON WAS ON HIS FACE, I WISHED I'D BEEN THE ONE TO DO IT...
ROADBUSTER... ARCEE...!
WHERE ARE YOU? WHAT...?
MY FAULT I LET HIM DO THAT TO ME... MY FAULT FOR FOLLOWING HIM, FOR NOT SEEING WHAT HE IS... MY FAULT FOR NOT BEING STRONG ENOUGH...
IT WAS BETTER TO DO IT WHILE THEY ALL SLEPT; THEY COULD HAVE GROWN UP TO BE ANYTHING...
THE ONLY TIME I'VE EVER KNOWN HAPPINESS WAS WHEN I WAS KILLING HIM, AGAIN, AND AGAIN, AND AGAIN...
IF I'D BEEN ABLE TO SWITCH MODES, I WOULD HAVE REACHED HIM FIRST... STOPPED HIM... I WOULDN'T HAVE HAD TO DO WHAT I DID LATER...
WHAT ARE YOU TALKING ABOUT? WHY ARE YOU SAYING...?
IT PAYS TO GO THAT ONE STEP FURTHER WITH THE WORK, PROWL. I NEVER KNEW WHAT YOU'D NEED NEXT, YOU SEE.
...NO...
...TARANTULAS...
THEY WEREN'T GOOD ENOUGH... THEY DIDN'T DESERVE TO BE THERE...SO I MADE IT LOOK LIKE AN ACCIDENT...
I'VE THOUGHT ABOUT SQUISHING ONE TO SEE WHAT SOUND IT MAKES...
SO WHEN YOU COMMISSIONED AEQUITAS—A COMPUTER THAT COULD ASCERTAIN GUILT—I HAD A VISION FOR WHAT COULD COME NEXT.
A COMPUTER THAT WOULD EXTRACT IT.
YOUR FRIENDS HAVE PROVEN MORE THAN ADEQUATE—IF LESS THAN WILLING—TEST-SUBJECTS FOR IMPETUS.
I'VE SAVED YOU A SEAT, PROWL.
COME: I WANT YOU TO SHOW ME SOMETHING NAUGHTY.

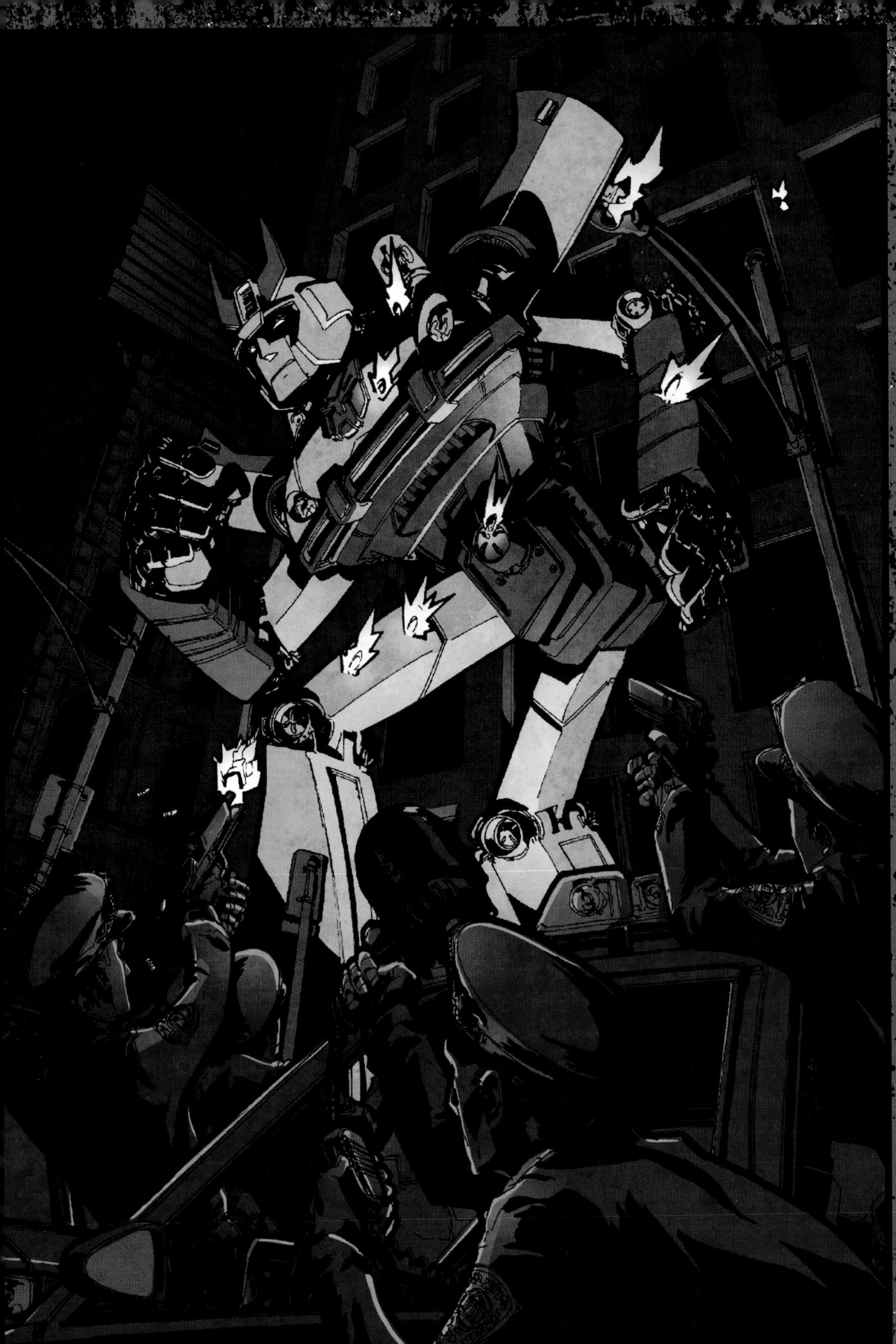

ART ANDY MACDONALD COLORS JOHN-PAUL BOVE

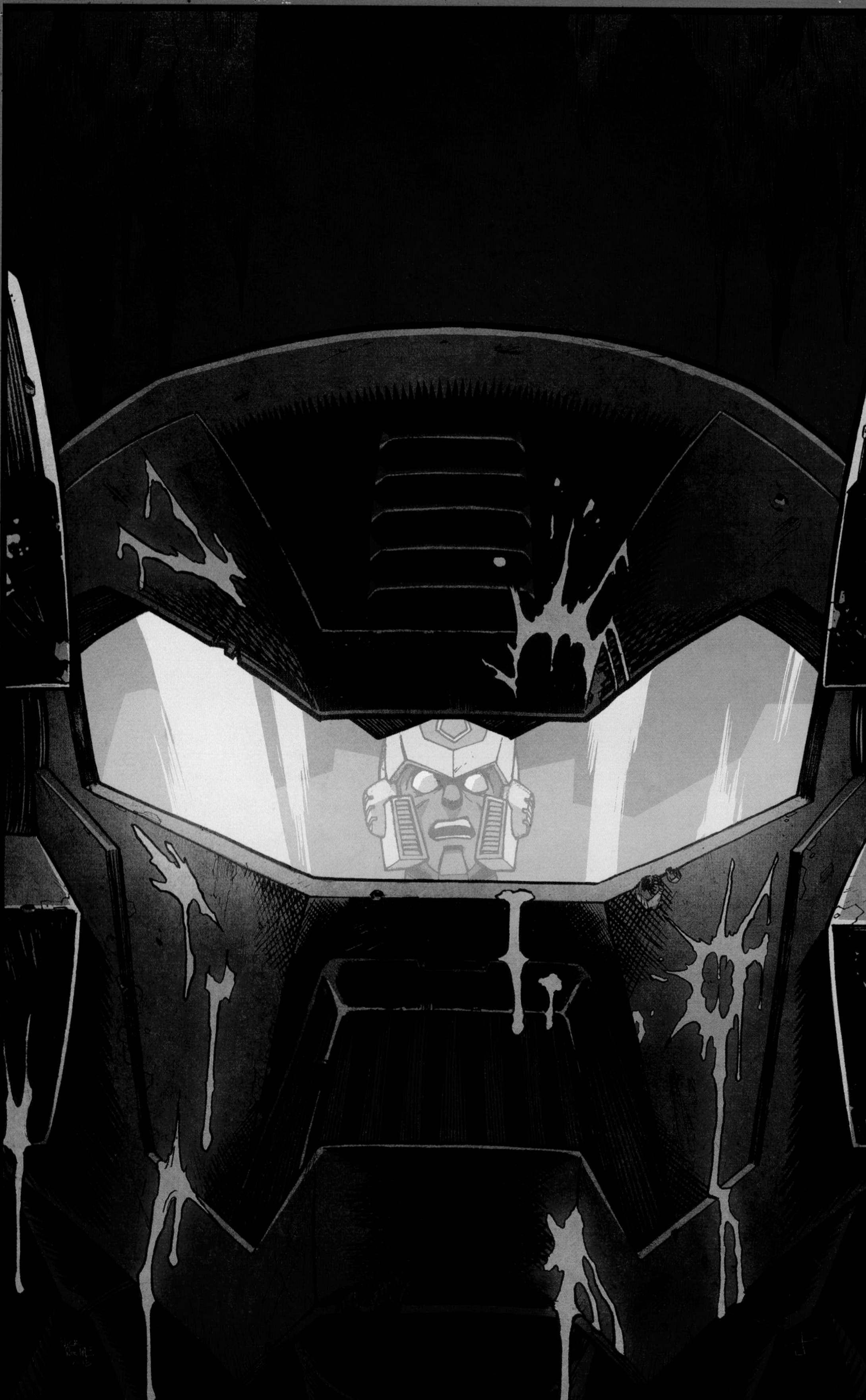

ART NICK ROCHE COLORS JOSH BURCHAM

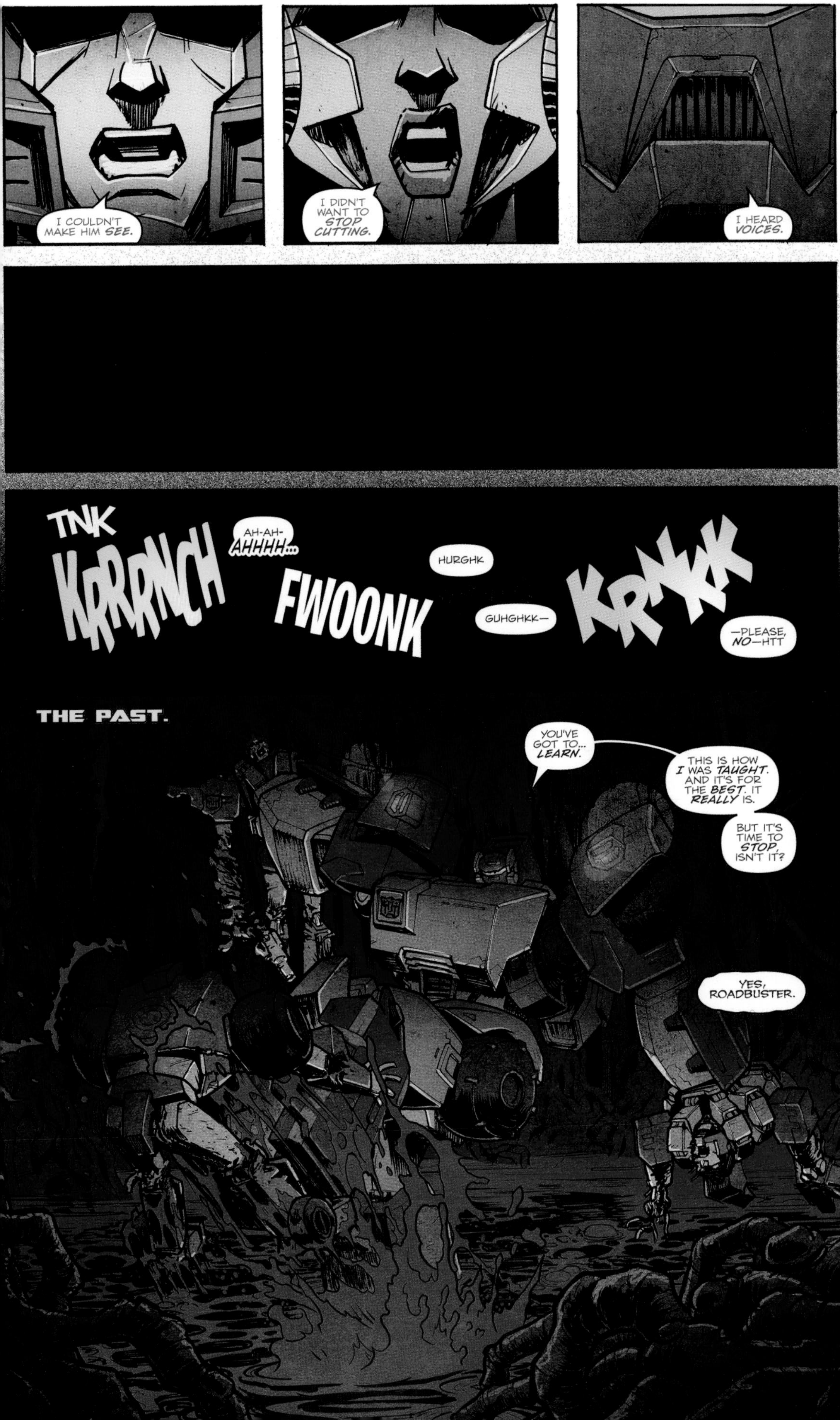
I COULDN'T MAKE HIM SEE.
I DIDN'T WANT TO STOP CUTTING.
I HEARD VOICES.
TNK
KRRRNCH
AH-AH-AHHHH...
FWOONK
HURGHK
GUHGHKK—
KRNKK
—PLEASE, NO—HTT
THE PAST.
YOU'VE GOT TO... LEARN.
THIS IS HOW I WAS TAUGHT. AND IT'S FOR THE BEST. IT REALLY IS.
BUT IT'S TIME TO STOP, ISN'T IT?
YES, ROADBUSTER.

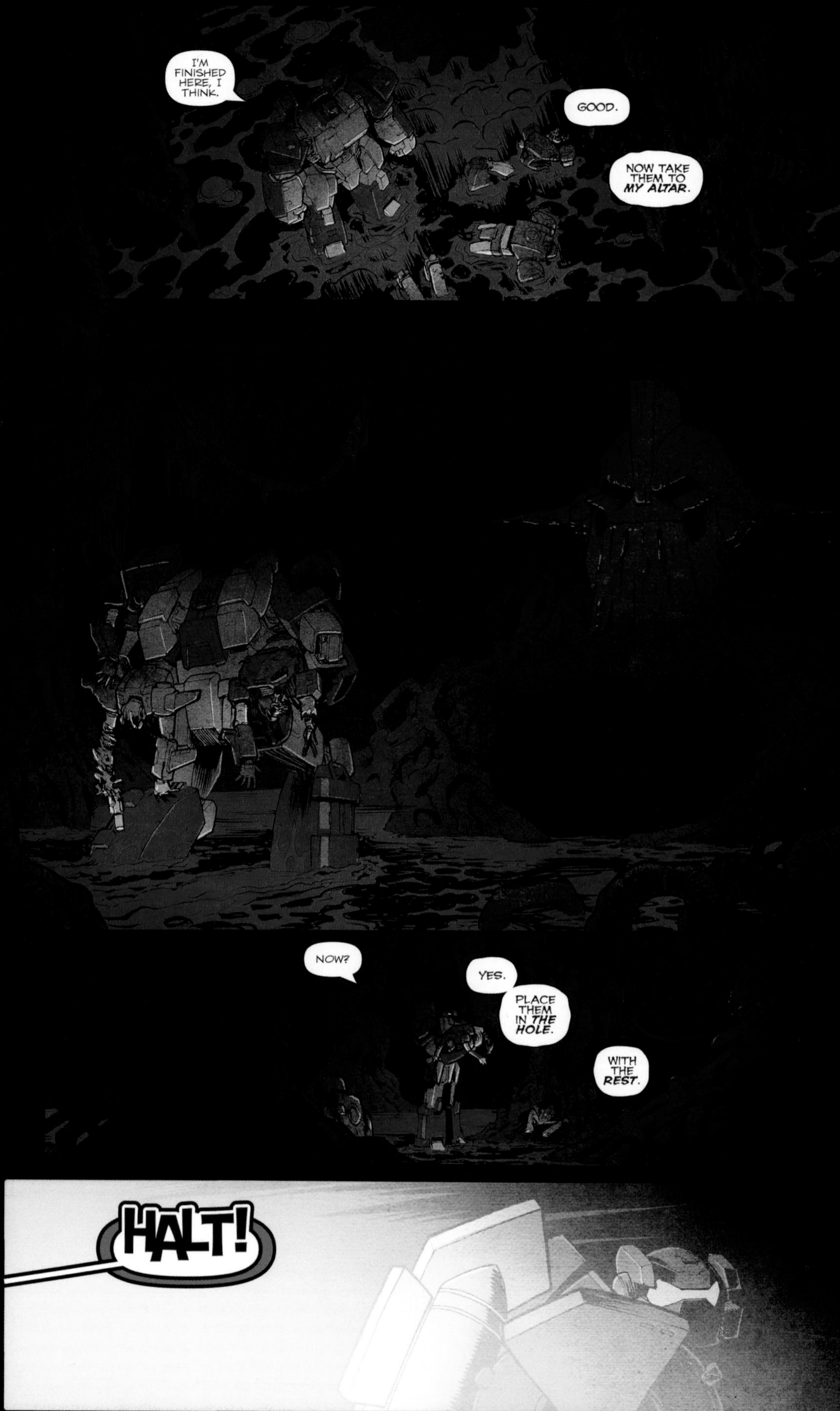
I'M FINISHED HERE, I THINK.
GOOD.
NOW TAKE THEM TO MY ALTAR.
NOW?
YES.
PLACE THEM IN THE HOLE.
WITH THE REST.
HALT!

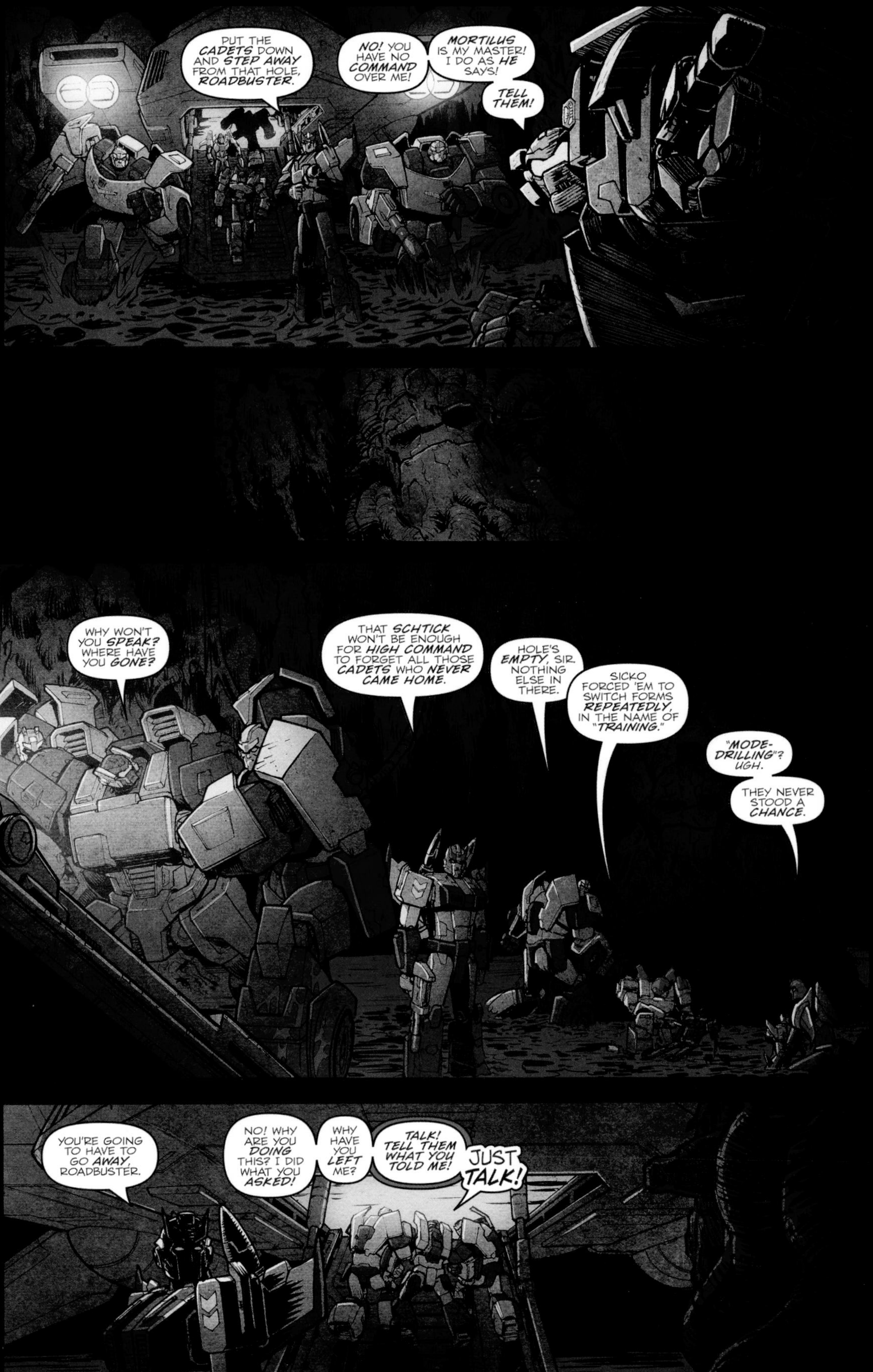
PUT THE CADETS DOWN AND STEP AWAY FROM THAT HOLE, ROADBUSTER.
NO! YOU HAVE NO COMMAND OVER ME!
MORTILUS IS MY MASTER! I DO AS HE SAYS!
TELL THEM!
WHY WON'T YOU SPEAK? WHERE HAVE YOU GONE?
THAT SCHTICK WON'T BE ENOUGH FOR HIGH COMMAND TO FORGET ALL THOSE CADETS WHO NEVER CAME HOME.
HOLE'S EMPTY, SIR. NOTHING ELSE IN THERE.
SICKO FORCED 'EM TO SWITCH FORMS REPEATEDLY, IN THE NAME OF "TRAINING."
"MODE-DRILLING"? UGH.
THEY NEVER STOOD A CHANCE.
YOU'RE GOING TO HAVE TO GO AWAY, ROADBUSTER.
NO! WHY ARE YOU DOING THIS? I DID WHAT YOU ASKED!
WHY HAVE YOU LEFT ME?
TALK! TELL THEM WHAT YOU TOLD ME!
JUST TALK!

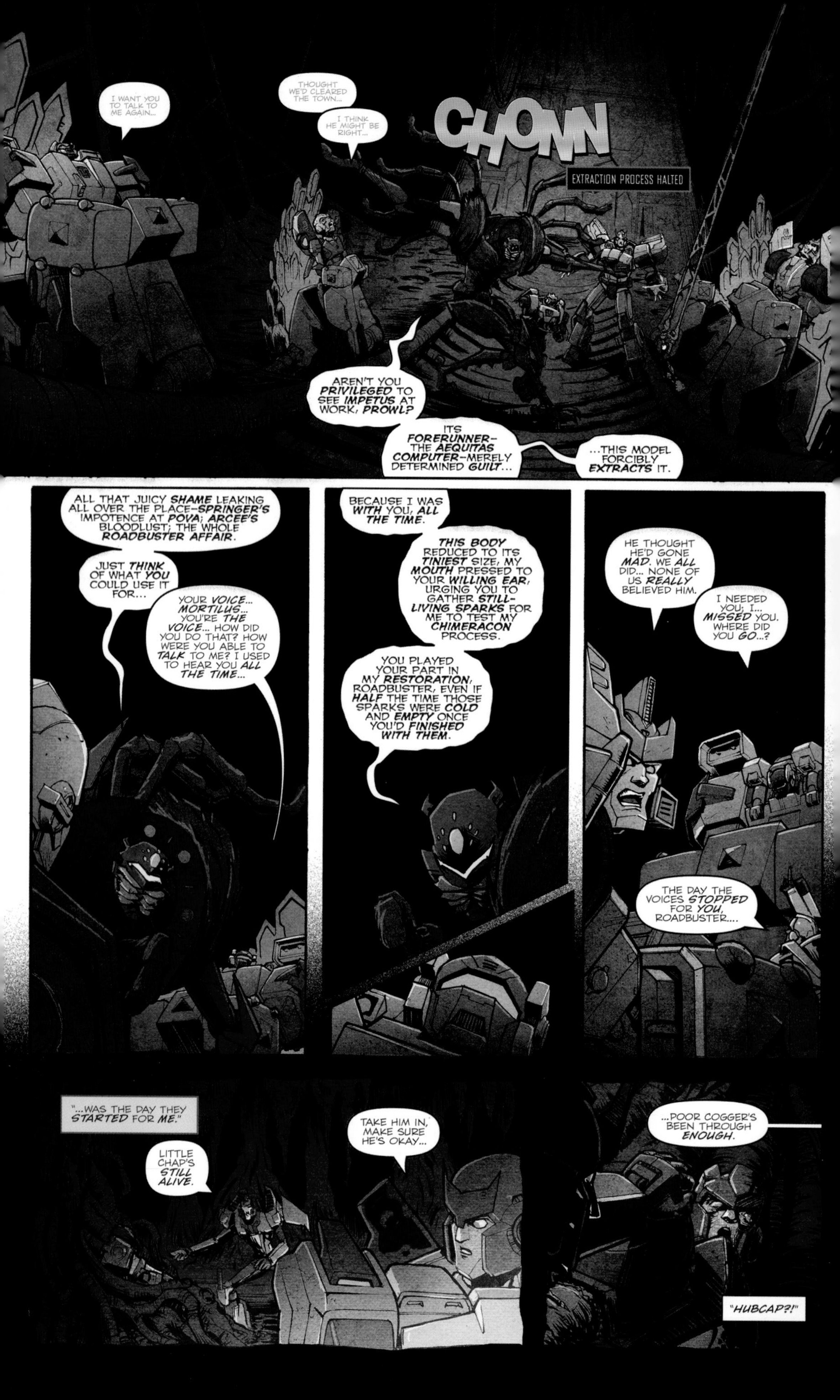

I WANT YOU TO TALK TO ME AGAIN...
THOUGHT WE'D CLEARED THE TOWN...
I THINK HE MIGHT BE RIGHT...
CHONN
EXTRACTION PROCESS HALTED
AREN'T YOU PRIVILEGED TO SEE IMPETUS AT WORK, PROWL?
ITS FORERUNNER–THE AEQUITAS COMPUTER–MERELY DETERMINED GUILT...
...THIS MODEL FORCIBLY EXTRACTS IT.
ALL THAT JUICY SHAME LEAKING ALL OVER THE PLACE–SPRINGER'S IMPOTENCE AT POVA; ARCEE'S BLOODLUST; THE WHOLE ROADBUSTER AFFAIR.
JUST THINK OF WHAT YOU COULD USE IT FOR...
YOUR VOICE... MORTILUS... YOU'RE THE VOICE... HOW DID YOU DO THAT? HOW WERE YOU ABLE TO TALK TO ME? I USED TO HEAR YOU ALL THE TIME...
BECAUSE I WAS WITH YOU, ALL THE TIME.
THIS BODY REDUCED TO ITS TINIEST SIZE, MY MOUTH PRESSED TO YOUR WILLING EAR, URGING YOU TO GATHER STILL-LIVING SPARKS FOR ME TO TEST MY CHIMERACON PROCESS.
YOU PLAYED YOUR PART IN MY RESTORATION, ROADBUSTER, EVEN IF HALF THE TIME THOSE SPARKS WERE COLD AND EMPTY ONCE YOU'D FINISHED WITH THEM.
HE THOUGHT HE'D GONE MAD. WE ALL DID... NONE OF US REALLY BELIEVED HIM.
I NEEDED YOU; I... MISSED YOU. WHERE DID YOU GO...?
THE DAY THE VOICES STOPPED FOR YOU, ROADBUSTER....
"...WAS THE DAY THEY STARTED FOR ME."
LITTLE CHAP'S STILL ALIVE.
TAKE HIM IN, MAKE SURE HE'S OKAY...
...POOR COGGER'S BEEN THROUGH ENOUGH.
"HUBCAP?!"

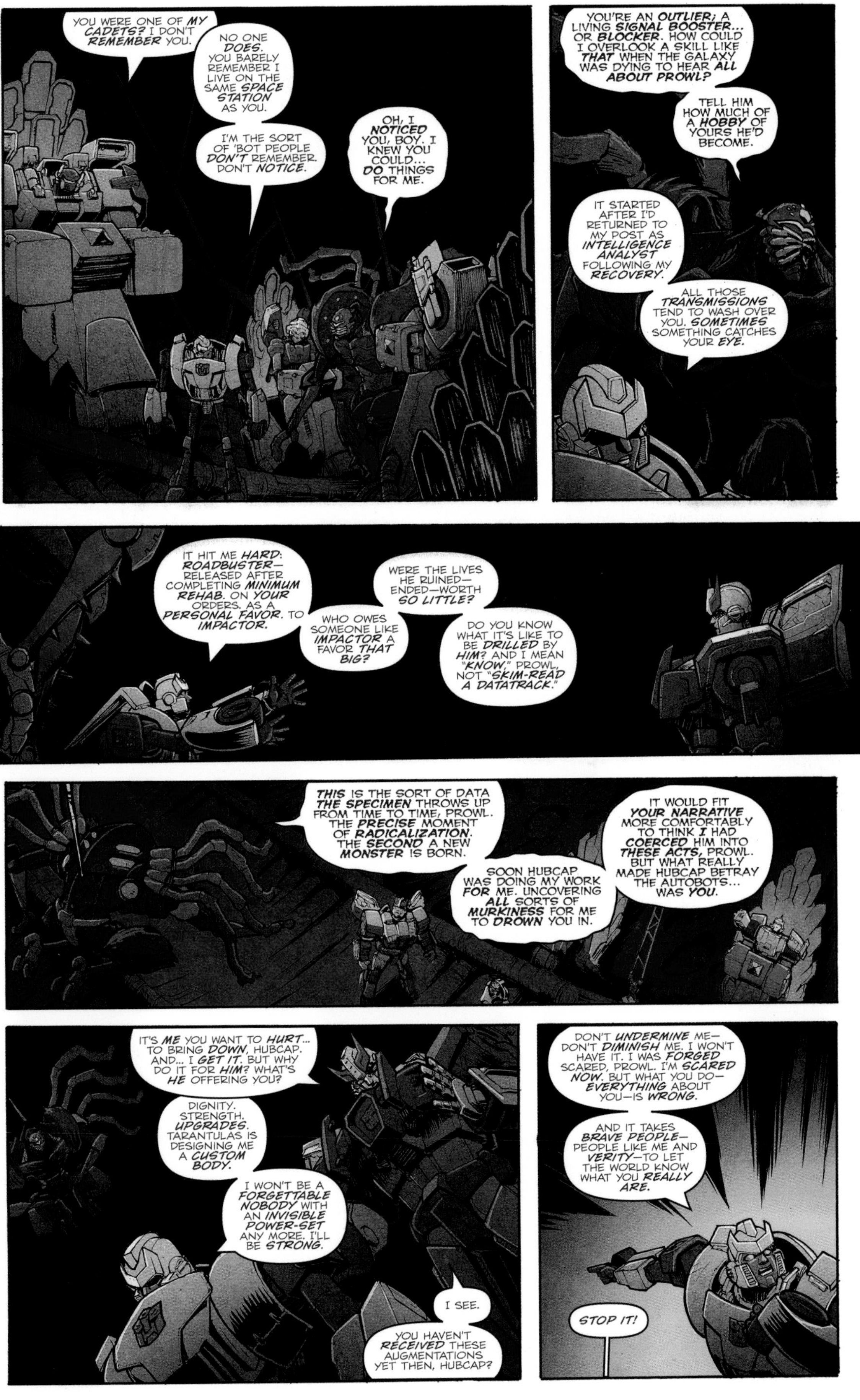
YOU WERE ONE OF MY CADETS? I DON'T REMEMBER YOU.
NO ONE DOES. YOU BARELY REMEMBER I LIVE ON THE SAME SPACE STATION AS YOU.
I'M THE SORT OF 'BOT PEOPLE DON'T REMEMBER. DON'T NOTICE.
OH, I NOTICED YOU, BOY. I KNEW YOU COULD... DO THINGS FOR ME.
YOU'RE AN OUTLIER; A LIVING SIGNAL BOOSTER... OR BLOCKER. HOW COULD I OVERLOOK A SKILL LIKE THAT WHEN THE GALAXY WAS DYING TO HEAR ALL ABOUT PROWL?
TELL HIM HOW MUCH OF A HOBBY OF YOURS HE'D BECOME.
IT STARTED AFTER I'D RETURNED TO MY POST AS INTELLIGENCE ANALYST FOLLOWING MY RECOVERY.
ALL THOSE TRANSMISSIONS TEND TO WASH OVER YOU. SOMETIMES SOMETHING CATCHES YOUR EYE.
IT HIT ME HARD: ROADBUSTER—RELEASED AFTER COMPLETING MINIMUM REHAB. ON YOUR ORDERS. AS A PERSONAL FAVOR. TO IMPACTOR.
WHO OWES SOMEONE LIKE IMPACTOR A FAVOR THAT BIG?
WERE THE LIVES HE RUINED—ENDED—WORTH SO LITTLE?
DO YOU KNOW WHAT IT'S LIKE TO BE DRILLED BY HIM? AND I MEAN "KNOW," PROWL, NOT "SKIM-READ A DATATRACK."
THIS IS THE SORT OF DATA THE SPECIMEN THROWS UP FROM TIME TO TIME, PROWL. THE PRECISE MOMENT OF RADICALIZATION. THE SECOND A NEW MONSTER IS BORN.
SOON HUBCAP WAS DOING MY WORK FOR ME. UNCOVERING ALL SORTS OF MURKINESS FOR ME TO DROWN YOU IN.
IT WOULD FIT YOUR NARRATIVE MORE COMFORTABLY TO THINK I HAD COERCED HIM INTO THESE ACTS, PROWL. BUT WHAT REALLY MADE HUBCAP BETRAY THE AUTOBOTS... WAS YOU.
IT'S ME YOU WANT TO HURT... TO BRING DOWN, HUBCAP. AND... I GET IT. BUT WHY DO IT FOR HIM? WHAT'S HE OFFERING YOU?
DIGNITY. STRENGTH. UPGRADES. TARANTULAS IS DESIGNING ME A CUSTOM BODY.
I WON'T BE A FORGETTABLE NOBODY WITH AN INVISIBLE POWER-SET ANY MORE. I'LL BE STRONG.
I SEE.
YOU HAVEN'T RECEIVED THESE AUGMENTATIONS YET THEN, HUBCAP?
DON'T UNDERMINE ME—DON'T DIMINISH ME. I WON'T HAVE IT. I WAS FORGED SCARED, PROWL. I'M SCARED NOW. BUT WHAT YOU DO—EVERYTHING ABOUT YOU—IS WRONG.
AND IT TAKES BRAVE PEOPLE—PEOPLE LIKE ME AND VERITY—TO LET THE WORLD KNOW WHAT YOU REALLY ARE.
STOP IT!

WHY DO YOU *KEEP SAYING* THAT?! I'M *NOT* BRAVE, I...

TELL THEM. OH, *PLEASE* TELL THEM. LET ME *STUDY* THEIR *REACTIONS.*

THE REASON I... IT'S BECAUSE... THE *REASON* I...

TELL THEM YOU'RE *DYING.*

YOU'RE A *LIAR,* TARANTULAS.

NO. HE'S *NOT.*

STAKEOUT— *GOD, STAKEOUT*— RAN THE *TESTS.*

OVER- EXPOSURE TO *"INTENSE ENERGY OF CYBERTRONIAN ORIGIN,"* HE SAID.

...NO...

HE WAS... *HALF-RIGHT.* I TOOK THE ENJOYABLE *LIBERTY* OF MAKING MY *OWN INSPECTION.*

"YOUR *CONDITION* ISN'T MERELY DOWN TO *DAY-TO-DAY CONTACT* WITH OUR KIND.

"THE *PARTICLE SIGNATURE* OF THE 'INTENSE ENERGY' THAT HAS SO *ERODED* YOUR *BODY* APPEARS TO ORIGINATE FROM *AEQUITAS ITSELF...*

"I SURMISE YOU MAY HAVE BEEN *PRESENT* FOR IT'S LESS-THAN- GRACEFUL *DOWNLOAD.*"

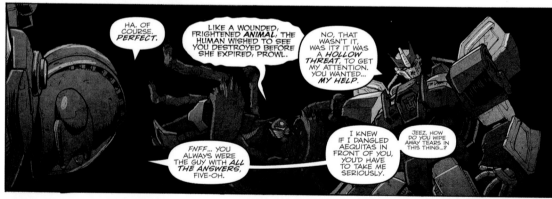

HA. OF COURSE. *PERFECT.*

LIKE A WOUNDED, FRIGHTENED *ANIMAL,* THE HUMAN WISHED TO SEE YOU DESTROYED BEFORE SHE EXPIRED, PROWL.

NO, THAT WASN'T IT, WAS IT? IT WAS A *HOLLOW THREAT,* TO GET MY ATTENTION. YOU WANTED... *MY HELP.*

FNFF... YOU ALWAYS WERE THE GUY WITH *ALL THE ANSWERS,* FIVE-OH.

I KNEW IF I DANGLED AEQUITAS IN FRONT OF YOU, YOU'D HAVE TO TAKE ME SERIOUSLY.

JEEZ, HOW DO YOU WIPE AWAY TEARS IN THIS THING...?

I WISH YOU HAD ASKED ME, VERITY.

AND GIVE YOU THE POWER TO SAY *NO?* LIKE, WHY *WOULD* YOU HELP ME, RIGHT?

NO. RIGHT THEN, I NEEDED SOME *CONTROL.* SOME *DIGNITY.*

ME AND *IRONFIST* HAD *BIG PLANS* FOR THAT DATA. *TRUTH; JUSTICE;* ALL THE *GOOD STUFF.*

BUT THEN I GOT SICKER... AND *SICKER.* AND AEQUITAS WAS ALL I HAD TO *BUY* MY WAY OUT.

IRONFIST WAS DYING THAT *WHOLE TIME,* AND HE JUST STUCK WITH THE PLAN. BE A GOOD *AUTOBOT*— THE *BEST* AUTOBOT— AND PUT *SAVING THE DAY* AHEAD OF YOUR *OWN* BUTT.

BUT I COULDN'T DO THAT. I DON'T KNOW WHAT IT'S LIKE FOR *YOU* GUYS, BUT ON *EARTH,* LIFE IS *SHORT* AND IT *FEELS* IT.

I'M *SORRY,* IRONFIST.

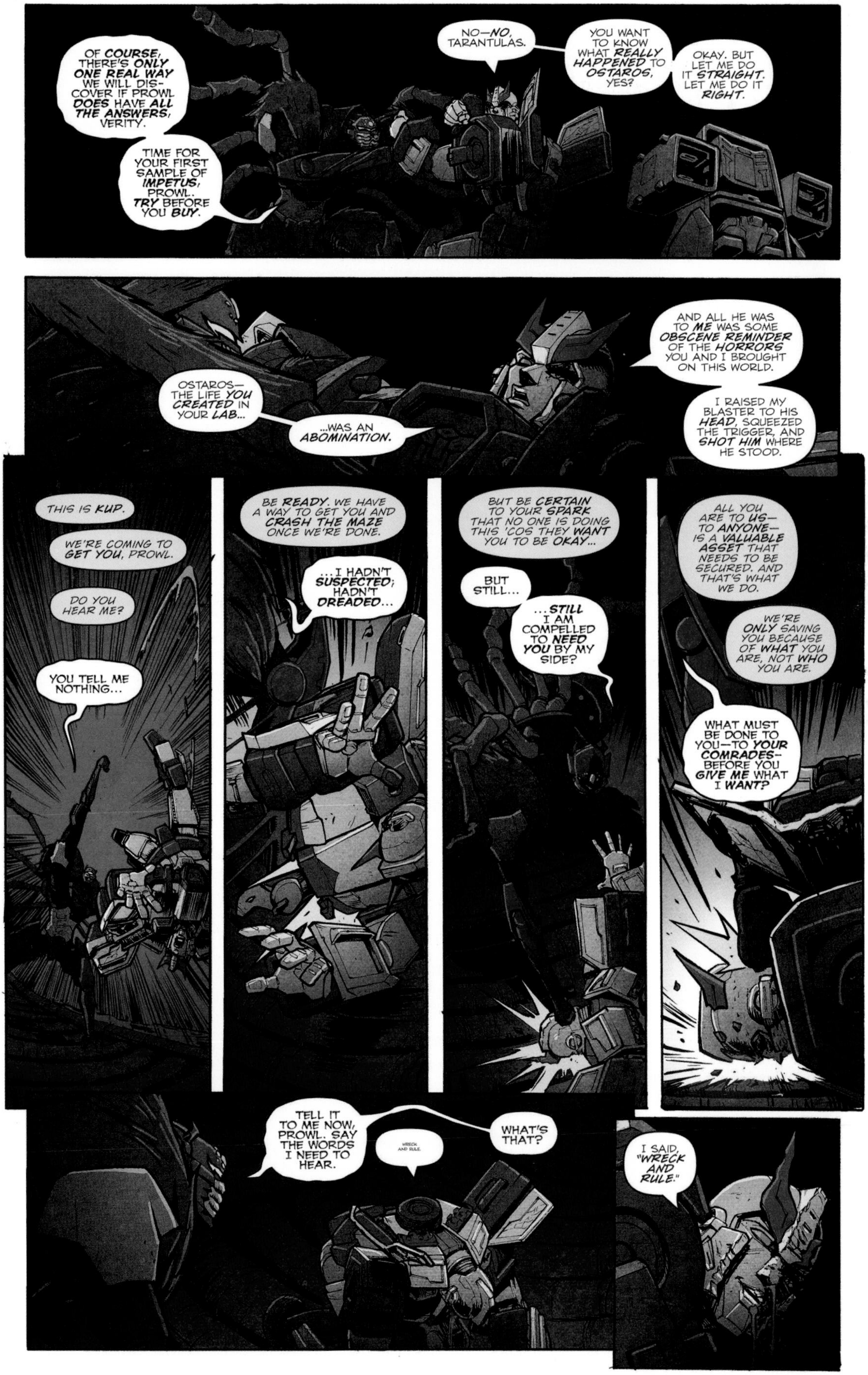
OF COURSE, THERE'S ONLY ONE REAL WAY WE WILL DISCOVER IF PROWL DOES HAVE ALL THE ANSWERS, VERITY.
TIME FOR YOUR FIRST SAMPLE OF IMPETUS, PROWL. TRY BEFORE YOU BUY.
NO—NO, TARANTULAS.
YOU WANT TO KNOW WHAT REALLY HAPPENED TO OSTAROS, YES?
OKAY. BUT LET ME DO IT STRAIGHT. LET ME DO IT RIGHT.
OSTAROS—THE LIFE YOU CREATED IN YOUR LAB...
...WAS AN ABOMINATION.
AND ALL HE WAS TO ME WAS SOME OBSCENE REMINDER OF THE HORRORS YOU AND I BROUGHT ON THIS WORLD.
I RAISED MY BLASTER TO HIS HEAD, SQUEEZED THE TRIGGER, AND SHOT HIM WHERE HE STOOD.
THIS IS KUP.
WE'RE COMING TO GET YOU, PROWL.
DO YOU HEAR ME?
YOU TELL ME NOTHING...
BE READY. WE HAVE A WAY TO GET YOU AND CRASH THE MAZE ONCE WE'RE DONE.
...I HADN'T SUSPECTED; HADN'T DREADED...
BUT BE CERTAIN TO YOUR SPARK THAT NO ONE IS DOING THIS 'COS THEY WANT YOU TO BE OKAY...
BUT STILL...
...STILL I AM COMPELLED TO NEED YOU BY MY SIDE?
ALL YOU ARE TO US—TO ANYONE—IS A VALUABLE ASSET THAT NEEDS TO BE SECURED. AND THAT'S WHAT WE DO.
WE'RE ONLY SAVING YOU BECAUSE OF WHAT YOU ARE, NOT WHO YOU ARE.
WHAT MUST BE DONE TO YOU—TO YOUR COMRADES—BEFORE YOU GIVE ME WHAT I WANT?
TELL IT TO ME NOW, PROWL. SAY THE WORDS I NEED TO HEAR.
WRECK AND RULE.
WHAT'S THAT?
I SAID, "WRECK AND RULE."

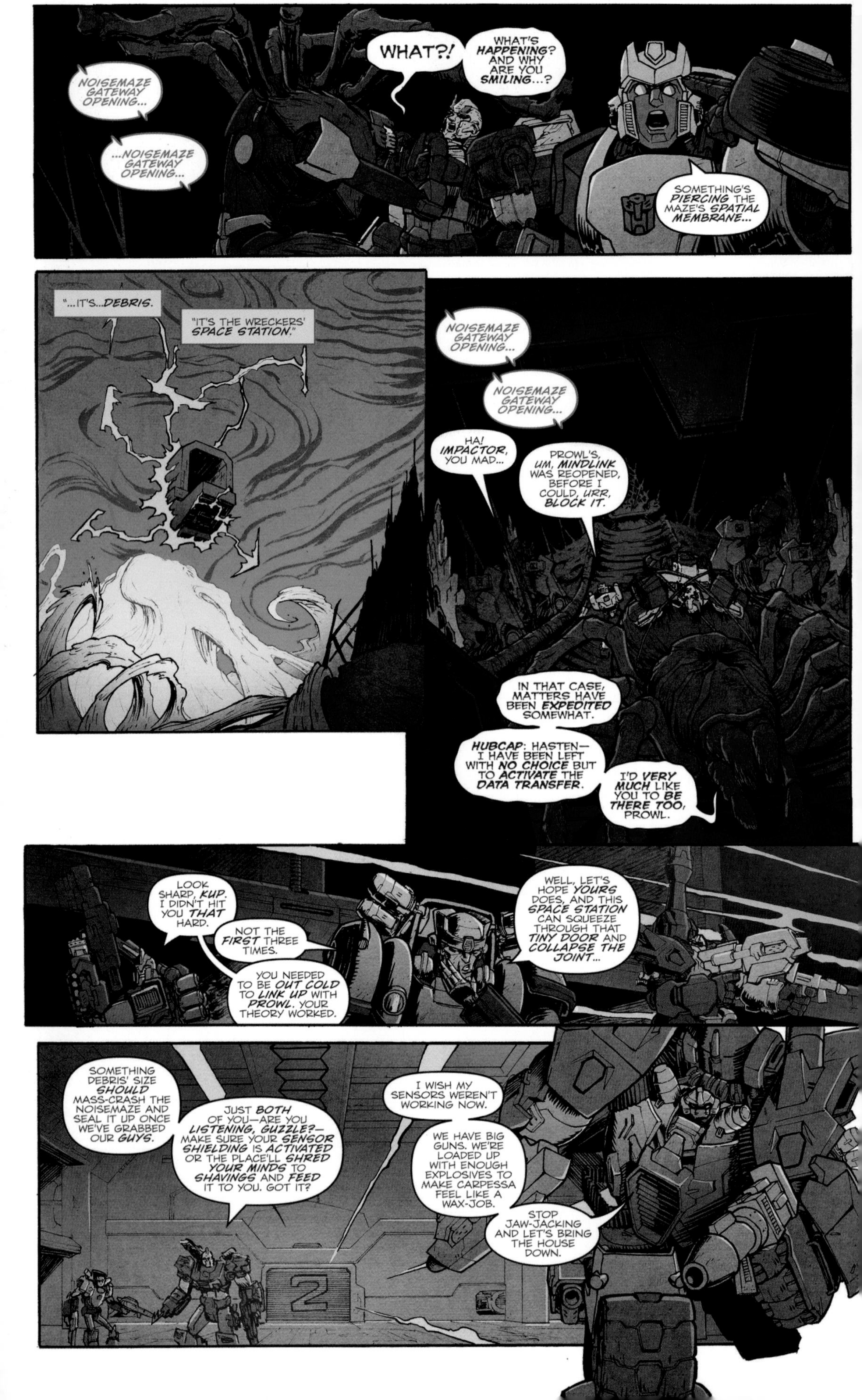
NOISEMAZE GATEWAY OPENING...
...NOISEMAZE GATEWAY OPENING...
WHAT?!
WHAT'S HAPPENING? AND WHY ARE YOU SMILING...?
SOMETHING'S PIERCING THE MAZE'S SPATIAL MEMBRANE...
"...IT'S...DEBRIS.
"IT'S THE WRECKERS' SPACE STATION."
NOISEMAZE GATEWAY OPENING...
NOISEMAZE GATEWAY OPENING...
HA! IMPACTOR, YOU MAD...
PROWL'S, UM, MINDLINK WAS REOPENED, BEFORE I COULD, URR, BLOCK IT.
IN THAT CASE, MATTERS HAVE BEEN EXPEDITED SOMEWHAT.
HUBCAP: HASTEN— I HAVE BEEN LEFT WITH NO CHOICE BUT TO ACTIVATE THE DATA TRANSFER.
I'D VERY MUCH LIKE YOU TO BE THERE TOO, PROWL.
LOOK SHARP, KUP. I DIDN'T HIT YOU THAT HARD.
NOT THE FIRST THREE TIMES.
YOU NEEDED TO BE OUT COLD TO LINK UP WITH PROWL. YOUR THEORY WORKED.
WELL, LET'S HOPE YOURS DOES, AND THIS SPACE STATION CAN SQUEEZE THROUGH THAT TINY DOOR AND COLLAPSE THE JOINT...
SOMETHING DEBRIS' SIZE SHOULD MASS-CRASH THE NOISEMAZE AND SEAL IT UP ONCE WE'VE GRABBED OUR GUYS.
JUST BOTH OF YOU—ARE YOU LISTENING, GUZZLE?— MAKE SURE YOUR SENSOR SHIELDING IS ACTIVATED OR THE PLACE'LL SHRED YOUR MINDS TO SHAVINGS AND FEED IT TO YOU. GOT IT?
I WISH MY SENSORS WEREN'T WORKING NOW.
WE HAVE BIG GUNS. WE'RE LOADED UP WITH ENOUGH EXPLOSIVES TO MAKE CARPESSA FEEL LIKE A WAX-JOB.
STOP JAW-JACKING AND LET'S BRING THE HOUSE DOWN.

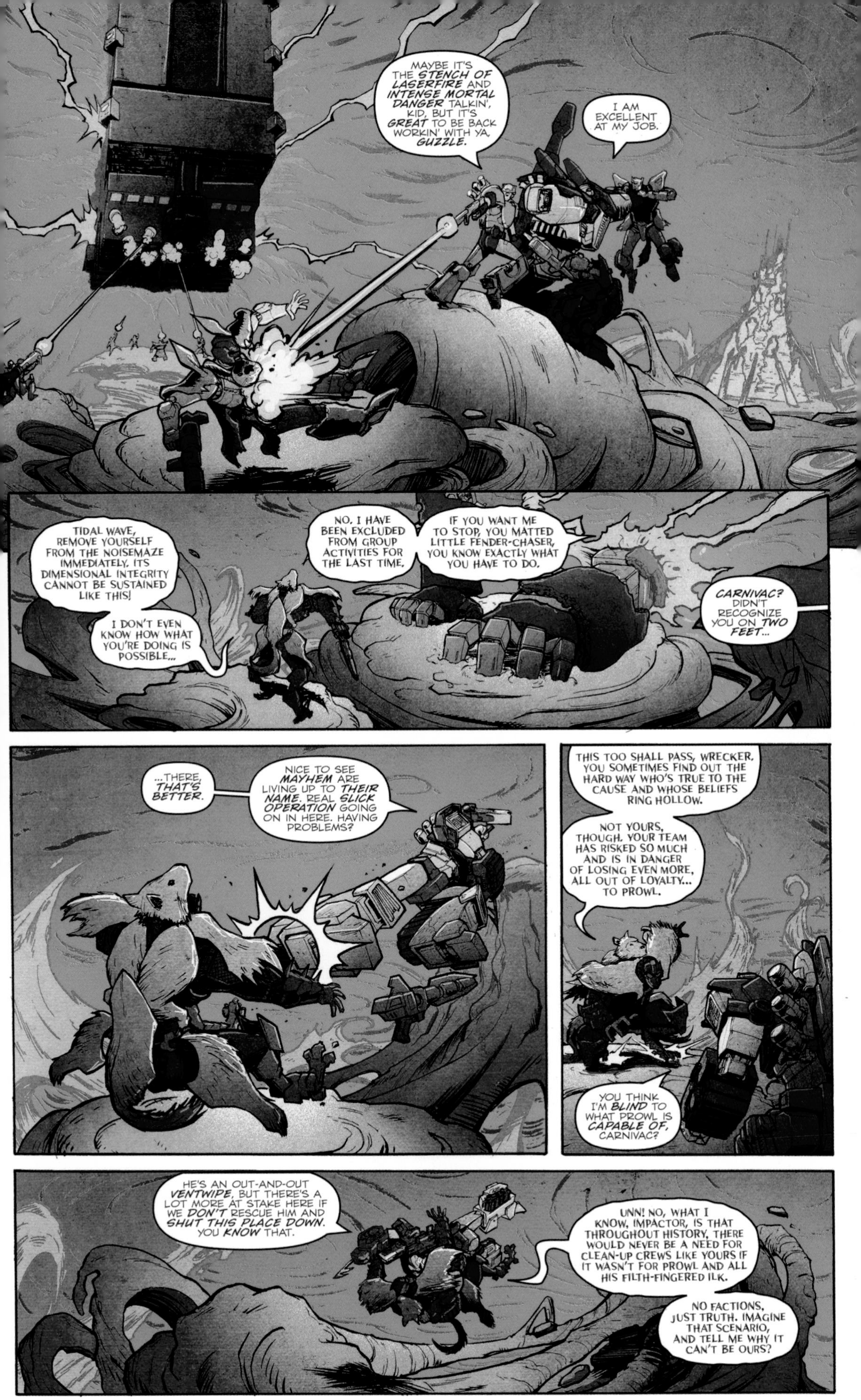
MAYBE IT'S THE STENCH OF LASERFIRE AND INTENSE MORTAL DANGER TALKIN', KID, BUT IT'S GREAT TO BE BACK WORKIN' WITH YA, GUZZLE.
I AM EXCELLENT AT MY JOB.
TIDAL WAVE, REMOVE YOURSELF FROM THE NOISEMAZE IMMEDIATELY. ITS DIMENSIONAL INTEGRITY CANNOT BE SUSTAINED LIKE THIS!
I DON'T EVEN KNOW HOW WHAT YOU'RE DOING IS POSSIBLE...
NO. I HAVE BEEN EXCLUDED FROM GROUP ACTIVITIES FOR THE LAST TIME.
IF YOU WANT ME TO STOP, YOU MATTED LITTLE FENDER-CHASER, YOU KNOW EXACTLY WHAT YOU HAVE TO DO.
CARNIVAC? DIDN'T RECOGNIZE YOU ON TWO FEET...
...THERE, THAT'S BETTER.
NICE TO SEE MAYHEM ARE LIVING UP TO THEIR NAME. REAL SLICK OPERATION GOING ON IN HERE. HAVING PROBLEMS?
THIS TOO SHALL PASS, WRECKER. YOU SOMETIMES FIND OUT THE HARD WAY WHO'S TRUE TO THE CAUSE AND WHOSE BELIEFS RING HOLLOW.
NOT YOURS, THOUGH. YOUR TEAM HAS RISKED SO MUCH AND IS IN DANGER OF LOSING EVEN MORE, ALL OUT OF LOYALTY... TO PROWL.
YOU THINK I'M BLIND TO WHAT PROWL IS CAPABLE OF, CARNIVAC?
HE'S AN OUT-AND-OUT VENTWIPE, BUT THERE'S A LOT MORE AT STAKE HERE IF WE DON'T RESCUE HIM AND SHUT THIS PLACE DOWN. YOU KNOW THAT.
UNN! NO, WHAT I KNOW, IMPACTOR, IS THAT THROUGHOUT HISTORY, THERE WOULD NEVER BE A NEED FOR CLEAN-UP CREWS LIKE YOURS IF IT WASN'T FOR PROWL AND ALL HIS FILTH-FINGERED ILK.
NO FACTIONS, JUST TRUTH. IMAGINE THAT SCENARIO, AND TELL ME WHY IT CAN'T BE OURS?

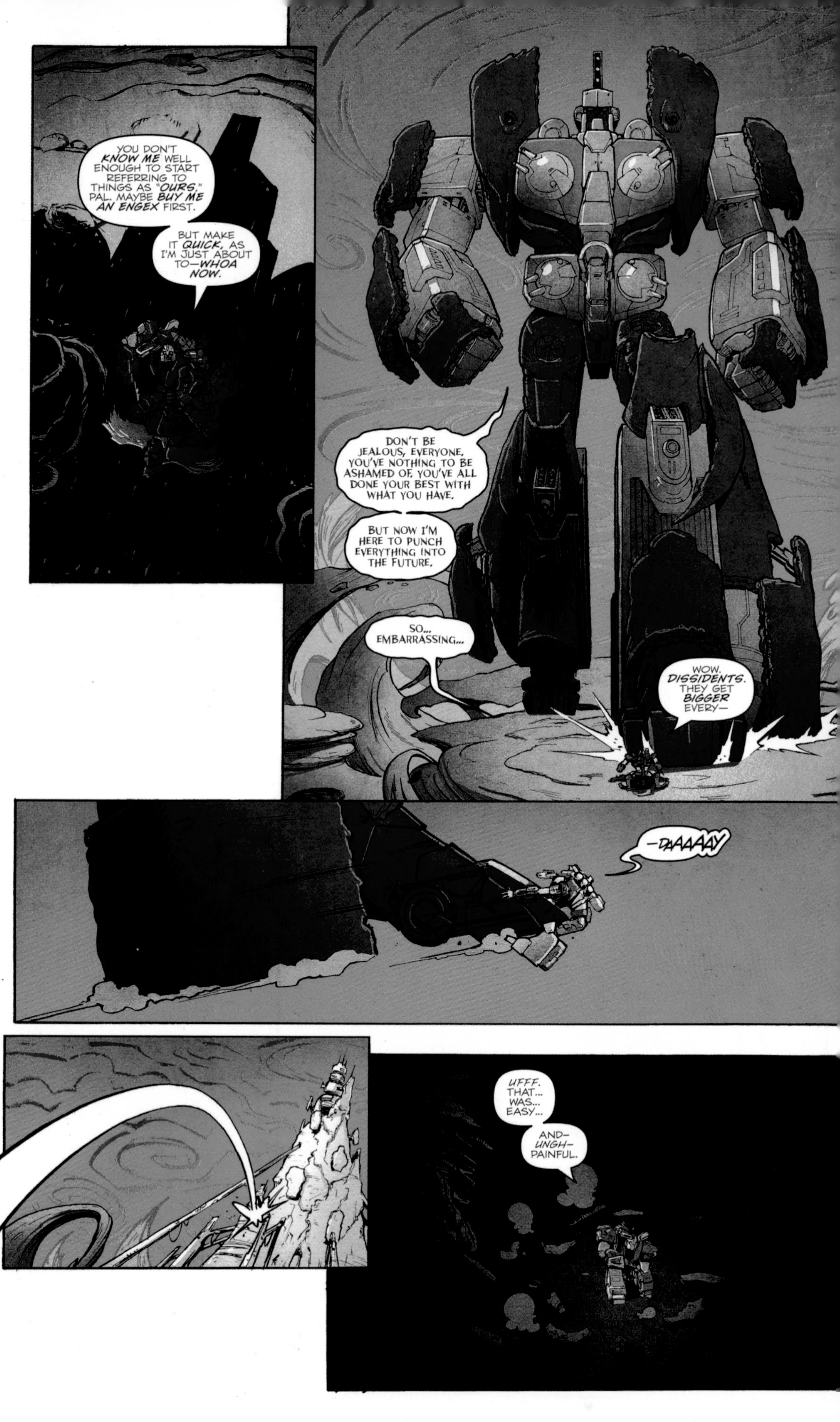
YOU DON'T KNOW ME WELL ENOUGH TO START REFERRING TO THINGS AS "OURS," PAL. MAYBE BUY ME AN ENGEX FIRST.
BUT MAKE IT QUICK, AS I'M JUST ABOUT TO—WHOA NOW.
DON'T BE JEALOUS, EVERYONE. YOU'VE NOTHING TO BE ASHAMED OF. YOU'VE ALL DONE YOUR BEST WITH WHAT YOU HAVE.
BUT NOW I'M HERE TO PUNCH EVERYTHING INTO THE FUTURE.
SO... EMBARRASSING...
WOW. DISSIDENTS. THEY GET BIGGER EVERY—
—DAAAAAY
UFFF. THAT... WAS... EASY...
AND— UNGH— PAINFUL.

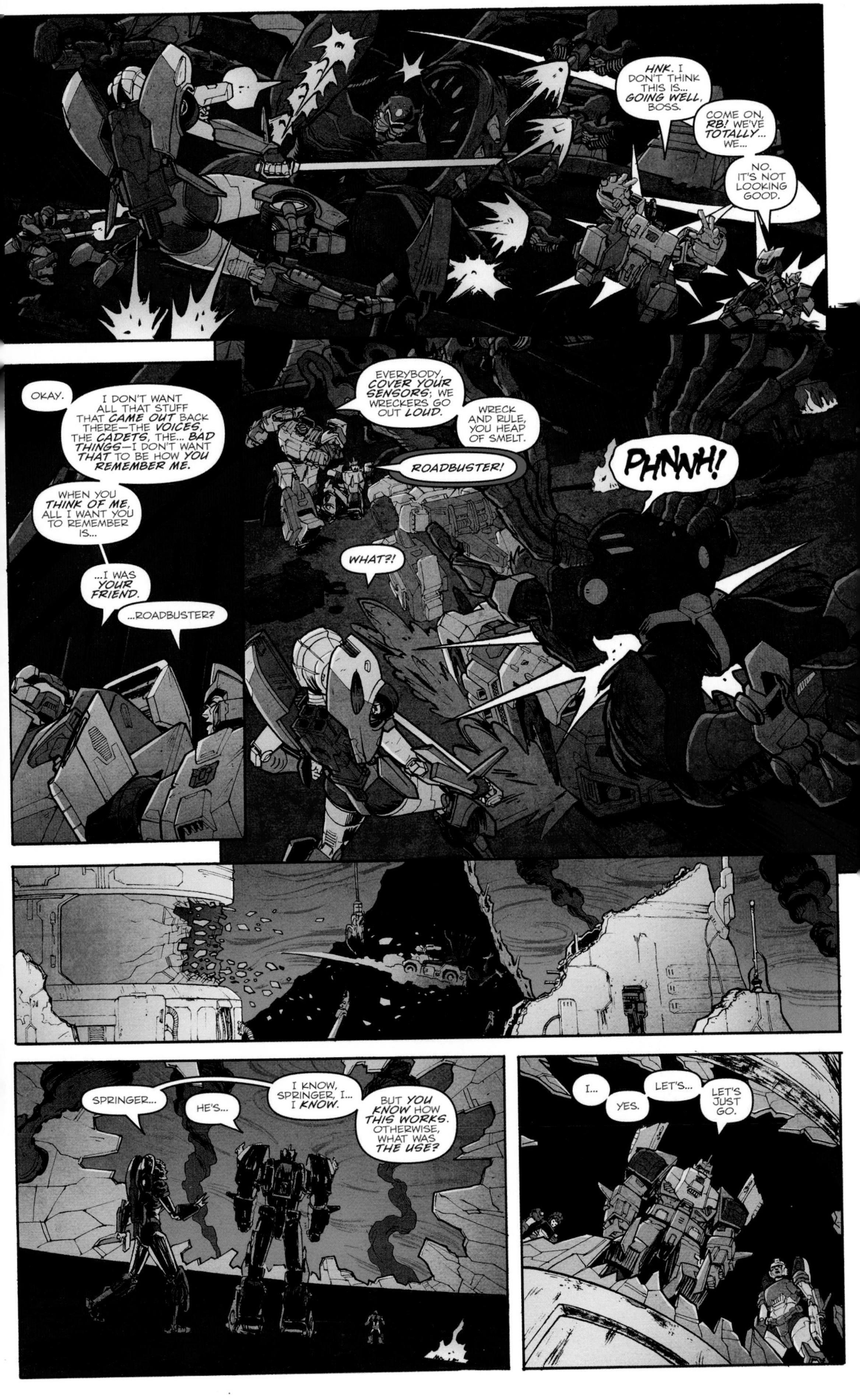

HNK. I DON'T THINK THIS IS... GOING WELL, BOSS.
COME ON, RB! WE'VE TOTALLY... WE...
NO. IT'S NOT LOOKING GOOD.
OKAY.
I DON'T WANT ALL THAT STUFF THAT CAME OUT BACK THERE—THE VOICES, THE CADETS, THE... BAD THINGS—I DON'T WANT THAT TO BE HOW YOU REMEMBER ME.
WHEN YOU THINK OF ME, ALL I WANT YOU TO REMEMBER IS...
...I WAS YOUR FRIEND.
...ROADBUSTER?
EVERYBODY, COVER YOUR SENSORS; WE WRECKERS GO OUT LOUD.
WRECK AND RULE, YOU HEAP OF SMELT.
ROADBUSTER!
PHNWH!
WHAT?!
SPRINGER...
HE'S...
I KNOW, SPRINGER, I... I KNOW.
BUT YOU KNOW HOW THIS WORKS. OTHERWISE, WHAT WAS THE USE?
I...
YES.
LET'S...
LET'S JUST GO.

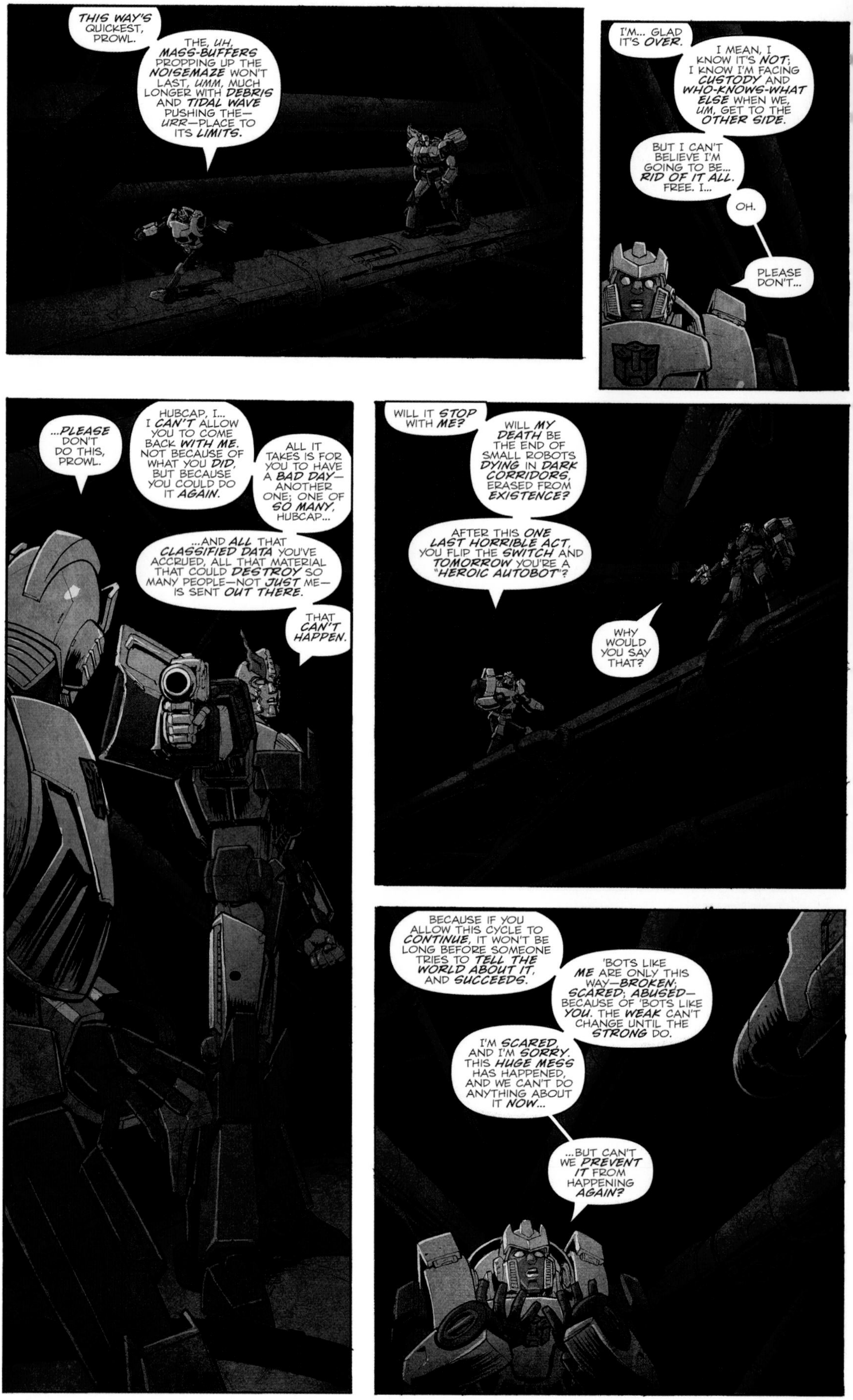
THIS WAY'S QUICKEST, PROWL.
THE, UH, MASS-BUFFERS PROPPING UP THE NOISEMAZE WON'T LAST, UMM, MUCH LONGER WITH DEBRIS AND TIDAL WAVE PUSHING THE—URR—PLACE TO ITS LIMITS.
I'M... GLAD IT'S OVER.
I MEAN, I KNOW IT'S NOT; I KNOW I'M FACING CUSTODY AND WHO-KNOWS-WHAT ELSE WHEN WE, UM, GET TO THE OTHER SIDE.
BUT I CAN'T BELIEVE I'M GOING TO BE... RID OF IT ALL. FREE. I...
OH.
PLEASE DON'T...
...PLEASE DON'T DO THIS, PROWL.
HUBCAP, I... I CAN'T ALLOW YOU TO COME BACK WITH ME. NOT BECAUSE OF WHAT YOU DID, BUT BECAUSE YOU COULD DO IT AGAIN.
ALL IT TAKES IS FOR YOU TO HAVE A BAD DAY—ANOTHER ONE; ONE OF SO MANY, HUBCAP...
...AND ALL THAT CLASSIFIED DATA YOU'VE ACCRUED, ALL THAT MATERIAL THAT COULD DESTROY SO MANY PEOPLE—NOT JUST ME—IS SENT OUT THERE.
THAT CAN'T HAPPEN.
WILL IT STOP WITH ME?
WILL MY DEATH BE THE END OF SMALL ROBOTS DYING IN DARK CORRIDORS, ERASED FROM EXISTENCE?
AFTER THIS ONE LAST HORRIBLE ACT, YOU FLIP THE SWITCH AND TOMORROW YOU'RE A "HEROIC AUTOBOT"?
WHY WOULD YOU SAY THAT?
BECAUSE IF YOU ALLOW THIS CYCLE TO CONTINUE, IT WON'T BE LONG BEFORE SOMEONE TRIES TO TELL THE WORLD ABOUT IT, AND SUCCEEDS.
'BOTS LIKE ME ARE ONLY THIS WAY—BROKEN; SCARED; ABUSED—BECAUSE OF 'BOTS LIKE YOU. THE WEAK CAN'T CHANGE UNTIL THE STRONG DO.
I'M SCARED, AND I'M SORRY. THIS HUGE MESS HAS HAPPENED, AND WE CAN'T DO ANYTHING ABOUT IT NOW...
...BUT CAN'T WE PREVENT IT FROM HAPPENING AGAIN?

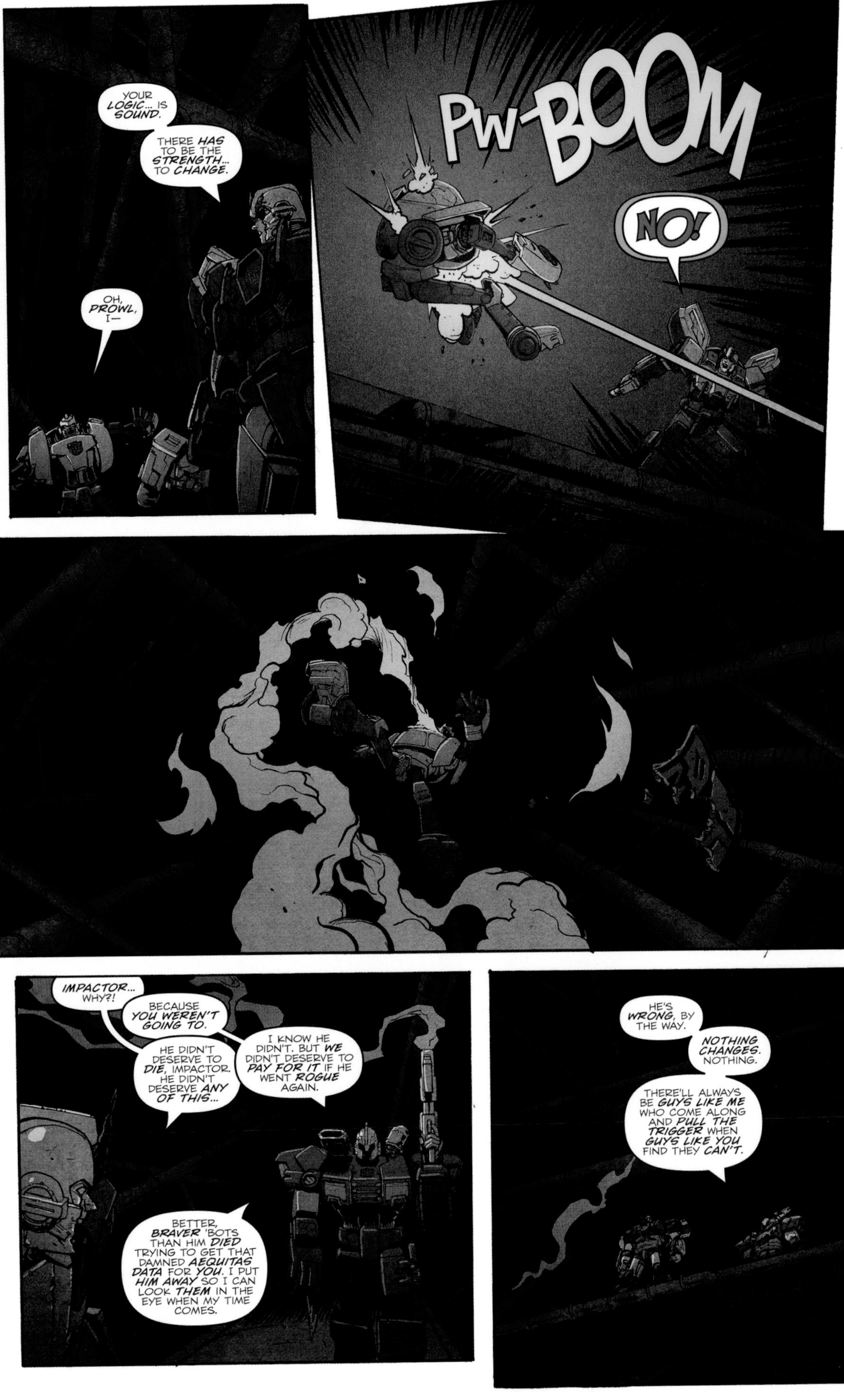

YOUR LOGIC... IS SOUND.
THERE HAS TO BE THE STRENGTH... TO CHANGE.
OH, PROWL, I—
PW-BOOM
NO!
IMPACTOR... WHY?!
BECAUSE YOU WEREN'T GOING TO.
HE DIDN'T DESERVE TO DIE, IMPACTOR. HE DIDN'T DESERVE ANY OF THIS...
I KNOW HE DIDN'T. BUT WE DIDN'T DESERVE TO PAY FOR IT IF HE WENT ROGUE AGAIN.
BETTER, BRAVER 'BOTS THAN HIM DIED TRYING TO GET THAT DAMNED AEQUITAS DATA FOR YOU. I PUT HIM AWAY SO I CAN LOOK THEM IN THE EYE WHEN MY TIME COMES.
HE'S WRONG, BY THE WAY.
NOTHING CHANGES. NOTHING.
THERE'LL ALWAYS BE GUYS LIKE ME WHO COME ALONG AND PULL THE TRIGGER WHEN GUYS LIKE YOU FIND THEY CAN'T.

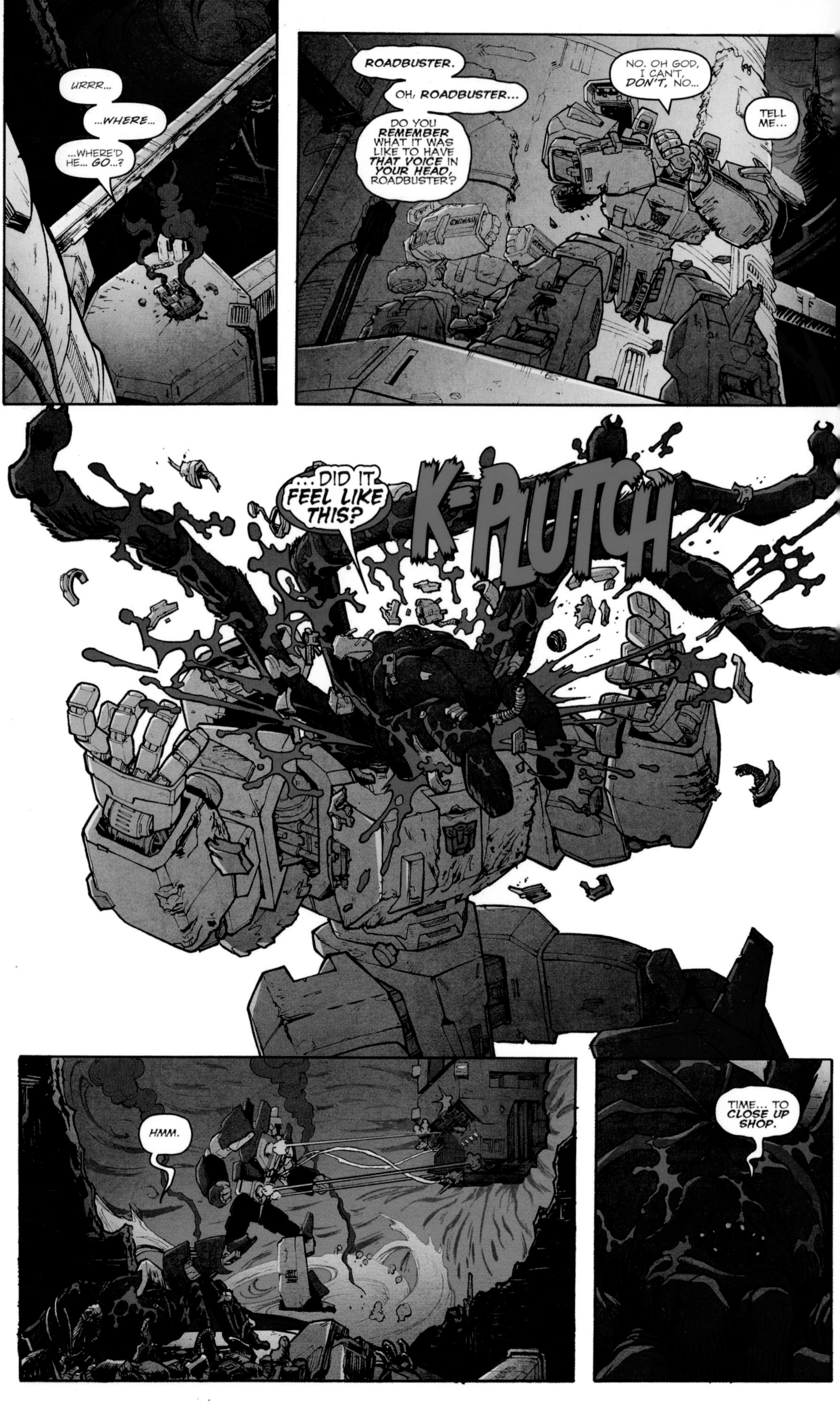
URRR...
...WHERE...
...WHERE'D HE... GO...?
ROADBUSTER.
OH, ROADBUSTER...
DO YOU REMEMBER WHAT IT WAS LIKE TO HAVE THAT VOICE IN YOUR HEAD, ROADBUSTER?
NO. OH GOD, I CAN'T, DON'T, NO...
TELL ME...
...DID IT FEEL LIKE THIS?
K-PLUTCH
HMM.
TIME... TO CLOSE UP SHOP.

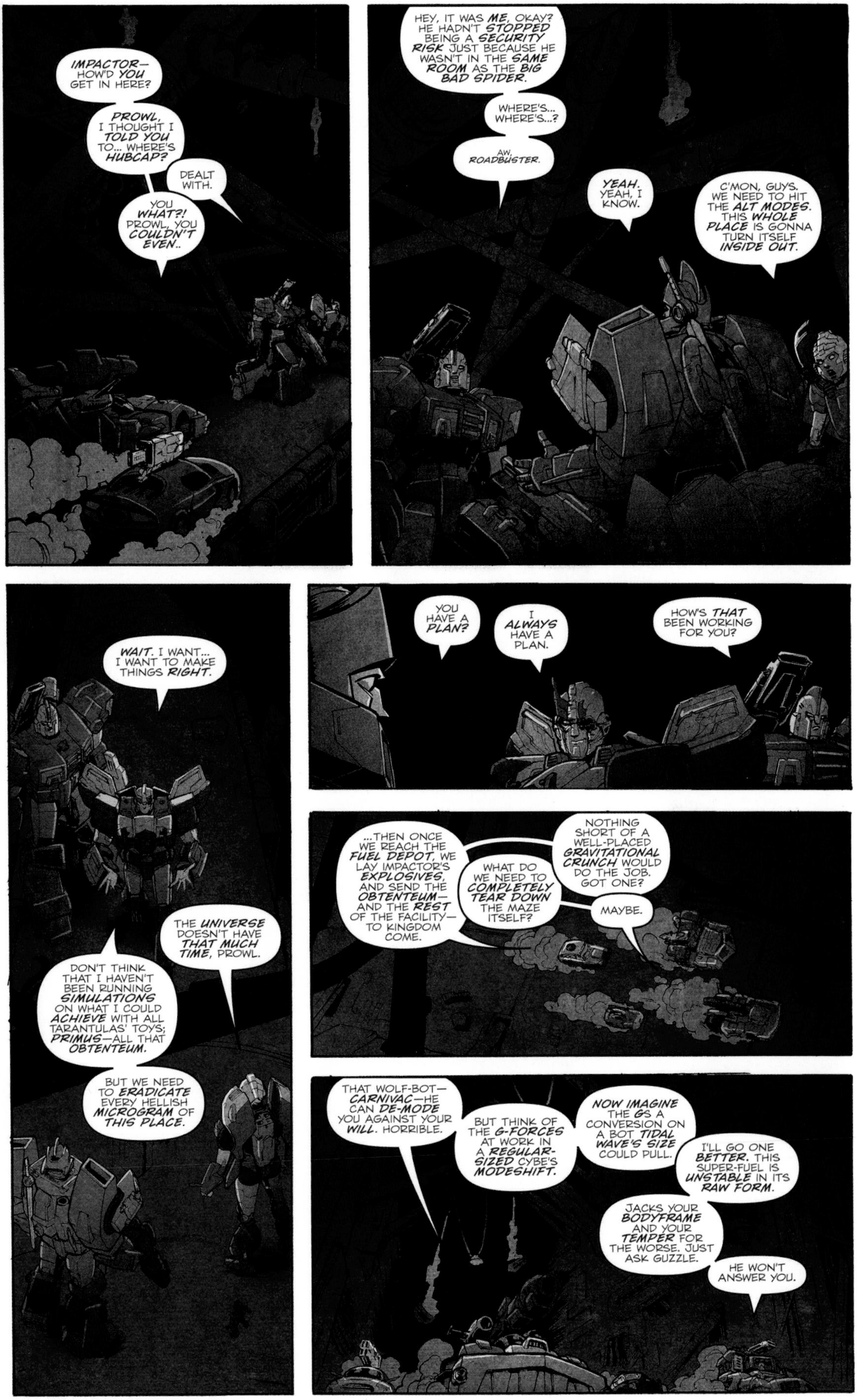
IMPACTOR— HOW'D YOU GET IN HERE?
PROWL, I THOUGHT I TOLD YOU TO... WHERE'S HUBCAP?
DEALT WITH.
YOU WHAT?! PROWL, YOU COULDN'T EVEN..
HEY, IT WAS ME, OKAY? HE HADN'T STOPPED BEING A SECURITY RISK JUST BECAUSE HE WASN'T IN THE SAME ROOM AS THE BIG BAD SPIDER.
WHERE'S... WHERE'S...?
AW, ROADBUSTER.
YEAH. YEAH, I KNOW.
C'MON, GUYS. WE NEED TO HIT THE ALT MODES. THIS WHOLE PLACE IS GONNA TURN ITSELF INSIDE OUT.
WAIT. I WANT... I WANT TO MAKE THINGS RIGHT.
THE UNIVERSE DOESN'T HAVE THAT MUCH TIME, PROWL.
DON'T THINK THAT I HAVEN'T BEEN RUNNING SIMULATIONS ON WHAT I COULD ACHIEVE WITH ALL TARANTULAS' TOYS; PRIMUS—ALL THAT OBTENTEUM.
BUT WE NEED TO ERADICATE EVERY HELLISH MICROGRAM OF THIS PLACE.
YOU HAVE A PLAN?
I ALWAYS HAVE A PLAN.
HOW'S THAT BEEN WORKING FOR YOU?
...THEN ONCE WE REACH THE FUEL DEPOT, WE LAY IMPACTOR'S EXPLOSIVES, AND SEND THE OBTENTEUM—AND THE REST OF THE FACILITY—TO KINGDOM COME.
WHAT DO WE NEED TO COMPLETELY TEAR DOWN THE MAZE ITSELF?
NOTHING SHORT OF A WELL-PLACED GRAVITATIONAL CRUNCH WOULD DO THE JOB. GOT ONE?
MAYBE.
THAT WOLF-BOT—CARNIVAC—HE CAN DE-MODE YOU AGAINST YOUR WILL. HORRIBLE.
BUT THINK OF THE G-FORCES AT WORK IN A REGULAR-SIZED CYBE'S MODESHIFT.
NOW IMAGINE THE GS A CONVERSION ON A BOT TIDAL WAVE'S SIZE COULD PULL.
I'LL GO ONE BETTER. THIS SUPER-FUEL IS UNSTABLE IN ITS RAW FORM.
JACKS YOUR BODYFRAME AND YOUR TEMPER FOR THE WORSE. JUST ASK GUZZLE.
HE WON'T ANSWER YOU.

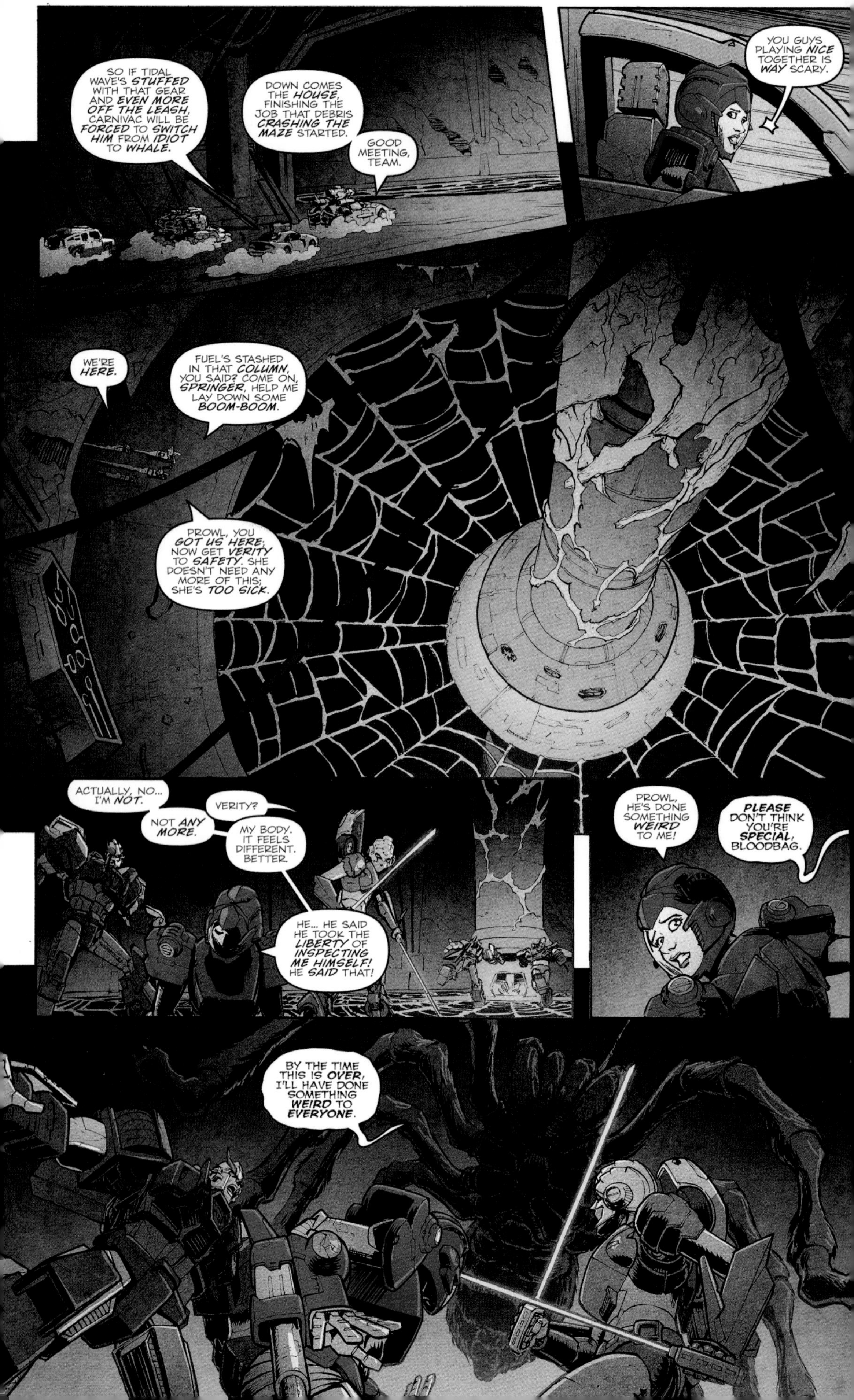
SO IF TIDAL WAVE'S STUFFED WITH THAT GEAR AND EVEN MORE OFF THE LEASH, CARNIVAC WILL BE FORCED TO SWITCH HIM FROM IDIOT TO WHALE.
DOWN COMES THE HOUSE, FINISHING THE JOB THAT DEBRIS CRASHING THE MAZE STARTED.
GOOD MEETING, TEAM.
YOU GUYS PLAYING NICE TOGETHER IS WAY SCARY.
WE'RE HERE.
FUEL'S STASHED IN THAT COLUMN, YOU SAID? COME ON, SPRINGER, HELP ME LAY DOWN SOME BOOM-BOOM.
PROWL, YOU GOT US HERE; NOW GET VERITY TO SAFETY. SHE DOESN'T NEED ANY MORE OF THIS; SHE'S TOO SICK.
ACTUALLY, NO... I'M NOT.
VERITY?
NOT ANY MORE.
MY BODY. IT FEELS DIFFERENT. BETTER.
HE... HE SAID HE TOOK THE LIBERTY OF INSPECTING ME HIMSELF! HE SAID THAT!
PROWL, HE'S DONE SOMETHING WEIRD TO ME!
PLEASE DON'T THINK YOU'RE SPECIAL, BLOODBAG.
BY THE TIME THIS IS OVER, I'LL HAVE DONE SOMETHING WEIRD TO EVERYONE.

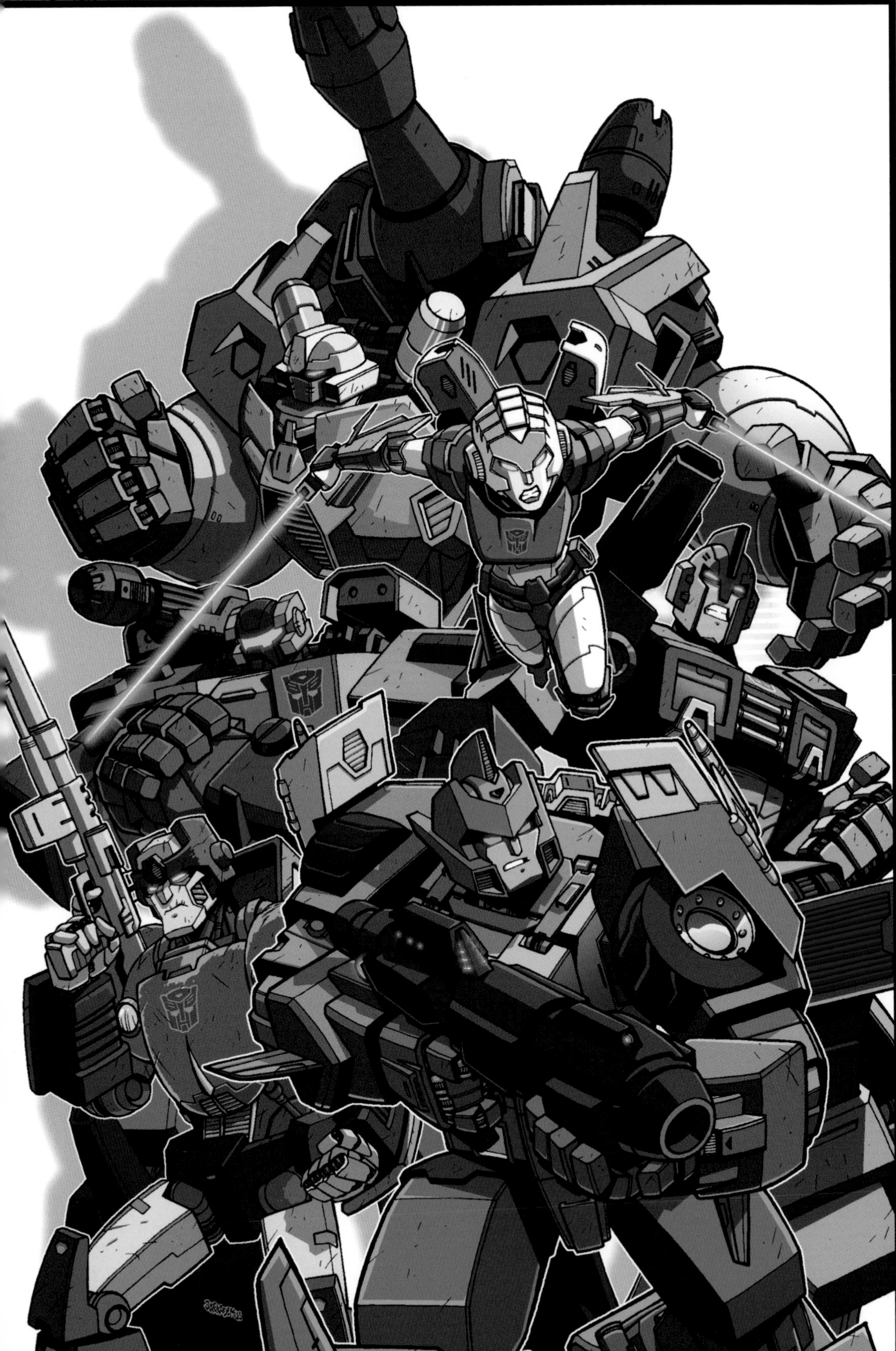

ART JACK LAWRENCE

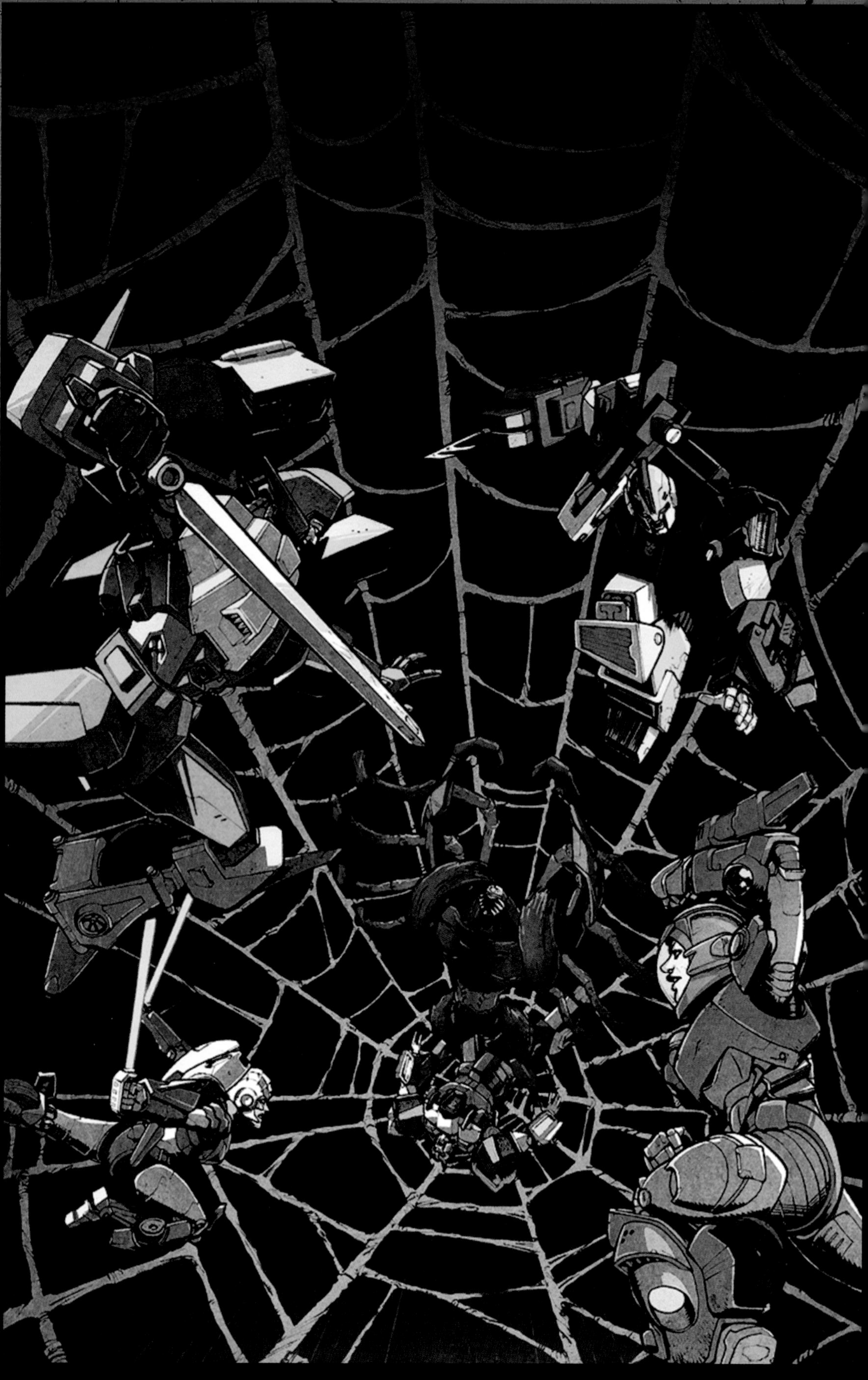

ART NICK ROCHE COLORS JOSH BURCHAM

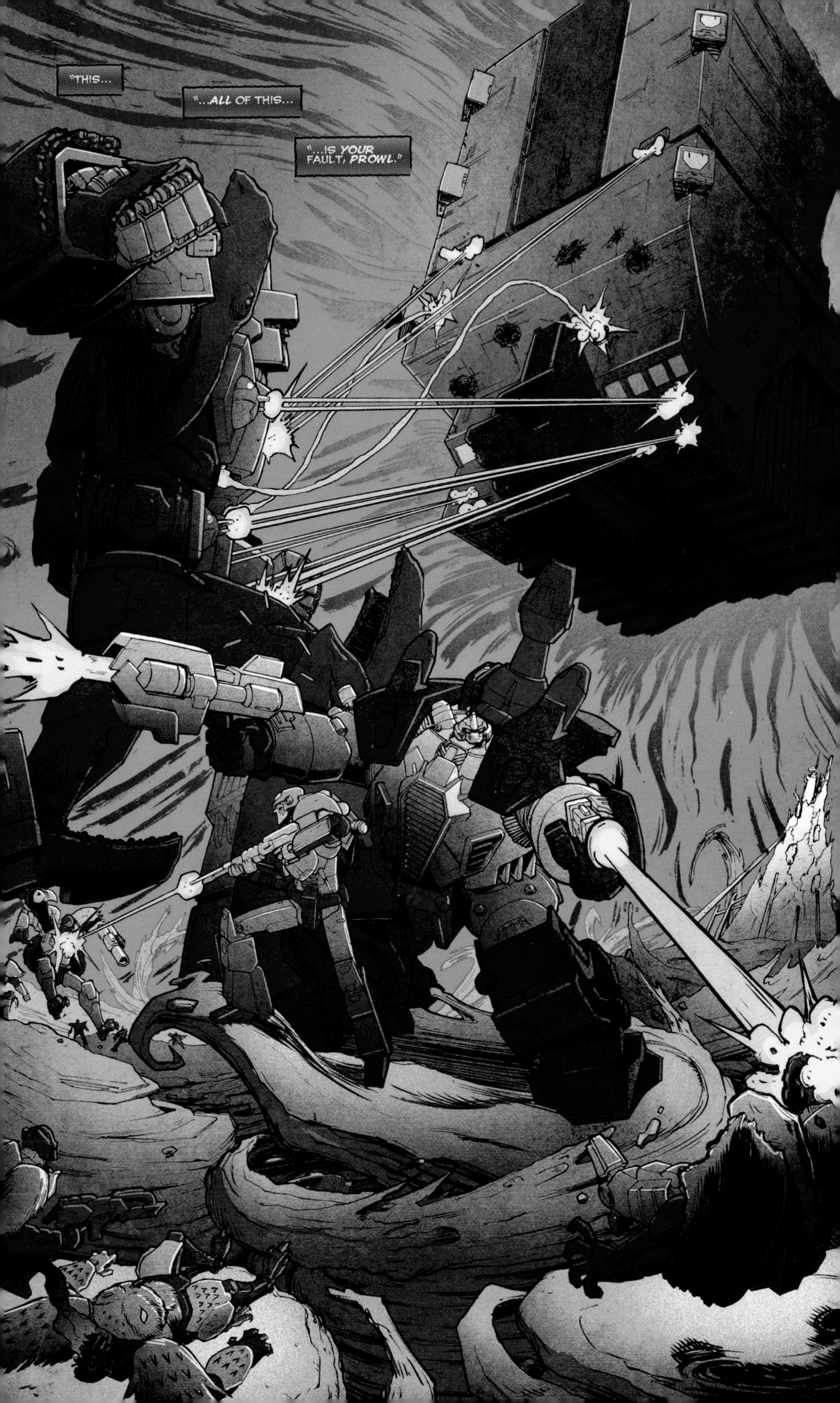
"THIS...
"...ALL OF THIS...
"...IS YOUR FAULT, PROWL."

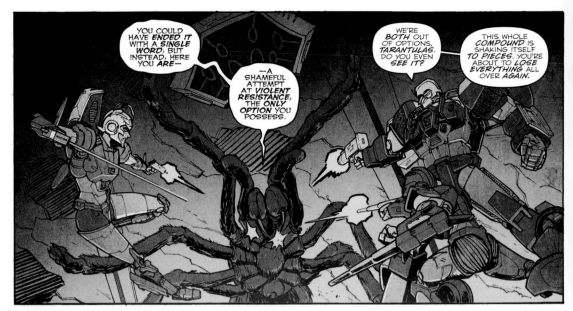

YOU COULD HAVE *ENDED IT* WITH A *SINGLE WORD*, BUT INSTEAD, HERE YOU *ARE*—

—A *SHAMEFUL ATTEMPT* AT *VIOLENT RESISTANCE*, THE *ONLY OPTION* YOU POSSESS.

WE'RE *BOTH* OUT OF OPTIONS, *TARANTULAS*. DO YOU EVEN *SEE* IT?

THIS WHOLE *COMPOUND* IS SHAKING ITSELF *TO PIECES*. YOU'RE ABOUT TO *LOSE EVERYTHING* ALL OVER *AGAIN*.

I DON'T REMEMBER YOU BEING THIS *WRONG* THIS *OFTEN*, PROWL.

Y'KNOW, YOU CAN HAVE TOO *MANY* PARTY *TRICKS*...

WE'RE GONNA NEED *BIGGER* SHOE...

I MADE SURE THERE'D BE A *BACK DOOR THIS TIME*, PROWL.

MY RESEARCH, MY DATA... MY *ENTIRE* FACILITY... IT'S ALL COMING *WITH ME*.

AND SO ARE *YOU*, ALL *THREE* OF YOU.

COMPOUND CONTRACTION INITIATED.

NOISEMAZE GATE OPENING.

AN *EX-TEST SUBJECT* OF *JHIAXUS'*; AN *"AUGMENTED" EARTH CREATURE*; AND YOU, *MY PROWL*.

THE THREE OF YOU, *INFINITE FODDER* FOR *MY STUDY*. HOW COULD I EVER GROW WEARY?

THIS *PLACE*... THIS *WHOLE PLACE*... IS *SHRINKING*...

MASS DISPLACEMENT HAS SO MANY USES, *BLOODBAG*.

THE NOISEMAZE MAY PERISH... BUT I HAVE A *WEALTH OF LOCATIONS* I COULD CHOOSE TO *MOURN IT* IN.

SPRINGER...

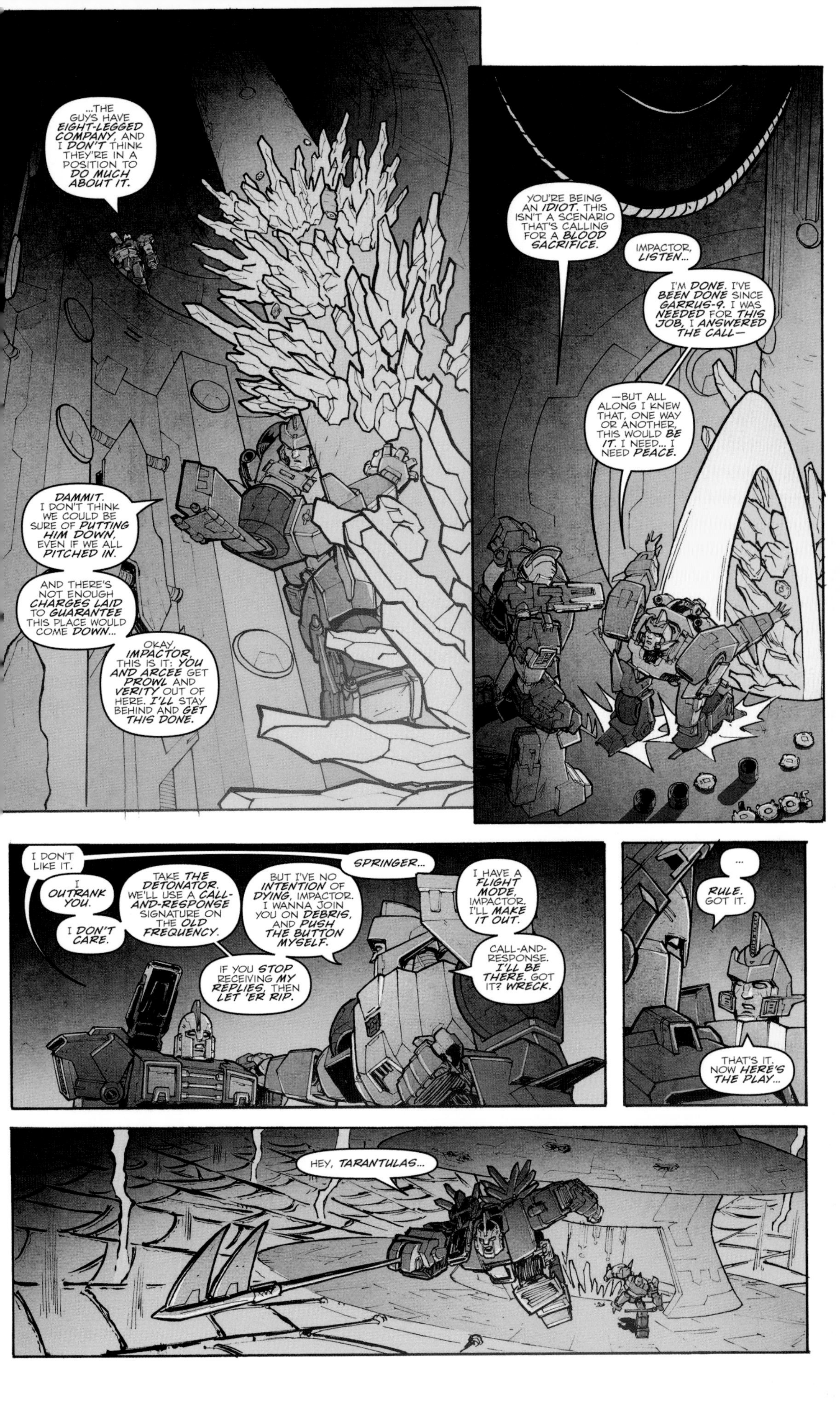
...THE GUYS HAVE EIGHT-LEGGED COMPANY, AND I DON'T THINK THEY'RE IN A POSITION TO DO MUCH ABOUT IT.
DAMMIT. I DON'T THINK WE COULD BE SURE OF PUTTING HIM DOWN, EVEN IF WE ALL PITCHED IN.
AND THERE'S NOT ENOUGH CHARGES LAID TO GUARANTEE THIS PLACE WOULD COME DOWN...
OKAY, IMPACTOR, THIS IS IT: YOU AND ARCEE GET PROWL AND VERITY OUT OF HERE. I'LL STAY BEHIND AND GET THIS DONE.
YOU'RE BEING AN IDIOT. THIS ISN'T A SCENARIO THAT'S CALLING FOR A BLOOD SACRIFICE.
IMPACTOR, LISTEN...
I'M DONE. I'VE BEEN DONE SINCE GARRUS-9. I WAS NEEDED FOR THIS JOB, I ANSWERED THE CALL—
—BUT ALL ALONG I KNEW THAT, ONE WAY OR ANOTHER, THIS WOULD BE IT. I NEED... I NEED PEACE.
I DON'T LIKE IT.
I OUTRANK YOU.
I DON'T CARE.
SPRINGER...
TAKE THE DETONATOR. WE'LL USE A CALL-AND-RESPONSE SIGNATURE ON THE OLD FREQUENCY.
IF YOU STOP RECEIVING MY REPLIES, THEN LET 'ER RIP.
BUT I'VE NO INTENTION OF DYING, IMPACTOR. I WANNA JOIN YOU ON DEBRIS, AND PUSH THE BUTTON MYSELF.
I HAVE A FLIGHT MODE, IMPACTOR. I'LL MAKE IT OUT.
CALL-AND-RESPONSE. I'LL BE THERE. GOT IT? WRECK.
...
RULE. GOT IT.
THAT'S IT. NOW HERE'S THE PLAY...
HEY, TARANTULAS...

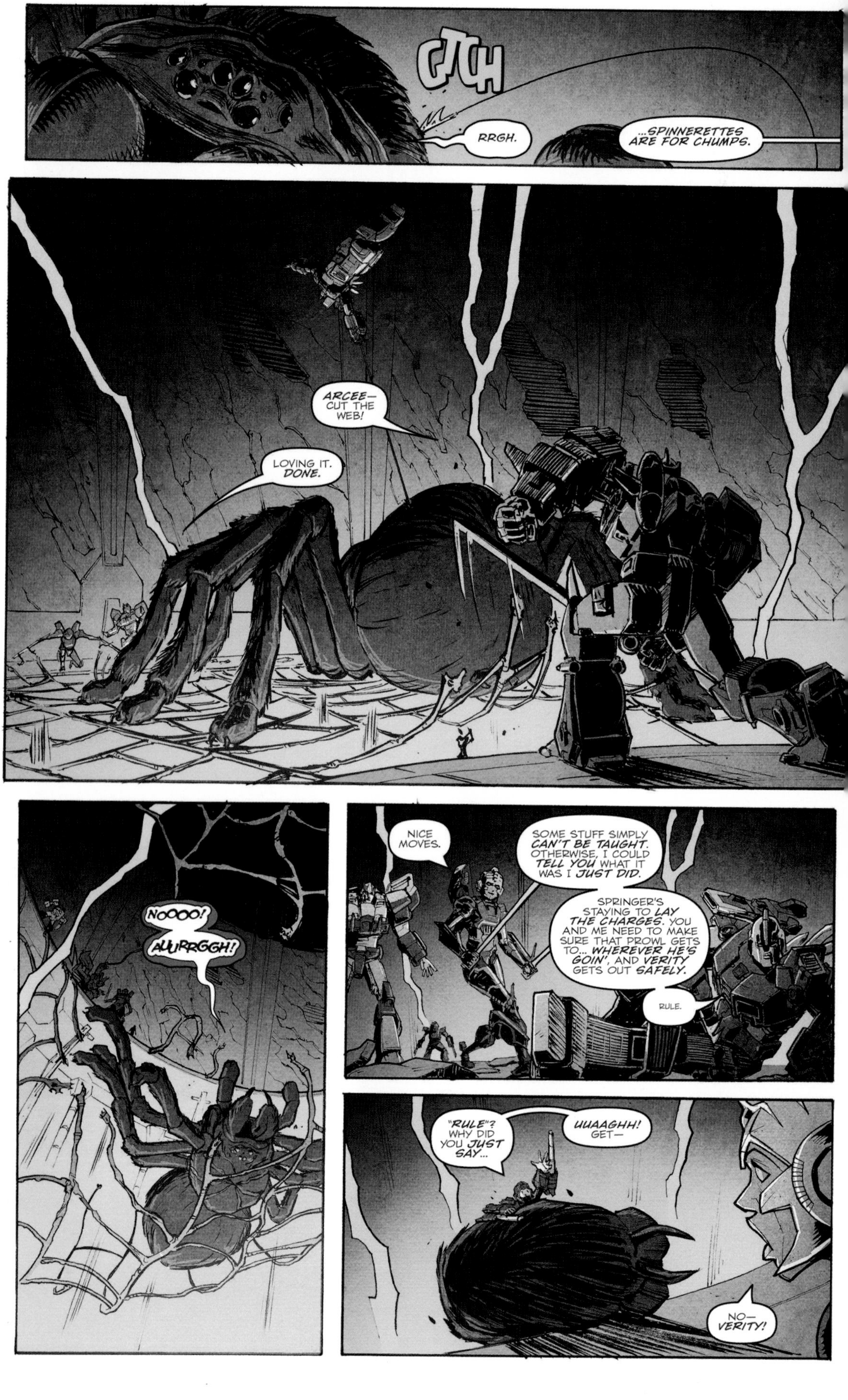
GTCH
RRGH.
...SPINNERETTES ARE FOR CHUMPS.
ARCEE— CUT THE WEB!
LOVING IT. DONE.
NOOOO!
AUURRGGH!
NICE MOVES.
SOME STUFF SIMPLY CAN'T BE TAUGHT. OTHERWISE, I COULD TELL YOU WHAT IT WAS I JUST DID.
SPRINGER'S STAYING TO LAY THE CHARGES. YOU AND ME NEED TO MAKE SURE THAT PROWL GETS TO... WHEREVER HE'S GOIN', AND VERITY GETS OUT SAFELY.
RULE.
"RULE"? WHY DID YOU JUST SAY...
UUAAGHH! GET—
NO— VERITY!

PLEASE—OH GOD OH GOD—THIS IS MORE THERAPY I CAN'T AFFORD!
STOP HIM...
YOU'RE NOT... HAVING HER...!
RULE.
YOUR COLLECTIVE CONCERN FOR THE FLESH-SACK SEEMS A LITTLE LATE, DON'T YOU THINK?
SHE WAS ALL BUT ABANDONED FOLLOWING HER CONTRIBUTION TO YOUR WAR; FOLLOWING HER SACRIFICES.
I WONDER WHAT IT WAS YOU SAW IN HER? A SENTINEL SPECIES, PERHAPS, DESIGNED TO TEST FOR HAZARDS?
A PET?
A MASCOT?
AGH.
I SAW A CREATURE, BROKEN IN SO MANY WAYS. A TINY CONUNDRUM; A KNOTTY LITTLE PUZZLE THAT I WISHED TO TEST MYSELF ON.
WITH ALL MY RESOURCES AND RESEARCH, THE BIO-TECH, THE DERMA-LOOM, THE NANO-SEALANTS, WHY WOULDN'T I PUT MY SKILLS TO THE TEST?
IT DOESN'T MAKE SENSE.
I DON'T EXPECT IT WOULD TO YOU, PROWL. A HELPLESS LIFE, CUT SHORT, IN NEED OF NURTURE AND CARE.
WHAT WOULD THAT MEAN TO YOU ANYWAY?
DO YOU NOT SEE? THIS IS WHAT I WAS CAPABLE OF TOO, PROWL. GIVING LIFE, INSTEAD OF TAKING IT.
THE HUMAN IS WHOLE AGAIN; REPAIRED. YOU COULD NEVER GIVE THAT GIFT. IN THIS WAY—A WAY THAT COUNTS—I WILL ALWAYS BE BETTER THAN YOU.
YOU DON'T GET TO DO THAT...! YOU DON'T GET TO PLAY WITH MY LIFE... MY BODY LIKE THAT, JUST TO SCORE A POINT!
PROWL SET THE RULES TO THIS GAME, BLOODBAG. HE COULD HAVE CALLED A HALT TO IT, YET CHOSE NOT TO. SO NOW I MAKE GOOD ON MY PROMISE.
EVERYTHING I CARED FOR, CRAFTED, LOVED, WAS TAKEN FROM ME. THAT'S SUFFERING. THAT'S WORSE THAN DEATH.
AND NOW I INTEND TO REPAY PROWL IN KIND, BACKDATED TO THE VERY SECOND HE SEALED ME INSIDE THE NOISEMAZE AND LEFT ME TO CRUMBLE.
RULE.
YOU SEEM SO SMART. INSANE, YEAH. CREEPILY DEPENDENT AND FIXATED, DEFINITELY.
BUT YOU COME ACROSS AS KNOWING ABOUT A LOT OF STUFF...

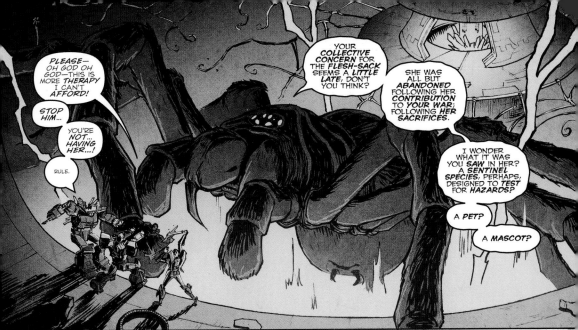

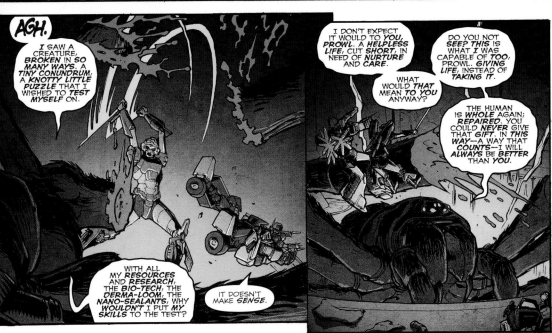

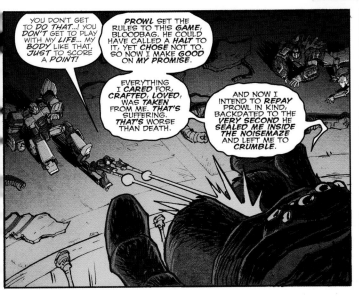

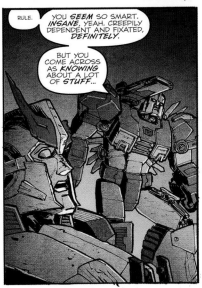

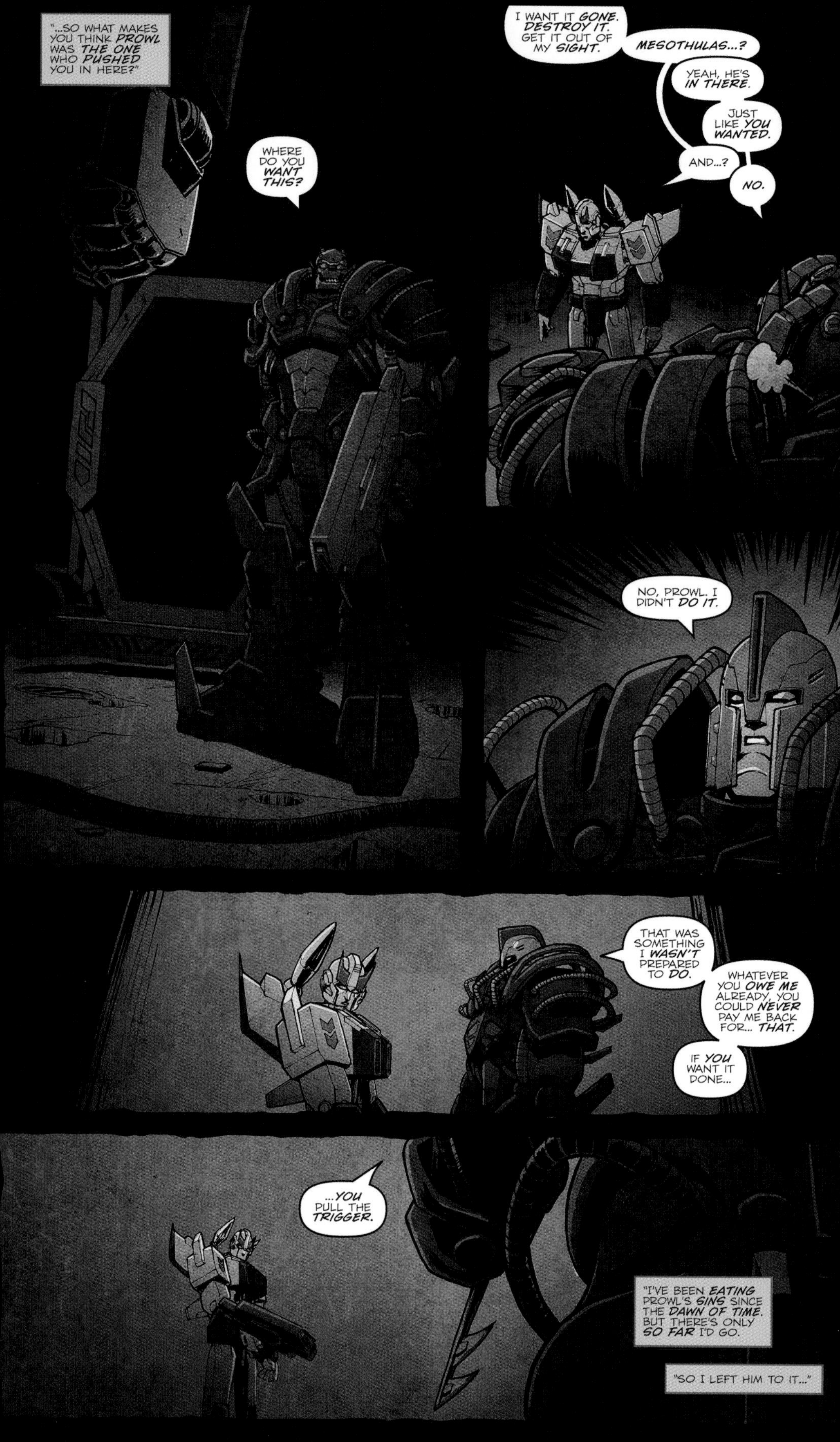
"...SO WHAT MAKES YOU THINK PROWL WAS THE ONE WHO PUSHED YOU IN HERE?"
WHERE DO YOU WANT THIS?
I WANT IT GONE. DESTROY IT. GET IT OUT OF MY SIGHT.
MESOTHULAS...?
YEAH, HE'S IN THERE.
JUST LIKE YOU WANTED.
AND...?
NO.
NO, PROWL. I DIDN'T DO IT.
THAT WAS SOMETHING I WASN'T PREPARED TO DO.
WHATEVER YOU OWE ME ALREADY, YOU COULD NEVER PAY ME BACK FOR... THAT.
IF YOU WANT IT DONE...
...YOU PULL THE TRIGGER.
"I'VE BEEN EATING PROWL'S SINS SINCE THE DAWN OF TIME. BUT THERE'S ONLY SO FAR I'D GO.
"SO I LEFT HIM TO IT..."

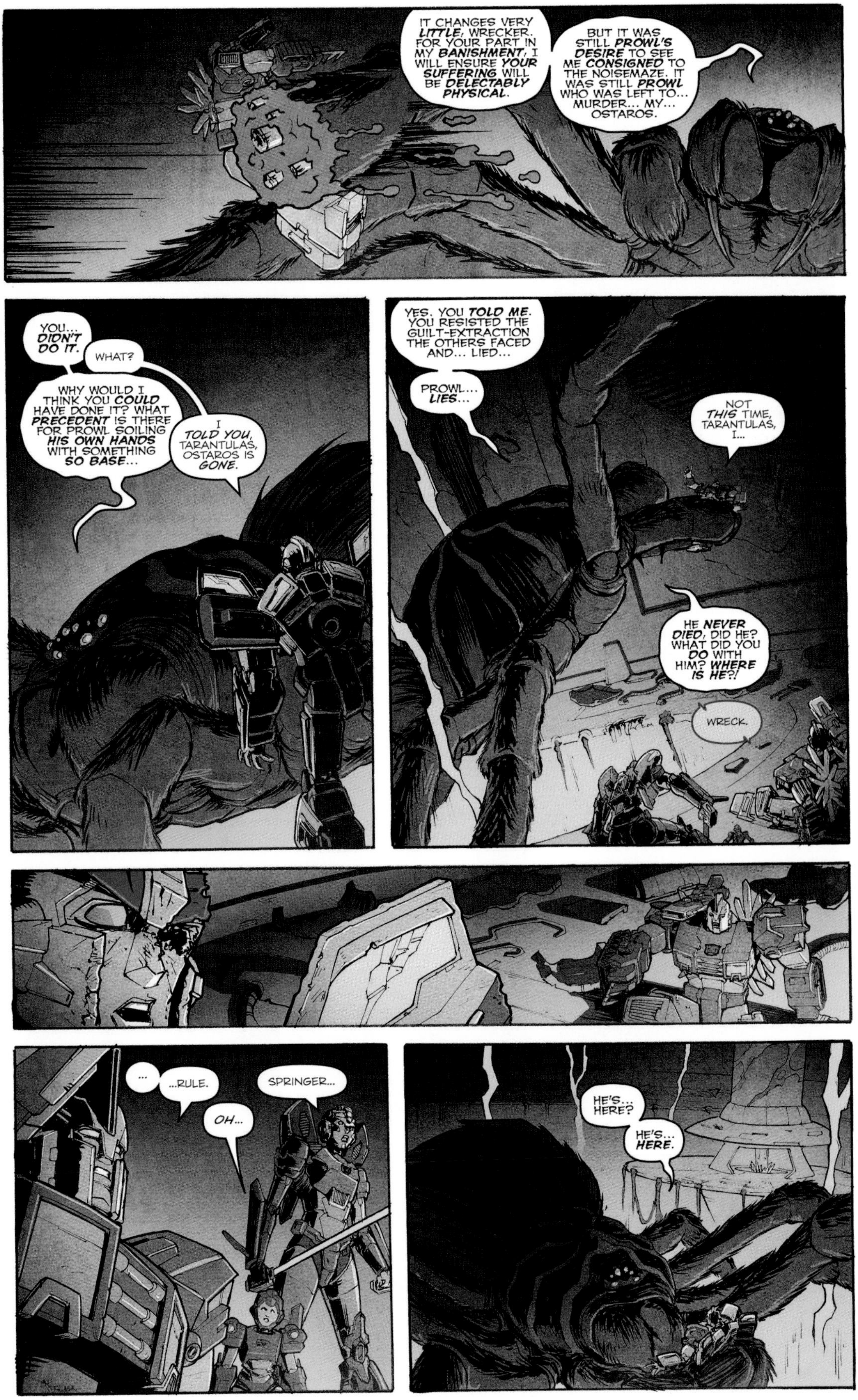

IT CHANGES VERY LITTLE, WRECKER. FOR YOUR PART IN MY BANISHMENT, I WILL ENSURE YOUR SUFFERING WILL BE DELECTABLY PHYSICAL.
BUT IT WAS STILL PROWL'S DESIRE TO SEE ME CONSIGNED TO THE NOISEMAZE. IT WAS STILL PROWL WHO WAS LEFT TO... MURDER... MY... OSTAROS.
YOU... DIDN'T DO IT.
WHAT?
WHY WOULD I THINK YOU COULD HAVE DONE IT? WHAT PRECEDENT IS THERE FOR PROWL SOILING HIS OWN HANDS WITH SOMETHING SO BASE...
I TOLD YOU, TARANTULAS, OSTAROS IS GONE.
YES. YOU TOLD ME. YOU RESISTED THE GUILT-EXTRACTION THE OTHERS FACED AND... LIED...
PROWL... LIES...
NOT THIS TIME, TARANTULAS, I...
HE NEVER DIED, DID HE? WHAT DID YOU DO WITH HIM? WHERE IS HE?!
WRECK.
...
...RULE.
OH...
SPRINGER...
HE'S... HERE?
HE'S... HERE.

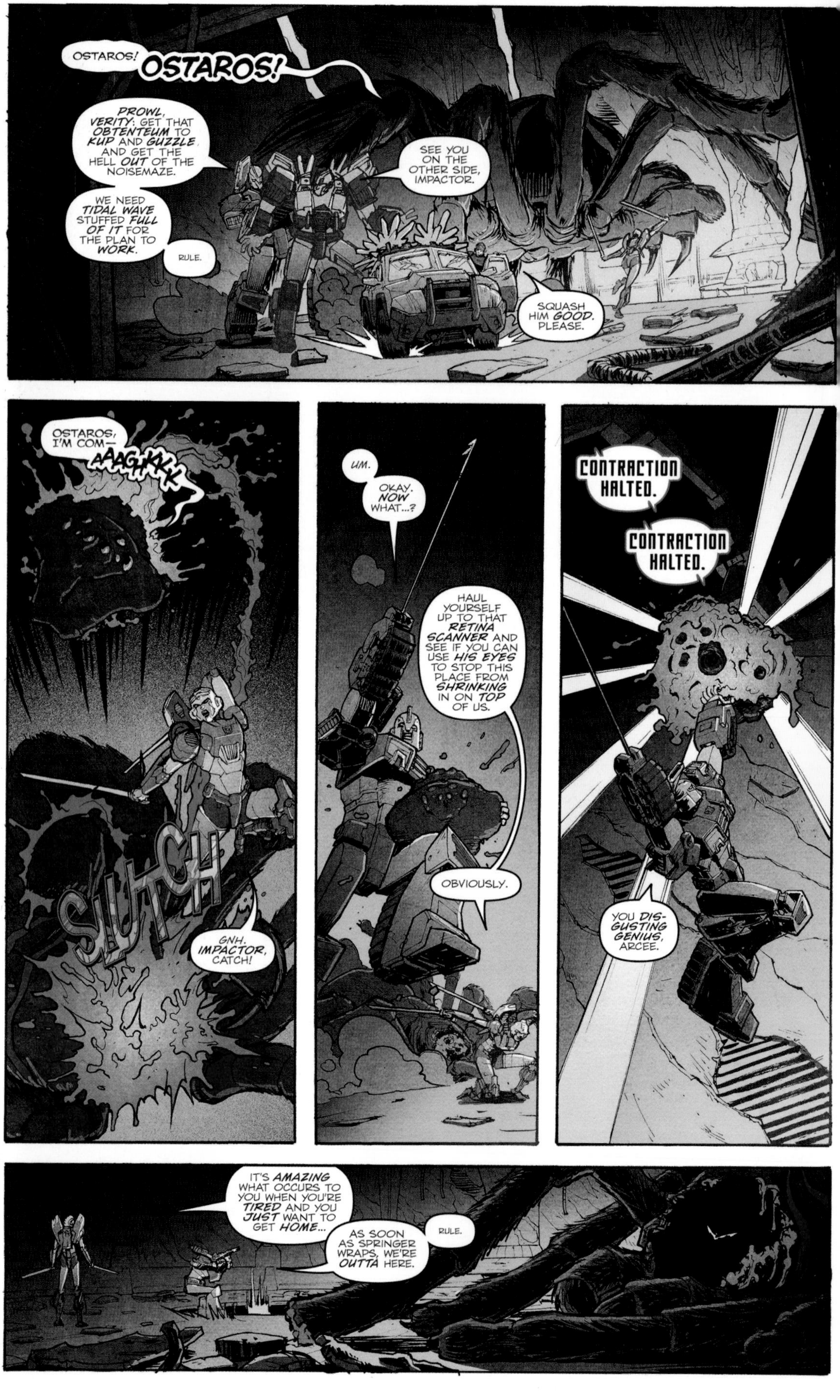
OSTAROS! OSTAROS!
PROWL, VERITY: GET THAT OBTENTEUM TO KUP AND GUZZLE AND GET THE HELL OUT OF THE NOISEMAZE.
WE NEED TIDAL WAVE STUFFED FULL OF IT FOR THE PLAN TO WORK.
RULE.
SEE YOU ON THE OTHER SIDE, IMPACTOR.
SQUASH HIM GOOD. PLEASE.
OSTAROS, I'M COM—AAAGHKKK
SLUTCH
GNH. IMPACTOR, CATCH!
UM.
OKAY. NOW WHAT...?
HAUL YOURSELF UP TO THAT RETINA SCANNER AND SEE IF YOU CAN USE HIS EYES TO STOP THIS PLACE FROM SHRINKING IN ON TOP OF US.
OBVIOUSLY.
CONTRACTION HALTED.
CONTRACTION HALTED.
YOU DISGUSTING GENIUS, ARCEE.
IT'S AMAZING WHAT OCCURS TO YOU WHEN YOU'RE TIRED AND YOU JUST WANT TO GET HOME...
RULE.
AS SOON AS SPRINGER WRAPS, WE'RE OUTTA HERE.

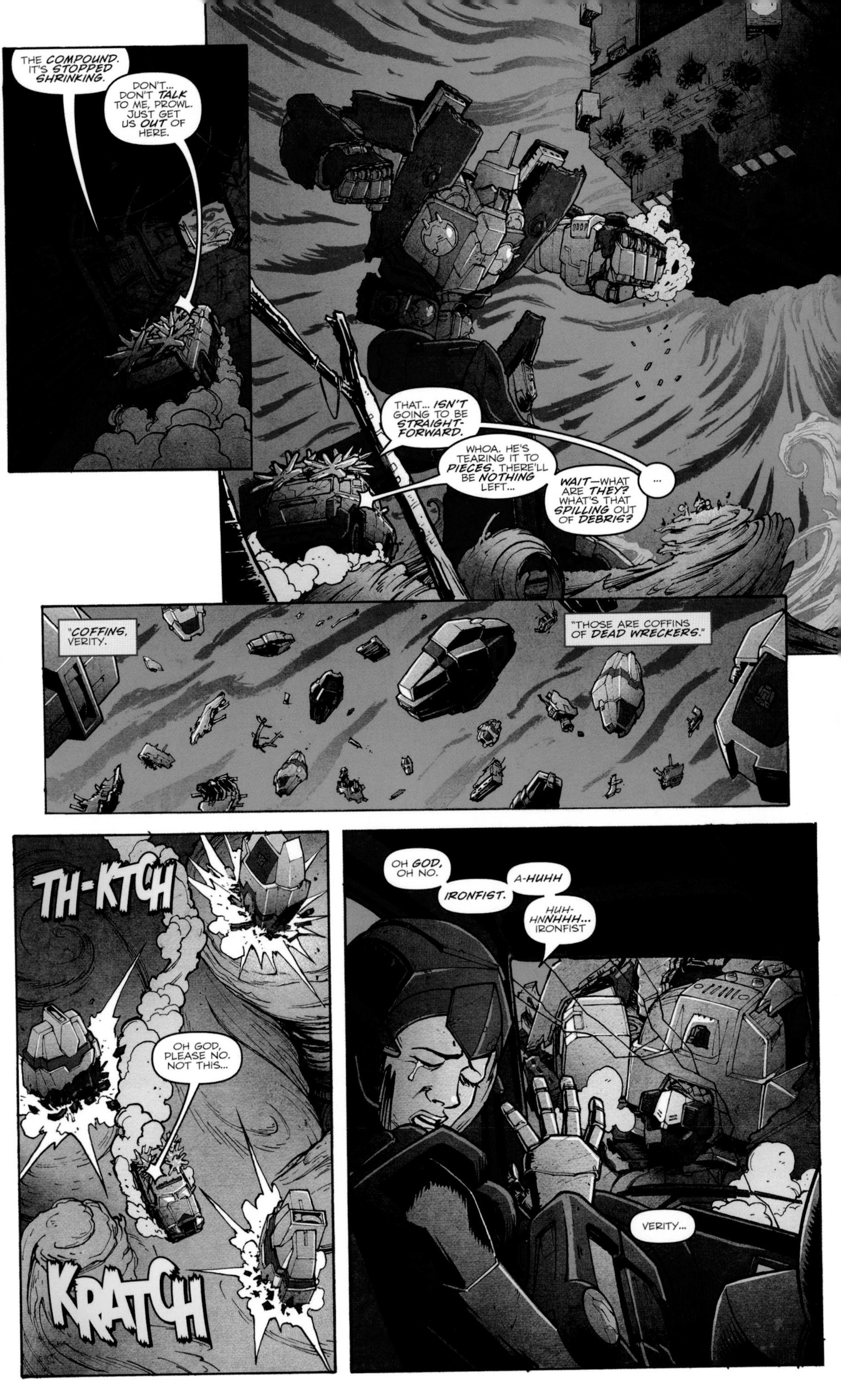

THE COMPOUND. IT'S STOPPED SHRINKING.
DON'T... DON'T TALK TO ME, PROWL. JUST GET US OUT OF HERE.
THAT... ISN'T GOING TO BE STRAIGHT-FORWARD.
WHOA. HE'S TEARING IT TO PIECES. THERE'LL BE NOTHING LEFT...
...
WAIT—WHAT ARE THEY? WHAT'S THAT SPILLING OUT OF DEBRIS?
"COFFINS, VERITY.
"THOSE ARE COFFINS OF DEAD WRECKERS."
TH-KTCH
OH GOD, PLEASE NO. NOT THIS...
KRATCH
OH GOD, OH NO.
IRONFIST.
A-HUHH
HUH-HNNHHH... IRONFIST
VERITY...

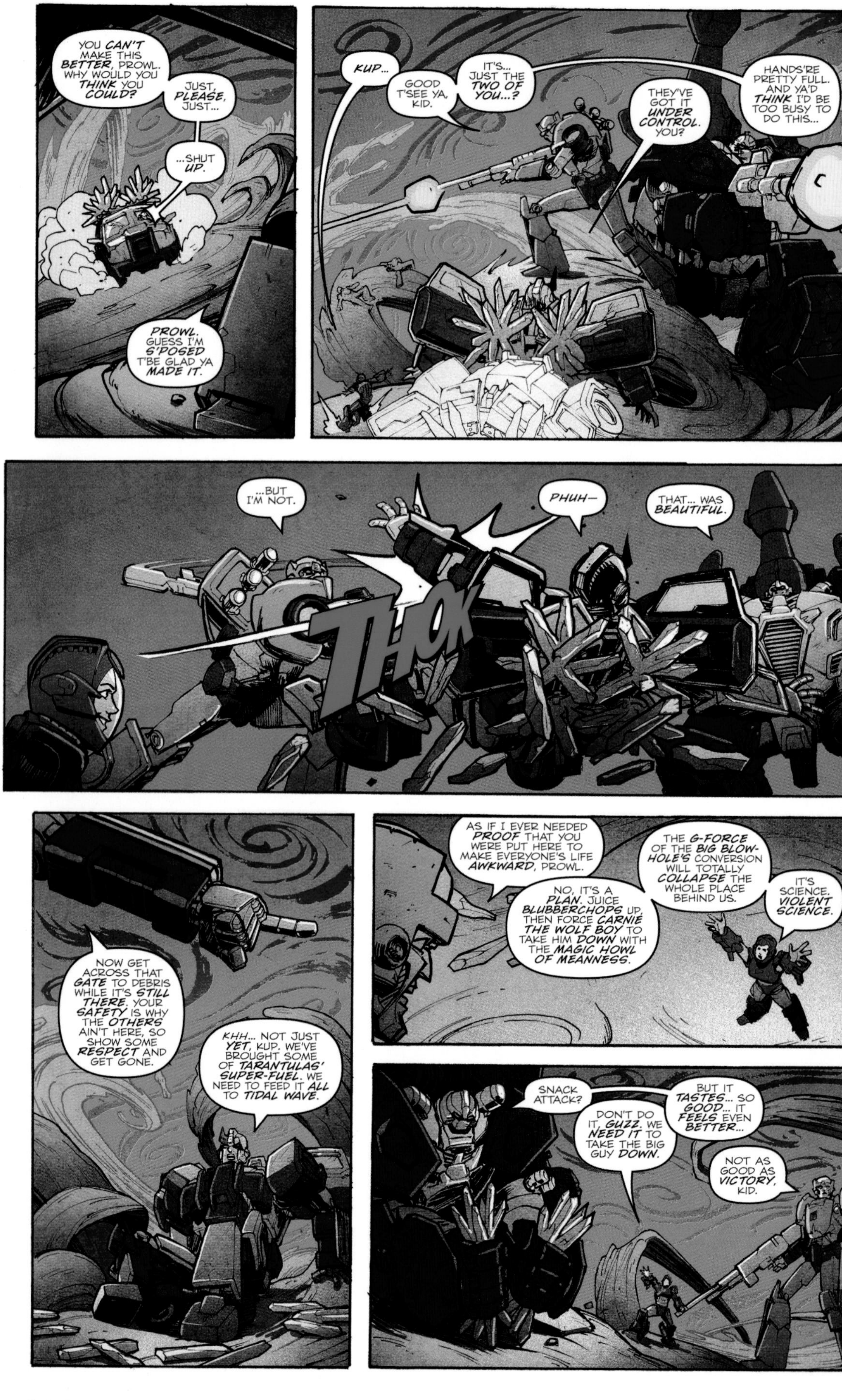

YOU CAN'T MAKE THIS BETTER, PROWL. WHY WOULD YOU THINK YOU COULD?
JUST, PLEASE, JUST...
...SHUT UP.
PROWL. GUESS I'M S'POSED T'BE GLAD YA MADE IT.
KUP...
GOOD T'SEE YA, KID.
IT'S... JUST THE TWO OF YOU...?
THEY'VE GOT IT UNDER CONTROL. YOU?
HANDS'RE PRETTY FULL. AND YA'D THINK I'D BE TOO BUSY TO DO THIS...
...BUT I'M NOT.
PHUH—
THAT... WAS BEAUTIFUL.
THOK
NOW GET ACROSS THAT GATE TO DEBRIS WHILE IT'S STILL THERE. YOUR SAFETY IS WHY THE OTHERS AIN'T HERE, SO SHOW SOME RESPECT AND GET GONE.
KHH... NOT JUST YET, KUP. WE'VE BROUGHT SOME OF TARANTULAS' SUPER-FUEL. WE NEED TO FEED IT ALL TO TIDAL WAVE.
AS IF I EVER NEEDED PROOF THAT YOU WERE PUT HERE TO MAKE EVERYONE'S LIFE AWKWARD, PROWL.
NO, IT'S A PLAN. JUICE BLUBBERCHOPS UP, THEN FORCE CARNIE THE WOLF BOY TO TAKE HIM DOWN WITH THE MAGIC HOWL OF MEANNESS.
THE G-FORCE OF THE BIG BLOW-HOLE'S CONVERSION WILL TOTALLY COLLAPSE THE WHOLE PLACE BEHIND US.
IT'S SCIENCE. VIOLENT SCIENCE.
SNACK ATTACK?
DON'T DO IT, GUZZ. WE NEED IT TO TAKE THE BIG GUY DOWN.
BUT IT TASTES... SO GOOD... IT FEELS EVEN BETTER...
NOT AS GOOD AS VICTORY, KID.

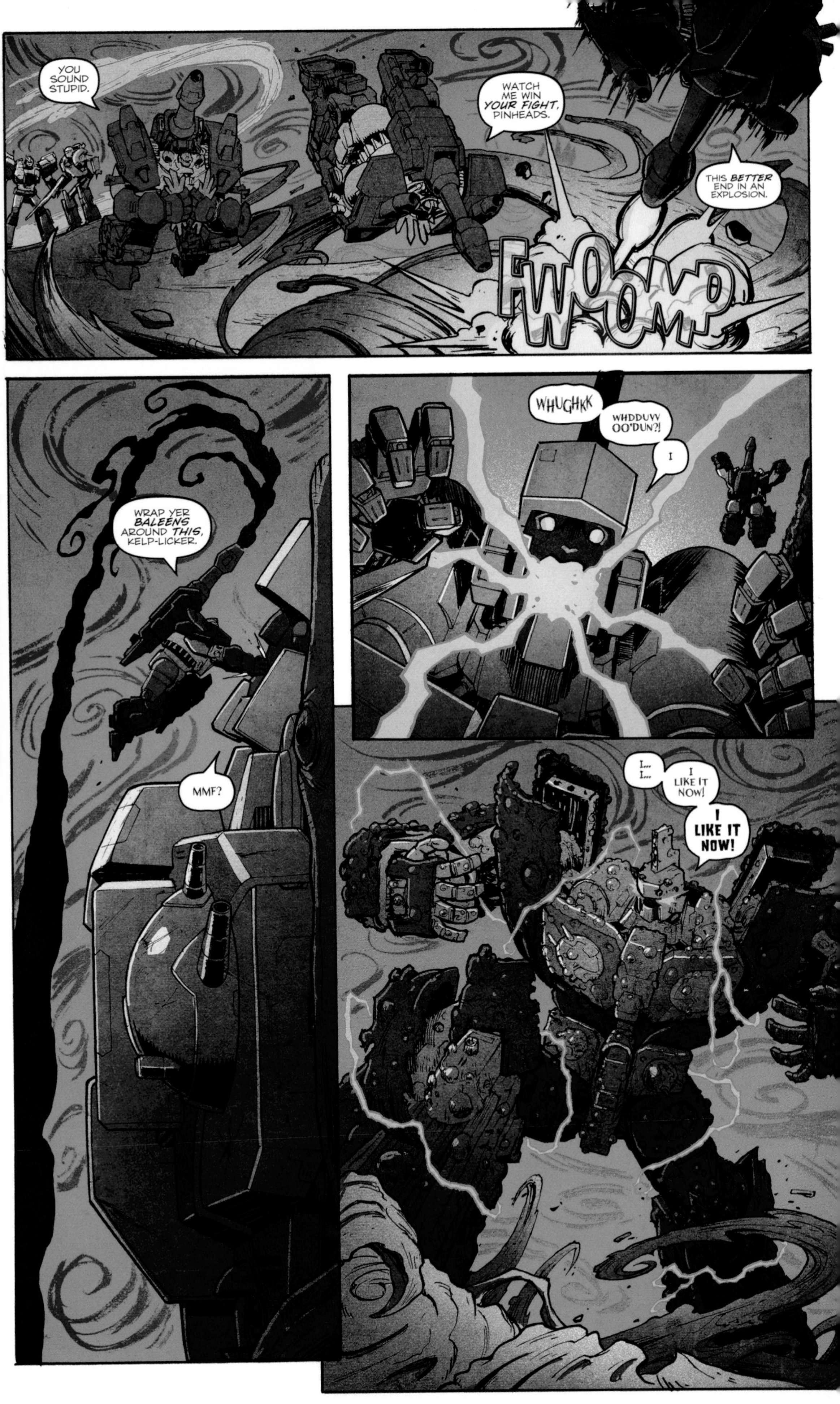
YOU SOUND STUPID.
WATCH ME WIN YOUR FIGHT, PINHEADS.
THIS BETTER END IN AN EXPLOSION.
FWOOMP
WRAP YER BALEENS AROUND THIS, KELP-LICKER.
MMF?
WHUGHKK
WHDDUVV OO'DUN?!
I
I... I...
I LIKE IT NOW!
I LIKE IT NOW!

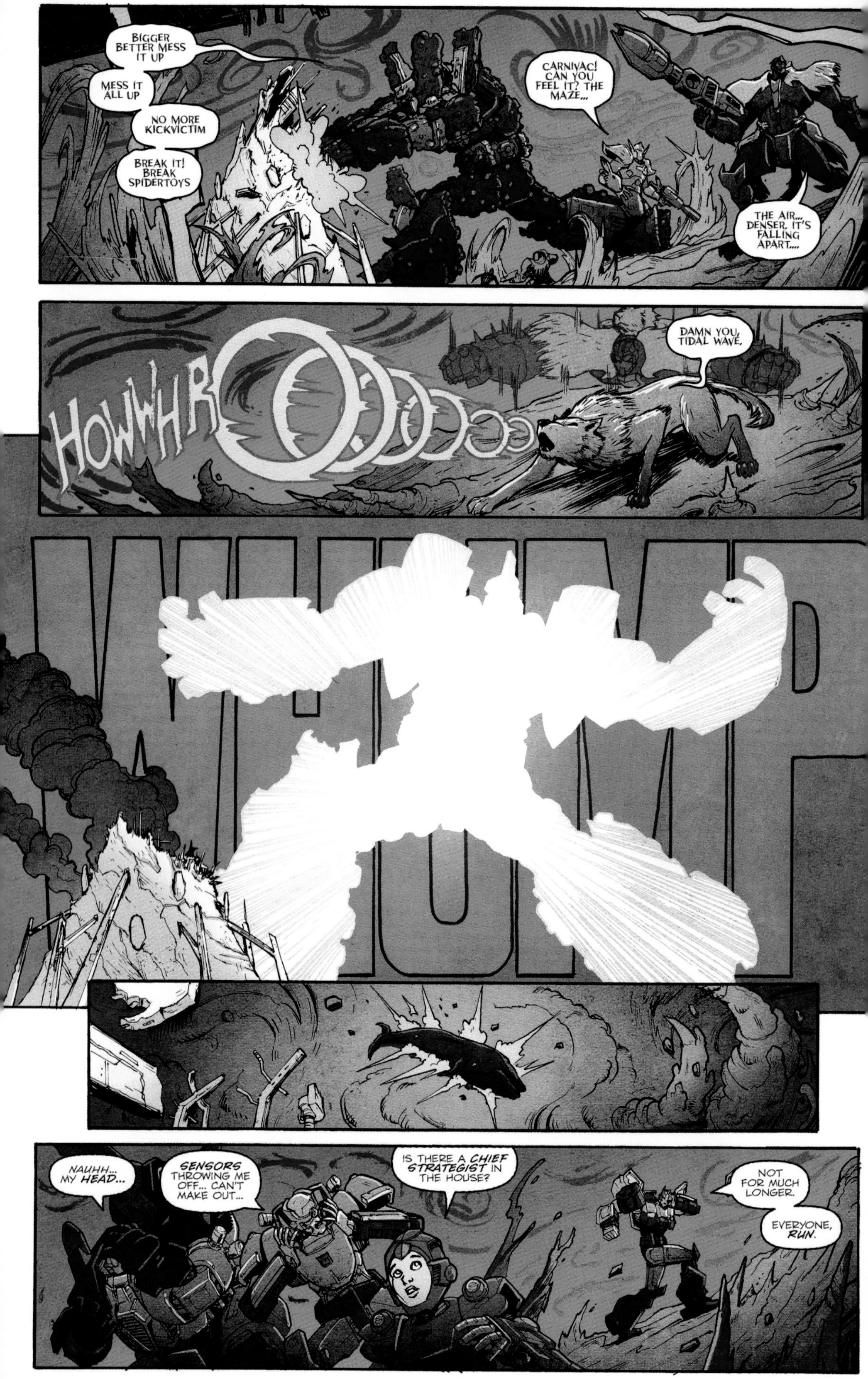
BIGGER BETTER MESS IT UP
MESS IT ALL UP
NO MORE KICKVICTIM
BREAK IT! BREAK SPIDERTOYS
CARNIVAC! CAN YOU FEEL IT? THE MAZE...
THE AIR... DENSER. IT'S FALLING APART....
HOWWHROOOOOOO
DAMN YOU, TIDAL WAVE.
WHUMP
NAUHH... MY HEAD...
SENSORS THROWING ME OFF... CAN'T MAKE OUT...
IS THERE A CHIEF STRATEGIST IN THE HOUSE?
NOT FOR MUCH LONGER.
EVERYONE, RUN.

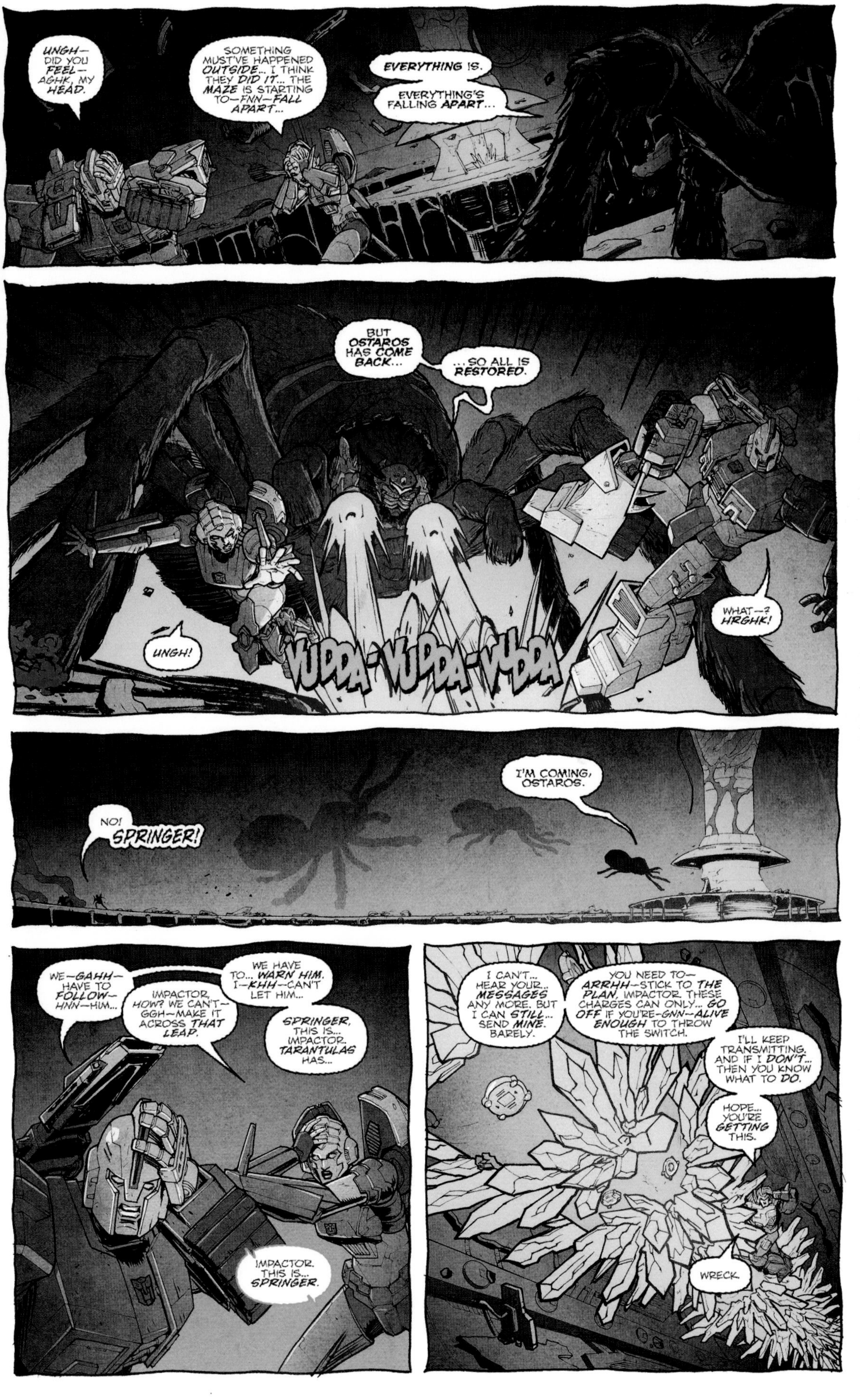
UNGH— DID YOU FEEL— AGHK, MY HEAD.
SOMETHING MUST'VE HAPPENED OUTSIDE... I THINK THEY DID IT... THE MAZE IS STARTING TO—FNN—FALL APART...
EVERYTHING IS.
EVERYTHING'S FALLING APART...
BUT OSTAROS HAS COME BACK...
...SO ALL IS RESTORED.
WHAT--? HRGHK!
UNGH!
VUDDA-VUDDA-VUDDA
I'M COMING, OSTAROS.
NO! SPRINGER!
WE—GAHH—HAVE TO FOLLOW—HNN—HIM...
IMPACTOR, HOW? WE CAN'T--GGH--MAKE IT ACROSS THAT LEAP.
WE HAVE TO... WARN HIM. I--KHH--CAN'T LET HIM...
SPRINGER, THIS IS... IMPACTOR. TARANTULAS HAS...
IMPACTOR. THIS IS... SPRINGER.
I CAN'T... HEAR YOUR... MESSAGES ANY MORE. BUT I CAN STILL... SEND MINE. BARELY.
YOU NEED TO— ARRHH--STICK TO THE PLAN, IMPACTOR. THESE CHARGES CAN ONLY... GO OFF IF YOU'RE--GNN--ALIVE ENOUGH TO THROW THE SWITCH.
I'LL KEEP TRANSMITTING. AND IF I DON'T... THEN YOU KNOW WHAT TO DO.
HOPE... YOU'RE GETTING THIS.
WRECK.

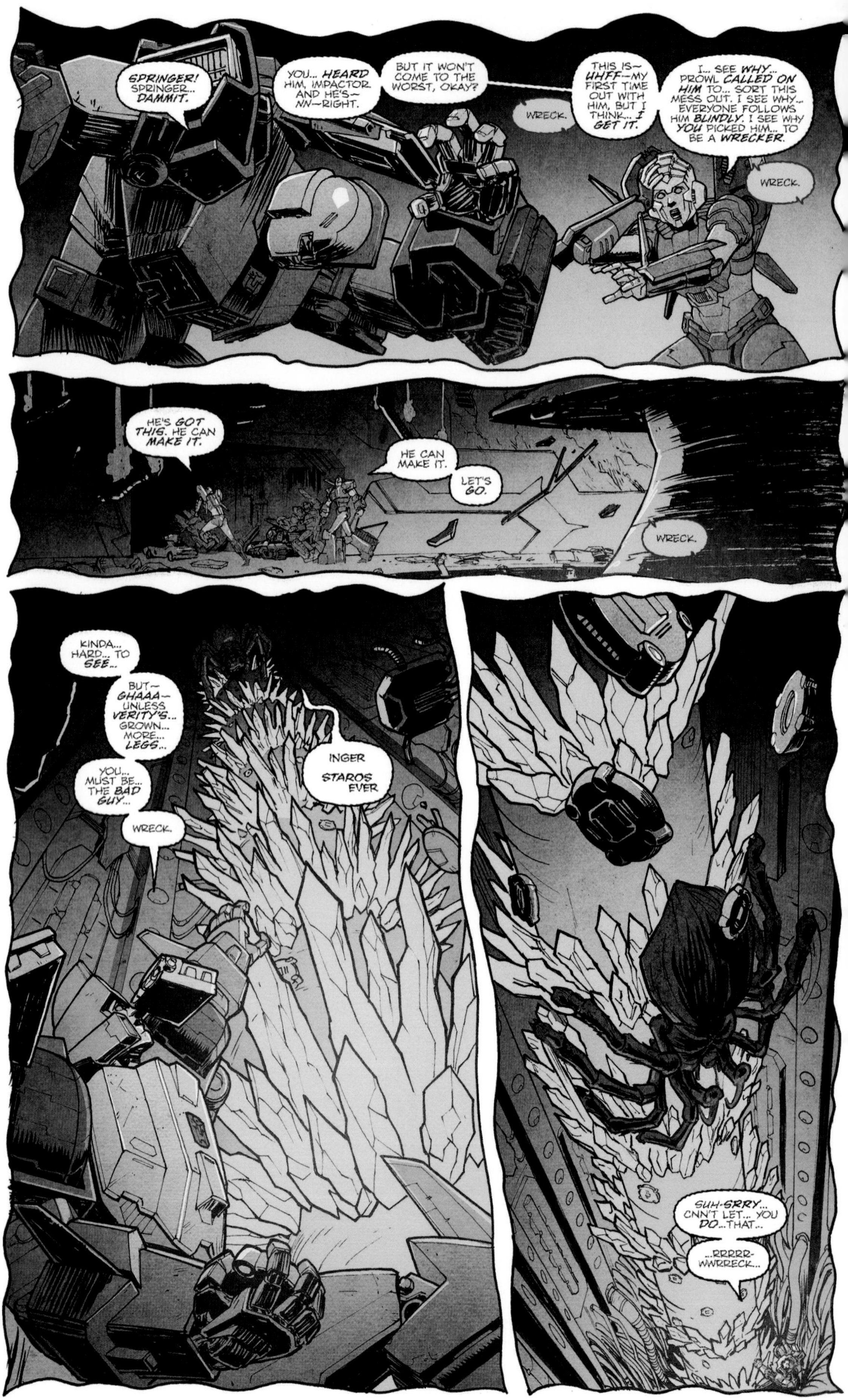
SPRINGER! SPRINGER... DAMMIT.
YOU... HEARD HIM, IMPACTOR. AND HE'S--NN--RIGHT.
BUT IT WON'T COME TO THE WORST, OKAY?
WRECK.
THIS IS-- UHFF--MY FIRST TIME OUT WITH HIM, BUT I THINK... I GET IT.
I... SEE WHY... PROWL CALLED ON HIM TO... SORT THIS MESS OUT. I SEE WHY... EVERYONE FOLLOWS HIM BLINDLY. I SEE WHY YOU PICKED HIM... TO BE A WRECKER.
WRECK.
HE'S GOT THIS. HE CAN MAKE IT.
HE CAN MAKE IT.
LET'S GO.
WRECK.
KINDA... HARD... TO SEE...
BUT-- GHAAA-- UNLESS VERITY'S... GROWN... MORE... LEGS...
YOU... MUST BE... THE BAD GUY...
WRECK.
INGER
STAROS EVER
SUH-SRRY... CNN'T LET... YOU DO...THAT...
...RRRRR-WWRRECK...

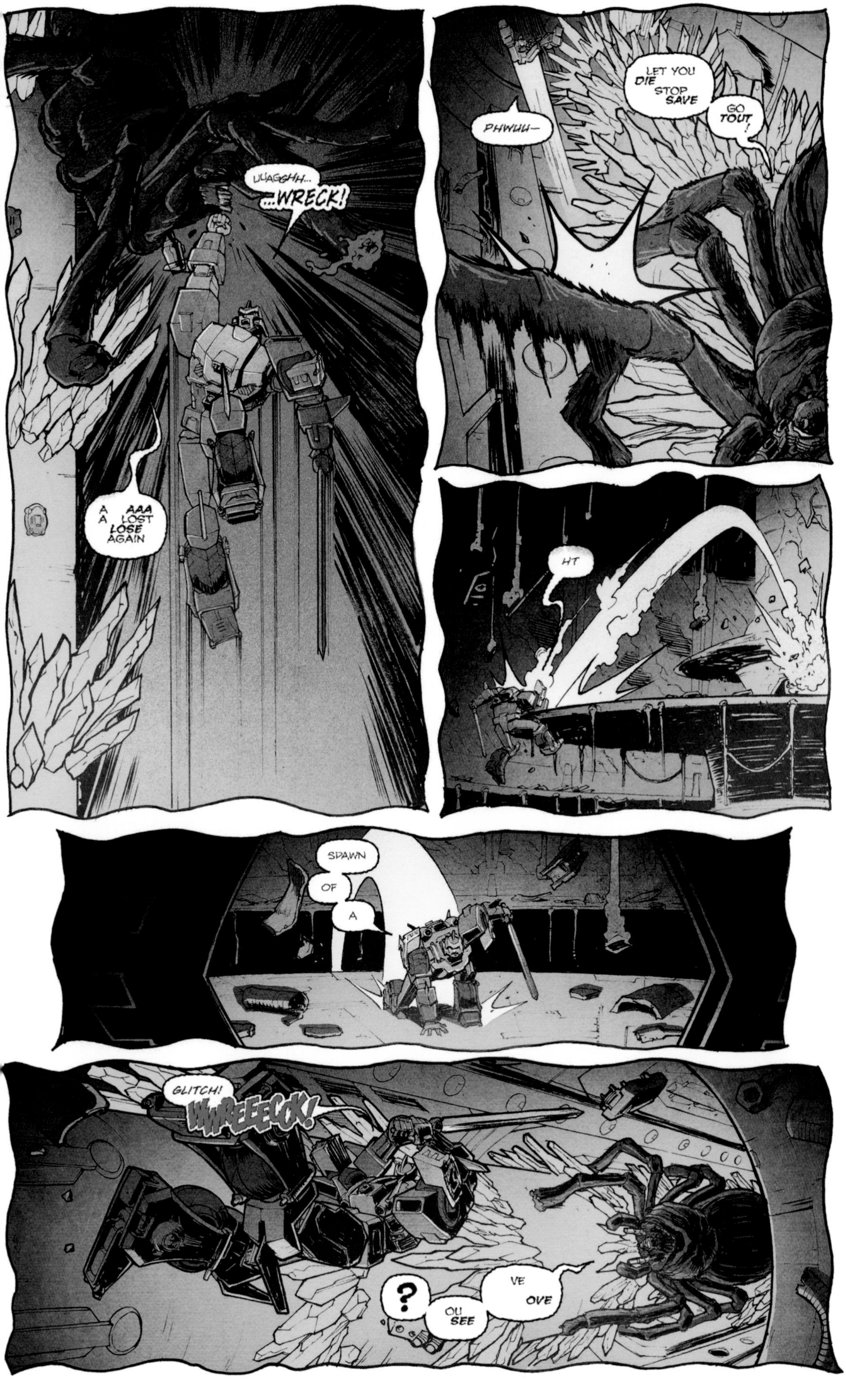

UUAGGHH...
...WRECK!
A AAA
A LOST
LOSE
AGAIN
PHWUU—
LET YOU
DIE
STOP
SAVE
GO
TOUT
!
HT
SPAWN
OF
A
GLITCH!
WWREEEECK!
?
OU
SEE
VE
OVE

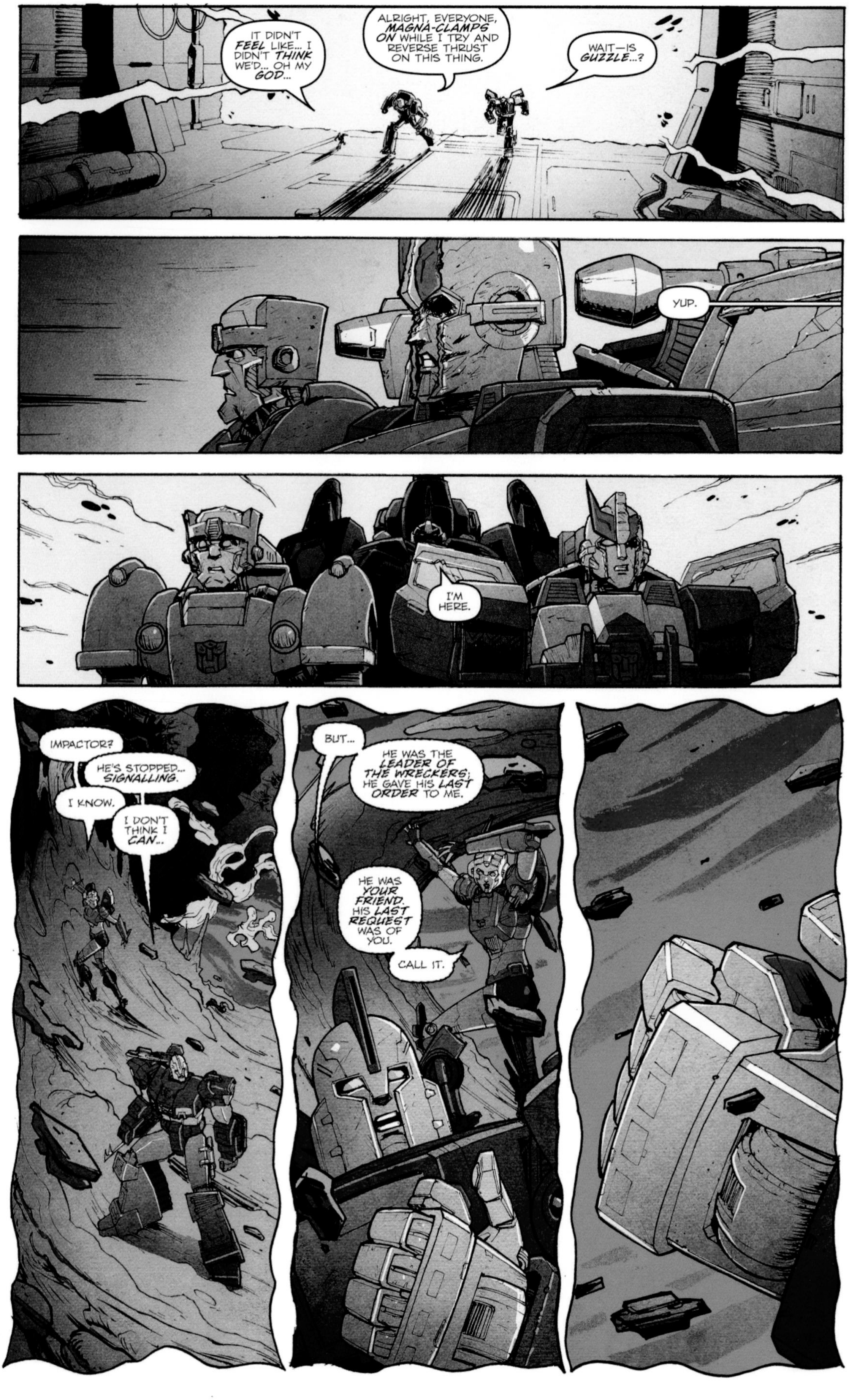

IT DIDN'T FEEL LIKE... I DIDN'T THINK WE'D... OH MY GOD...
ALRIGHT, EVERYONE, MAGNA-CLAMPS ON WHILE I TRY AND REVERSE THRUST ON THIS THING.
WAIT—IS GUZZLE...?
YUP.
I'M HERE.
IMPACTOR?
HE'S STOPPED... SIGNALLING.
I KNOW.
I DON'T THINK I CAN...
BUT...
HE WAS THE LEADER OF THE WRECKERS; HE GAVE HIS LAST ORDER TO ME.
HE WAS YOUR FRIEND. HIS LAST REQUEST WAS OF YOU.
CALL IT.

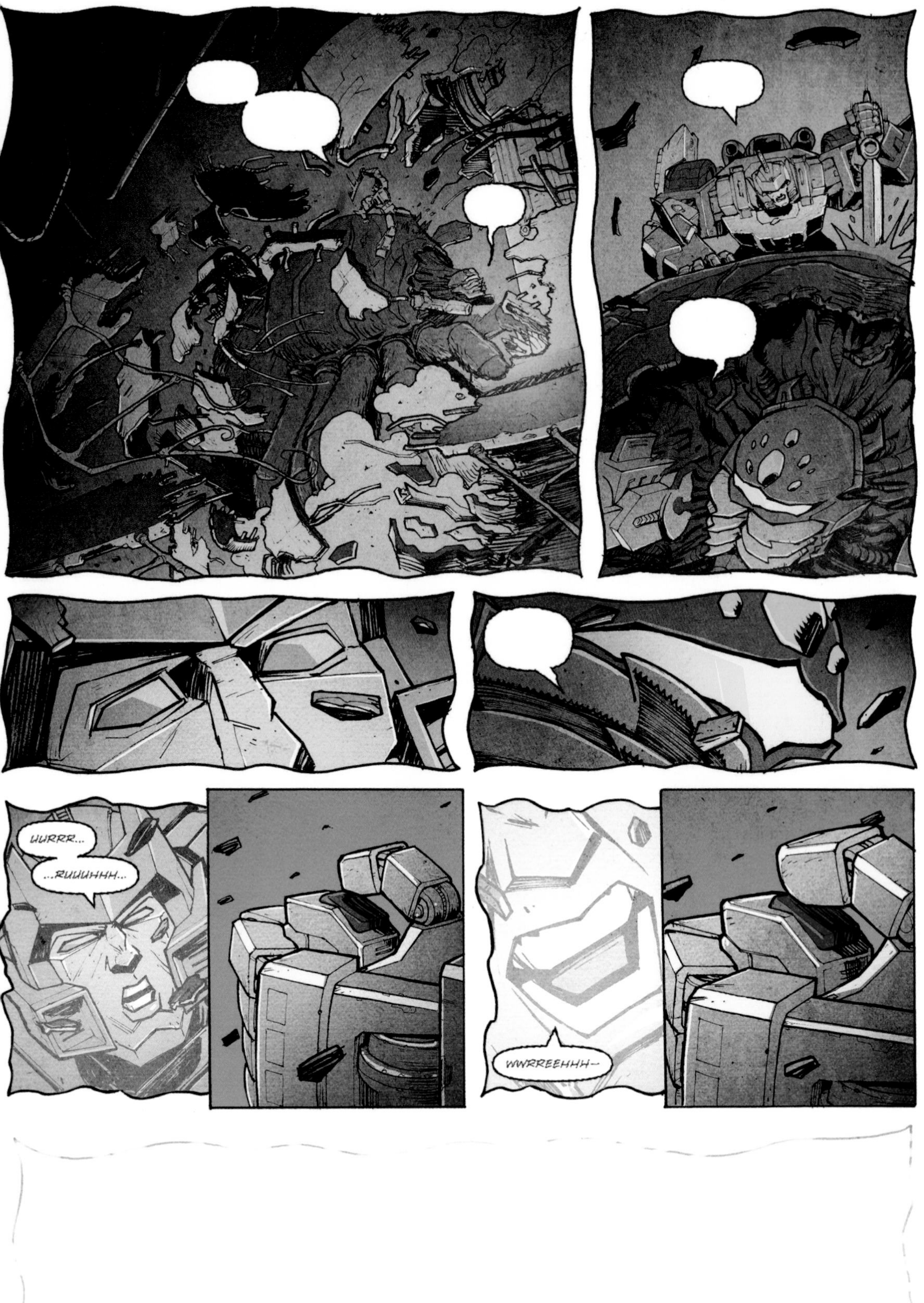
UURRR...
...RUUUHHH...
WWRREEHHH--

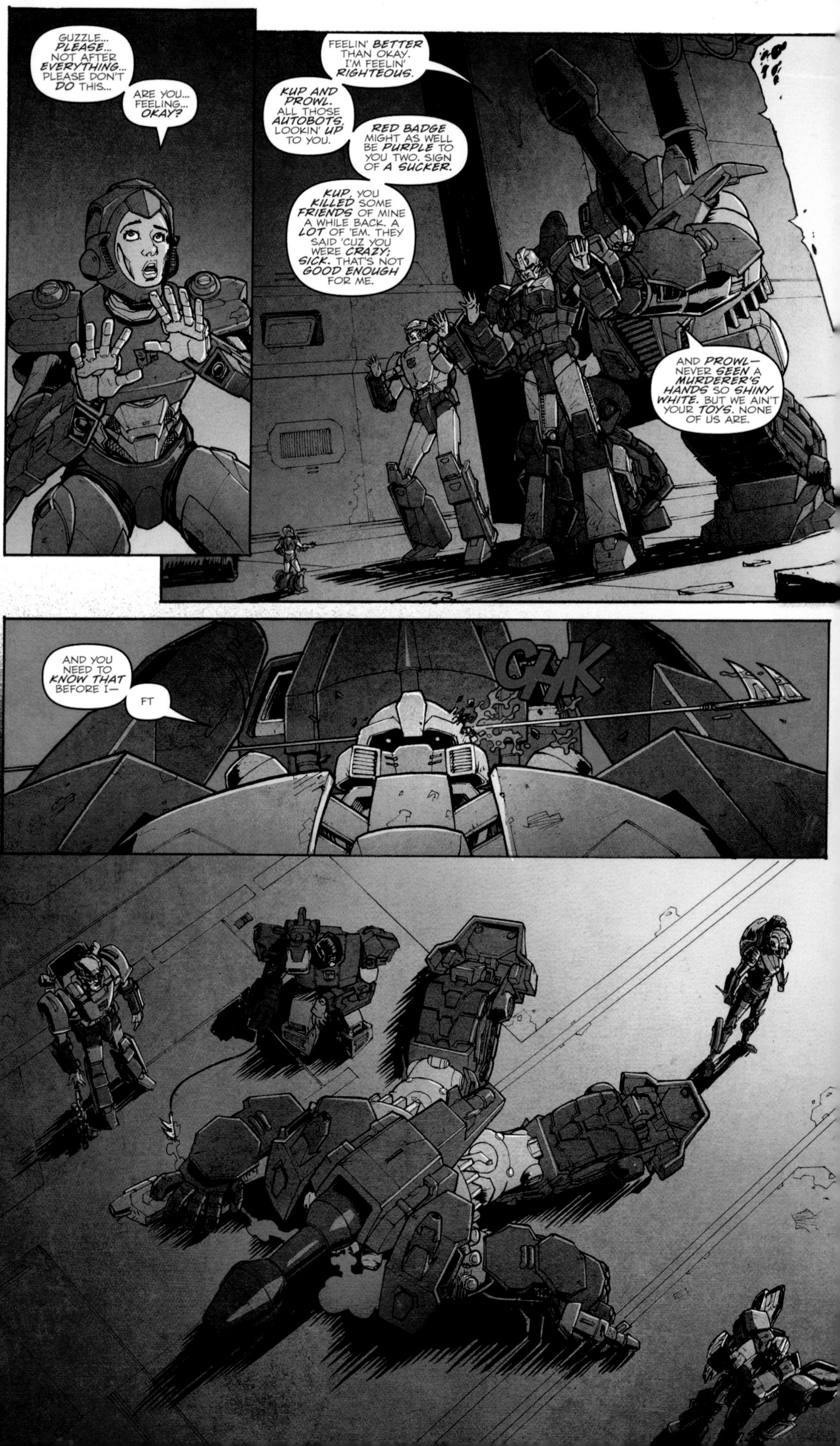
GUZZLE... PLEASE... NOT AFTER EVERYTHING... PLEASE DON'T DO THIS...
ARE YOU... FEELING... OKAY?
FEELIN' BETTER THAN OKAY. I'M FEELIN' RIGHTEOUS.
KUP AND PROWL. ALL THOSE AUTOBOTS, LOOKIN' UP TO YOU.
RED BADGE MIGHT AS WELL BE PURPLE TO YOU TWO. SIGN OF A SUCKER.
KUP, YOU KILLED SOME FRIENDS OF MINE A WHILE BACK. A LOT OF 'EM. THEY SAID 'CUZ YOU WERE CRAZY; SICK. THAT'S NOT GOOD ENOUGH FOR ME.
AND PROWL— NEVER SEEN A MURDERER'S HANDS SO SHINY WHITE. BUT WE AIN'T YOUR TOYS. NONE OF US ARE.
AND YOU NEED TO KNOW THAT BEFORE I—
FT
CHK

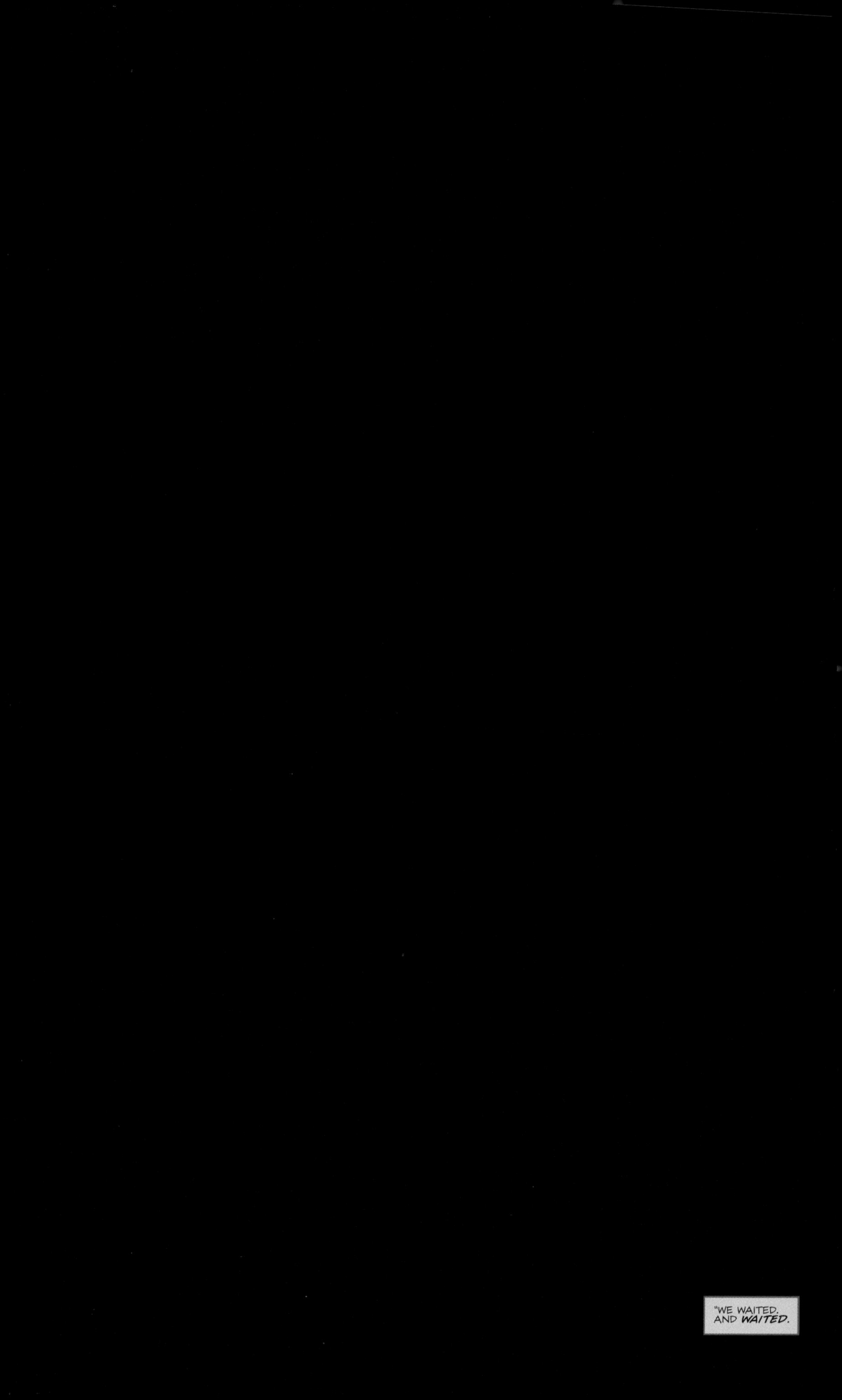
"WE WAITED. AND WAITED.

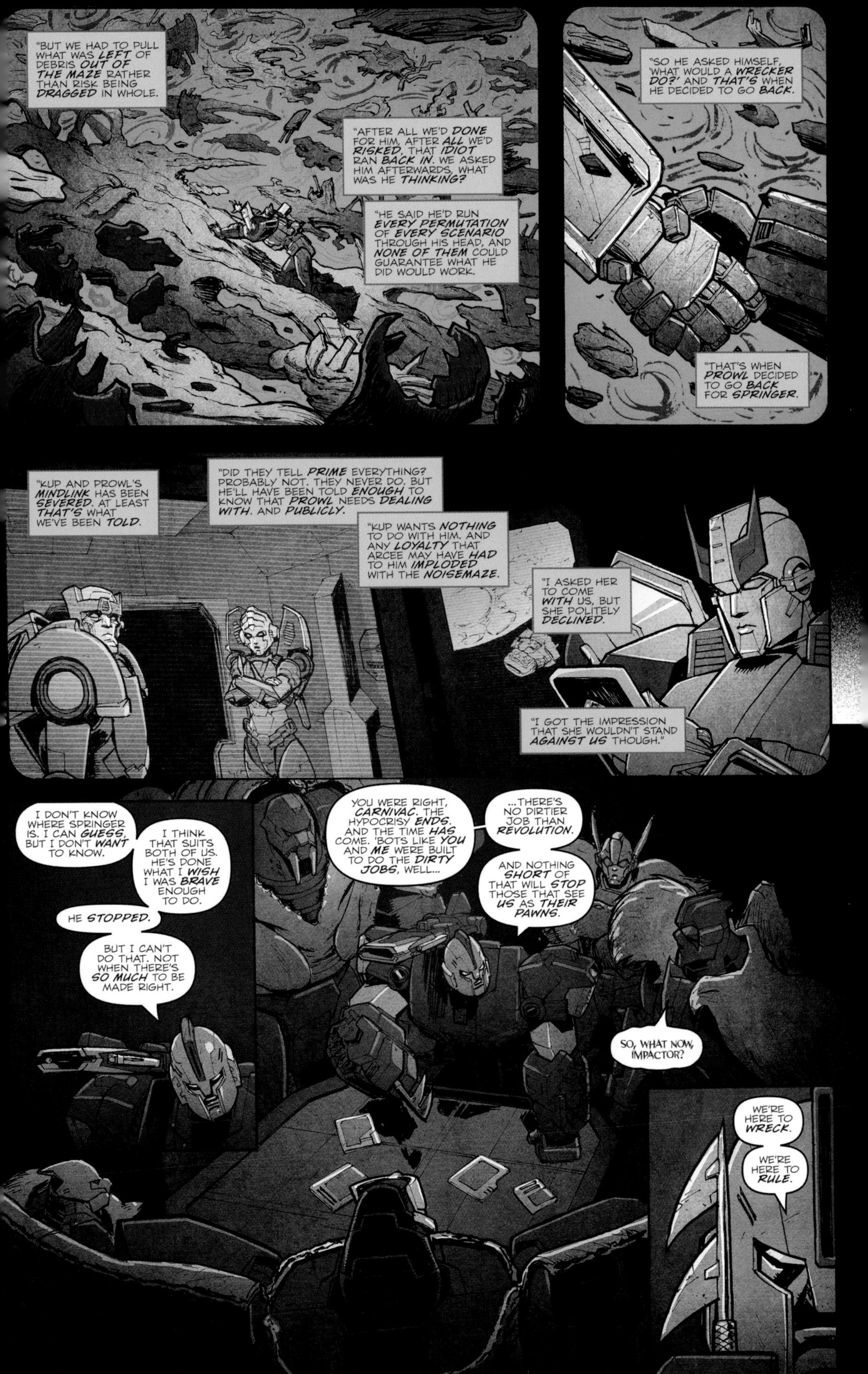
"BUT WE HAD TO PULL WHAT WAS LEFT OF DEBRIS OUT OF THE MAZE RATHER THAN RISK BEING DRAGGED IN WHOLE.
"AFTER ALL WE'D DONE FOR HIM, AFTER ALL WE'D RISKED, THAT IDIOT RAN BACK IN. WE ASKED HIM AFTERWARDS, WHAT WAS HE THINKING?
"HE SAID HE'D RUN EVERY PERMUTATION OF EVERY SCENARIO THROUGH HIS HEAD, AND NONE OF THEM COULD GUARANTEE WHAT HE DID WOULD WORK.
"SO HE ASKED HIMSELF, 'WHAT WOULD A WRECKER DO?' AND THAT'S WHEN HE DECIDED TO GO BACK.
"THAT'S WHEN PROWL DECIDED TO GO BACK FOR SPRINGER.
"KUP AND PROWL'S MINDLINK HAS BEEN SEVERED. AT LEAST THAT'S WHAT WE'VE BEEN TOLD.
"DID THEY TELL PRIME EVERYTHING? PROBABLY NOT. THEY NEVER DO. BUT HE'LL HAVE BEEN TOLD ENOUGH TO KNOW THAT PROWL NEEDS DEALING WITH. AND PUBLICLY.
"KUP WANTS NOTHING TO DO WITH HIM. AND ANY LOYALTY THAT ARCEE MAY HAVE HAD TO HIM IMPLODED WITH THE NOISEMAZE.
"I ASKED HER TO COME WITH US, BUT SHE POLITELY DECLINED.
"I GOT THE IMPRESSION THAT SHE WOULDN'T STAND AGAINST US THOUGH."
I DON'T KNOW WHERE SPRINGER IS. I CAN GUESS, BUT I DON'T WANT TO KNOW.
I THINK THAT SUITS BOTH OF US. HE'S DONE WHAT I WISH I WAS BRAVE ENOUGH TO DO.
HE STOPPED.
BUT I CAN'T DO THAT. NOT WHEN THERE'S SO MUCH TO BE MADE RIGHT.
YOU WERE RIGHT, CARNIVAC. THE HYPOCRISY ENDS. AND THE TIME HAS COME. 'BOTS LIKE YOU AND ME WERE BUILT TO DO THE DIRTY JOBS, WELL...
...THERE'S NO DIRTIER JOB THAN REVOLUTION.
AND NOTHING SHORT OF THAT WILL STOP THOSE THAT SEE US AS THEIR PAWNS.
SO, WHAT NOW, IMPACTOR?
WE'RE HERE TO WRECK.
WE'RE HERE TO RULE.

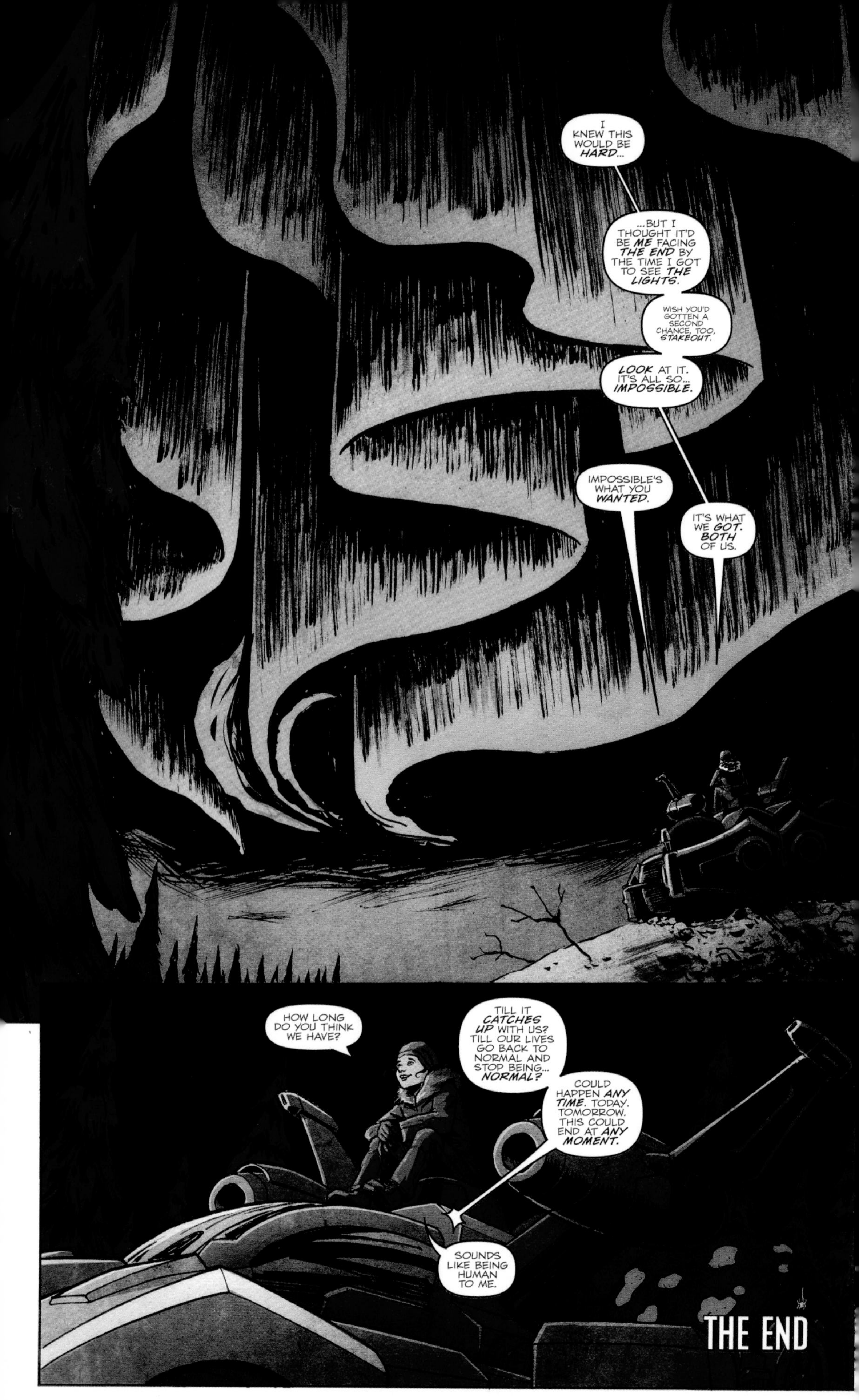
I KNEW THIS WOULD BE HARD...
...BUT I THOUGHT IT'D BE ME FACING THE END BY THE TIME I GOT TO SEE THE LIGHTS.
WISH YOU'D GOTTEN A SECOND CHANCE, TOO, STAKEOUT.
LOOK AT IT. IT'S ALL SO... IMPOSSIBLE.
IMPOSSIBLE'S WHAT YOU WANTED.
IT'S WHAT WE GOT. BOTH OF US.
HOW LONG DO YOU THINK WE HAVE?
TILL IT CATCHES UP WITH US? TILL OUR LIVES GO BACK TO NORMAL AND STOP BEING... NORMAL?
COULD HAPPEN ANY TIME. TODAY. TOMORROW. THIS COULD END AT ANY MOMENT.
SOUNDS LIKE BEING HUMAN TO ME.
THE END

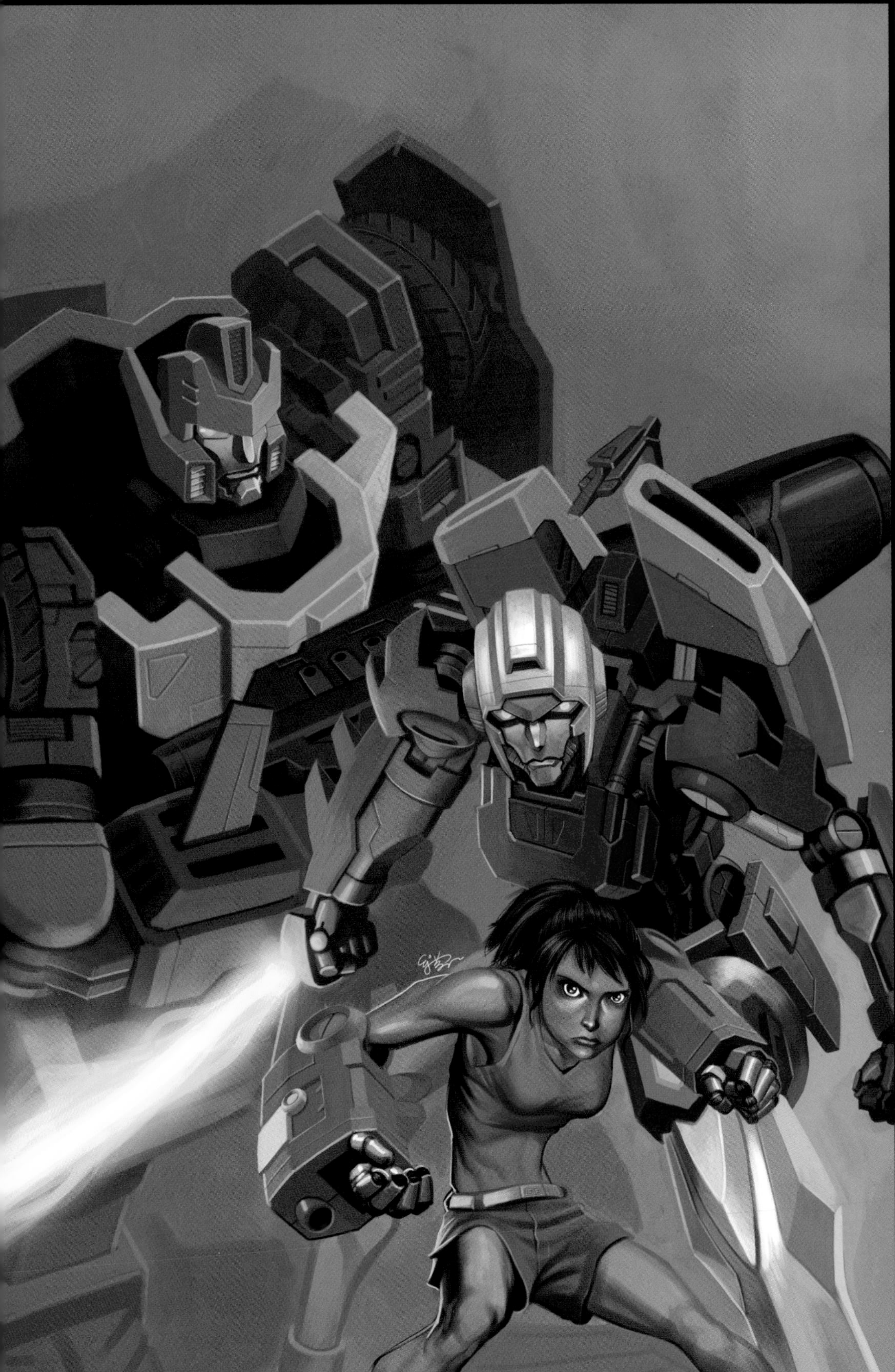

ART **EJ SU**

REQUIEM OF THE WRECKERS

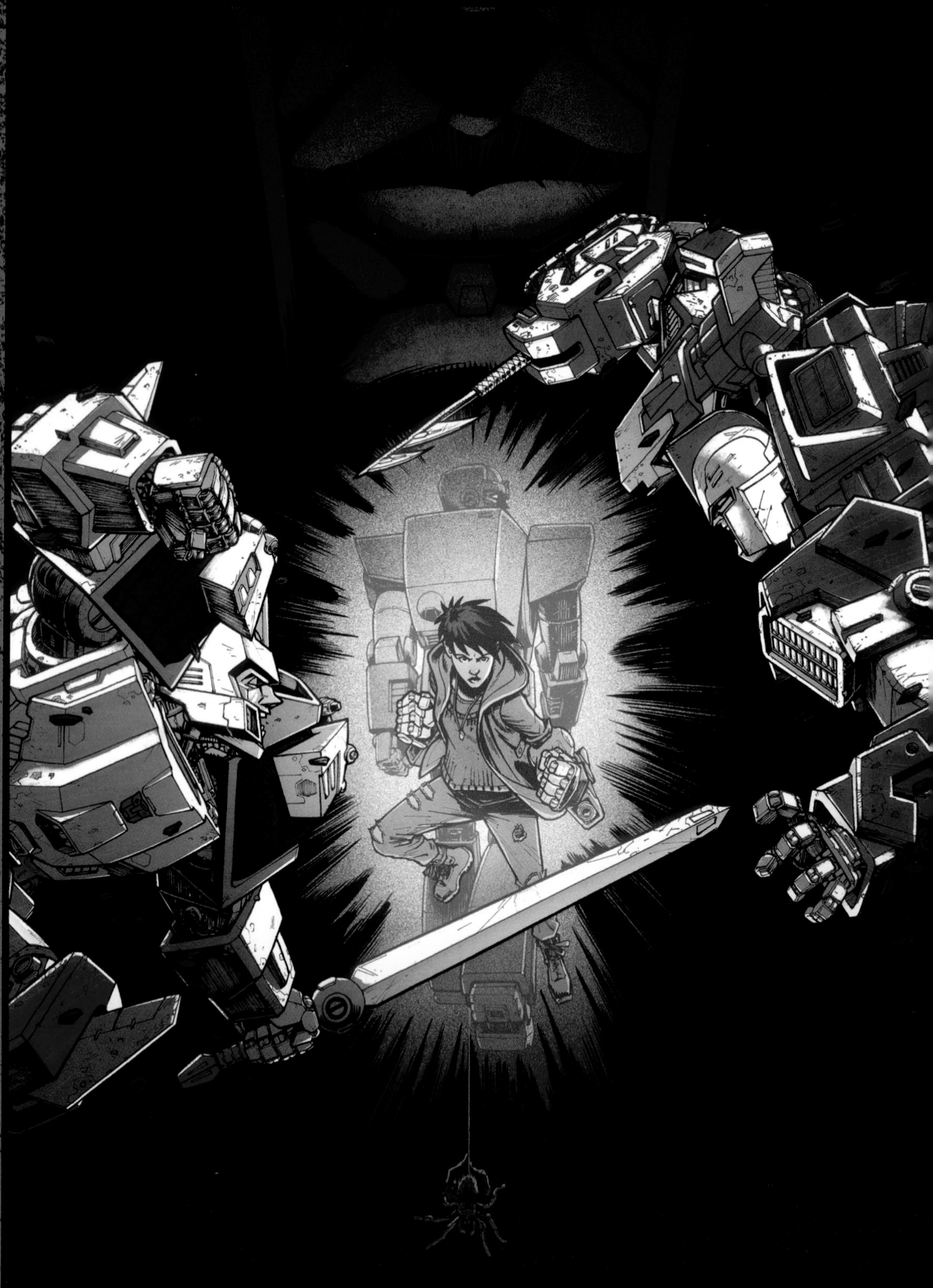

ART NICK ROCHE COLORS JOSH BURCHAM

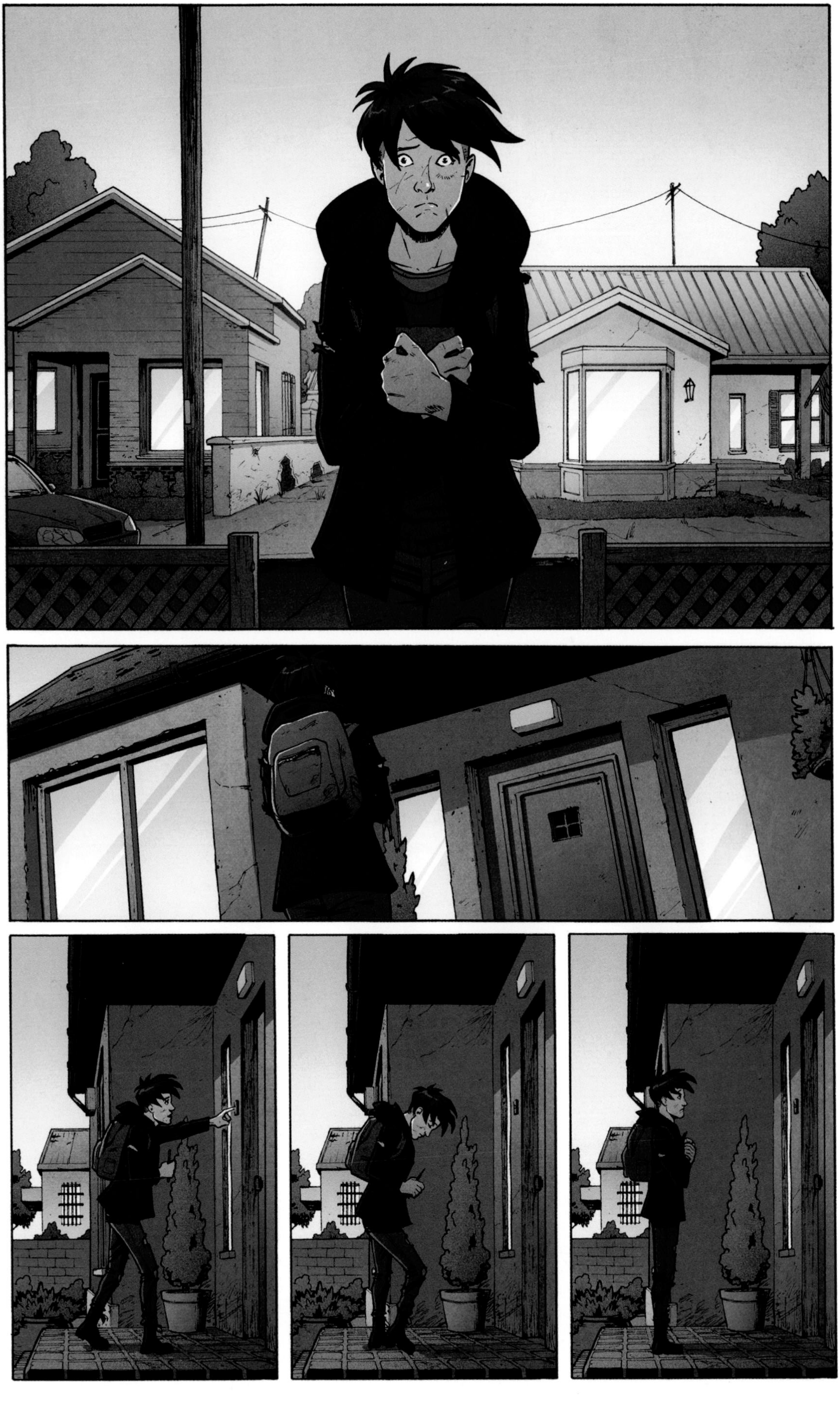

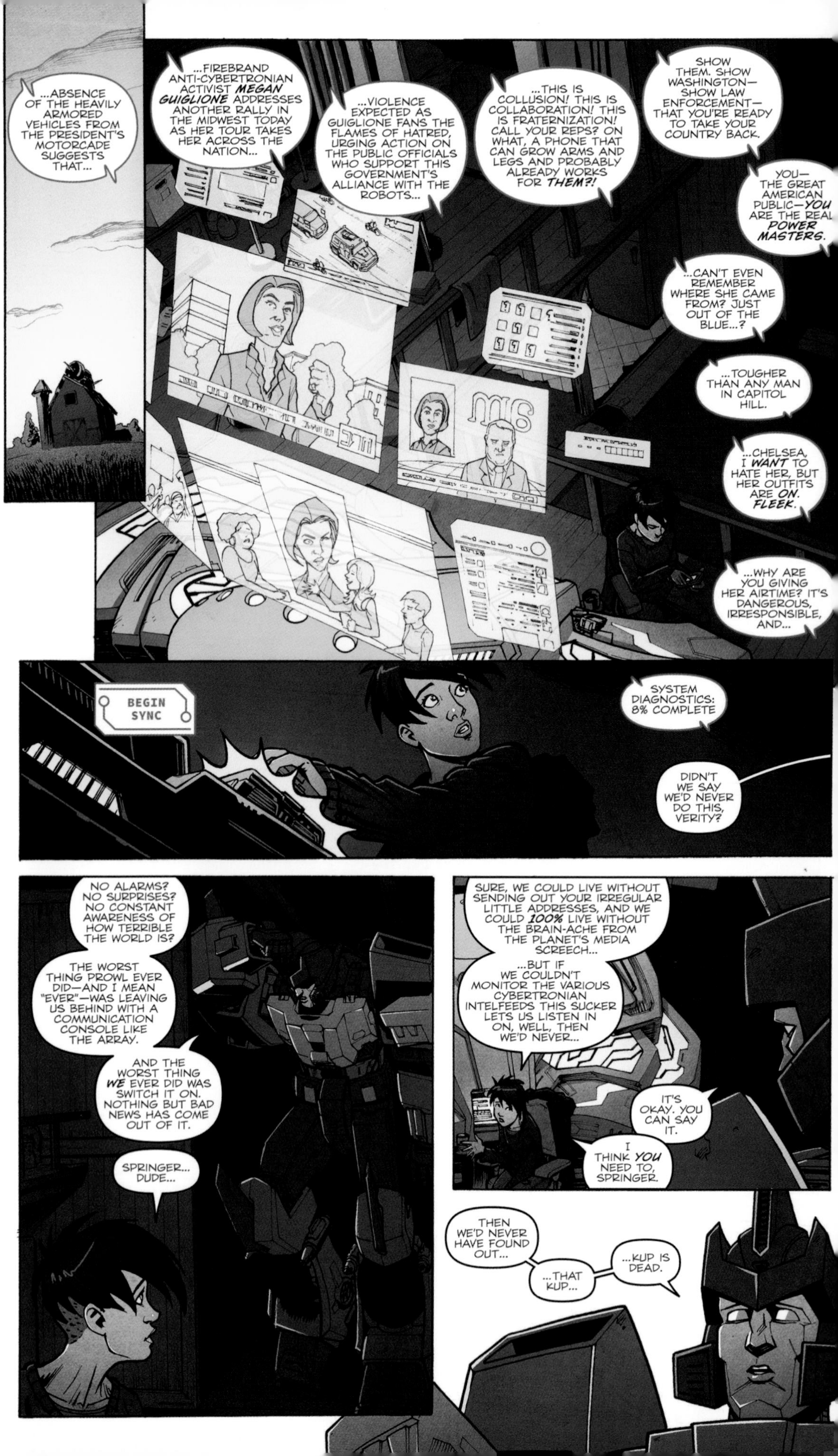
...ABSENCE OF THE HEAVILY ARMORED VEHICLES FROM THE PRESIDENT'S MOTORCADE SUGGESTS THAT...
...FIREBRAND ANTI-CYBERTRONIAN ACTIVIST MEGAN GUIGLIONE ADDRESSES ANOTHER RALLY IN THE MIDWEST TODAY AS HER TOUR TAKES HER ACROSS THE NATION...
...VIOLENCE EXPECTED AS GUIGLIONE FANS THE FLAMES OF HATRED, URGING ACTION ON THE PUBLIC OFFICIALS WHO SUPPORT THIS GOVERNMENT'S ALLIANCE WITH THE ROBOTS...
...THIS IS COLLUSION! THIS IS COLLABORATION! THIS IS FRATERNIZATION! CALL YOUR REPS? ON WHAT, A PHONE THAT CAN GROW ARMS AND LEGS AND PROBABLY ALREADY WORKS FOR THEM?!
SHOW THEM. SHOW WASHINGTON—SHOW LAW ENFORCEMENT—THAT YOU'RE READY TO TAKE YOUR COUNTRY BACK.
YOU—THE GREAT AMERICAN PUBLIC—YOU ARE THE REAL POWER MASTERS.
...CAN'T EVEN REMEMBER WHERE SHE CAME FROM? JUST OUT OF THE BLUE...?
...TOUGHER THAN ANY MAN IN CAPITOL HILL.
...CHELSEA, I WANT TO HATE HER, BUT HER OUTFITS ARE ON. FLEEK.
...WHY ARE YOU GIVING HER AIRTIME? IT'S DANGEROUS, IRRESPONSIBLE, AND...
BEGIN SYNC
SYSTEM DIAGNOSTICS: 8% COMPLETE
DIDN'T WE SAY WE'D NEVER DO THIS, VERITY?
NO ALARMS? NO SURPRISES? NO CONSTANT AWARENESS OF HOW TERRIBLE THE WORLD IS?
THE WORST THING PROWL EVER DID—AND I MEAN "EVER"—WAS LEAVING US BEHIND WITH A COMMUNICATION CONSOLE LIKE THE ARRAY.
AND THE WORST THING WE EVER DID WAS SWITCH IT ON. NOTHING BUT BAD NEWS HAS COME OUT OF IT.
SPRINGER... DUDE...
SURE, WE COULD LIVE WITHOUT SENDING OUT YOUR IRREGULAR LITTLE ADDRESSES, AND WE COULD 100% LIVE WITHOUT THE BRAIN-ACHE FROM THE PLANET'S MEDIA SCREECH...
...BUT IF WE COULDN'T MONITOR THE VARIOUS CYBERTRONIAN INTELFEEDS THIS SUCKER LETS US LISTEN IN ON, WELL, THEN WE'D NEVER...
IT'S OKAY. YOU CAN SAY IT.
I THINK YOU NEED TO, SPRINGER.
THEN WE'D NEVER HAVE FOUND OUT...
...THAT KUP...
...KUP IS DEAD.

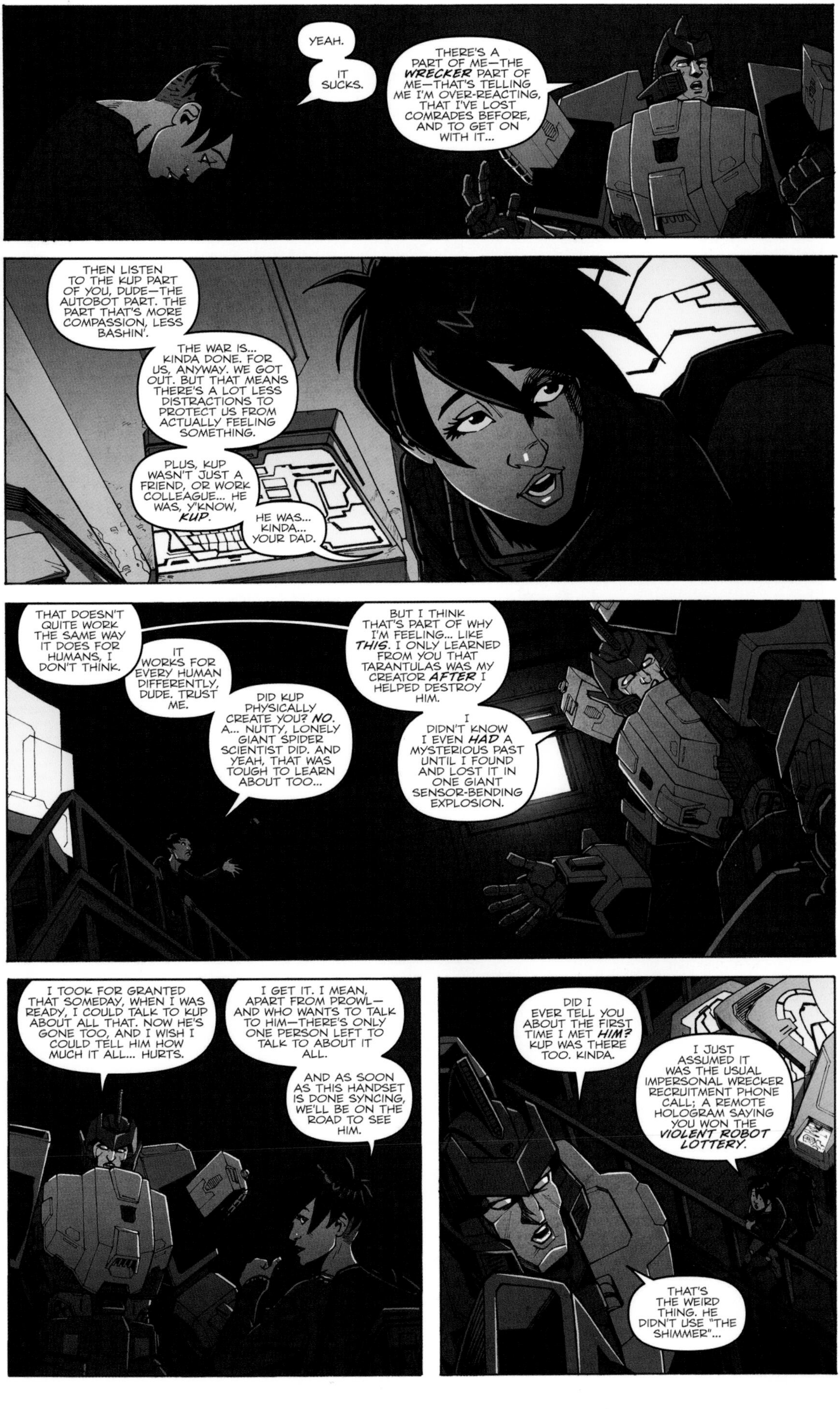
YEAH.
IT SUCKS.
THERE'S A PART OF ME—THE WRECKER PART OF ME—THAT'S TELLING ME I'M OVER-REACTING, THAT I'VE LOST COMRADES BEFORE, AND TO GET ON WITH IT...
THEN LISTEN TO THE KUP PART OF YOU, DUDE—THE AUTOBOT PART. THE PART THAT'S MORE COMPASSION, LESS BASHIN'.
THE WAR IS... KINDA DONE. FOR US, ANYWAY. WE GOT OUT. BUT THAT MEANS THERE'S A LOT LESS DISTRACTIONS TO PROTECT US FROM ACTUALLY FEELING SOMETHING.
PLUS, KUP WASN'T JUST A FRIEND, OR WORK COLLEAGUE... HE WAS, Y'KNOW, KUP.
HE WAS... KINDA... YOUR DAD.
THAT DOESN'T QUITE WORK THE SAME WAY IT DOES FOR HUMANS, I DON'T THINK.
BUT I THINK THAT'S PART OF WHY I'M FEELING... LIKE THIS. I ONLY LEARNED FROM YOU THAT TARANTULAS WAS MY CREATOR AFTER I HELPED DESTROY HIM.
IT WORKS FOR EVERY HUMAN DIFFERENTLY, DUDE. TRUST ME.
DID KUP PHYSICALLY CREATE YOU? NO. A... NUTTY, LONELY GIANT SPIDER SCIENTIST DID. AND YEAH, THAT WAS TOUGH TO LEARN ABOUT TOO...
I DIDN'T KNOW I EVEN HAD A MYSTERIOUS PAST UNTIL I FOUND AND LOST IT IN ONE GIANT SENSOR-BENDING EXPLOSION.
I TOOK FOR GRANTED THAT SOMEDAY, WHEN I WAS READY, I COULD TALK TO KUP ABOUT ALL THAT. NOW HE'S GONE TOO, AND I WISH I COULD TELL HIM HOW MUCH IT ALL... HURTS.
I GET IT. I MEAN, APART FROM PROWL—AND WHO WANTS TO TALK TO HIM—THERE'S ONLY ONE PERSON LEFT TO TALK TO ABOUT IT ALL.
AND AS SOON AS THIS HANDSET IS DONE SYNCING, WE'LL BE ON THE ROAD TO SEE HIM.
DID I EVER TELL YOU ABOUT THE FIRST TIME I MET HIM? KUP WAS THERE TOO. KINDA.
I JUST ASSUMED IT WAS THE USUAL IMPERSONAL WRECKER RECRUITMENT PHONE CALL; A REMOTE HOLOGRAM SAYING YOU WON THE VIOLENT ROBOT LOTTERY.
THAT'S THE WEIRD THING. HE DIDN'T USE "THE SHIMMER"...

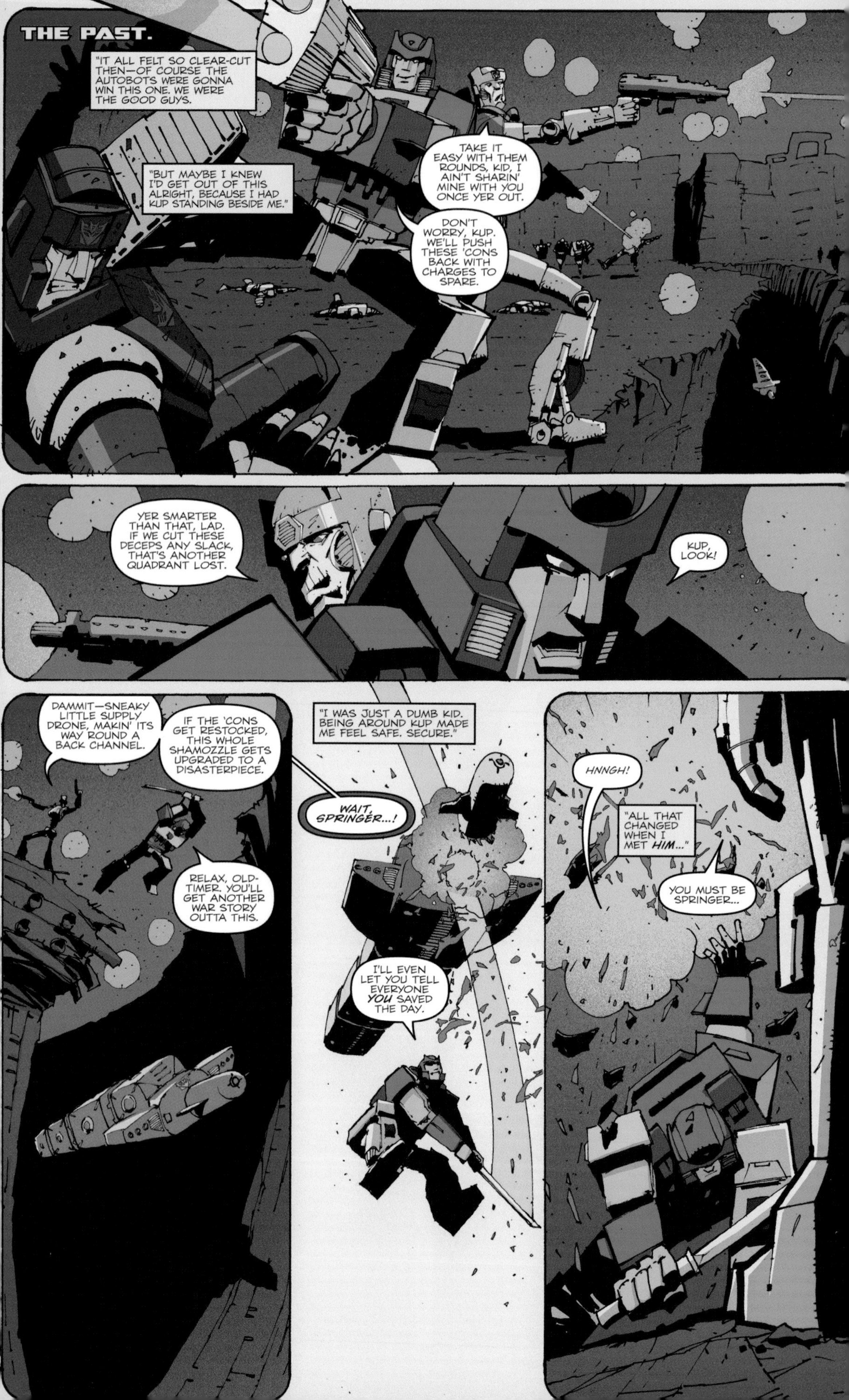
THE PAST.
"IT ALL FELT SO CLEAR-CUT THEN—OF COURSE THE AUTOBOTS WERE GONNA WIN THIS ONE. WE WERE THE GOOD GUYS.
"BUT MAYBE I KNEW I'D GET OUT OF THIS ALRIGHT, BECAUSE I HAD KUP STANDING BESIDE ME."
TAKE IT EASY WITH THEM ROUNDS, KID, I AIN'T SHARIN' MINE WITH YOU ONCE YER OUT.
DON'T WORRY, KUP. WE'LL PUSH THESE 'CONS BACK WITH CHARGES TO SPARE.
YER SMARTER THAN THAT, LAD. IF WE CUT THESE DECEPS ANY SLACK, THAT'S ANOTHER QUADRANT LOST.
KUP, LOOK!
DAMMIT—SNEAKY LITTLE SUPPLY DRONE, MAKIN' ITS WAY ROUND A BACK CHANNEL.
IF THE 'CONS GET RESTOCKED, THIS WHOLE SHAMOZZLE GETS UPGRADED TO A DISASTERPIECE.
RELAX, OLD-TIMER. YOU'LL GET ANOTHER WAR STORY OUTTA THIS.
"I WAS JUST A DUMB KID. BEING AROUND KUP MADE ME FEEL SAFE. SECURE."
WAIT, SPRINGER...!
I'LL EVEN LET YOU TELL EVERYONE YOU SAVED THE DAY.
HNNGH!
"ALL THAT CHANGED WHEN I MET HIM..."
YOU MUST BE SPRINGER...

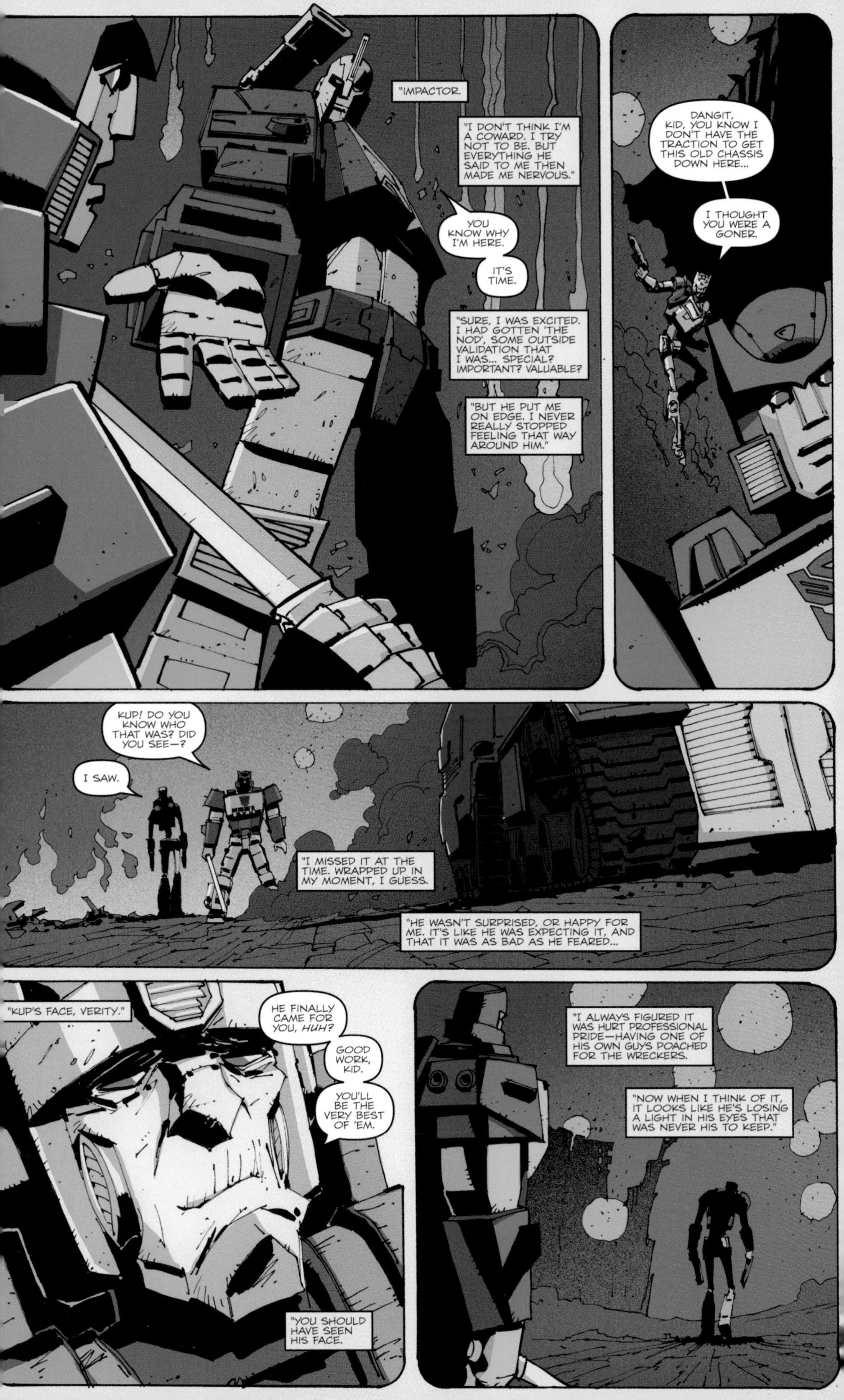

"IMPACTOR.
"I DON'T THINK I'M A COWARD. I TRY NOT TO BE. BUT EVERYTHING HE SAID TO ME THEN MADE ME NERVOUS."
YOU KNOW WHY I'M HERE.
IT'S TIME.
"SURE, I WAS EXCITED. I HAD GOTTEN 'THE NOD', SOME OUTSIDE VALIDATION THAT I WAS... SPECIAL? IMPORTANT? VALUABLE?
"BUT HE PUT ME ON EDGE. I NEVER REALLY STOPPED FEELING THAT WAY AROUND HIM."
DANGIT, KID, YOU KNOW I DON'T HAVE THE TRACTION TO GET THIS OLD CHASSIS DOWN HERE...
I THOUGHT YOU WERE A GONER.
KUP! DO YOU KNOW WHO THAT WAS? DID YOU SEE—?
I SAW.
"I MISSED IT AT THE TIME. WRAPPED UP IN MY MOMENT, I GUESS.
"HE WASN'T SURPRISED, OR HAPPY FOR ME. IT'S LIKE HE WAS EXPECTING IT, AND THAT IT WAS AS BAD AS HE FEARED...
"KUP'S FACE, VERITY."
HE FINALLY CAME FOR YOU, HUH?
GOOD WORK, KID.
YOU'LL BE THE VERY BEST OF 'EM.
"YOU SHOULD HAVE SEEN HIS FACE.
"I ALWAYS FIGURED IT WAS HURT PROFESSIONAL PRIDE—HAVING ONE OF HIS OWN GUYS POACHED FOR THE WRECKERS.
"NOW WHEN I THINK OF IT, IT LOOKS LIKE HE'S LOSING A LIGHT IN HIS EYES THAT WAS NEVER HIS TO KEEP."

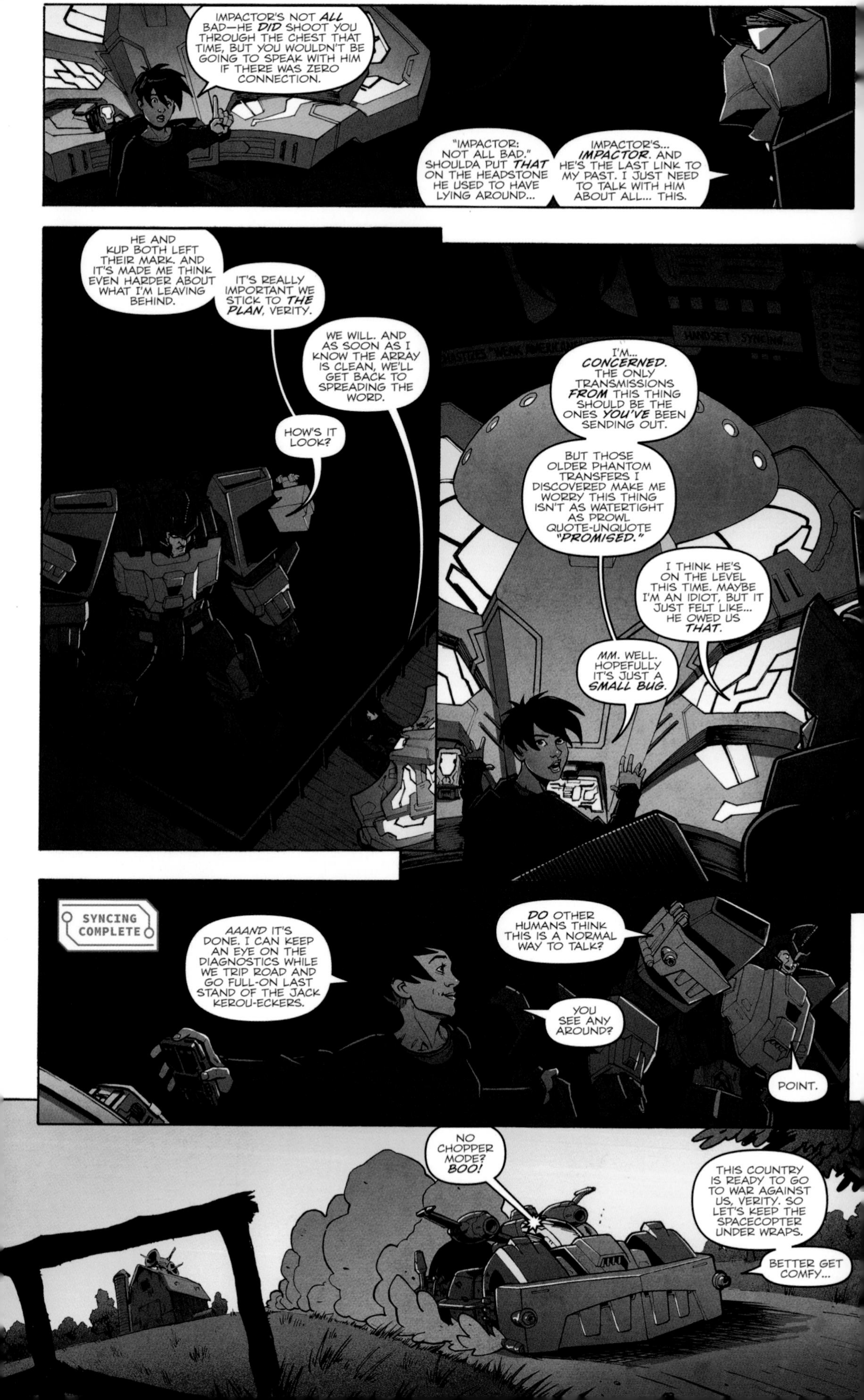
IMPACTOR'S NOT ALL BAD—HE DID SHOOT YOU THROUGH THE CHEST THAT TIME, BUT YOU WOULDN'T BE GOING TO SPEAK WITH HIM IF THERE WAS ZERO CONNECTION.
IMPACTOR'S... IMPACTOR. AND HE'S THE LAST LINK TO MY PAST. I JUST NEED TO TALK WITH HIM ABOUT ALL... THIS.
"IMPACTOR: NOT ALL BAD." SHOULDA PUT THAT ON THE HEADSTONE HE USED TO HAVE LYING AROUND...
HE AND KUP BOTH LEFT THEIR MARK. AND IT'S MADE ME THINK EVEN HARDER ABOUT WHAT I'M LEAVING BEHIND.
IT'S REALLY IMPORTANT WE STICK TO THE PLAN, VERITY.
WE WILL. AND AS SOON AS I KNOW THE ARRAY IS CLEAN, WE'LL GET BACK TO SPREADING THE WORD.
HOW'S IT LOOK?
I'M... CONCERNED. THE ONLY TRANSMISSIONS FROM THIS THING SHOULD BE THE ONES YOU'VE BEEN SENDING OUT.
BUT THOSE OLDER PHANTOM TRANSFERS I DISCOVERED MAKE ME WORRY THIS THING ISN'T AS WATERTIGHT AS PROWL QUOTE-UNQUOTE "PROMISED."
I THINK HE'S ON THE LEVEL THIS TIME. MAYBE I'M AN IDIOT, BUT IT JUST FELT LIKE... HE OWED US THAT.
MM. WELL. HOPEFULLY IT'S JUST A SMALL BUG.
SYNCING COMPLETE
AAAND IT'S DONE. I CAN KEEP AN EYE ON THE DIAGNOSTICS WHILE WE TRIP ROAD AND GO FULL-ON LAST STAND OF THE JACK KEROU-ECKERS.
DO OTHER HUMANS THINK THIS IS A NORMAL WAY TO TALK?
YOU SEE ANY AROUND?
POINT.
NO CHOPPER MODE? BOO!
THIS COUNTRY IS READY TO GO TO WAR AGAINST US, VERITY. SO LET'S KEEP THE SPACECOPTER UNDER WRAPS.
BETTER GET COMFY...

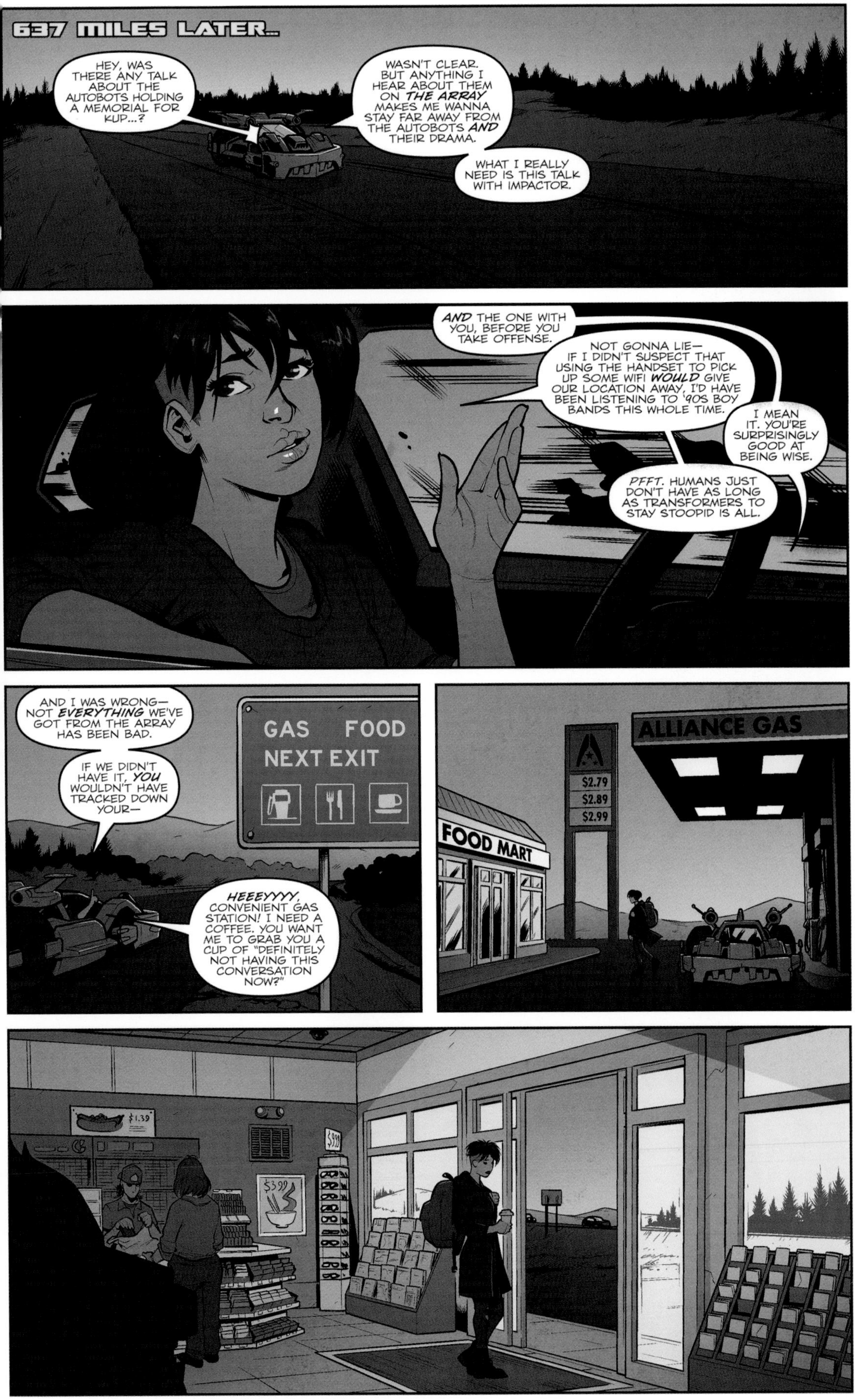
637 MILES LATER...
HEY, WAS THERE ANY TALK ABOUT THE AUTOBOTS HOLDING A MEMORIAL FOR KUP...?
WASN'T CLEAR. BUT ANYTHING I HEAR ABOUT THEM ON THE ARRAY MAKES ME WANNA STAY FAR AWAY FROM THE AUTOBOTS AND THEIR DRAMA.
WHAT I REALLY NEED IS THIS TALK WITH IMPACTOR.
AND THE ONE WITH YOU, BEFORE YOU TAKE OFFENSE.
NOT GONNA LIE— IF I DIDN'T SUSPECT THAT USING THE HANDSET TO PICK UP SOME WIFI WOULD GIVE OUR LOCATION AWAY, I'D HAVE BEEN LISTENING TO '90S BOY BANDS THIS WHOLE TIME.
I MEAN IT. YOU'RE SURPRISINGLY GOOD AT BEING WISE.
PFFT. HUMANS JUST DON'T HAVE AS LONG AS TRANSFORMERS TO STAY STOOPID IS ALL.
AND I WAS WRONG— NOT EVERYTHING WE'VE GOT FROM THE ARRAY HAS BEEN BAD.
IF WE DIDN'T HAVE IT, YOU WOULDN'T HAVE TRACKED DOWN YOUR—
GAS FOOD
NEXT EXIT
HEEEYYYY, CONVENIENT GAS STATION! I NEED A COFFEE. YOU WANT ME TO GRAB YOU A CUP OF "DEFINITELY NOT HAVING THIS CONVERSATION NOW?"
ALLIANCE GAS
$2.79
$2.89
$2.99
FOOD MART
$1.39
$3.99

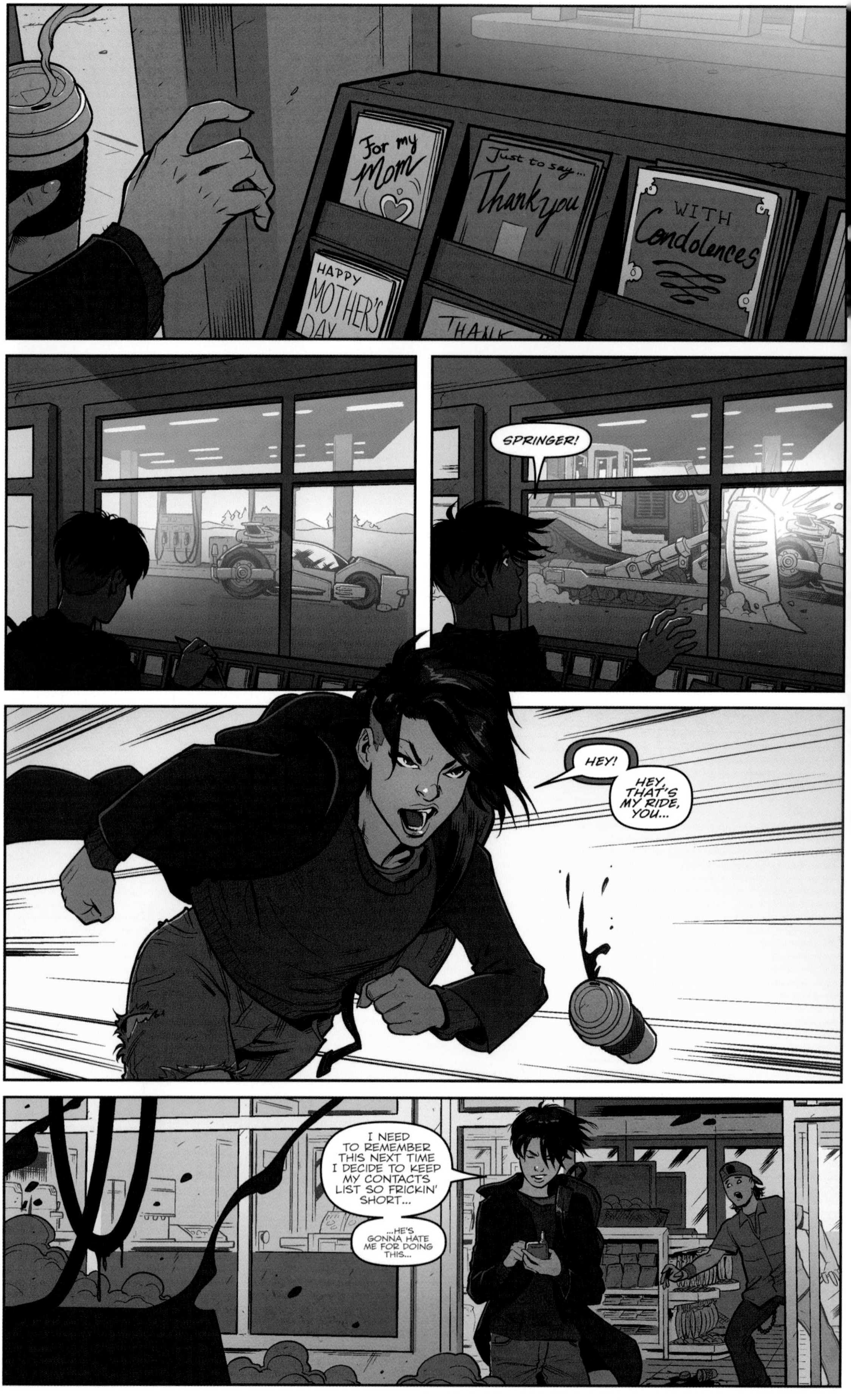

For my Mom
Just to say... Thank you
WITH Condolences
HAPPY MOTHER'S DAY
SPRINGER!
HEY!
HEY, THAT'S MY RIDE, YOU...
I NEED TO REMEMBER THIS NEXT TIME I DECIDE TO KEEP MY CONTACTS LIST SO FRICKIN' SHORT...
...HE'S GONNA HATE ME FOR DOING THIS...

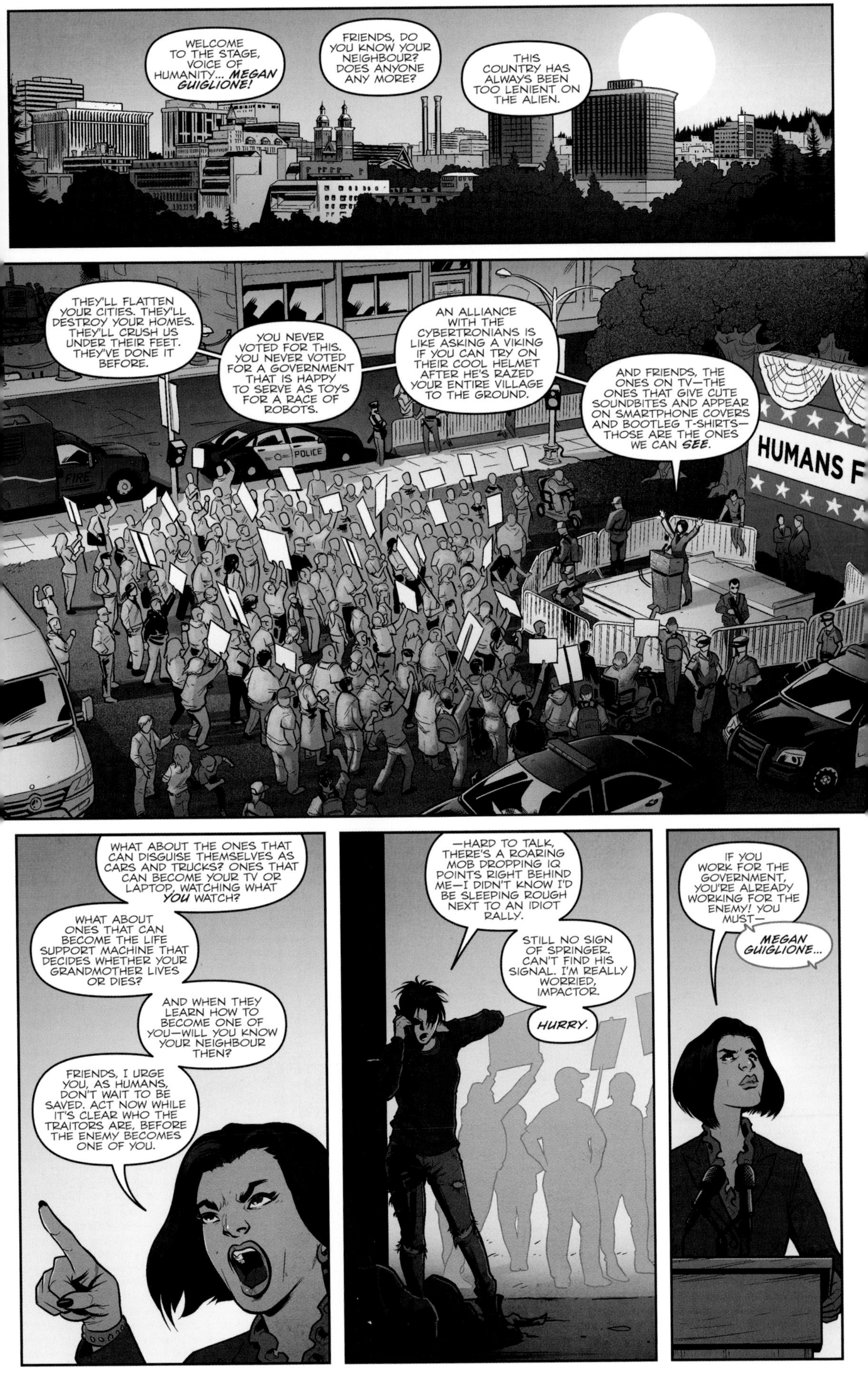
WELCOME TO THE STAGE, VOICE OF HUMANITY... MEGAN GUIGLIONE!
FRIENDS, DO YOU KNOW YOUR NEIGHBOUR? DOES ANYONE ANY MORE?
THIS COUNTRY HAS ALWAYS BEEN TOO LENIENT ON THE ALIEN.
THEY'LL FLATTEN YOUR CITIES. THEY'LL DESTROY YOUR HOMES. THEY'LL CRUSH US UNDER THEIR FEET. THEY'VE DONE IT BEFORE.
YOU NEVER VOTED FOR THIS. YOU NEVER VOTED FOR A GOVERNMENT THAT IS HAPPY TO SERVE AS TOYS FOR A RACE OF ROBOTS.
AN ALLIANCE WITH THE CYBERTRONIANS IS LIKE ASKING A VIKING IF YOU CAN TRY ON THEIR COOL HELMET AFTER HE'S RAZED YOUR ENTIRE VILLAGE TO THE GROUND.
AND FRIENDS, THE ONES ON TV—THE ONES THAT GIVE CUTE SOUNDBITES AND APPEAR ON SMARTPHONE COVERS AND BOOTLEG T-SHIRTS—THOSE ARE THE ONES WE CAN SEE.
POLICE
FIRE
HUMANS F
WHAT ABOUT THE ONES THAT CAN DISGUISE THEMSELVES AS CARS AND TRUCKS? ONES THAT CAN BECOME YOUR TV OR LAPTOP, WATCHING WHAT YOU WATCH?
WHAT ABOUT ONES THAT CAN BECOME THE LIFE SUPPORT MACHINE THAT DECIDES WHETHER YOUR GRANDMOTHER LIVES OR DIES?
AND WHEN THEY LEARN HOW TO BECOME ONE OF YOU—WILL YOU KNOW YOUR NEIGHBOUR THEN?
FRIENDS, I URGE YOU, AS HUMANS, DON'T WAIT TO BE SAVED. ACT NOW WHILE IT'S CLEAR WHO THE TRAITORS ARE, BEFORE THE ENEMY BECOMES ONE OF YOU.
—HARD TO TALK, THERE'S A ROARING MOB DROPPING IQ POINTS RIGHT BEHIND ME—I DIDN'T KNOW I'D BE SLEEPING ROUGH NEXT TO AN IDIOT RALLY.
STILL NO SIGN OF SPRINGER. CAN'T FIND HIS SIGNAL. I'M REALLY WORRIED, IMPACTOR.
HURRY.
IF YOU WORK FOR THE GOVERNMENT, YOU'RE ALREADY WORKING FOR THE ENEMY! YOU MUST—
MEGAN GUIGLIONE...

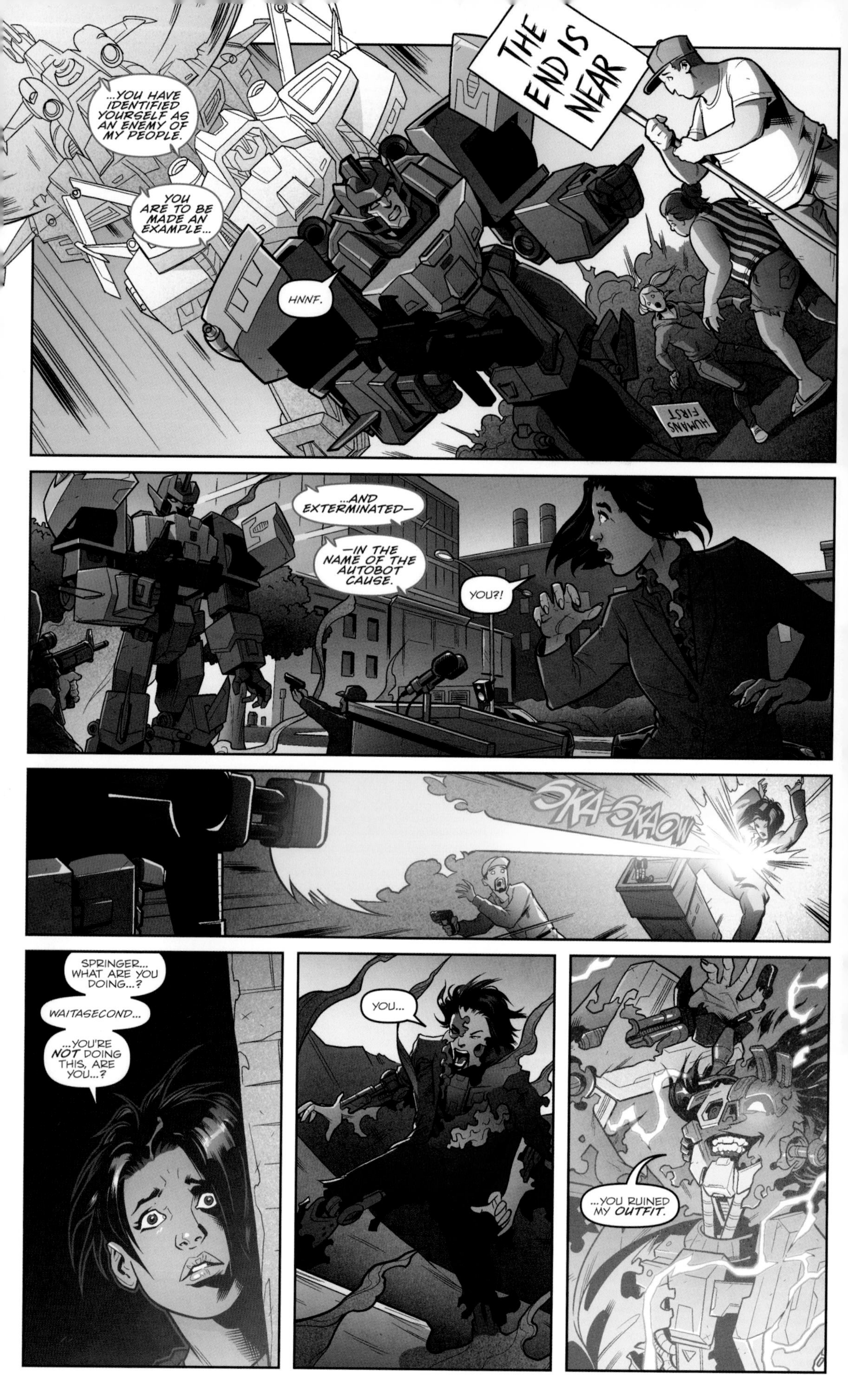
THE END IS NEAR
...YOU HAVE IDENTIFIED YOURSELF AS AN ENEMY OF MY PEOPLE.
YOU ARE TO BE MADE AN EXAMPLE...
HNNF.
HUMANS FIRST
...AND EXTERMINATED—
—IN THE NAME OF THE AUTOBOT CAUSE.
YOU?!
SKA-SKAOW
SPRINGER... WHAT ARE YOU DOING...?
WAITASECOND...
...YOU'RE NOT DOING THIS, ARE YOU...?
YOU...
...YOU RUINED MY OUTFIT.

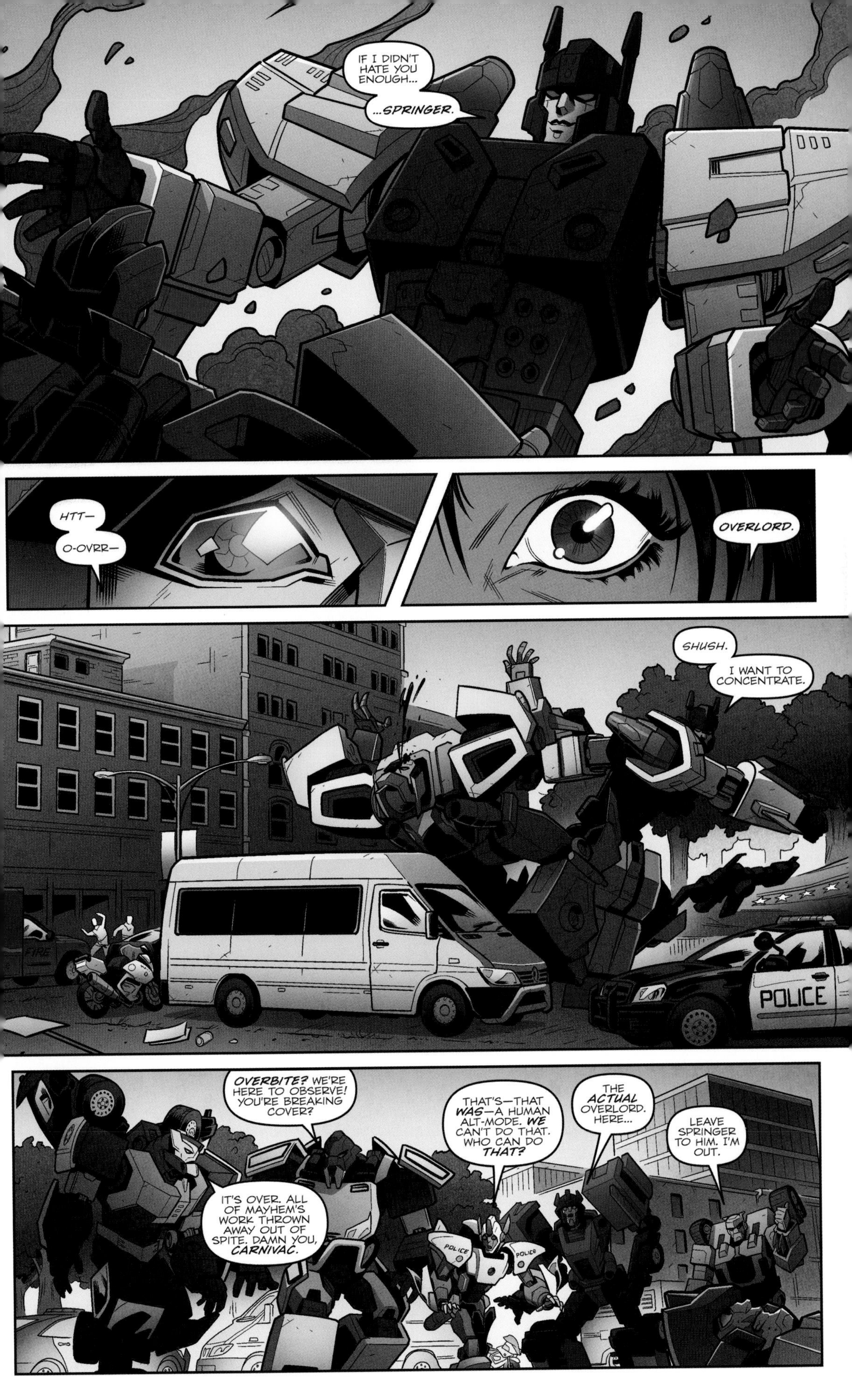
IF I DIDN'T HATE YOU ENOUGH...
...SPRINGER.
HTT—
O-OVRR—
OVERLORD.
SHUSH.
I WANT TO CONCENTRATE.
OVERBITE? WE'RE HERE TO OBSERVE! YOU'RE BREAKING COVER?
IT'S OVER. ALL OF MAYHEM'S WORK THROWN AWAY OUT OF SPITE. DAMN YOU, CARNIVAC.
THAT'S—THAT WAS—A HUMAN ALT-MODE. WE CAN'T DO THAT. WHO CAN DO THAT?
THE ACTUAL OVERLORD. HERE...
LEAVE SPRINGER TO HIM. I'M OUT.
POLICE
FIRE

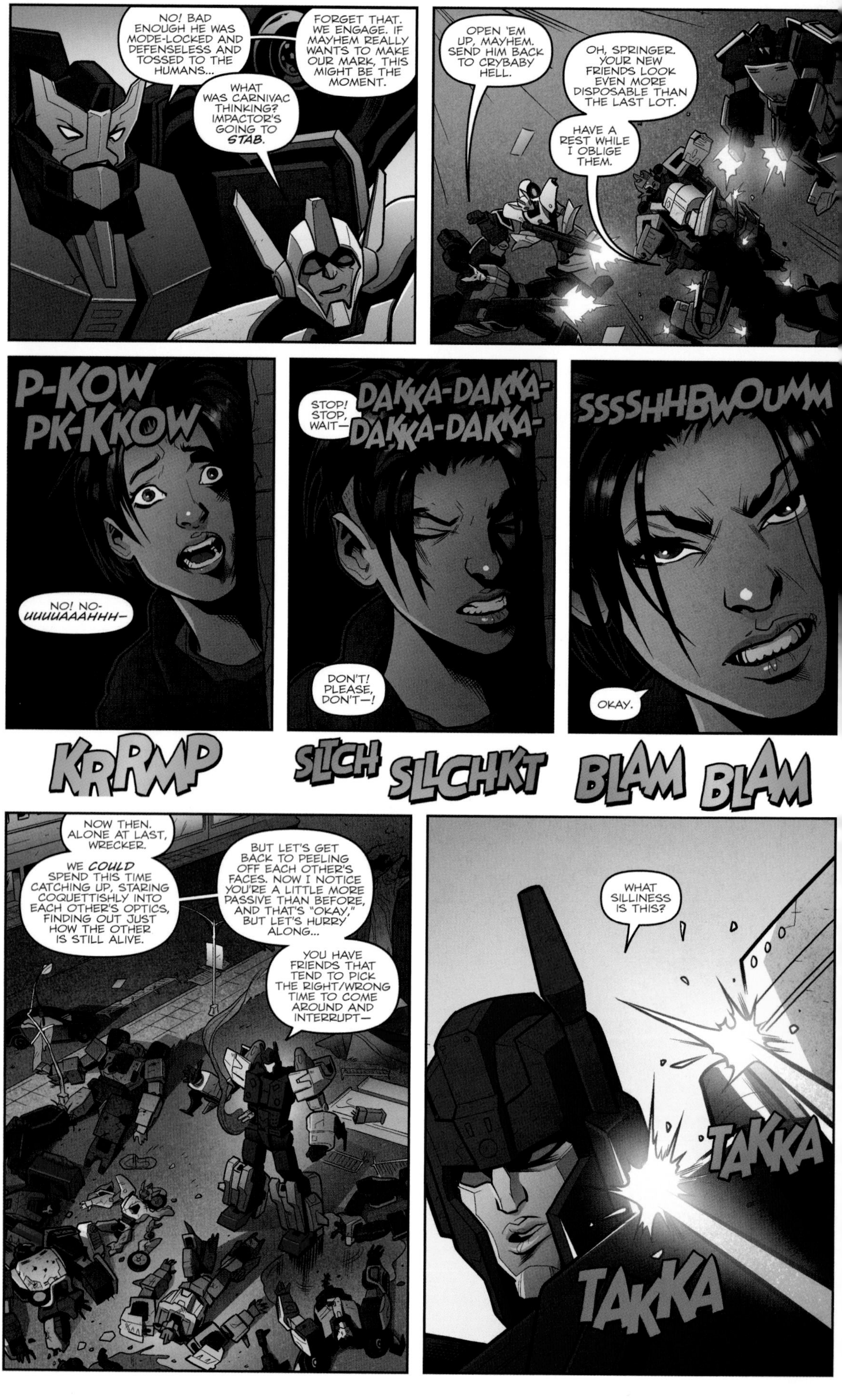
NO! BAD ENOUGH HE WAS MODE-LOCKED AND DEFENSELESS AND TOSSED TO THE HUMANS...
WHAT WAS CARNIVAC THINKING? IMPACTOR'S GOING TO STAB.
FORGET THAT. WE ENGAGE. IF MAYHEM REALLY WANTS TO MAKE OUR MARK, THIS MIGHT BE THE MOMENT.
OPEN 'EM UP, MAYHEM. SEND HIM BACK TO CRYBABY HELL.
OH, SPRINGER. YOUR NEW FRIENDS LOOK EVEN MORE DISPOSABLE THAN THE LAST LOT.
HAVE A REST WHILE I OBLIGE THEM.
P-KOW PK-KKOW
NO! NO-UUUUAAAHHH—
STOP! STOP, WAIT—
DAKKA-DAKKA-DAKKA-DAKKA-
DON'T! PLEASE, DON'T—!
SSSSHHBWOUMM
OKAY.
KRRMP
SLTCH SLLCHKT
BLAM BLAM
NOW THEN. ALONE AT LAST, WRECKER.
WE COULD SPEND THIS TIME CATCHING UP, STARING COQUETTISHLY INTO EACH OTHER'S OPTICS, FINDING OUT JUST HOW THE OTHER IS STILL ALIVE.
BUT LET'S GET BACK TO PEELING OFF EACH OTHER'S FACES. NOW I NOTICE YOU'RE A LITTLE MORE PASSIVE THAN BEFORE, AND THAT'S "OKAY," BUT LET'S HURRY ALONG...
YOU HAVE FRIENDS THAT TEND TO PICK THE RIGHT/WRONG TIME TO COME AROUND AND INTERRUPT—
WHAT SILLINESS IS THIS?
TAKKA
TAKKA

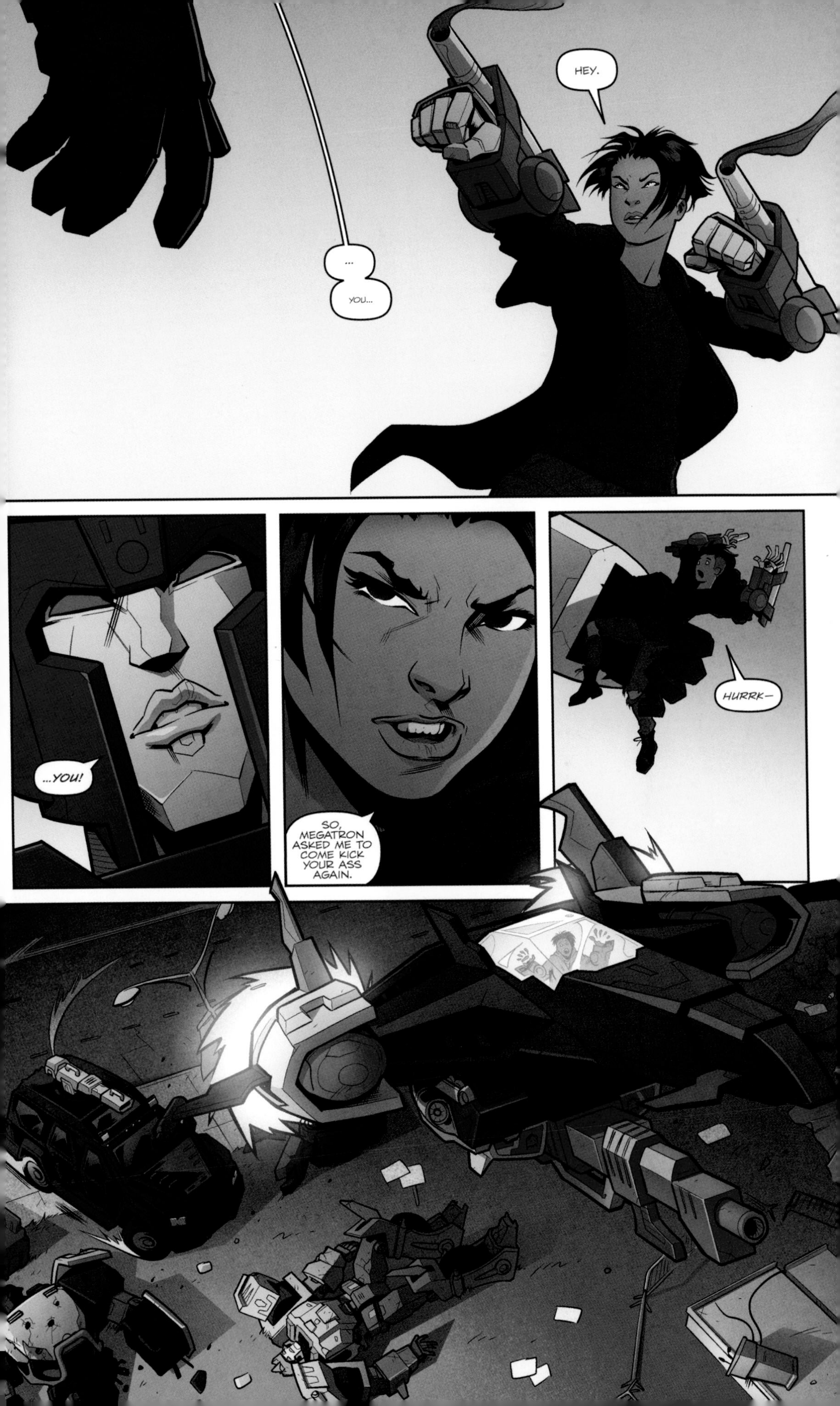

HEY.
...
YOU...
...YOU!
SO, MEGATRON ASKED ME TO COME KICK YOUR ASS AGAIN.
HURRK—

OVERLORD...?

HNN... HHH—IMPACTOR... HE TOOK HER...

SPRINGER—IT'S OKAY. I'M HERE... I'M HERE...

CARNIVAC!

CARNIVAC, I KNOW YOU'RE HERE!

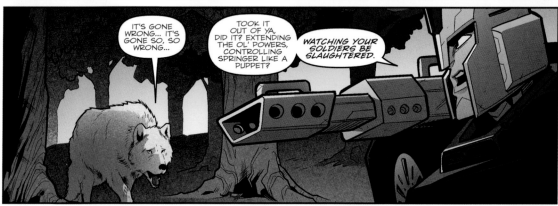

IT'S GONE WRONG... IT'S GONE SO, SO WRONG...

TOOK IT OUT OF YA, DID IT? EXTENDING THE OL' POWERS, CONTROLLING SPRINGER LIKE A PUPPET?

WATCHING YOUR SOLDIERS BE SLAUGHTERED.

I TOOK THE CHANCE, IMPACTOR.

YOU TOOK ADVANTAGE. YOU CHOSE TO REASSERT YOUR CONTROL OF MAYHEM WHILE I WAS UNDER DEEP COVER.

I BELIEVED IN YOU, CARNIVAC. I WANTED THE SAME THINGS YOU DID. BUT USING SPRINGER AS THE PATSY, WHAT—TO GET AT ME? TO SETTLE A SCORE?

TO GET OUR FRIENDS KILLED? WAS IT WORTH IT, CARNIVAC?

WAS. IT. WORTH. IT?

THE HUMANS ARE SENDING A STRIKE AGAINST US. SOON THE AUTOBOTS WILL BE HERE.

BUT I'M GETTING US BACK TO BASE, WHERE I'M GOING TO TRY AND SAVE MY FRIEND, AND GET YOU REPAIRED.

AND THEN I'M GOING TO KILL YOU.

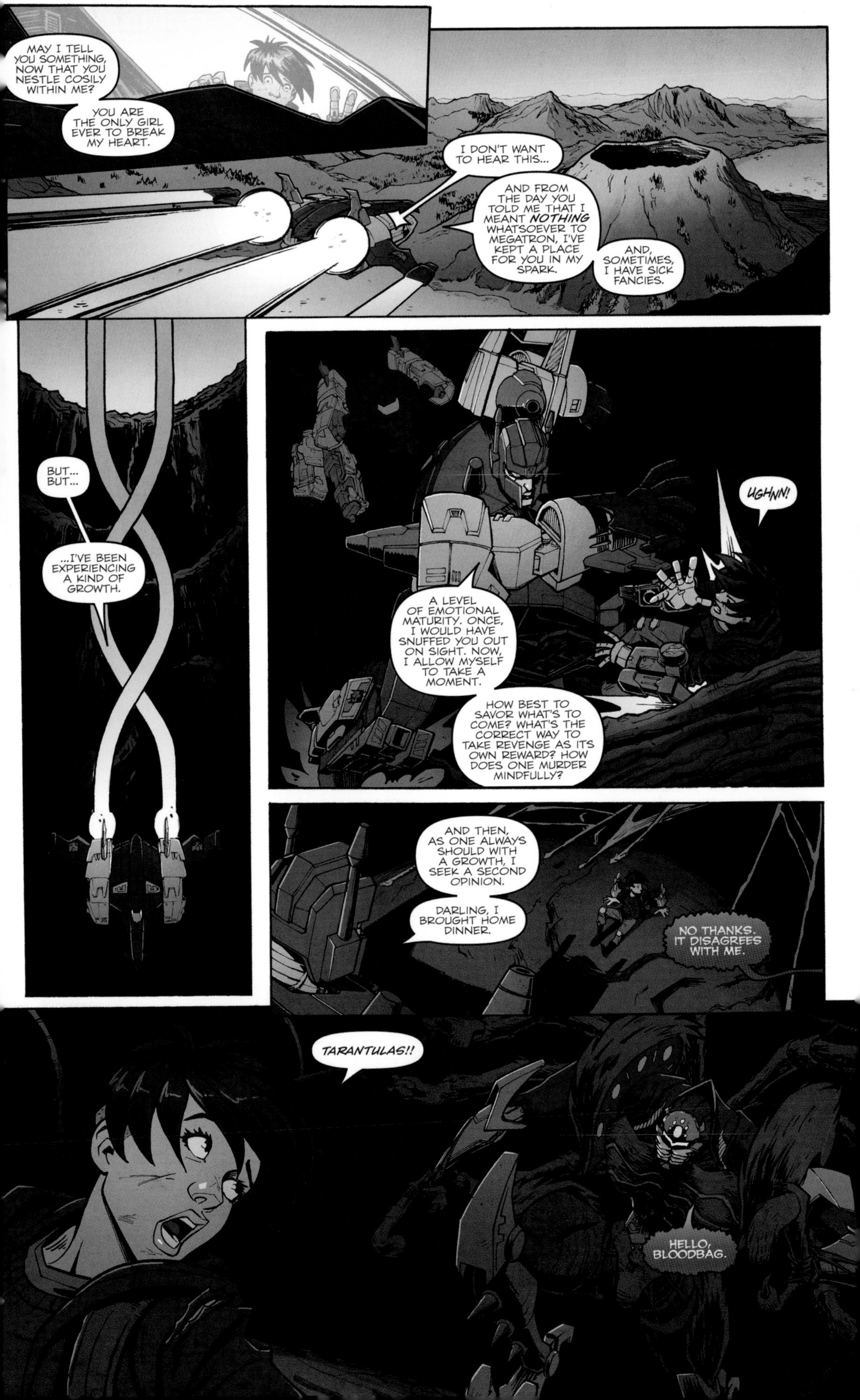

MAY I TELL YOU SOMETHING, NOW THAT YOU NESTLE COSILY WITHIN ME?
YOU ARE THE ONLY GIRL EVER TO BREAK MY HEART.
I DON'T WANT TO HEAR THIS...
AND FROM THE DAY YOU TOLD ME THAT I MEANT NOTHING WHATSOEVER TO MEGATRON, I'VE KEPT A PLACE FOR YOU IN MY SPARK.
AND, SOMETIMES, I HAVE SICK FANCIES.
BUT... BUT...
...I'VE BEEN EXPERIENCING A KIND OF GROWTH.
UGHNN!
A LEVEL OF EMOTIONAL MATURITY. ONCE, I WOULD HAVE SNUFFED YOU OUT ON SIGHT. NOW, I ALLOW MYSELF TO TAKE A MOMENT.
HOW BEST TO SAVOR WHAT'S TO COME? WHAT'S THE CORRECT WAY TO TAKE REVENGE AS ITS OWN REWARD? HOW DOES ONE MURDER MINDFULLY?
AND THEN, AS ONE ALWAYS SHOULD WITH A GROWTH, I SEEK A SECOND OPINION.
DARLING, I BROUGHT HOME DINNER.
NO THANKS. IT DISAGREES WITH ME.
TARANTULAS!!
HELLO, BLOODBAG.

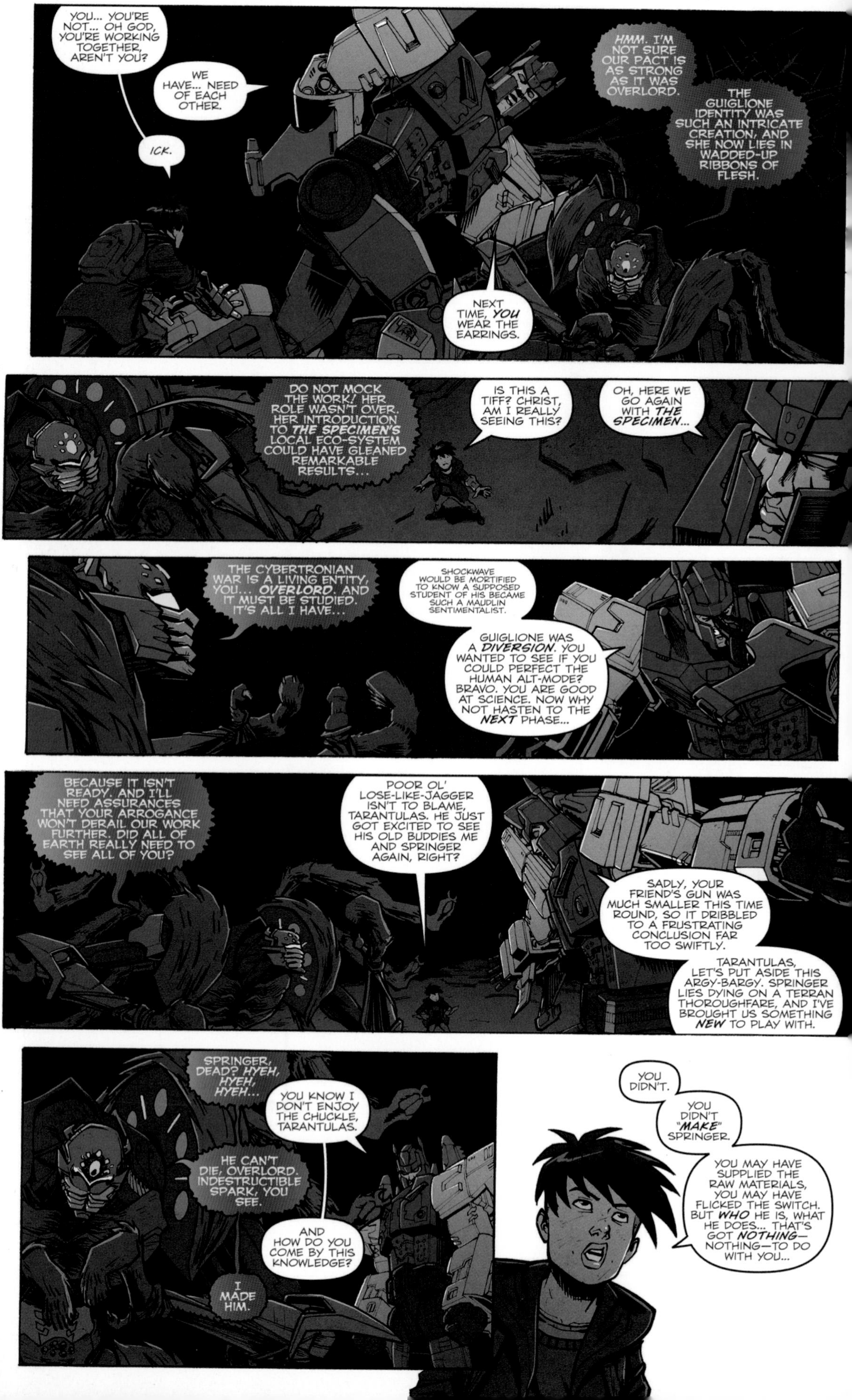
YOU... YOU'RE NOT... OH GOD, YOU'RE WORKING TOGETHER, AREN'T YOU?
WE HAVE... NEED OF EACH OTHER.
ICK.
HMM. I'M NOT SURE OUR PACT IS AS STRONG AS IT WAS OVERLORD.
THE GUIGLIONE IDENTITY WAS SUCH AN INTRICATE CREATION, AND SHE NOW LIES IN WADDED-UP RIBBONS OF FLESH.
NEXT TIME, YOU WEAR THE EARRINGS.
DO NOT MOCK THE WORK! HER ROLE WASN'T OVER. HER INTRODUCTION TO THE SPECIMEN'S LOCAL ECO-SYSTEM COULD HAVE GLEANED REMARKABLE RESULTS...
IS THIS A TIFF? CHRIST, AM I REALLY SEEING THIS?
OH, HERE WE GO AGAIN WITH THE SPECIMEN...
THE CYBERTRONIAN WAR IS A LIVING ENTITY, YOU... OVERLORD. AND IT MUST BE STUDIED. IT'S ALL I HAVE...
SHOCKWAVE WOULD BE MORTIFIED TO KNOW A SUPPOSED STUDENT OF HIS BECAME SUCH A MAUDLIN SENTIMENTALIST.
GUIGLIONE WAS A DIVERSION. YOU WANTED TO SEE IF YOU COULD PERFECT THE HUMAN ALT-MODE? BRAVO. YOU ARE GOOD AT SCIENCE. NOW WHY NOT HASTEN TO THE NEXT PHASE...
BECAUSE IT ISN'T READY. AND I'LL NEED ASSURANCES THAT YOUR ARROGANCE WON'T DERAIL OUR WORK FURTHER. DID ALL OF EARTH REALLY NEED TO SEE ALL OF YOU?
POOR OL' LOSE-LIKE-JAGGER ISN'T TO BLAME, TARANTULAS. HE JUST GOT EXCITED TO SEE HIS OLD BUDDIES ME AND SPRINGER AGAIN, RIGHT?
SADLY, YOUR FRIEND'S GUN WAS MUCH SMALLER THIS TIME ROUND, SO IT DRIBBLED TO A FRUSTRATING CONCLUSION FAR TOO SWIFTLY.
TARANTULAS, LET'S PUT ASIDE THIS ARGY-BARGY. SPRINGER LIES DYING ON A TERRAN THOROUGHFARE, AND I'VE BROUGHT US SOMETHING NEW TO PLAY WITH.
SPRINGER, DEAD? HYEH, HYEH, HYEH...
YOU KNOW I DON'T ENJOY THE CHUCKLE, TARANTULAS.
HE CAN'T DIE, OVERLORD. INDESTRUCTIBLE SPARK, YOU SEE.
AND HOW DO YOU COME BY THIS KNOWLEDGE?
I MADE HIM.
YOU DIDN'T.
YOU DIDN'T "MAKE" SPRINGER.
YOU MAY HAVE SUPPLIED THE RAW MATERIALS, YOU MAY HAVE FLICKED THE SWITCH. BUT WHO HE IS, WHAT HE DOES... THAT'S GOT NOTHING— NOTHING—TO DO WITH YOU...

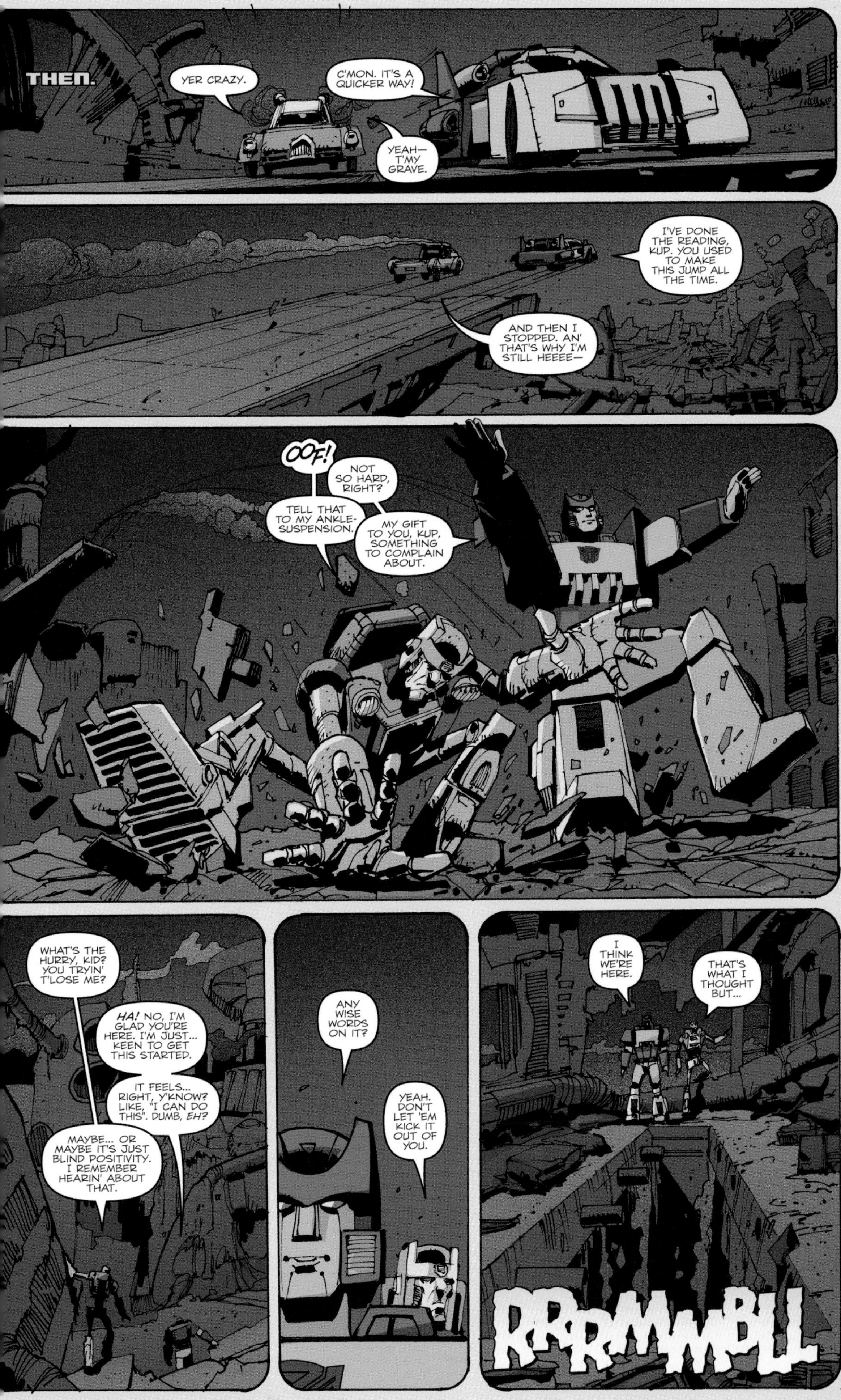
THEN.
YER CRAZY.
C'MON. IT'S A QUICKER WAY!
YEAH— T'MY GRAVE.
I'VE DONE THE READING, KUP. YOU USED TO MAKE THIS JUMP ALL THE TIME.
AND THEN I STOPPED. AN' THAT'S WHY I'M STILL HEEEE—
OOF!
NOT SO HARD, RIGHT?
TELL THAT TO MY ANKLE-SUSPENSION.
MY GIFT TO YOU, KUP, SOMETHING TO COMPLAIN ABOUT.
WHAT'S THE HURRY, KID? YOU TRYIN' T'LOSE ME?
HA! NO, I'M GLAD YOU'RE HERE. I'M JUST... KEEN TO GET THIS STARTED.
IT FEELS... RIGHT, Y'KNOW? LIKE, "I CAN DO THIS". DUMB, EH?
MAYBE... OR MAYBE IT'S JUST BLIND POSITIVITY. I REMEMBER HEARIN' ABOUT THAT.
ANY WISE WORDS ON IT?
YEAH. DON'T LET 'EM KICK IT OUT OF YOU.
I THINK WE'RE HERE.
THAT'S WHAT I THOUGHT BUT...
RRRMMBLL

GLAD YOU MADE IT, SPRINGER. NOT ALL OF 'EM DO, BUT I FIND 'EM IN THE END.

THESE ARE THE WRECKERS. WELCOME TO YOUR FIRST DAY OF TRAINING. *REAL* TRAINING.

KUP.

IMPACTOR.

HA! NO, I... HE JUST CAME ALONG BECAUSE WE... HE'S BEEN GOOD TO ME, SIR.

"GOOD?" GOOD AT WHAT—PUMPIN' YOUR TIRES, SPIT-SHININ' YOUR CANOPY, THAT SORTA "GOOD?"

SIR...?

'COS I TELL YOU ONE THING: HE'S NO GOOD AT GOODBYES...

SORRY, ONLY WRECKERS BEYOND THIS POINT.

THINK YOU CAN MANAGE THE STEPS ON YOUR OWN, KID?

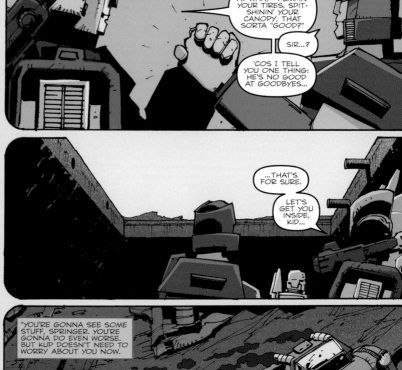

...THAT'S FOR SURE.

LET'S GET YOU INSIDE, KID...

"YOU'RE GONNA SEE SOME STUFF, SPRINGER. YOU'RE GONNA DO EVEN WORSE. BUT KUP DOESN'T NEED TO WORRY ABOUT YOU NOW.

"YOU'RE A WRECKER AND I PROMISE TO TAKE GOOD CARE OF YOU..."

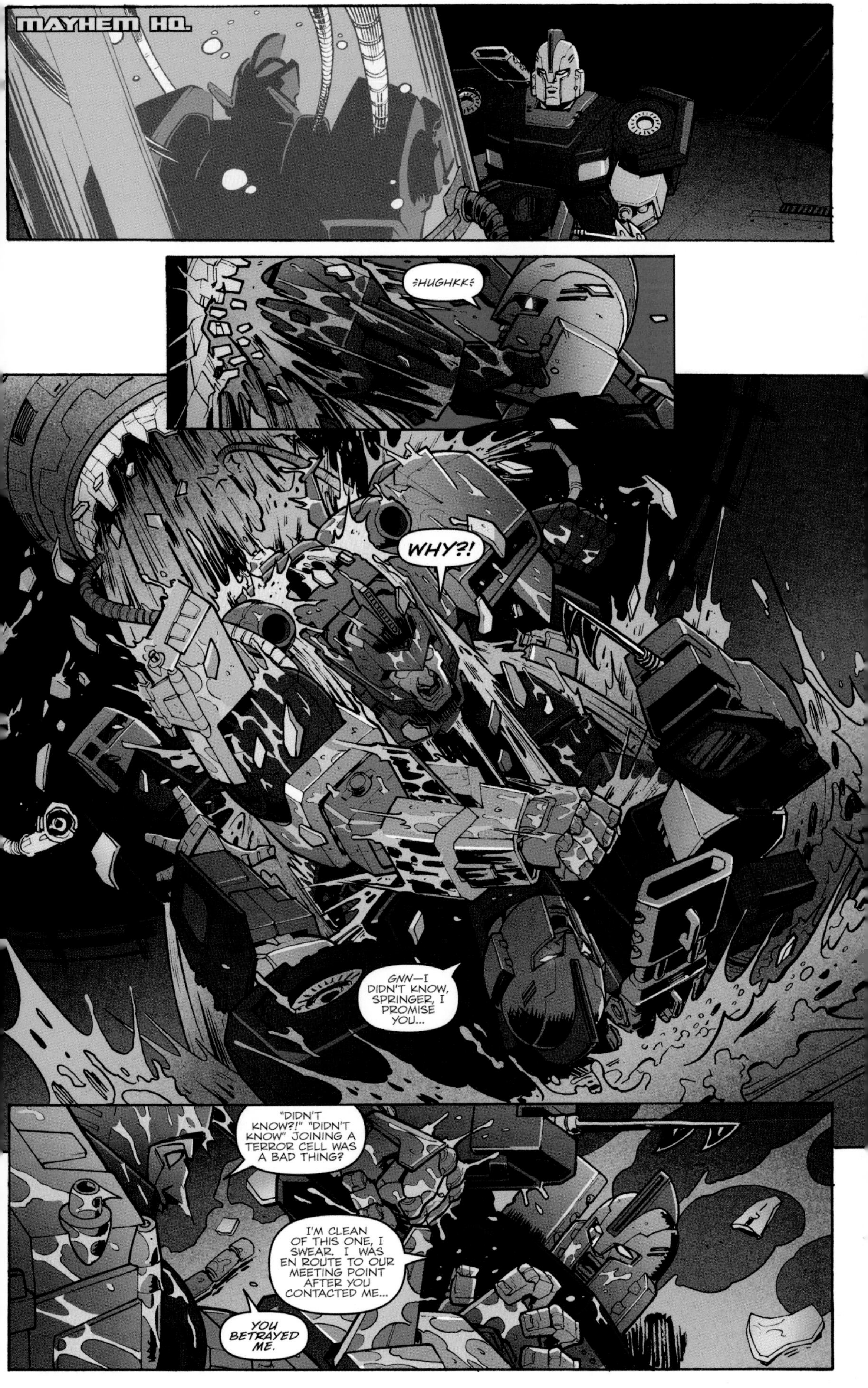
MAYHEM HQ.
HUGHKK
WHY?!
GNN—I DIDN'T KNOW, SPRINGER, I PROMISE YOU...
"DIDN'T KNOW?!" "DIDN'T KNOW" JOINING A TERROR CELL WAS A BAD THING?
I'M CLEAN OF THIS ONE, I SWEAR. I WAS EN ROUTE TO OUR MEETING POINT AFTER YOU CONTACTED ME...
YOU BETRAYED ME.

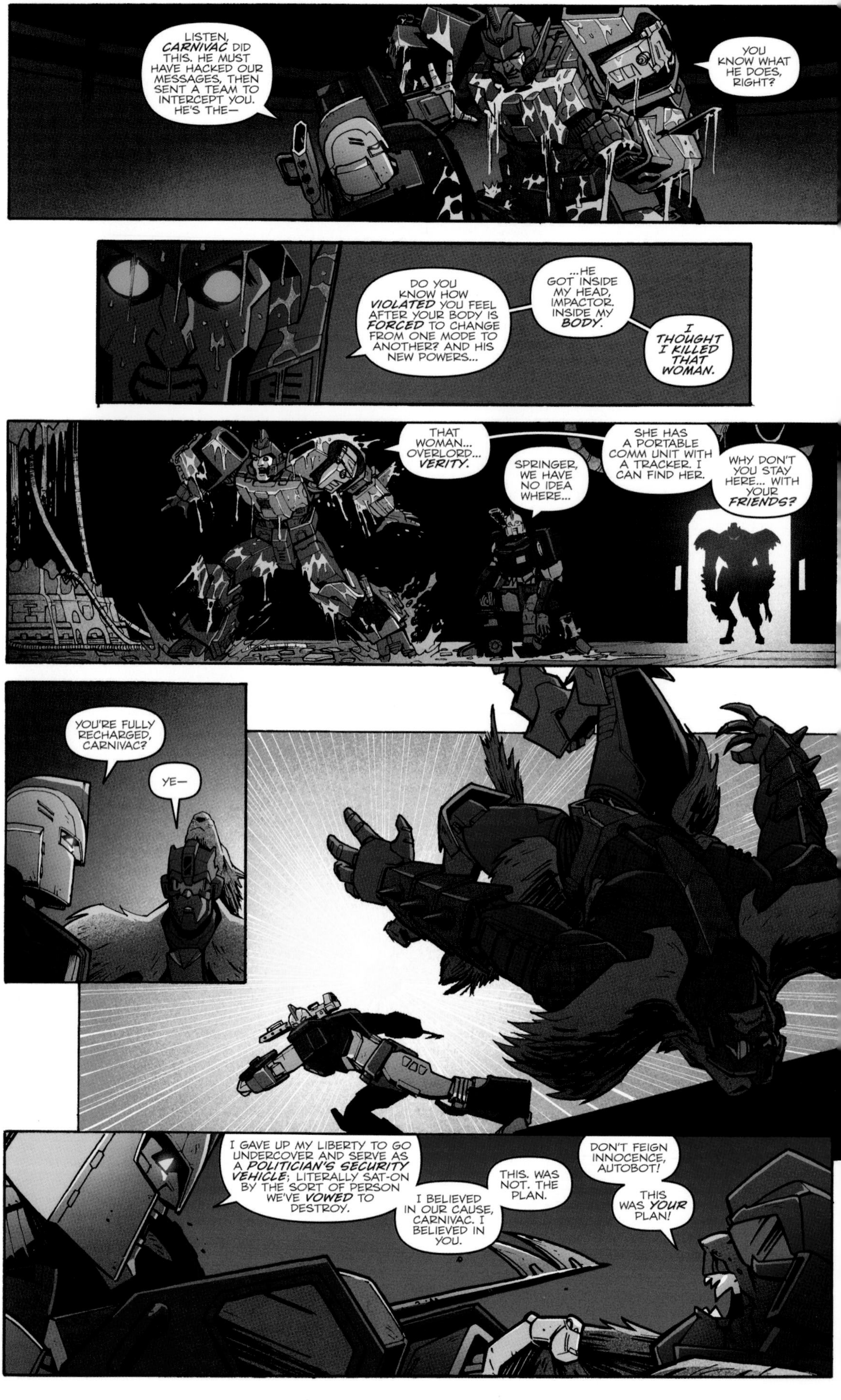
LISTEN, CARNIVAC DID THIS. HE MUST HAVE HACKED OUR MESSAGES, THEN SENT A TEAM TO INTERCEPT YOU. HE'S THE—
YOU KNOW WHAT HE DOES, RIGHT?
DO YOU KNOW HOW VIOLATED YOU FEEL AFTER YOUR BODY IS FORCED TO CHANGE FROM ONE MODE TO ANOTHER? AND HIS NEW POWERS...
...HE GOT INSIDE MY HEAD, IMPACTOR. INSIDE MY BODY.
I THOUGHT I KILLED THAT WOMAN.
THAT WOMAN... OVERLORD... VERITY.
SPRINGER, WE HAVE NO IDEA WHERE...
SHE HAS A PORTABLE COMM UNIT WITH A TRACKER. I CAN FIND HER.
WHY DON'T YOU STAY HERE... WITH YOUR FRIENDS?
YOU'RE FULLY RECHARGED, CARNIVAC?
YE—
I GAVE UP MY LIBERTY TO GO UNDERCOVER AND SERVE AS A POLITICIAN'S SECURITY VEHICLE; LITERALLY SAT-ON BY THE SORT OF PERSON WE'VE VOWED TO DESTROY.
I BELIEVED IN OUR CAUSE, CARNIVAC. I BELIEVED IN YOU.
THIS. WAS NOT. THE PLAN.
DON'T FEIGN INNOCENCE, AUTOBOT!
THIS WAS YOUR PLAN!

IMPACTOR...?

HOW BEST TO DESTABILIZE THE PEACE PROCESS AND SHATTER THE SHACKLES GRIPPED BY OUR COMMANDERS? HOW BEST TO DESTROY HUMAN/CYBERTRONIAN RELATIONS? "SIMPLE," YOU SAID.

"A COP *KILLED* BY AN AUTOBOT LEAVES A *SCAR*; A PUBLIC FIGURE *MARTYRED* BY ONE OPENS A *WOUND* THAT MUST NEVER BE ALLOWED TO HEAL."

MY GOD.

BUT NOT MY—NOT *SPRINGER*.

AND NOT WITHOUT MY GO-AHEAD. FRAMING AN AUTOBOT WAS ONE THING...

I PICKED AN AUTOBOT WHOSE ACTIONS MEAN SOMETHING!

THINK OF THE FALLOUT IF A "HERO" LIKE HIM TOOK A HUMAN LIFE AT SUCH A CRITICAL MOMENT...

NO. THAT'S NOT *IT*. THAT'S NOT WHY YOU FRAMED SPRINGER.

YOU'RE STILL HURT HE TURNED YOU AND MAYHEM DOWN. YOU'RE HURT BECAUSE YOU'RE NOT IN CHARGE ANY MORE.

THAT'S WHY YOU DESTROY OUR COVER... OUR *CAUSE*... BECAUSE OF YOUR PETTY PRIDE.

I DON'T HAVE TIME FOR THIS. YOU BOTH MAKE ME SICK.

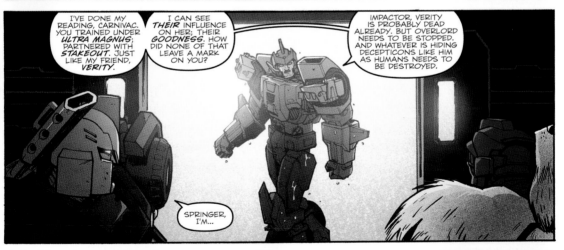

I'VE DONE MY READING, CARNIVAC. YOU TRAINED UNDER *ULTRA MAGNUS*; PARTNERED WITH *STAKEOUT*. JUST LIKE MY FRIEND, *VERITY*.

I CAN SEE *THEIR* INFLUENCE ON HER; THEIR *GOODNESS*. HOW DID NONE OF THAT LEAVE A MARK ON YOU?

IMPACTOR, VERITY IS PROBABLY DEAD ALREADY. BUT OVERLORD NEEDS TO BE STOPPED. AND WHATEVER IS HIDING DECEPTICONS LIKE HIM AS HUMANS NEEDS TO BE DESTROYED.

SPRINGER, I'M...

FINE. STAY AND BEAT CARNIVAC UP ALL YOU WANT. BUT DESPITE WHAT HE THINKS, YOU CAN'T FORCE PEOPLE TO CHANGE.

YOU JUST PROVED THAT.

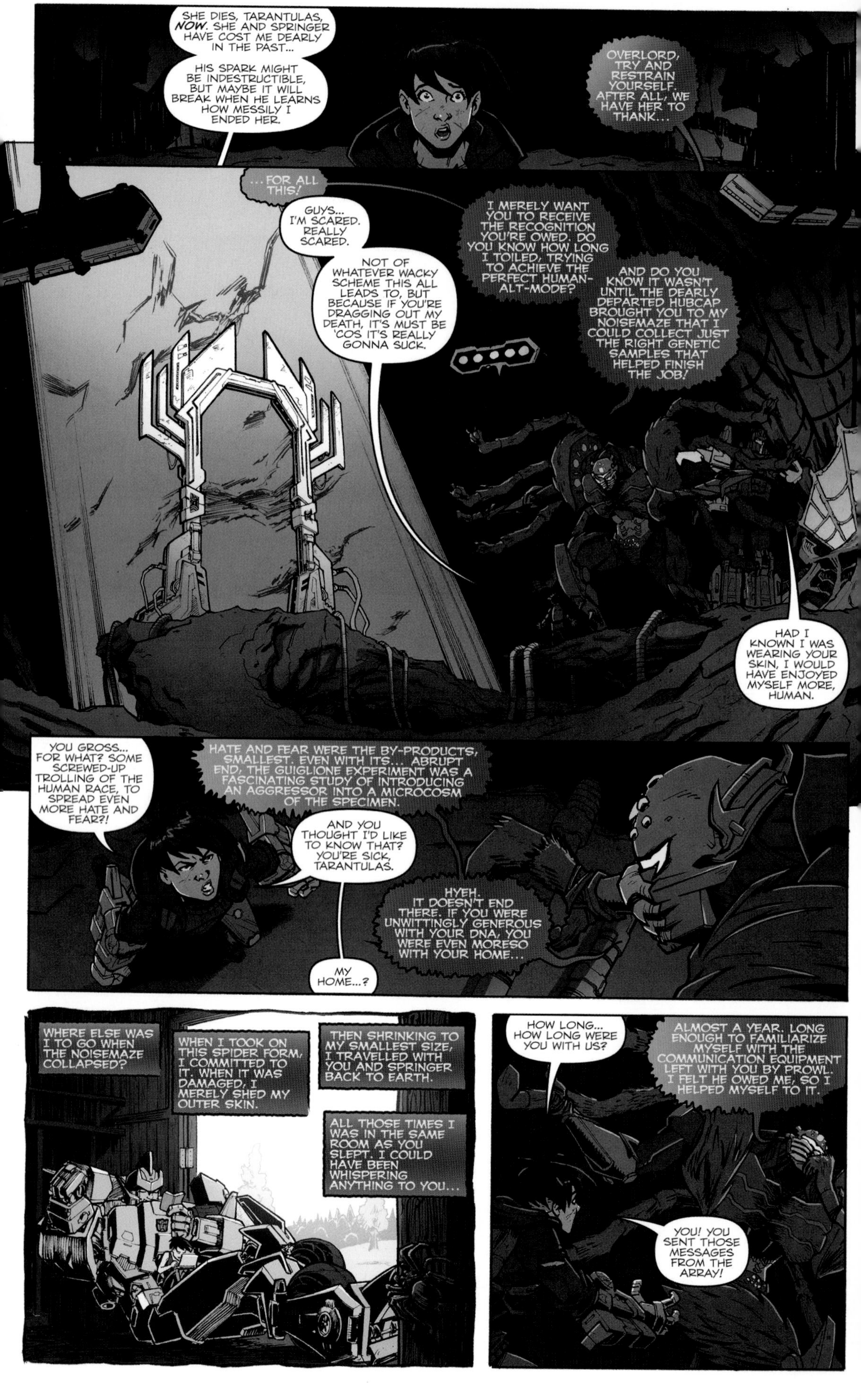
SHE DIES, TARANTULAS, NOW. SHE AND SPRINGER HAVE COST ME DEARLY IN THE PAST...
HIS SPARK MIGHT BE INDESTRUCTIBLE, BUT MAYBE IT WILL BREAK WHEN HE LEARNS HOW MESSILY I ENDED HER.
OVERLORD, TRY AND RESTRAIN YOURSELF. AFTER ALL, WE HAVE HER TO THANK...
...FOR ALL THIS!
GUYS... I'M SCARED. REALLY SCARED.
NOT OF WHATEVER WACKY SCHEME THIS ALL LEADS TO, BUT BECAUSE IF YOU'RE DRAGGING OUT MY DEATH, IT'S MUST BE 'COS IT'S REALLY GONNA SUCK.
I MERELY WANT YOU TO RECEIVE THE RECOGNITION YOU'RE OWED. DO YOU KNOW HOW LONG I TOILED, TRYING TO ACHIEVE THE PERFECT HUMAN-ALT-MODE?
AND DO YOU KNOW IT WASN'T UNTIL THE DEARLY DEPARTED HUBCAP BROUGHT YOU TO MY NOISEMAZE THAT I COULD COLLECT JUST THE RIGHT GENETIC SAMPLES THAT HELPED FINISH THE JOB!
HAD I KNOWN I WAS WEARING YOUR SKIN, I WOULD HAVE ENJOYED MYSELF MORE, HUMAN.
YOU GROSS... FOR WHAT? SOME SCREWED-UP TROLLING OF THE HUMAN RACE, TO SPREAD EVEN MORE HATE AND FEAR?!
HATE AND FEAR WERE THE BY-PRODUCTS, SMALLEST. EVEN WITH ITS... ABRUPT END, THE GUIGLIONE EXPERIMENT WAS A FASCINATING STUDY OF INTRODUCING AN AGGRESSOR INTO A MICROCOSM OF THE SPECIMEN.
AND YOU THOUGHT I'D LIKE TO KNOW THAT? YOU'RE SICK, TARANTULAS.
HYEH. IT DOESN'T END THERE. IF YOU WERE UNWITTINGLY GENEROUS WITH YOUR DNA, YOU WERE EVEN MORESO WITH YOUR HOME...
MY HOME...?
WHERE ELSE WAS I TO GO WHEN THE NOISEMAZE COLLAPSED?
WHEN I TOOK ON THIS SPIDER FORM, I COMMITTED TO IT. WHEN IT WAS DAMAGED, I MERELY SHED MY OUTER SKIN.
THEN SHRINKING TO MY SMALLEST SIZE, I TRAVELLED WITH YOU AND SPRINGER BACK TO EARTH.
ALL THOSE TIMES I WAS IN THE SAME ROOM AS YOU SLEPT. I COULD HAVE BEEN WHISPERING ANYTHING TO YOU...
HOW LONG... HOW LONG WERE YOU WITH US?
ALMOST A YEAR. LONG ENOUGH TO FAMILIARIZE MYSELF WITH THE COMMUNICATION EQUIPMENT LEFT WITH YOU BY PROWL. I FELT HE OWED ME, SO I HELPED MYSELF TO IT.
YOU! YOU SENT THOSE MESSAGES FROM THE ARRAY!

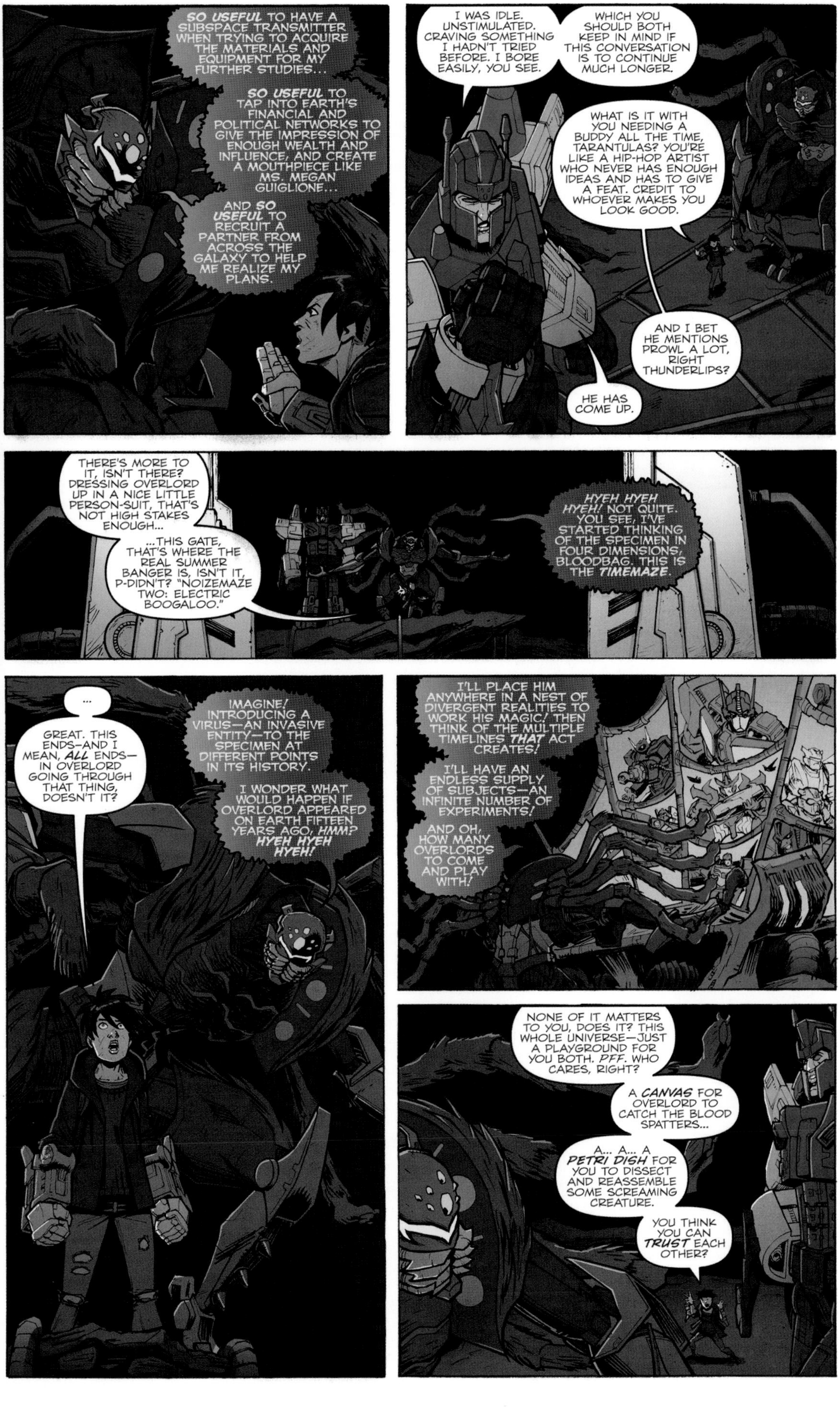
SO USEFUL TO HAVE A SUBSPACE TRANSMITTER WHEN TRYING TO ACQUIRE THE MATERIALS AND EQUIPMENT FOR MY FURTHER STUDIES...
SO USEFUL TO TAP INTO EARTH'S FINANCIAL AND POLITICAL NETWORKS TO GIVE THE IMPRESSION OF ENOUGH WEALTH AND INFLUENCE, AND CREATE A MOUTHPIECE LIKE MS. MEGAN GUIGLIONE...
AND SO USEFUL TO RECRUIT A PARTNER FROM ACROSS THE GALAXY TO HELP ME REALIZE MY PLANS.
I WAS IDLE. UNSTIMULATED. CRAVING SOMETHING I HADN'T TRIED BEFORE. I BORE EASILY, YOU SEE.
WHICH YOU SHOULD BOTH KEEP IN MIND IF THIS CONVERSATION IS TO CONTINUE MUCH LONGER.
WHAT IS IT WITH YOU NEEDING A BUDDY ALL THE TIME, TARANTULAS? YOU'RE LIKE A HIP-HOP ARTIST WHO NEVER HAS ENOUGH IDEAS AND HAS TO GIVE A FEAT. CREDIT TO WHOEVER MAKES YOU LOOK GOOD.
AND I BET HE MENTIONS PROWL A LOT, RIGHT THUNDERLIPS?
HE HAS COME UP.
THERE'S MORE TO IT, ISN'T THERE? DRESSING OVERLORD UP IN A NICE LITTLE PERSON-SUIT, THAT'S NOT HIGH STAKES ENOUGH...
...THIS GATE, THAT'S WHERE THE REAL SUMMER BANGER IS, ISN'T IT, P-DIDN'T? "NOIZEMAZE TWO: ELECTRIC BOOGALOO."
HYEH HYEH HYEH! NOT QUITE. YOU SEE, I'VE STARTED THINKING OF THE SPECIMEN IN FOUR DIMENSIONS, BLOODBAG. THIS IS THE TIMEMAZE.
...
GREAT. THIS ENDS—AND I MEAN, ALL ENDS—IN OVERLORD GOING THROUGH THAT THING, DOESN'T IT?
IMAGINE! INTRODUCING A VIRUS—AN INVASIVE ENTITY—TO THE SPECIMEN AT DIFFERENT POINTS IN ITS HISTORY.
I WONDER WHAT WOULD HAPPEN IF OVERLORD APPEARED ON EARTH FIFTEEN YEARS AGO, HMM? HYEH HYEH HYEH!
I'LL PLACE HIM ANYWHERE IN A NEST OF DIVERGENT REALITIES TO WORK HIS MAGIC! THEN THINK OF THE MULTIPLE TIMELINES THAT ACT CREATES!
I'LL HAVE AN ENDLESS SUPPLY OF SUBJECTS—AN INFINITE NUMBER OF EXPERIMENTS!
AND OH, HOW MANY OVERLORDS TO COME AND PLAY WITH!
NONE OF IT MATTERS TO YOU, DOES IT? THIS WHOLE UNIVERSE—JUST A PLAYGROUND FOR YOU BOTH. PFF. WHO CARES, RIGHT?
A CANVAS FOR OVERLORD TO CATCH THE BLOOD SPATTERS...
A... A... A PETRI DISH FOR YOU TO DISSECT AND REASSEMBLE SOME SCREAMING CREATURE.
YOU THINK YOU CAN TRUST EACH OTHER?

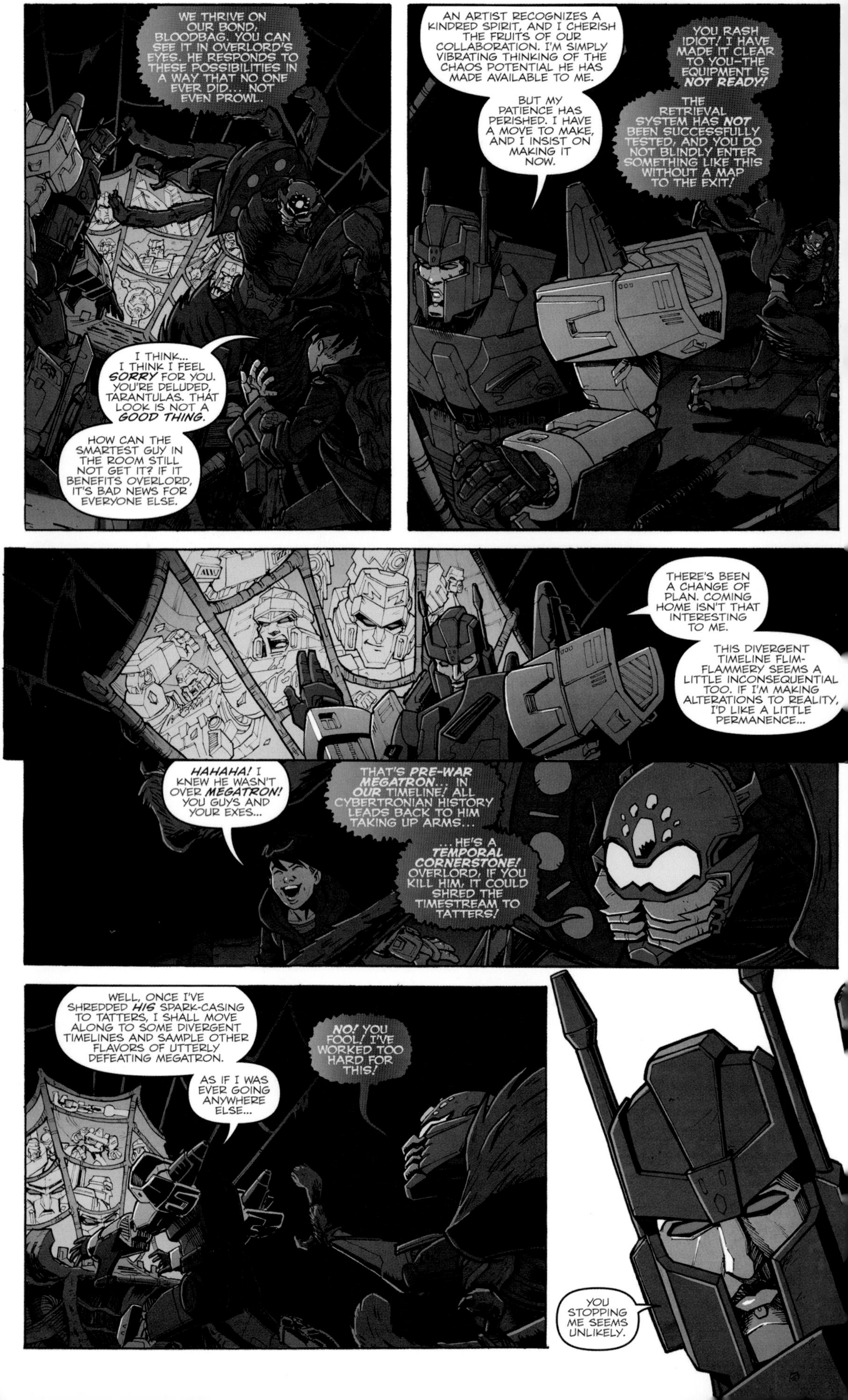
WE THRIVE ON OUR BOND, BLOODBAG. YOU CAN SEE IT IN OVERLORD'S EYES. HE RESPONDS TO THESE POSSIBILITIES IN A WAY THAT NO ONE EVER DID... NOT EVEN PROWL.
I THINK... I THINK I FEEL SORRY FOR YOU. YOU'RE DELUDED, TARANTULAS. THAT LOOK IS NOT A GOOD THING.
HOW CAN THE SMARTEST GUY IN THE ROOM STILL NOT GET IT? IF IT BENEFITS OVERLORD, IT'S BAD NEWS FOR EVERYONE ELSE.
AN ARTIST RECOGNIZES A KINDRED SPIRIT, AND I CHERISH THE FRUITS OF OUR COLLABORATION. I'M SIMPLY VIBRATING THINKING OF THE CHAOS POTENTIAL HE HAS MADE AVAILABLE TO ME.
BUT MY PATIENCE HAS PERISHED. I HAVE A MOVE TO MAKE, AND I INSIST ON MAKING IT NOW.
YOU RASH IDIOT! I HAVE MADE IT CLEAR TO YOU–THE EQUIPMENT IS NOT READY!
THE RETRIEVAL SYSTEM HAS NOT BEEN SUCCESSFULLY TESTED, AND YOU DO NOT BLINDLY ENTER SOMETHING LIKE THIS WITHOUT A MAP TO THE EXIT!
THERE'S BEEN A CHANGE OF PLAN. COMING HOME ISN'T THAT INTERESTING TO ME.
THIS DIVERGENT TIMELINE FLIM-FLAMMERY SEEMS A LITTLE INCONSEQUENTIAL TOO. IF I'M MAKING ALTERATIONS TO REALITY, I'D LIKE A LITTLE PERMANENCE...
HAHAHA! I KNEW HE WASN'T OVER MEGATRON! YOU GUYS AND YOUR EXES...
THAT'S PRE-WAR MEGATRON... IN OUR TIMELINE! ALL CYBERTRONIAN HISTORY LEADS BACK TO HIM TAKING UP ARMS...
...HE'S A TEMPORAL CORNERSTONE! OVERLORD, IF YOU KILL HIM, IT COULD SHRED THE TIMESTREAM TO TATTERS!
WELL, ONCE I'VE SHREDDED HIS SPARK-CASING TO TATTERS, I SHALL MOVE ALONG TO SOME DIVERGENT TIMELINES AND SAMPLE OTHER FLAVORS OF UTTERLY DEFEATING MEGATRON.
AS IF I WAS EVER GOING ANYWHERE ELSE...
NO! YOU FOOL! I'VE WORKED TOO HARD FOR THIS!
YOU STOPPING ME SEEMS UNLIKELY.

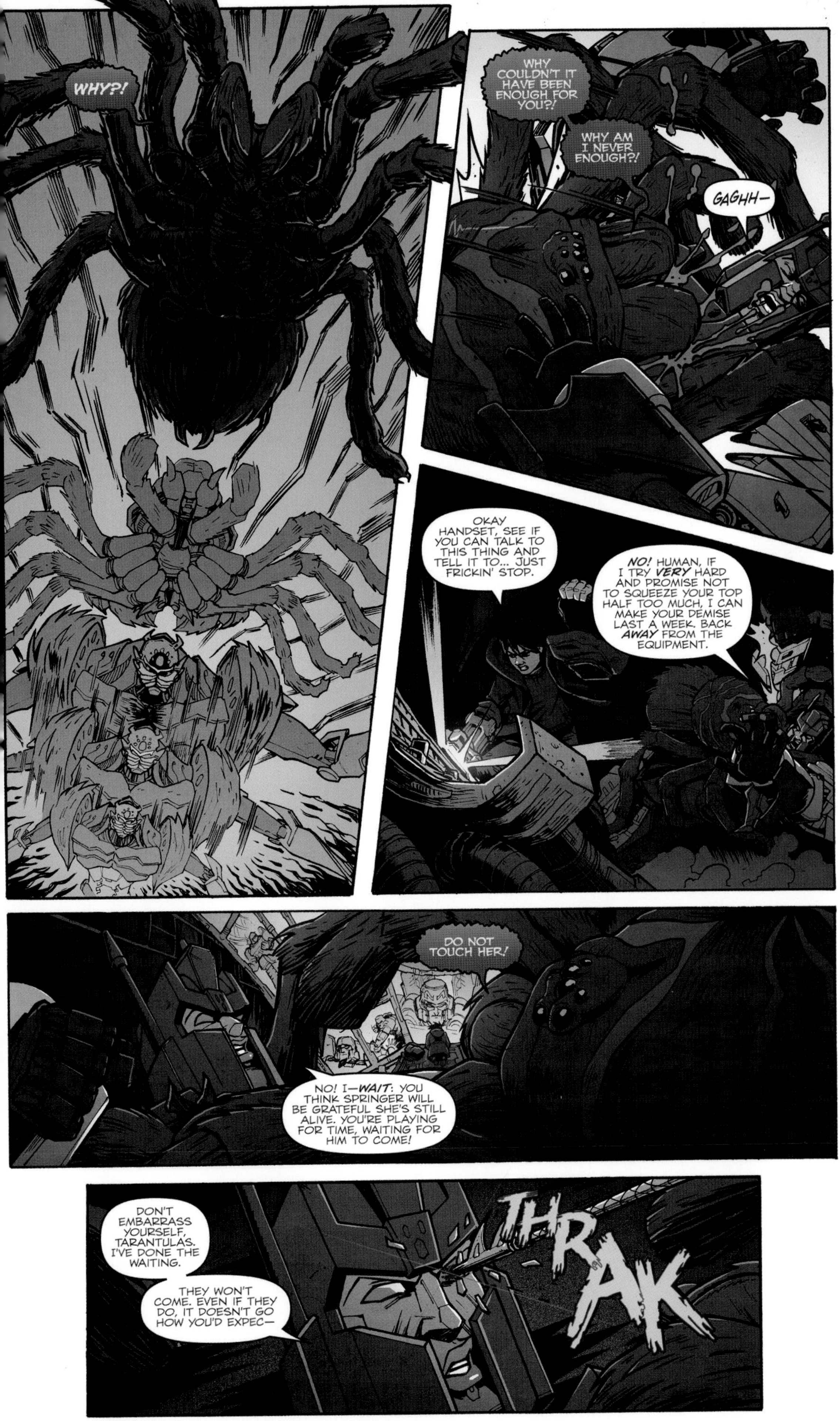
WHY?!
WHY COULDN'T IT HAVE BEEN ENOUGH FOR YOU?!
WHY AM I NEVER ENOUGH?!
GAGHH—
OKAY HANDSET, SEE IF YOU CAN TALK TO THIS THING AND TELL IT TO... JUST FRICKIN' STOP.
NO! HUMAN, IF I TRY VERY HARD AND PROMISE NOT TO SQUEEZE YOUR TOP HALF TOO MUCH, I CAN MAKE YOUR DEMISE LAST A WEEK. BACK AWAY FROM THE EQUIPMENT.
DO NOT TOUCH HER!
NO! I—WAIT: YOU THINK SPRINGER WILL BE GRATEFUL SHE'S STILL ALIVE. YOU'RE PLAYING FOR TIME, WAITING FOR HIM TO COME!
DON'T EMBARRASS YOURSELF, TARANTULAS. I'VE DONE THE WAITING.
THEY WON'T COME. EVEN IF THEY DO, IT DOESN'T GO HOW YOU'D EXPEC—
THRAK

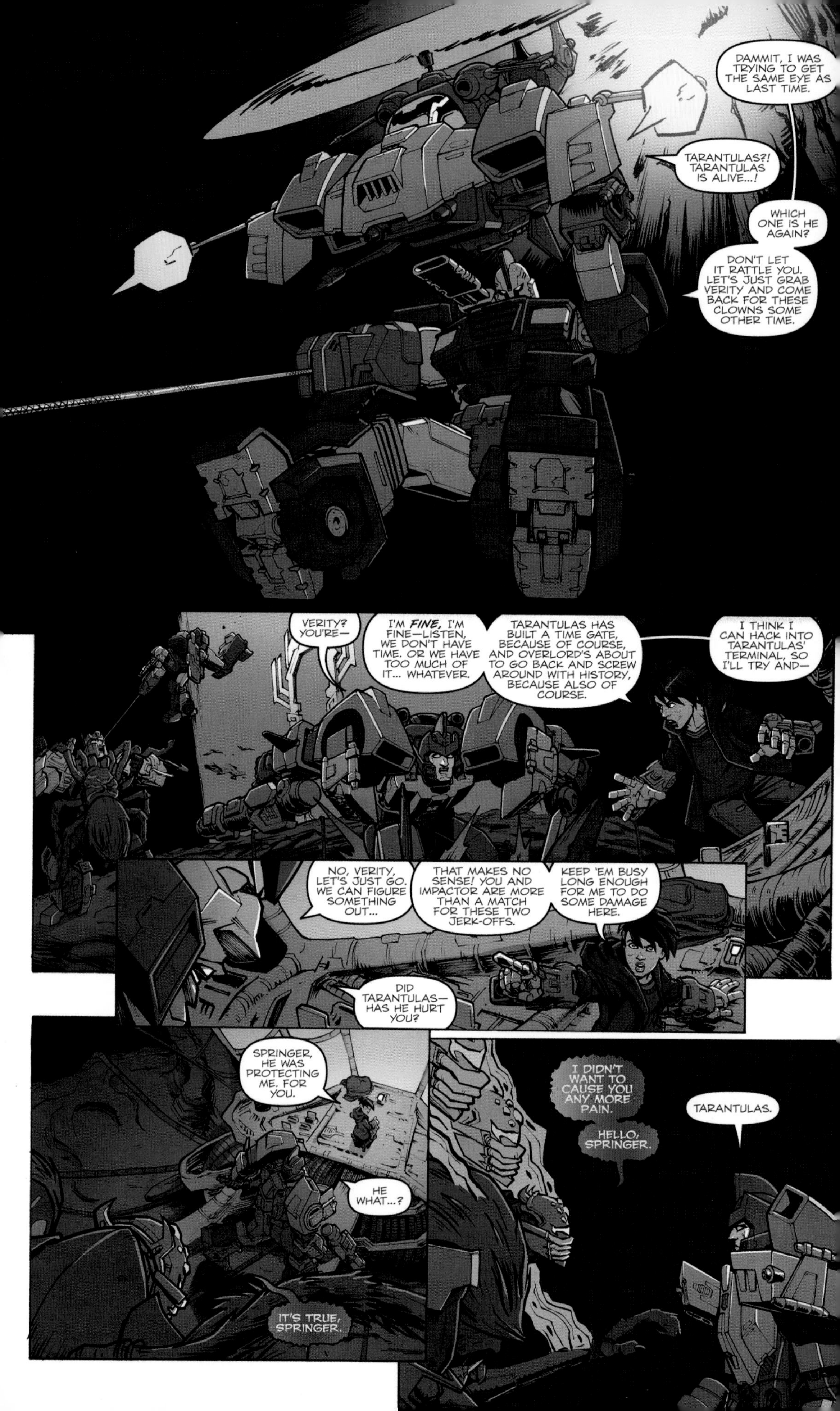
DAMMIT, I WAS TRYING TO GET THE SAME EYE AS LAST TIME.
TARANTULAS?! TARANTULAS IS ALIVE...!
WHICH ONE IS HE AGAIN?
DON'T LET IT RATTLE YOU. LET'S JUST GRAB VERITY AND COME BACK FOR THESE CLOWNS SOME OTHER TIME.
VERITY? YOU'RE—
I'M FINE, I'M FINE—LISTEN, WE DON'T HAVE TIME. OR WE HAVE TOO MUCH OF IT... WHATEVER.
TARANTULAS HAS BUILT A TIME GATE, BECAUSE OF COURSE, AND OVERLORD'S ABOUT TO GO BACK AND SCREW AROUND WITH HISTORY, BECAUSE ALSO OF COURSE.
I THINK I CAN HACK INTO TARANTULAS' TERMINAL, SO I'LL TRY AND—
NO, VERITY, LET'S JUST GO. WE CAN FIGURE SOMETHING OUT...
THAT MAKES NO SENSE! YOU AND IMPACTOR ARE MORE THAN A MATCH FOR THESE TWO JERK-OFFS.
KEEP 'EM BUSY LONG ENOUGH FOR ME TO DO SOME DAMAGE HERE.
DID TARANTULAS— HAS HE HURT YOU?
SPRINGER, HE WAS PROTECTING ME. FOR YOU.
HE WHAT...?
IT'S TRUE, SPRINGER.
I DIDN'T WANT TO CAUSE YOU ANY MORE PAIN.
HELLO, SPRINGER.
TARANTULAS.

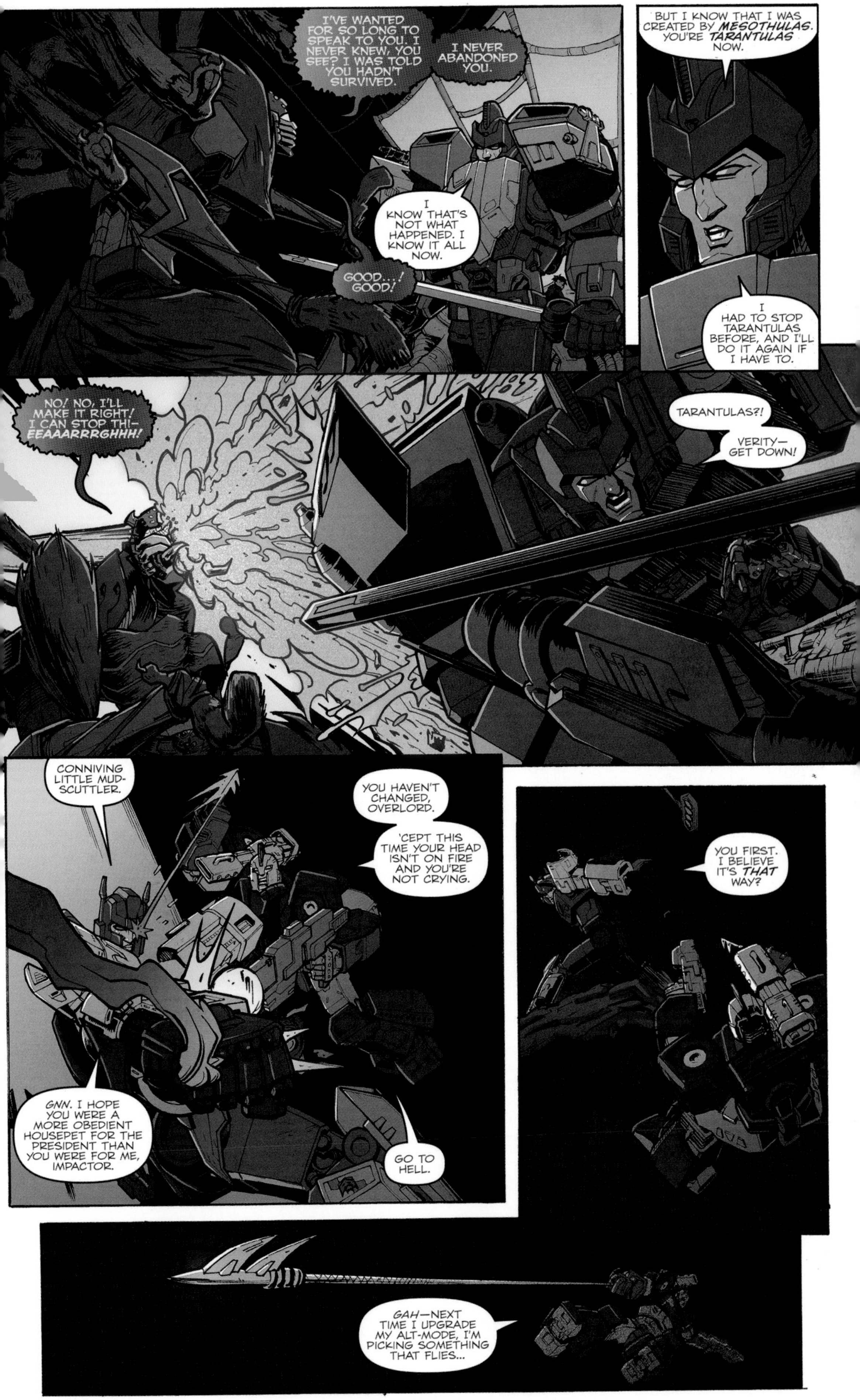

I'VE WANTED FOR SO LONG TO SPEAK TO YOU. I NEVER KNEW, YOU SEE? I WAS TOLD YOU HADN'T SURVIVED.
I NEVER ABANDONED YOU.
I KNOW THAT'S NOT WHAT HAPPENED. I KNOW IT ALL NOW.
GOOD...! GOOD!
BUT I KNOW THAT I WAS CREATED BY MESOTHULAS. YOU'RE TARANTULAS NOW.
I HAD TO STOP TARANTULAS BEFORE, AND I'LL DO IT AGAIN IF I HAVE TO.
NO! NO, I'LL MAKE IT RIGHT! I CAN STOP THI– EEAAARRRGHHH!
TARANTULAS?!
VERITY— GET DOWN!
CONNIVING LITTLE MUD-SCUTTLER.
YOU HAVEN'T CHANGED, OVERLORD.
'CEPT THIS TIME YOUR HEAD ISN'T ON FIRE AND YOU'RE NOT CRYING.
GNN. I HOPE YOU WERE A MORE OBEDIENT HOUSEPET FOR THE PRESIDENT THAN YOU WERE FOR ME, IMPACTOR.
GO TO HELL.
YOU FIRST. I BELIEVE IT'S THAT WAY?
GAH—NEXT TIME I UPGRADE MY ALT-MODE, I'M PICKING SOMETHING THAT FLIES...

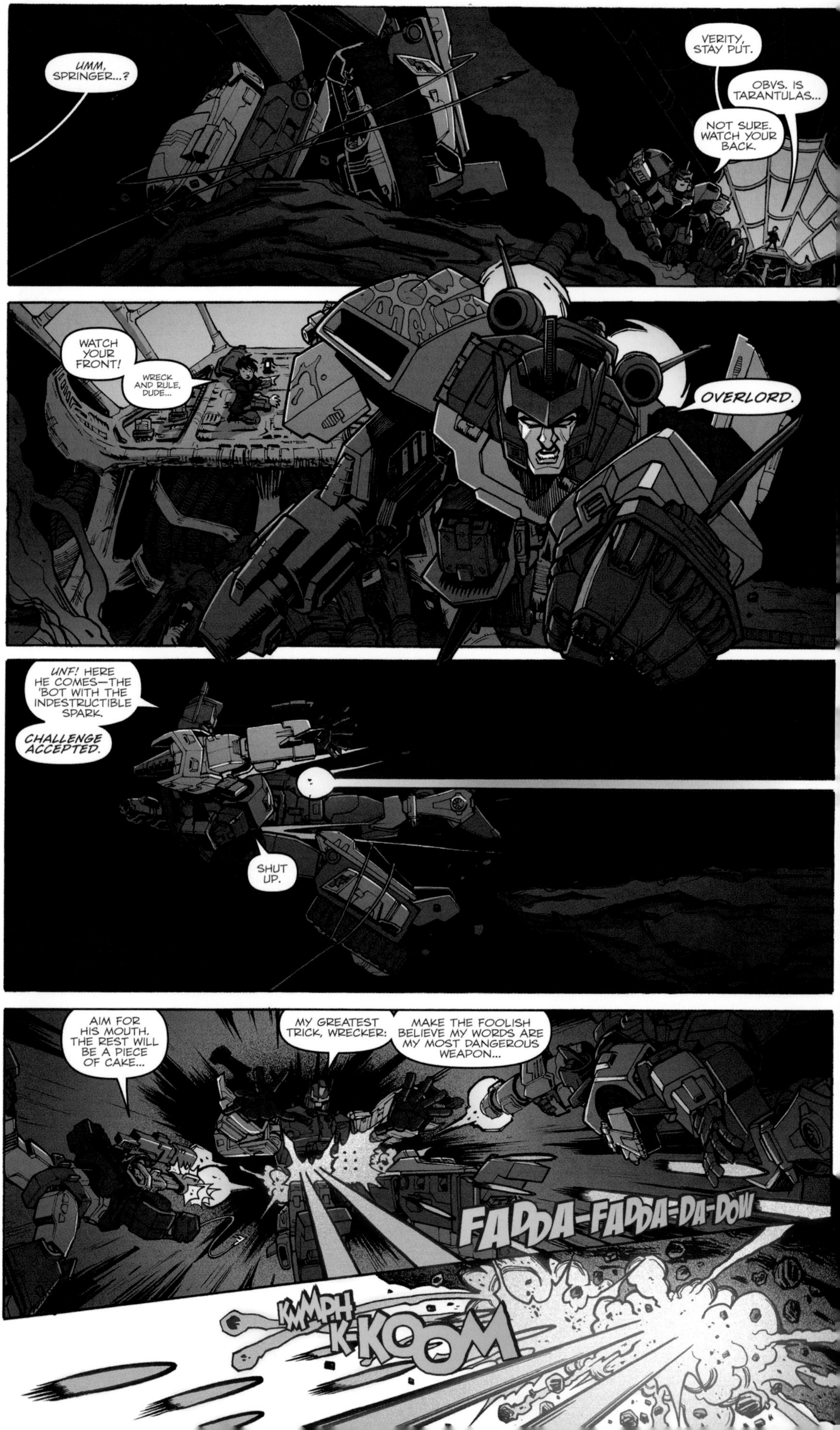
UMM, SPRINGER...?
VERITY, STAY PUT.
OBVS. IS TARANTULAS...
NOT SURE. WATCH YOUR BACK.
WATCH YOUR FRONT!
WRECK AND RULE, DUDE...
OVERLORD.
UNF! HERE HE COMES—THE 'BOT WITH THE INDESTRUCTIBLE SPARK.
CHALLENGE ACCEPTED.
SHUT UP.
AIM FOR HIS MOUTH. THE REST WILL BE A PIECE OF CAKE...
MY GREATEST TRICK, WRECKER:
MAKE THE FOOLISH BELIEVE MY WORDS ARE MY MOST DANGEROUS WEAPON...
FADDA-FADDA-DA-DOW
KWMPH K-KOOM

SPRINGER, WATCH OUT, IT'S COMING DOW—

≠KOFF≠

SPRINGER...?

SPRINGER, YOU THERE...?

YEAH.

I MADE IT. YOU'RE...

NEVER BETTER, PAL.

WATCH OUT, I'LL START MOVING THESE...

WHOA! SPRINGER, YOU'RE NUTS. YOU'LL BRING IT ALL DOWN.

MAN. WHEN I ASKED TO MEET YOU, I DIDN'T EXPECT IT TO GO LIKE THIS.

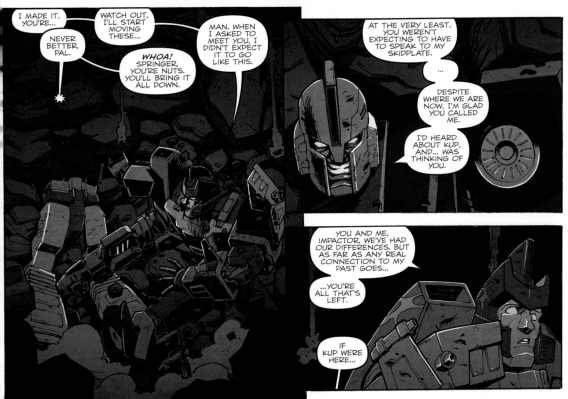

AT THE VERY LEAST, YOU WEREN'T EXPECTING TO HAVE TO SPEAK TO MY SKIDPLATE.

...

DESPITE WHERE WE ARE NOW, I'M GLAD YOU CALLED ME.

I'D HEARD ABOUT KUP, AND... WAS THINKING OF YOU.

YOU AND ME, IMPACTOR, WE'VE HAD OUR DIFFERENCES. BUT AS FAR AS ANY REAL CONNECTION TO MY PAST GOES...

...YOU'RE ALL THAT'S LEFT.

IF KUP WERE HERE...

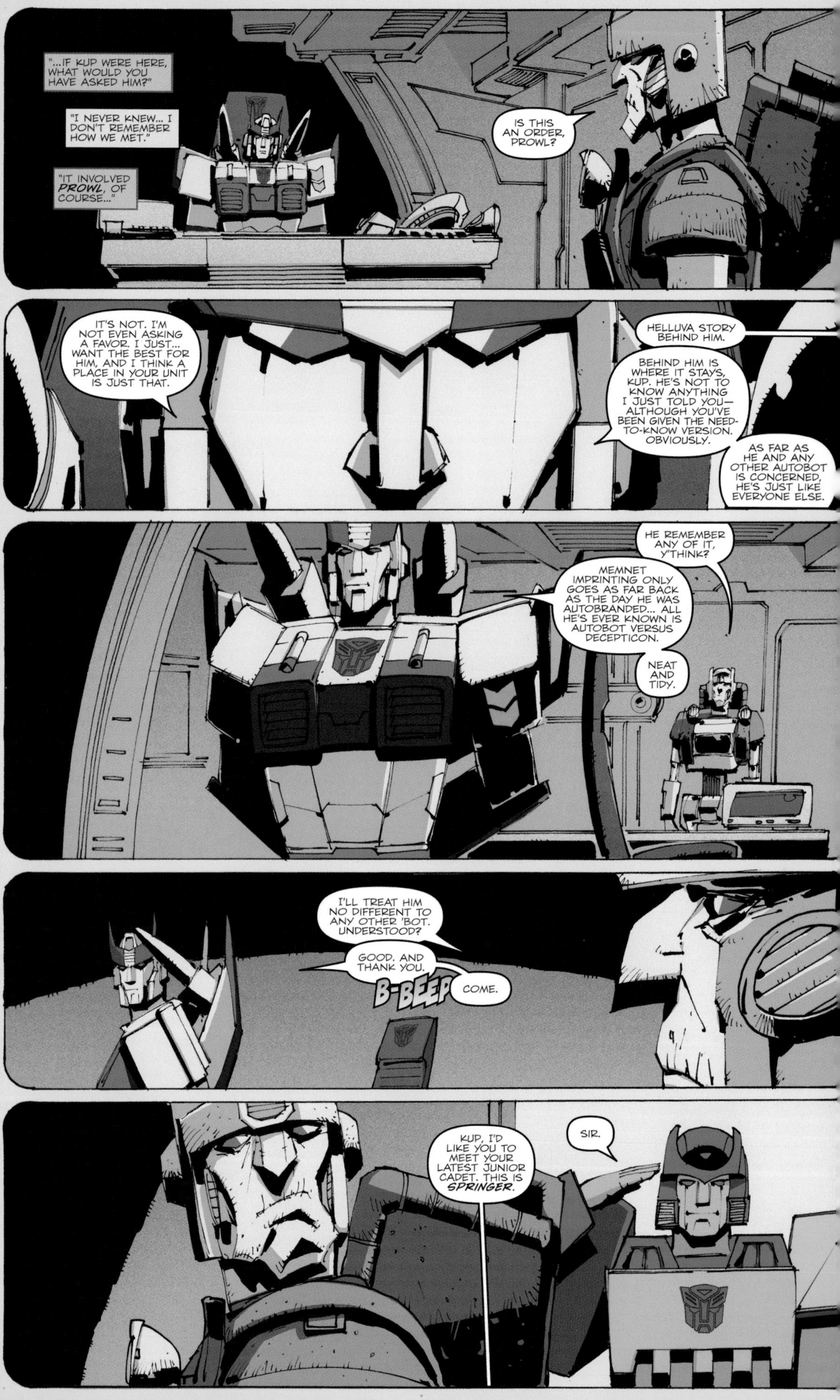
"...IF KUP WERE HERE, WHAT WOULD YOU HAVE ASKED HIM?"
"I NEVER KNEW... I DON'T REMEMBER HOW WE MET."
"IT INVOLVED PROWL, OF COURSE..."
IS THIS AN ORDER, PROWL?
IT'S NOT. I'M NOT EVEN ASKING A FAVOR. I JUST... WANT THE BEST FOR HIM, AND I THINK A PLACE IN YOUR UNIT IS JUST THAT.
HELLUVA STORY BEHIND HIM.
BEHIND HIM IS WHERE IT STAYS, KUP. HE'S NOT TO KNOW ANYTHING I JUST TOLD YOU— ALTHOUGH YOU'VE BEEN GIVEN THE NEED-TO-KNOW VERSION. OBVIOUSLY.
AS FAR AS HE AND ANY OTHER AUTOBOT IS CONCERNED, HE'S JUST LIKE EVERYONE ELSE.
HE REMEMBER ANY OF IT, Y'THINK?
MEMNET IMPRINTING ONLY GOES AS FAR BACK AS THE DAY HE WAS AUTOBRANDED... ALL HE'S EVER KNOWN IS AUTOBOT VERSUS DECEPTICON.
NEAT AND TIDY.
I'LL TREAT HIM NO DIFFERENT TO ANY OTHER 'BOT. UNDERSTOOD?
GOOD. AND THANK YOU.
B-BEEP
COME.
KUP, I'D LIKE YOU TO MEET YOUR LATEST JUNIOR CADET. THIS IS SPRINGER.
SIR.

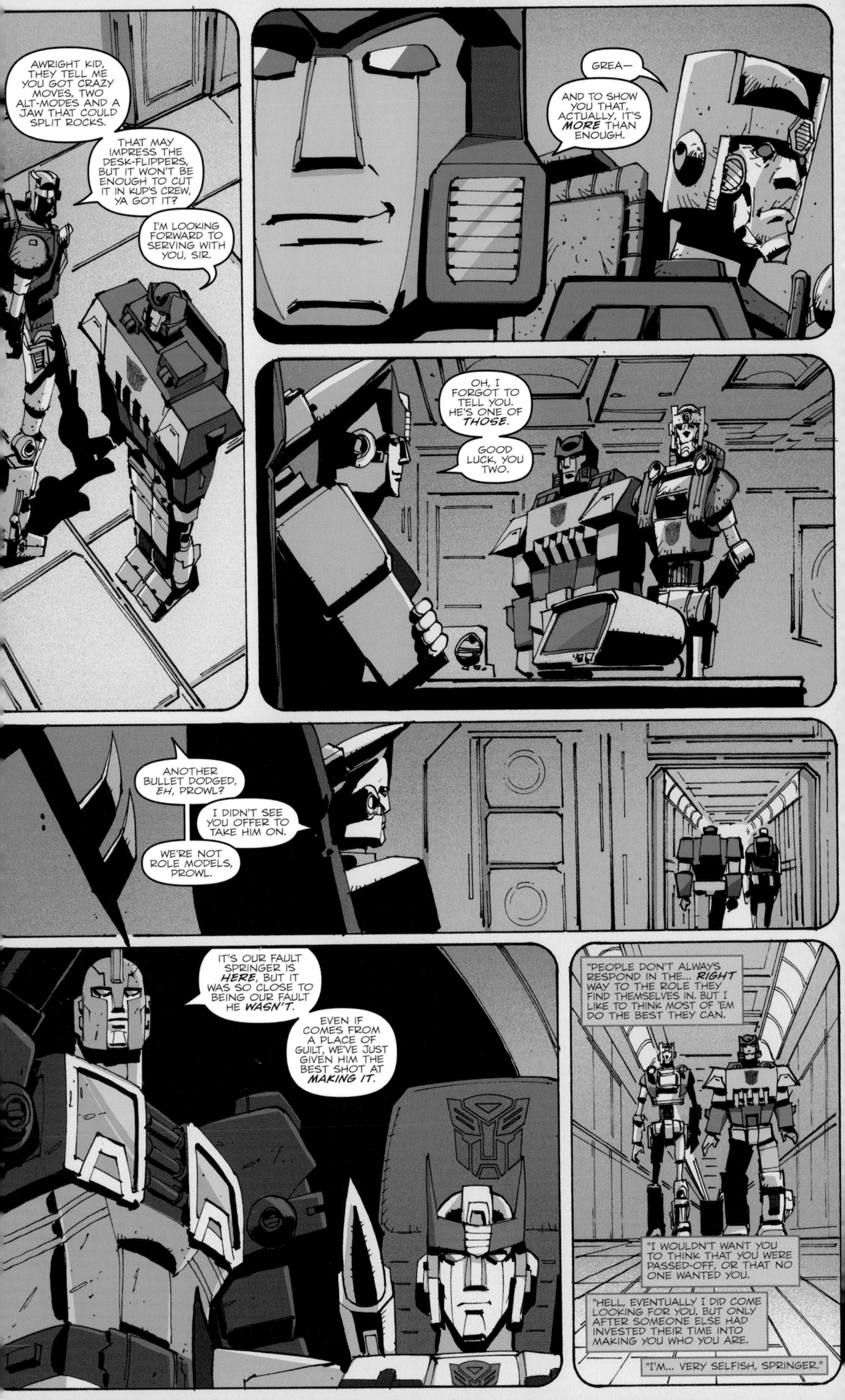
AWRIGHT KID, THEY TELL ME YOU GOT CRAZY MOVES, TWO ALT-MODES AND A JAW THAT COULD SPLIT ROCKS.
THAT MAY IMPRESS THE DESK-FLIPPERS, BUT IT WON'T BE ENOUGH TO CUT IT IN KUP'S CREW, YA GOT IT?
I'M LOOKING FORWARD TO SERVING WITH YOU, SIR.
GREA—
AND TO SHOW YOU THAT, ACTUALLY, IT'S MORE THAN ENOUGH.
OH, I FORGOT TO TELL YOU. HE'S ONE OF THOSE.
GOOD LUCK, YOU TWO.
ANOTHER BULLET DODGED, EH, PROWL?
I DIDN'T SEE YOU OFFER TO TAKE HIM ON.
WE'RE NOT ROLE MODELS, PROWL.
IT'S OUR FAULT SPRINGER IS HERE, BUT IT WAS SO CLOSE TO BEING OUR FAULT HE WASN'T.
EVEN IF COMES FROM A PLACE OF GUILT, WE'VE JUST GIVEN HIM THE BEST SHOT AT MAKING IT.
"PEOPLE DON'T ALWAYS RESPOND IN THE... RIGHT WAY TO THE ROLE THEY FIND THEMSELVES IN. BUT I LIKE TO THINK MOST OF 'EM DO THE BEST THEY CAN.
"I WOULDN'T WANT YOU TO THINK THAT YOU WERE PASSED-OFF, OR THAT NO ONE WANTED YOU.
"HELL, EVENTUALLY I DID COME LOOKING FOR YOU, BUT ONLY AFTER SOMEONE ELSE HAD INVESTED THEIR TIME INTO MAKING YOU WHO YOU ARE.
"I'M... VERY SELFISH, SPRINGER."

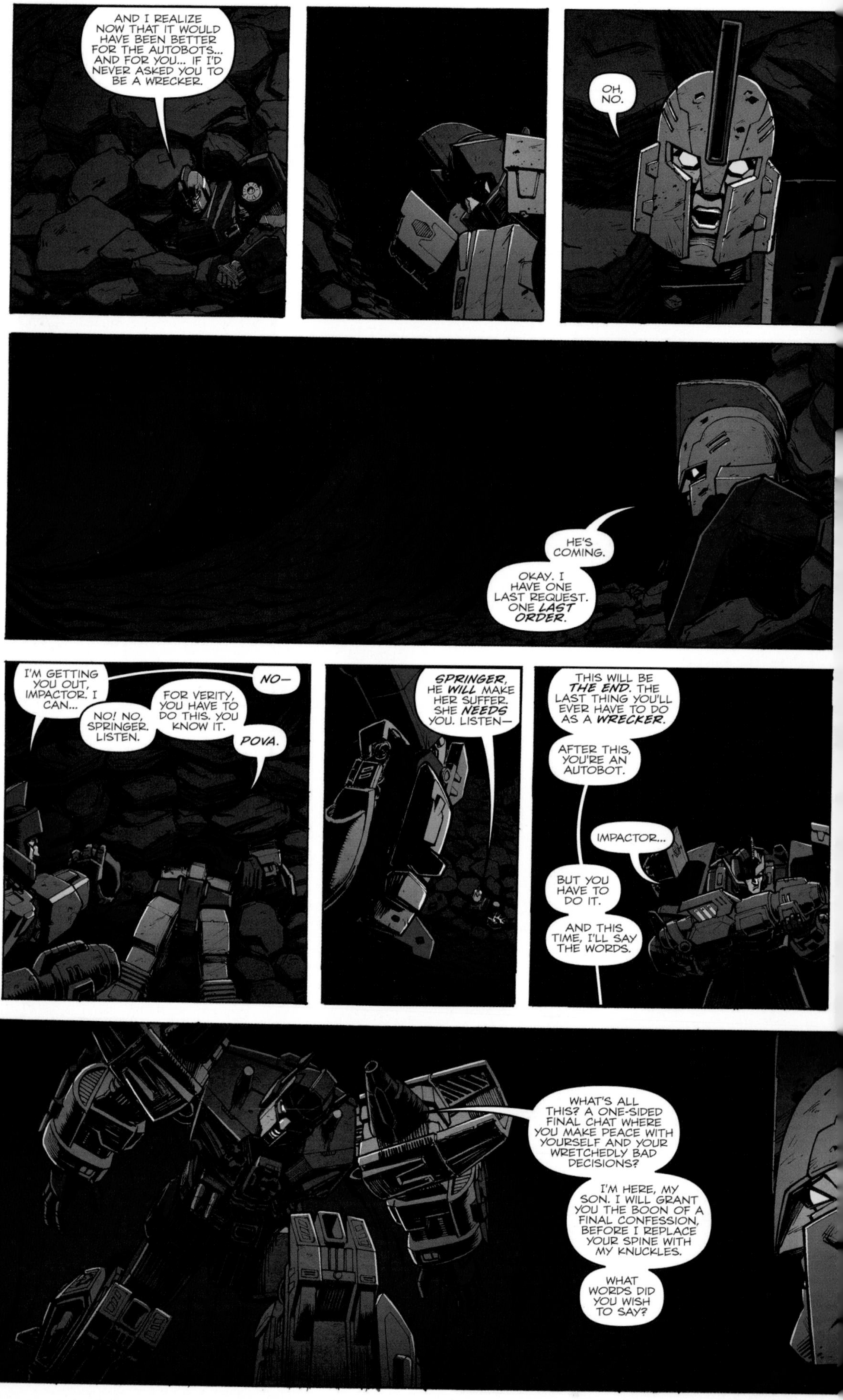
AND I REALIZE NOW THAT IT WOULD HAVE BEEN BETTER FOR THE AUTOBOTS... AND FOR YOU... IF I'D NEVER ASKED YOU TO BE A WRECKER.
OH, NO.
HE'S COMING.
OKAY. I HAVE ONE LAST REQUEST. ONE LAST ORDER.
I'M GETTING YOU OUT, IMPACTOR. I CAN...
NO—
NO! NO, SPRINGER. LISTEN.
FOR VERITY, YOU HAVE TO DO THIS. YOU KNOW IT.
POVA.
SPRINGER, HE WILL MAKE HER SUFFER. SHE NEEDS YOU. LISTEN—
THIS WILL BE THE END. THE LAST THING YOU'LL EVER HAVE TO DO AS A WRECKER.
AFTER THIS, YOU'RE AN AUTOBOT.
IMPACTOR...
BUT YOU HAVE TO DO IT.
AND THIS TIME, I'LL SAY THE WORDS.
WHAT'S ALL THIS? A ONE-SIDED FINAL CHAT WHERE YOU MAKE PEACE WITH YOURSELF AND YOUR WRETCHEDLY BAD DECISIONS?
I'M HERE, MY SON. I WILL GRANT YOU THE BOON OF A FINAL CONFESSION, BEFORE I REPLACE YOUR SPINE WITH MY KNUCKLES.
WHAT WORDS DID YOU WISH TO SAY?

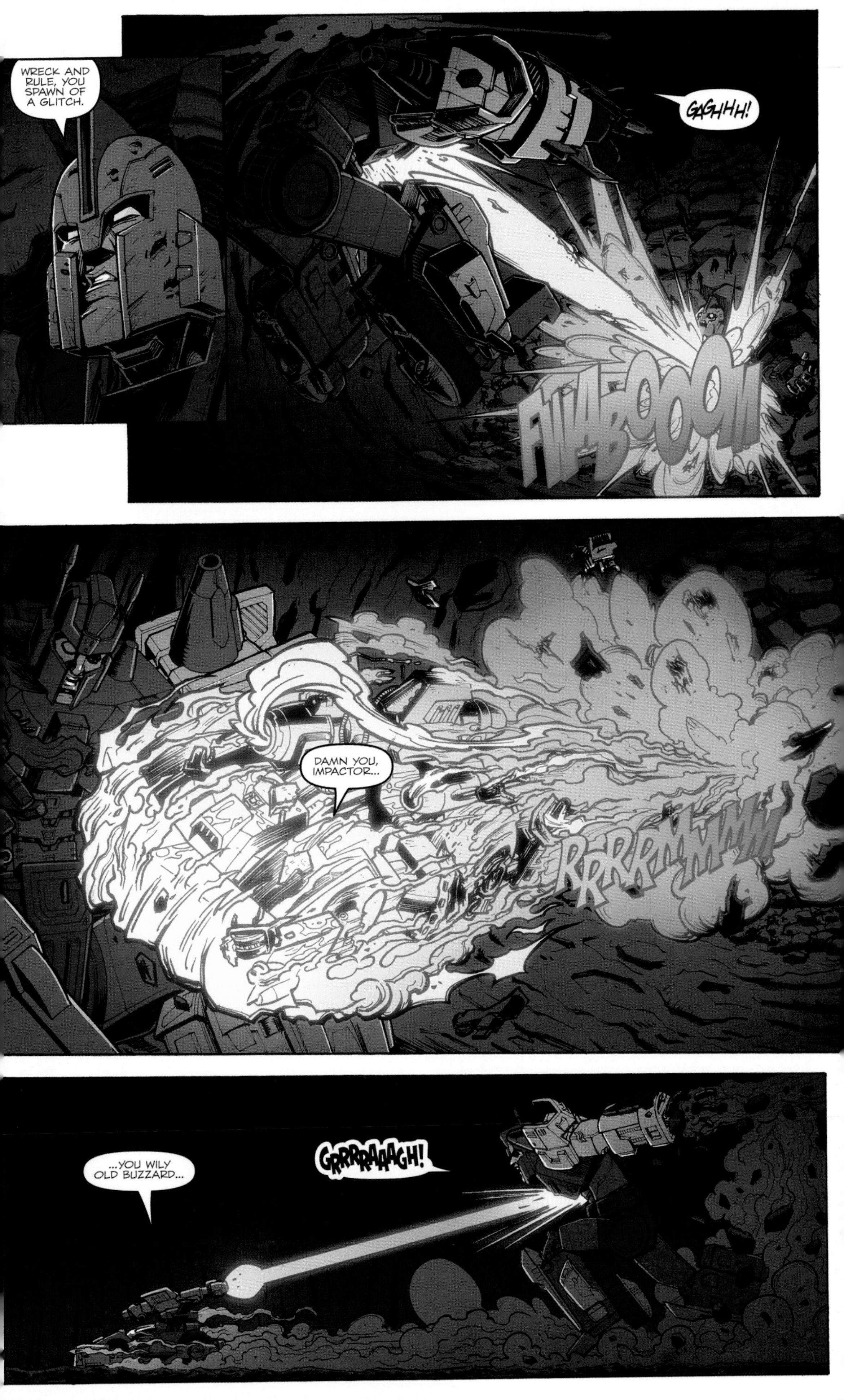
WRECK AND RULE, YOU SPAWN OF A GLITCH.
GAGHHH!
FWABOOOM
DAMN YOU, IMPACTOR...
RRRRMMMM
...YOU WILY OLD BUZZARD...
GRRRRAAAGH!

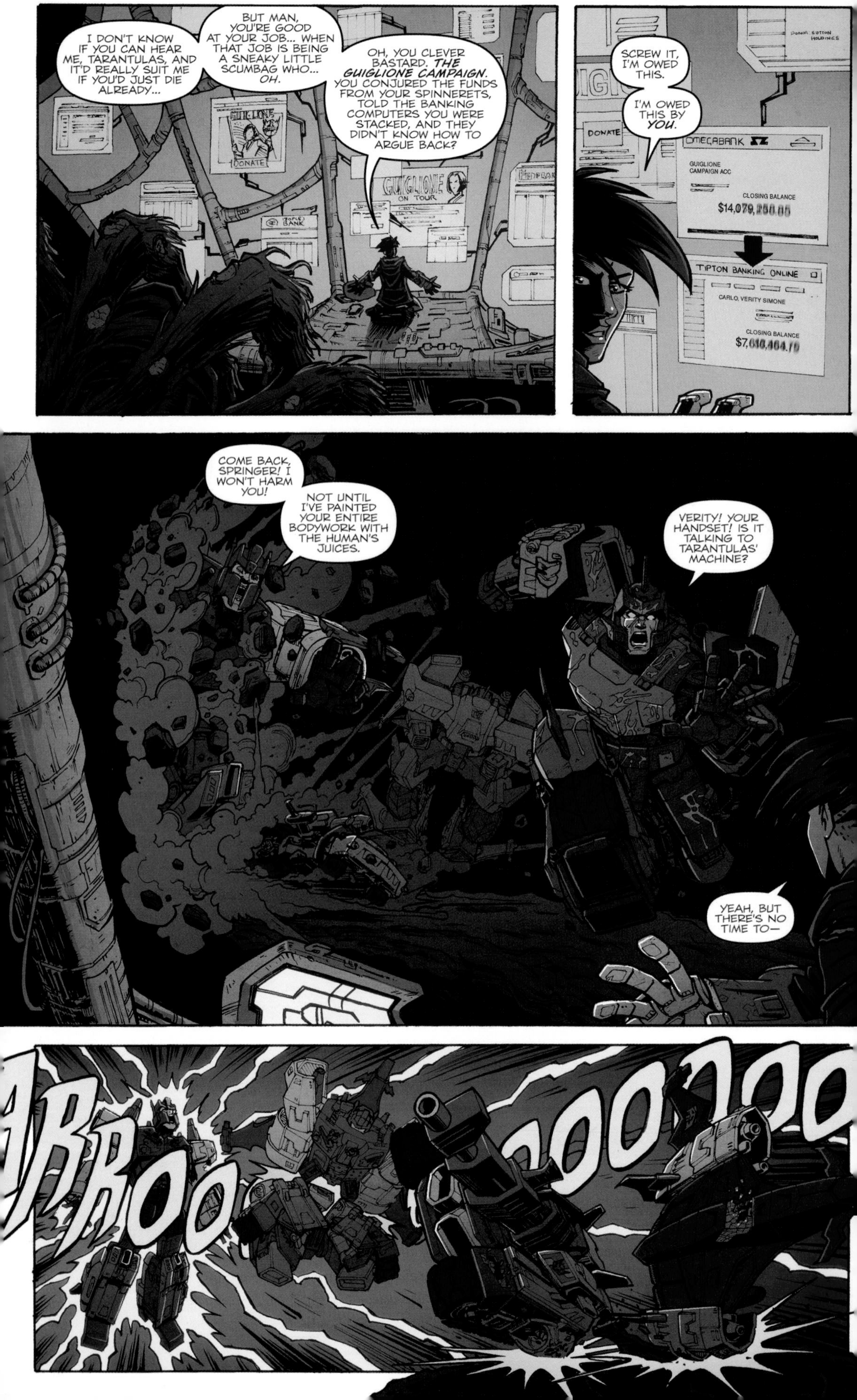
I DON'T KNOW IF YOU CAN HEAR ME, TARANTULAS, AND IT'D REALLY SUIT ME IF YOU'D JUST DIE ALREADY...
BUT MAN, YOU'RE GOOD AT YOUR JOB... WHEN THAT JOB IS BEING A SNEAKY LITTLE SCUMBAG WHO... OH.
OH, YOU CLEVER BASTARD. THE GUIGLIONE CAMPAIGN. YOU CONJURED THE FUNDS FROM YOUR SPINNERETS, TOLD THE BANKING COMPUTERS YOU WERE STACKED, AND THEY DIDN'T KNOW HOW TO ARGUE BACK?
GUIGLIONE
DONATE
GUIGLIONE ON TOUR
SCREW IT, I'M OWED THIS.
I'M OWED THIS BY YOU.
DONATE
OMEGABANK
GUIGLIONE CAMPAIGN ACC
CLOSING BALANCE
TIPTON BANKING ONLINE
CARLO, VERITY SIMONE
CLOSING BALANCE
COME BACK, SPRINGER! I WON'T HARM YOU!
NOT UNTIL I'VE PAINTED YOUR ENTIRE BODYWORK WITH THE HUMAN'S JUICES.
VERITY! YOUR HANDSET! IS IT TALKING TO TARANTULAS' MACHINE?
YEAH, BUT THERE'S NO TIME TO—
ARROOOOOOOOOO

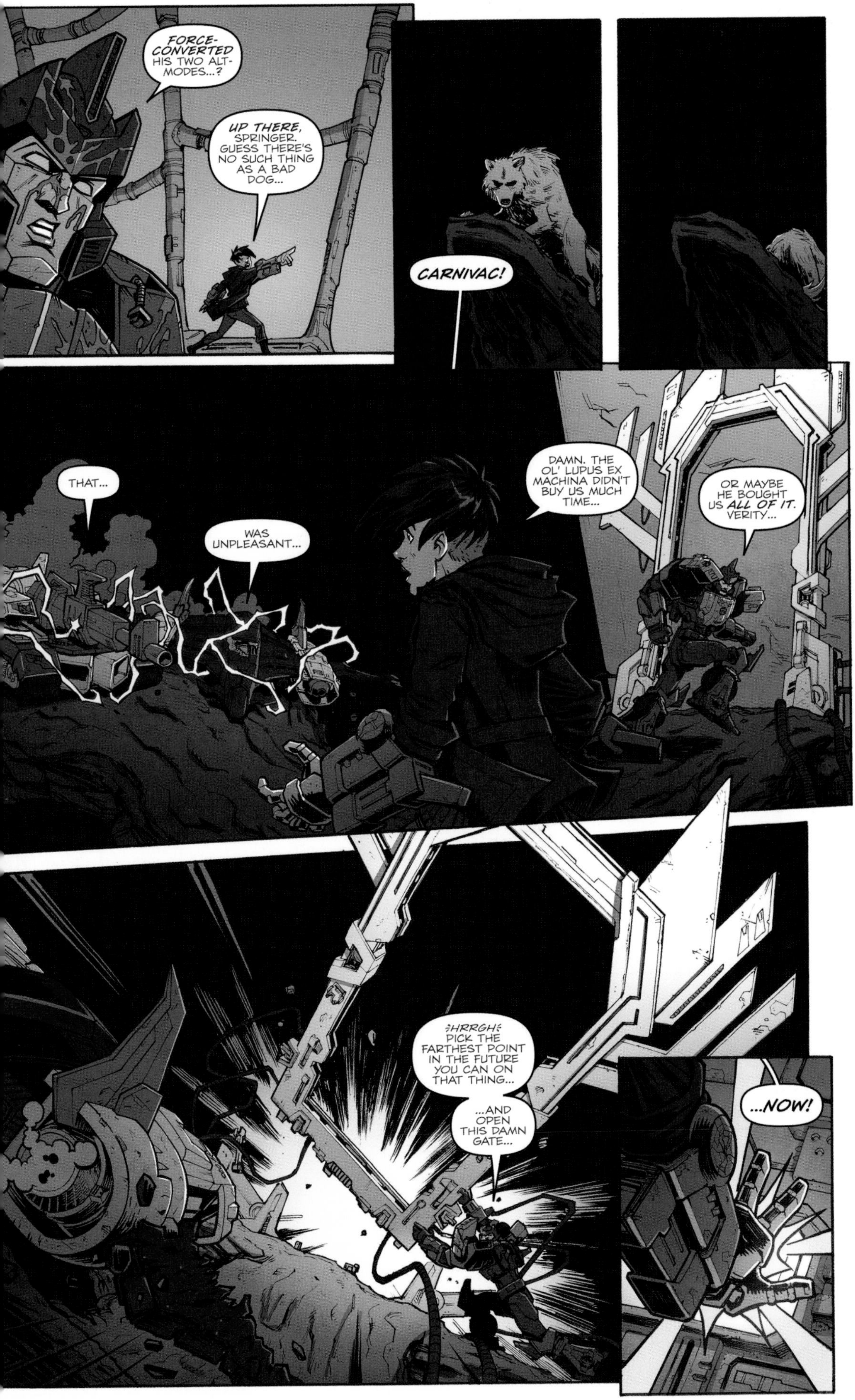
FORCE-CONVERTED HIS TWO ALT-MODES...?
UP THERE, SPRINGER. GUESS THERE'S NO SUCH THING AS A BAD DOG...
CARNIVAC!
THAT...
WAS UNPLEASANT...
DAMN. THE OL' LUPUS EX MACHINA DIDN'T BUY US MUCH TIME...
OR MAYBE HE BOUGHT US ALL OF IT. VERITY...
HRRGH PICK THE FARTHEST POINT IN THE FUTURE YOU CAN ON THAT THING...
...AND OPEN THIS DAMN GATE...
...NOW!

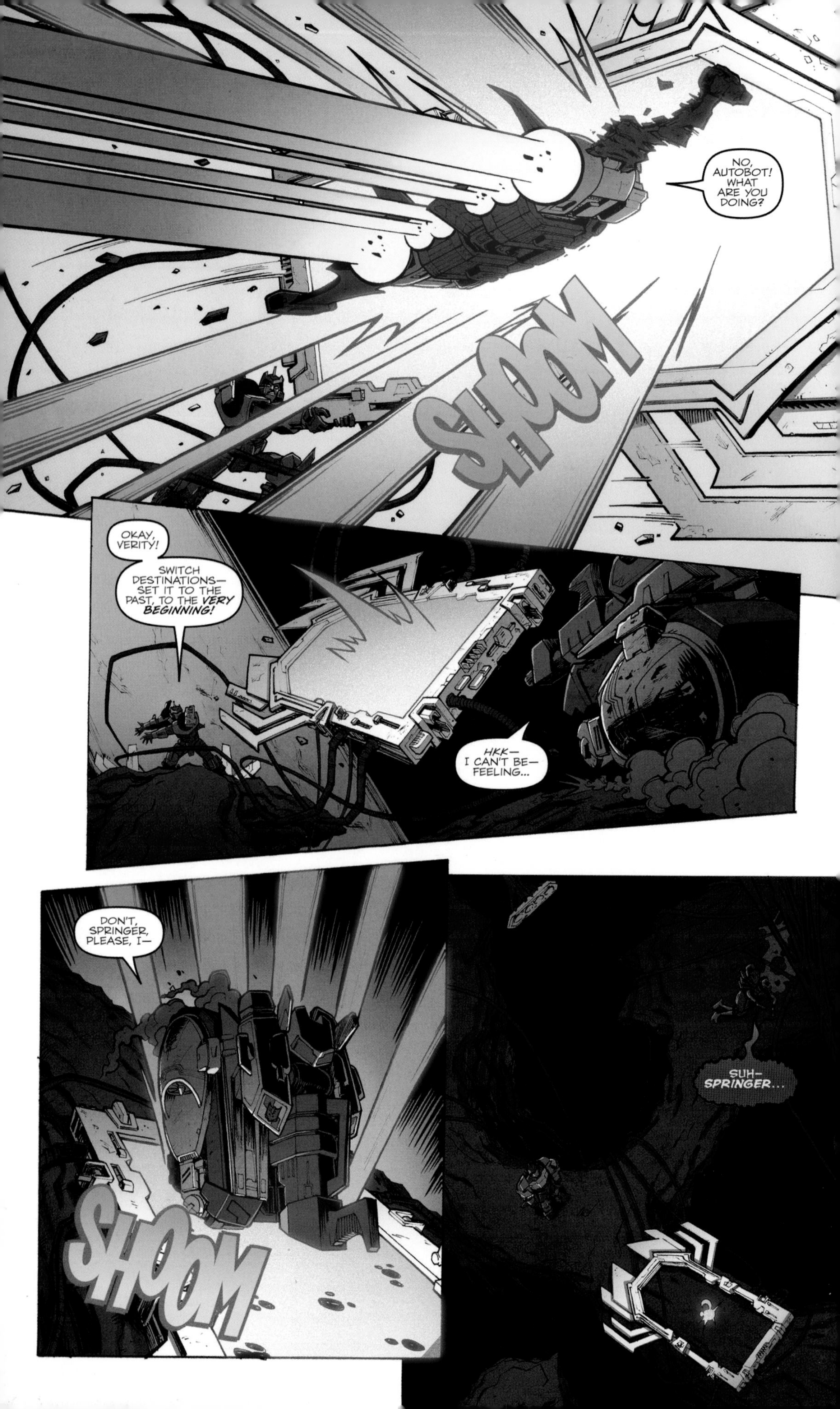
NO, AUTOBOT! WHAT ARE YOU DOING?
SHOOM
OKAY, VERITY!
SWITCH DESTINATIONS— SET IT TO THE PAST, TO THE *VERY BEGINNING!*
HKK— I CAN'T BE— FEELING...
DON'T, SPRINGER, PLEASE, I—
SHOOM
SUH-SPRINGER...

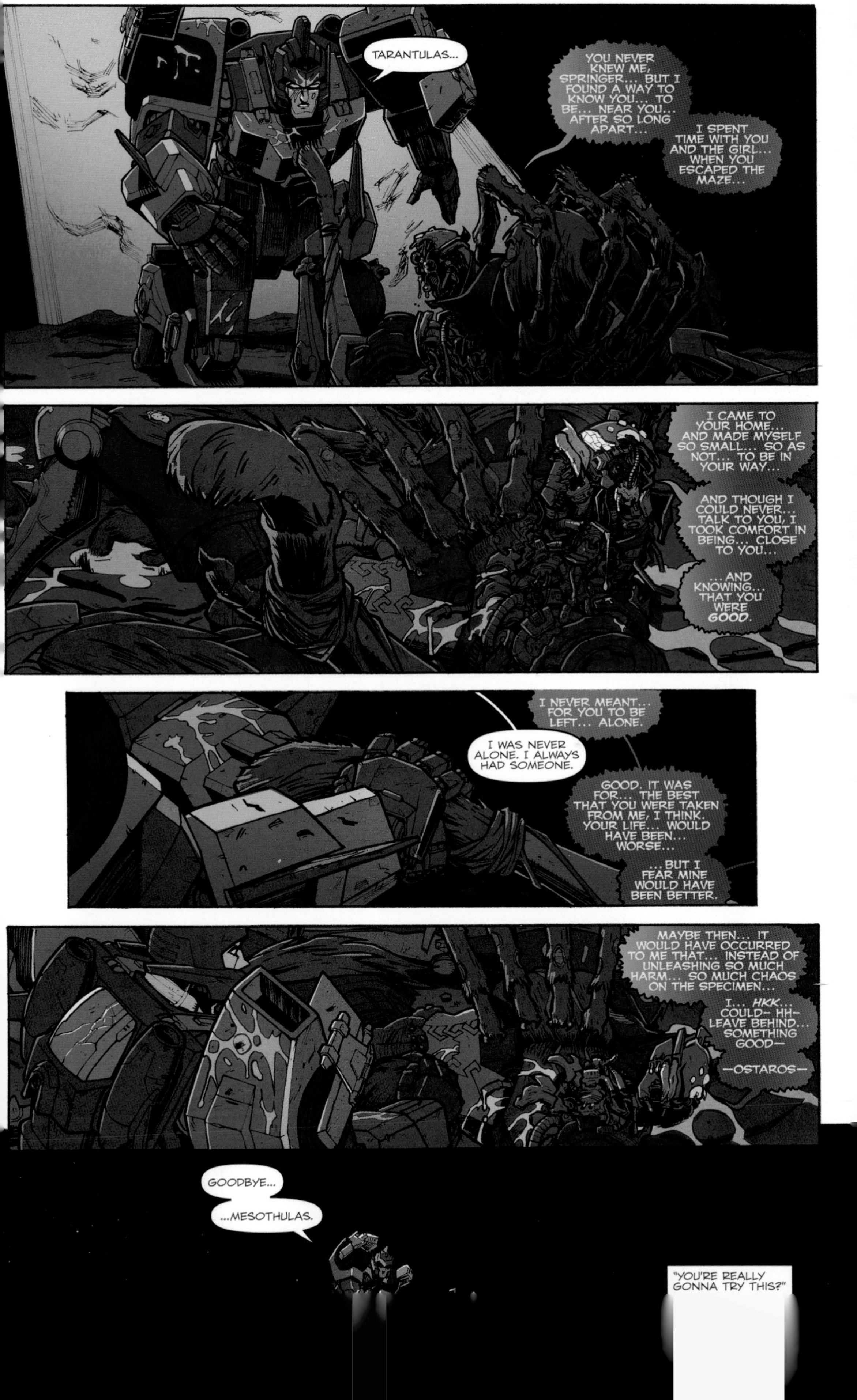
TARANTULAS...
YOU NEVER KNEW ME, SPRINGER... BUT I FOUND A WAY TO KNOW YOU... TO BE... NEAR YOU... AFTER SO LONG APART...
I SPENT TIME WITH YOU AND THE GIRL... WHEN YOU ESCAPED THE MAZE...
I CAME TO YOUR HOME... AND MADE MYSELF SO SMALL... SO AS NOT... TO BE IN YOUR WAY...
AND THOUGH I COULD NEVER... TALK TO YOU, I TOOK COMFORT IN BEING... CLOSE TO YOU...
...AND KNOWING... THAT YOU WERE GOOD.
I NEVER MEANT... FOR YOU TO BE LEFT... ALONE.
I WAS NEVER ALONE. I ALWAYS HAD SOMEONE.
GOOD. IT WAS FOR... THE BEST THAT YOU WERE TAKEN FROM ME, I THINK. YOUR LIFE... WOULD HAVE BEEN... WORSE...
...BUT I FEAR MINE WOULD HAVE BEEN BETTER.
MAYBE THEN... IT WOULD HAVE OCCURRED TO ME THAT... INSTEAD OF UNLEASHING SO MUCH HARM... SO MUCH CHAOS ON THE SPECIMEN...
I... HKK... COULD— HH— LEAVE BEHIND... SOMETHING GOOD—
—OSTAROS—
GOODBYE...
...MESOTHULAS.
"YOU'RE REALLY GONNA TRY THIS?"

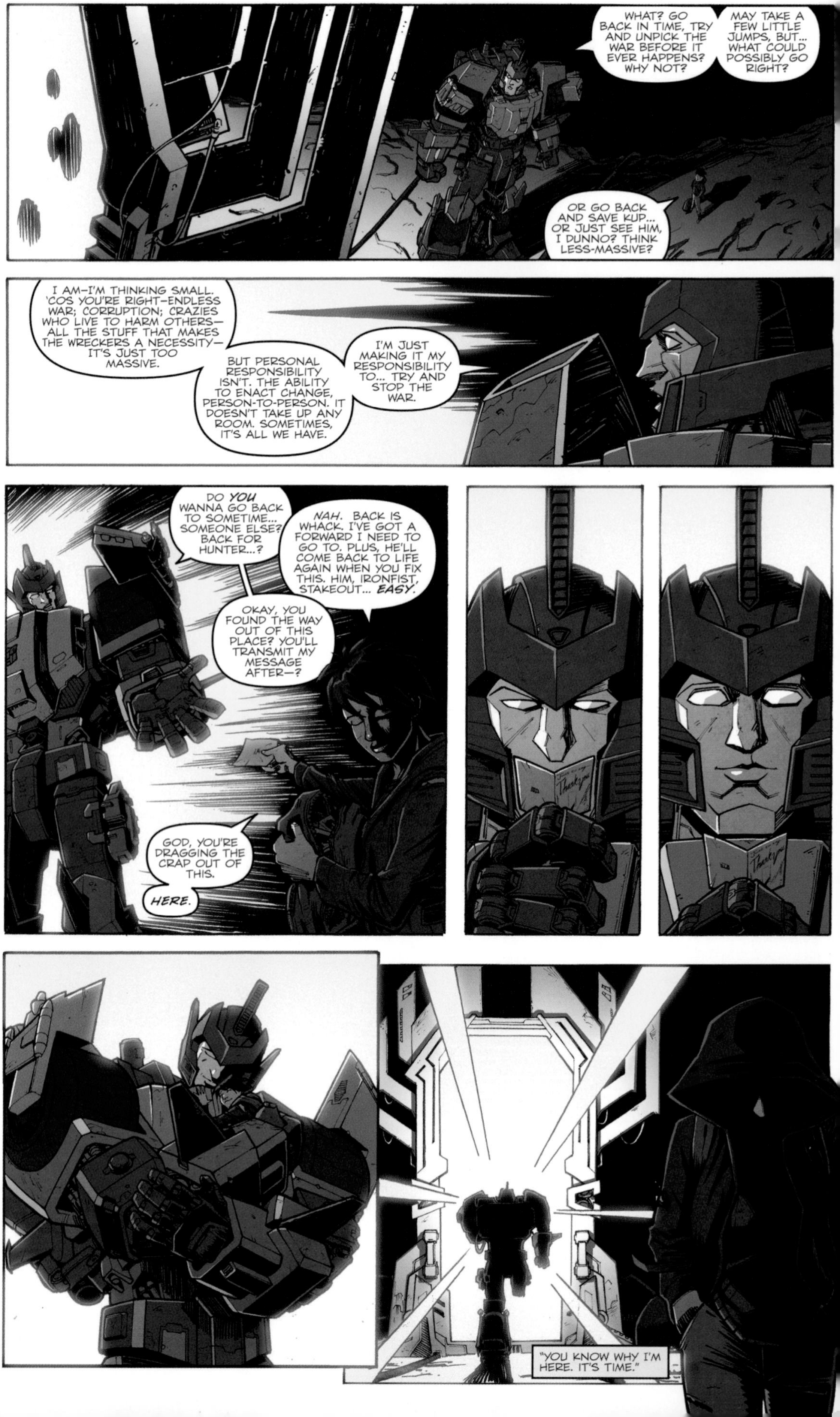
WHAT? GO BACK IN TIME, TRY AND UNPICK THE WAR BEFORE IT EVER HAPPENS? WHY NOT?
MAY TAKE A FEW LITTLE JUMPS, BUT... WHAT COULD POSSIBLY GO RIGHT?
OR GO BACK AND SAVE KUP... OR JUST SEE HIM, I DUNNO? THINK LESS-MASSIVE?
I AM–I'M THINKING SMALL. 'COS YOU'RE RIGHT–ENDLESS WAR; CORRUPTION; CRAZIES WHO LIVE TO HARM OTHERS–ALL THE STUFF THAT MAKES THE WRECKERS A NECESSITY–IT'S JUST TOO MASSIVE.
BUT PERSONAL RESPONSIBILITY ISN'T. THE ABILITY TO ENACT CHANGE, PERSON-TO-PERSON. IT DOESN'T TAKE UP ANY ROOM. SOMETIMES, IT'S ALL WE HAVE.
I'M JUST MAKING IT MY RESPONSIBILITY TO... TRY AND STOP THE WAR.
DO *YOU* WANNA GO BACK TO SOMETIME... SOMEONE ELSE? BACK FOR HUNTER...?
NAH. BACK IS WHACK. I'VE GOT A FORWARD I NEED TO GO TO. PLUS, HE'LL COME BACK TO LIFE AGAIN WHEN YOU FIX THIS. HIM, IRONFIST, STAKEOUT... ***EASY.***
OKAY, YOU FOUND THE WAY OUT OF THIS PLACE? YOU'LL TRANSMIT MY MESSAGE AFTER–?
GOD, YOU'RE DRAGGING THE CRAP OUT OF THIS.
HERE.
Thank you
"YOU KNOW WHY I'M HERE. IT'S TIME."

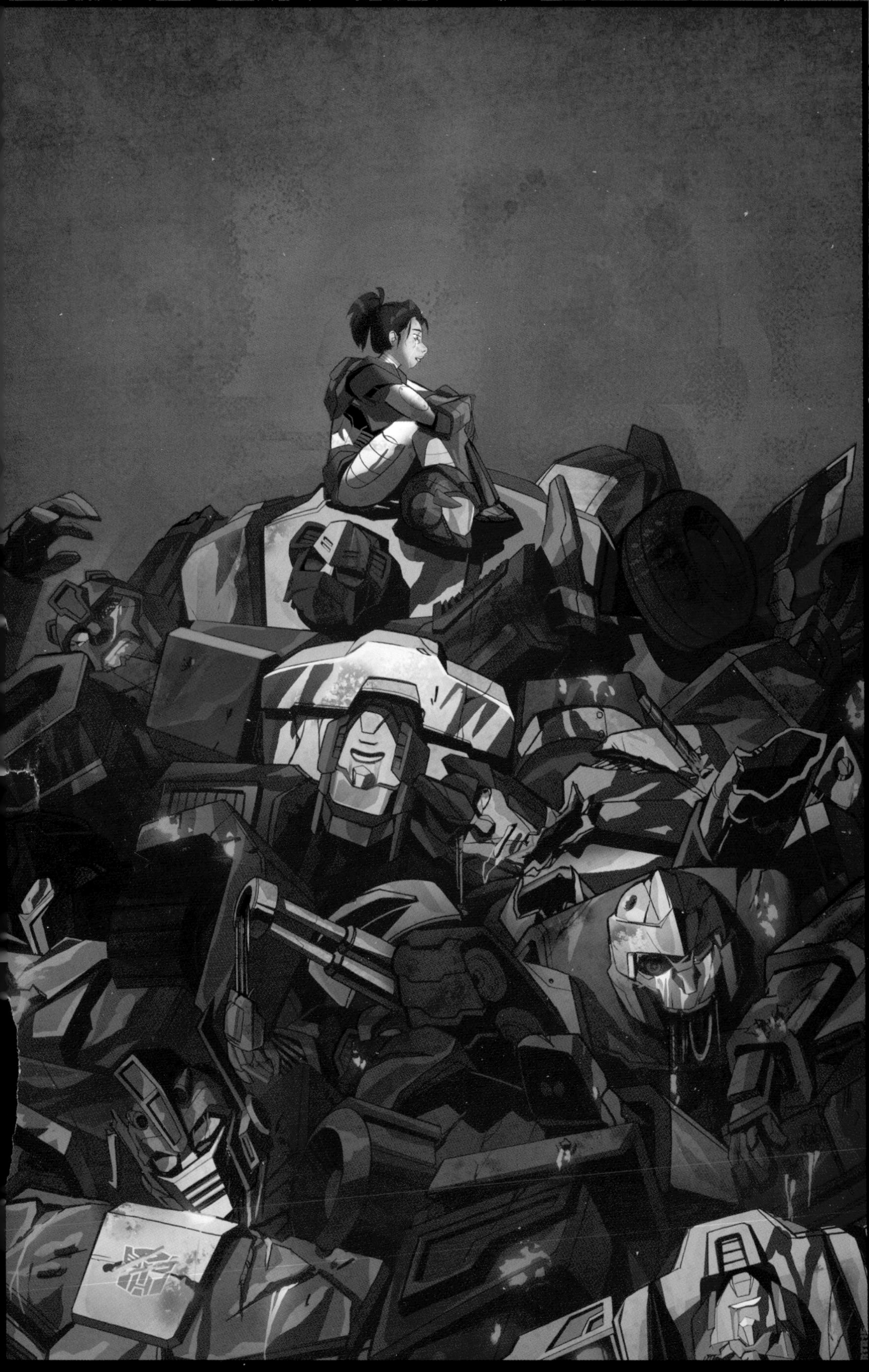

ART PRISCILLA TRAMONTANO

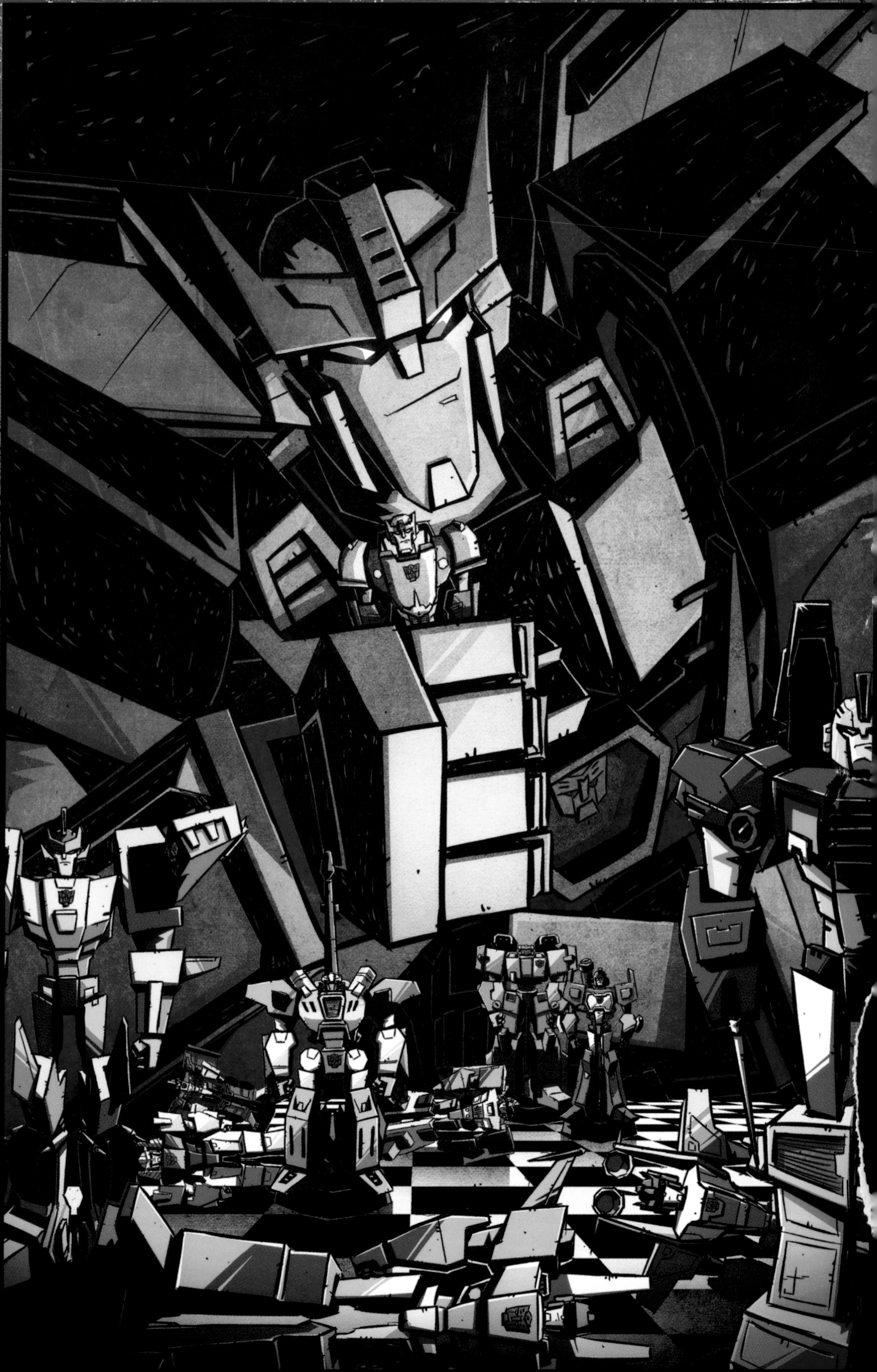

ART JOSH BURCHAM

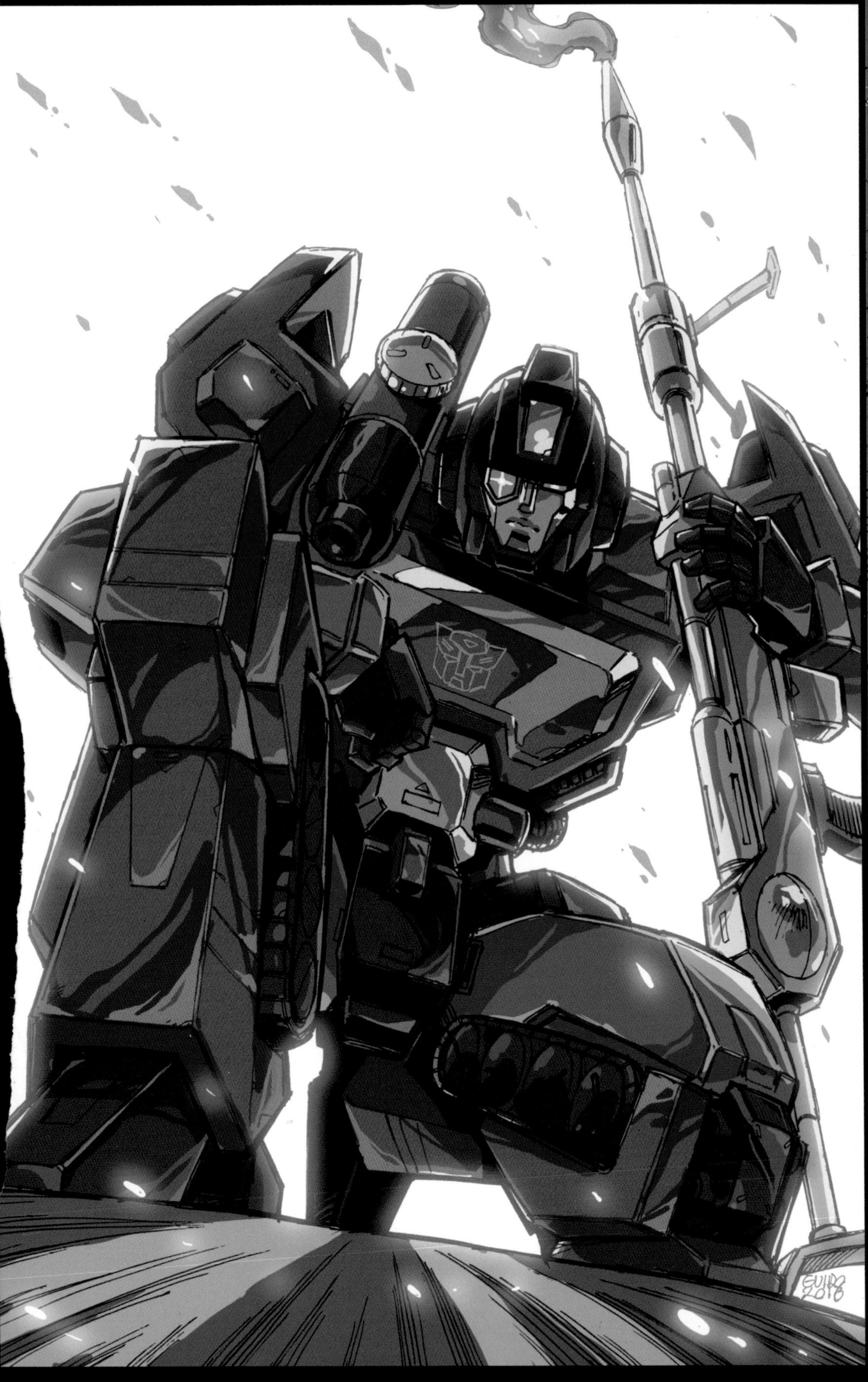
GUIDO 2018

ART GUIDO GUIDI

ART **NICK ROCHE** COLORS **JOSH BURCHAM**

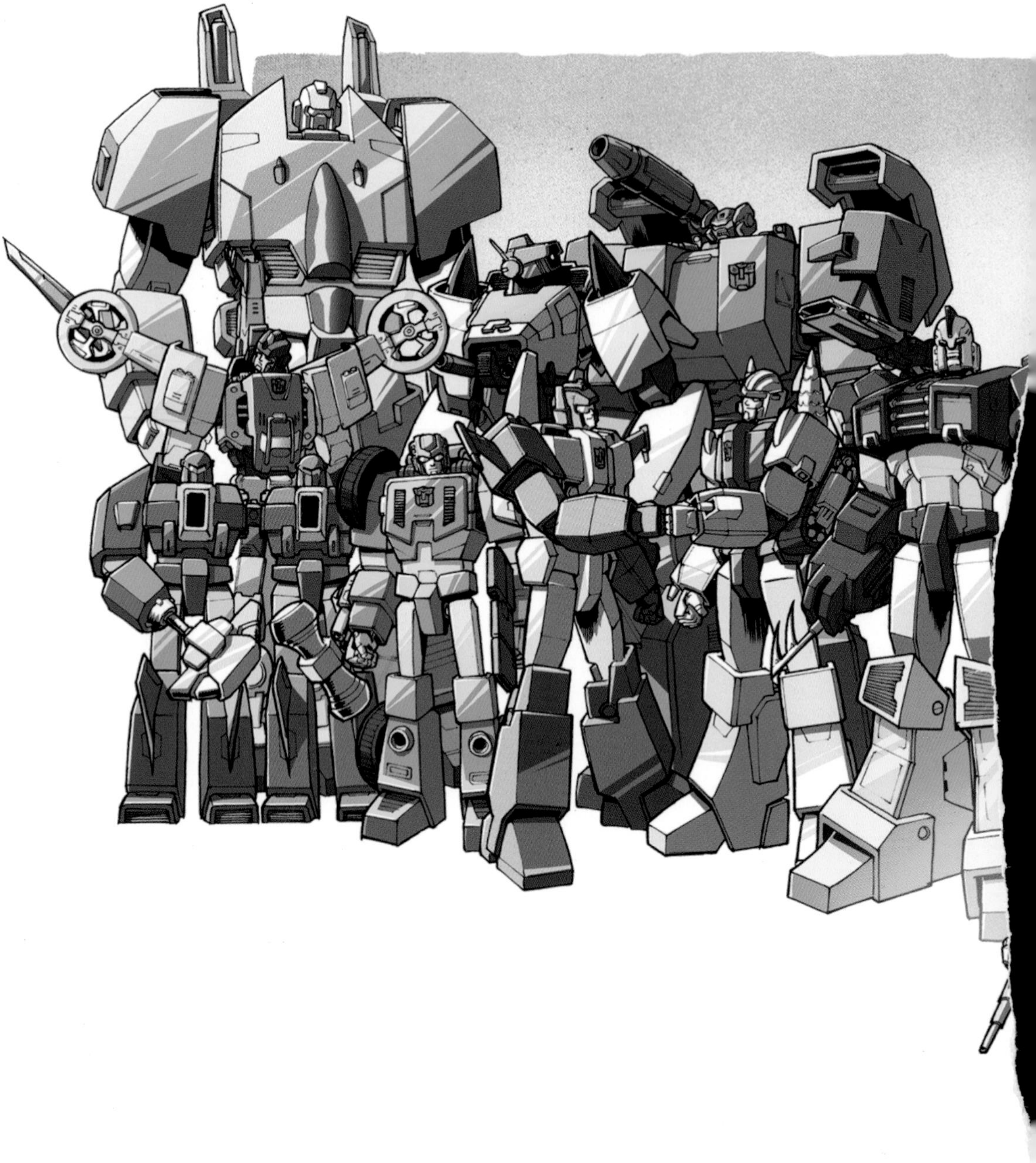